Third Edition, Revised and Enlarged

PUTTING FOOD BY

Ruth Hertzberg
Beatrice Vaughan
Janet Greene

A JANET GREENE BOOK

The Stephen Greene Press
Brattleboro, Vermont · Lexington, Massachusetts

1957
25TH
1982

Third Edition
First Edition published January 1973, five printings through July 1974.
Second Edition published July 1975, five printings through June 1981.

This book is manufactured in the United States of America. It is designed by Irving Perkins Associates and published by The Stephen Greene Press, Fessenden Road, Brattleboro, Vermont 05301.

Some parts of Chapter 21, "Drying," appeared in different form in the August 1981 issue of *Blair & Ketchum's Country Journal.*

All photographs and drawings not otherwise credited are from the U.S. Department of Agriculture. The exceptions are: drawings on page 45—John Devaney; photographs on pages 29, 30, 110, 271—Allan Seymour; drawings on pages 29, 51, 144, 146, 147, 239, 304, 383, 397, 419, 424—Norman Rogers; photograph on page 404—Self Reliance Foundation; drawings on pages 7, 15, 264, 300, 373, 381, 382, 427, 428, 432—Irving Perkins Associates.

Library of Congress Cataloging in Publication Data

Hertzberg, Ruth
    Putting food by

    "A Janet Greene book."
    Bibliography: p. 505
    Includes index
       1. Food—Preservation.   I. Vaughan, Beatrice
  II. Greene, Janet C.   III. Title
  TX601.H54 1982   641.4   82-9176
  ISBN 0-8289-0468-5   AACR2
  ISBN 0-8289-0469-3 (pbk.)

The cover painting of Putting Food By's *bountiful canning jar is by W. Kenneth Frederick.*

CONTENTS

ACKNOWLEDGMENTS   v

1.   IS IT WORTH IT?   1

2.   WHY PUT-BY FOODS SPOIL   5

3.   THE CANNING METHODS   13

4.   ON GUARD!   62

5.   CANNING FRUITS   72

6.   CANNING TOMATOES   103

7.   CANNING VEGETABLES   114

8.   CANNING MEATS   140

9.   CANNING SEAFOOD   158

10. CANNING CONVENIENCE FOODS   170

11. GETTING AND USING A FREEZER   186

12. FREEZING FRUITS   197

13. FREEZING VEGETABLES   218

14. FREEZING MEATS   236

15.	FREEZING SEAFOOD	243
16.	FREEZING CONVENIENCE FOODS, EGGS AND DAIRY PRODUCTS	249
17.	COMMON INGREDIENTS AND HOW TO USE THEM	273
18.	JELLIES, JAMS AND OTHER SWEET THINGS	292
19.	PICKLES, RELISHES AND OTHER SPICY THINGS	331
20.	CURING: SALT AND SMOKE	355
21.	DRYING	376
22.	ROOT-CELLARING	421
23.	SPROUTS AND OTHER GOOD THINGS	440
24.	COOKING	458
25.	WHERE TO FIND THINGS	505
	INDEX	515

ACKNOWLEDGMENTS

"Acknowledgment" is a temperate word for the thanks the authors owe for the above-and-beyond kindness given this Third Edition of *PFB* by Ruth N. Klippstein of Cornell University; Margy Woodburn, microbiologist of Oregon State University, Corvallis; Jane Keely of the Good Housekeeping Institute; Isabel D. Wolf of the University of Minnesota; Pat Kendall of Colorado State University; Dr. Evelyn Johnson of Washington, D.C.; F. Aline Coffey of the University of Vermont; Isabelle Downey, formerly of Auburn University, Alabama; Mildred S. Bradsher of the University of Missouri, Columbia; Reba K. Hendren of the University of Tennessee, Knoxville; Kirby Hayes of the University of Massachusetts, Amherst; Mae Martha Johnson of New Mexico State University, Las Cruces; Bonita Wyse of Utah State University; and Paulette DeJong of the University of California, Davis.

Experts in many fields have always been generous with help and information, none more so than Alexis Nason, geologist and chemist; pharmacologists Ralph Howe, Jr., and Kenneth Carpenter; Val Dubal, D.V.M., and Paul Miner, D.V.M., of the Vermont state and the Federal governments, respectively; George Pollak and George Papritz of Consumers Union; Alex Wilson of the New England Solar Energy Association and Ed Walkinstik of the Solar Chariot; Miss Wolan Harsanyi of the FDA; Dianne Leipold of Hercules, Inc.; David Strietelmeier of Morton Salt; Diane Metz Cline and Laura Rittenhouse of Best Foods; Doris Koch of General Foods; Mary Lou Williamson, formerly of the Ball Corporation; Peter Johnson of Dominion Glass Company, Ltd., Canada.

Scientists at America's land-grant colleges and universities have spurred as well as safeguarded advances in food technology and nutrition, as the authors know well from direct experience with Jo Anne Barton of Virginia Polytechnic Institute and State University; R. P. Bates of the University of Florida; Nancy Brockel–Kaufman of North Dakota; Audrey C. Burkart and Nicholas Pintauro of Rutgers University; Eleanor B. Coats of Mississippi State; Frederick J. Francis of Massachusetts, Amherst; Kenneth N. Hall of Connecticut, Storrs; Francille K. Johnson of the University of Arkansas, Auburn; Nancy Johnson of the University of Wisconsin; Palemón Martinez and Roberta Rios of Santa Fe, New Mexico; I. E. McCarty of the University of Tennessee; Von Mendenhall and Gary Richardson of Utah State University; Penny K. Ross of Georgia; Marguerite Stetson of the University of Alaska; Marjorie Stevenson of Nevada; Marilyn A. Swanson of Idaho; Nadine F. Tope of North Carolina State University, Raleigh.

For their contributions the authors are grateful to Helen and Kent Ruth of Oklahoma and Betty Armstrong of Albuquerque, New Mexico; Pat Baca for advice about materials published under the aegis of The Church of Jesus Christ of Latter-day Saints; Charlotte C. Blume of Dixie Canner Equipment Company. To Frances Bond; master builder Guy Brunton; Hepper and John Caldwell, Lona B. Chatterton; Mary Clark and Marjorie Goss of Garden Way Living Center; apple-grower William H. Darrow Jr.; Albert and Mildred Dupell, Larry Feldman, Barbara Fungaroli, Donna Lee Funk, Mary Lou Gould, Jane Grass, Jennifer and Stephanie Greene, Margaret Gunnell, Thure Hertzberg, Florence Howe of Agway, Jari Jasinoski, Ann C. Johnson, Merrill Lawrence, Jonathan Leff, Jeanne Lesem of UPI, John McLeod of Gage Publishing, Ltd., Canada, Robert L. McShinsky, Sr., Susan Mahnke, Claudette and Norman Marcotte, Russell Marena, Bishop Charles James Mullins of The Church of Jesus Christ of Latter-day Saints, Samuel R. Ogden, Susan Osgood, Annette Pestle, Gabrielle Pike, Paul Putnam, "Skip" Reardan, Norman Rogers, Francis Rohr, naturalist Ronald Rood, the Sea Garden, Sumi Schreyer, Irene Bartlett Sherman, Kathleen Shulga, Yuri and Satoru Sugimura, Esther Munroe Swift, Mikkie Van der Graaf of The Netherlands, and Betty Wenstadt of National Presto Industries, Inc.

And this book would not be here if it weren't for Irene F. Gilbert, and for Mary Metcalf of The Stephen Greene Press.

This book is in praise of
Miss Gertrude Russell
—and of all self-reliant people like
her, everywhere, who want to save good
food and know what's in it.

(To "put by" is an old, deep-country way of saying to "save something you don't have to use now, against the time when you'll need it." Putting food by is the antidote for running scared.   J.G.)

IS IT WORTH IT?

Early each spring, sure as crocuses, there comes a bigger-than-ever crop of articles forecasting a greater-than-ever number of backyard vegetable gardens in the United States. By the start of the 1980's it was predicted that more than half the nation's households would be eating some produce of their own raising, and there would be Americans growing a favorite vegetable or two in window boxes, in tubs on a patio, in trays warmed by a passive solar collector.

The gardens would be planted, most writers felt, to help family food budgets not only by providing beautifully fresh vegetables and small fruits in season, but also to assure an abundance to preserve—at a saving over store-bought—for meals during the rest of the year. The seed cataloguers agree, for they list canning and freezing equipment, even crop dryers, along with other specialties.

But does a garden truly effect a saving?—does it, in the authors' phrasing, stretch the family's food dollar? Two eminent nutritionists whose jobs oblige them to be unswervingly practical carried out studies to find the answer.

Back in the mid–1970's Evelyn Johnson of the Extension Service headquarters in Washington, D.C., made the first top-level survey to see if people should be encouraged to start growing vegetables and fruits at home in order to save money. Her report was dispassionate, and, being written for fellow food specialists, factual indeed. And the impact of Dr. Johnson's report was that householders anxiously watching their food budgets would do better to keep track of sales of wholesome canned food at their supermarkets, and sales of frozen food *if* they already possessed adequate freezer storage. Or they perhaps could take part in a co-operative buying effort whereby good plain food could be bought at a discount because of buying in large quantities, and the savings then would be shared.

Dr. Johnson's study was sensible and forthright, and showed the pitfalls of starting to raise food without considering the capital investment needed to preserve it and store it—the buying of Pressure Canners and Boiling–Water Bath canners, and jars or cans; buying freezers and freezing materials; and paying the utility bills.

In the summer of 1979 Ruth N. Klippstein of Cornell University was the author of a study made much more for the general public titled *The True Cost of Home Food Preservation.* Like Dr. Johnson, Professor Klippstein also

1

talks about energy costs and whether it's gas or electricity that is firing the canner or running the freezer. Clearly, warmly, she discusses the time required, aside from the human energy, to put by green beans, tomatoes, and peaches, both for the freezer and in jars to go on the pantry shelves.

"Mrs. K," as her graduate students and so many county Extension Service home economists across New York State call her, has a small and beautifully managed vegetable garden of her own. She had access, as well, to experimental vegetable garden plots of Cornell's College of Agriculture in Freeville, New York. A number of charts and explicit costs and comparisons make this report extremely interesting to the professional and the layman alike.

The Effect of Intangibles

The conclusions in both Dr. Johnson's and Professor Klippstein's bulletins agree that, from a straight dollars-and-cents standpoint, the answer to the original question is No.

But there's another consideration that must be factored into the calculations about whether it is or is not worth the money and the effort to put by food at home; and this is the matter of satisfaction. Satisfaction to Ruth Klippstein means that one has the pleasure of growing the food, sharing it if there is a surplus, eating it while it is fresh and most nutritious. Through the garden and later preserving, one teaches one's children that planting (birth), growing and harvesting (maturing) and cutting-back and plowing-under (dying) are the continuity of all living things, and nothing ever is a waste.

When the food is taken from the jar or the freezer, or from the cannister where it was held dry or from the brining crock, there is a deep and special pleasure in cooking it and serving it forth. And we know what is in it.

MISS RUSSELL'S WAY

We doubt very much if Miss Gertrude Russell has ever read either of these bulletins just discussed, or, if she did have them available, whether they would make her operations very different. Miss Russell lives in a house about a hundred years old in a small town in New England—she truly lives on the High Street—and her backyard extends nearly to the center of the block. She has a small business, her own beauty parlor, on the ground floor. The house is spacious enough to allow her a good apartment for herself and of course a full cellar underneath. Upstairs is a seven- or eight-room tenement. "Tenement" in the area where Miss Russell lives refers to any premises, either modest or grand, that are leased to a tenant; the word has no connotation of ghetto.

Miss Russell sees no reason to discuss her age beyond saying that she has been entitled to social security for some years now. She has a little trouble with her knee. Her complexion is fine-grained and clear and very fresh; her eyes are blue, her hair is dark with a charming little flair of white outlining the natural curl that falls on her forehead. She works five days a week, taking Wednesdays off and working Saturdays. Her clientele is seemingly unchangeable; her ladies are of a certain age, and she sees that their hair is kept healthy and becomingly dressed.

Living alone as she does, Miss Russell finds the separate freezer in the top of her refrigerator—it is about 3 cubic feet—adequate for her needs. The cellar has an earthen floor. At one end are the furnaces that heat her part of the house and the tenant's part, and at the other end are the various bins for holding root-crops over the winter. Upstairs is a cool pantry where she holds her apples. It is near here, too, that she stores her canned goods.

Behind the house with its wide veranda is her garden. It is 50 feet long and 30 feet wide, and in it are the perennial Jerusalem artichokes, raspberry and blackberry bushes and currants, and the herbs—including chives and tarragon—that carry over from year to year.

The end of April or the first day of May, Miss Russell has her garden rototilled. At that time is chopped into the soil the winter rye she has sowed the preceding fall when she put her garden to bed; for this first and deep tilling she adds manure and compost, and lime if necessary. Every year or so she has the County Agent test the soil of her garden, and the report is invariably that it is uncommonly friable, and able to grow good food.

Usually she starts a few summer squash and string beans under hot-caps so she can have them early. She has carrots and beets. From seed that she harvests from one plant at the end of each season she raises half a bushel of the great Gilfeather turnip (a strain originated by the family of that name in Wardsboro, Vermont, and which in 1981 for the first time "went national"). For greens she has endive and chard and a hybrid called celtuce; she also plants zucchini and tomatoes. Table cucumbers she grows on sunflower stalks, and before the summer is out the vines will reach almost as high as the great golden heads.

She plants nearly the same vegetables every year but each season she tries a different thing. Sometimes the innovation is a success and she adds it to her repertoire, and sometimes it's a flop, so she doesn't do it the next year. She had a good time recently experimenting with which winter squash she likes the best aside from acorn squash.

Miss Russell takes her main meal in the middle of the day in the old-fashioned and most healthful manner. She's very fond of potatoes, so she runs out to the kitchen about 11 o'clock in the morning and puts on her potatoes so she will have a baked potato when her last customer is finished at noon. She may bake a frozen meat patty, seasoning it with herbs that she has dried herself.

Before she goes out to pick her salad—and what a salad it will be!—Miss Russell will take from her refrigerator one of the large beets that she has baked whole earlier. She will peel it and cut off the remains of the stem and the roots and slice what she wants with a bit of butter and put it in a pan on the stove; this she will eat as one of her two vegetables, besides potatoes, that she will have in a very few minutes. In the garden she will start collecting her salad. Depending upon what time of the season it is, there will be a leaf here and there of several different kinds of lettuce, some endive, a leaf or two of spinach (spinach for its own sake; it's not her favorite green, but she often has some to use in salads), and there will be some chard perhaps, and a few young tender beet greens. These she usually dresses with the spiced vinegar from a jar of her homemade pickles. In season she has raspberries or blackberries from her garden, or strawberries or blueberries that she has picked from a nearby farm open to the public for harvesting. She relies on fruit for her dessert year round, including her own applesauce and her own canned Bartlett pears. She is not much of a hand for sweets.

When she goes to the market she buys milk and other dairy products, ground meat, blade steak, beef stew meat, turkey or chicken breasts, sometimes a whole roasting chicken, pork liver, ham, chicken livers, pork chops. She buys cream-style corn in cans and canned peas—she doesn't grow peas herself and she doesn't like frozen ones. One purchase she makes always is popcorn, for like many people of her generation and part of the country she regards popcorn as a special treat for Sunday night supper.

She also buys about 60 pounds of Green Mountain potatoes in the fall and two bushels of Northern Spy apples, which she considers by far and away the finest apple God ever put on Earth. One bushel she eats, storing it in the cool pantry instead of down cellar because apples respire so much and she doesn't want them to interfere with the potatoes. The other she cans as applesauce. She buys two bushels of Bartlett pears that she cans right away, going into a cookbook for the proportions of sweetener to water but cutting down further on the sweetness. She substitutes corn syrup for the white sugar called for, and once in a while she adds a touch of cinnamon for a little difference.

Pears and applesauce are the only things she cans in quarts because her planning-ahead is done in pints. She figures on two pints of each vegetable for a week; out of a pint she might get two meals and she might get three. From counting how many pints she would use in a week she goes on to how many she will need so they will last through to the summer until the new vegetables are ready to pick from her garden. At the end of a harvest she will have about 46 jars of pints and ½-pints of ripe cucumber pickles (she got most of these cucumbers from a cousin); 8 quarts of applesauce, 23 quarts of pears, 11 pints of assorted produce left over from the preceding season and which she will start the new autumn eating; 32 pints of carrots, 18 pints of stringbeans, 14 pints of beets, 23 pints of greens, 12 pints of tomatoes, 20 pints of blueberries and she will have frozen 16 half-pints of strawberries.

Is it worth it?

Yes. It is.

2

WHY PUT-BY FOODS SPOIL

What can spizzy tomato juice have in common with a slippery pickle—or moldy popcorn with a tired chocolate mousse?—or, for that matter, soft frozen beans with a warm chicken pot pie?

Answer: All of them could be spoiled.

They're likely to be spoiled by mishandling when the materials were being prepared or by being processed in the wrong way, and their type of spoilage will range from merely unpleasant or unappetizing to downright sickening, even deadly.

Four kinds of things cause spoilage in preserved food: (1) *enzymes,* which are naturally occuring substances in living tissues, and are necessary to complete growth and reproduction; and three types of micro-organisms—(2) *molds,* (3) *yeasts* and (4) *bacteria.* All these micro-organisms are present in the soil, water and air around us. They can be controlled adequately by care in choosing ingredients, scrupulous cleanliness in handling them, and faithful good sense in following the established safe procedures for putting food by at home.

For thousands of years people have been drying food to preserve it; by all indications, they've been salting it or fermenting it for just about as long. Some foods by their own nature require no special treatment or process: root crops, for instance, need only be held under reasonably controlled temperature and humidity to last until the next harvest. Canning—holding cooked food in airtight containers—is less than two centuries old, and freezing is the youngest method of the lot.

Everything in this chapter applies to every safe method of preserving food at home, as you will see as *PFB* describes each process for each individual food. Meanwhile here follow the basic principles that are amplified throughout the rest of the book. They are corralled here for ready reference because we feel so strongly that any newcomer to canning, freezing, making preserves, drying, root-cellaring, or curing can always keep the *How* of food safety in mind if the *Why* is clear and handy.

Metric Conversions for Why Put-by Foods Spoil

Full metric conversions, with the arithmetic for refining them, are given at the start of Chapter 17 ("Common Ingredients and How to Use Them"). For simplicity in this chapter's discussion, metric temperatures have been rounded off.

• • •

Temperatures @ sea-level zone (up to 1000 feet/305 meters): 32 F/Zero C——40 F/4 C——45 F/7 C——50 F/10 C——70 F/21 C——80 F/27 C——85 F/29 C——100 F/38 C——110 F/43 C——120 F/49 C——140 F/60 C——190 F/88 C——212 F/100 C——240 F/116 C——250 F/121 C.

Hᴏᴡ Eɴᴢʏᴍᴇѕ Aᴄᴛ

Nature has designed each plant or animal with the ability to program the production of its own enzymes, which are the biochemicals that help the organism to ripen and mature—in short, enzymes promote the organic changes necessary to the life cycle of all growing things. However, their action is reversible: they can turn around and cause decomposition, thereby causing changes in color, flavor, and texture, and making food unappetizing.

Their action slows down in cold conditions, increases most quickly between around 85 to 120 degrees Fahrenheit/29 to 49 degrees Celsius, and begins to be destroyed at about 140 F/60 C. However, the heat resistance of enzymes in a vinegar-loaded—and hence strong-acid—food like pickles can be stiffer than the opposition inherent in bacteria or molds or yeasts in the same type of food. The natural enzymes in cucumbers are especially tough.

Hᴏᴡ Mᴏʟᴅѕ Aᴄᴛ

Molds are microscopic fungi whose dry spores (seeds) alight on food and start growing silken threads that can become slight streaks of discoloration in food or cover it with a mat of fuzz.

It used to be felt that "a little mold won't hurt you," but modern research has disclosed that only the mold introduced deliberately into the "blue" cheeses like Roquefort, Gorgonzola or Stilton is trustworthy. The others, as they grow in food, are capable of producing substances called mycotoxins, and some of them can be hurtful indeed.

In addition, molds eat natural acid present in food, thereby lowering the acidity that is protection against more actively dangerous poisons—but we'll have more to say about this in a minute.

Molds are alive but don't grow below 32 degrees Fahrenheit/Zero Celsius; they start to grow above freezing, have their maximum acceleration between 50 and 100 F/10 and 38 Celsius, and then taper off to inactivity beginning around 120 F/49 C; they die with increasing speed at temperatures from 140 to 190 F/60 to 88 C.

TEMPERATURE *vs.* THE SPOILERS

F = Fahrenheit/C = Celsius

(At sea level to 1000 feet/305 meters altitude)

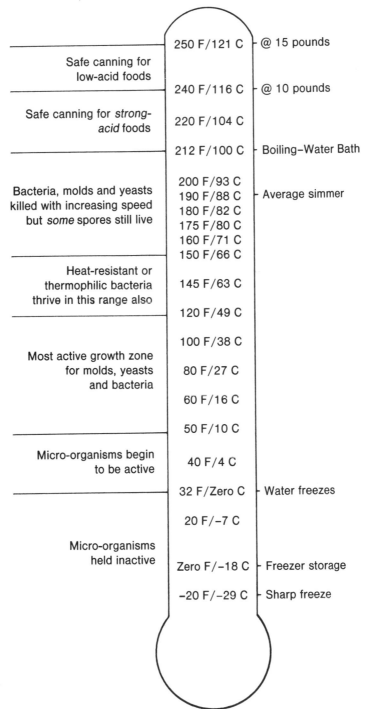

	250 F/121 C	@ 15 pounds
Safe canning for low-acid foods		
	240 F/116 C	@ 10 pounds
Safe canning for *strong-acid* foods	220 F/104 C	
	212 F/100 C	Boiling–Water Bath
Bacteria, molds and yeasts killed with increasing speed but *some* spores still live	200 F/93 C	
	190 F/88 C	Average simmer
	180 F/82 C	
	175 F/80 C	
	160 F/71 C	
	150 F/66 C	
Heat-resistant or thermophilic bacteria thrive in this range also	145 F/63 C	
	120 F/49 C	
Most active growth zone for molds, yeasts and bacteria	100 F/38 C	
	80 F/27 C	
	60 F/16 C	
	50 F/10 C	
Micro-organisms begin to be active	40 F/4 C	
	32 F/Zero C	Water freezes
	20 F/–7 C	
Micro-organisms held inactive	Zero F/–18 C	Freezer storage
	–20 F/–29 C	Sharp freeze

HOW YEASTS ACT

The micro-organisms we call yeasts are also fungi grown from spores, and they cause fermentation—which is delightful in beer, necessary in sauerkraut, and horrid in applesauce. As with molds, severe cold holds them inactive, 50 to 100 F/10 to 38 C hurries their growth, and 140 to 190 F/60 to 88 C destroys them.

HOW BACTERIA ACT

Bacteria also are present in soil and water, and their spores, too, can be carried by the air. But bacteria are often far tougher than molds and yeasts are; certain ones actually thrive in heat that kills these fungi, and in some foods there can exist bacterial spores which can make hidden toxins. These spores will be destroyed in a reasonable time only if the food is heated at from 240 to 250 degrees Fahrenheit/116 to 121 Celsius—*at least 28 degrees higher than the boiling temperature for water AT SEA-LEVEL CLASSIFICATION*, and *obtainable only under pressure.*

Of the disease-causing bacteria we're concerned with mainly, the most fragile are members of the genus Salmonella, which are transmitted by pets, rodents, insects and human beings, in addition to existing in our soil and water. Salmonellae live in frozen food, are inactive up to 45 F/7 C, and are killed when held at 140 F/60 C, with destruction much quicker at higher temperatures.

> • • Where, in any discussion of the spoilers, does "ptomaine" poisoning come in?
>
> The answer is: Nowhere, really.
>
> For many generations—starting in 1870, when the term first came into use, on up until fairly recently—"ptomaine" was regarded as a substance that, in its own right, was responsible for most cases of food poisoning. Now it is known that many potent toxins are built up by specific micro-organisms, and are not the sole product that results from putrefaction and used to be called "ptomaine."

The transmittable bacteria that cause "staph" poisoning, the *Staphlococcus aureus,* are responsible for the most common type of food-borne illness, the sort formerly attributed to "ptomaines." The prevalence of the poisoning is traced to the fact that most meats and dairy foods carry the bacterium but its presence is not known unless the foods are allowed to sit unrefrigerated at room temperature; it is specially widespread during the summer, when picnic food is spread out, and it is found in meats kept warm for serving to a crowd. The staph bacteria are halted in their tracks fairly easily at temperatures that kill Salmonellae. However, their toxin is destroyed only by many hours of boiling or 30 minutes at 240 F/116 C; the growth of the bacteria themselves is checked if the food is kept above 140 F/60 C or below 45 F/7 C.

Most dangerous of the bacteria is the tough *Clostridium botulinum,* which deserves a section of its own.

Botulism

The scientific books describe *C. botulinum* as a "soil-borne, mesophilic, spore-forming, anaerobic bacterium." Which, translated into everyday language, means that it is present in soil that is carried into our kitchens on raw foods, on implements, on clothing, on our hands—you name it. Next, it thrives best in the middle range of heat—beginning at about room temperature, 70 degrees Fahrenheit/21 Celsius, on up to 110 F/43 C. Next, it produces spores that are extremely durable: Whereas the bacterium is destroyed in a relatively short time at 212 F/100 C, the temperature of briskly boiling water at sea level, the *spores* are not destroyed unless they are subjected to at least 240 degrees F/116 C for a sustained length of time. And finally, the bacterium lives and grows in the *absence* of air (and also in a very moist environment; these combined conditions exist in a container of canned food).

This description does not mention the poison thrown off by the bacteria as they grow: the toxin is so powerful that one teaspoon of the pure substance could kill hundreds of thousands of people.

The grave illness caused by eating toxin present in preserved food is comparatively rare—rare in relation to the cases of "staph" or salmonellosis—but, unlike them, it is often fatal unless life-support care is given right away. The symptoms are blurred vision, slurred speech, inability to hold up the head, and eventual respiratory arrest unless the victim is given help to breathe until the body can reverse the progress of the illness with the aid of medication. Between 1899 and 1949 the case-fatality rate of food-borne botulism was 60 percent. Since then it has declined markedly and steadily, thanks to quicker diagnosis and great improvements in intensive care at the outset. The *case* rate took a brief upward spurt in the mid–'70's, however, because a whole generation of people went in for food preservation, especially home-canning, without having the information or equipment needed for a safe product.

The botulinum toxin can be destroyed by brisk boiling in an open vessel. This is why, throughout this book, we warn people to boil hard—for the time demanded by its density and acidity—any home-canned food *about which there is the slightest safety problem.*

C. botulinum is held inactive at freezing and comes into its own at room temperatures, as mentioned earlier. Type E, the comparatively rare food-borne strain that is found on sea- and freshwater seafoods, begins to grow at refrigeration temperatures.

As with all micro-organisms, a moisture content of below 35 percent directly inhibits its growth.

DEALING WITH THE SPOILERS

ENTER pH—THE ACIDITY FACTOR

The strength of the acid in any food determines to a great extent which of the spoilage micro-organisms can grow in each food. Therefore acidity is a built-in directive that tells us what temperatures are necessary to destroy these spoilers within it, and make it safe to eat. (Heat alone, not natural acidity, controls the action of enzymes.)

pH Ratings

This listing indicates in a general way the natural acid strength of common foods on the *pH* scale. Different varieties of the same food will have different ratings, of course, as will identical varieties grown under different conditions. The Food and Drug Administration now uses a *pH* rating of 4.6 as the dividing point that dictates the preserving techniques to use: most notably, which canning method is right. Thus foods rated 2.2 (some lemons) on up to 4.6 (virtually every tomato, but see Chapter 6) *PFB* calls *strong-acid*—inserting "strong" as a sharper workable distinction than merely "acid," the customary designation. Foods over 4.6 up to Neutral 7 are always specified as *low-acid*.

Lemons	2.2–2.8	Beets	4.9–5.8
Gooseberries	2.8–3.0	Squash	5.0–5.4
Plums	2.8–4.0	Beans, string, green, wax	5.0–6.0
Apples	2.9–3.7	Spinach	5.1–5.9
Grapefruit	3.0–3.7	Cabbage	5.2–5.4
Strawberries	3.0–3.9	Turnips	5.2–5.6
Oranges	3.0–4.0	Peppers, green, bell	5.3
Rhubarb	3.1–3.2	Sweet potatoes	5.3–5.6
Blackberries	3.2–4.0+	Asparagus	5.4–5.8
Cherries	3.2–4.2	Potatoes, white	5.4–6.0
Raspberries	2.8–3.6	Mushrooms	5.8–5.9
Blueberries	3.3–3.5	Peas	5.8–6.5
Sauerkraut	3.4–3.7	Tuna fish	5.9–6.1
Peaches	3.4–4.0+	Beans, Lima	6.0–6.3
Apricots	3.4–4.4+	Corn	6.0–6.8
Pears	3.6–4.4+	Meats	6.0–6.9
Pineapple	3.7	Salmon	6.1–6.3
Tomatoes	4.0+–4.6	Oysters	6.1–6.6
Pimientos	4.6–5.2	Milk, cow's	6.3–6.6
Pumpkin	4.8–5.2	Shrimp	6.8–7.0
Carrots	4.9–5.4	Hominy	6.8–8.0

Acid strength is measured on the *pH scale,* which starts with strongest acid at 1 and declines to strongest alkali at 14, with the Neutral point at 7, where the food is considered neither acid nor alkaline. The *pH* ratings appear to run backwards, since the larger the number, the less the acid, but it may help to think of the ratings as like sewing thread: Size 100 cotton thread is smaller (finer) than Size 60.

The term *"pH"* is an abbreviation in chemistry for "potential of hydrogen," traced by a sophisticated laboratory device. Crude indications can be made by litmus-like test papers gettable from supply houses like the Fisher company (see Chapter 25, "Where to Find things," under Chapter 17 listing).

THE IMPORTANCE OF SANITATION

Even though the spoilage micro-organisms in a food are rendered inactive by cold, they start functioning with a vengeance as soon as they warm up.

Or, adequately preheated food can be contaminated by airborne spores while it, or its unfilled container, stands around unprotected; and, unless it is cooled quickly or refrigerated, the new batch of spoilers can start growing— and growing fast. In this connection, it's interesting to trace back the notion that one must not put hot food in a refrigerator in order to cool it quickly. This idea is a holdover from the days of the wooden ice chest, which was kept cool by a big block of ice: Of course the hot food warmed the inside of the ice chest, and there was a long lag before the ice (or what was left of it) could reduce the internal temperature of the cabinet to a safe-holding coolness. With modern refrigerators, though, a container of warm food merely causes the thermostat to kick on, and the cooling machinery goes to work immediately.

Another good way to deal with the spoilers is simply to wash them off the food as carefully as possible, and to keep work surfaces and equipment sanitary at every stage in the procedure. Food scientists refer to the "bacterial load" in describing the almost staggering rate of increase in bacteria if the food is handled in an unsanitary manner or allowed to remain at the optimum growing temperature for the spoilers. The procedures described in this book have been established after years of research by food scientists, and naturally there is an allowance made for extra micro-organisms that must be destroyed. But in many cases the food would have to be processed almost beyond palatability if the bacterial load had been allowed to increase geometrically to an enormous extent; the alternative of course would be that the treatment was not intensified, so the food spoiled after all.

HOUSEHOLD DISINFECTANTS

Boiling water can destroy many organisms *if* it is indeed boiling and *if* it has long enough contact with a contaminated surface after it has dropped a hair below the boiling point. Cleaning work surfaces with boiling water is a cumbersome exercise, though; better to use a good household disinfectant. Which, for our money, is the liquid chlorine bleach on hand in most kitchens. An extremely strong solution of such bleach is 1 : 4, or 1 part bleach to each 4 parts water; this should do a virtually instantaneous job of destroying bacteria—the drawback is that if the water is hot the fumes are strong enough to be unpleasant, even dangerous in large amounts.

A good workable solution is ¼ cup chlorine bleach to each 4 cups of water, or 1 : 16 (1 part bleach to 16 parts water). Wipe this on the surfaces, let it sit for 5 minutes or so, wipe off with fresh water; dry.

Easiest of all is to have a clean piece of cotton toweling wrung out in hot water; hold it tight against the mouth of the bleach bottle and slosh some full-strength bleach against the cloth. Wipe the surfaces.

Chlorine dissipates after a while: when you can smell it in the air, it is dissipating. (The best way to rid big-city tap water of too much chlorine is merely to draw a pitcher/bottle of water and let it sit uncovered in the refrigerator for several hours.)

The carbolic-acid-based disinfectants, generally pine-scented, and always milky in solution, are likely to leave their flavor on surfaces.

HEAT + ACIDITY = CANNING SAFETY

Combining (1) the temperatures that control life and growth of spoilage micro-organisms with (2) the *pH* acidity factor of the foods that are particularly hospitable to certain spoilers, gives the conscientious home-canner this rule to go by: *It is safe to can strong-acid foods at 212 F/100 C (at sea level to 1000 feet) in a Boiling–Water Bath, but low-acid/nonacid foods must be canned at 240 F/116 C (again, at sea-level zone)—a temperature possible only in a Pressure Canner at 10 pounds' pressure—if they are to be safe.*

Processing times vary according to acidity and density of the food concerned. Adequate temperature and length of processing time are given in the specific instructions for individual foods.

3

THE CANNING METHODS

What is regarded as the world's first canning factory was opened near Paris in 1806 by one Nicolas Appert, who in 1810 won a government prize for his efforts to preserve food for the French army and navy during the Napoleonic wars. From its beginning, horrendous spoilage occurred—horrendous, that is, by modern standards. And why not, since Louis Pasteur didn't establish that bacteria were the cause of spoilage until the 1860's?

The first widespread method for canning at home was a simpler procedure than Appert's. It was called "open-kettle," whereby hot jars were filled to brimming with hot, fully cooked food, then the lids were clapped on, and a vacuum was expected to form an airtight seal, proof against contamination, as the contents cooled. In its youth open-kettle was used primarily for the home-canning of fruit, tomatoes (botanically a fruit) and vinegared things like pickles and relishes. Because of this generally observed limitation, the method continued to be sanctioned, but only for strong-acid foods, until World War II. By the mid-Forties, though, microbiologists and food scientists had started chipping away at its reputation for safety, and today jams, pickles and relishes are given a further boiling in the jars. This added treatment is a relatively short stay in a Boiling–Water Bath (q.v. shortly); without it, open-kettle is considered able to protect only cooked fruit jellies. Even so, the near-boiling jelly must be poured into sterilized jars and topped with a sterile covering in order to ensure safety from spoilers. In regions with poor storage conditions the extra boiling bath is recommended to increase shelf life of jellies *sealed without paraffin.*

Relevant Metric Conversions for Canning Methods

Full metric conversions, with the arithmetic for refining them, are given at the start of Chapter 17 ("Common Ingredients and How to Use Them"), but here follow some measurements, rounded off, most commonly used in this general discussion of canning. Soon in this chapter will come the subsection "Correcting for Altitude," with extremely important help for all householders who live *above* the sea-level designation, which means *over* 1000 feet/305 meters.

• • •

Temperatures @ sea-level zone (up to 1000 feet/305 meters): 145 F/63 C——165 F/74 C——170 F/77 C——180 F/82 C——190 F/88 C——200 F/93 C——212 F/100 C——220 F/104 C——228 F/109 C——240 F/116 C——250 F/121 C.

Volume: ½ cup = 125 mL—¾ cup = 200 mL——½ pint = 250 mL——1 pint = 500 mL——1 quart = 1 L——21 quarts = 20 L——33 quarts = 31 L.

Length: ¼ inch = 0.64 cm——½ inch = 1.27 cm——1 inch = 2.54 cm——2 inches = 5.1 cm——5 inches = 12.7 cm——9 inches = 22.9 cm.

The two methods for canning everything else at home are the *Boiling–Water Bath* and *Pressure–processing:* the first is for strong-acid foods; the latter, for low-acid ones. Together, these procedures make canning the means most often used in North America by householders preserving perishable foodstuffs.

For its effectiveness, canning relies on sterilization and the exclusion of air. Both these functions are accomplished by heat, which destroys the things in the food that cause spoilage or poisoning, and drives out air from the contents; thus is created a condition that will form the vacuum that seals the containers against outside contamination during storage.

How *much heat* depends on the acidity of each particular food we intend to can, as was discussed at some length in Chapter 2. In our kitchens this means that every carefully prepared food with a *pH* rating of 4.6 or below may be canned safely in a Boiling–Water Bath at 212 Fahrenheit/100 Celsius at the sea-level zone (which includes up to 1000 feet/305 meters; we'll deal with higher altitudes in a minute). Every carefully prepared food with a rating of higher than 4.6 *pH* must be processed in a Pressure Canner—which at sea level produces temperatures ranging from 1 degree hotter than the boiling point of water on up to 250 F/121 C, and beyond.

The *type of heat* is vitally important, because the ability to transfer heat varies between wet heat and dry heat. Illustration: Hold your hand in a steady, strong flow of steam from the spout of a teakettle for one minute, and it will be burned enough to blister badly; hold it in the dry air of an oven at the same temperature-reading for a minute and it will be pleasantly warmed. To carry the idea further, the 240 F/116 C steam in a Pressure Canner at 10 pounds *psi* (per square inch) at sea level has a much greater effect on the heat transfer process than does the atmosphere of an oven operating at 240 F/116 C.

• • **So Never Forget This:**   Only under *GREATER THAN ATMOSPHERIC PRESSURE* can you produce *wet heat that is hotter than the boiling point of water at your altitude.*

And you will need wet heat under pressure to reach deep enough inside a container of low-acid food to destroy the spoilers that can make it nasty, even dangerous, to eat.

If you remember this *Why,* you'll always be able to keep track of the *How* in canning food at home.

In their University of Minnesota *Extension Bulletin 413, Home Canning—Fruits, Vegetables, and Meats,* Isabel Wolf and Edmund Zottola cite both the rate of heat penetration and the acidity of the food (discussed in Chapter 2) as the criteria for determining the length of time needed to process food safely when it's canned at home.

HOW HEAT PENETRATES A CONTAINER OF FOOD

Heat from outside the jar or can comes through the wall of the container and moves deep into the contents either by *conduction,* i.e., by being passed from one particle of food to another particle next to it; or by *convection*—being carried, almost swirled, by currents within the container. Usually both types of heat are involved, of course in varying proportions, when adequate processing occurs.

CONDUCTION

In closely packed food, and with relatively little fluid, heat is passed from the surface of the container inward from top, bottom and sides, leaving a spot in the center as the last place that will heat. There is extra worry when the food is low in acid. Strained pumpkin and mashed winter squash are extreme examples of low-acid food that would process mainly by conducted heat—and in Chapter 7 *PFB* recommends NOT to try canning them at home. Reason: The

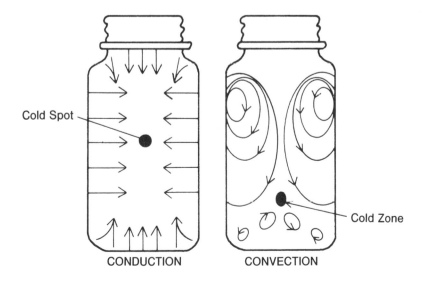

Cold Spot

Cold Zone

CONDUCTION   CONVECTION

outer areas of the pack would be sadly overcooked in order to make certain that the part in the "cold" area would be heated enough—and long enough—to be safe. Raw meat ground fine and packed without liquid offers the same sort of problem—but at least its own juices add some degree of convection to the processing.

CONVECTION

Cut vegetables with added liquid and fruits in syrup of their own lavish juice depend greatly on convection for safe processing. In such packs, the heat seems to spiral inward from the sides, the swirls growing larger as they circle down and back up and closer toward each other, until eventually they touch and expand down to deal with the cold zone; this cold area, in convection, has lain in the center of the bottom one-fourth of the container.

OTHER FACTORS IN HEAT PENETRATION

There are still more considerations to be dealt with before the *length of the heat* can be specified.

1) How big is the container—and is it slender, or squat? These are questions concerning procedure, not prettiness. Naturally a big jar or can will take longer to heat through than a smaller one; and a short, chunky shape may have a cold zone that takes longer to heat than does a tall, slim one with greater actual volume.

2) How densely or loosely is the food packed inside the container? The less liquid in the container, the more worry you have that the food will be processed safely. (Remember the strained pumpkin that's not for home-canning.) There is a limit, though, on the size of container that can be processed successfully at home, and we're coming to that soon. For now, just the warning that density also regulates how large a container you can use—as witness in Chapter 7 that Cream-style Corn is limited to pint jars or No. 2 cans, whereas Whole-kernel Corn (which has a good deal of free liquid) is O.K. canned in quarts and No. 2½ cans.

3) If you're canning meat or a combination/convenience food: is it as lean and free of fat as possible? Fat insulates against heat just as it does against cold, and the more fat there is in a food, the slower the penetration by any heat.

The temperatures and processing times demanded for each food—strong-acid or low-acid, densely textured, loosely or firmly packed, in large containers or small—are given in the individual instructions contained in Chapters 5 through 10.

Basic Equipment for Home–Canning

Some specialized canning equipment is essential for turning out *safe* and attractive products in return for your efforts, and it includes large canners for processing filled containers, and the containers (with their fittings), which are made to withstand the required heat treatments, and to seal well. These few special items—and their *Why's*—are described fully in the following pages; for all the rest, your regular kitchen utensils will be adequate.

A deep Water–Bath Canner for processing strong-acid foods

A steam Pressure Canner for processing low-acid foods: with gauge(s) of tested accuracy

6- to 8-quart enameled or stainless-steel kettle for precooking or blanching foods to be canned

Jars or "tin" cans in prime condition, with lids/sealers/gaskets ditto

Sealing machine (hand-operated), if you're using cans

Alarm clock, to time processing longer than 1 hour—

   plus a minute-timer with warning bell (more accurate than an alarm clock and better for processing less than 1 hour)—

   plus a clock with a sweep second-hand (if you go in for quite brief 15-psi processing)

Pencil-shaped glass food thermometer (you'll need it for meats, poultry and seafoods in jars, and for all foods in cans)

Shallow pans (dishpans will do)

Wire basket or cheesecloth to hold foods for blanching

Ladle or dipper

Perforated ladle or long-handled slotted spoon, for removing food from its precooking kettle

Wide-mouth funnel for filling jars

Jar-lifter

Food mill, for puréeing (or a blender; a food processor is ultimate luxury)

Sieve or strainer

Colander, for draining

Large measuring cups, and measuring spoons

Muslin bag, for straining juices

Plenty of clean, dry potholders, dish cloths and towels

Long-handled fork

Household scales

Large trays

• SHOPPING NOTE: If you're looking for a new cookstove and like the idea of a double-oven range whose upper oven partially overhangs the cooking-top, check the clearance above the burners before you buy. Some models don't have room for a really big double-boiler—much less a canner tall enough to process quart jars on the back *or* front burners.

Community Canning Kitchens

In the middle of the 1970's, which saw so great a renaissance in home canning, two community canning kitchens were set up within an hour's drive from *PFB*'s bailiwick, and neither is in existence in 1982. Instead, one has combined its efforts with those of a center farther upstate, and there its operators are developing several canned specialties for sale within the state; the other lacked the consistent volume of brought-in produce to make the operation feasible, and folded. However, scarcities or brutally high food prices—and they often go together—have always stimulated interest in the community canning kitchen, just as they inspire the householder to grow his own produce or to join his neighbors in a community garden project, as witness the co-operative ventures during the Great Depression and the Victory gardens and kitchens of World War II.

FEASIBILITY TEST

A workable, equable neighborhood garden requires thoughtful co-operation to be a success, and a safe and truly thrifty community canning kitchen demands even more in the way of clearheaded dedication from the people involved. Therefore several questions must be answered with a resounding Yes before any group undertakes to start one up.

Food supply. Is there a large enough amount of fresh, in-season food coming into your town or county to make the kitchen worth its cost in time, effort and money?

Beneficiaries. Are there enough people benefiting to make it worth while?

Location and space. Because the type of project we're talking about is a lot more sophisticated than the occasional work bee in one's home, is there available a convenient institutional-size kitchen where the equipment can be set up and used regularly? (A school that prepares hot lunches, say, or a well-equipped grange hall or church.) And is there plenty of good running water, and enough space for counters and work tables?

Stove. Will the stove-top accommodate two 2-to-2½ feet-in-diameter processing vats (two at least, to avoid waiting around between batches)? Can the stove's heat be regulated easily to ensure correct processing at every stage?

• • **Equipment for community canning kitchens** is gettable from two main sources. One is the Ball Food Preservation System, which uses glass canning jars, and was originated by the Ball Corporation of Muncie, Indiana, several generations ago. By 1980 the system had been donated by the parent company to the World Ministry of Brethren Churches. Information about procedures and costs may be obtained from Brethren Service Center, 500 Main Street, Box 188, New Windsor, Maryland 21776. The director of information went from Ball to the Center with the system he had been instrumental in developing.

The other organization outfits community canning kitchens *with "tin" cans* and the hardware for sealing and processing them. Inquire of Dixie Canner Equipment

Company, P.O. Box 1348, Athens, Georgia 30603. The information department for the Community Food Processing Centers was helpful with catalogs, specifications and requirements for serving large or small groups.

THE PEOPLE TO WORK IT

A well-trained leader is essential if the kitchen is to turn out *safe* canned products in a consistently smooth, economical manner. This person must have a number of competencies: (1) thorough grounding in the bacteriology of food spoilage—either from contaminants in food itself, or in the course of handling or processing it; (2) experience in preparing and processing large batches of food, and in managing large-scale equipment; and (3) the ability to organize the work-flow, ranging from the preparation of raw materials to packing to processing to cooling to storage (and including cleaning all equipment and work surfaces at the end of each session).

Next on the list of key personnel is *one qualified, regular operator per shift* to handle the actual processing—and in addition to the duties of timing and temperature control, this "brewmaster" should be strong enough to heft the vats and remove their contents to cooling tubs of water if cans are used, or to counters for jars.

A team to examine and prepare containers for filling.

A team whose duties are broken down to *sorting, paring/cutting* and *packing the food* in containers.

A clean-up team.

And of course a clerk-of-the-works to *check in supplies, keep records, and distribute allotments of canned food.*

CORRECTING FOR ALTITUDE

Acidity and heat penetration dictate how long a food must be processed when it is being canned at home. With these factors in mind we choose the Boiling–Water Bath or Pressure–processing, and——

And a lot of us run smack into the problem of Altitude.

At a guess, more North Americans who preserve food in some manner live below 1000 feet/305 meters—in the sea-level zone—than live higher. But there remain a great many householders who, to ensure that their home-canned goods are safe, must compensate for the perceptible *decrease* in atmospheric pressure as the altitude *increases.* It's one thing to have a roast pork unhappily undercooked and yet dry; it's another thing to court food poisoning in a cannerful of green beans.

Before we go any further, we must consider Altitude.

• • WE HAVE TO JUMP THE GUN: Detailed descriptions of the methods and equipment for the Boiling–Water Bath (strong-acid food, at 212 F/100 C in the sea-level zone) and for Pressure–processing (low-acid food at higher than sea-level boiling temperature on up to 250 F/121 C, and hotter) won't come for a while, but we must mention them in context with Altitude in this section. You'll see why.

Also, at the end of this major section will be thumbnail *Why's* and *How's* for other procedures at high altitudes—jelly-making, baking, roasting, etc. They're not that germane to Canning, but they are part of Altitude. Best to have them gathered under this heading, with cross-references sprinkled throughout the rest of the book as needed, than the other way round.

BOILING: WHAT IS IT?

Boiling is the process by which a liquid (for our purposes here the liquid is water) becomes a vapor, and this conversion is produced by heat. We put water into a pot, and put the pot over a source of heat, and soon the water boils. In boiling, bubbles of vapor are created at the bottom of the vessel near the heat; and they rise to the surface and break and waft into the air as steam, which is the gaseous form of water. As they rise, the bubbles agitate the water: gently as in a simmer, or violently as in a full boil.

When water is boiling—and by this we mean a thrashing, rolling boil—it looks the same at different altitudes *but it is not boiling at the same temperature.* The temperature is different because the blanket of air around us, called atmospheric pressure, is lighter when we live higher; and *the lighter the air the lower the boiling point of water.* At sea level our blanket of air weighs 14.7 pounds per square inch (psi), but at 10,000 feet/3048 meters the atmospheric pressure is only 10.1 psi; this difference of 4.6 psi will be the basis for a looks-dandy-on-paper tabulation that we think is too persnickety to follow with the usual household equipment.

However, back to boiling. Water at sea level, and for simplicity's sake up to 1000 ft/305 m, boils at 212 F/100 C; at 5000 ft/1524 m, boiling point is rounded to 203 F/95 C; and at 10,000 ft/3048 m, water boils at a mere 194 F/90 C. Right away you see that this makes it harder for us to apply a heat treatment that will deal with bad micro-organisms in the food we intend to can. Say that *Bacterium xyz* is destroyed if the container of strong-acid food (*pH* of 4.6 or lower) is held at 212 F/100 C for 35 minutes—but we live above the sea-level zone. What do we do?

We add processing *time.* Up to a feasible, sensible point, that is.

What if the food is low-acid (*pH* higher than 4.6) and of course we use a

Pressure Canner to achieve the heat needed to destroy *Clostridium botulinum* spores, but we live well up in the mountains?

We add *Pressure.*

Metric Equivalents for Altitude and Water's Boiling Point			
ALTITUDE FEET/METERS	WATER BOILS FAHRENHEIT/CELSIUS	ALTITUDE FEET/METERS	WATER BOILS FAHRENHEIT/CELSIUS
Sea Level: 0+/0+	212.0/100		
1000/305	210.0/98.9	5000/1524	202.6/94.8
1500/457	209.1/98.4	5500/1676	201.7/94.3
2000/610	208.2/97.9	6000/1829	200.7/93.7
2500/762	207.1/97.3	6500/1982	199.8/93.2
3000/914	206.2/96.8	7000/2134	198.7/92.6
3500/1067	205.3/96.3	7500/2286	198.0/92.2
4000/1219	204.4/95.8	8000/2438	196.9/91.6
4500/1372	203.4/95.2	10,000/3048	194.0/90.0

Time out for "Simmer" and "Pasteurize"

There's no easy way to put these below-boiling terms later, so this interruption does get them recorded for future reference, and indexing.

The descriptions of *simmer* range from the French cook's "making the pot smile" on up to the one we mean when we say to simmer: which is 185 to possibly 200 F/85 to 93 C at sea level. In this range small bubbles rise gently from the bottom of the pot, and the surface merely quivers, instead of dancing as in the full boil at 212 F/100 C.

We mention this now because we use a *Hot*-Water Bath in processing a number of canned fruit juices. The individual instructions specify the simmer temperature needed—most often it's 190 F/88 C—but again this is at sea-level, so at higher altitudes increase H–W Bath processing time for such foods.

Pasteurization is the *partial* sterilization of food, and it was devised in the nineteenth century by Louis Pasteur as a means of controlling the fermentation of wine. As applied to milk, one method raises the temperature to 142 to 145 F/61 to 63 C, holds it there for 30 minutes, then quickly reduces the temperature to well below 50 F/10 C, where is is held for storage. The other way—called the "flash" method and used commercially by dairies—raises the temperature to 160 to 165 F/71 to 74 C for a mere 15 seconds, followed by rapid cooling to well below 50 F/10 C.

The longer time at the lower temperature range is the method given in the instruction for pasteurizing milk in Chapter 23 because we think it is less hair-trigger, and therefore less chancy, for the average homemaker to use for achieving the result desired.

In addition we use the term *pasteurizing* in connection with the *Hot*–Water Bath for processing canned fruit juices (Chapter 5); and also in Chapter 21 in recommending a "finishing" treatment by dry heat at 175 F/80 C for foods dried in open-air/sun.

Which Answer for Altitude?

We'll start with the compensations-table that *PFB* (which does its canning at around 2400 ft/c. 732 m) finds hard to apply; then go to what leading makers say about increasing pressure; and add a few words of advice given us by some of the most practical people we know—Extension home economists working among their neighbors in the high country of the Rockies.

Then it's over to your good sense, and what your County Agent can tell you.

A Not-Very-Helpful Table of Altitude Adjustments

The following recommendations are offered in most manuals for canning food at home. In the list of equipment coming later we suggest a clock with a sweep second-hand if you hope to go in for almost hair-trigger processing.

For the B–W Bath you *add minutes* to processing time—how many, depends on whether the sea-level time required is *20 minutes or less,* or *more than 20 minutes.* For Pressure–processing you *add pounds*—but not varying the progression even though the sea-level pressure required is 5 or 10 (used most often) or 15 pounds. Thus:

The Marginally Helpful Adjustment Table

In B–W Bath Add:		At These Altitudes:		In Pressure Canner Raise Pounds To:		
IF 20 MINS OR LESS	IF OVER 20 MINS	FEET	METERS	IF 5 LBS	IF 10 LBS	IF 15 LBS
1 min	2 mins	1000	305	5½ lbs	10½ lbs	15½ lbs
2 mins	4 mins	2000	610	6 lbs	11 lbs	16 lbs
3 mins	6 mins	3000	914	6½ lbs	11½ lbs	16½ lbs
4 mins	8 mins	4000	1219	7 lbs	12 lbs	17 lbs
5 mins	10 mins	5000	1524	7½ lbs	12½ lbs	17½ lbs
6 mins	12 mins	6000	1829	8 lbs	13 lbs	18 lbs
7 mins	14 mins	7000	2134	8½ lbs	13½ lbs	18½ lbs
8 mins	16 mins	8000	2438	9 lbs	14 lbs	19 lbs
9 mins	18 mins	9000	2743	9½ lbs	14½ lbs	19½ lbs
10 mins	20 mins	10,000	3048	10 lbs	15 lbs	20 lbs

The drawbacks to using these adjustments is that, though our kitchens are well enough equipped, we can't guarantee to add *accurately* 1 minute more to our Boiling–Water Bath time; and with our Pressure Canners we certainly can't make ½-pound increments for every 1000 feet above the sea-level zone we happen to be canning in. (This is where you remember that the difference between the psi around sea level is *c.* 4.5 higher than at 10,000 ft/3048 m, with the implied adjustment being to add ½ pound for each additional 1000 ft/305 m in altitude.)

PFB's dial gauges are no more or less refined than those of other householders; we do keep them checked, and replace them rather than fiddle with mental calibrations to offset the fact that they register significantly off from the actual internal pressure. Our wristwatches have sweep hands and the cookie-timers work and we have a choice of rather well-managed heat sources: electric or gas or wood-burning ranges. We try hard to follow directions, even our own.

There just happens to be a world of difference between the testing laboratory and an everyday kitchen.

IMPORTANT NOTES FOR *PFB* FROM MAKERS OF PRESSURE CANNERS

Several times we had seen written that the makers of Pressure Canners will modify their standard 5–10–15 psi (pounds per square inch) weighted gauges to accommodate householders whose high altitudes do not fall neatly into these three expectable psi slots. So *PFB* called the home economics/consumer service officers at the U.S.A.'s two largest manufacturers of Pressure Canners for home use: National Presto Industries, Inc., and Mirro Corporation (for their addresses see Chapter 25 under the subsection listing for this Chapter 3). Only their comments that apply to altitude canning in general are clumped here; their other valuable tips are cited where the information is most relevant to the point being discussed.

First: Both makers say that they DO NOT make dead-weight gauges other than in the regular 5–10–15 psi controls for home Pressure Canners. Parenthetically, we like their term "dead-weight gauge" better than the usual "weighted gauge": more precise.

Second: It is possible to get large Pressure Canners that have both a dead-weight *and* a dial gauge—a combination that deals well with high-altitude canning. We bought our big Presto with its two gauges from wonderful McGuckin's in mile-high Boulder, Colorado.

Third: Each Pressure Canner has an operating manual that describes how its dead-weight/weighted gauge indicates when the chosen operating pressure has been reached. Meanwhile, for the record: Mirro's dead-weight gauge *jiggles* and dances; Presto's *rocks.*

15–Pound Canning at More Than a Mile

The following abbreviated table is taken from the National Presto Industries, Inc., pamphlet AD78–3449B (for more of its content and the address to write for it, see Chapter 25 under the listing for this chapter). We offer these excerpts because this handling at 15 psi at *under* 10,000 ft/3048 m not only was developed by food scientists in kitchen-laboratory conditions, but also is the clearheaded approach used by Extension Service home economists working out in the field with householders from a wide variety of cultural, climatic and economic backgrounds.

Occasionally, a food may be overprocessed—color on the drab side, texture perhaps a bit soft. However, you can be much more certain that you will have food safety.

Just follow the commonsensical procedures outlined in detail soon, and repeated with the handling of each type of food in its own chapter.

	IN LARGE PRESSURE CANNERS (12–QT OR MORE) AT 15 PSI		
		BETWEEN	
	ALTITUDE	**3000 FT/914 M**	**ALTITUDE**
	UNDER	**AND**	**OVER**
	3000FT/914 M	**7000 FT/2134 M**	**7000 FT/2134 M**
FOOD	MINUTES	MINUTES	MINUTES
Asparagus	15	25	35
Beans, shell	30	60	85
Beans, snap	15	30	45
Beets, sliced	15	30	45
Carrots	15	30	45
Corn, whole-kernel	50	90	135
Greens, all kinds	35	65	95
Mushrooms (½-pt)	20	40	60
Okra	15	30	45
Peas, green	30	60	85
Squash, cubed	20	40	60
Meat cut/precooked	50	90	135
Game meat	50	90	135
Poultry with bone	30	60	85

The Consumer Center of Mirro Corporation has a simpler rule-of-thumb for altitude correction for Pressure Canners that varies slightly from the recent "Marginally Helpful Table," and is simply this: Above 2000 ft/610 m, if the procedure says to Pressure–process at 5 psi, process *at 10 psi* for the specified time. If the procedure says 10 psi, process *at 15 psi* for the specified time. If the procedure specifies 15 psi, increase the Pressure–processing time *slightly* (italics ours).

Mrs. Betty Wenstadt of Presto agreed with her colleague at Mirro. Both experts stressed that low-acid food *may NOT be canned in a pressure saucepan* at altitudes over 3000 ft/914 m. Evaporation increases greatly at higher altitudes, and these small cookers cannot hold enough water to allow for the long processing needed for high-protein foods.

Notes from "the Field"

Pat Kendall of Colorado State University, Fort Collins, and Roberta Rios of Santa Fe County Extension Service, New Mexico, helped *PFB* to get a cross-bearing on practical ways to deal with high altitudes. Both live and work at more than a mile high on the eastern slopes of the Rockies.

ACROSS-THE-BOARD 15 PSI

Minnesota's *Bulletin 413, Home Canning: Fruits, Vegetables, and Meats* (Revised 1980) by Isabel Wolf and Edmund Zottola gives Pressure–processing times for fruits at 5 psi and for low-acid foods at 15 psi, even though research was done in the sea-level zone. (See Chapter 25 for where to write for it, and Chapters 5 through 8.)

Roberta Rios, whose territory of Santa Fe averages better than 7000 ft/2134 m above the sea, says that she advises many of her householders and residents of nearby pueblos to go directly to Pressure–processing at 15 psi, bypassing the Boiling–Water Bath as being far too tedious to achieve the needed result.

PFB opts for 15 psi for altitudes 3500 ft/1067 m and more: *and for the same processing time as is given for the individual foods at 10 psi (240 F/116 C).* Exception: above 8000 ft/2438 m, where your home economics County Agent will advise the amount of processing time to add.

SUMMARIZING: WAYS TO DEAL WITH ALTITUDE

Because water boils at lower temperatures the higher we go above sea level—and therefore is less effective as a destroyer of micro-organisms with every increase in altitude—we should:

1) Add processing time in a Boiling–Water Bath as the USDA advises (given recently in this section), *but*—and this recommendation is our own, based on interview material—*only up to 2500 ft/762 m.* There and higher, go to Pressure–processing. Updated instructions for using your Pressure Canner will help here; otherwise you could apply the rules-of-thumb in "Important Notes ... from Makers, etc.," earlier. *PFB* arrived at this opinion after talking with experts whose jobs are to handle everyday problems posed by everyday people. Research scientists have our wholehearted respect; our feeling for workers out in the field comes from the difference between "making do" as opposed to what's called in the deep country "having everything to do *with*."

2) Remember that gas (steam) expands more at higher altitudes, so we allow extra room for it inside our canning jars. This is called headroom, and it's discussed in "General Steps in Canning" later on. If we did not increase headroom, the contents of the jars would erupt out between the lid and the sealing rim. Bad business.

3) The virtues and drawbacks of dial gauges compared with dead-weight/weighted gauges are matters for later discussion. But unless you'd bet your life on the accuracy of your dial—and maybe you are, at that—it's safer and easier to go along with the 5–10–15 psi of the dead-weight gauge at high altitudes.

Other Bothers with Altitude

Jelly-making and cooking syrups for candy and cake frosting are affected by lowered boiling points as you go higher. What happens is, that water in the juice/syrup evaporates faster as the altitude increases. So if you are counting on the jelly stage being reached at 8 F/4.4 C above the boiling point of water at sea level—or a reading of 220 F/104. 4 C—you'd have some mighty stiff jelly. To deal with this, Pat Kendall says to lower the final cooking temperature by around 2 F/1.1 C for each 1000 ft/305 m in elevation. Quickly from Fahrenheit, then, the temperature would be 218 at 2000 feet, 216 at 3000, 214 at 4000, and so on.

Maybe the sheeting test (Chapter 18, "Jellies, Jams and Other Sweet Things") is your best bet.

Just plain boiling food to cook it will take longer—and the pot might be in danger of going dry: again, the problems are lower boiling points plus greater evaporation. These factors also must be considered in cooking by steaming.

Blanching before freezing or drying. Hard to make an across-the-board recommendation here, because so much depends on the food (certainly all vegetables) being treated—age, tenderness, cut size. Leaf vegetables are usually better boiled than steamed, because they tend to mat in the steam basket, but can roll around if gathered loosely in cheesecloth and popped into water at a thrashing boil. For steam-blanching above 2000 ft/610 m, for every additional 1000 ft/305 m add 1 minute to the specified sea-level-zone time; boiling, add 30 seconds for the same increases in altitude.

Baking: Yeast-bread doughs rise very quickly, thus allowing less time for flavor to develop; Professor Kendall suggests letting yeast-leavened mixtures rise twice. The gases from baking powder also expand more, as does the trapped air in beaten egg whites.

Roasting at high altitudes can result in an expensive chunk of meat's being dry outside and woefully underdone inside.

Deep-frying: Temperature of the fat must be reduced the higher you go, she says. Above 3000 ft/914 m, temperature of the fat could be lowered 3 F/1.7 C for each added 1000 ft/305 m as a way to avoid outsides too dark and insides not fully cooked.

Using a double-boiler can be tricky because water boils at so much lower a temperature that many starchy thickeners are not activated to do their job. Better, Pat Kendall says, to use a fine, heavy, enameled saucepan over well-managed direct heat.

THE BOILING–WATER BATH

The Boiling–Water Bath has limitations: It is suitable *only for canning strong-acid foods*—vinegared things, and fruits, which include tomatoes—and for "finishing" pickles, relishes, etc., and cooked sweet fruit garnishes like jams on through butters to conserves. With such foods, the B–W Bath does these things *if it is used correctly:*

- In raw or blanched (just partly precooked) strong-acid foods, it destroys yeast and molds and the bacteria that cannot live at the temperatures reached in the middle of the containers of food. Thus it deals with the food, as well as all inner parts of the containers that could have got contaminated by airborne spoilers while waiting to be filled and capped.
- Drives out the air naturally present in the tissues of the foods and in the canning liquid (air bubbles trapped in the container as it was filled are removed before capping.) Air can prevent a perfect seal and permit spoilage.
- Creates a vacuum that enables the *jars to seal themselves.* (As we'll see, *cans* are sealed by hand after the air in the food's tissues and in the added liquid is exhausted; then they go in the B–W Bath, which kills organisms in the contents.)

The B–W Bath Canner

People with long memories recall the copper washboiler on the wood stove in the summer kitchen. These lovely vessels are collectors' items now; today we buy our B–W Bath canner from the housewares sections of hardware, farm supply or department stores.

It is round, usually made of heavy enameled ware (also called "granite" ware)—and this finish is a blessing because it allows us to use the canner for cooking or treating loose foods that are acid or heavily salted. Stainless steel is good too, but it's more expensive; aluminum, while fine for processing filled containers, will react with acid or salt in loose food.

It has a cover.

It has a rack to hold containers off the bottom of the kettle, thus letting boiling water circulate under them as they process. The large-size canners often have a second rack that's supposed to hold a second tier of containers. Sometimes the racks are like shallow baskets with folding handles that let you lift out bodily the entire batch of containers you have processed.

There are many B–W Bath canners offered for sale, and it should be easy to get one that's right—but often it isn't.

It's Got to Be Deep Enough

The most popular sizes are billed as 21-quart and 33-quart, and *PFB* uses both of them. These capacities actually mean loose contents; which is fair enough, since the labels also say, of the respective sizes, "7-jar rack" and "9-jar rack."

But this 7-jar/9-jar bit is *not* fair, because the reasonable inference is that they hold 7 pints or quarts, or 9 pints or quarts, and *even the 33-quart one is not deep enough to process quart jars correctly*—meaning, for our money, *safely.* When you're in a store looking at canners, and if the salesperson has enough experience with canning to point out that a particular kettle is too shallow for certain jars, pay attention—and ignore what the manufacturer's label implies.

Here's the arithmetic. Starting at the bottom of the 33-quart canner, you should have ¾ to 1 inch between the holding rack and the bottom of the kettle—call it 1 inch for simplicity. Then you must have between 1 and 2 inches of boiling water covering the tops of your containers: 2 is better, so call it 2. Now you have 3 inches accounted for.

Then you must have a *minimum* of 1 more inch of "boiling room" between the bubbling surface of the water and the rim of the kettle. If you don't, the briskly boiling water will keep slopping out onto your stove-top and drenching the well of your heating element (making a mess even if it doesn't extinguish a gas flame, and offering a temptation to reduce your boil to a polite, and inadequate, simmer). Be cagey and remember that the close-fitting cover on your canner will increase its tendency to slop over: allow 1½ inches for headroom to boil in. Now you have 4½ inches—and your containers haven't even gone in yet.

The height of a quart jar (we'll use jars here, as the manufacturer and the great majority of home-canners do) is 7 inches if it's a modern mason with a 2-piece screwband lid, or 7½ inches if it's the old bailed type with a domed glass lid.

Add 4½ inches and 7 to 7½ inches and you get 11½ to 12 inches.

But the inside depth of our 33-quart Boiling–Water Bath canner is only a scant 10 inches. Therefore—though it's O.K. for pints, which are 5 to 5½ inches tall, and of course for the even shorter ½-pint jars—*we cannot use it for processing quart jars.*

There are canners around, but you have to insist first on depth when you're looking for a B–W Bath kettle. Know the height of your jars, add 4½ to 5 inches, and measure the height of every canner you see. Stick to your guns, and you'll find the one that will do the job right.

Other B–W Bath Canner Possibilities

The question readers asked *PFB* most often during its first decade was where to get a B–W Bath canner that was deep enough (next most-frequent query: where to find low-methoxyl pectin for making special jelly).

A leading maker of the big spotted-enamel kettles just mentioned has turned to making what is called an "atmospheric steam canner"—and it's discussed in detail in Chapter 4, "On Guard!" Gist of the comments there is that the principle is O.K., but that the operating directions with any processor of this type on the market early in 1982 do not make such canners live up to their billing. There is an aluminum version, more fragile; it has the same sort of directions for use that have been criticized by food scientists and nutritionists across the country. Keep nagging, though: someone out there is bound to hear you.

You can always sail right on past the inadequate B–W Bath canners and buy a stockpot. The maker of graniteware kettles noted above has come out with a stockpot that is taller and more slender and has a lid, and there's no reason why this would not work well as a canner. There is a heavy-duty aluminum stockpot that would do a good job for safe processing of strong-acid foods; it could not double as a preserving kettle for brined or vinegared things because, being aluminum, the metal would react with the acid. Most glorious of all are the stainless-steel stockpots. They're relatively expensive, but they do come in many sizes; and they are impervious to acid, as enamelware is. See Chapter 25 for where to write or what to ask for.

A third idea is to use a Pressure Canner for a B–W Bath. Put in enough water to come up to the shoulders of the jars you'll process; start the water heating. Put in the filled jars, taking care lest they touch the sides or each other; of course they're on a rack that holds them off the bottom of the pot. Then *lay* the

The cutaway drawing shows the room needed above jar tops for correct processing in a Boiling–Water Bath; the canner at right is too shallow for the quart jar (even though it was sold as O.K. for quarts): There's only 1 inch between jar top and kettle rim. At left below, jars are wedged tight together and boiling water can't circulate around them. Guy Brunton's sturdy canner-racks are made of hardware cloth stapled to ¾- x-¾-inch strips of untreated softwood—untreated because the paint, etc., can cook off and gum up the containers of food and the inside of the canner.

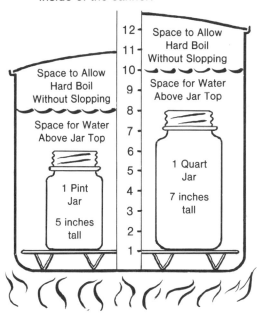

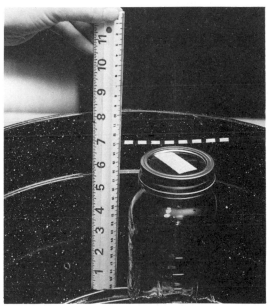

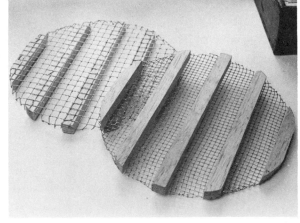

heavy lid on the sealing rim of the canner, but *do not lock it.* Leave the vent open. (These terms come up in the complete descriptions of the anatomy and operation of the Pressure Canner soon; meanwhile this much of them belongs here because we're talking about B–W Baths, not Pressure–processing.) After a strong flow of escaping steam is established, start timing as for the B–W Bath recommended for the strong-acid food you are treating.

If you lock the lid, you will get 1 to 1½ pounds of pressure, even with the vent open. At *PFB*'s altitude, this is good. We use it only to ensure that our B–W Bath is hot enough; *it's not any alternative to correct Pressure–processing.*

How to Use the B–W Bath

Put the canner on the stove and fill it halfway with water; put a rack in the bottom; turn on the heat. If the food you're canning takes relatively little time to prepare for packing in the containers, start heating a large teakettle of extra water now too.

Prepare the food for canning according to the individual instructions, packing it in clean, scalded containers and putting on lids as directed.

Jars of *raw* (cold) food *must not be put in boiling water,* lest they crack; you may need to add cool water to the canner. However, if the food in the jars is very hot, the filled jars may go into boiling water without fear of breakage. Cans will always be hot, because they've just been exhausted.

Process in each load only *one type of food,* in *one size of container.*

Use your jar-lifter to lower jars/cans into the hot water. Place them away

Use these to lift hot jars from canners. Left to right below: usual small kitchen tongs, big barbecue tongs (their extreme tips bent slightly inward to ensure that they catch under the flange of the jar's neck); below, a patented gadget that pulls snug with the weight of the jar, then a fine old-style lifter that's again being made, now with plastic-coated wire to protect boiling-hot jars; and finally a desperation lifter made from a very stout coathanger. At right, another view shows the coathanger bent so it will grab under the jar's flange; just hold it upright over the jar, squeezing a wire loop "handle" tight in each hand to get enough purchase—and lift.

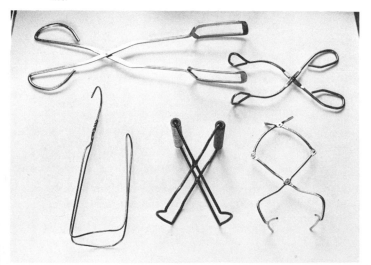

from the sides of the canner and about 1 inch apart, so the boiling water will be able to circulate freely around them. Don't jam them in or even let them touch: jars might break as they expand ever so slightly while processing. If your batch is too small to make a full canner-load, submerge open mayonnaise jars, or whatever, in the empty spaces to keep your capped jars of food from shifting around as they boil.

If your canner is tall enough to let you process two tiers of small jars/cans at a time, use a wire cake-cooling rack—or one of Guy Brunton's—to hold the upper layer of containers. Ensure adequate circulation by staggering them as you do when baking on several racks in your oven.

Pour enough more hot water around the jars/cans to bring the level 2 inches above the tops of all containers; be careful not to dump boiling water smack on top of jars, particularly if their contents are cool.

WHAT TO DO ABOUT RACKS

The racks that come in store-bought B–W Bath kettles can be infuriating. Made of heavy-gauge wire, they may resemble a flimsy wagon wheel or they look like the skeleton of a basket; at any rate the "spokes" or dividers are so wide apart that even pint jars sometimes fall between them, instead of resting on them. Some lack support strong enough to hold containers high enough off the bottom of the canner. Many actually cause jars to teeter and topple—and you have broken glass to contend with.

So buy several large round cake-cooling racks. Their wire is more fragile, but it's closely crisscrossed; and for support toward the middle, cluster on the bottom of the kettle five or six screwbands that have become slightly rusted or bent, and therefore aren't fit to use on jar lids. Measure the bottom diameter of your B–W Bath canner (not the top, which usually is about an inch larger), and choose your racks accordingly: ½ inch of leeway all around is about right.

Our favorites are the racks made for us by Guy Brunton, who cut ¾-x-¾-inch softwood in graduated lengths, the longest being 1 inch shorter than the bottom diameter of the canner. He laid them parallel a couple of inches apart, the longest in the center and the outer ones diminishing in size, and on them he staple-gunned a larger circle of ½-inch or ¼-inch hardware cloth, which he bent down to make a smooth finish around the edge. Guy predicted that the racks were likely to warp after a while, being made with untreated softwood scraps instead of the harder-to-get poplar or butternut. The weight of the filled jars held them flat for some time, though; after that, we whomped the replacements together ourselves.

Hot–Water Bath (Pasteurization)

We have bent over backwards in referring to the *Boiling-*Water Bath because it's necessary to distinguish clearly between the B–W—which maintains a real 212 F/100 C boil at sea-level—and the *simmering* Hot–Water version, which is a form of pasteurizing.

The Hot–Water Bath is recommended *only for certain sweet, acid fruit juices.* Despite the casual swapping of these terms in some older manuals, the processes themselves are not interchangeable.

THE *WHY* OF PRESSURE CANNING

Even in the sea-level zone, every plain vegetable except tomatoes (q.v.), every meat, every seafood that is canned at home—and every mixture containing these—MUST BE CANNED IN A PRESSURE CANNER.
Or put it this way:
Pressure Canning is the ONLY process that is able to destroy the tough spores of bacteria like *Clostridium botulinum* which can grow and produce deadly poison in jars or cans of *any* low-acid food.
Or this way:
Dangerous spoilers can live through even a day-long Boiling–Water Bath at 212 F/100 C in containers of low-acid food with a natural acidity rating of a *pH* higher than 4.6, but *they are killed by the higher temperatures reached only in a Pressure Canner.*

Please look at the *pH* ratings of selected foods and the section called "Dealing with the Spoilers" in Chapter 2.
And before we talk about how to use a Pressure Canner, we'll make three points:

1. The Pressure Canner we're talking about is not to be confused with a *steamer*—either the old-style arrangement that swirled steam at Zero pounds/212 F/100 C around containers of food, or today's compartmented kettles for cooking clams or lobsters, or the "atmospheric canner" described in Chapter 4.
2. The Pressure Canner we're talking about is an honest-to-goodness, regular, conventional *big* Pressure *Canner*—not the 4–, 6– or 8–quart pressure saucepan that you may already use for cooking loose food. *PFB* is leery of processing any containers of low-acid food in such a saucepan. (It's also a worry that manufacturers, and even some food specialists, keep using the term "pressure *cooker*" for both the Canner and the saucepan—adding to the chances for a slip-up.) We're distrustful because:

   Being so much smaller, the *saucepans'* heating-up and cooling-down periods are a good deal shorter than those of the Pressure Canners. These heating/cooling spans are factors in over-all processing under pressure, and the differences must be reconciled if the product is to be safe.
   Gauges, vents and gaskets of *saucepans* may not be checked as carefully or often, as the sensible householder will do with a Pressure Canner during the season. Less than perfect operation while cooking a Swiss steak is no big deal, but a hitch during pressure-canning could mean food poisoning when the contents of the containers are eaten several months later.
   Many a cook has cooled a pressure *saucepan* quickly in order to inspect

the progress of loose food being cooked, but doing such a thing is totally wrong when containers of food are being processed to destroy harmful micro-organisms, create a seal, and ensure a decent shelf life in storage.

And anyway this quick cooling usually draws contents out of caning jars, ruining the batch and making a Grade A mess.

Canning instructions for saucepans in some makers' manuals may assume that beginners know the full *Why* and *How* of Pressure–processing in a full-size, *big* kettle—and this assumption can lead to trouble for the householder (who inadvertantly takes short cuts).

So follow the maker's directions for *mechanical operation* of the saucepan, but follow the directions published by the USDA and the Canada Department of Agriculture—or the ones in this or any other complete and carefully researched body of instructions—*for the actual canning procedures for each food.*

However, if one of these saucepans is the only thing you have for canning low-acid foods, go ahead and use a pressure *saucepan—with these stipulations:*

Process nothing larger than a 1-pint jar or a No. 2 can.

Don't let the containers touch each other inside the pan; and of course the jars/cans will be on a rack that holds them up from the bottom of the pan.

Let the pan vent as for a Pressure Canner—see "The Pressure Canner at Work" a few pages later on. Then close the vent and start counting the minutes required for safe processing.

Add 20 minutes to the processing times given in later chapters for individual foods being pressure-canned (again, this is to compensate for shorter heating/cooling times in the smaller pot).

Consult "Correcting for Altitude" earlier in this chapter for the adjustments to make in *pressure* if you live above 1000 feet/305 meters. *However, if you live higher than 3000 ft/914 m, the two leading makers of pressure pots warn against processing low-acid food in one of these saucepans. Reason: Water needed for extra processing time at altitude will evaporate before the food is adequately treated.*

When processing time is over, remove the saucepan from heat and let it cool by itself if you're using jars. Do not open the vent or remove the weighted gauge if the food is in jars: with such an abrupt change in pressure, contents will be forced out, wrecking the seal, or the glass could break.

You may release steam to lower pressure quickly *if the food is in cans.*

See "Post–Processing Jobs" later in this chapter for how to handle newly canned food.

3. Independent food scientists, who truly have no axes to grind, recommend 10 pounds in the sea-level zone (240 F/116 C) as the safest and most effective pressure to use for low-acid foods. Even in their instruc-

tions for the person who feels comfortable only with pressure-canned plain tomatoes, they prefer 10 pounds to some manufacturers' 5 pounds (228 F/109 C) as more likely to do a safe job of processing.

As for 15 pounds (250 F/121 C), this is very seldom given for sea level/1000 feet; it is, though, the common-sense pressure for high altitudes (q.v., earlier).

Buying a Pressure Canner

Pressure Canners are usually made of cast aluminum. Like B–W Bath kettles, they come in sizes measured according to loose-contents capacity; unlike B–W Bath kettles, though, their diameters are all roughly the same: it's their height that varies. The most popular sizes are 16-quart (actually taking 7 quart jars or 9 pint jars), and 22-quart (actually taking 7 quarts, or 18 pints in two layers, or 34 ½-pints stacked in three tiers).

They're expensive, but they do their job for years and years if you take good care of them and keep their sealing rims and pressure gauges and safety vents in good working order.

It may make economic sense to buy a Pressure Canner if you plant a good-sized garden or can get lots of fresh produce cheaply in season, and have surplus meat to put by. But if your family is small and you have just a few surplus foodstuffs to store, maybe your answer is freezing in the separate and genuine, though small, freezer unit of your modern refrigerator (for the procedures see Chapters 11 through 16).

Borrowing?—usually not feasible. But something that is: Go shares with a thoroughly compatible friend in buying a large one (estimating the size carefully beforehand) and pool your resources and energies for canning bees. (See also "Community Canning Kitchens," earlier in this chapter.)

The Anatomy of a Pressure Canner

The base, or kettle, is covered with a tight-fitting lid that contains the controls. The lid is fastened down with clamps or a system of interlocking ridges and grooves. It may or may not have a rubber gasket.

Controls are: (1) a pressure gauge—a dial, or a weight like those usually seen with pressure saucepans that has 5/10/15-pound holes that seat on the vent; (2) an open vent to let air and steam exhaust before processing time begins, and is closed with a petcock or separate weight (if gauge is a dial) or with the dead-weight gauge, to start raising pressure; and (3) a safety valve/plug that blows if pressure gets unsafe.

The canner also will have a shallow removable rack to keep jars/cans from touching the kettle bottom, or a strong wire basket that serves as a rack and lets you lift all the hot containers out in one fell swoop.

Servicing Your Pressure Canner

First, read the operating manual that comes with it.

Next, clean the canner according to directions, to remove any factory dust or gunk. Use hot sudsy water for the kettle, avoiding strong cleaners or scouring powders. Do *not* immerse dial in water: instead, wipe lid clean with a soapy cloth, and follow with a clean damp one to remove the soap.

Check the openings of the vent, safety valve and pressure gauge to make sure they're unclogged and clean. Take a small sharp-pointed tool (like a large darning needle or a bodkin) to the openings if they need it; clean the vent by drawing a narrow strip of cloth through it.

Be sure the sealing surfaces of kettle and lid are smoothly clean, so they'll lock completely tight and not allow any pressure, in the form of steam, to escape. If your canner has a rubber gasket, replace it when it shows signs of losing its gimp or getting hard or tired; it should be as limber as a good jar rubber. The kind of hardware store that has replacement dial gauges is likely to have gaskets as well, so take your canner lid with you to make sure of the right size (and don't forget a fresh safety plug if yours has hardened and cracked).

CHECKING THE DIAL GAUGE

Each year well before canning season, or more often if you put by large quantities, you should have the dial gauge of your Pressure Canner checked for accuracy against a master gauge. Just because the dial may rest at 2 pounds pressure when the canner is not in use does not necessarily mean that the gauge is simply 2 pounds high, or that it is uniformly 2 pounds off throughout its range: *have it checked.*

The problem is to find the nearest master gauge and the people able to make the test. But first unscrew the gauge at home—carefully, so the threads do not strip—and have it ready to mail off or to take by in person. Likely sources of help or information are the manufacturer's instruction booklet. A store that carries your brand of canner (it should have catalog material and a listing of the nearest regional sales or servicing centers). Or call the Vocational or the Practical Arts department of a district high school: someone in either section might be able to steer you. The home economics department at your state technical college is another idea.

Telephone your county Agricultural Extension Service offices. The County Agent in home economics there is likely to have the equipment to do it for you—or at least she can tell you where to go. The director of the EFNEP (Expanded Food and Nutrition Education Program) center for your area might be able to offer similar information.

DEALING WITH A FAULTY GAUGE

In earlier editions of this book we relayed faithfully the recommendations from older official publications about how to compensate for a dial gauge that misrepresented the actual psi inside an operating Pressure Canner. Now we edit this advice ruthlessly, because newer research and equipment are asking for more refined measurements. Surely if you want to try the (almost) revolutionary Minnesota 15-psi-at-sea-level for processing low-acid foods—see Chapter 25, under the heading for this chapter—you need an impeccably accurate gauge, either dial or dead-weight/weighted.

So. Have your dial gauge checked. If it is off by more than 1 pound, get a new one. This is not the big deal that you might think. McGuckin Hardware of Boulder, Colorado, carries replacement dial gauges, as well as gaskets, etc. Nor does your hardware store need to be a giant that serves 14 Western states: Brown & Roberts on the Main Street of small Brattleboro, Vermont, is an old-fashioned emporium whose know-how and variety of supplies include dial gauges and gaskets for Pressure Canners. Just take in the lid of your canner, and make sure that the model number is with it; sometimes the number is on a plate on the top, sometimes it's near the sealing rim, sometimes it's on the bottom. (Pressure saucepans generally have their model numbers on their handles.)

Or send to the maker of your canner, enclosing model number: again, see Chapter 25. Or maybe you're lucky and have hardware stores with housewares sections like our favorites.

Meanwhile: Use your faulty dial gauge for only a called-for pressure of 10 psi. If it has been declared to be registering 1 pound too low, process at 11 pounds for the time required. If it is 1 pound too high, process at 9 pounds for the time required. Earlier editions of *PFB,* and a major canning guide as recently as 1979, were giving a rundown for compensations up to 4 pounds either way; and some USDA or EFNEP publications also give this information. Go to any of these if you're more confident than we are about dealing with wide discrepancies. And meanwhile get your new dial gauge ordered.

THE PRESSURE CANNER AT WORK

Here are the mechanics of using a Pressure Canner (directions for filling jars/cans come in the big subsection "About Jars and Cans" later, and of course in the instructions for each individual food in Chapters 5 through 10). And a common-sense rule: don't leave your canner unattended while it's doing its job.

WATER IN—

Put about 1½ inches of warm water in the thoroughly clean canner. If you know that your canner leaks steam slightly when the vent is closed, add an extra inch of water to ensure that the canner will not boil dry if the processing time is more than 30 minutes.

START IT HEATING—

Place the uncovered kettle (bottom section) over heat high enough to raise the pressure quickly *after* the lid is clamped tight. (See how to estimate this heat in "Leery of Pressure Canners?"—coming in a minute.)

COVER ON TIGHT—

When the batch is loaded, put the lid in position, matching arrows or other indicators. Turn the cover to the Closed position or tighten knobs, clamps, etc., to fasten the closure so no steam can escape at the rim.

Two "musts": time carefully, and open lid away from you.

LET IT VENT—

It is important to consider the *Why* of this next step, because sometimes it isn't stressed hard enough in the instruction booklet that comes with your canner—and your processing could be thrown off whack.

Air that is trapped in your Pressure Canner will expand and exert extra pressure—that is, pressure in addition to that of the steam—and your gauge will give you a false indication of the actual temperature inside your canner. Therefore you must make sure that *all air is displaced by steam before you close your petcock or vent.*

For canners with either type of gauge, leave the vent open on the locked-in-place lid until steam has been issuing from it in a *strong, steady* stream—*7 minutes* for small canners, *10 minutes for larger ones.* Use your minute-timer here. And don't get stuck on the telephone or something: after 10 minutes of strong venting, internal pressure can reach 1 to 3 pounds (enough to affect processing time). When your canner has vented, close the vent by the means specified for dial or weighted gauge.

MANAGE THE CONTROLS—

Follow carefully the manufacturer's instructions. For processing adjustments at altitudes higher than 1000 feet/305 meters, see the section "Correcting for Altitude," and especially the passages about recommendations from makers and from workers "in the field."

For a canner with a *dial-faced gauge,* close the vent and let pressure rise quickly inside the kettle until the dial registers about ½ pound *under* the processing pressure that is called for. At this point, reduce the heat moderately under your canner to slow down the rate at which the pressure is climbing: in a minute the gauge will have reached the exact poundage you want, so you adjust the heat again to keep pressure steady at the correct poundage.

For a canner with a *dead-weight-weighted gauge* (harder to monitor than a dial is), set the gauge on the vent and then carry on as for the canner with a dial gauge—but of course keep track of the frequency of the jiggles as the maker's instructions say to do.

Watch the Gauge—

Pressure, once the right level is reached, *must be constant.*

You're using a Pressure Canner so your food will be safe, so if the pressure sags you should bring it back up to the mark and start timing again from scratch. Don't guess—turn your timer right back to the full processing period. Your food will be overcooked, of course—but next time you'll keep your eye on the pressure, right?

Fluctuating pressure also can cause liquid to be drawn from jars. And this in turn can prevent a perfect seal.

And Watch the Clock—

Count the processing time from the moment pressure reaches the correct level for the food being canned. *Be accurate:* at this high temperature even a few minutes too much can severely overcook the food.

Reduce to Zero

At the end of the required processing time turn off the heat or remove the canner from the stove. It's heavy and hot, so take care.

If you're using *glass jars,* let the canner cool until the pressure drops back to Zero. Then open the vent very slowly.

CAUTION: If the vent is opened suddenly or before the pressure inside the canner has dropped to Zero, liquid will be pulled from jars, or the sudden change in pressure may break them.

If you're using *tin cans,* the pressure does not need to fall naturally to Zero by cooling: open the vent gradually when processing is over and the canner is off heat, to let steam out slowly until pressure is Zero.

Lift the Lid—

Never remove the lid until after steam has stopped coming from the vent. Open lid clamps or fastenings.

Raise the farther rim of the cover first, tilting it to direct remaining heat and steam *away* from you.

Take Out Jars or Cans Promptly—

If the canner doesn't have a basket rack, use a jar-lifter and *dry* potholders (wet ones get unbearably hot in a wink) to remove jars/cans promptly. Promptness is important. Certain bacteria *like* heat, remember, and some types of spoilage are thermophilic.

Cool *cans* quickly in cold water.

Ignore the "afterboil" still bubbling in jars and complete seals if necessary.

Stand jars on a wood surface, or one padded with cloth or paper, to cool away from drafts.

Test seals when containers have cooled overnight.

Leery of Pressure Canners?

If you're a beginner, and fearful, prepare the canner and take it through a practice run on your stove before processing any food in it. Thus:

Put a couple of inches of water in it, secure the cover, and put it on heat; exhaust the air by allowing a steady flow of steam through the vent for 10 minutes. Close the vent and watch the gauge until it reaches 10 pounds pressure (the pressure used most often in canning low-acid food in the sea-level zone (up to 1000 feet/305 meters), and hold it there—fiddling with the heat under the canner to determine how much is needed to hold a steady 10 pounds—for at least five minutes, to get the feel of it. Then slide the canner off heat, let pressure fall back to Zero, open the vent to release any last gasp of steam, and remove the cover, tilting it away from you.

You've done it! Now you'll know what to expect, and you know you can boss the beast.—R.H.

• **SUMMARIZING:** Pressure Canners are nothing to be afraid of if you treat them with respect and follow the manufacturer's directions exactly. Much research by government and private agencies has determined the best techniques for Pressure–processing: *don't try short cuts.*

MAVERICK CANNING METHODS—*NO!*

There's nothing like the *Morbidity and Mortality Weekly Report* for discouraging nostalgic ways of canning food at home, because in almost every account of an outbreak of food-borne botulism, the Editorial Note deduces that "inadequate processing" or "inadequate heating" allowed the toxin to form.

Spelling it out, this means that low-acid foods that should have been Pressure-processed were merely given a Boiling–Water Bath; and that strong-acid foods—which should have been given a B–W Bath to sterilize container and heat contents adequately—were canned instead by "open-kettle," or were treated with dry heat in an oven, or were put in a tank affair and surrounded by swirls of steam *not* under pressure.

NO to Old "Open-kettle"

The first page of this Chapter 3 describes the origin of what was called open-kettle canning, a method whereby hot food—presumably fully cooked—was put into hot jars that once were sterile and were capped with hot lids that also once were sterile, and then usually a vacuum was formed as the contents cooled, helping to form the seal.

You see the problems. Jars, lids, sealing-rims probably were sterilized carefully by being filled with, or lying in, boiling water. Fine. But then they sat for seconds or minutes in the open air of the kitchen while the contents were ladled in, and air-borne spoilers, some potentially deadly, contaminated the inside of jars and covers. The hot food simply was not able to re-sterilize the container; and indeed it may not have cooked quite long enough to destroy the bacteria that *like* heat approaching 212 F/100 C at the sea-level zone.

Mold is one of the leaders in the air-borne danger brigade, and it can settle on the underside of a canning lid, and grow. In the process of growing it can metabolize the safe margin of acid just enough to allow surviving *C. botulinum* spores to develop and throw off their wicked toxin. So your jar of supposedly "safe" open-kettle-canned tomatoes—or dill pickles or jams or condiments or pears or peaches, all of which traditionally have been regarded as strong-acid enough to be protected—may not be really safe at all. And aside from botulism, there is also the dreaded aflatoxin from mold itself (see "A Little Mold Won't Hurt You" in the chapter following this one).

The foods in Chapters 5 and 6—fruits and tomatoes—must be fully processed in a Boiling-Water Bath, unless high altitude requires that they be Pressure-processed. Several generations ago it was considered O.K. to can these by open-kettle—but a lot of research and a lot of public health statistics have proved otherwise. As for the cooked jams and the pickles and relishes in Chapters 18 and 19: *They all should have a finishing Boiling-Water Bath to sterilize the jars and lids* once the jars are filled and capped. Even unwaxed jellies, for good shelf life in warm climates.

And *NO* to Old "Oven-canning"

The folklore of homemaking has another bad method that continues to surface: trying to process foods by baking them. Please look back at "How Heat Penetrates a Container of Food," early in this chapter. Dry heat just plain cannot produce the same effect as boiling water, either at atmospheric pressure or under extra pressure, can.

In addition to the danger of inadequate processing, there is also the likelihood that a jar of food will burst in your face as you open the oven door.

Quite early in the marketing of microwave ovens to the general public, one maker touted his product as able to can fruits. In very short order the manufacturer discontinued such a claim for his oven. Now all responsible makers of microwave ovens warn against using them for canning.

- **But note:** Blanching produce as a preliminary treatment before freezing or drying may be done in a microwave. The way to blanch in these ovens is described in each section where the treatment is needed.

And *NO* to Old "Steamer-canning"

As far as we can discover, steamer-canning (NOT to be confused with Pressure-processing—*please*) was carried out in a tank arrangement that let plain steam waft around the jars placed on racks inside it. The outfit was not on the market very long: apparently too many canning failures from letting jars of food putter along in the steamer. ("But steam is *steam,* isn't it?" Nope. It isn't. As any youngster taking practical science in grade-school can tell us.)

Rigging up a clam-steamer, stockpot, even an honest B–W Bath kettle and trying to process with steam in it—*Don't!*

Not like the old-time steam tank, above, is the fairly new "atmospheric steam canner": we say our say about this one in Chapter 4, and we mentioned it briefly a minute ago.

ABOUT JARS AND CANS

Either glass jars *specially made for home-canning* or metal cans may be used for putting food by.

Overall, canning jars are more versatile than cans are: (1) anything that is canned in cans may also be canned in glass; (2) Boiling–Water Bath and Pressure–processing are used for either jars or cans of food; but (3) there are certain foods that should be home-canned only in glass—the individual instructions later on will tell you which ones, but among them are jellies, preserves, pickles, relishes, a couple of fruits and vegetables, and all seafoods.

Another advantage of jars is that they usually require one less step in the packing procedure than cans do; the step is called "exhausting," and will be described in detail in a minute.

Still another plus-mark for jars is that they're generally a lot easier to get, being sold in hardware and farm stores and supermarkets all over the country.

And of course jars show off their contents, and hence are a requisite for exhibiting your food at the fair. Jars of food must be stored in a cool, dry place that's also dark, otherwise the contents will fade in the light.

And last, jars are re-usable as long as they have no nicks or scratches, even minute ones, and as long as you can get the proper fittings for them.

Aside from having to be special-ordered from the distributor, cans require an expensive hand-operated machine for crimping their lids onto the sides to form a perfect seal. Also, certain foods need cans with special enameled linings.

Cans are not re-usable.

But *cans* of food require only dry, cool storage—not darkness, since the contents are not exposed to light. And cans stack easily. Further, when they're piping hot from the processing kettle they don't need to be handled so gingerly as glass does. (It's a mistake to be rough with them, though: a dented rim can mean a damaged seal.)

THE TYPES OF JARS FOR HOME-CANNING

The jars recommended for use to North American householders are all alike in three highly important respects:

1. *The jars are manufactured specifically for canning food AT HOME.* Generally speaking, this means that they are designed to withstand more cavalier treatment during filling, processing and storage than their commercial counterparts undergo at the hands of industrial processors and shippers. Compared to the jars that we buy mayonnaise and peanut butter, etc., in, jars made specially for home-canning have slightly heavier glass, and have been given higher heat-tempering.

    North America's largest makers of home-canning jars—which means in Canada and the U.S.A.—have told *PFB* that, though they also make commercial glass containers, their jars for salad dressing or whatever are "one-trip" containers, and therefore are not reliable for re-use in canning food at home.

2. *The canning jars come in ½-pint, 1-pint, 1½-pint, 1-quart and ½-gallon sizes;* of these, the ½-gallon does not have a wide-mouth version.

    We do not give instructions for processing ½-gallons, because dense and low-acid foods do not heat well enough in them to be safe. And strong-acid foods could be safe, perhaps, but *the outside would be cooked to smithereens before the cold spot was done right.* These jars would be too tall for your canner anyway.

    Unless specified otherwise, ½-pints are processed like 1-pint jars, and 1½-pint jars are processed like 1-quart jars.

3. *The jars have types of closures (described below) for which fresh sealers are available at the start of each canning season.* And our filling/processing/sealing instructions take these closures into account.

Modern Mason with 2-Piece Screwband Metal Lid

"Mason" goes back to the name of the originator of the screwtop canning jar, and denotes any jar with a neck threaded to take a closure that is screwed down.

Today's modern mason is the highly refined home-canning jar being produced in the millions each year by manufacturers in the United States and Canada.

The jar mostly has standard and wide-mouth openings, and, depending on the maker, has a variety of shapes and sizes. The straight-sided and wide-mouth jars are especially handy for large pieces of food that you'd like to remove more or less intact.

The cartons will say which of these jars is O.K. for freezing.

The jars come packed with their closures. The lids also are sold separately, with or without screwbands.

How the 2-Piece Metal Closure Works

The lid—called "dome" or "self-sealing" or "snap" by the individual makers, but of one basic design—is a flat metal disc with its edge flanged to seat accurately on the *rim* of the jar's mouth; the underside of the flange has a rubber-like sealing compound; the center surface next to the food is enameled, often white.

The lid is sterilized (more about this in a minute), placed on the clean-wiped rim of the jar of food, and then is held in place by the screwband, which is screwed down on the neck of the jar *firmly tight—AND IS NEVER TIGHTENED FURTHER.* "Firmly tight" means screwed down completely but without using full force, or without being yanked around as with a wrench.

The capped jar is processed, during which the "give" in the metal lid allows air in the contents to be forced out. As the jar cools, the pliant metal will be sucked down by the vacuum until the lid is slightly concave. You often hear the small *plink* as the lid snaps down, thus indicating that the jar is sealed.

• **Note:** For a while in the mid-'70's one maker varied the sealing compound on the inside rim of the disc lid, and, because of the change, felt obliged to recommend tightening the screwband further when the jar was removed from the canner. However, since then this maker returned to a sealer that does *not* require any more tightening after the jar is processed.

To be on the safe side, though, pay attention to each maker's instructions as given in the package of closures.

Sterilizing Jars and 2-Piece Lids

Wash jars, screwbands and lids in hot soapy water, rinse well in scalding water. Containers and closures that will be processed in a Boiling–Water Bath or Pressure Canner need not be sterilized further: but do let them stand filled/covered with the hot water until used, to protect them from dust and airborne spoilers.

Containers for food that will not be processed or "finished" in a B–W Bath at *212 F/100 C at the sea-level zone* must be sterilized (and this goes for jars and lids to be used for fruit juices, q.v., and perhaps jelly). Wash jars and closures as above. Stand open jars upright in a big kettle, fill with hot water until the jars are submerged; bring the whole thing to boiling, and boil for 15 minutes. Remove the kettle from heat but let jars stay in the hot water.

Clean and scald the screwbands the way you do jars.

But scald, or boil, *the metal lids according to the manufacturer's directions.* This isn't a cop-out: the makers give different instructions here, and all of us consumers must assume that they know what's best for their own product. The result in every case is to sterilize, though; and all the lids are left in the hot water as a protection against dust, etc.

What Is Re-usable

You should *NEVER use the lid itself again* for canning: the sealing compound on the lid will not seal right a second time around. And besides, it is ever so slightly warped now because you pried it off (and it may be punctured to boot). Even when a lid looks unbent after it comes off, we scratch a big fat "X" on its enameled or painted outside surface, then it's washed and tossed in a catch-all drawer to use sometime on a refrigerator-storage jar.

You of course can use the jars over and over again as long as they have perfectly smooth sealing rims, and have no cracks or scratches anywhere.

You can use the screwbands again for canning—*unless* they're rusted, or bent, or the threads are marred. (Screwbands too tired to be safe in canning can hold foil or plastic wrap tight on jars of food in the refrigerator, and the like. We often use "retired" screwbands for extra support under a springy wire rack in the bottom of our B–W Bath kettle, or to hold jars well apart in the canner.)

Old-style Zinc Caps for Modern Masons

The one-piece threaded zinc cap with its porcelain liner was last catalogued by the Ball Corporation's 1979 *Blue Book*. Shortly thereafter the company began phasing out the lids, and they were not offered to the market after the 1982 canning season. In case you have found a supply, here's how they work:

The zinc cap has a porcelain disc attached in the head where the metal would otherwise come in contact with food in the jar. It fits a modern standard-mouth mason, screwing down to rest on a separate and cushioning rubber ring that you have put around the neck of the jar *at the base of the threads* near the shoulder. (Unlike the flat metal lid of the 2-piece screwband combination, whose rubber-like compound encircles the under-edge to form a seal with the rim of the jar, the zinc cap's seal occurs on the jar rubber low on the neck of the container.) Jar rubbers are always gettable, in standard and wide-mouth sizes, to use with the bailed jars described in a minute.

Of course your jars and caps are sound and unchipped—the caps, particularly, must be uncorroded and with porcelain intact. Wash jars, caps and rubbers in hot soapy water, rinse well. Unless the food is to be processed at 212 F/100 C or higher, sea-level zone, you will sterilize the jars as described earlier, and sterilize the clean caps by boiling for 15 minutes and letting them remain covered by the very hot water until each is used. But *do not boil the jar rubbers;* instead, pour briskly boiling water over them in a shallow pan and let them sit there, hot, until used.

Next, gently—but only slightly—stretch the rubber, now more pliable and still wet from being held in hot water, and ease it over the neck of the jar to seat flat around the narrow ledge of glass below the threads. Fill the container (how, in detail later), wipe any dribbles from the rubber, screw the cap down *tight* on the rubber ring—*and then give it a ¼-inch COUNTER-turn* for a slight loosening that will allow air in the jar/contents to vent during processing.

As you remove the jars from the processing kettle, *RE-tighten the cap slowly*—slowly, because a quick jerk is likely to shift the rubber, thus breaking the seal; and never tighten the cap again, especially after the jar has cooled. This gentle retightening when the jar is taken from the kettle is the action referred to later in the individual instructions as "complete the seals if necessary."

Only perfect caps and perfect jars are re-usable. Rubbers lose their sealing ability in just one use: *discard rubbers.*

Old-style Bailed Jars with Glass Lids

These haven't been manufactured since the early 1960's as far as we know, but there are still countless thousands of these sturdy performers around. Sometimes called "lightning" or "ideal" type, they have a domed glass lid cushioned on a separate rubber ring that seats on a glass ledge a scant ¼-inch down on the neck of the jar. The lid is held in place during processing by the longer hoop of the two-part wire clamp.

As you remove the jars from the canner after processing, snap down the shorter spring-section of the clamp so it rests on the shoulder of the jar. Therefore this is another case where *"complete the seals if necessary"* applies in the individual instructions.

Fittings for Bailed Jars

The glass lids and the two-part wire bail are no longer made, but occasionally you can find a trove of unused glass lids or separate bails in the storeroom of an old-fashioned neighborhood store.

Discard any lids that have rough or chipped rims, or whose top-notch (which holds the longer loop in place) is worn away.

Sometimes the wire bails are so rusted or old or tired that they have lost their gimp and can't hold the lid down tightly. *Please* don't go in for makeshift tightening by bending the wires or padding the lids. Retire the jars.

Rubbers are still sold in boxes of twelve, and come in standard and wide-mouth sizes. *Never re-use rubbers,* or use old, stale rubbers that have been hanging around for years. Stretch rubbers gently and only enough so they'll go over the neck of the jar.

To sterilize. Boil jars and lids for 15 minutes, and let them wait, covered by the hot water, until used. But *don't boil rubbers:* Wash well, then put them in a shallow pan, cover with boiling water, and let stand till used.

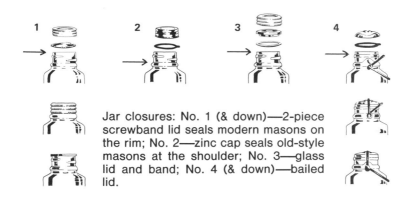

Jar closures: No. 1 (& down)—2-piece screwband lid seals modern masons on the rim; No. 2—zinc cap seals old-style masons at the shoulder; No. 3—glass lid and band; No. 4 (& down)—bailed lid.

Masons with 3-Piece Glass Lids

These are like the modern mason with the 2-piece screwband *metal* lid, and are still made in Canada. The center of the glass lid protrudes down inside the jar; the seal occurs on the *rim* of the jar, where the edge of the lid is cushioned by a separate rubber ring applied, wet, to the lid.

The screwband is turned down *tight, then given a ¼-inch counter-turn* (as with the one-piece zinc cap above) to allow air in the contents to vent during processing. *Retighten the band carefully as you remove each jar* from the processing kettle, and never retighten it further. (Another example of what you do to "complete seals if necessary.")

—But Don't Use These

Supplies of new, good, home-canning jars and fittings are beginning to catch up with the demand, even though local stocks may be sold out when August rolls around. So be forehanded. Start looking in *March.* Ask your friendliest storekeeper to let you know when he expects a shipment. And protect your family by using only the jars and fittings that are GRAS, as the Food and Drug Administration might put it (meaning "generally recognized as safe"). Don't be stampeded into using unreliable or makeshift closures (see "Checklist for Safe Canning-Jar Closures," in a minute).

(1) Any jars imported from Europe or Asia *for which you don't have full and explicit directions* that live up to USDA or Agriculture Canada standards of safety. We have a number of such jars from several countries. They're charming—as cannisters, but they're too bulky for safe processing of many dense, Raw-packed strong-acid foods; in addition, they are *not O.K.'d as heat-tempered for Pressure-processing* low-acid foods. Further, their sides are often too fragile for routine handling (just used as cannisters, two got cracked merely by being pressed strongly together). As for their sealing arrangements, most jars like these have a stiff latch like the one on footlockers; such a clamp is so strong that either the necessary venting is impossible during processing, or the seal is created by the latch's external pressure and not by formation of a proper vacuum; we were only 50 percent successful with the squat ½-liter (pint) size. And there's one brand that claims its rubber sealer is re-usable!

(2) Commercial glass containers—the one-trip jars holding baby food, salad dressing, peanut butter, pickles, fancy fruit, whatever. Not even if good, safe, modern home-canning closures will fit them (and especially not if we'd have to re-use the commercial closure—which cannot seal safely a second time).

(3) Very old jars for which new fittings/closures are not gettable. There are a number of books about antique canning jars—like the ones for collectors of old bottles—and you may have some real prizes (to keep or to sell, but not to can in). Look in the *Readers' Guide to Periodical Literature,* at every library, for articles in antiques magazines.

JARS IN AND OUT OF THE CANNER

Don't put cold jars of food into very hot water; don't fill a canner with jars of boiling-hot food and then slosh cold water into the canner. Don't clunk filled jars against each other—especially if they're filled with boiling-hot food.

After processing time is up, remove jars at once from the B–W Bath, but let the Pressure Canner return to Zero naturally before you lift out the jars. Take care that you don't knock the jars against each other as you unload them. Complete seals if necessary. Then set them on a rack, a wooden surface, or one padded with cloth or newspaper, and be sure it's not in a draft of cold air. And *never* invert processed jars in the mistaken idea that you're helping the seal— quite the contrary!

Cooling. Jars must cool naturally: *Don't* drape a towel over them with the idea of protecting them from air currents, because keeping them warm will invite flat sour. Let them sit undisturbed for 12 hours before you check the seals and perform the other chores described in "Post-processing Jobs," later in this chapter.

CHECKLIST FOR SAFE CANNING–JAR CLOSURES

In the mid–1970's there was a scary shortage of canning-jar lids—scary, because it brought forth a number of fly-by-night producers in addition to some new and conscientious ones. In case such a crisis occurs again, here are the things to look for in a new product; and they apply to equipment other than jar lids.

Good Directions for Use?

The most experienced hands at safe home-canning pay attention to the instructions for using any new product, and they read with really critical attention if the product has an unusual feature.

First, *are* there any directions, either printed on the container or on a separate sheet/folder inside the package?

(A *responsible* manufacturer—one who knows home-canning, and has food safety in mind—will want us to use his closure in the way that gets good, wholesome results which store well.)

Next, if there are directions, do they make sense? Although they may be terse, do they cite with helpful clarity the steps required for using that *particular closure successfully?*

Then, do the directions say how to handle the particular closure after the processed jar of food comes from the canner? Do they tell us explicitly *how this closure looks* when the cooled jar has a good seal? Or whether, if it's a conventional 2-piece screwband type, the band may/may not be removed before storing?

(One brand of jars newly marketed in our area never mentioned the distinctive appearance which the top of the lid should have after the seal was accomplished. This sort of lapse is no help to a first-time canner who might think a jar has sealed when it hasn't, and store it away—to spoil. Phooey to such directions.)

And finally, do the directions say clearly that the steps they give cover only the procedure for using *that closure?* Do they therefore tell the home-canner to use an established guide for complete instructions on packing and processing specific foods? (Makers of canning-jar closures have an obligation to the people who use their products, and it takes only a few lines of print to give an address we can write to for a government bulletin—or for their own home-canning booklet, if they've been in the business long enough to have one. See Chapter 25.

Acceptable Characteristics for Its Type?

If the new entry seems to be of a design almost identical to the familiar standbys for modern mason jars described on page 42, it has a separate metal lid with a ring of sealing compound bonded to its underside, and during processing (either in a Pressure or in a Boiling–Water Bath canner) a screw-on band holds it firmly in place on the sealing rim of the jar. The lid may not be re-used: and it was the replacements for once-used lids that were so scarce during the 1975 canning season.

Among the individual tops we found and used were a couple of newly marketed *one*-piece screw-on closures that incorporate the conventional metal lid and the band. Therefore the characteristics noted below for an acceptable, separate lid would also hold true for such one-piece closures.

Is it well made and of durable material, able to withstand high heat for a maximum processing period without distorting?
   (A sleazy lid is unlikely either to behave well in a Pressure Canner at 240 F/116 C or to retain a seal after months on the jar.)
Does it have a ring of sealing compound that's evenly applied? And sufficiently wide to cover *amply* the jar's sealing rim?
Does the top have a degree of flexibility—meaning springiness—in the center?
   (On a well-sealed modern mason, all lids of this type will be slightly depressed in the center, which is pulled down by the strong vacuum created as the food cools after correct processing.)
Does it have a tiny down-turning flange that lets it seat securely, and properly centered, on the jar's rim *before* the lid is held down by the band?
   (A piping-hot lid that slides back and forth on the jar requires some extra manipulation when we put on a piping-hot screwband. And the lid section of every two-piece closure *must* be set separately on the jar rim before the band is applied; even the most terse manufacturers' directions make a point of doing this. *Never* clap the lid inside the band and then screw the whole business on as if it were the top to a peanut-butter jar, because the ring of sealing compound on the separate lid may not be wide enough to compensate for such treatment—which could force the lid so badly off-center that it fails to hold a good seal.)

THE TYPES OF CANS FOR HOME-CANNING

The containers called "tin cans" are made of steel and merely coated with tin inside and outside. This tin coating is satisfactory for use with most foods. These are called *plain* cans.

But certain deeply colored acid foods will fade when they come in long contact with plain tin coating, so for them there is a can with an inner coating of special acid-resistant enamel that prevents such bleaching of the food. This is called an *R-enamel* can.

Then we have still other foods that discolor the inside tin coating—perhaps because some of them are high in sulfur, and act on the tin the way eggs tarnish silver; or because some are so low in acid as to nudge or straddle the Neutral line. Although there's no record of any damage to these foods from tin coating, there's a can for them that is lined with *C-enamel*.

A leading manufacturer of cans for home-canning says that we may use *plain* cans and *C-enamel* cans interchangeably—except for meats, which always take *plain* cans—with the sole detriment that sometimes the insides of plain cans will be discolored.

- **NOTE:** Although there are many sizes of canned foods on supermarket shelves, the cans used in putting by food at home are: *No. 2*—which holds about 2½ cups; and *No. 2½*—which holds about 3½ cups. (The difference in measure between No. 2 and pints, and No. 2½ and quarts accounts in part for the difference in processing time given for jars and cans.) A No. 303 can (16 ounces) is mentioned only rarely for home-canning; it's processed like a No. 2.

WHAT FOODS TO CAN IN WHICH

Throughout the individual instructions we've included the type of can—plain, R-enamel or C-enamel—to use if you use cans at all.

However, here's a rule-of-thumb to go by if you're canning a food we don't go into:

R-enamel. Think of "R" as standing for "red" and you'll have the general idea: beets, all red berries and their juices, cherries and grapes and their juices, plums, pumpkins and winter squash, rhubarb and sauerkraut (which is very acid).

C-enamel. Think of "C" as standing for "corn" (which has no acid) and for "cauliflower" (whose typically strong flavor indicates sulfur) and you get: corn—and hominy, very low-acid Lima and other light-colored shell beans (and, combined with corn, succotash); cauliflower—and things with such related taste as plain cabbage, Brussels sprouts, broccoli, turnips and rutabagas; plus onions, seafood and tripe.

Plain. This is the catch-all, and may take these foods, as well as others: most fruits, tomatoes, meats, poultry, greens, peas, and green/snap/string/wax beans, and certain made dishes (like baked beans, etc.).

If you're canning mixed vegetables, use *C-enamel for preference* if one or more of the ingredients would go in C-enamel by itself.

Remember, though, that the heavens won't fall if you mix up *plain* and *C-enamel* for fruits and vegetables. Nor will "red" acid foods be bad if they're not canned in *R-enamel:* they just won't have their full color.

What's Re-usable?

Answer: Only the sealer apparatus.

No damaged, rusted, dented, bent *new* can or lid may ever be used in the first place.

No can or lid may be *re-used* at all.

Where to Get Cans and Can-sealers

Freund Can Company
155 West 84th Street
Chicago, Illinois 60620
(Distributor for American Can and Continental Can)

Ives-Way Products, Inc.
820 Saratoga Lane
Buffalo Grove, Illinois 60090
(Formerly Rowe Automatic Can Sealer)

Dixie Canner Equipment Company
786 East Broad Street
P.O. Box 1348
Athens, Georgia 30601
(More about this company under "Community Canning Kitchens," earlier.)

In the Dominion, two possible sources are: Continental Can of Canada Ltd., P.O. Box 4021 Terminal A, Toronto, Ontario; and American Can of Canada Ltd., One International Boulevard, Rexdale, Toronto, Ontario.

Preparing Cans, Lids & Sealer

If cans and lids are to be processed in a Boiling–Water Bath (212 F/100 C) or Pressure–processed, they need not be sterilized before filling.

Wash cans in clear hot water, scald; drain upside down on sterile cloths so air in the room cannot contaminate the inside of the can. To sterilize, wash, submerge in hot water and bring to boiling, and boil for 15 minutes; remove and drain as above.

The gaskets of some lids could be of a material that *must not be wetted* or it won't seal right; other gaskets are of a rubber-like composition that must be treated as carefully as the compound on nonboilable metal screwband lids. Therefore be sure to ask your supplier for explicit instructions for sterilizing the lids.

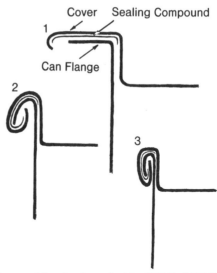

A can of food exhausted to 170 F / 77 C (hence the dry cloth pad to protect fingers) will be sealed with the rolling seam shown in stages at right.

Until you know how to sterilize lids, reserve your cans for use only in the B–W Bath and Pressure Canner. Wipe factory dust from the lids with a scrupulously clean damp cloth immediately before sealing them to the can.

Adjust the sealer according to the manufacturer's directions, and test its efficiency by sealing a can that's partly filled with water, then submerge the can in boiling water: if any air bubbles rise from the can after a few seconds, the lid is not seamed tightly enough. Adjust the chucks of your sealer until you have a perfect seam joining the lid to the can.

In and Out of the Canner

Unlike jars, cans do not vent during processing: they are sealed completely before they go into the B–W Bath or Pressure Canner. Therefore air in the food's tissues and in the canning liquid must be driven out *before* the lid is crimped on perfectly tight—otherwise you wouldn't end up with a vacuum when the cans are cooled.

So *all* cans of food require an extra intermediate step that may be bypassed with most jars (the exceptions being jars of meat, poultry and seafood), and we'll deal with it now before we turn to the Raw and Hot packs in the general procedure for filling any container with food to be canned.

THE EXTRA STEP: "EXHAUSTING"

To drive out enough air to make the desired vacuum, you heat the food to a minimum of 170 F/77 C at the center of the filled can or jar. You achieve this temperature either by bringing loose food to boiling in a kettle and then ladling it into the container, or by heating the container of raw or cold food until a glass food thermometer thrust into the middle of the contents registers 170 F/77 C (or the 180 F/82 C preferred by the Ohio Extension Service, if you live in the Buckeye State).

Fill the cans according to the instructions for the specific food and put them, still open, on a rack in a large kettle; add hot water to about 2 inches *below* the tops of the cans. Cover the kettle and boil the whole business until your pencil-shaped food thermometer, stuck down in the center of the food until its bulb is halfway to the bottom of the can, registers 170 F/77 C. You can get the same result by boiling open cans in a Pressure Canner at Zero pounds pressure (as described for jars in "Canning Seafood," Chapter 9).

The individual directions will repeat the need to "exhaust to 170 F/77 C" even with cans just filled with boiling-hot food. This deliberate repetition is our way of emphasizing the importance of checking the contents with your pencil thermometer: it's easy to let food get cool as you turn to sealing the cans, and the given processing times depend on having the food at 170 F/77 C when the sealed cans go into the canner.

Cooling the Cans

Cans *must be cooled quickly* after their processing time is up, lest their contents cook further (this is why, if you're using cans, you vent your Pressure Canner to hasten its return to Zero pounds).

Fill your sink or a washtub with very cold water and drop the processed cans into it. As each can is removed from the canner its ends should be slightly convex, bulging from the pressure of the hot food inside it; if the ends don't bulge, it means that the can was imperfectly sealed before it went into the processing kettle. The ends will flatten to look slightly concave when the contents have cooled and shrunk, indicating that the desired vacuum has formed inside.

Change the water when it warms, or add ice, to hasten cooling. Remove cans when they're still warm so they'll air-dry quickly.

GENERAL STEPS IN CANNING

Let's see how to fill the jars/cans with food before they go into the Boiling–Water Bath or the Pressure Canner, and how to treat them afterward.

RAW PACK AND HOT PACK

Many foods may be packed in their containers either *Raw* (in some manuals also designated as "Cold") or *Hot*. The food is trimmed, cleaned, peeled, cut up, etc., in the same manner for both packs. The same amount of canning liquid is added to the container of solid food, regardless of whether it's Hot pack or Raw—roughly ½ to ¾ cup for pints or No. 2 cans, 1 to 1½ cups for quarts or

No. 2½ cans; also the liquid should always be very hot. The optional seasoning is added just before processing either pack. And with both packs the containers are handled identically after being removed from the canner and cooled.

Raw Pack

Foods of relatively low density tend to hold their shape better and be firmer with the Raw pack (this is what *PFB* recommends for canning *whole* tomatoes, for example). The basic reason for this is an enzymatic action early in processing as the temperature rises slowly. There's more about this in Chapter 7, "Canning Vegetables," in the directions for Beans—green/snap/string.

Boiling syrup, juice or water is added to raw foods that require added liquid for processing.

Jars of Raw-packed food must start their processing treatment in hot *but never boiling* water, otherwise they're likely to crack. Even when a jar has been exhausted, the water in the processing kettle should not be at a full boil.

Raw-packed foods usually take longer than Hot packs to process in a Boiling–Water Bath; this is especially true for the denser foods.

Hot Pack

Food that is precooked a little or almost fully is made more pliable, and so permits a closer pack. (Foods differ in the amount of preheating they need, though: spinach is merely wilted before it's packed Hot, but green string beans boil for 5 minutes.)

Fruit that is canned without sweetening is always packed Hot.

Pressure–processing will condense this Raw pack of summer squash a great deal, even after it's tamped down and given generous headroom.

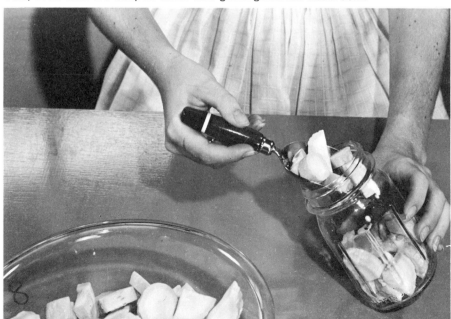

In a Boiling–Water Bath, Hot-packed food generally requires less processing time than Raw does, because it is thoroughly hot beforehand. However, there generally is no difference in the time required for Pressure Canning either pack: by the time you start counting—the minute pressure reaches 10 pounds (240 F/116 C)—Raw-packed food has become as hot as if it had been packed Hot to begin with. (One of the interesting exceptions is summer squash, which needs *longer* Pressure-processing for Hot pack, because the precooked squash is much more dense in the container than the crisp raw pieces are.)

LEAVING HEADROOM

In packing jars of food that will be processed in a Hot–Water Bath, Boiling–Water Bath or Pressure Canner, there must be some leeway left between the lid and the top of the food or its liquid. This space—called *headroom* in the instructions that follow later—allows for expansion of solids or the bubbling-up of liquid during processing. Without it, some of the contents would be forced out with the air, thus leaving a deposit of food on sealing surfaces, and ruining the seal.

Too much headroom may cause food at the top to discolor—*and* could even prevent a seal, unless processing time was long enough to exhaust all the excess amount of air.

> • • **Important altitude note:** Steam in the headroom expands more at high altitudes than it does in the sea-level zone (1000 feet/305 meters), so we suggest that you increase headroom by ⅛ inch for every 1000 ft/305 m above the sea-level zone, but not to exceed 1¾ inches for quarts, 1 inch for pints, ¾ inch for ½-pints.
>
> Also, Pressure–processing has steam at higher temperature than a B–W Bath does, and steam expands more when it's hotter.
>
> All of which means that you should be prepared to make your own arithmetical adjustments if you live at, say 7000 ft/2134 m, and process at 15 psi.

The right headroom *in the sea-level zone* for each food and its processing liquid is specified in the individual instructions, with more headroom given to starchy foods—Lima/shell beans, green peas, corn, etc.—because they swell in the canner.

> • **Note:** In the older 3-piece closure for mason jars (glass lids + separate rubber ring + metal screwband to hold things in place), the center of the glass lid protrudes a bit down into the jar. With these glass lids, therefore, we recommend that you add from ¼ to ½ inch *more* to the headroom given in the directions, in order to compensate for space lost in the neck of the jar.

Cans generally require no headroom between liquid and lid: all air is driven out in the exhausting step, and the lids are sealed on, before the cans are processed.

FILLING, BUBBLING & CAPPING

Whether it's in cans or jars, you pack most raw food firmly (except for the starchy vegetables that expand, mentioned above), and most hot foods rather loosely.

Have your clean, scalded containers and sealers ready. If you're using old-style masons with porcelain-lined caps, or bailed jars with rounded glass tops, gently fit the wet rubber rings around the necks of the jars, stretching them as little as possible; make sure they rest snugly on the ledge of glass that supports them. (Fittings that seal on the rim of the jar, and of course can lids, are put on after the containers are filled.)

Prepare and fill only one container at a time—don't set them up in a row, standing open to airborne spoilers. Set the jar/can in a clean pie dish, or whatever, to catch spills and overflows.

As you pack Raw, shake the container or tunk it on the bottom to settle the pieces of food; use a slender rubber spatula to make room for chunks you're fitting in; don't compress the food so much that it will spring up again, though, and invade the headroom. Pour in your boiling liquid—syrup, water, juice—to the desired level, keeping track of the headroom you must leave.

Follow directions for headroom in Hot pack. Your wide-mouth funnel is most handy here for controlling dribbles of food that must be wiped away completely.

Examples of headroom in canning in jars larger than 1 pint: left, 1 inch for chicken packed Raw, and exhausted; and right, ¼ inch for whole-kernel corn packed Hot in cans, with boiling precooking liquid added right up to the brim.

Removing Bubbles

In either pack in any container, run the blade of a table knife down between the food and the side of the jar/can at several points. There is likely to be more air trapped in the liquid between pieces of food in Raw pack than in Hot; but use your knife with both. Take care not to stir or to fold in more air.

For insurance, use your knife again—but sparingly—when you "top up" a can with boiling liquid after exhausting it to 170 F/77 C.

Capping

With a scrupulously clean cloth wrung out in boiling water, wipe the sealing rim of cans to remove any liquid, food tissue or fatty substance, because any of these can interfere with the seal. Wrap a clean, damp cloth around the body of the hot can to make it comfortable to hold; set the can in the sealer. Wipe the lid (rinse it quickly in hot water if, in some way, it has become dusty—and this is the *first* time it may be wetted), place it on the sealing rim of the can, and crimp it in place according to the directions for making the seal complete. Set the can in the processing kettle, and deal with the next one.

Wipe the sealing edges of the jars—*rim* of the glass, if you're using 2-piece screwband metal lids or the 3-piece glass closure; *rubber ring* around the neck of the jar, if it's a bailed closure or takes a porcelain-lined cap. Remove every vestige of food or other substance that would prevent a perfect seal.

Set the metal lid of your modern masons on the rim of the jar, *sealing compound next to the glass;* screw down the band *firmly tight.* Put the jar in the canner.

Set a wet rubber ring on the rim of the jar that takes a 3-piece glass closure; seat the glass lid on the rubber so the center of the lid protrudes down into the headroom; screw the metal band down tight, then give it a ¼-inch counterturn to allow the jar to vent during processing. (You'll retighten it after the jar is processed.)

Screw the porcelain-lined zinc cap down tight on the rubber-padded shoulder of the old-style mason jar, then give it a ¼-inch counterturn to allow for venting. (You'll retighten it after the jar is processed.)

Set the rounded glass lid of your bailed jar on the rubber ring, turning the cap so the notch in the top will catch the wire most securely; push the longer hoop up over the top of the lid until it's held firmly in the notch. (But *don't* snap the lower bail down on the shoulder of the jar: you'll do this after the jar is processed.)

POST–PROCESSING JOBS

Your B–W Bath kettle is off the heat, your Pressure Canner has returned to Zero—but not until tomorrow will today's canning be finished.

As you remove *cans* to drop them in cold water, mark the ones with poor seals. Right now, hot from the canner, their ends *should* bulge from internal pressure sealed in; and in the cooling tub, tiny bubbles must *not* appear around the lids. Therefore flat ends or bubbles mean pinpoint gaps in the sealing seam.

On the other hand, your *jars* seal themselves as they cool. Of course you never tighten the modern "dome"/"snap"/"self-sealing" 2-piece screwband metal closures. But when you "complete seals if necessary" by flipping down bails or screwing down caps or glass lids that have separate rubber rings, *you* are not actually making the seal: you're merely securing the lids firmly in place so the ensuing vacuum can complete the seal.

For this reason, *don't open the jar* to add liquid if you notice one whose liquid has partly boiled out during processing. Simply treat the jar normally and stand it up beside the others. After cooling undisturbed overnight, it might have a good, safe seal.

Two more things. Cans aren't shockproof just because they're already sealed and are made of metal, so don't bump them around or transport them until they have cooled and rested overnight. And don't invert or shake—or even tilt—jars before they're cold and sealed.

Checking Seals

The day after canning is the time for checking the seals of your containers, and preparing them for storage. And *this is your ONLY chance to salvage food* that has failed to seal; once it is stored, a bad seal means that you must destroy it.

Can Seals

By now the ends of your cans should be pulled slightly inward, proving that there is a vacuum inside. However, if the end of a can has not collapsed, press it hard: if it stays in, the seal is O.K.

Be right finicky as you check your cans, because at this early stage a poor seal will not have had time to become dramatic. Therefore the ends won't be bulging 'way out (certainly not even so much as they did right after the cans were processed yesterday); nor will the seams be leaking gassy, spoiled food (although traces of food at any seam are an obvious sign, since the cans got well rinsed by the water in which they cooled).

Springy ends and bits of food mean bad seals. Open the cans and refrigerate the contents, to serve or reprocess.

Jar Seals

First, don't be dumped if there's a haze of dried canning liquid on the outside of some jars. All your jars vented in the processing kettle, remember; and several may have lost liquid, which clouded the water in the canner and so left a slight deposit on the jars.

Food particles lodged around the base of the closure could mean trouble, though. You'll know for sure when you check your seals.

On your modern mason jars, the metal lids of the 2-piece screwband closure will have snapped down, pulled in by the vacuum that means a good seal. If you find a lid that is not concave, press it: if it springs back, the seal is gone; if it stays down, well and good—but set this jar to one side for a tougher test you'll give questionable jars in a minute.

Test bailed jars and the old-style masons with porcelain-lined zinc caps by tilting them far enough so the food presses against the closure. If bubbles start at the lids and rise through the contents, the seal is poor. Moisture appearing at the sealing point is a bad sign too.

Test your flat glass lids by *gently* removing the screwbands that hold them down on their rubber rings. If the band is reluctant to turn, for heaven's sake don't force it—this could shift the lid enough to break the seal right there. A hot cloth held around the band is usually enough to make it expand and come free. Tilt the jar: any seepage or bubbles that mean a poor seal?

The really tough second test can be applied to all your jars except for old masons with the zinc cap. Take a jar you have doubts about—modern mason with its metal lid, any with a glass lid, any with a bailed closure—and remove the screwband or release the bail, including the longer hoop that holds the rounded glass top in place. Set the jar in a pan that's padded with a perfectly clean towel *and lift the jar by its sealed-on lid.* If the seal is weak, the weight of the jar will break it and the jar will drop and spill, leaving the metal disc or glass lid in your fingers. (The towel protects the fallen jar from cracking; collect the spilled contents to serve or reprocess.)

Checklist for Poor Seals

One poor seal out of a full canner batch is a disappointment, but not a worry. Nor is the food in only one container worth reprocessing, which means getting cranked up to start over from scratch with a fresh jar or can and a fresh closure, and repeating, with utmost care this time, every step in the whole canning procedure. Best to eat it right away.

But two poor seals?—not so good. And more than two seal failures in one canner batch will tell you that you're making at least one mistake in your canning technique. For your family's sake, see if it's one of these:

Short cuts in sanitation or preparing food "because it will sterilize anyway."
  Manufacturers' directions not followed in preparing closures.
Imperfect or makeshift containers/closures. Sealing edges of jars, permanent closures (glass tops/lids, porcelain-lined zinc caps) have nicks/cracks/warps. Jars are "one-trip" commercial containers, plus commercial lids from peanut butter, mayonnaise, pickle, etc., or baby-food jars. Rusty or bent bails on old jars (with extra padding to take up slack?). Re-used sealers (rubber rings or metal lids with sealing compound). Dented/bent cans or can lids.
Haphazard filling, exhausting, capping of containers. Packing too tightly or too loosely. Too much or too little headroom. Trapped air not removed. Cans not properly exhausted before capping. Sealing rims not wiped clean after filling. Screwbands of modern 2-piece lids not "firmly tight" to hold lids snugly on and in place during processing; other jar lids not allowed necessary venting. Cans not properly exhausted before sealing. Can-sealer not tested/adjusted.

Processing kettle mismanaged. Water in B–W Bath not 2 inches over tops of containers; Pressure Canner not vented long enough to remove air (or, if used unlocked as a substitute B–W Bath kettle, not vented long or strongly enough before starting to time processing period). True boil not reached and maintained in B–W Bath; called-for pressure not reached (gauge unchecked?) or maintained; full processing time not used. Maker's instructions for mechanical operation not followed. Pressure allowed to fluctuate, so contents lost from jars and trapped between jar rim and lid—thus preventing good seal.

Processing method inadequate. Maverick or makeshift method used. Adjustments for altitude above sea-level zone (up to 1000 ft/305 m) not made. Incorrect venting or return-to-Zero of Pressure Canner (made to cool quickly? lid removed before Zero?).

Containers mishandled after processing. Modern two-piece screwband lids were fiddled with (notable offense being brisk tightening of the screwband, which usually loosens slightly during processing); seals not completed as needed for other closures.

Cans not cooled quickly enough; but jars left in B–W kettle after processing time is done OR were wrapped to slow down natural cooling.

Jars inverted to cool: wrong and unnecessary but maybe prompted by misconceived notion of how post–World War II closures work.

Jars/cans roughly stacked for storage or in other ways knocked around, thus hurting seals.

Cleaning & Labeling

Wipe all jars carefully with a clean, damp cloth, paying special attention to the area around the seals.

Some experts say to remove the screwbands from the 2-piece modern mason closure. Certainly you should take them off if there are signs of food lodged underneath (but presumably you've done this already with jars you suspected of having poor seals). But *never force* a reluctant screwband: hold a hot cloth around it to make it loosen by expanding; if this doesn't work, mark the jar for special watching while it is stored, and turn to the next jar.

The modern metal closure doesn't need a screwband to ensure the seal, of course—but the band does protect the seal in case you plan to transport the jars or stack them. *Don't replace the screwbands if you take them off,* because you could twist the lid just enough so the torque will break the seal.

Clean thoroughly any screwbands you remove and dry them thoroughly before storing for future use.

The glass lids of 3-piece closures are especially vulnerable to jostling and bumping, so weigh carefully the possibility of broken seals before removing bands here.

Label each container with the name of the food, the date it was canned, and any special treatment you gave the food (the last information will be mighty handy if the product is notably good or notably bad when you come to serve it).

STORING

Storage for all canned food must be cool and dry and—if the food is in jars—dark. Even when home-canned foods are adequately processed, they will lose Vitamin C, carotene, thiamine, riboflavin and niacin at temperatures above 50 degrees Fahrenheit/10 C; and light hastens oxidation of fats and oils, destroys fat-soluble and light-sensitive vitamins, and fades the color of the food.

"Cool" means 32 to 50 F/Zero to 10 C. Containers must not freeze, lest the food expand and break the seal. Canned food that is held in storage too warm can still spoil, because certain thermoduric bacteria can re-activate and grow at room temperature or higher. Therefore keep canned food away from heating pipes or cozy nooks behind furnaces, etc.

Damp or humid storage can corrode or rust the metal of cans and closures, and thereby endanger the seals.

Berries and fruits are especially likely to bleach in jars exposed to light, but other foods, too, can become pale and unappetizing if stored in the light. "Cool" and "dry" have priority over "dark," so you may have to protect jars of food from light by wrapping them individually in paper, or putting them in the cartons the jars came in (be sure to put cardboard dividers between the jars).

Put any containers with suspect seals in a special place so you will use them first or be able to keep an eye on them easily.

Arrange your food on the storage shelves so "last in" is "last out"—this way you'll keep a good rotation.

And do check your canned food periodically for signs of spoilage that have developed during storage.

SIGNS OF SPOILAGE AND WHAT TO DO

Before a container is opened, you can see signs of spoilage that indicate the food is unfit or actually dangerous to eat:

- Seeping seams, bulging ends on cans.
- Seepage around the seal, even though it seems firmly seated.
- Mold around the seal or visible in the contents.
- Gassiness (small bubbles) in the contents.
- Cloudy or yeasty liquid.
- Shriveled or spongy-looking food.
- Food an unnatural color (often very dark).

When the container is opened, these are additional signs of spoilage:

- Spurting liquid, pressure from inside as the container is opened.
- Fermentation (gassiness).

- Food slimy, or with too soft a texture.
- Musty or disagreeable or downright nasty odor.
- Mold, even a fleck, on the underside of the lid or in the contents.

If any such signs are evident in unopened or opened containers DESTROY THE CONTENTS SO THEY CANNOT BE EATEN BY PEOPLE OR ANIMALS. Burn the food if you can—it is sometimes not safe from animals if you bury it. If you can't burn or bury the contents, dump them into a large kettle, adding water to prevent scorching, and boil the spoiled food hard for 15 minutes to destroy toxins, and then flush down the toilet whatever will not clog the plumbing. Soak all metal cans, lids, jars, closures in the very strong disinfecting solution of 1 part household chlorine bleach to 4 parts tepid water for at least 15 minutes. Discard the sterilized metal cans and closures, and all sealers. Sterilized jars and glass lids may be used again if they are perfect and undamaged. In a fresh 1:4 solution of chlorine bleach and water, wash all utensils, cloths and surfaces that might have come in contact with the spoiled food.

• • BEFORE TASTING ANY CANNED LOW–ACID FOOD: You must be unshakably certain that your Pressure Canner was operated correctly—pressure gauge accurate and/or dead-weight gauge signaling properly—and that requirements for times and corrections for altitude were followed.

Unless you are sure that these safeguards were observed, a margin of protection is added by boiling the canned low-acid food hard for 15 minutes to destroy any hidden toxins (corn and greens require 20 minutes), and stirring to distribute the heat. If the food foams unduly or smells bad during boiling, destroy it completely so it cannot be eaten by people or animals.

P.S. At least two groups whose work *PFB* respects have studied additional ways to destroy toxins that cause illness (the toxins here have not, obviously, given such advance warnings as bad smell, foaminess, etc.). One is a team made up of Oregon State University's noted microbiologist Dr. Margy Woodburn and researchers at the University of Wisconsin; the other was led by Mrs. Betty Wendstadt of National Presto Industries. Their addresses, so you can inquire about recent published material, are given in Chapter 25, "Where to Find Things": Mrs. Wenstadt's under the listing for Chapter 3, "The Canning Methods," and Dr. Woodburn's under the listing for Chapter 9, "Canning Seafood."

4

ON GUARD!

A number of things have come along since the last revised edition of this book in 1975—some new equipment, some new questions or paraphrases of old ones—and they deserve discussion in a chapter of their own. Also, because we feel so strongly that if you remember the *Why* you can keep track of the *How,* it makes sense to recap in one place a few of the warnings against using particular procedures or utensils; the warnings have been uttered, but they're strung through the sequence of the preserving methods described. Finally, for good measure we'll add worries that keep cropping up in letters to *PFB.*

The items are offered in no special rank of scariness, though we'll start with ones that haven't been cited before. A few more years of research may solve the problems anyway.

THE ATMOSPHERIC STEAM CANNER

There came on the market in the late 1970's a canner devised to be a substitute for the adequately deep Boiling–Water Bath kettle that manufacturers of routine housewares had been so slow to produce in quantity at a reasonable price. (The question *PFB* gets asked most often is where to find affordable B–W Bath canners that live up to recognized standards for processing safely.)

This newcomer is referred to as an "atmospheric steam" canner, and it *must NEVER be confused with the traditional Pressure Canner.*

The atmospheric canner gets its name because the kettle is not sealed, and therefore the saturated steam inside it—not being under significantly more pressure per square inch than the air in the room outside—cannot get hotter than the boiling point of water in a utensil with an unsecured cover.

In contrast, after the cover of a Pressure Canner is clamped on tight and the free air inside the vessel is exhausted in a strong plume for 10 minutes, the vent is then closed, thus sealing the canner so that the internal pressure can build. From 212 F/100 C at sea level under no extra pressure, the steam temperature rises to better than 215 F/102 C at 1 pound, to 228 F/109 C at 5 pounds, to 240 F/116 C at 10 pounds, to 250 F/121 C at 15 pounds (naturally, it can go higher, but 15 pounds is the maximum pressure considered wise to use with home equipment and conditions).

The use of atmospheric steam for home-canning apparently got its first sizable push after World War I. Advertisements around the late 1920's/early '30's showed big boxy affairs called "steamer canners" holding tiers of jars on racks inside; steam was expected to wend through and around the layers to process the food. They had a relatively short life as home-canning equipment. Their cost during the Depression years, the advances in food technology, and, as a result, development of the Pressure Canner for home use, combined to force them out of the scene.

The modern version we're talking about resembles a giant top-of-the-stove sterilizer for babies' nursing bottles. It comes in three sections: a shallow bottom to hold water that will boil hard to produce steam around the jars; a rack set just above the water to hold the jars of fruit or pickles; and a tall, domed lid that inverts to come down over the jars and rest on the lip around the edge of the bottom. Small holes at the rim of the cover let steam escape near the base of the jars while they're being processed.

So far as *PFB* can tell without sidetracking on who-did-what-first, April 1976 saw perhaps the earliest publication of results from investigating a substitute for the B–W Bath kettle. This is the date of *Circular 226, Use of Low Water Level in Boiling Water Bath Canning,* Agricultural Experiment Station, Auburn University, Auburn, Alabama. In their introduction the authors—a professor of horticulture and a graduate in food science—say that ". . . Products will heat as well with a low level of boiling water as with a high level, provided the canning vessel is equipped with a close-fitting cover to hold saturated steam around and over the jars."

What spurred the research we don't know. The energy crunch was a vivid concern; so was the fact that the number of people canning their food was nearly three times greater than in the 1960's (and evidenced by such a shortage of decent jar lids that *The New Yorker* magazine had a cartoon of cocktail-party chatter about canning lids). We like to think the study was prompted by consumer frustration at the dearth of canners that would do the job right.

The important thing in considering atmospheric steam canners here and now is that *Circular 226* devotes itself to documenting the steps taken to apply physics to the technical problem, with a lucid and brief discussion of convected and conducted heat— ". . . Factors affecting heating rate [of food in the jars being processed—J.G.] should be understood. While this research has demonstrated that low-water level in a covered BWB canner does not slow the heating rate of the product, certain other factors do affect the heating rate."

The vessels used in the Auburn study were kettles tall enough to hold jars of food and possessed tight-fitting covers of varied design. The report does not recommend processing times for foods canned at home in atmospheric kettles.

Nor does it describe procedures for everyday use beyond murmuring that "In the case of atmospheric canning, jar covers should be tightened firmly but not excessively. Jars closed in this manner with the two-piece covers will self-exhaust during heating."

Notable, too, is the restraint of the authors when they say: "Use of low-water method would greatly reduce time and heat-energy requirements for *preheating canning vessels and water* [italics supplied], reduce the amount of heat liberated to the kitchen, and provide a basis for a wider choice of vessels for BWB canning."

This is thumbnail background, and rough; and not meant to be more.

But it does show that the Auburn researchers made no claim that their atmospheric process would "cut in half the canning time" for fruits and other strong-acid foods. Yet this is part of the sales pitch for a domed aluminum canner put on the market later in the '70's, and developed, reportedly, at a Middle Western university. In some stories the inventor was quoted as saying that his canner could create a temperature of around 190 degrees Fahrenheit in the center of jars of fruit (and by inference in other strong-acid foods normally processed in a B–W Bath). Nevertheless, the maker's ads chose to stress "canning time cut in half"—a copy-line echoed by merchants when a heavier-duty and larger graniteware domed atmospheric canner came along.

It's ironic that the enameled atmospheric canner is made by a company that was sluggish about supplying a conventional B–W Bath canner needed so sorely for processing quart jars; as was explained in Chapter 3, such a vessel would have to be 4½ to 5 inches deeper than the height of the capped canning jar. (And meanwhile alert householders have been buying heavy-duty restaurant stockpots from "gourmet" kitchenware shops, and using the mighty kettles as canners.)

A number of the nation's most listened-to food scientists have been frustrated by the new atmospheric steam canner. The physics of it are sound, and it worked under the controlled conditions of laboratories/test kitchens. And Lord knows a good canner is needed for strong-acid food. So why did these experts urge mail-order outlets to hold off on cataloguing it? Or refuse to give it their blessing? Even to warn outright against it?

Because at this writing no one has yet produced comprehensive and sound and workable directions for using such a canner at home. The directions would have to be supported by an adequate research base, and one that any sensible person can trust and follow with safety.

Certainly the 1981 congress in Chicago of top-flight food scientists and nutritionists has had an impact on testing, and will have an impact on publishing respectable instructions for the average buyer of a new atmospheric fruit canner. The directions should include these things:

How long to exhaust the canner before starting to count the processing time?

How long should actual processing time be for each strong-acid food—including dense ones tightly packed (requiring conduction heat), and ones with looser texture, and suspended in more liquid (requiring convection heat)?

When/how to check if the water level is right for processing a particular food? (Something more is required than the quaint old trick of putting marbles in the water so they'll bounce with the boil: you can wreck a whole batch by letting the heat fluctuate drastically as you add water for the migs and cat's-eyes.) Wouldn't it make sense to refill the water compartment after each batch is through processing?

What more, if anything, is needed for a safe translation for atmospheric canners of the processing times and procedures that have been developed—oh, so carefully over the years!—for the good old Boiling–Water Bath, provided the criteria for making and maintaining saturated steam are met?

Wait. You'll get the answer.

In the meantime you can turn back to the preceding chapter, and see how to convert a Pressure Canner, with its vent open, into a safe kettle for processing strong-acid foods.

SO WHAT'S A LITTLE BIT OF MOLD . . .

A mold is a fungus, and the fungi include mushrooms like truffles or the elegant morel, and yeasts, plus the specially cultured growths that trace blue veins in a noble Stilton cheese and or give us the means of producing streptomycin and penicillin. Surely these molds can't be said to hurt you.

But then there are the fungi that embrace toadstools and mildew, and the mold on fruits and vegetables and grains and nuts and seeds, and on food too long in the refrigerator, and in foods improperly canned or sealed. Inhale spores from some of these molds and you can develop allergies or suffer injury to your bronchia and lungs. As they grow, some molds throw off poisons called mycotoxins (much like the way spores of *Clostridium botulinum* make the deadly toxin that causes botulism); of the mycotoxins, the one with the most and worst publicity is aflatoxin. Aflatoxin occurs naturally on nuts and peanuts and corn and wheat and millet and rice and cottonseed among other things, and none of the usual means of destroying a poison like, say, botulinum toxin is able to faze it.

Mold grows in warmish temperatures on foodstuffs exposed to moisture and oxygen. These are the reasons why grains must be stored dry and kept cool, and fresh vegetables and fruit must be kept cool, and canned food must be kept sealed after it has been processed (and processed correctly in the first place, to destroy mold spores in the food and in the containers). In addition to attacking plant materials, molds in a refrigerator will invade preserves and ham and cold cuts and dairy products and cake and bread; they just take longer to do so in cool storage.

So far molds have been a matter for routine good handling. *PFB* is especially harsh about molds because they can get into an apparently well-sealed jar of canned food in the 4.5 or 4.6 *pH* range—that is, in foods rated as strong-acid—and they can consume just enough acid to make the contents tip over into the low-acid category, thus giving any undestroyed spores of *C. botulinum* a medium in which they can flourish. And as these spores multiply, they make the dreaded poison; and as they make their poison, they can produce a different sort of acid in minuscule amounts. But apparently these amounts can add up to enough acidity to restore the *pH* rating that should guarantee safety IF the food had been canned with reliable procedures in the first place.

This is not a scenario made up to be scary. It actually occurred in the early 1970's when tomatoes were canned by the old open-kettle method, long in disrepute. Canned juice, even canned pears, also caused an outbreak of botulism. In the last case it was considered that specks of food lodged on the sealing-rim of the jar, preventing a true seal—and thereby giving mold a chance to eat its way into the contents. Or maybe a bad sealing-ring was used by a cook who wasn't much bothered by mold.

USING SPACE–AGE PLASTICS

In Chapter 21, "Drying," *PFB* warns against using any plastic for storing food of any kind unless the wrap/bag/box is rated as *food-grade*. So how to find out if one of these plastic things is O.K. to use with food, when the labels don't tell you NOT to do it?

First, really examine the label. Just as certain wraps and bags are quick to tell you that they're "ideal for freezing" or that they're intended for use in freezers in the first place, so will wrappings that are food-grade tell you to use them to protect food.

If the blurb or the label does not mention food, consider that the plastics are *not O.K.'d* for use with food. Such plastics are those used in making waste bins or trash cans, in liners for waste-collectors, and lawn/leaf/trash bags. The best-known makers of plastics for such use are the chemical division of Mobil, and Union Carbide. Both these giants take the trouble to warn *against* using their trash plastics for food. Neither company has asked the Food and Drug Administration to approve these particular plastic products for use with food; we understand that they're not about to, either. Both, along with Dow, make highly publicized lines of food-grade plastic containers and wraps.

Their trash plastics contain a chemical toughener, and usually a substance called a "plasticizer" added to the ingredients to allow the goop to extrude readily in the form desired (as a sheet, or as toothbrush handles or as cat boxes or whatever). These plasticizer chemicals often contain cadmium—definitely not a thing for human beings to mess with, much less ingest, since all its soluble compounds are poisonous. As are the garbage bags with built-in germicides.

Cobalt 60 and Your Cut-up Fryer

If consumers, the Congress, the FDA and the food industry ever run short of contention, they can always turn to the matter of commercial irradiation of foods, a problem to keep all parties busy for years.

This irradiation has nothing whatever to do with handling food at home or with methods discussed in *PFB:* instead, it's an esoteric treatment designed to purify rather than to preserve by processing, and it would use a radiation source like Cobalt 60 to sterilize fresh or packaged food. This short-term bombardment, which in some ways resembles an X-ray treatment, would be to give the treated foods a much longer storage life.

Ruth Hertzberg first saw radiation tested in the 1960's at the U.S. Army Research Center at Natick, Massachusetts, where food processing and preparation methods were being developed and refined for the armed services and the NASA program. Freeze-drying, Ruth points out, is an example of the results achieved there.

By Congressional definition the source of radiation is regarded as a food additive; and, as an additive, is investigated and monitored and evaluated by the Food and Drug Administration. Both the Congress and the FDA agree that an enormous campaign of public education must be mounted if this sort of irradiation is ever to be used on our food supply. Meanwhile, in mid–December of 1981 the FDA granted conditional permission to a San Jose, California, company to treat fruit threatened with infestation by the Mediterranean fruit fly.

However, there's no move—or prediction of a move—to offer that the average household in the U.S.A. be furnished with do-it-yourself radiation sources for treating food at home. Remember back in the '60's the far-out prediction that Americans would rush to equip their homes with small reactors in the cellar to furnish heat and light? —J.G.

DEALING WITH HIGH TECHNOLOGY

While we're on the subject of space-age innovations, now is as good a time as any to take a stand against things that keep cropping up in our mail. In a minute we'll be talking about mistaken ideas from the past; the following, most of them dramatically wrong, are taken from the living present.

It is not possible to can food in a modern automatic electric dishwasher. Heaven knows where this notion first surfaced, but like several other suggestions that are equally hairy, *PFB* encountered the idea in several reader-participation columns of publications with wide circulation. It would be interesting to chart the thought processes behind such a procedure, since deluxe models reach an atmospheric heat of 140+ F/60+ C only when they're set for extra hot cycles. In a home dishwasher the temperature reached inside a container of food could only help produce a bacterial load that nobody needs.

Perhaps correspondents bemused by the novelty were thinking: "(1) We see steam sometimes coming under the door just when the drying cycle starts; (2) wait a minute—don't the experts say steam is good for canning food?; and (3) hey!—we'll put those jars of tomatoes in with the other things right at the start of the cycles, and when we take out the dishes we'll have some canned tomatoes ready to put down cellar."

Lord!

It is impossible to can safely in a microwave oven. A number of years ago when one of the big makers of microwave ovens was launching its product with a lot of fanfare, it suggested that fruits, being strong-acid, could be canned in their oven. *PFB* saw this early literature and did its share of making a fuss about the recommendation. The company was good about such protests, and jerked the idea from its promotion. *Neither this company nor any other responsible manufacturer sanctions the idea that food may be canned in their microwave ovens.*

Blanching vegetables or fruits in a microwave oven to prepare them for freezing or drying is all right, though: the directions for operating each model specify how to blanch in it. In general there is a quite small amount of food in each batch; not much water is used; and the food is turned or stirred at least once to allow it to precook evenly. (Simpler, on the whole, to dunk each 1 pound of prepared vegetables in 1 gallon of briskly boiling water; or steam the food according to individual instructions.)

You cannot can food in a crockpot. We don't know who could have advocated this, since we have never seen any such claims in print by the makers of crockpots. But it has come up several times in letters to *PFB,* usually from writers who say they hope it's safe, because they felt that slow-cooking was more likely to preserve nutrients than subjecting the food to heats like 240 F/116 C. All we need to say about a crockpot is that if it's on a long low-heat setting, chances are that the nastier micro-organisms will be encouraged to grow and breed like mad, and what else should you expect?

It is interesting that the people asking about crockpot canning do not think in terms of pasteurizing milk by heating it for 30 minutes at 142 F/61 C *vs.* for 15 seconds at 160 F/71 C. Both these treatments do the same job in destroying bacteria they're aimed at ("aimed at," because pasteurization destroys only certain micro-organisms), but more vitamins remain in the milk at the higher temperature for 15 seconds than are left after lower heat for half an hour.

Vacuum sealer. One of the more lavish gift catalogs that comes our way often lists housewares for those people who "have everything" including lots and lots of money. A featured item in late 1981 was a table-top vacuum chamber—about a foot in diameter and slightly taller—in which, the advertisement said, one could put a (closed?) container of food, press a button, and in seconds have an airtight seal. The vessel is praised as being particularly good as a way of fighting inflation by preventing the waste of food, because *air is the major cause of spoiling* (italics ours). H'm-m-m. Then later comes the flat assertion that the utensil can be *an invaluable aid to canning* because it *saves time and assures a tighter, safer seal.* (Horrified italics supplied because the statement IGNORES THE MATTER OF ACIDITY, and THE NEED FOR HEAT–PRO-CESSING to destroy bad micro-organisms, etc., etc.—ed.)

Know your canner at 15 pounds. This is not hair-raising, like the preceding ideas; it's a plea for vigilance and good sense. Talking about Pressure Canners in Chapter 3, we cited publication late in the 1970's of the University of Minnesota's curtailed-at-15-pounds processing for low-acid foods; in later chapters specifics are mentioned as they apply. We mentioned the report as innovative: not because the concept for dealing with tomatoes, vegetables, meats, poultry and seafood was new, but because the procedures were the first we had seen that spelled out particulars and times—and were backed by the Minnesota Extension Service's reputation for impeccable research.

PFB feels a responsibility, though, to warn *beginners* at home-canning to hold off on processing at 15 pounds for the shorter periods. Householders must have completely reliable gauges—no mental calibrations, PLEASE, for a dial that could be off by a pound or two; and they must know how many jiggles or rockings per minute is correct for the dead-weight gauges of their canners. And what altitude they live at, and how to compensate for atmospheric pressure. And they should have a clock with sweep second- and minute-hands, not only a cookie-timer.

They should know their stuff as well as know their canners.

BACTERIAL LOAD

Everyone careful in handling food knows that the best way to have safe food is to start with clean food; and that the utensils and boards and holding vessels must be immaculate, or they will supply contamination. Above all, the food-handler knows that it's not merely O.K. it's *absolutely necessary* to refrigerate food that's not going to be held at 140 F/60 C or above until it is eaten. *PFB* is leery of any steam-table unless it is supervised by a professional, and generally we deplore casual "keeping something warm" at home. For several generations now, the refrigerator has been capable of kicking its motor on automatically to cool any warm food put into it; certainly it's no trick to reheat quickly any dish to be served. (A case of botulism was traced to a frozen pot pie that was not completely cooked when the oven was turned off; it stayed in the oven until the next day, as we recollect the report; and then it was reheated and eaten by a hungry teenager—who recovered after intensive care in the hospital.)

PFB also is stiff-necked about refreezing thawed food, especially poultry and seafood—actually, any low-acid thing that has not been thoroughly cooked. When you look at the thermometer-chart in Chapter 2, you see the range where bacteria begin to grow and where they thrive. When the package goes back into the freezer, the micro-organisms don't die—they just become inactive. Then if that piece of food is thawed on a countertop before being cooked, and the way it finally is cooked doesn't take care of the manifold increase of bacteria . . .

Salmonella food poisoning is nothing like the killer that *C. botulinum* can be, but it's all too commonplace in poultry and eggs, etc., etc.

HOME–CURING PORK

Professionals should do the slaughtering of meat animals, and the carcasses should be correctly hung and bled and chilled. *PFB* got a letter, restrained under the circumstances, from a reader who'd followed our directions for preparing the cure, and applying it, and holding the hams and bacon properly and at 38 F/3 C. She was clear and definite about the temperature; they'd used an old refrigerator, kept a thermometer inside, and checked it often. Despite such care the meat spoiled: it discolored and a nasty liquid collected in the bottom of the container.

We took the problem to various Agriculture Department experts, all of whom agreed that our directions were correct, and they offered these reasons for the spoilage:

The carcass had not been bled immediately or fully.

The carcass had been improperly chilled. This can mean either that the flesh had been allowed to freeze to some extent, thereby making it less capable of absorbing salt; or it had not been cooled adequately and quickly enough, and so the bacterial load had increased to such an extent that the cure could not offset its progress.

Perhaps the cure had contained ingredients that are not food-grade. Standard commercial mixtures are food-grade (even though some consumers jib at the nitrites), but an ice-melting type of salt might have been introduced into the cure.

Perhaps sea salt—which could mean solar salt, dried in beds (see Chapters 17 and 20) had been part of the cure. Even if it is food-grade and O.K. to ingest, apparently sea salt can contain substances that react poorly with other natural chemicals in the raw meat (of special interest, because we'd not been told this before). Salt sold commercially as *solar* is loaded with impurities.

COZY OLD–TIME WAYS

Don't try to can food in a conventional oven. Dry heat cannot penetrate a container of food well enough to do the job: boiling water or saturated steam for strong-acid food, or steam under pressure for low-acid food—these are for canning. (And the jars can explode in your hands.) Sterilize jelly glasses in an oven, before they're filled with hot jelly. But this is the extent of it.

Words from the Top. Among the pleasures of compiling Chapter 25, "Where to Find Things," were—still are—the varied styles and flavors of writing by the nation's foremost experts on food safety. Here are two examples:

From Ruth Klippstein, Professor of Nutritional Sciences at Cornell University, concerning material sent out to the county agents in home economics across New York State:

"[Apropos *very* old-time instructions from a number of sources] they are either very imprecise, or use what is now an expensive ingredient, or result in a product which by modern standards is not acceptable."

And from Isabel D. Wolf, Associate Professor and Food Science and Nutrition Extension Specialist, University of Minnesota, under the heading "Home Canning Recipes":

". . . Avoid following the home-canning advice of celebrities, old cookbooks, 'back to nature' publications, and out-of-date home canning leaflets. Some potentially dangerous instructions can be found in old official publications, even those of this state!"

"Canning pills" went out with corset-covers. Old manuals might suggest that salicylic acid (read this "aspirin") be dropped in each canning jar before it was capped. Such things never helped then and would not help now.

No preservative added can offset dirty handling or inadequate processing.

Let canned food cool upright at room temperature. Several generations ago there were cooks who removed their jars from the processing kettle, swaddled each in towels or newspapers and then planted them upside-down to cool. Keeping hot glass jars out of drafts is one thing; wrapping them merely slows down the cooling and can lead to spoilage on the shelf. As for upending them, more seals are broken by such a practice than are helped: the seal has begun by the time the jar is taken from the canner. (In 1981 directions were distributed with a certain preserving aid that recommended jars be turned on their tops to cool; the seals didn't break, but the jelly just stuck to the caps and left head-room at the bottom of the jars.)

The 2 inches of boiling water in a B–W Bath helps keep liquid from being drawn from the containers during processing—aside from helping to ensure a safe product.

Don't leave processed food in a Pressure Canner more than 20 minutes after pressure is back to Zero. The canner can create a seal inside itself if not allowed the final quick venting as the lid is removed; this seal can break the seal on jars.

5

CANNING FRUITS

Canned fruits have a major place in any family food plan, so there's no apology needed for canning fruit and using it, unadorned, to complement a meal. The newcomer to food preservation usually starts with canning fruits, unless she/he already has a freezer—or is bemused by the current popularity of so-called dehydrating and therefore dries it for snacks. And people will always keep on putting it into jellies or jams or conserves . . .

Certainly some fruits are less satisfactory canned than frozen: strawberries are a prime example. Yet when you think of beautiful peaches (which do much better in jars and cans than they do in freezers as a general rule), and a compôte from containers on the pantry shelf, and tart berries or mixtures that are the "timber" for pies and cobblers in the wintertime, and pears that are light and charming as salad makings or to end a meal—when you think of these you have a hint of the versatility of fruits canned at home.

And as any conscientious parent will point out, infants thrive on natural fruit purées without additives (if you can them at home you know darned well what is *not* in them), and the taste for fruit's simplicity continues through to any age. Healthy is the youngster who is pleased with applesauce for dessert instead of a fistful of junk food.

We predict a resurgence of interest in canning fruit, now that it has been made inescapably plain that the average diet in the United States contains far too much sugar. The old idea that canned fruit must wallow in heavy syrup in order to be acceptable is a concept long discredited. Indeed, fruit may be canned without any added sweetness, because the amount of sweetening put into canned fruits is merely there to help hold color or to enhance flavor: it has no virtue to speak of as a preservative. So what does one use in place of a syrup, especially since water alone may be too blah for words?—Fruit juice. It takes only a little more thought and a bit more time to extract it from fruit set apart for the purpose. The result is delightful.

As with all food that is being put by, fruit and berries must be in fine condition before they are canned. Therefore use only firm just-ripe fruits and berries. They must be fresh—strictly fresh. They must be processed within hours of being brought into the house, or they must be refrigerated overnight.

If they are merely a shade overripe they have lost some of their natural acid content—and they'll also be more likely to float to the top of the jar.

If they are extremely overripe they have lost a critical amount of acid, and, aside from the fact that their flavor and texture are disappointing, they might not be able to discourage growth of spoilers.

Never use "drops"—drops being fruit that has fallen from the tree or been shaken from the bush. These are on the verge of rotting, and they can all but ruin a good batch of food.

The individual instructions that follow use the Boiling–Water Bath at 212 F/100 C at the sea-level zone, with, occasionally for juice, the pasteurizing *Hot*-Water Bath at 190 F/88 C at sea level. To people living at high altitudes we recommend another look at "Correcting for Altitude" in Chapter 3; and we've inserted just ahead of the specifics for each fruit a reminder about increasing headroom above 1000 ft/305 m, and especially for Pressure-processing.

• NOTE: Procedures for canning Tomatoes—which are classed botanically as fruit—are given separately in their own Chapter 6.

NO SHORT CUTS

You simply must follow carefully all the right steps for selecting, preparing and processing fruits: There have been cases reported of botulism poisoning from home-canned apricots, blackberries, figs, huckleberry juice, peaches and pears—even though these are all in the traditional strong-acid grouping. Records of these cases indicate that there was careless handling somewhere along the line. (See "Dealing with the Spoilers" in Chapter 2).

Relevant Metrics for Canning Fruits

Full metric conversions, with the arithmetic for refining them, are given at the start of Chapter 17 ("Common Ingredients and How to Use Them"), but the following—rounded off—apply in this chapter.

If you live above the sea-level zone (i.e., *over* 1000 ft/305 m), consult the subsection "Correcting for Altitude" in Chapter 3. (And do pay attention to the need for extra headroom in jars at high altitudes.)

• • •

Temperatures (@ sea level): 170 F/77 C——190 F/88 C——200 F/93 C——212 F/100 C.

Volume: 1 teaspoon = 5 mL——1 tablespoon = 15 mL——2 tablespoons = 30 mL——½ cup = 125 mL——¾ cup = 200 mL——1 cup = 250 mL——½ pint = 250 mL——1 pint = 500 mL——1 quart = 1 L.

Length: ¼ inch = 0.64 cm——½ inch = 1.27 cm——1 inch = 2.54 cm.

In case you find a tempting old recipe that relies on the "open-kettle" procedure now proven to be inadequate, here is how to translate it for the B–W Bath. Prepare and cook the fruit according to the old recipe. Pack the boiling-hot fruit and its juice in clean jars, leaving correct headroom for container size and altitude. Adjust lids, and process in a B–W Bath for the time given for Hot pack in the directions for that sort of food, later in this chapter.

Liquids for Canning Fruits

Sugar is not necessary as a preservative in canning fruit. The amounts of sugar given in the syrup proportions that follow, or that are used in commercial canning, or are found in the old manuals—all these amounts of sugar or comparable sweeteners are used to retain the texture and color of canned fruit. That the added sugar cannot act as a preservative is borne out by the disquieting appearance of mold and fermentation in opened jars of fruit that have remained too long in the refrigerator.

Commercial canners in the past have leaned toward Heavy syrup, except in the so-called diet pack that declares that the fruit is canned in its own juices, or it is mentioned on the label contents that water is added to the pack. Usually these ostensible diet packs were found only in the special sections of supermarkets devoted to low-sodium, low- or non-sugar products. More recently, though, the Calorie-conscious shopper has been insisting on having fruit canned in its own juices or with Very Light syrup on sale in the regular sections of canned fruit.

Now the emphasis for health is even more explicit: Nutrition surveys report that Americans, per capita, eat 100 pounds of sugar each year—a great deal too much. One of the best ways to promote healthy eating habits, especially in youngsters, is to top off a pleasant meal with fruit. Out of season, the fruits are either too expensive; or they require thawing if they have been frozen. It is much easier to take a jar off the shelf and serve it, knowing that the family's taste and the family's health are being served along with it.

Heavy syrup has not been used very much by home-canners for some time. The instructions for individual fruits recommend which syrups to use—but remember, please, that if you prefer to can without any sweetening, it is perfectly safe to do so. The recommendation of syrups are merely for flavor and texture, and this fact cannot be emphasized too much.

Boiling water is the easiest liquid to add: it is poured into the jars after the fruit has been packed; then, as with all packs involving added liquid, a table knife or a very thin spatula is moved around the inside of the jar to release any bubbles of air that are trapped when the fruit was packed with the water.

• **Altitude note:** At sea level the usual headroom for fruits is a scant ½ inch for ½-pint jars (not used very often unless they are for special diets, which are discussed later). Standard headroom for fruit in pints or quarts in a B–W Bath at sea level is ½ inch. At high altitudes—especially above

3,000 feet, and *always at 5,000 or more feet*—extra headroom must be added because steam in the jars as the atmospheric pressure gets *lower,* expands as the altitude gets higher. Therefore a housewife in Santa Fe would can a 1-pint jar of fruit with up to 1 inch of headroom (and most likely in a pressure canner). Do look again at "Correcting for Altitude" in Chapter 3.

How Much Liquid

Roughly estimate up to ½ to ¾ cup of syrup/liquid for each pint or No. 2 can, and increase the allowance proportionally for larger containers; this means that quarts would take from 1 to 1½ cups of added liquid, with the same amount estimated for No. 2½ cans. The middle-sized 1½-pint jars—and tapered wide-mouth—would take an in-between amount.

Because you don't want to hold up the parade by stopping to make syrup or extract juices when you're in the throes of packing your fruit in jars, it's a good idea to do your fruit juice/syrups before you actually start preparing your fruit for canning; of course the syrup can be made several days in advance and refrigerated. If you take a quick look at the yield chart for fresh fruits to can you'll find that the *pounds* needed per 1 quart jar are the most sensible measurement to go by. (Not many people buy grapes or apricots by the bushel any more; cherries and the smaller fruits are bought by the pound and, unless you have your own fruit trees or berry plants, you're watching the cost as you go along.) However, a whole bushel of peaches, one that averages 48 pounds in weight, will produce 18 to 24 quarts, depending on whether the fruit is packed as halves or quarters or slices. With this in mind, you can make and store in the refrigerator a number of quarts of syrup.

The rules-of-thumb are: For Thin syrup use 4 cups of water or other liquid and 2 cups of sugar to make 5 cups.

For Medium, use 4 cups of water or other liquid and 3 cups of sugar to make 5½ cups.

For Heavy, use 4 cups of water or other liquid and 4¾ cups of sugar to get 6½ cups.

To make any of these, mix the sugar with the water/liquid in the proportions given, heat them together until the sugar is dissolved, skimming if necessary. Skimming is sometimes needed because of perfectly edible substances in the sugar that can make a small amount of opaque froth as the syrup is heated.

Using Juice for Canning Liquid

The best source for estimating the yield of juice from fruit is in Chapter 18, "Jellies, Jams and Other Sweet Things"; or the leaflet that comes with any commercial pectin to be used for making jelly and jam at home. Naturally these juices that are the base for jellies are likely to overpower fruit if they are used full strength as canning liquid; therefore, if you make up a batch of clear, strained juice as if it were for jelly, you will want to dilute it with an equal amount of water, or to suit the family's taste. Try mixing maverick juices for unusual and delicious flavors. However, generally ground spices change flavor too much or cloud the liquid.

Either buy extra fruit from which you'll make the juice, or set aside a portion of a large amount, like a bushel, that you already have. Pick over the fruit carefully (reserving the perfect examples for canning and using the homelier ones for making juice). Wash these and cut away all blemishes, bruises, gouges; certainly any areas where spoilage has started must be cut out drastically. It is not necessary to peel the fruit to be used in the canning liquid, but just make sure that your fruit is impeccably clean, and has been cut in small pieces after all blemishes have been removed. Put the prepared fruit in an enameled or stainless-steel kettle with an equal amount of water. Bring to simmering and, when the fruit is softened, crush it with a potato masher or pastry blender or some such thing. Then bring it to a boil and boil it for a couple of minutes. The fruit pulp need not be put through a real jelly bag (again, see Chapter 18) if you are in a hurry. Still, it is nice to have a reasonably clear liquid surrounding your nice canned fruit, so flop your pulp around in a sieve to get all the juice you can and then—because the juice is much less concentrated than it would be for making jelly—pour it through a standard coffee filter into a series of clean, hot quart jars. Our favorite for fast filtering is a large circle that folds into quarters, but any filter paper will do as liners for smaller sieves that hold the cone in place to let the hot juice drip through very quickly. Cap with the sterile lid and store in the refrigerator, not longer than 3 or 4 days.

THE SWEETENERS TO USE

Chapter 17, "Common Ingredients and How to Use Them," offers details of the relative sweetening powers of natural and artificial ingredients (and also comments on their virtues in special diets). Meanwhile, *fructose,* which is fruit sugar, could be substituted for standard sucrose (table sugar)—*if* you can afford to do so. Commercial canners use the "HFS" (high fructose syrup) that is not available to the general public. If you are drawn to fructose, it would be better economy to add it when the fruit is served.

Light corn syrup may be substituted for up to ½ the white sugar called for in making the syrups described above.

Mild-flavored honey also may be used for up to ½ the regular sugar in the syrup ingredients. Honey is getting more expensive all the time, and it may not be feasible except for very special bland fruits like pears, which might benefit from the addition of honey. Use only a mild honey, lest a pronounced flavor mask that of the fruit.

Maple syrup, another natural sweetener whose cost is likely to be prohibitive, should take the place of only ¼ the sugar noted in the syrup above, because of its pronounced flavor even when it is a Fancy or Grade A.

Brown sugar, which used to be termed "raw" although it wasn't, may be substituted for part of the white sugar according to the family's preference or if some special result is desired. Usually, though, its molasses-y flavor is too much for regular canned fruits.

Sorghum and *molasses* are both too overpowering in their own right to be satisfactory in canned fruit.

STEPS IN CANNING ALL FRUITS

Make your syrup ahead of time, in an amount based on the quantity of fruit you intend to can (discussed at length in "Liquid for Canning Fruits" earlier).

Next, collect your utensils and containers. It's vital to have scrupulously clean utensils, cloths and work surfaces, including cutting-boards and counters, and a good supply of fresh water of drinking quality.

Jars/cans and their sealers must be perfect and perfectly clean. They need not be sterilized, since the adequate Boiling–Water Bath will sterilize the inside of containers during processing. Prepare containers and their sealers as in "About Jars and Cans" in Chapter 3.

To Prevent Canned Fruit from Discoloring

Work with only one canner batch at a time. Wash the fruit thoroughly in fresh drinking water, but don't let it soak. Lift it from the water to allow sediment to settle at the bottom of the wash water. Be extra gentle with berries. Remove stems, hulls, pits, skins, cores as described in instructions for individual fruits. Cut away all soft or bruised spots and any places where skin is broken: such blemishes can spoil your batch.

Cut apples, apricots, nectarines, peaches and pears discolor in air. Either coat the cut pieces well as you go along with a solution of 1 teaspoon crystalline ascorbic acid (Vitamin C, the best anti-oxidant) to each 1 cup water; OR drop the pieces in a solution of 2 tablespoons salt and 2 tablespoons vinegar for each 1 gallon of cold water— but not for longer than 20 minutes, lest nutrients leach out too much—then rinse and drain the pieces well before packing the Raw or Hot way. Optional: to prevent their darkening while in the containers, add ¼ teaspoon Vitamin C to each 1 quart during packing—IF they haven't been treated with ascorbic acid as they were being prepared. (See also "Anti-discoloration Treatments" in Chapter 17.)

And remember: Fruit canned with too much headroom or too little liquid will tend to darken at the top of the container.

Packing, Processing and All the Rest . . .

We refer you to the blow-by-blow "General Steps in Canning" in Chapter 3, instead of offering a quick paraphrase here. Everything in that detailed account applies to packing, processing, checking and storing jars or cans of fruit.

Each step is essential to successful canning, but if we had to assign a No. 1 priority as most critical for food safety (assuming that the containers are sound and the food is appetizing), it would be: *Adequate processing*—meaning full heat for the full time in a Pressure Canner for low-acid foods, or in a B–W Bath for strong-acid ones.

CANNED FRUIT TROUBLES AND WHAT TO DO

The only time you can tinker SAFELY with a container of canned food is during the 24 hours after it comes from the canner and before it is stored away.

If you find a faulty seal during this lull, repack and reprocess the fruit from scratch according to the original instructions, cutting no corners. There of course will be a loss in quality, especially in texture, from doing it over; and if there's only one poor seal it's probably simpler to eat the fruit right away or refrigerate it for a day or so, then serve it.

Examples: failing to exhaust the contents of a can to a minimum of 170 F/77 C, or leaving insufficient headroom in jars (the latter can cause bits of food to be forced out during the processing period, with resulting poor seals). Heat the food—exhausting if in cans, or as Hot pack—in clean containers, *with fresh, new lids/sealers,* and reprocess for the full time. However, several poor seals warn you that something was dangerously wrong with your packing or processing, and the failure could affect the whole batch.

Failing to keep at least 2 inches of boiling water over the tops of the containers, and not keeping the water in the canner at a full boil from beginning to end of the processing period—both are fairly common causes of loss of liquid in the jars, and poor seals. Repack in clean containers with fresh, new sealers, and reprocess for the full time.

But, if, after the containers have been stored away, you find any of the following, DESTROY THE CONTENTS SO THAT THEY CANNOT BE EATEN BY PEOPLE OR ANIMALS. Then follow the procedures in "Signs of Spoilage and What to Do" in Chapter 3 (i.e., 15-minute soak for containers and closures in a 1:4 household bleach solution; discarding all closures except *sound* all-glass lids for bail-type jars, and discarding all cans, metal caps, rubber rings and sealers). If sound, the jars may be used again.

- Broken seals, bulging lids on cans.
- Seepage around the seal, even though it seems firmly seated.
- Mold, even a fleck, in the contents or around the seal or on the underside of the lid.
- Gassiness (small bubbles) in the contents.
- Spurting liquid, pressure from inside as the container is opened.
- Spongy or slimy food.
- Cloudy or yeasty liquid.
- Off-odor, disagreeable smell, mustiness.

Not Prize-Winning, But Edible

If the containers and contents offer none of the signs of spoilage noted above, and if the storage has been properly cool, you still can have these less-than-perfect fruits that still are O.K. to eat.

Floating fruit. The fruit was overripe, or it was packed too loosely, or the syrup was too heavy.

Darker fruit at the top of the container. Too much headroom above the liquid.

Bleached-looking berries. With no signs of spoilage present, this could mean that jars were exposed to light in the storage area; wrap the jars in paper or stash them in closed cartons if the storage isn't dark.

CANNING EACH FRUIT

Altitude and headroom reminders: Do look at "Correcting for Altitude" in Chapter 3 for adjustments you must make in times, or even in the processing procedure, required. And remember that, if you have elected to use Pressure–processing according to the makers' most recent instructions (Chapter 25 for sources) instead of the Boiling–Water Bath, you should increase slightly the amount of headroom, because the air (gas) inside the jar expands more at the greater heat of the Pressure Canner. If you remain with the B–W Bath and merely add processing *time,* you still should increase headroom for altitudes of more than, say, 3000 feet/914 meters: ¾ inch for pints is not too much in this case.

Apples

Even with root-cellaring and drying (see both), you'll want some apples put by as sauce, dessert slices or pie timber. And of these, probably the handiest thing is to can applesauce and slices done in syrup, and to freeze the slices you'll use for pies, q.v. in Chapters 12 and 16. There's a handy rule for Apple Pie Filling, and for the method/uses of Boiled Cider, in Chapter 10, "Canning Convenience Foods." How to do Apple Cider is described later in this chapter, under "Canning Juices."

GENERAL HANDLING

Boiling–Water Bath. Use Hot pack only. Use jars or plain cans. Process with Thin Syrup, plain water, or with natural juice as desired.

Because apples oxidize in the air, work quickly with only one canner batch at a time. Wash, peel and core apples (save peels and cores for jelly, as described in Applesauce, in a minute); treat prepared pieces with either of the anti-discoloration solutions described in Chapter 17. Drain, and carry on with the specific handling.

SLICES (HOT PACK ONLY)

Rinse drained, prepared pieces. Cover with hot Thin Syrup or water, boil gently for 5 minutes. Lift out and drain, saving cooking syrup or water. Pack hot.

Yields in Canned Fruit

Since the legal weight of a bushel of fruits differs between States, the weights given below are average; the yields are approximate.

FRUITS	FRESH	QUARTS CANNED
Apples	1 bu (48 lbs)	16–20
	2½–3 lbs	1
Apple juice	1 bu (48 lbs)	10
Applesauce	1 bu (48 lbs)	15–18
	2½–3½ lbs	1
Apricots	1 bu (50 lbs)	20–24
	2–2½ lbs	1
Berries (excluding strawberries)	24-qt crate	12–18
	5–8 cups	1
Cherries, as picked	1 bu (56 lbs)	22–32
	2–2½ lbs	1
Figs	2–2½ lbs	1
Grapes	28-lb lug	7–8
	4 lbs	1
Grapefruit	4–6 fruit	1
Nectarines	18-lb flat	6–9
	2–3 lbs	1
Peaches	1 bu (48 lbs)	18–24
	2–2½ lbs	1
Pears	1 bu (50 lbs)	20–25
	2–2½ lbs	1
Pineapple	2 average	1
	5 lbs	2
Plums and Prunes	1 bu (56 lbs)	24–30
	2–2½ lbs	1
Rhubarb	15 lbs	7–11
	2 lbs	1
Strawberries	24-qt crate	12–16
	6–8 cups	1

In jars. Fill clean, hot jars, leaving ½ inch of headroom. Add boiling-hot canning liquid of your choice, leaving ½ inch of headroom; adjust lids. Process in a Boiling–Water Bath (212 F/100 C)—pints for 15 minutes, quarts for 20 minutes. Remove jars; complete seals if necessary.

In plain cans. Fill, leaving only ¼ inch of headroom. Add boiling-hot Thin Syrup or water to the top of the can. Exhaust to 170 F/77 C (c. 10 minutes); seal. Process in a B–W Bath (212 F/100 C)—10 minutes for either No. 2 or No. 2½ cans. Remove cans; cool quickly.

APPLESAUCE (HOT PACK ONLY)

Prepare by your favorite rule and according to how you'll use it—chunky or strained smooth; sweetened or not; with spices (cinnamon, nutmeg, whatever) or plain. Because of complete precooking and being packed so hot, processing time is relatively short and is designed to ensure sterilization and a good seal.

Pare crisp, red apples, cut in quarters or eighths and remove core parts; drop pieces in anti-discoloration solution. (*Don't throw away the peels and cores: save them to boil up for a beautiful juice for jelly.*) Put about 1 inch of water in a large enameled or stainless-steel kettle, fill with well-rinsed apple pieces to within 2 inches of the top. Bring to a boil, stirring now and then to prevent sticking, and cook until apples are tender. Leave as is for chunky sauce, or put it through a sieve or food mill for smoothness. Sweeten to taste if you like (see "Sweeteners" in Chapter 17); bring it briefly to boiling to dissolve any sweetening. Pack very hot.

In jars. Fill clean, hot jars with piping-hot sauce, leaving ½ inch of headroom; adjust lids. Process in a Boiling–Water Bath (212 F/100 C)—20 minutes for either pints or quarts. Remove jars; complete seals if necessary.

In plain cans. Pack to the top with hot sauce. Exhaust to 170 F/77 C (c. 10 minutes); seal. Process in B–W Bath (212 F/100 C)—20 minutes for either No. 2 or No. 2½ cans. Remove cans; cool quickly.

BAKED APPLES (HOT PACK ONLY)

Sometimes people can baked apples. Prepare them in a favorite way and bake until *half done;* pack hot in wide-mouth jars or plain cans as for Apple Slices, adding hot Thin Syrup. Adjust jar lids or exhaust and seal cans. Process in a Boiling–Water Bath (212 F/100 C)—20 minutes for either pint or quart jars, 10 minutes for either No. 2 or 2½ cans (reaching 170 F/100 C by exhausting shortens processing time). Complete seals if necessary for jars; cool cans quickly.

Apricots

Can these exactly as you would Peaches (q.v.), but leave the skins on if you like. Some varieties tend to break up when they're heated, so handle them very gently. Hot pack preferred.

Berries, See the major subsection following the brief "Fruit for Special Diets," later in this chapter.

Cherries, Sour (for Pie)

Because these are used primarily as pie timber, they may be canned in water—but they have better flavor in Thin Syrup. Either way, you'll add the extra sweetening at the time you thicken the juice when you're building the pie.

General Handling

Boiling–Water Bath. Use Raw or Hot pack. Use jars or R-enamel cans. Prepare Thin Syrup for Raw pack; heat in their own juice with sugar for Hot pack.

Wash, stem and pit cherries. (Use a small sterilized hairpin or the looped end of a paper clip if you don't have a pitting gadget.) Shake fruit down in the containers for a firm pack.

Raw Pack

In jars. Jog cherries down several times during packing; leave ½ inch of headroom. Add boiling syrup, leaving ½ inch of headroom; adjust lids. Process in a Boiling–Water Bath (212 F/100 C)—pints for 20 minutes, quarts for 25 minutes. Remove jars; complete seals if necessary.

In R-enamel cans. Make a firm pack, leaving only ¼ inch of headroom. Add boiling syrup to top. Exhaust to 170 F/77 C (*c.* 10 minutes); seal. Process in a B–W Bath (212 F/100 C)—No. 2 cans for 20 minutes, No. 2½ cans for 25 minutes. Remove cans; cool quickly.

Preferred: Hot Pack

Measure pitted cherries and put them in a covered kettle with ½ cup of sugar for every 1 quart of fruit. There should be enough juice to keep the cherries from sticking. Set on lowest burner. Cover the kettle, and bring fruit very slowly to a boil to bring out the juice. Be prepared to add a little boiling water to each jar if you haven't enough juice to go around.

In jars. Fill with hot fruit and juice, leaving ½ inch of headroom; adjust lids. Process in a Boiling–Water Bath (212 F/100 C)—pints for 10 minutes, quarts for 15 minutes. Remove jars; complete seals if necessary.

In R-enamel cans. Fill to the top with hot fruit and juice. Exhaust to 170 F/77 C (*c.* 10 minutes); seal. Process in a B–W Bath (212 F/100 C)—No. 2 cans for 15 minutes, No. 2½ for 20 minutes. Remove cans; cool quickly.

Cherries, Sweet

General Handling

Boiling–Water Bath. Use Raw or Hot pack. Use jars or cans (plain cans for light varieties like Royal Ann; R-enamel for dark red or "black" types like Bing).

If you're going to serve these as is, or combined with other fruits in a compôte, you don't pit them (they'll hold their shape better unpitted); but do prick each cherry with a needle to keep it from bursting while it's processed. Use Medium or Heavy Syrup for Raw pack; for Hot pack add more sugar than for Sour Cherries.

Wash cherries, checking for blemishes, and discard any that float (they may be wormy); remove stems. Shake down for a firm pack.

Raw Pack

In jars. Fill firmly, leaving ½ inch of headroom. Add boiling syrup, leaving ½ inch of headroom; adjust lids. Process in a Boiling–Water Bath (212 F/100 C)—pints for 20 minutes, quarts for 25 minutes. Remove jars; complete seals if necessary.

In plain or R-enamel cans. Make a firm pack, leaving only ¼ inch of headroom. Fill to top with boiling syrup. Exhaust to 170 F/77 C (*c.* 10 minutes); seal. Process in a B–W Bath (212 F/100 C)—No. 2 cans for 20 minutes, No. 2½ cans for 25 minutes. Remove cans; cool quickly.

Preferred: Hot Pack

Measure washed and pricked cherries into a covered kettle, adding ¾ cup of sugar for every 1 quart of fruit. Because there is not much juice in the pan, add a little water to keep fruit from sticking as it heats. Cover and bring very slowly to a boil, shaking the pan gently a few times (instead of stirring, which breaks the fruit). Heat some Medium or Heavy Syrup to have on hand in case there's not enough juice to go around when you fill the containers.

In jars. Proceed and process as for Raw pack.

In plain or R-enamel cans. Proceed and process as for Raw pack.

Dried Fruits

Feasibility

Any dried fruit may be freshened and canned. But why do it, when they keep so well as is (see "Drying," Chapter 21)—unless you foresee a particular need for a few servings of them stewed up ready for the table?

General Handling

Boiling–Water Bath only. Use Raw or Hot pack. Use jars or plain cans.

Freshen by covering with cold water and letting stand overnight. Drain, saving the soaking water (heated to boiling) to use in processing, and proceed with Raw pack.

If you're in a hurry, cover with water, bring to a boil, and simmer until the fruit is plumped. Drain, saving the cooking water for processing, and proceed with Hot pack.

Raw Pack

In jars. Fill, leaving ½ inch of headroom. Add 2 to 4 tablespoons sugar (depending on sweetness of fruit) to pints, 4 to 6 tablespoons to quarts. Add boiling soaking water, leaving ½ inch of headroom; adjust lids. Process in a Boiling–Water Bath (212 F/100 C)—pints for 20 minutes, quarts for 25 minutes. Remove jars; complete seals if necessary.

In plain cans. Fill, leaving only ¼ inch of headroom Add 2 to 4 tablespoons sugar to No. 2 cans, 4 to 6 tablespoons to No. 2½ cans. Fill to top with boiling soaking water. Exhaust to 170 F/77 C (*c.* 15 minutes); seal. Process in B–W Bath (212 F/100 C)—No. 2 cans for 15 minutes, No. 2½ for 20 minutes. Remove cans; cool quickly.

Preferred: Hot Pack

In jars. Fill with hot fruit, sweeten and add hot cooking water as for Raw pack. Process in a B–W Bath (212 F/100 C)—pints for 15 minutes, quarts for 20 minutes. Remove jars; complete seals if necessary.

In plain cans. Fill with hot fruit, sweeten, and add hot cooking water as for Raw pack. Process in a B–W Bath (212 F/100 C)—No. 2 cans for 15 minutes, No. 2½ for 20 minutes. Remove cans; cool quickly.

Canning Frozen Fruits and Berries

For delivery in early fall, large farm-supply chain stores (look under "Feeds" or "Grain" in the Yellow Pages) often have good buys in multi-gallon containers of frozen fruits and berries—good buys because you order them ahead, and they usually cost no more than the going price of store-bought fresh fruit; and all the washing and peeling and slicing is already done, to boot. A list from one such outfit offers sweet or sour cherries, strawberries, halved purple plums, sliced peaches, sliced Spy apples and applesauce, all with sugar; and blueberries, blackberries, red raspberries, rhubarb and crushed pineapple, all without sugar.

The hitch: You must take delivery when they come in, and hence be prepared to can your order immediately (unless you have a freezer big enough to hold the bulk packages). And you should be a serious canner: a 4-gallon chunk of prepared fruit is a lot to deal with in one swoop, and requires organizing the time and utensils for the job.

Handling: Boiling–Water Bath only. Use Hot pack only. Use jars or cans—plain or R-enamel as recommended for the specific raw food (q.v.).

Defrost fruit slowly in the unopened package. Drain off all juice and measure it: if the fruit was unsugared, add sweetening in proportion to make Thin or Medium syrup, as desired; if it was sugared, add more sweetener to taste if you want to. Bring juice to boiling. Add fruit and boil it gently for 2 or 3 minutes. Proceed with hot-packing and processing in a Boiling–Water Bath as for the specific fresh fruit (you may need to add some boiling water to each container if there's not enough juice to go around).

Figs

The green-colored Kadota variety makes a particularly attractive product, but whatever kind you use should be tree-ripened yet still firm.

Some casual old instructions would have you soften (or even remove) fig skins by treating the fruit with a strong soda solution—*but don't do it.* Any such alkaline will counteract some of the acidity upon which we rely to make the stipulated Boiling–Water Bath efficient.

GENERAL HANDLING

Long Boiling–Water Bath. Use Hot pack only. Use jars or plain cans. Prepare Thin Syrup.

Wash ripe, firm figs; do not peel or remove stems. Cover with boiling water and let simmer for 5 minutes. Drain and pack hot, not too tightly.

HOT PACK ONLY

In jars. Fill with hot figs, leaving ½ inch of headroom for pints, 1 inch of headroom for quarts. Add 1 tablespoon lemon juice to pints, 2 tablespoons lemon juice to quarts (an optional very thin slice of fresh lemon may also be added to each jar for looks). Add boiling syrup, retaining headroom. Adjust lids. Process in a Boiling–Water Bath (212 F/100 C)—pints for 85 minutes, quarts for 90 minutes. Remove jars; complete seals if necessary.

In plain cans. Fill with hot fruit, leaving only ¼ inch of headroom. Top off with boiling syrup and 2 teaspoons lemon juice to No. 2 cans, 4 teaspoons lemon juice to No. 2½ cans (an optional very thin slice of fresh lemon may also be added to each can for looks). Exhaust to 170 F/77 C (*c.* 10 minutes); seal. Process in a B–W Bath (212 F/100 C)—No. 2 cans for 85 minutes, No. 2½ cans for 90 minutes. Remove cans; cool quickly.

Grapes

Tight-skinned seedless grapes are the ones to can if you can any—for fruit cocktail, compôtes, gelatin desserts and salads (but grapes for juice may be any sort you have plenty of).

GENERAL HANDLING

Boiling–Water Bath. Use Raw or Hot pack. Use jars or cans (plain, or R-enamel cans if it's a dark grape).

Sort, wash and stem.

RAW PACK

In jars. Fill tightly but without crushing grapes, leaving ½ inch of headroom. Add boiling Medium Syrup, leaving ½ inch of headroom; adjust lids. Process in a Boiling–Water Bath (212 F/100 C)—pints for 15 minutes, quarts for 20 minutes. Remove jars; complete seals if necessary.

In cans (plain or R-enamel). Fill, leaving ¼ inch of headroom. Add boiling Medium Syrup to top. Exhaust to 170 F/77 C (*c.* 10 minutes); seal. Process in a B–W Bath (212 F/100 C)—No. 2 cans for 20 minutes, No. 2½ for 25 minutes. Remove cans; cool quickly.

Preferred: Hot Pack

Prepare as for Raw pack. Bring to a boil in Medium Syrup. Drain, reserving syrup, and pack.

In jars. Pack with hot grapes, leaving ½ inch of headroom. Add boiling syrup, leaving ½ inch of headroom; adjust lids. Process in a Boiling–Water Bath (212 F/100 C)—pints for 15 minutes, quarts for 20 minutes. Remove jars; complete seals if necessary.

In cans (plain or R-enamel). Fill with hot grapes, leaving ¼ inch of headroom. Add boiling syrup to the top. Exhaust to 170 F/77 C (c. 10 minutes); seal. Process in B–W Bath (212 F/100 C)—No. 2 cans for 20 minutes, No. 2½ for 25 minutes. Remove cans; cool quickly.

Grapefruit (or Orange) Sections

Feasibility

Only if you have a good supply of tree-ripened fruits is canning worthwhile—but canning makes an infinitely handier product than freezing does. Don't overlook Mixed Fruit; and don't forget marmalades and conserves (q.v.).

General Handling

Boiling–Water Bath only. Use Raw pack only. Use jars only (cans could give a metallic taste to home-canned citrus).

Wash fruit and pare, removing the white membrane as you go. Slip a very sharp thin-bladed knife between the dividing skin and pulp of each section, and lift out the section without breaking. Remove any seeds from individual sections. Prepare Thin Syrup.

Raw Pack Only

In jars only. Fill hot jars with sections, leaving ½ inch of headroom. Add boiling Thin Syrup, leaving ½ inch of headroom; adjust lids. Process in a Boiling–Water Bath (212 F/100 C)—10 minutes for either pints or quarts. Remove jars; complete seals if necessary.

Juices, see grouped handling at the end of Fruits section.

Peaches

Feasibility

The benefits and pleasures of canning are exemplified in peaches: home-canned peaches are full of flavor, are versatile, and are considered by many cooks to be better than frozen ones. See also Chapter 21 ("Drying"), Chapter 18 ("Jellies, Jams and Other Sweet Things"), and the relevant recipes in Chapter 24 ("Cooking").

GENERAL HANDLING

Boiling–Water Bath only. Use Raw or Hot pack. Use jars or plain cans.

Wash; slip off skins after a quick dip in boiling water, with immediate dunk in cold. Cut, pit; from the cavity scrape away dark fibers, which may turn dark in canning. Hold peeled fruit in an anti-discoloration solution as for Apples; rinse and drain before packing. Use Thin or Medium Syrup, or a combination of juice and water/syrup (see "Liquids," earlier).

For Peach Melba—and see Melba Sauce—pack as halves, Raw for best texture, in wide-mouth jars. Light corn syrup is good here: see "Liquids."

RAW PACK

In jars. Pack halves or slices attractively, leaving ½ inch of headroom. Add boiling syrup, leaving ½ inch of headroom; adjust lids. Process in a Boiling–Water Bath (212 F/100 C)—pints for 25 minutes, quarts for 30 minutes. Remove jars; complete seals if necessary.

In plain cans. Fill carefully, leaving only ¼ inch of headroom. Add boiling syrup to the top. Exhaust to 170 F/77 C (*c.* 10 minutes); seal. Process in a B–W Bath (212 F/100 C)—No. 2 cans for 30 minutes, No 2½ for 35 minutes. Remove cans; cool quickly.

PREFERRED: HOT PACK

Simmer prepared peaches in hot syrup for 2 minutes. Drain, reserving syrup.

In jars. Fill with hot peaches, leaving ½ inch of headroom. Add boiling syrup, leaving ½ inch of headroom; adjust lids. Process in a Boiling–Water Bath (212 F/100 C)—pints for 20 minutes, quarts for 25 minutes. Remove jars; complete seals if necessary.

Skins come easily off scalded peaches, below left, and cut fruit is held in an anti-darkening solution; right, boiling syrup must cover the beautifully packed peaches with headroom to spare.

In plain cans. Fill with hot peaches, leaving only ¼ inch of headroom. Add boiling syrup to the top. Exhaust to 170 F/77 C (*c.* 10 minutes); seal. Process in a B–W Bath (212 F/100 C)—No. 2 cans for 25 minutes, No. 2½ for 30 minutes. Remove cans; cool quickly.

Peaches, Brandied

GENERAL HANDLING

Boiling–Water Bath only. Use Hot pack only. Use jars only (because they look so pretty: which is part of their fun).

The peaches should be small to medium in size, firm-ripe, and with attractive color; blemish-free of course. Wash. Using a coarse-textured towel, rub off all their fuzz. Weigh them.

For every 1 pound of peaches, make a Heavy Syrup of 1 cup sugar to 1 cup water. Bring syrup to boiling and, when sugar is dissolved, add the whole peaches and simmer them for 5 minutes. Drain; save the syrup and keep it hot.

HOT PACK ONLY, IN JARS ONLY

Without crushing, fit peaches in hot jars, leaving ½ inch of headroom. Pour 2 tablespoons of brandy over the peaches in each 1-pint jar, using proportionately more brandy for quarts. Fill jars with hot syrup, leaving ½ inch of headroom; adjust lids. Process in a Boiling–Water Bath (212 F/100 C)—pints for 15 minutes, quarts for 20 minutes. Remove jars; complete seals if necessary.

Pears

Bartlett pears are ideal for canning, to serve alone or as a salad or in a compôte. They will be too soft for successful canning, though, if they've ripened on the tree: use ones that were picked green (but full grown) and allowed to ripen in cool storage, between 60 and 65 F (16 and 18 C).

Very firm-fleshed varieties like Seckel and Kieffer are generally spiced or pickled; they make a satisfactory product if ripened in storage and simmered in water till nearly tender before packing with syrup. The so-called winter pears—such as Anjou and Bosc—are usually eaten fresh; they are cold-stored much the way apples are, but they are not likely to keep as long (see "Root–Cellaring," Chapter 22).

GENERAL HANDLING

Use a Boiling–Water Bath. Hot pack preferred. Use jars or plain cans.

Wash; cut in halves or quarters. Remove stems, core (a melon-ball scoop is handy for this); pare. Treat pieces against oxidation with either of the solutions described for apples.

Make Thin or Medium Syrup.

Small pears may be canned whole: pare them, but leave the stems on. It takes about 9 small whole pears to fill a pint jar or a No. 2 can.

RAW PACK

In jars. Pack halves or quarters attractively, leaving ½ inch of headroom. Add boiling syrup, leaving ½ inch of headroom; adjust lids. Process in a Boiling–Water Bath (212 F/100 C)—pints for 25 minutes, quarts for 30 minutes. Remove jars; complete seals if necessary.

In plain cans. Fill carefully, leaving only ¼ inch of headroom. Add boiling syrup to the top. Exhaust to 170 F/77 C (c. 10 minutes); seal. Process in a B–W Bath (212 F/100 C)—No. 2 cans for 30 minutes, No. 2½ for 35 minutes. Remove cans; cool quickly.

HOT PACK PREFERRED

Simmer fruit in syrup for 2 minutes; drain, reserving hot syrup.

In jars. Fill with hot pears, leaving ½ inch of headroom. Add boiling syrup, leaving ½ inch of headroom; adjust lids. Process in a Boiling–Water Bath (212 F/100 C)—pints for 20 minutes, quarts for 25 minutes. Remove jars; complete seals if necessary.

In plain cans. Fill with hot pears, leaving only ¼ inch of headroom. Add boiling syrup to the top. Exhaust to 170 F/77 C (c. 10 minutes); seal. Process in a B–W bath (212 F/77 C)—No. 2 cans for 25 minutes, No. 2½ for 30 minutes. Remove cans; cool quickly.

MINT VARIATION

Prepare as above; the pears may be cut up or left whole. To Medium Syrup, add enough natural peppermint extract and green food coloring to give the desired taste and color.

Simmer the pears in this syrup for 5 to 10 minutes, depending on size and firmness of fruit, before packing Hot and processing in a B–W Bath as above.

Pears, Spiced

Seckel, Kieffer and similar hard varieties are best for spicing. Bartletts or other soft pears may be used if they are underripe.

GENERAL HANDLING

Use a Boiling–Water Bath. Use Hot pack only. Use jars only (like Brandied Peaches, these are very attractive to look at; and you could take a ribbon at the fair!).

Wash, peel and core 6 pounds of pears. Gently boil them covered in 3 cups of water until they start to soften.

Make a very heavy syrup of 4 cups sugar and 2 cups white vinegar. Tie in a small cloth bag 3 or 4 3-inch sticks of cinnamon, ¼ cup whole cloves, and 4 teaspoons cracked ginger. Simmer the spice bag in the syrup for 5 minutes.

Add the pears and the water in which they were partially cooked to the spiced syrup, and simmer for 4 minutes. Drain pears, saving the hot syrup and discarding the spice bag.

Hot Pack Only, in Jars Only

Pack hot pears attractively in clean hot jars. Add spiced syrup, leaving ½ inch of headroom; adjust lids. Process in a Boiling–Water Bath (212 F/100 C)—pints for 15 minutes, quarts for 20 minutes. Remove jars; complete seals if necessary.

Pineapple

Fresh pineapple is as easy to can as any fruit—and may be packed in any plain or minted and colored syrup (see also "Canning Frozen Fruits," earlier in this chapter).

General Handling

Use a Boiling–Water Bath. Use Hot pack only. Use jars or plain cans.

Scrub firm, ripe pineapples. Cut a thin slice from each end. Cut like a jelly roll in ½-inch slices, or in 8 lengthwise wedges. Remove the skin, the "eyes" and the tough-fiber core from each piece. Leave in slices or wedges, or cut small or chop: Let future use guide your hand.

Simmer pineapple gently in Light or Medium Syrup for about 5 minutes. Drain; save the hot syrup for packing.

Hot Pack Only

In jars. Fill with fruit, leaving ½ inch headroom. Add hot syrup, leaving ½ inch of headroom; adjust lids. Process in a Boiling–Water Bath (212 F/100 C)—pints for 15 minutes, quarts for 20 minutes. Remove jars; complete seals if necessary.

In plain cans. Fill with fruit, leaving ¼ inch of headroom. Add hot syrup to the top of the cans. Exhaust to 170 F/77 C (*c.* 10 minutes); seal. Process in a B–W Bath (212 F/100 C)—No. 2 cans for 20 minutes, No. 2½ for 25 minutes. Remove cans; cool quickly.

Plums (and Italian Prunes)

General Handling

Use Boiling–Water Bath. Use Raw or Hot pack. Use jars or cans—R-enamel for red plums, plain for greenish-yellow varieties.

Firm, meaty plums (such as the Greengage) hold their shape better for canning whole than the more juicy types do. Freestone plums and prunes are easily halved and pitted for the tighter pack.

Choose moderately ripe fruit. Wash. If fruit is kept whole, the skins should be pricked several times with a large needle to prevent the fruit from bursting. Halve and pit the freestone varieties. Prepare Medium or Heavy Syrup, and have it hot.

RAW PACK

In jars. Fill with raw fruit, leaving ½ inch of headroom. Add boiling syrup, leaving ½ inch of headroom; adjust lids. Process in a Boiling–Water Bath (212 F/100 C)—pints for 20 minutes, quarts for 25 minutes. Remove jars; complete seals if necessary.

In cans (R-enamel for red fruit, plain for light-colored). Pack raw fruit, leaving ¼ inch of headroom. Add boiling syrup to the top of the can. Exhaust to 170 F/77 C (c. 10 minutes); seal. Process in a B–W Bath (212 F/100 C)—No. 2 cans for 15 minutes, No. 2½ for 20 minutes. Remove cans; cool quickly.

PREFERRED: HOT PACK

Heat prepared plums to boiling in syrup. If they're halved and are very juicy, heat them slowly to bring out the juice; measure the juice, and for each 1 cup juice add ¾ cup sugar—give or take a little, according to your taste—to make a Medium Syrup. Reheat to boiling for just long enough to dissolve the sugar. Drain fruit, saving the hot syrup. Have some hot plain Medium Syrup on hand for eking out sweetened juice.

In jars. Pack hot fruit, leaving ½ inch of headroom. Add boiling syrup, leaving ½ inch of headroom; adjust lids. Process in a Boiling–Water Bath (212 F/100 C)—pints for 20 minutes, quarts for 25 minutes. Remove jars; complete seals if necessary.

In cans (R-enamel for red fruit, plain for light-colored). Pack hot fruit, leaving ¼ inch of headroom. Fill to top with boiling syrup. Exhaust to 170 F/77 C (c. 10 minutes); seal. Process in a B–W Bath (212 F/100 C)—No. 2 cans for 15 minutes, No. 2½ for 20 minutes. Remove cans; cool quickly.

Rhubarb (or Pie Plant)

Never eat rhubarb LEAVES: they are high in oxalic acid, which is poisonous.
Safe to eat are the tart, red stalks of this plant, which are excellent pie timber, make a tangy dessert sauce, are a favorite ingredient in old-time preserves. However, your best use would be to can sweetened sauce by the method given below, and to freeze the raw pieces for pies. Rhubarb juice makes a good hot-weather drink. See under "Beverages" in Chapter 24.

GENERAL HANDLING AS SAUCE

Use a Boiling–Water Bath. Use Hot pack. Use jars or R-enamel cans.
For best results, can it the same day you cut it. If the stalks are young enough, they need not be peeled (their red color makes an attractive product). *Discard leaves,* trim away both ends of the stalks, and wash; cut stalks in ½-inch pieces. Measure. Put rhubarb in an enameled kettle (because of the tartness), mixing in ½ cup of sugar for each 1 quart (4 cups) of raw fruit. Let it stand,

covered, at room temperature for about 4 hours to draw out the juice. Bring slowly to a boil; let boil no more than 1 minute (or the pieces will break up). (*Alternative:* Bake sugared rhubarb in a heavy, covered pan in a slow oven, *c.* 275 F/135 C, for 1 hour.)

HOT PACK ONLY

In jars. Fill with hot fruit and its juice, leaving ½ inch of headroom; adjust lids. Process in a Boiling–Water Bath (212 F/100 C)—10 minutes for either pints or quarts. Remove jars; complete seals if necessary.

In R-enamel cans. Pack hot fruit and juice to the top of the cans. Exhaust to 170 F/77 C (*c.* 10 minutes); seal. Process in a B–W Bath (212 F/100 C)—10 minutes for either No. 2 or No. 2½ cans. Remove cans; cook quickly.

Fruit for Special Diets

For canning large pieces of fruit without sugar or other sweetener, follow individual instructions given earlier, but in addition to omitting sugar *use Hot pack only,* and eke out the natural liquid with extra unsweetened boiling juice (not water) if necessary to fill containers.

Pint jars (½-pints for infants or the person with a small appetite) are usually the best size to use unless you're canning sugarless fruit for several people in the family. Processing time is the same for pint and ½-pint jars.

Fruit Purées

Infants and those on low-residue diets require fruit whose natural fiber has been reduced to tiny particles in a sieve, food mill, blender or food processor with the steel blade in place (in the last instance, the purée will be runniest, and this looseness can be reduced by longer precooking). These purées are generally processed without sweetening—certainly the strained fruits for babies are unsweetened.

Any favorite fruit may be canned as a purée, because the only limiting factor would be an above-average amount of fiber to deal with. Apples, apricots, peaches and pears are the most popular for purées.

Use Boiling–Water Bath. Use Hot pack only. Use standard ½-pint canning jars with appropriate closures (*not* commercial babyfood jars, whose sealers are not re-usable).

APPLE PURÉE

Follow directions for Applesauce earlier, but omit sweetening; sieve, pack and process as for Apricot Purée, below.

Apricot Purée (or Peach or Pear)

Use perfectly sound, ripe fruit. Wash, drain; pit and slice. In a large kettle crush a 1-inch layer of fruit to start the juice, then add the rest of the prepared fruit; if there seems not to be enough juice to keep the fruit from sticking or scorching, add no more than ¼ cup water for every firmly packed 1 cup of fruit. Simmer over medium heat, stirring as needed, until the fruit is soft—about 20 minutes. Push the cooked fruit through a sieve or food mill; or whirl briefly in a blender at a high setting, or in a processor, and strain. Measure, and add 1 tablespoon fresh lemon juice for each 2 cups of pulp. Reheat to a 200 F/93 C simmer. Pack hot.

Hot pack only, in ½-pint standard canning jars. Pour hot purée into clean, scalded ½-pint jars, leaving ½ inch of headroom. Adjust lids. Process in a Boiling–Water Bath (212 F/100 C) for 10 minutes. Remove jars, complete seals if necessary.

CANNING BERRIES

Don't get so taken up with making jellies and jams in berry-time that you forget to can some too: they may be done for serving solo and in compôtes and salads; or, with slightly different handling, for use in cobblers, pies and puddings. See "Cooking" (Chapter 24) and also look at "Freezing" (Chapter 12), and "Drying" (Chapter 21).

For purposes of general handling, berries—except for strawberries, which are a law unto themselves—are divided in two categories: *soft* (raspberries, blackberries, boysenberries, dewberries, loganberries and youngberries), and *firm* (blueberries, cranberries, currants, elderberries, gooseberries and huckleberries). The texture usually determines which pack to use; but some of the firm ones may be dealt with in more than one way, and such variations are described separately below for the specific berries.

It goes without saying that you'll want to use only perfect berries that are ripe without being at all mushy. Pick them over carefully, wash them gently and drain; stem or hull them as necessary. Work with only a couple of quarts at a time because all berries, particularly the soft ones, break down quickly by being handled.

General Procedure for Most Berries

All berries are acid, so a Boiling–Water Bath for the prescribed length of time is the best process for them.

Use Raw pack generally for *soft* berries, because they break down so much in precooking.

A Hot pack in general makes a better product of most *firm* berries.

Use jars or cans—R-enamel cans for all red berries, but plain cans for gooseberries.

All may be canned either with sugar or without—but just a little sweetening helps hold the flavor even of berries you intend to doll up later for desserts. Thin and Medium Syrups are used more often than Heavy, with Medium usually considered as giving a better table-ready product than Thin.

RAW PACK (SOFT BERRIES)

In jars. Fill clean, hot jars, shaking to settle the berries for a firm pack; leave ½ inch of headroom. Add boiling Thin or Medium Syrup, leaving ½ inch of headroom; adjust lids. Process in a Boiling–Water Bath (212 F/100 C)—pints for 15 minutes, quarts for 20 minutes. Remove jars; complete seals if necessary.

In R-enamel cans. Fill, shaking for a firm pack; leave only ¼ inch of headroom. Add boiling Thin or Medium Syrup to the top of the can. Exhaust to 170 F/77 C (*c.* 10 minutes); seal. Process in a B–W Bath (212 F/100 C)—No. 2 cans for 15 minutes, No. 2½ for 20 minutes. Remove cans; cool quickly.

STANDARD HOT PACK (MOST FIRM BERRIES)

Measure berries into a kettle, and add ½ cup of sugar for each 1 quart of berries. On lowest burner, bring very slowly to a boil, shaking the pan to prevent berries from sticking (rather than stirring, which breaks them down). Remove from heat and let them stand, covered, for several hours. *This plumps up the berries and keeps them from floating to the top of the container when they're processed.* For packing, reheat them slowly. As insurance, have some hot Thin or Medium Syrup on hand in case you run short of juice when filling the containers.

In jars. Fill with hot berries and juice, leaving ½ inch of headroom. Proceed and process as for Raw pack.

In R-enamel or plain cans. Fill to the top with hot berries and juice, leaving no headroom. Proceed and process as for Raw pack.

UNSWEETENED HOT PACK (MOST FIRM BERRIES)

This is often used for sugar-restricted diets; it is also another way of canning berries intended for pies.

Pour just enough cold water in a kettle to cover the bottom. Add the berries and place over very low heat. Bring to a simmer until they are hot throughout, shaking the pot—not stirring—to keep them from sticking.

Pack hot fruit and its juice, leaving headroom as above; remove any air bubbles by running a knife blade around the inner side of the container. Process as for Raw pack.

Specific Berries—except Strawberries

BLACKBERRIES

Raw pack. Usually considered soft, so for over-all versatility use Raw pack under the General Procedure above. With boiling water or Thin or Medium Syrup—but Medium Syrup if you want them table-ready. In jars or R-enamel cans.

BLUEBERRIES

Though in the firm category, they actually break down too much in the standard Hot pack (but they make a lovely sauce for ice cream, etc., if you want to can them by Hot pack with a good deal of extra sweetening). Old-timers dried them (q.v.) to use like currants in fruit cake.

Raw pack. With boiling water or syrup (Medium recommended). In jars or R-enamel cans. Proceed and process under "General Procedure" above.

Raw pack variation. If you want to hold them as much like their original texture and taste as possible when canned (to use like fresh berries in cakes, muffins, pies), you must blanch them. Put no more than 3 quarts of berries in a single layer of cheesecloth about 20 inches square. Gather and hold the cloth by the corners, and dunk the bundle to cover the berries in boiling water until juice spots show on the cloth—*about 30 seconds.* Dip the bundle immediately in cold water to cool the berries. Drain them.
    Fill jars, leaving ½ inch of headroom. Add no water or sweetening; adjust lids. Process as for standard Raw pack under "General Procedure" above.

BOYSENBERRIES

Soft; in Raw pack as under "General Procedure." Use jars or R-enamel cans.

CRANBERRIES

These hold so well fresh in proper cold storage (see "Root-Cellaring," Chapter 22) or in the refrigerator, and they also freeze (q.v.), so they probably make the most sense canned if they're done as whole or jellied sauce.
    Use jars only.

For about 6 pints Whole Sauce. Boil together 4 cups sugar and 2 cups water for 5 minutes. Add 8 cups (about 2 pounds) of washed, stemmed cranberries, and boil without stirring until the skins burst. Pour boiling hot into clean *hot jars,* leaving ½ inch of headroom, and run a sterile knife or spatula around the inner side of the jar to remove trapped air.
    Boiling–Water Bath. After filling with ½ inch of headroom, *adjust* lids, and process pints in a B–W Bath (212 F/100 C) for 10 minutes. Remove jars; complete seals if necessary.

For 4 pints Jellied Sauce. Boil 2 pounds of washed, stemmed berries with 1 quart of water until the skins burst. Push berries and juice through a food mill or strainer. Add 4 cups sugar to the resulting purée, return to heat, and boil almost to the jelly stage (see "Testing for Doneness" in Jelly section for jellies, in Chapter 18). Pour hot into sterilized straight-sided jars (so it will slip out easily); seal with sterilized lids as for any jelly.

CURRANTS

Currants are a novelty in certain sections of the United States where, during the 1920's, the bushes were uprooted because they harbored a fungus destructive to the white pine. If you are fortunate enough to have some, by all means make jelly with them. Turn extra ones into dessert sauce; dry some; and they freeze.

Classed as firm berries, they can by Hot pack under "General Procedure"; in jars or R-enamel cans.

DEWBERRIES

Soft; in Raw pack as under "General Procedure." Use jars or R-enamel cans.

ELDERBERRIES

Best use is for jelly or wine.

If you do can them, use a Hot pack under "General Procedure"—and add 1 tablespoon lemon juice for each 1 quart of berries, to improve their flavor. In jars or R-enamel cans.

On the outside chance that you'd want to use them in muffins and cakes, experiment with blanching and the Raw pack variation described under Blueberries.

GOOSEBERRIES

Another scarce fruit in many sections of the country because, like the currant, they harbored the white-pine blister rust fungus, and were eradicated as a conservation measure. But they make such heavenly old-fashioned pies, tarts and preserves!

Although they're firm, they do well in Raw pack with very sweet syrup. Or they may be done with Hot pack (where they hold their shape less well).

Wash; pick them over, pinch off stem ends and tails. Some cooks prick each berry with a sterile needle to promote a better blending of sweetening and juice (but we can't imagine a quicker way to drive ourselves up the wall; we'll leave it to osmosis).

Raw pack. Heavy Syrup is recommended for these very tart berries. And they'll probably pack better if you put ½ cup of hot syrup in the bottom of the container before you start filling. Use jars or plain cans. Process as in "General Procedure" above.

Hot pack. Follow the steps given earlier for a standard Hot pack—but you may want to increase the sugar to ¾ cup for each 1 quart of berries. Process.

Huckleberries

Being cousins of the blueberry, these firm berries are handled like Blueberries (q.v.).

Loganberries

They're soft, so pack Raw as under "General Procedure."

Raspberries

Tenderest of the soft berries, these really do better if they're frozen. Put by some as jam or jelly, of course; try canning some sauce or juice. And if you have them in your garden, please don't forget to take a basket of fresh-picked raspberries to some older person who doesn't have a way to get them any more.

If you can them, use Raw pack and Medium Syrup. Use jars or R-enamel cans. Follow the General Procedure above.

Youngberries

Another softie. Raw pack, as under "General Procedure."

Strawberries

The most popular berry in the United States, these nevertheless are often a disappointment when canned, because they will fade and float if they are handled in the standard way recommended for most other soft berries. Here's how to have a blue-ribbon product—and no short cuts, please.

General Handling

Use a Boiling–Water Bath. Use Hot pack only (even though they're soft). Use jars or R-enamel cans.

Wash and hull perfect berries that are red-ripe, firm, and without white or hollow centers. Measure berries. Using ½ to 1 cup sugar for each 4 cups of berries, spread the berries and sugar in shallow pans in thin alternating layers. Cover with waxed paper or foil if necessary as a protection against insects, and let stand at room temperature for 2 to 4 hours. Then turn into a kettle and simmer for 5 minutes in their own juice. Have some boiling Thin Syrup on hand if there's not enough juice for packing.

HOT PACK ONLY

In jars. Fill, leaving ½ inch of headroom (adding a bit of hot syrup if needed); adjust lids. Process in a Boiling–Water Bath (212 F/100 C)—pints for 10 minutes, quarts for 15 minutes. Remove jars; complete seals if necessary.

In R-enamel cans. Fill to the top with hot berries and juice. Exhaust to 170 F/77 C (*c.* 10 minutes); seal. Process in a B–W Bath (212 F/100 C)—No. 2 cans for 15 minutes, No. 2½ for 20 minutes. Remove cans; cool quickly.

FOR A NICE SAUCE

Some ½-pint jars of strawberries will be welcome for toppings on ice cream or puddings.

Prepare the berries as above, but use 1 to 1¼ cups sugar to each 4 cups of berries. Process the ½-pints in a B–W Bath (212 F/100 C) for 10 minutes. Remove jars; complete seals if necessary.

CANNING FRUIT JUICES

It might seem a marginal use of time and material to can fruit juices, but they may be used to advantage in several ways: as beverages at breakfast or in place of commercial soft drinks for the family, or as the base for punches served by a country caterer (a Grange group, for instance); or the juices may be put by for future jelly-making.

Beverage juices will have better flavor if they are presweetened at least partially. Use sugar, or the sweetener of your choice. (But for sugar-restricted diets, *use only the non-nutritive artificial sweetener approved by your doctor.* And unless you have had success in cooking with it, postpone adding the sweetener until serving time—some of these sugar substitutes leave an aftertaste if heated.)

Juices intended for jelly are not sweetened until you are making your jelly.

Fruit (and berry) syrups, which are concentrated, are better made from regular canned juice at the time you'll be wanting to use them, because you could run into a problem with pectin in some cases and end up with something too gooey for your purpose.

General Procedure for Most Juices

Because boiling temperature (212 F/100 C at sea level) can impair the fresh flavor of almost all fruit juices, these are usually processed by the *Hot*-Water Bath (given as 190 F/88 C), which is pasteurization. Be sure there is at least 1 to 2 inches of definitely simmering water above the tops of the containers throughout the processing time, as for the B–W Bath.

The various nectars are processed in a Boiling–Water Bath (212 F/100 C) because of their greater density.

Use Hot pack only. Use jars or cans (R-enamel suggested).

Choose firm-ripe, blemish-free fruit or berries; wash carefully, lifting the fruit from the water to let any sediment settle, and to avoid bruising. Then stem, hull, pit, core, slice—whatever is needed for preparing the particular fruit. *Simmer* the fruit until soft; strain through a jelly bag to extract clear juice (see "Equipment for Jellies, Jams, Etc." in Chapter 18).

Containers for Canned Juices

Modern glass home-canning jars with fresh sealers are your best choice for juices or nectars because they're made to withstand heat-processing and years of re-use, and they provide a good seal *if* filling and processing are done conscientiously.

Cans also are suitable for juices. One manufacturer recommends R-enamel cans for all juices, even though the fruits from which they are made do not lose color in plain cans. Juices in cans, which are light-proof, need not be stored in the dark as do glass jars.

The manufacturers of commercial containers for several name-brands of mayonnaise, peanut butter and salad dressing have told *PFB* that they regard such jars and bottles (with their closures) as "one-trip containers," and therefore *do not recommend them for re-use* in home-canning.

Also not suitable for re-use in heat-processing at home are soft-drink bottles; nor would crimped-on caps be satisfactory.

APPLE CIDER (BEVERAGE)

Get cider fresh from the mill and process it without delay (though it can be held in a refrigerator in sterilized covered containers for 12 hours, if necessary). To prepare, strain it through a clean, dampened jelly bag, and in a large kettle bring it to a good simmer at 200 F/93 C, *but do not boil.* Pack hot.

Hot pack only, in jars. Pour strained fresh cider into hot sterilized jars, leaving ½ inch of headroom; adjust lids. Process in a Hot–Water Bath at 190 F/88 C, for 30 minutes for either pints or quarts. Remove jars; complete seals if necessary.

Hot pack only, in cans (R-enamel suggested). Fill to the top with strained fresh cider leaving no headroom. Exhaust to 170 F/77 C (*c.* 15 minutes); seal. Process in a H–W Bath at 190 F/88 C, for 30 minutes for either No. 2 or No. 2½ cans. Remove cans; cool quickly.

Apple Juice (for Jelly Later)

Add some underripe apples to the batch for more pectin. Wash and cut up apples, discarding stem and blossom ends. *Do not peel or core* (you may even use the peels left over from making Applesauce). Barely cover with cold water and bring to a boil over moderate heat, and simmer until apples are quite soft—about 30 minutes. Strain hot through a dampened jelly bag.

Reheat to 200 F/93 C and pack *hot;* process as for Apple Cider, above.

Apricot Nectar

Nectars—most often made from apricots, peaches and pears—are simply juices thickened with *finely* sieved pulp of the fruit; usually they are "let down" with ice water when served. For sweetening, which is optional, honey or corn syrup may be substituted (see earlier in this chapter for proportions); artificial non-nutritive sweetening, if wanted, should be added at serving time to avoid a flavor change caused by heat-processing.

Use a Boiling–Water Bath. Use Hot pack only. Use ½-pint or pint jars or No. 2 cans (R-enamel suggested).

Wash, drain; pit and slice. Measure, and treat with an anti-oxidant if desired (see "General Handling for All Fruits" earlier in this chapter). In a large enameled kettle add 1 cup boiling water to each 4 cups of prepared fruit, bring to simmering, and cook gently until fruit is soft. Put through a fine sieve or food mill. Measure again, and to each 2 cups of fruit juice–plus-pulp add 1 tablespoon lemon juice and about ½ cup sugar, or sweetening to taste. Reheat and simmer until sugar is dissolved. Pack hot.

Hot pack only, in jars. Pour hot nectar into ½-pint or pint jars, leaving ½ inch of headroom; adjust lids. Process in a Boiling–Water Bath (212 F/100 C)—15 minutes for either ½-pints or pints. Remove jars; complete seals if necessary.

Hot pack only, in No. 2 cans (R-enamel suggested). Fill No. 2 cans to the top with simmering nectar, leaving no headroom; seal. Process in a Boiling–Water Bath (212 F/100 C)—for 15 minutes. Remove cans; cool quickly.

Berry Juices

Crush and simmer berries in their own juice until soft; strain through a jelly bag—allow several hours for draining. If you twist the bag for a greater yield, the juice should be strained again through clean cloth to make it clear.

Measure, and to each 4 quarts of strained juice add 4 tablespoons lemon juice, plus sugar to taste—usually 1 to 2 cups. (If the juice is for jelly later, omit lemon juice and sugar at this time.) Reheat juice to a 200 F/93 C simmer. Pack.

Hot pack only, in jars. Pour simmering juice into hot scalded jars, leaving ½ inch of headroom; adjust lids. Process in a Hot–Water Bath at 190 F/88 C, for 30 minutes for either pints or quarts. Remove jars; complete seals if necessary.

Hot pack only, in R-enamel cans. Fill cans to the top with hot juice, leaving no headroom; seal (at simmering stage it will already be more than 170 F/77 C, so exhausting is not necessary). Process in a H–W Bath at 190 F/88 C, for 30 minutes for either No. 2 or No. 2½ cans. Remove cans; cool quickly.

CHERRY JUICE

Prepare as for Berry Juices. To each 4 quarts of strained juice add 2 tablespoons lemon juice, but adjust sweetening to the tartness of the cherries. (If the juice is for jelly later, omit lemon juice and sugar at this time.) Reheat juice to a 200 F/93 C simmer. Pack hot. Process in a Hot–Water Bath at 190 F/88 C, for 30 minutes for either pint or quart jars or for No. 2 or No. 2½ cans.

CRANBERRY JUICE

Boiling–Water Bath only. Hot pack only. Use jars only.

Pick over the berries and wash. Measure, and add an equal amount of water. Bring to boiling in an enameled kettle and cook until berries burst. Strain through a jelly bag (squeezing the bag adds to the yield: re-strain if you want beautifully clear juice). Add sugar to taste, and bring just to boiling. Pack hot.

If you're canning this juice only for special-diet reasons, omit sugar. Add the artificial non-nutritive sweetener *prescribed by your doctor* just before serving, lest heat-processing give the sweetener an unwanted aftertaste.

Hot pack only, in jars only. Pour boiling juice into clean hot jars, leaving ½ inch of headroom; adjust lids. Process in a B–W Bath (212 F/100 C)—10 minutes for either pints or quarts. Remove jars; complete seals if necessary.

CURRANT JUICE

Prepare and process as for Berry Juices, above.

GRAPE JUICE

Hot–Water Bath only. Use Hot pack only. Use jars or R-enamel cans.

The extra intermediate step of refrigerating the juice will prevent crystals of tartaric acid (harmless, but not beautiful) in the finished product. It's easier to work with not more than 1 gallon of grapes at a time.

Select firm-ripe grapes; wash, stem. Crush and measure into an enameled or stainless-steel kettle; add 1 cup water for each 4 quarts of crushed grapes. Cook gently *without boiling* until fruit is very soft—about 10 minutes. Strain through a jelly bag, squeezing it for a greater yield.

Refrigerate the juice for 24 hours. Then strain again for perfect clearness, being mighty careful to hold back the sediment of tartaric acid crystals in the bottom of the container.

Add ½ cup sugar for each 1 quart of juice (or omit sweetening), and heat to a 200 F/93 C simmer.

Hot pack only, in jars. Pour simmering juice into hot scalded jars, leaving ½ inch of headroom; adjust lids. Process in a Hot–Water Bath at 190 F/88 C, for 30 minutes for either pints or quarts. Remove jars; complete seals if necessary.

Hot pack only, in R-enamel cans. Fill cans to the top with simmering juice, leaving no headroom; seal (the step of exhausting to 170 F/77 C is not necessary when juice is simmering-hot). Process in a H–W Bath at 190 F/88 C— 30 minutes for either No. 2 or No. 2½ cans. Remove cans; cool quickly.

Peach Nectar

Prepare and process as for Apricot Nectar, above.

Pear Nectar

Prepare and process as for Apricot Nectar, above.

Plum Juice (and Fresh Prune)

Hot–Water Bath only. Use Hot pack only. Use jars or R-enamel cans.

Choose firm-ripe plums with attractive red skins. Wash; stem; cut in small pieces. Measure. Put in an enameled or stainless-steel kettle, add 1 cup water for each 1 cup prepared fruit. Bring slowly to simmering, and cook gently until fruit is soft—about 15 minutes. Strain through a jelly bag. Add ¼ cup sugar to each 2 cups juice, or to taste. Reheat just to a 200 F/93 C simmer.

Pack and process as for Berry Juices, above.

Rhubarb Juice

This makes good sense if you have extra rhubarb, because it can be used for a delicious quencher, and was the main ingredient of a hill-country wedding punch in olden days (see Chapter 24). And rhubarb is said to be good for our teeth.

Boiling–Water Bath only. Use Hot pack only. Use jars or R-enamel cans.

Wash and trim fresh young red rhubarb, but *do not peel.* Cover the bottom of the kettle with ½ inch of water, add rhubarb cut in ½-inch pieces. Bring to simmering, and cook gently until soft—about 10 minutes. Strain through a jelly bag. Reheat juice, adding ¼ cup sugar to each 4 cups of juice to hold the flavor, and simmer at 200 F/93 C until sugar is dissolved.

Hot pack, in jars. Pour simmering juice into hot scalded jars, leaving ½ inch of headroom; adjust lids. Process in a B–W Bath (212 F/100 C)—10 minutes for either pints or quarts. Remove jars; complete seals if necessary.

Hot pack, in R-enamel cans. Fill cans to the top with simmering juice; seal (exhausting is not necessary if juice is simmering-hot). Process in a B–W Bath (212 F/100 C)—10 minutes for either No. 2 or No. 2½ cans. Remove cans; cool quickly.

CANNING TOMATOES

In 1974 the Center for Disease Control of the U.S. Public Health Service dropped a bomb: It reported that in the first half of the year there were two verified cases of botulism from eating home-canned tomatoes or tomato juice. Alert consumer activists publicized the CDC's report, quite rightly. The widespread scare that followed was not helped by the fact that for several previous years the big seed catalogs had been advertising and describing various hybrid tomatoes as "low-acid" table tomatoes. The inference drawn by the public at large was that, in the course of developing tomatoes especially suitable for slicing and serving as a cold vegetable, the hybridizers had eliminated the safety factor of the tomato's acidity. It is this acidity which allows them to be canned in a Boiling–Water Bath in complete safety.

Meanwhile the public-health officers were doing their own quiet investigating. And they discovered that the canned tomatoes identified in the cases of botulism were the result of a two-step problem: Common bacteria or molds grew in the food in the jars and thereby reduced the acidity (because the natural acid in the tomatoes was metabolized by the micro-organisms as they grew and developed). It was established after compassionate, but thorough, investigation that the common bacteria or molds survived either because the tomatoes were canned by the discredited open-kettle method, or entered under the lid of a jar that wasn't adequately sealed.

It also was clarified in fairly quick order by the various USDA Agricultural Experiment and investigation units, that the term "low-acid" as used in the seedsmen's catalogs referred to the fact that the tomatoes were *sweeter,* rather than that they are less acid. This acid *vs.* sweetness relationship is one that we'll see from time to time throughout most methods of preserving food at home. Especially, you will see in Chapter 19, which tells about making pickles, that we must *never reduce the amount of vinegar* in a recipe dealing with such a low-acid vegetable as cucumbers; instead we must *increase the sugar* to offset the bite and sharpness of the vinegar. The developers of "low acid table tomatoes" were hybridizing with this principle in mind, and the result was varieties with more sugar, but not with less acid. When the big scare came, the catalog-writers were hard put to it to explain to a bright public that their varieties truly were safe for canning by traditional methods, and did not require anything drastic in the way of new treatment. (There may be some tomato varieties that are a shade lower in acid than the ones the public buys in the raw state, but these are grown and produced solely for commercial canners, who have extremely strict control over the process at every stage.)

Government researchers now allow a *pH* of 4.7 as the limit for tomatoes, rather than 4.6, which is the limit for other fruits (see Chapter 2, "Why Foods Spoil," and especially *"pH* the Acidity Factor"). If you have any fear that the tomatoes you are dealing with are, nevertheless, of a lower acid content—as indicated by a *higher pH rating*—you may add a bit of acid in the packing step of canning. This acid is not a crutch, and should never take the place of scrupulous cleanliness or rigid adherence to times and heat required for safe processing.

• **Summarizing:** There is no need, then, to be frightened of canning tomatoes. So long as the fruit is not overripe, damaged or mishandled on its way into the jars/cans at home, it may be canned with confidence by established procedures.

WHY THEY'RE SO POPULAR

Tomatoes are by far and away the most popular food for canning at home. One of the reasons for their popularity is that they are so versatile, since canned tomatoes in various forms can be served plain, or titivated, or used as the base for any number of nutritious, family-pleasing and inexpensive main dishes. Another attribute is their abundance, because they are grown at home in every likely corner of North America, and they're sold in vast quantities by professional truck gardeners from uncountable roadside stands.

The average bushel of tomatoes weighs about 53 pounds/c. 25 kilos, and will yield from 15 to 20 quarts of canned tomatoes that are cut up. It takes 2½ to 3 pounds of fresh tomatoes to do 1 quart. If you plan to add hot tomato juice as canning liquid instead of any boiling water, the yield in jars canned will be a bit smaller because you are using some tomatoes for juicing.

Their third great virtue has been that they are easy to can—so easy that many a householder considered them to be just about foolproof. And this presumed dependability, regardless of handling or canning method, was ascribed to the fact that traditionally they had always been grouped with fruits on the *pH* scale. The average homemaker believed, therefore, that canned tomatoes were too strong-acid ever to permit the growth of certain bacteria, including the dread toxin-producing spores of *C. botulinum.*

. . . BUT THE *CARE* NEVER VARIES

No matter which strain of tomato you can in which form—whole, stewed or puréed; as juice, chili sauce or ketchup—any sloppiness, any cutting of corners will result in tomato products that are disappointing or even nasty or possibly downright dangerous.

The federal, state and non-government experts whom *PFB* has consulted since the "great tomato revolution" of '74 agree 100 percent that clean, careful handling, and due respect for the *Why's* of good packing and processing, are the primary safeguards in canning tomatoes of all varieties.

Selecting the fruit. Use only *firm*-ripe, unblemished tomatoes, ones that have not quite reached the table-ready stage wanted for slicing and serving raw.

Discard any that have rotten spots or mold. (The regulations governing commercial canning regard *just one decomposed tomato per 100 sound fruit* as reason enough to condemn the entire lot as unfit for human consumption.)

Discard any that have open lesions.

Washing. Wash the fruit carefully in fresh water of drinking quality. If many are spattered with field dirt, or have not been staked or mulched in your own garden, add a little mild detergent and 4 teaspoons of 5 percent chlorine bleach to each 1 gallon of wash water; rinse well in fresh water. (This thoroughness cuts down bacterial load.)

Peeling and cutting. You will be working with clean equipment and cutting surfaces—just as you do when handling any food you're putting by. Peel tomatoes by dipping a few at a time in briskly boiling water, then dunking immediately in cold, clean water: the skins will strip off.

Without cutting into the seed cavity, ream out the stem end and core (the point of an apple-corer does a good job). Cut off the blossom end. Cut off any green shoulders to ensure a product of uniform tenderness and flavor. Cut out any bruises, no matter how small.

Cut/chop as individual instructions say to.

Packing. Pack in clean, scalded containers, leaving appropriate headroom. Cap with clean, scalded closures that have been treated according to the maker's instructions (see "About Jars and Cans" in Chapter 3).

Add boiling juice to Raw-packed whole tomatoes. All other tomato products are packed Hot, with the contents of cans exhausted to a minimum of 170 F/77 C if the tomatoes have cooled after precooking.

Leave the right amount of headroom.

Processing. Old-style open-kettle canning—with its opportunities for wicked airborne spoilers to contaminate food and the interiors of containers and lids, and with its unreliable temperature control—has been considered the reason for some cases of botulism in supposedly strong-acid foods in years past: DO NOT USE THE OLD OPEN-KETTLE METHOD.

Whether you process in a Boiling–Water Bath or in a Pressure Canner, *time the processing accurately:* from return to the full boil in a B–W Bath; or after 10 pounds is reached, following a 7-to-10-minute strong flow of steam from the vent (depending on the size of the canner) to ensure adequate pressure inside.

Removing and cooling containers. Follow instructions given toward the end of Chapter 3. Complete the seals on bail-type jar lids as you take them from the canner. NEVER RE-TIGHTEN 2-PIECE SCREWBAND LIDS. AT ANY TIME. EVER.

Remember that *hastening* the cooling of jars can cause them to break; *retarding* the natural cooling of jars can cause thermophilic spoilage (like "flat sour") to develop in the contents. But cool *cans* quickly.

Check, clean, label and store containers according to "Handling after Processing" and "Storing All Canned Foods," given in Chapter 3.

Relevant Metrics for Canning Tomatoes

Full metric conversions, with the arithmetic for refining them, are given at the start of Chapter 17 ("Common Ingredients and How to Use Them"), but the following—rounded off—apply in this chapter.

If you live above the sea-level zone (i.e., *over* 1000 ft/305 m) consult the subsection "Correcting for Altitude" in Chapter 3. (And do pay attention to the need for extra headroom in jars at high altitudes.)

• • •

Temperatures (@ sea level): 170 F/77 C——212 F/100 C——228 F/109 C——240 F/116 C——250 F/121 C.

Volume: ¼ teaspoon = 1.25 mL——½ teaspoon = 2.5 mL——1 teaspoon = 5 mL——1 tablespoon = 15 mL——½ pint = 250 mL——1 pint = 500 mL.

Length: ¼ inch = 0.64 cm——½ inch = 1.27 cm——1 inch = 2.54 cm.

THE CHOICE BETWEEN PROCESSING METHODS

Until the extensive research on lower-acid tomatoes is completed and the reports are correlated, there can be no consensus that says tomatoes must be Pressure-processed to ensure a safe home-canned food. In the meantime each householder must make a judgment call.

If you have reason to think your tomatoes are not quite within the acid range for the B–W Bath (a *pH* rating more than 4.6, or even the 4.7 cutoff some experts sanction)—because of the way they were grown, or if you're stuck with fruit that's past its ideal condition—then just let informed good sense choose between:

Either (1) increasing the acid content of the pack yourself (how, is told below), and use a proper B–W Bath (212 F/100 C) for the time specified.

Or (2) processing at 5 or 10 pounds pressure (228 F/109 C, or 240 F/116 C) for the length of time given for the individual tomato products.

Or (3) processing at 15 pounds pressure (250 F/121 C) because you live at high altitude that requires it (see "Correcting for Altitude" in Chapter 3).

Or (4) processing at 15 pounds pressure for barely a moment in a procedure researched at the University of Minnesota and reported by Isabel D. Wolf and Edmund A. Zottola. *PFB* is edgy about describing this method from instructions given in the University of Minnesota's Food Science and Nutrition *Fact Sheet No. 13, Home Canning Tomatoes* (1976, with a 1980 updated notation in the Minnesota *Extension Bulletin 413*, for which see Chapter 25 under the subheading for this chapter). Success with this method from a research project relies on the abilities of the householder and an impeccably accurate and faultlessly operated Pressure Canner. Chapter 25 tells where to get your own copy.

(And there's always *freezing*, q.v. in Chapter 16, "Freezing Convenience Foods," in a space-saving form like sauce.)

Good Company

Adding acid to tomatoes is not new. Nor is it gastronomical vandalism in the eyes of French cooks, who are famed for snubbing all but the naturally best ingredients for their dishes. Here's something from one of our favorite older cookbooks, *Nos amis les légumes, recettes de Marie* (Édition Valmorin-Andrieux, no date). "Choissez des tomates moyennes bien rouges et fermes. Épluchez-les après les avoir passées quelques secondes dans de l'eau bouillante. Mettez-les dans les bocaux, remplissez avec de l'eau salée dans la proportion de 1 cuillerée à café par litre d'eau, *ajoutez le jus d'un citron.* Remplissez les bocaux jusqu' à 3 centimètres du bord. Faites stériliser . . ." etc., etc.

Added Acid + B–W Bath

Adding acid is NOT A CRUTCH. Increasing the acidity DOES NOT MEAN THAT YOU CAN SHORT-CUT ANY STEP in safe canning procedure.

Remember that the temperature of your kitchen during canning season allows most bacteria to *double* their populations *every 15 to 30 minutes.* So if your tomatoes are not carefully selected and washed, and your work surfaces and utensils are not sanitary, the result can be a bacterial load that your processing method can't deal with completely.

As for how much of what acid to add in order to bring the *pH* rating of your tomatoes within the safety range for the B–W Bath, in late April 1975 the head nutritionists of the USDA Extension Service issued their recommendation: ¼ teaspoon of pure crystalline citric acid (U.S.P.) to each pint or No. 2 can, ½ teaspoon of the powdered citric acid to each quart or No. 2½ can—right on top of the tomatoes before the containers are capped/sealed (just as we add the salt for seasoning, which is optional). We also give a workable equivalent in white (distilled) vinegar. (See "Acids" in Chapter 17, for more information.)

Adjust lids on jars; exhaust the contents of cans to 170 F/77 C if the tomatoes have cooled below that temperature in packing. In the B–W canner the jars/cans are covered with a *minimum* of 1 to 2 inches of water; the water is brought to a brisk boil—212 F/100 C at sea level, with compensation for high altitudes (according to the table in Chapter 3)—and boiled continuously *by the clock for the full time required.* Remove containers: with jars, complete seals if necessary and cool naturally out of drafts; pop cans in cold water to cool quickly.

After 24 hours, when containers are checked, cleaned and labeled, store your canned tomatoes in a cool, dark, dry place.

Enjoy.

Pressure–Processing for Tomatoes

It is easy to cite Pressure–processing as the alternative method for canning tomatoes safely at home. However, a sound and well-tested timetable—a time-table of the reasoned sort we all rely on now for canning other foods—will take a good while to establish.

Meanwhile, for the householder who feels secure only with tomatoes done in a Pressure Canner, we offer the following stopgap. First, though, five things:

1. Pressure–processing is NOT A CRUTCH. It DOES NOT MEAN THAT YOU CAN SHORT–CUT ANY STEP of good canning procedure—careful selection, sanitation, correct packing, maintaining pressure, accurate timing, ensuring seals, proper storage.
2. Nutrients in some degree and of course texture to a greater extent will suffer more than they do in a Boiling–Water Bath. The tender flesh of tomatoes will disintegrate more (unless a firming additive is included: q.v. calcium hydroxide in "Firming Agents," Chapter 17), and an excessive amount of juice is likely to separate from the tissues.
3. Independent food scientists around the country agree that *5 pounds pressure is TOO LOW* to get the result desired from Pressure-processing plain tomatoes.
4. The processing times given below are for *cut-up plain tomatoes ONLY.* The times are not long enough to deal safely with a mixture of tomatoes and lower-acid vegetables like onions, celery, green peppers, or whatever (see Stewed Tomatoes, in Chapter 10).
5. The processing vessel used is a conventional Pressure *Canner—NOT a pressure saucepan,* even though it might hold several pint jars. The much smaller size of the saucepan plays hob with any pressure timetable (for why, see under "Canning Methods," Chapter 3). And anyway such a little saucepan-size batch of cut-up plain tomatoes would be better converted to Plain Sauce (q.v.) and done in the proper Boiling–Water Bath.

These points made, for Pressure–canning cut-up plain tomatoes: Use Hot pack only. Use jars or plain cans (if necessary, exhausting the contents to a minimum of 170 F/77 C after packing). Vent the heated canner 7 minutes for medium-size kettles, 10 minutes for large ones. Time the processing after internal pressure of the canner has reached *10 pounds* (240 F/116 C)—15 minutes for pint jars, 20 minutes for quarts, 15 minutes for No. 2 cans, 20 minutes for No. 2½ cans. Complete jar seals if necessary, cool naturally; remove cans, cool quickly in cold water.

> • • BEFORE TASTING CANNED FOOD WITH ANY LOW-ACID IN-
> GREDIENTS: You must be unshakably certain that your
> Pressure Canner was operated correctly—pressure
> gauge accurate and dead-weight gauge signaling prop-
> erly—and that the Boiling–Water Bath kept the neces-
> sary water at a full boil around and over the containers of
> food; and that requirements for times and corrections for
> altitude were followed.
>
> Unless you are sure that these safeguards were ob-
> served, a margin of protection is added by boiling the
> canned food hard for 15 minutes to destroy any hidden
> toxins and stirring to distribute the heat. If the food foams
> unduly or smells bad during boiling, destroy it completely
> so it cannot be eaten by people or animals.

CANNED TOMATO TROUBLES AND WHAT TO DO

New developments bring new strictness, so canned tomatoes in your store-room should be examined for the same signs that mean vegetables are unfit, or dangerous, to eat:

- Broken seals.
- Bulging cans.
- Seepage around the seal.
- Mold, the tiniest spot, around the seal or on the underside of the lid or in the contents.
- Gassiness in the contents, spurting liquid from pressure inside any container when it is opened.
- Cloudy or yeasty liquid.
- Unnatural color.
- Unnatural or unpleasant odor.

If any of these indications is present in the smallest degree, play safe and *do not even taste the tomatoes before boiling them for 15 minutes to destroy hidden toxins. Then, during boiling, if they foam or smell bad, destroy them so they can-not be eaten by people or animals.* Wash the containers and sealers in hot soapy water, then cover with fresh water and boil hard for 15 minutes; salvage only sterilized jars—destroy cans and all closures, etc.

SPECIFIC TOMATO PRODUCTS

Unless you can pick with finicky selectiveness from a well-managed small garden of your own, there is bound to be a range of ripeness, size and condition in any good-size batch of tomatoes you're getting ready to can. So pick them over carefully, of course discarding any rotten or banged-up ones, and let size and degree of acceptable ripeness dictate the form you'll can them in.

Perfect just *firm-ripe*—better underripe than overripe—uniform and small enough to slip easily down into the jar—these are the ones for canning whole to use in salads. Misshapen or overly large fruit are cut to stewing size—quarters, eighths or chunks—and are canned plain or with added vegetables for flavor; they also go for sauce or juice.

Regardless of the form or whether they're to be processed in a Boiling–Water Bath or a Pressure Canner, prepare the tomatoes according to the general di-rections given earlier in this chapter under ". . . But the Care Never Varies" and "Added Acid + B–W Bath."

Whole Tomatoes (Salad Style)

Serve these filled with a salad mixture of chopped vegetables or tuna fish or chicken. (Or try this: In a glass or china bowl combine with each 1 pint of to-matoes-plus-juice ¼ to ⅓ cup thinly sliced red onion, ¼ cup vinaigrette French dressing, perhaps 1 teaspoon Worcestershire sauce, maybe ¼ teaspoon dried basil or oregano; turn gently to mix; cover well and refrigerate several hours or overnight. Serve chilled as a side dish instead of salad.)

Troubles galore after six months in storage. There may have been too much headroom; or the sealing rim wasn't wiped clean. Whatever the cause, the seal was poor. So the tomatoes fermented, forcing material to ooze out under the lid (and turning the contents an unnatu-ral brown). Destroy.

HANDLING

Use a Boiling–Water Bath. Use Raw pack (and this is the only style we prefer Raw-packed). Use jars only.

In advance prepare enough Tomato Juice (q.v. below) to be the canning liquid for the batch—figure on ½ to ¾ cup of hot juice for each pint jar, 1 to 1½ cups of juice for each quart. Hold the juice in a covered container until you're ready to heat it to fill the jars. (*Caution:* Don't dilute the acidity of the pack by eking out the tomato juice with boiling water—be ready to use canned juice if your planning went wrong.)

Peel select, thoroughly washed tomatoes by dunking them in briskly boiling water for about 30 seconds, then in cold water; handle gently as you strip off the skins and core the fruit.

Raw pack, in jars only. Fit whole tomatoes snugly—but without pressing so much that you break them—into clean scalded jars, leaving ½ inch of headroom for pints, 1 inch for quarts. Add ¼ teaspoon fine crystalline citric acid *or* 1 tablespoon white vinegar to pints, add ½ teaspoon citric acid *or* 2 tablespoons white vinegar to quarts. (Optional: Add ½ teaspoon salt to pints, 1 teaspoon salt to quarts.)

Add boiling juice, leaving ½ inch of headroom for both pints and quarts (hold the tomatoes away from the jar's side with the blade of a table knife to let the hot liquid fill all gaps). Adjust lids. Process in a Boiling–Water Bath (212 F/100 C)—40 minutes for pints, 50 minutes for quarts. Remove jars, complete seals if necessary.

Cut-up Plain Tomatoes

Boiling–Water Bath preferred (but for Pressure–canning see times, etc., in the general introduction for this chapter). Use Hot pack only. Use jars or plain cans.

Select, wash, peel, according to general handling earlier; cut in quarters or eighths, saving all juice possible. In a large enameled kettle bring cut tomatoes to a boil in their own juice, and cook gently for 5 minutes, stirring so they don't stick. Pack.

• **NOTE:** Individual food scientists around the country do not agree that 5 pounds' pressure is enough to get the result desired from Pressure–processing Plain Tomatoes, especially at altitudes above 3000 feet/914 meters. Nor do they agree across-the-board on B–W Bath timing in every case: check with your regional Extension Service for special handling in your area.

HOT PACK ONLY

B–W Bath, in jars. Fill clean scalded jars with boiling-hot tomatoes and their juice, leaving ½ inch of headroom. Add ¼ teaspoon crystalline citric acid (or 1 tablespoon white vinegar) to pints, ½ teaspoon citric acid (or 2 tablespoons white vinegar) to quarts. (Optional: Add ½ teaspoon salt to pints, 1 teaspoon salt to quarts.) Adjust lids. Process in a Boiling–Water Bath (212

F/100 C)—15 minutes for pints, 20 minutes for quarts. Remove jars. Complete seals if necessary.

B–W Bath, in plain cans. Fill to the rim with boiling-hot tomatoes and juice. Add ¼ teaspoon citric acid (or 1 tablespoon white vinegar) to No. 2 cans, ½ teaspoon citric acid (or 2 tablespoons white vinegar) to No. 2½ cans. Fill to the top with boiling juice. (Optional: Add ½ teaspoon salt to No. 2 cans, 1 teaspoon salt to No. 2½ cans.) If the tomatoes have cooled unavoidably, exhaust to 170 F/77 C (*c.* 10 minutes); seal. Process in a B–W Bath (212 F/100 C)—15 Minutes for No. 2 cans, 20 minutes for No. 2½ cans. Remove cans. Cool quickly.

Stewed Tomatoes with Added Vegetables, see Chapter 10, "Canning Convenience Foods."

Plain Tomato Sauce (Purée)

This is a handy way indeed to can tomatoes, and it makes a better base for red Italian-style pasta sauces than does Tomato Paste (which Americans often tend to use too much of in such sauces anyway). The texture should fall about halfway between juice and paste.

Do not add onions or celery, etc., now *or you must* Pressure–process the sauce (see Stewed Tomatoes).

HANDLING

Use a Boiling–Water Bath. Use Hot pack only. Use ½-pint or pint jars only.
Prepare and sieve the fruits as for Tomato Juice (below). In a large enameled kettle bring the juice to boiling, and boil gently until thickened but not so stiff as Tomato Paste—about 1 hour or a little longer. Stir often so it doesn't stick.

Hot pack only, in ½-pint or pint jars. Pour into clean scalded jars, leaving ¼ inch of headroom in ½-pints, ½ inch in pints. Add ⅛ teaspoon citric acid (or 1½ teaspoons white vinegar), and (Optional: add ½ teaspoon salt to ½-pints); add ¼ teaspoon citric acid (or 1 tablespoon vinegar), and (Optional: add ½ teaspoon salt to pints). Adjust lids. Process in a B–W Bath (212 F/100 C)—30 minutes for either ½-pints or pints. Remove jars; complete seals if necessary.

Tomato Paste

If you're canning many tomatoes, you'll surely want a few little jars of paste put by too. Work with small batches, because it scorches easily during the last half of cooking. And forgo onions, garlic, celery, etc., because such flavors may not be wanted in delicate sauces you merely want to color with the paste.

HANDLING

Use a Boiling–Water Bath. Use Hot pack only. Use ½-pint jars only.
Carefully wash, peel, trim and chop the tomatoes saving all the juice possible (4 to 4½ pounds of tomatoes will make about 4 ½-pint jars of paste). In an

enameled kettle bring the chopped tomatoes to a boil, then reduce heat and simmer for 1 hour, stirring to prevent sticking. Remove from heat and put the cooked pulp and juice through a fine sieve or food mill. Measure, return to the kettle, and for every 2 cups of sieved tomatoes add ¼ teaspoon citric acid (or 1 tablespoon white vinegar). (Optional: add ½ teaspoon salt.) Reheat, and continue cooking very slowly, stirring frequently, until the paste holds its shape on the spoon—about 2 hours more.

Hot pack only, in ½-pint jars. Ladle hot paste into clean hot jars, leaving ¼ inch of headroom. Adjust lids, and process in a B–W Bath (212 F/100 C) for 35 minutes. Remove jars; complete seals if necessary.

Chili Sauce and **Tomato Ketchup,** see toward the end of Chapter 19.

Tomato Juice

Time out for an interesting point: Preparing juice from *uncooked* tomatoes— in a blender at high speed, or in a food processor—gives a thin product that separates (enzyme action is the reason).

Canned tomato juice is noted for encouraging growth of the highly heat-resistant bacillus that causes *flat-sour* spoilage, a sneaky and nasty-tasting condition indeed. However, even though the organism is very hard to destroy, it can be avoided quite easily: just follow carefully all the requirements for handling food in a sanitary way.

This care extends from every piece of sterilized equipment to the tomatoes themselves. Choose only firm-ripe, red, perfect tomatoes—no injured ones, none with soft spots or broken skins. Wash them thoroughly. With a stainless-steel knife cut away stem and blossom ends and cores. Cut the fruit in eighths and put it in an enameled kettle (which won't react with the acid of the tomatoes), and simmer it, stirring often, until soft. Put the tomatoes through a fine sieve or food mill: the finer the pulp, the less likely that the juice will separate during storage. Measure the juice into the kettle, and for each 4 cups of juice add ½ teaspoon citric acid (or see Chapter 17). (Optional: Add ½ teaspoon salt to pints, 1 teaspoon salt to quarts.) Reheat all to simmering. Pack hot.

Hot pack only, in jars. Fill clean, hot jars with the very hot juice, leaving ½ inch of headroom; adjust lids. Process in a Boiling–Water Bath—15 minutes for either pints or quarts. Remove jars, complete seals if necessary.

Hot pack only, in plain cans. Fill to the top with boiling juice, leaving no headroom: seal (juice already 170 F/77 C or over doesn't need further exhausting). Process in a B–W Bath (212 F/100 C) for 20 minutes for either No. 2 or No. 2½ cans. Remove cans; cool quickly.

CANNING VEGETABLES

"Credibility" became a buzzword at the beginning of the 1980's, and it acquired several overtones alongside its original meaning of plain truth-telling. It took on a subjective "Do I believe this?" in addition to "Do they believe what they're saying?" on through to "*X* says it's right and *Y* says it's wrong—so which can you believe?"

It's hard all round, this business of getting a straightforward message across, and having it trusted. Hard for the newcomer to food preservation to be convinced of the safest method to use, and hard for the people who usually can food by hearsay practices to be induced to switch to more mindful ways of doing it. And Heaven knows it's hard for *PFB* to persuade without being deliberately frightening, or getting shrill, or, worse, becoming aloof: "The correct procedure was laid down once and for all, so why harp on the *Why's* and *what-ifs* . . ."

Anyone who has the enterprise to can vegetables at home is likely to have the gumption to want to can them safely. *Because all fresh natural* (as opposed to pickled) *vegetables are low-acid, they MUST be processed in a regular Pressure Canner.* And no short cuts, no scamping.

The outbreaks of food-borne botulism have fallen off from their peak in the mid-1970's, when hundreds of thousands of Americans were discovering canning, but still at least 90 percent of the traceable sources of this dreaded type of poisoning is laid to *home*-canned low-acid food. And inadequate processing is the cause named in virtually every case investigated by public-health teams.

The spores of *C. botulinum*—and it's the spores that make the toxin, remember—can survive 5 hours or more of boiling at 212 F/100 C, even though the vegetative form of the bacterium is much more fragile. Therefore anything less than adequate Pressure–processing is a monstrous gamble. People who count on getting away with processing natural vegetables in a Boiling–Water Bath are playing for stakes too high.

Relevant Metrics for Canning Vegetables

Full metric conversions, with the arithmetic for refining them, are given at the start of Chapter 17 ("Common Ingredients and How to Use Them"), but the following—rounded off—apply in this chapter.

If you live above the sea-level zone (i.e., *over* 1000 ft/305 m), consult the subsection "Correcting for Altitude" in Chapter 3. (And do pay attention to the need for extra headroom in jars at high altitudes.)

• • •

Temperatures (@ sea level): *170 F/77 C——180 F/82 C——228/109 C——240 F/116 C——250 F/121 C—275 F/132 C.*

Volume: *⅛ teaspoon = 0.62 mL——½ teaspoon = 2.5 mL——1 teaspoon = 5 mL——1 tablespoon = 15 mL——½ pint = 250 mL——1 pint = 500 mL——1 quart = 1 L——1 gallon = 4 L.*

Length: *¼ inch = 0.64 cm——½ inch = 1.27 cm——1 inch = 2.54 cm.*

EQUIPMENT FOR CANNING VEGETABLES

All the utensils and standard kitchen furnishings that you used for fruits (see the list at the start of Chapter 5) will do, with two exceptions:

1) Use only a *standard Pressure Canner* for processing. In Chapter 3, "The Canning Methods," we went on record as not liking pressure *saucepans* no matter how much adjustment in operating time is made in order to compensate for the problems created by their smallness. (In all fairness, though, some specialists allow using them if proper safeguards are followed. But all responsible authorities agree that you should never use a 4- or 6-quart pressure saucepan for low-acid foods at an altitude above 3000 feet/914 meters: such pots simply can't hold enough water to process low-acid food for the longer time demanded.)

And the other exception, 2): You will need a blanching basket or some other means of holding prepared vegetables loosely in boiling water for the partial precooking in Hot pack. Blanching may be done in a microwave oven or in steam (for how, see especially Chapter 13, "Freezing Vegetables," and Chapter 21, "Drying"), but it is handier to precook in boiling water, which you can then use as the canning liquid—thereby saving nutrients.

CANNED VEGETABLE TROUBLES AND WHAT TO DO

It goes without saying that every conscientious canner will select only prime vegetables; will prepare them carefully, pack them and Pressure–process them right; will check seals, and will store them in a cool, dark, dry place 24 hours after they have been canned.

But if, after they have been in storage, you find any of the following, *destroy the contents so that they cannot be eaten by people or animals.* Wash containers and closures (and rubbers, if used) in a disinfectant chlorine solution. Then throw away the cans, lids, sealing discs and rubbers; if sound, the jars may be used again.

Yields in Canned Vegetables

Since the legal weight of a bushel of vegetables differs between States, the weights given below are average; the yields are approximate.

Vegetables	Fresh	Quarts Canned
Asparagus	1 bu (45 lbs)	11
	3–4 lbs	1
Beans, Lima, in pods	1 bu (32 lbs)	6–8
	4–5 lbs	1
Beans, snap/green/wax	1 bu (30 lbs)	15–20
	1½–2 lbs	1
Beets, without tops	1 bu (52 lbs)	17–20
	2½–3 lbs	1
Broccoli	25-lb crate	10–12
	2–3 lbs	1
Brussels sprouts	4 qts	1–1½
	1 lb	½
Carrots, without tops	1 bu (50 lbs)	16–20
	2½–3 lbs	1
Cauliflower	2 medium heads	1½
	1 bu (12 lbs)	4–6
Corn, in husks	1 bu (35 lbs)	8–9
	4–5 lbs	1
Eggplant	2 average	1
Kale	1 bu (18 lbs)	6–9
	2–3 lbs	1
Okra	1 bu (26 lbs)	17
	1½ lbs	1
Peas, green (pods)	1 bu (30 lbs)	6–8
	2–2½ lbs	½
Potatoes, white	1 bu (50 lbs)	20
	2½–3 lbs	1
Potatoes, sweet (and yams)	1 bu (50 lbs)	20
	2½–3 lbs	1
Pumpkin	50 lbs	15
	3 lbs	1
Spinach (most greens)	1 bu (18 lbs)	6–9
	2–3 lbs	1
Squash, summer	1 bu (40 lbs)	16–20
	2–2½ lbs	1
Squash, winter (chunks)	3 lbs	1½

- Broken seal.
- Bulging cans.
- Seepage around the seal.
- Mold, even a speck, in the contents or around the seal or on the underside of the lid.
- Gassiness (small bubbles) in the contents.
- Spurting liquid, pressure from inside the container as it is opened.
- Cloudy or yeasty liquid.
- Unnatural or unpleasant odor.

> • • BEFORE TASTING ANY CANNED LOW-ACID FOOD: You must be unshakably certain that your Pressure Canner was operated correctly—pressure gauge accurate and dead-weight gauge signaling properly—and that requirements for times and corrections for altitude were followed.
>
> Unless you are sure that these safeguards were observed, a margin of protection is added by boiling the canned low-acid food hard for 15 minutes to destroy any hidden toxins (corn and greens require 20 minutes), and stirring to distribute the heat. If the food foams unduly or smells bad during boiling, destroy it completely so it cannot be eaten by people or animals.

- IMPORTANT: We refer you to the special table by the Presto people under· "15-Pound Canning at Higher Than a Mile" in Chapter 3's big subsection on how to compensate for the effects of Altitude.

Some Special Considerations

Salt added to vegetables in canning is merely a seasoning and therefore *of course is optional.* Pure canning salt is ideal, but the amounts called for are so small that the fillers, etc., in your regular table salt won't cloud the canning liquid. However, salt substitutes should *not* be added to the pack before processing, lest the finished product have an unwanted aftertaste: add your salt substitute to the heated vegetable just before serving.

Starchy vegetables swell during processing, especially so if they are packed Raw, so they need double the headroom usually supplied to non-starchy foods. Be particularly careful about shell beans of all kinds, green peas, and whole-kernel corn (hominy, being long-cooked before canning, does not swell further during processing).

Add extra headroom at altitudes above 2000 feet/610 meters (see "Correcting for Altitude" in Chapter 3), because the lower atmospheric pressure allows the steam inside the jars to expand more. Also, the greater temperatures in Pressure–processing mean that the steam will expand more than in boiling not under pressure.

Some precooking water can be bitter. This of course depends on the hardness of the water to begin with, and to some extent on the growing conditions of the vegetable. However, water in which asparagus, some greens, and members of the turnip family are precooked for Hot pack can be bitter; taste the water, and if it is too strong or has a bitterness, substitute boiling water as the canning liquid.

Asparagus

Asparagus keeps more spring flavor if you freeze it; but it cans easily—whole or cut up. See Recipes below.

GENERAL HANDLING

Only Pressure Canning for asparagus: it has even less acid than string beans. Use Raw or Hot pack. Use jars or plain cans.

Wash; remove large scales that may have sand behind them; break off tough ends; wash again. If you're canning it whole, sort spears for length and thickness, because you'll pack them upright; otherwise cut spears in 1-inch pieces.

RAW PACK

In jars. Whether asparagus is whole (spears packed upright) or cut up, leave ½ inch of headroom. (Optional: Add ½ teaspoon salt to pints, 1 teaspoon salt to quarts.) Add boiling water, leaving ½ inch of headroom; adjust lids.

Pressure–process at 10 pounds (240 F/116 C)—pints for 25 minutes, quarts for 30 minutes. Remove jars; complete seals if necessary.

In plain cans. Pack as for jars, leaving only ¼ inch of headroom. Add ½ teaspoon salt to No. 2 cans, 1 teaspoon to No. 2½. Fill to top with boiling water. Exhaust to 170 F/77 C (*c.* 10 minutes); seal. Pressure–process at 10 pounds (240 F/116 C)—20 minutes for either No. 2 or No. 2½. Remove cans; cool quickly.

PREFERRED: HOT PACK

Whole spears—stand upright in a wire blanching basket and dunk it for 3 minutes in boiling water up to *but not covering* the tips; drain and pack upright (tight but not squudged). Cut-up—cover clean 1-inch pieces with boiling water for 2 to 3 minutes; drain and pack.

The added processing liquid can be the boiling-hot blanching water—if it's free of grit—instead of fresh boiling water.

In jars. Complete the pack and Pressure-process as for Raw pack, above.

In plain cans. Complete the pack and Pressure–process as for Raw pack, above.

Beans, "Butter," see Beans, Lima (fresh)

Beans—Green/Italian/Snap/String/Wax

Perhaps next to tomatoes, these beans are the most popular vegetable canned by American householders. They also are established as being the single most likely source of botulism poisoning among home-canned foods.

But please don't forgo canning them: just process them in a Pressure Canner for the time stipulated, making any needed adjustment for altitude (q.v. earlier in this chapter, and in Chapter 3 under "Correcting for Altitude").

They freeze well, especially the young ones whose seeds have barely begun to form bumps; freeze some of these, and can the more mature ones. Look up these beans in Chapter 21, "Drying": old-timers called them Leather Britches.

BEFORE WE START—A WORD ABOUT MUSHINESS

People have written to *PFB* often about how to avoid having mushy canned green beans, and the answer first and always is *never cut down on the Pressure-processing time.* The warning holds true regardless of the part of North America the query comes from, and regardless of the varieties, growing conditions, and hardness or softness of the water for canning.

Variety is the least important factor in the result, actually. If you grow your own you might plant an old-fashioned pole bean. But do ask your County Agricultural Agent for varieties that do well for canning in your area; especially look at some of the tender new hybrids—these are likely to be more satisfactory when frozen.

The hardness or softness of the water in your area of course has a bearing on the texture of the finished product. Rainwater, or water chemically treated to be very soft, can make the beans slough or get soft very quickly when brought to a full, rolling boil for serving at the table. This is the reason why commercial canners sometimes give their beans a meticulously controlled low-temperature blanch for a few minutes before proceeding to Hot-pack and Pressure–process them (a pre-treatment that sets the calcium pectate in the beans' outer tissues). You can achieve much the same result by Raw-packing your beans: much the same thing occurs as with the commercial blanch, and you get a firmer finished bean.

Harder-than-average water is likely to toughen beans, a result that has been proved by blanching beans in hard water before freezing them. Given a choice between soft and hard, opt for the hard water as your canning liquid. However, don't tinker with the hardening chemicals often advocated by old-time cooks to make their pickles, etc., crisper (see under "Firming Agents" in Chapter 17).

Perhaps the most sensible solution: Simply choose beans for canning that are a little more mature than you'd use immediately for the table or for freezing. *PFB* was given this tip by several plant scientists, who added that signs of bumpiness indicate that the bean seeds are starting to develop and fill the pods, and the tissues therefore will be more likely to stay firm in canning.

GENERAL HANDLING

Pressure Canning only. Use Raw or Hot pack (Hot makes them supple and permits a more solid pack). Use jars or plain cans.

The name "snap" comes from the crisp way the young ones break when they're fresh-picked; if you must hold them overnight before canning, refrigerate them in bags. Wash, trim ends. Sort roughly for size: you may want some whole in a fancy pack (upright like asparagus spears), or others frenched or cut on a slant in 1-inch pieces. If you're stuck with doing some bigger, older ones, though, break off tips and tails, unzip their strings along their length, cut them in small pieces, and pack them by themselves. There's plenty of use for all types.

RAW PACK

In jars. Fill as tightly as you can, leaving ½ inch of headroom. (Optional: Add ½ teaspoon salt to pints, 1 teaspoon salt to quarts.) Add boiling water, leaving ½ inch headroom. Adjust lids. Pressure–process at 10 pounds (240 F/116 C)—pints for 20 minutes, quarts for 25 minutes. Remove jars; complete seal if necessary.

In plain cans. Pack as tightly as you can, leaving only ¼ inch of headroom. (Optional: Add ½ teaspoon salt to No. 2 cans, 1 teaspoon salt to No. 2½.) Fill to top with boiling water. Exhaust to 170 F/77 C (*c.* 10 minutes); seal. Pressure–process at 10 pounds (240 F/116 C)—No. 2 cans for 25 minutes, No. 2½ for 30 minutes. Remove cans; cool quickly.

PREFERRED: HOT PACK

Cover clean, trimmed beans with boiling water and boil 5 minutes. Drain, keeping the hot cooking water. Pack whole beans upright; use a wide-mouth funnel to pack the cut ones.

In jars. Fill with hot beans, leaving ½ inch of headroom. (Optional: Add ½ teaspoon salt to pints, 1 teaspoon salt to quarts.) Add boiling-hot cooking water, leaving ½ inch of headroom. Adjust lids. Pressure–process at 10 pounds (240 F/116 C)—pints for 20 minutes, quarts for 25 minutes. Remove jars; complete seals if necessary.

In plain cans. Fill loosely with hot beans, leaving only ¼ inch of headroom. (Optional: Add ½ teaspoon salt to No. 2 cans, 1 teaspoon salt to No. 2½.) Fill to top with boiling-hot cooking water. Exhaust to 170 F/77 C (*c.* 10 minutes); seal. Pressure–process at 10 pounds (240 F/116 C)—No. 2 cans for 25 minutes, No. 2½ for 30 minutes. Remove cans; cool quickly.

Beans, fresh Lima (Shell beans)

Pressure Canning only. Use Raw or Hot pack. Use jars or C-enamel cans.

Deal with one variety at a time: different-sized types require different amounts of headroom and perhaps processing.

Shell the beans and wash them before packing. They must be packed loosely because, like all starchy legumes, they swell.

RAW PACK

In jars. If it's a small variety, leave 1 inch of headroom for pints, 1½ inches of headroom for quarts; if it's a large variety, leave ¾ inch of headroom for pints, 1¼ inches of headroom for quarts. *Do not press or shake the beans down.* (Optional: Add ½ teaspoon salt to pints, 1 teaspoon salt to quarts.) Add boiling water, leaving ½ inch of headroom (the water will be well over the top of the beans); adjust lids. Pressure–process at 10 pounds (240 F/116 C)—pints for 40 minutes, quarts for 50 minutes. Remove jars; complete seals if necessary.

In C-enamel cans. Fill with beans, leaving ¾ inch of headroom for either No. 2 or No. 2½ cans; *don't press or shake down.* (Optional: Add ½ teaspoon salt to No. 2 cans, 1 teaspoon salt to No. 2½.) Fill cans to top with boiling water. Exhaust to 170 F/77 C (*c.* 10 minutes); seal. Pressure–process at 10 pounds (240 F/116 C)—40 minutes for either No. 2 or No. 2½. Remove cans; cool quickly.

PREFERRED: HOT PACK

Cover shelled, washed beans with boiling water and cook 1 minute after water returns to boiling. Drain, saving the hot cooking water.

In jars. Fill loosely with drained hot beans, leaving 1 inch of headroom for either pints or quarts. (Optional: Add ½ teaspoon salt to pints, 1 teaspoon salt to quarts.) Add boiling-hot cooking water, leaving 1 inch of headroom; adjust lids. Pressure–process at 10 pounds (240 F/116 C)—pints for 40 minutes, quarts for 50 minutes. Remove jars; complete seals if necessary.
In C-enamel cans. Fill loosely with drained hot beans, leaving only ½ inch of headroom. (Optional: Add ½ teaspoon salt to No. 2 cans, 1 teaspoon salt to No. 2½.) Fill to the top with boiling-hot cooking water. Exhaust to 170 F/77 C. (*c.* 10 minutes); seal. Pressure–process at 10 pounds (240 F/116 C)—40 minutes for either No. 2 or 2½. Remove cans; cool quickly.

Beets

Beets keep well in a root cellar (q.v.). Between canning and freezing, can them: they can beautifully. Use canned beets plain, titivated as a relish, in Red Flannel Hash (see Chapter 24).

GENERAL HANDLING

Only Pressure Canning for beets: they rank with home-canned string beans as carriers of *C. Botulinum* toxin. Because they're firm-fleshed, use Hot pack only. Use jars or R-enamel cans.

Sort for size; leave on tap root and 2 inches of stem (otherwise they bleed out their juice before they get in the containers). Wash carefully. Cover with boiling water and boil until skins slip off easily (15 to 25 minutes, depending on size/age). Drop them in cold water for just long enough to be able to slip off skins; skin, trim away roots, stems, any blemishes. Leave tiny beets whole; cut larger ones in slices or dice. Now they are ready to pickle or can.

Hot Pack Only

In jars. Fill with hot beets, leaving ½ inch of headroom. (Optional: Add ½ teaspoon salt to pints, 1 teaspoon salt to quarts.) Add fresh boiling water, leaving ½ inch of headroom; adjust lids. Pressure–process at 10 pounds (240 F/116 C)—pints for 30 minutes, quarts for 35 minutes. Remove jars; complete seals if necessary.

In R-enamel cans. Fill with hot beets, leaving only ¼ inch of headroom. (Optional: Add ½ teaspoon salt to No. 2 cans, 1 teaspoon salt to No. 2½.) Cover to top with boiling water. Exhaust to 170 F/77 C (*c.* 10 minutes); seal. Pressure–process at 10 pounds (240 F/116 C)—30 minutes for either No. 2 or No. 2½ cans. Remove cans; cool quickly.

Beets, Pickled

Boiling–Water Bath (vinegar makes them so acid that a B–W Bath is quite O.K.). Use Hot pack only. Use jars only.

Scrub; leave the tap root and a bit of stem to help prevent "bleeding." Boil until tender—how long, depends on size—in unsalted water (if wanted, salt may be added later). Dunk in cold water to handle; trim, strip off skins, slice. While beets are cooking, make a Pickling Syrup of equal parts of vinegar and sugar, adding 25 percent more sugar if you like a less-sharp pickle: Remember that you counteract acidity *by increasing sweetness, NOT* by lowering acidity— especially for a low-acid food like beets. Figure on ½ to ¾ cup syrup for each pint jar; larger containers of course need more, so allow for this; and leftover syrup can be refrigerated until used in any number of ways.

Fill clean, hot jars with hot beet slices, leaving ½ inch of headroom for pints, 1 inch for quarts. (Optional: Add ½ teaspoon salt to pints, 1 teaspoon salt to quarts.) Add boiling Pickling Syrup, leaving ½ inch headroom in pints, 1 inch in quarts. Adjust lids. Process in a Boiling–Water Bath (212 F/100 C)—30 minutes for either pints or quarts. Remove jars; complete seals if necessary.

Broccoli

Broccoli and similarly strong-flavored vegetables—Brussels sprouts, cabbage (unless it's done as Sauerkraut, and see also "Root-Cellaring," Chapter 22) and cauliflower—usually discolor when canned and grow even stronger in flavor. But here's how you can broccoli and the others if you have to.

GENERAL HANDLING

Pressure Canning only. Use Hot pack only. Use jars or C-enamel cans.

Wash all-green spears, trimming off leaves, any old blossoms, and woody parts of the stems. Soak in cold salt water (1 tablespoon salt to 1 quart water) for 10 minutes to drive out bugs, etc. Drain and wash in fresh water. Cut in 2-inch pieces, splitting thick stalks; or size as you like.

HOT PACK ONLY

Cover trimmed, clean, cut broccoli with boiling water and boil 3 minutes; drain.

In jars. Pack, leaving 1 inch of headroom. (Optional: Add ½ teaspoon salt to pints, 1 teaspoon salt to quarts.) Add boiling water, leaving 1 inch of headroom; adjust lids. Pressure–process at 10 pounds (240 F/116 C)—pints for 30 minutes, quarts for 35 minutes. Remove jars; complete seals if necessary.

In C-enamel cans. Pack, leaving only ½ inch of headroom. (Optional: Add ½ teaspoon salt to No. 2 cans, 1 teaspoon salt to No. 2½.) Fill to top with boiling water. Exhaust to 170 F/77 C (*c.* 10 minutes); seal. Pressure–process at 10 pounds (240 F/116 C)—30 minutes for either No. 2 or No. 2½ cans. Remove cans; cool quickly.

Brussels Sprouts

These really should be frozen (they're hateful soggy and watery). But if canning, treat them like Broccoli, making a special point of the salt-water soak because they may have worms.

Cabbage

This really should be root-cellared. Or put by as Sauerkraut (q.v.).

If canned as is, see Broccoli, but Pressure–process cans at 10 pounds (240 F/116 C) for *40* minutes.

Carrots

Like beets, carrots can be harvested late in the season to can when weather is cooler. Don't bother with overlarge, woody ones.

GENERAL HANDLING

Only Pressure Canning. Raw or Hot pack. In jars or C-enamel cans.

Sort for size. Wash, scrubbing well, and scrape. (An energetic scrub with your stiffest brush often will do for the very small ones; or parboil them just enough to loosen the skins, dunk them in cold water, slip off their skins, then use Hot pack.) Slice, dice, cut in strips—whatever.

RAW PACK

In jars. Fill tightly, leaving 1 inch of headroom. (Optional: Add ½ teaspoon salt to pints, 1 teaspoon salt to quarts.) Add boiling water, leaving ½ inch of headroom (water comes above the carrots); adjust lids. Pressure–process at 10 pounds (240 F/116 C)—pints for 25 minutes, quarts for 30 minutes. Remove jars; complete seal if necessary.

In C-enamel cans. Fill tightly, leaving ½ inch of headroom. (Optional: Add ½ teaspoon salt to No. 2 cans, 1 teaspoon salt to No. 2½.) Add boiling water to top. Exhaust to 170 F/77 C (*c.* 10 minutes); seal. Pressure–process at 10 pounds (240 F/116 C)—No. 2 cans for 25 minutes, No. 2½ for 30 minutes. Remove cans; cool quickly.

PREFERRED: HOT PACK

Cover clean, scraped, cut or whole carrots with boiling water, bring again to a full boil; drain, but save the water to put in the jars for processing.

In jars. Pack hot carrots, leaving just ½ inch of headroom. Proceed as for Raw pack, using the cooking water for the added processing liquid.

In C-enamel cans. Pack, leaving only ¼ inch of headroom. Proceed as for Raw pack, using cooking water as the processing liquid, and reducing Pressure–process time—No. 2 cans for 20 minutes, No. 2½ for 25 minutes.

Cauliflower

Immeasurably better frozen; but can it like Broccoli.

Celery

Pressure Canning only. Use Hot pack only. Use jars or plain cans.
Wash thoroughly, trim off leaves (but if it's destined for stew, a few bits of chopped leaf are good flavor), cut stalks in 1-inch pieces. Cover with boiling water, boil 3 minutes. Drain, saving the cooking water.

HOT PACK ONLY

In jars. Fill with hot celery, leaving 1 inch of headroom. (Optional: Add ½ teaspoon salt to pints, 1 teaspoon salt to quarts.) Add boiling-hot cooking water, leaving 1 inch of headroom; adjust lids. Pressure–process at 10 pounds (240 F/116 C)—pints for 30 minutes, quarts for 35 minutes. Remove jars; complete seals if necessary.

In plain cans. Fill with hot celery, leaving ½ inch of headroom. (Optional: Add ½ teaspoon salt to No. 2 cans, 1 teaspoon salt to No. 2½.) Fill to top with boiling cooking water. Exhaust to 170 F/77 C (*c.* 10 minutes); seal. Pressure–process at 10 pounds (240 F/116 C)—30 minutes for either No. 2 or No. 2½ cans. Remove cans; cool quickly.

Corn, Cream Style

Canning is the better, and certainly handier, way of putting by cream-style corn. Its density demands that it be home-canned *only in pint jars or No. 2 cans:* an extremely low-acid vegetable, it would be pressure-cooked to death for the much longer time needed to process the interior of larger containers.

General Handling

Pressure Canning only. Use Raw or Hot pack. Use pint jars or No. 2 C-enamel cans.

Get it ready by husking, de-silking and washing the ears. Slice the corn from the cob *halfway through the kernels,* then scrape the milky juice that's left on the cob in with the cut corn (this is where the "cream" comes in).

Raw Pack

In pints jars only. Fill with corn-cream mixture, leaving 1½ inches of headroom (more space than usual is needed for expansion). (Optional: Add ½ teaspoon salt.) Add boiling water, leaving ½ inch of headroom (water will be well over the top of the corn); adjust lids. Pressure–process at 10 pounds (240 *F/116 C) for 95 minutes. Remove jars; complete seals if necessary.*

In No. 2 C-enamel cans only. Fill without shaking or pressing down, leaving ½ inch of headroom. (Optional: Add ½ teaspoon salt.) Fill to top with boiling water. Exhaust to 170 F/77 C (*c.* 25 minutes); seal. Pressure–process at 10 pounds (240 F/116 C) for 105 minutes. Remove cans; cool quickly.

Preffered: Hot Pack

Prepare as for Raw pack. To each 4 cups of corn-cream mixture, add 2 cups boiling water. Heat to boiling, stirring, over medium heat (it scorches easily).

In pint jars only. Fill with boiling corn and liquid, leaving 1 inch of headroom. (Optional: Add ½ teaspoon salt.) Adjust lids. Pressure–process at 10 pounds (240 F/116 C) for 85 minutes. Remove jars; complete seals if necessary.

In No. 2 C-enamel cans only. Fill to the top with boiling corn and liquid. (Optional: Add ½ teaspoon salt.) Exhaust to 170 F/77 C (*c.* 10 minutes); seal. Pressure–process at 10 pounds (240 F/116 C) for 105 minutes. Remove cans; cool quickly.

Corn, Whole Kernel

Pressure Canning only. Use Raw or Hot pack. Use jars or C-enamel cans. Less dense than cream-style corn, it may be canned in quarts and No. 2½ cans just as well as in pints and No. 2 cans.

Husk, de-silk and wash fresh-picked ears. Cut from the cob at about ⅔ the depth of the kernels (this is deeper than for cream-style, but still avoids getting bits of cob).

Raw Pack

In jars. Fill, leaving 1 inch of headroom—and don't shake or press down. (Optional: Add ½ teaspoon salt to pints, 1 teaspoon salt to quarts.) Add boiling water, leaving ½ inch of headroom (water will come well over top of corn); adjust lids. Pressure–process at 10 pounds (240 F/116 C)—pints for 55 minutes, quarts for 85 minutes. Remove jars; complete seals if necessary.

In C-enamel cans. Fill, leaving ½ inch of headroom—and don't shake or press down. (Optional: Add ½ teaspoon salt to No. 2 cans, 1 teaspoon salt to No. 2½.) Add boiling water to top. Exhaust to 170 F/77 C (*c.* 10 minutes); seal. Pressure–process at 10 pounds (240 F/116 C)—60 minutes for either No. 2 or No. 2½ cans. Remove cans; cool quickly.

Preferred: Hot Pack

Prepare as for Raw pack. To each 4 cups of kernels, add 2 cups boiling water. Bring to boiling over medium heat, stirring so it won't scorch. Drain, saving the hot liquid.

In jars. Fill with kernels, leaving 1 inch of headroom. (Optional: Add ½ teaspoon salt to pints, 1 teaspoon salt to quarts.) Add boiling-hot cooking liquid, leaving 1 inch of headroom; adjust lids. Pressure–process at 10 pounds (240 F/116 C)—pints for 55 minutes, quarts for 85 minutes. Remove jars; complete seals if necessary.

In C-enamel cans. Fill with hot kernels, leaving ½ inch of headroom. (Optional: Add ½ teaspoon salt to No. 2 cans, 1 teaspoon salt to No. 2½.) Add boiling-hot cooking liquid to top (water will come well over top of corn). Exhaust to 170 F/77 C (*c.* 10 minutes); seal. Pressure–process at 10 pounds (240 F/116 C)—60 minutes for either No. 2 or No. 2½ cans. Remove cans; cool quickly.

Eggplant

This loses its looks when it's canned, but freezes well enough for casseroles (see Chapters 13 and 24).

GENERAL HANDLING

Pressure Canning only. Use Hot pack only. Use jars or plain cans.

Wash, pare and slice or cube eggplant. Sprinkle lightly with salt and cover with cold water (to help draw out its juice). Let soak 45 minutes; drain. In fresh water, boil for 5 minutes. Drain, and pack hot without adding salt.

In jars. Fill clean hot jars, leaving 1 inch of headroom. Add boiling water, leaving 1 inch of headroom; adjust lids. Pressure–process at 10 pounds (240 F/116 C)—pints for 30 minutes, quarts for 40 minutes. Remove jars; complete seals if necessary.

In plain cans. Pack, leaving only ¼ inch of headroom. Fill to top with boiling water. Exhaust to 170 F/77 C (*c.* 10 minutes); seal. Pressure–process at 10 pounds (240 F/116 C)—No. 2 cans for 35 minutes, No. 2½ for 40 minutes. Remove cans; cool quickly.

Greens—Spinach, etc., and Wild

All garden greens—spinach, chard, turnip or beet tops—can nicely; so do wild ones like dandelions and milkweed (fiddleheads and cowslips are usually such treats that they're eaten as they come in). Greens freeze well, and with more garden freshness.

GENERAL HANDLING

Pressure Canning only. Use Hot pack only (to make greens solid enough in the container). Use jars or plain cans.

Using spinach as the example *for garden greens:* Remove bits of grass, poor leaves, etc., from just-picked leaves; cut out tough stems and coarse midribs. Wash thoroughly, lifting from the water to let any sediment settle. Put about

2½ pounds of clean, wet leaves in a large cheesecloth, tie the top, and steam the spinach for about 10 minutes—or until well wilted, and pack.

Prepare *wild greens*—dandelions, milkweed and fiddleheads—according to directions given for the individual greens in Chapter 24, "Cooking."

HOT PACK ONLY

In jars. Fill with greens, leaving ½ inch of headroom. (Optional: Add ½ teaspoon salt to pints, 1 teaspoon salt to quarts.) Add boiling water, leaving ½ inch of headroom; adjust lids. Pressure–process at 10 pounds (240 F/116 C)—pints for 70 minutes, quarts for 90 minutes. Remove jars; complete seals if necessary.

In plain cans. Fill with greens, leaving only ¼ inch of headroom. (Optional: Add ½ teaspoon salt to No. 2 cans, 1 teaspoon salt to No. 2½.) Cover to top with boiling water. Exhaust to 170 F/77 C (*c.* 10 minutes); seal. Pressure–process at 10 pounds (240 F/116 C)—No. 2 cans for 65 minutes, No. 2½ for 75 minutes. Remove cans; cool quickly.

Hominy (Alkali-hulled Corn)

This traditional Southern vegetable is made from dried whole-kernel corn after the hulls are removed by cooking in a solution of lye—or of pickling lime or washing soda, even of the leachings from wood ashes (for the processes, see Chapter 23). After the hulls have been removed, the kernels are cooked in several fresh waters until the kernels are soft; this precooking causes the hominy to swell, so extra headroom is not needed when it is Hot-packed. This strong alkaline treatment destroys almost all the Vitamin C and many of the B vitamins in the corn.

Hominy is tasty served hot with butter as a side dish; or substitute the more easily bought grits (although canned hominy is gettable at most large supermarkets). In the American Southwest, buy it hulled and swollen, though dry, as *posole:* Cook it in a stew with pork, chili, onions, etc.—but be sure to add the salt late in cooking lest the kernels fail to reach their full plumpness.

HOT PACK ONLY

In jars. Fill, leaving ½ inch of headroom. (Optional: Add ½ teaspoon salt to pints, 1 teaspoon salt to quarts.) Add boiling water, leaving ½ inch of headroom; adjust lids. Pressure–process at 10 pounds (240 F/116 C)—pints for 60 minutes, quarts for 70 minutes. Remove jars; complete seals if necessary.
In C-enamel cans. Fill, leaving only ¼ inch of headroom. (Optional: Add ½ teaspoon salt to No. 2 cans, 1 teaspoon salt to No. 2½.) Fill to top with boiling water. Exhaust to 170 F/77 C (*c.* 10 minutes); seal. Pressure–process at 10 pounds (240 F/116 C)—No. 2 cans for 60 minutes, No. 2½ for 70 minutes. Remove cans; cool quickly.

Mixed Vegetables (in General)

Pressure Canning only. Hot pack only. Use jars or plain or C-enamel cans (for which type of can, see "About Jars and Cans" in Chapter 3).

Rule-of-thumb for processing: Choose the time required by the single ingredient requiring the longest processing (viz. Stewed Tomatoes with Added Vegetables in Chapter 10).

Wash, trim vegetables, peeling if necessary. Cut to uniform size. Cover with boiling water, boil 10 minutes. Drain; save the cooking water for processing.

Hot Pack Only

In jars. Fill with hot mixed vegetables, leaving ½ inch of headroom. (Optional: Add ½ teaspoon salt to pints, 1 teaspoon salt to quarts.) Add boiling water (fresh, or the cooking water), leaving ½ inch of headroom; adjust lids. Pressure–process at 10 pounds (240 F/116 C)—pints for 60 minutes, quarts for 70 minutes. Remove jars; complete seals if necessary.

In plain or C-enamel cans. Fill with hot mixed vegetables, leaving ½ inch of headroom. (Optional: Add ½ teaspoon salt to No. 2 cans, 1 teaspoon salt to No. 2½.) Fill to the top with boiling water (fresh, or the cooking water). Exhaust to 170 F/77 C (*c.* 10 minutes); seal. Pressure–process at 10 pounds (240 F/116 C)—No. 2 cans for 60 minutes, No. 2½ for 70 minutes. Remove cans; cool quickly.

Mixed Corn and Beans (Succotash)

Pressure Canning only. Use Hot pack only. Use jars or C-enamel cans.

Boil freshly picked ears of corn for 5 minutes; cut kernels from cobs (as for Whole-Kernel Corn, *without* scraping in the milk). Prepare fresh lima beans or green/snap beans, and boil by themselves for 3 minutes. Measure and mix hot corn with ½ to an equal amount of beans.

Hot Pack Only

In jars. Fill with hot corn-and-bean mixture, leaving 1 inch of headroom. (Optional: Add ½ teaspoon salt to pints, 1 teaspoon salt to quarts.) Add boiling water, leaving 1 inch of headroom; adjust lids. Pressure–process at 10 pounds (240 F/116 C)—pints for 60 minutes, quarts for 85 minutes. Remove jars; complete seals if necessary.

In C-enamel cans. Fill with hot mixture, leaving ½ inch of headroom. (Optional: Add ½ teaspoon salt to No. 2 cans, 1 teaspoon salt to No. 2½.) Fill to the top with boiling water. Exhaust to 170 F/77 C (*c.* 10 minutes); seal. Pressure–process at 10 pounds (240 F/116 C)—No. 2 cans for 70 minutes, No. 2½ for 95 minutes. Remove cans; cool quickly.

Mushrooms

Canned mushrooms have a bad track record as carriers of *C. botulinum* toxin, so use only fresh edible mushrooms—preferably those grown in presterilized soil.

General Handling

Pressure Canning only. Use Hot pack only. Use ½-pint or pint jars, plain No. 2 cans.

Soak them in cold water for 10 minutes to loosen field dirt, then wash well. Trim blemishes from caps and stems. Leave small buttons whole; cut larger ones in button-size pieces. In a covered saucepan simmer them gently for 15 minutes.

Hot Pack Only

In jars. Fill with hot mushrooms, leaving ½ inch of headroom. (Optional: Add ¼ teaspoon salt to ½-pints, ½ teaspoon salt to pints.) To prevent color change, add ¹⁄₁₆ teaspoon of crystalline ascorbic acid to ½-pint jars, ⅛ teaspoon to pints. Add boiling water, leaving ½ inch of headroom; adjust lids. Pressure–process at 10 pounds (240 F/116 C)—30 minutes for either ½-pints or pints. Remove jars; complete seals if necessary.

In plain No. 2 cans. Fill with hot mushrooms, leaving ½ inch of headroom. (Optional: Add ½ teaspoon salt to No. 2 cans.) Add ⅛ teaspoon crystalline ascorbic acid. Fill to top with boiling water. Exhaust to 170 F/77 C (*c.* 10 minutes); seal. Pressure–process at 10 pounds (240 F/116 C) for 30 minutes. Remove cans; cool quickly.

Nut Meats

Nuts are an important source of protein for vegetarian main dishes, and are a popular touch in baked goods, candies, salads, etc. All nuts are rather fatty, and it's this fat that turns rancid and spoils the meats (even nuts in the shell can spoil after a while). Freeze them too.

General Handling

Pressure Canning or Boiling–Water Bath. Use *dry* Hot pack only (nut meats are oven-dried before canning). Use dry, sterilized jars no larger than pints, and with *self-sealing lids* (see "About Jars and Cans" in Chapter 3).

Spread a shallow layer of nut meats in baking pans, and bake in a very slow oven—not more than 275 F/135 C—watching the nuts carefully and stirring once in a while, until they are dry but not browned: they must not scorch. Keep hot for packing.

Dry Hot Pack Only

In self-sealing jars. For pints (or ½-pints), fill dry, sterilized jars, leaving ½ inch of headroom; adjust lids. Pressure–process at 5 pounds (228 F/109

C)—10 minutes for ½-pints or pints. OR process in a Boiling–Water Bath—*but with the water level well below the top of the jars*—for 20 minutes. Remove jars; remove bands from self-sealing lids after jars have cooled 12 hours.

Okra (Gumbo)

This vegetable popular in Southern, Creole and West Indian cooking cans and freezes equally well: if you plan to use it cut up in soups and stews, it's probably handier canned.

GENERAL HANDLING

Pressure Canning only. Use Hot pack only. Use jars or plain cans.

Wash tender young pods; trim stems but don't cut off caps. Cover with boiling water and boil 1 minute; drain. Leave whole with cap, or cut in 1-inch pieces, discarding cap.

HOT PACK ONLY

In jars. Fill with hot okra, leaving ½ inch of headroom. (Optional: Add ½ teaspoon salt to pints, 1 teaspoon salt to quarts.) Add boiling water, leaving ½ inch of headroom; adjust lids. Pressure–process at 10 pounds (240 F/116 C)—pints for 25 minutes, quarts for 40 minutes. Remove jars; complete seals if necessary.

In plain cans. Fill with hot okra, leaving only ¼ inch of headroom. (Optional: Add ½ teaspoon salt to No. 2 cans, 1 teaspoon salt to No. 2½.) Fill to top with boiling water. Exhaust to 170 F/77 C (*c.* 10 minutes); seal. Pressure–process at 10 pounds (240 F/116 C)—No. 2 cans for 25 minutes, No. 2½ for 35 minutes. Remove cans; cool quickly.

Onions, White

Onions that are properly cured and stored (see "Drying," Chapter 21) carry over so well that many cooks don't bother to can them—on top of which home-canned onions are apt to be dark in color and soft in texture. They are often canned in combinations (see Mixed Vegetables, earlier in this chapter, for rule-of-thumb).

GENERAL HANDLING

Pressure Canning only. Use Hot pack only. Use jars or C-enamel cans.

Sort for uniform size—1 inch in diameter is ideal—and wash. Peel, trimming off roots and stalks. (If you push a hole downward through the middle with a slender finishing nail, their centers will cook with less chance of shucking off outer layers.) Cover with boiling water, parboil gently for 5 minutes. Drain, saving the cooking water for processing.

HOT PACK ONLY

In jars. Fit whole onions in closely, leaving ½ inch of headroom. (Optional: Add ½ teaspoon salt to pints, 1 teaspoon salt to quarts.) Add boiling cooking liquid, leaving ½ inch of headroom; adjust lids. Pressure–process at 10 pounds (240 F/116 C)—pints for 25 minutes, quarts for 30 minutes. Remove jars; complete seals if necessary.

In C-enamel cans. Fit whole onions closely, leaving ¼ inch of headroom. (Optional: Add ½ teaspoon salt to No. 2 cans, 1 teaspoon salt to No. 2½.) Fill to brim with boiling cooking water. Exhaust to 170 F/77 C (*c.* 10 minutes); seal. Pressure–process at 10 pounds (240 F/116 C)—No. 2 cans for 25 minutes, No. 2½ for 30 minutes. Remove cans; cool quickly.

Parsnips

This is probably the only vegetable that actually improves by wintering over in frozen ground—so why take the shine off it as the "first of spring" treat?

But if you can't keep them in a garden or a root cellar: wash, trim, scrape, and cut them in pieces, then proceed as for Broccoli (q.v.).

Peas, Black-eyed (Cowpeas, Black-eyed Beans)

Pressure Canning only. Use Raw or Hot pack. Use jars or C-enamel cans. Shell and wash before packing. Take care *not* to shake or press down the peas when you pack the containers: they swell in the containers.

RAW PACK

In jars. Fill with raw peas, leaving 1½ inches of headroom in pints, 2 inches of headroom in quarts. (Optional: Add ½ teaspoon salt to pints, 1 teaspoon salt to quarts.) Add boiling water, leaving ½ inch of headroom (water will come well over the top of the peas); adjust lids. Pressure–process at 10 pounds (240 F/116 C)—pints for 35 minutes, quarts for 40 minutes. Remove jars; complete seals if necessary.

In C-enamel cans. Fill with raw peas, leaving ¾ inch of headroom. (Optional: Add ½ teaspoon salt to No. 2 cans, 1 teaspoon salt to No. 2½.) Add boiling water, leaving ¼ inch of headroom. Exhaust to 170 F/77 C (*c.* 10 minutes); seal. Pressure–process at 10 pounds (240 F/116 C)—No. 2 cans for 35 minutes, No. 2½ for 40 minutes. Remove cans; cool quickly.

PREFERRED: HOT PACK

After shelling and washing, cover with boiling water, bring to a full, high boil. Drain, saving the blanching water for processing.

In jars. Pack hot, leaving 1¼ inches of headroom in pints, 1½ inches of headroom in quarts. (Optional: Add ½ teaspoon salt to pints, 1 teaspoon salt to quarts.) Add boiling water (or blanching liquid), leaving ½ inch of headroom in either size of jar; adjust lids. Pressure–process at 10 pounds (240 F/116 C)—pints for 35 minutes, quarts for 40 minutes. Remove jars; complete seals if necessary.

In C-enamel cans. Pack hot, leaving ½ inch of headroom for either size of can. (Optional: Add ½ teaspoon salt to No. 2 cans, 1 teaspoon salt to No. 2½.) Add boiling water, leaving ¼ inch of headroom. Exhaust to 170 F/77 C (*c.* 10 minutes); seal. Pressure–process at 10 pounds (240 F/116 C)—No. 2 cans for 30 minutes, No. 2½ for 35 minutes. Remove cans; cool quickly.

Peas, Green

Shell and wash. *Don't shake or press down in packing:* peas swell.

Edible-pod and *Snow* varieties. Unstring young edible-pod ones, proceed to pack Hot and process like Beans, Green, earlier. If too mature, these peas may be shelled and treated as in "Preferred: Hot Pack," below. Snow peas are much better frozen, but if you must can them, do them like Beans, Green, with Hot pack.

RAW PACK

In jars. Fill, leaving 1 inch of headroom. (Optional: Add ½ teaspoon salt to pints, 1 teaspoon salt to quarts.) Add boiling water to within 1½ inches of the top of the jar (water will come well below the top of the peas); adjust lids. Pressure–process at 10 pounds (240 F/116 C)—40 minutes for both pints and quarts. Remove jars; complete seal if necessary.

In plain cans. Fill, leaving only ¼ inch of headroom. (Optional: Add ½ teaspoon salt to No. 2 cans, 1 teaspoon salt to No. 2½.) Fill to top with boiling water. Exhaust to 170 F/77 C (*c.* 10 minutes); seal. Pressure–process at 10 pounds (240 F/116 C)—No. 2 cans for 30 minutes, No. 2½ for 35 minutes. Remove cans; cool quickly.

PREFERRED: HOT PACK

Cover peas with boiling water, return to a full boil; save the water.

In jars. Fill loosely with hot drained peas, leaving 1 inch of headroom. (Optional: Add ½ teaspoon salt to pints, 1 teaspoon salt to quarts.) Add boiling water or blanching liquid, leaving 1 inch of headroom; adjust lids. Pressure–process at 10 pounds (240 F/116 C)—40 minutes for either pints or quarts. Remove jars; complete seals if necessary.

In plain cans. Fill loosely with hot peas, leaving only ¼ inch of headroom. (Optional: Add ½ teaspoon salt to No. 2 cans, 1 teaspoon salt to No. 2½.) Fill to brim with boiling water or blanching liquid. Exhaust to 170 F/77 C (*c.* 10 minutes); seal. Pressure–process at 10 pounds (240 F/116 C)—No. 2 cans for 30 minutes, No. 2½ for 35 minutes. Remove cans; cool quickly.

Peppers, Green (Bell, Sweet)

Pressure Canning only. Hot pack only. Use jars or plain cans.

Wash, remove stems, cores and seeds. Cut in large pieces or leave whole. Put in boiling water and boil 3 minutes. Drain and pack. (If you like them peeled, take them from the boiling water, dunk in cold water to cool just enough for handling, and strip off the skins; pack.)

Acid is added to green peppers in order to can them safely.

HOT PACK ONLY

In jars. Pack hot peppers flat, leaving 1 inch of headroom in pints, 1¼ inches of headroom in quarts. Add 1 tablespoon white vinegar to pints, 2 tablespoons vinegar to quarts; pour in boiling water, leaving ½ inch of headroom in pints, ¾ inch in quarts, so that water covers the peppers. (Optional: Add ½ teaspoon salt to pints, 1 teaspoon salt to quarts.) Adjust lids. Pressure–process at 10 pounds (240 F/116 C)—pints for 35 minutes, quarts for 45 minutes. Remove jars; complete seals if necessary.

In plain cans. Pack flat, leaving ½ inch of headroom for both No. 2 cans and No. 2½ cans. Add 1 tablespoon white vinegar to No. 2 cans, 2 tablespoons to No. 2½ cans. (Optional: Add ½ teaspoon salt to No. 2 cans, 1 teaspoon salt to No. 2½ cans.) Fill to the top of the container with boiling water. Exhaust to 170 F/77 C (*c.* 10 minutes); seal. Pressure–process at 10 pounds (240 F/116 C)—No. 2 cans for 20 minutes, No. 2½ cans for 20 minutes. Remove cans; cool quickly.

Pimientos

Pressure Canning only. Use Hot pack only. Use ½-pint or pint jars, or No. 2 plain cans.

Warning note: It used to be permissible to can tightly packed or densely textured food without added liquid: *no longer.* Pimientos are among the foods that now require added liquid.

Wash, cover with boiling water, and simmer until skins can be peeled off—4 to 5 minutes. Dunk in cold water so they can be handled, trim stems, blossom ends, and skin them like Green Peppers, above; pack hot, adding acid for safety as indicated.

HOT PACK ONLY

In jars. Pack flat in clean, hot ½-pint or pint jars, leaving ¾ inch of headroom. Add 1½ teaspoons white vinegar to ½-pints, 1 tablespoon vinegar to pints. (Optional: Add ¼ teaspoon salt to ½-pint jars, ½ teaspoon salt to pints.) Pour in just enough boiling water to cover pimientos, leaving ½ inch of headroom in both ½-pints and pints. Adjust lids. Pressure–process at 10 pounds (240 F/116 C)—20 minutes for either ½-pints or pints. Remove jars; complete seals if necessary.

In No. 2 plain cans. Pack flat, leaving only ⅛ inch headroom. Add 1 tablespoon white vinegar, and just enough boiling water to cover the pimientos. (Optional: Add ½ teaspoon salt to No. 2 cans of pimientos.) Exhaust to 170 F/77 C (c. 10 minutes); seal. Pressure–process at 10 pounds (240 F/116 C) for 20 minutes. Remove cans; cool quickly.

Potatoes, Sweet (and Yams)

Updated research says that these, too, must be canned with some liquid added, to let heat penetrate safely. For glazing: Remove pieces whole from the container, pat off moisture and finish drying them on foil in a slow oven for a few minutes, turning once; then glaze.

GENERAL HANDLING

Pressure Canning only. Hot pack only; Wet pack only. Use jars or plain cans.
Sort for size, wash; boil or steam until only half cooked, and the skins come off easily—20 minutes or so. Dunk in cold water so they can be handled, slip off skins, cut away blemishes. Cut large potatoes in pieces lengthwise.

HOT PACK—WET ONLY

In jars. Pack loosely; upright if you'll glaze them later. Leave 1 inch of headroom in both pints and quarts. (Optional: Add ½ teaspoon salt to pints, 1 teaspoon salt to quarts.) Add boiling water or Medium Syrup (see "Liquids for Canning Fruits" in Chapter 5), leaving 1 inch of headroom; adjust lids. Pressure–process at 10 pounds (240 F/116 C)—pints 55 minutes, quarts 90 minutes. Remove jars; complete seals if necessary.

In plain cans. Fill loosely, leaving ¼ inch of headroom. (Optional: Add ½ teaspoon salt to No. 2 cans, 1 teaspoon salt to No. 2½.) Fill to top with boiling water or Medium Syrup (refer above). Exhaust to 170 F/77 C (c. 10 minutes); seal. Pressure–process at 10 pounds (240 F/116 C)—No. 2 cans for 70 minutes, No. 2½ cans for 90 minutes. Remove cans; cool quickly.

Potatoes, White ("Irish")

These potatoes don't home-freeze at all well (unless they're partially pre-cooked in a combination dish, q.v.)—so cold-store them (see "Root-Cellaring," Chapter 22). But it's possible for them to be too immature to store without spoiling—so you can them. Delicate tiny, new potatoes can well, and are good served hot with parsley butter or creamed.

GENERAL HANDLING

Pressure Canning only. Use Raw or Hot Pack. Use jars or plain cans. If around 1 to 1½ inches in diameter, they may be canned whole; dice the larger ones.
Wash and scrape just-dug new potatoes, removing all blemishes. (If you're dicing them, prevent darkening during preparation by dropping the dice in a solution of 1 teaspoon salt for each 1 quart of cold water.) Drain before packing by either method.

Raw Pack

In this pack, *diced get 5 minutes longer processing time,* because they're more dense in the containers than whole ones are.

In jars. Fill with whole or diced potatoes, leaving ½ inch of headroom. (Optional: Add ½ teaspoon salt to pints, 1 teaspoon salt to quarts.) Add boiling water, leaving ½ inch of headroom; adjust lids. Pressure–process at 10 pounds (240 F/116 C)—*whole,* pints or quarts for 40 minutes; *diced,* pints or quarts for 45 minutes. Remove jars; complete seals if necessary.

In plain cans. Fill, leaving only ½ inch of headroom. (Optional: Add ½ teaspoon salt to No. 2 cans, 1 teaspoon salt to No. 2½.) Fill to the top with boiling water. Exhaust to 170 F/77 C (*c.* 10 minutes); seal. Pressure–process at 10 pounds (240 F/116 C)—*whole,* No. 2 cans for 40 minutes, No. 2½ for 45 minutes; *diced,* No. 2 for 45 minutes, No. 2½ for 50 minutes. Remove cans; cool quickly.

Preferred: Hot Pack

Cover clean, scraped *whole* potatoes with boiling water, boil 10 minutes; drain. Drain anti-discoloration solution off *diced* potatoes; cover them with boiling fresh water, boil 2 minutes; drain.

In jars. With whole or diced potatoes, leave ½ inch of headroom. (Optional: Add ½ teaspoon salt to pints, 1 teaspoon salt to quarts.) Add boiling water, leaving ½ inch of headroom; adjust lids. Pressure–process at 10 pounds (240 F/116 C)—*whole,* pints for 30 minutes, quarts for 40 minutes; *diced,* pints for 35 minutes, quarts for 40 minutes. Remove jars; complete seals if necessary.

In plain cans. Fill with whole or diced potatoes, leaving only ¼ inch of headroom. (Optional: Add ½ teaspoon salt to No. 2 cans, 1 teaspoon salt to No. 2½.) Fill to top with boiling water. Exhaust to 170 F/77 C (*c.* 10 minutes); seal. Pressure–process at 10 pounds (240 F/116 C)—*whole* or *diced*— No. 2 cans for 35 minutes, No. 2½ for 40 minutes. Remove cans; cool quickly.

Pumpkin (and Winter Squash)

Pressure Canning only. Hot pack only. Use jars or R-enamel cans. Cube it only: heat transfer fails in strained foods of this type.

Dry-fleshed pumpkin (or winter squash) is best for canning: test it with your thumbnail—it's dry enough if your nail won't cut the surface skin easily.

Hot Pack—Cubed

Wash, cut in manageable hunks, pare and remove seeds; cut in 1-inch cubes. Cover with water and bring to boiling. Drain, reserving hot liquid, and pack hot.

In jars. Fill with hot cubes, leaving ½ inch of headroom. (Optional: Add ½ teaspoon salt to pints, 1 teaspoon salt to quarts.) Add boiling cooking water, leaving ½ inch of headroom; adjust lids. Pressure–process at 10 pounds (240 F/116 C)—pints for 55 minutes, quarts for 90 minutes. Remove jars; complete seals if necessary.

In R-enamel cans. Fill, leaving only ¼ inch of headroom. (Optional: Add ½ teaspoon salt to No. 2 cans, 1 teaspoon salt to No. 2½.) Fill to brim with boiling cooking water. Exhaust to 170 F/77 C (*c.* 10 minutes); seal. Pressure–process at 10 pounds (240 F/116 C)—No. 2 cans for 50 minutes, No. 2½ for 75 minutes. Remove cans; cool quickly.

Rutabagas (and White Turnips)

Root-cellaring is best (q.v.), but rutabagas are good to ferment like Sauerkraut (see how in "Curing," Chapter 20)—in which case they are canned like Sauerkraut, below.

However, if you do want *to can them fresh:* Wash, peel, cube; pack in jars/C-enamel cans, and Pressure–process as for Broccoli (q.v.).

Salsify (Oyster Plant)

Like parsnips and horseradish, this delicately flavored, old-fashioned vegetable is able to winter in the ground, and it may be root-cellared. With a little extra attention so it won't discolor, it cans well. (See Chapter 24 for recipe.)

GENERAL HANDLING

Pressure Canning only. Use Hot pack only. Use jars or C-enamel cans.

Its milky juice turns rather rusty when it hits the air, and you may prevent discoloration of the vegetable by either one of two ways: (1) Scrub roots well, scrape as for carrots, and slice, dropping each slice immediately in a solution of 2 tablespoons vinegar and 2 tablespoons salt for each 1 gallon of cold water; rinse well, cover quickly with boiling water, boil for 2 minutes; pack hot. Or (2) scrub roots; in a solution of 1 tablespoon vinegar to each 1 quart of water, boil whole until skins come off easily—10 to 15 minutes; rinse well in cold water, skin, leave whole or slice; pack hot.

HOT PACK ONLY

In jars. Fill, leaving 1 inch of headroom. And fresh boiling water, leaving 1 inch of headroom; adjust lids. Pressure–process at 10 pounds (240 F/116 C)—pints for 30 minutes, quarts for 35 minutes. Remove jars; complete seals if necessary.

In C-enamel cans. Fill, leaving ½ inch of headroom; add fresh boiling water to brim. Exhaust to 170 F/77 C (*c.* 10 minutes); seal. Pressure–process at 10 pounds (240 F/116 C)—30 minutes for both No. 2 and No. 2½ cans. Remove cans; cool quickly.

Sauerkraut (Fermented Cabbage)

By all means can your sauerkraut—unless you are able to guarantee cool enough storage for the crock after it is fermented.

General Handling

Boiling–Water Bath processing is adequate for a food as acid as this. Hot pack only. Use jars or R-enamel cans.

Hot Pack Only

Heat to simmering—180 to 210 F (82 to 99 C)—*do not boil,* and pack as directed below. If you don't have enough sauerkraut juice, eke it out with a brine made of 1½ tablespoons salt for each 1 quart of water.

In jars. Fill clean, hot jars, leaving ½ inch of headroom. Add hot juice (or hot brine, above), leaving ½ inch of headroom; adjust lids. Process in a Boiling–Water Bath—pints for 15 minutes, quarts for 20 minutes. Remove jars; complete seals if necessary.

In R-enamel cans. Pack hot, leaving only ½ inch of headroom. Fill to the brim with hot juice or brine (again, as above). Exhaust to 170 F/77 C (*c.* 10 minutes); seal. Process in a Boiling–Water Bath—25 minutes for either No. 2 or No. 2½ cans. Remove cans; cool quickly.

Soybeans

Although not particularly interesting by themselves, soybeans are a splendid *natural* high-protein addition—aside from being an economical "stretcher"— for ground meats, stews, chowders, casseroles, etc. They are good keepers when dried and they also freeze well.

General Handling

Use shelled, fully developed but still tender, *green* soybeans (old, light-colored ones are better dried, after which they're handled like any dried bean for baking, or whatever).
Pressure Canning only. Hot pack only. Use jars or C-enamel cans. Pack loosely, allowing the extra amount of headroom because they swell.

Hot Pack Only

Prepare and process like Lima Beans (q.v.), except *increase the processing time* at 10 pounds (240 F/116 C) to—*55 minutes* for pint jars, *65 minutes* for quart jars; *50 minutes* for No. 2 cans, *60 minutes* for No. 2½ cans.

Spinach, see Greens

Squash—Chayote, Summer, Zucchini

Pressure Canning only. Use Raw or Hot pack. Use jars or plain cans.
Wash, trim ends but do not peel. Cut in ½-inch slices; halve or quarter the slices to make the pieces uniform.

RAW PACK

In jars. Pack tightly in clean, hot jars, leaving 1 inch of headroom. (Optional: Add ½ teaspoon salt to pints, 1 teaspoon salt to quarts.) Add boiling water, leaving ½ inch of headroom (water will come over the top of the squash); adjust lids. Pressure–process at 10 pounds (240 F/116 C)—pints for 25 minutes, quarts for 30 minutes. Remove jars; complete seals if necessary.

In plain cans. Pack tightly, leaving ½ inch of headroom. (Optional: Add ½ teaspoon salt to No. 2 cans, 1 teaspoon salt to No. 2½.) Fill to the brim with boiling water. Exhaust to 170 F/77 C (*c.* 10 minutes); seal. Pressure–process at 10 pounds (240 F/77 C)—20 minutes for either No. 2 or No. 2½ cans. Remove cans; cool quickly.

PREFERRED: HOT PACK

Prepare as for Raw pack. Cover with boiling water, bring to a boil. Drain, saving the hot cooking liquid for processing.

In jars. Pack hot squash loosely, leaving ½ inch of headroom. Proceed as for Raw pack, but Pressure–process pints for 30 minutes, quarts for 40 minutes. (Hot squash is more dense than raw, so it requires longer processing.) Remove jars; complete seals if necessary.

In plain cans. Pack hot squash loosely, leaving ¼ inch of headroom. Proceed as for Raw pack, Pressure–processing both No. 2 and No. 2½ cans for 20 minutes (exhausting to 170 F/77 C gives several minutes' advantage here). Remove cans; cool quickly.

Squash, Winter, see Pumpkin

Tomatoes, see Chapter 6.

Turnips, White, see Rutabagas

8

CANNING MEATS

It is easier to freeze meat than to can it. Given equally fresh, wholesome meat or poultry, in the first instance you trim and cut to any useful size; package in the right sort of wrapping; label, and put it in the appropriate spot to freeze well and most quickly; cold enough, it is moved the next day or so to a different part of the freezer for storage.

In canning, you trim and cut to fit your containers as well as your serving preferences; then precook or pack Raw—plus always exhaust even in jars (as well as in cans); apply the lids, and Pressure–process in a relatively long session; remove the containers, let them cool naturally if they're jars; next day check the seals, clean and label and store the containers in a dry, dark place that's not going to let them freeze or get too warm.

And at this point the weight of comparison starts to shift a bit toward the benefit of canning. The meat, correctly handled, packed and processed, need only be heated—unless it will be served in a salad or in sandwiches or as cold cuts. This is why meats are included in Chapter 10, "Canning Convenience Foods." This is why householders with a desire for self-reliance sometimes put meat by in cans even though they also have it in freezers.

WHERE TO GET YOUR MEAT

More people each year are either raising food animals themselves, or are bespeaking part of a beef or a pig or a lamb grown by a country neighbor, because they hope to save money over what they would pay at supermarket special sales. Whether they do indeed get a bargain is not always predictable, and depends upon how the animal was weighed, the costs for slaughtering and butchering—and if the meat was cut with professional economy and minimal waste. In addition to knowing the grower, therefore, it is equally important to be certain that the meat was handled with adequate refrigeration and scrupulous cleanliness at every stage. *C. botulinum* can be introduced by careless treatment. More often, though, it's the Salmonellae that contaminate meat, with the meat of poultry being the most common source for this nasty form of gastro-intestinal illness.

140

All in all, your safest buy is from a meat-seller whose goods are purchased under the regulations that now require all meat sold in, as well as between, States to be inspected, and the premises where it was dealt with checked regularly. Such inspections have eliminated most parasites and diseases carried by the meat; an exception is *Trichina spiralis*—especially in pork (and also found often in bear meat)—for which the USDA does not conduct inspections.

Relevant Metrics for Canning Meat

Full metric conversions, with the arithmetic for refining them, are given at the start of Chapter 17 ("Common Ingredients and How to Use Them"), but the following—rounded off—apply in this chapter.

If you live above the sea-level zone (i.e., *over* 1000 ft/305 m), consult the subsection "Correcting for Altitude" in Chapter 3. (And do pay attention to the need for extra headroom in jars at high altitudes.)

• • •

Temperatures (@ sea level): 32 F to 38 F/Zero C to 3 C—— 170 F/77 C——240 F/116 C——250 F/121 C——350 F/177 C.

Volume: ¼ teaspoon = 1.25 mL——½ teaspoon = 2.5 mL——1 teaspoon = 5 mL——1 tablespoon = 15 mL——1 cup = 250 mL——1 pint = 500 mL——1 quart = 1 L.

Length: ¼ inch = 0.64 cm——½ inch = 1.27 cm——¾ inch = 1.9 cm——1 inch = 2.54 cm.

Warning about Game

Any wild game may be diseased or carry parasites. Bear, for example, often have trichinosis, and a number of cases are reported to the Center for Disease Control each year; and the University of Georgia, Athens advises handling rabbit with utensils and rubber gloves as safeguards against tularemia.

So if you are a successful hunter, or have been given a present of wild meat *do not eat it cooked Rare.* Roasted or grilled until Well Done, or cooked long in a stew: these are the insurance.

Pressure Canning at 10 pounds (240 F/116 C) at the sea-level zone or at 15 pounds (250 F/121 C) at higher altitudes—and for the length of time required for large pieces, small pieces, or ground meat, respectively—is the only safe way for canning game.

The State Biologist in the headquarters of your Fish and Game Department will tell you of any disease problems with game in your area. A quicker source of such information is likely to be one of your county game wardens.

GENERAL PROCEDURES FOR CANNING MEATS

Beef, pork, lamb and chicken are the most popular meats for canning. Domestic rabbits and small-game animals are canned like Poultry. Choose only good meat for canning, and handle it quickly and with total cleanliness, because bacteria grow at a frightening rate in meats and poultry if given half a chance. Any meat picks up bacteria so don't keep it waiting at room temperature until you can handle it. If you have a large amount to do, temporarily store the part you're not working on in the refrigerator or a meat cooler (32 to 38 F/Zero to 3 C). Can first thing *tomorrow* what you could not can today.

Process all canned animals and birds only in a Pressure Canner at 10 or 15 pounds (240 F/116 C or 250 F/121 C) to destroy bacteria—including the *spores of C. botulinum*. The 15 psi processing is specially recommended to offset the effects of high altitude. By all means see the Presto and Mirro companies' chart and rule-of-thumb in "15–Pound Canning at Higher Than a Mile" under the big Altitude subsection in Chapter 3.

Equipment and Its Care

A Pressure Canner is essential. And you'll need a pencil-shaped glass food thermometer *for exhausting jars* as well as cans.

Containers may be jars—we recommend the modern straight-sided ones, because they're easier to get the meat out of—or plain cans (meat sometimes makes the coating flake off the interiors of enameled cans: harmless, but unattractive).

Use good-sized sharp knives, including a 3- to 4-inch boning knife.

Wooden cutting-boards and surfaces can be very handsome and they are easier on knives than harder surfaces are, but *PFB* uses a heavy-duty skidproof acrylic panel whose side supports of metal can be extended to straddle a sink. Easy to work on, much easier to keep reasonably free of the sort of bacteria that are likely to be harbored in the pores of wood.

If you plan to do large quantities of meat, you should have a high-sided roasting pan and a very big kettle (as large as your Boiling–Water Bath kettle).

All tools and utensils must be scrubbed in hot soapy water and rinsed well with fresh boiling water before each use.

To control bacteria, cutting-boards and wooden working surfaces must be scrubbed hard in hot soapy water *both before and after* you handle meat on them, and must be disinfected with a solution of ¼ cup chlorine bleach to 4 cups of lukewarm water; leave it on for several minutes, then rinse off with fresh water. Or leave on the surface for 15 minutes a solution of 2 tablespoons chlorine bleach in 4 cups of water; rinse with boiling water.

Signs of Spoilage and What to Do

The fats in meat, plus its high protein content, make it more susceptible to spoilage than vegetables are. Follow the procedures for examining vegetables ("Canned Vegetable Troubles and What to Do," Chapter 7). In addition, take this warning to heart:

• • BEFORE TASTING HOME–CANNED MEAT AND POULTRY, AND THEIR BROTHS: You must be unshakably certain that your Pressure Canner was operated correctly—pressure gauge accurate and dead-weight/weighted gauge signaling properly—and that requirements for times and "Correcting for Altitude" in Chapter 3 were followed.

Unless you are sure that these safeguards were observed, a margin of protection is added by boiling the food hard for 20 minutes to destroy possible hidden toxins, stirring to distribute the heat and adding water if necessary. If the food foams unduly or smells bad during boiling, destroy it completely so it cannot be eaten by people or animals. (See also "A Quieter Method of Destroying Botulism Toxin" in Chapter 9.)

AND ABOUT SALT

Salt is merely an optional seasoning in canned meat and poultry; it may be omitted.

If you use salt, your regular table salt will do.

Salt substitutes for special diets can leave an unwanted aftertaste when used in canning: wait to add these seasonings when the food is heated for serving.

STEPS IN CANNING MEAT

CUTS OF MEAT FROM LARGE ANIMALS

Know what a whole, half or quarter of an animal will yield in the way of cuts before you buy one. There is 20 to 25 percent waste to start with, and usually there will be more pounds of stewing and/or ground meat than pounds of steaks and roasts and chops. Various USDA publications, and an article in the September 1974 issue of *Consumer Reports* are helpful about actual yield.

Cutting the Meat

Have the carcass cut in serving pieces by a professional meat-cutter to get the most out of your investment.

If you wish to tackle the job yourself, ask your County Extension Service office for a copy of *Farmers Bulletin No. 2209, Slaughtering, Cutting and Pro-*

cessing Beef on the Farm, and for a copy of *Farmers Bulletin No. 2265, Slaughtering, Cutting and Processing Pork on the Farm.*

Audrey Alley Gorton's *The Venison Book, How to Dress, Cut up and Cook Your Deer* is a helpful guide to field-dressing and butchering large game.

CANNING LARGE PIECES OF MEAT

Pressure Canning only. Use Raw or Hot pack (we prefer Hot pack). Use straight-sided jars or plain cans.

Unlike the canning procedures for Vegetables, in certain instances the air in food in *jars*—as well as cans—is exhausted before processing.

Prime cuts of beef, pork, lamb, veal and large game are best canned in large pieces. The less choice parts are good for stews and ground meats.

MAJOR CUTS OF BEEF (or ELK or MOOSE)

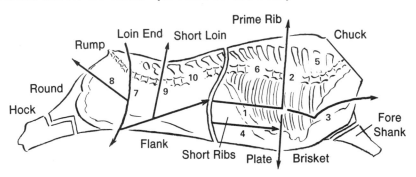

The following USDA pictures show the efficient sequence—and with a minimum of waste—for breaking down a side of beef into major anatomical cuts. From these large basic pieces the householder will cut the pot roasts, oven roasts, steaks, pieces for stewing and grinding—some to be served soon, the rest to put by. Use a meat saw for bones, wickedly sharp knives for cutting tissue.

First, the fore- and hindquarter are separated just behind the last rib in the

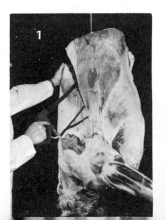
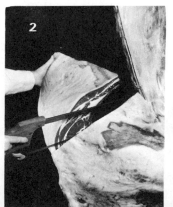
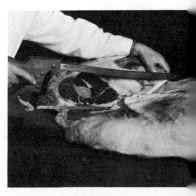

manner indicated by the gap in the diagram. Photos 1–6 deal with the fore-quarter. *Photos 1 and 2:* removing the prime-rib section. *Photo 3:* separating the plate-and-brisket section from the chuck (foreshank already removed). *Photo 4:* cutting short ribs from the plate. *Photo 5:* cutting chuck steaks. *Photo 6:* dividing the prime-rib section into standing rib roasts.

Turning to the hindquarter, *Photo 7:* having marked the cutting line to end at a point four vertebrae forward from the root of the tail, separate round-and-rump section from the loin. *Photo 8:* separating rump from round. *Photo 9:* having removed the flank (which will go into flank steaks or ground meat), divide the loin into short loin and loin end (which makes eventual sirloin roasts or steaks). *Photo 10:* cutting Porterhouse steaks from the short loin.

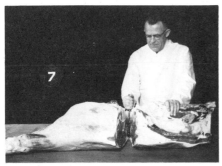
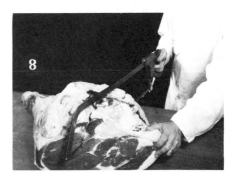
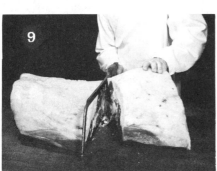
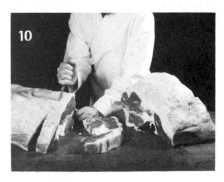

MAJOR CUTS OF PORK

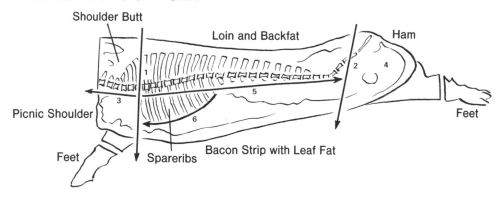

The USDA pictures below show the large basic cuts from a side of pork; they will be broken down to suit the family's purpose. Use a meat saw on bones, use long *sharp* knives for cutting tissue.

Photo 1: having removed the head (for head cheese or sausage), cut down between the second and third ribs to separate shoulder section from loin-and-bacon midsection. *Photo 2:* remove the square-top ham with a cut at right angles to the shank. *Photo 3:* separating picnic shoulder and shoulder butt (both usually cured and smoked). *Photo 4:* trimming the ham. *Photo 5:* separating the loin from the bacon strip and leaf fat. *Photo 6:* cutting spareribs from the bacon strips.

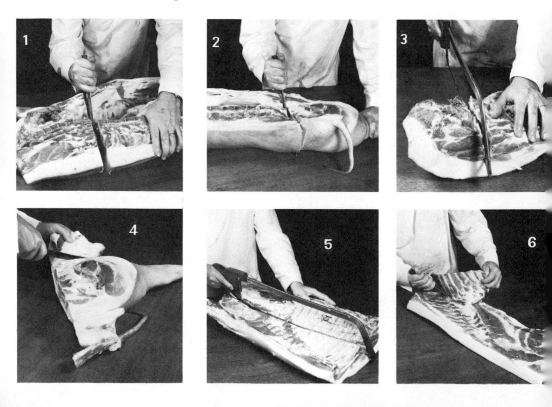

MAJOR CUTS OF LAMB (OR GOAT)

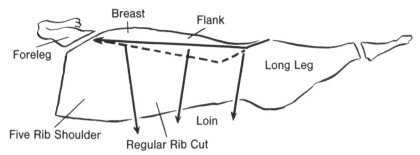

To cut up lamb or goat. The carcass is handled whole, not split lengthwise like the larger beef, pork, elk, etc. Also, the USDA photos show finished cuts (except for chops).

Photo 1: removing breast and flank (both for stew) and foreleg; for rib chops with shorter bone, cut at the dotted line. *Photo 2:* cuts for *A, B, C* and *D* will give, left to right, a five-rib shoulder, regular rib cut, loin and long leg. *Photo 3:* splitting the preceding cuts along the backbone gives *AA*—two shoulder roasts (or to become chops); *BB*—for rib chops; *CC*—for loin chops; *DD*—two leg roasts.

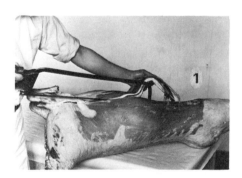

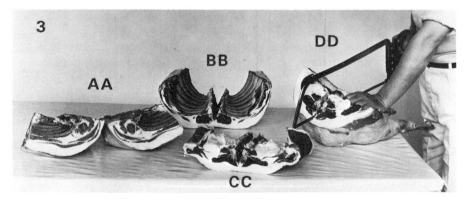

PACKING AND PROCESSING LARGE CUTS

PFB is indebted to the University of Minnesota for underscoring a long-harbored worry of ours about Raw pack for meats. Their *Extension Bulletin 413* (Revised 1980) states that research done at the university shows that meat and poultry are *satisfactorily canned ONLY by Hot pack* (italics ours).

Some people nevertheless want to pack Raw: and for them we include the procedure in this chapter.

Prepare and Pack Raw

Wipe raw meat with a clean damp cloth. Remove bones *and all surface fat* (fat in canned meat is likely to shorten its storage life, and fat is a Number One seal-spoiler).

Cut in jar/can lengths, with the grain running the long way of the container.

IN STRAIGHT-SIDED JARS

Push the long pieces into the jars, leaving 1 inch of headroom. *Add no liquid:* there will be enough juice. Exhaust jars in a slow-boil bath to 170 F/77 C (*c.* 70 minutes). Remove jars from exhaust bath. (Optional: Add ½ teaspoon salt to pints, 1 teaspoon salt to quarts). Adjust lids.

Pressure–process at 10 pounds (240 F/116 C)—pints for 75 minutes, quarts for 90 minutes. Remove jars; complete seals if necessary.

IN PLAIN CANS

Push long pieces into the cans, leaving *no* headroom. *Add no liquid:* there will be enough juice. Exhaust cans in a slow-boil bath to 170 F/77 C (*c.* 70 minutes). Remove from exhaust bath. (Optional: Add ½ teaspoon salt to No. 2 cans, ¾ teaspoon salt to No. 2½ cans); seal.

Pressure–process at 10 pounds (240 F/116 C)—No. 2 cans for 65 minutes, No. 2½ cans for 90 minutes. Remove cans; cool quickly.

Preferred: Pack Hot (Precooked)

Put large cut-to-measure pieces of boned, de-fatted meat (see Raw pack preparation, above) in a large, shallow pan. Add just enough water to keep meat from sticking; cover, and cook slowly on top of the stove or in a 350 F/177 C oven until the meat is Medium done, turning it now and then so it precooks evenly.

IN STRAIGHT-SIDED JARS

Pack hot meat loosely, leaving 1 inch of headroom. (Optional: Add ½ teaspoon salt to pints, 1 teaspoon salt to quarts.) Add boiling meat juice (extended with boiling water if necessary), leaving 1 inch of headroom. Wipe jar rims carefully to remove any fat. Adjust lids.

Pressure–process at 10 pounds (240 F/116 C)—pints for 75 minutes, quarts for 90 minutes. Remove jars; complete seals if necessary.

In Plain Cans

Pack hot meat loosely, leaving ½ inch of headroom. (Optional: Add ½ teaspoon salt to No. 2 cans, ¾ teaspoon salt to No. 2½ cans.) Fill cans to the top with boiling meat juice (extended with boiling water if necessary), leaving *no* headroom. Wipe can rims carefully to remove any fat; seal (no exhausting is necessary, because long precooking has driven air from the meat).

Pressure–process at 10 pounds (240 F/116 C)—No. 2 cans for 65 minutes, No. 2½ cans for 90 minutes. Remove cans; cool quickly.

- **Note:** You may also roast large pieces of meat as for the table until it is Medium done; pack as above (extending pan juices with boiling broth or water if necessary), and Pressure–process at 10 pounds (240 F/116 C) for the full time required above.

CANNING SMALL PIECES OF MEAT

Use the less choice parts of the animal for future use in stews, main-dish pies. Pressure Canning only. Use Raw or Hot (precooked) pack. Use straight-sided jars or plain cans.

Prepare and Pack Raw

Remove all surface fat from clean meat. Cut the meat off any bones. As you cut in stewing-size pieces, remove any interior bits of fat; cut away any tough muscle-sheath.

In Straight-sided Jars

Pack, leaving 1 inch of headroom. *Add no liquid:* there will be enough juice. Exhaust jars in a slow-boil bath to 170 F/77 C (*c.* 70 minutes). Remove from exhaust bath. (Optional: Add ½ teaspoon salt to pints, 1 teaspoon salt to quarts.) Wipe jar rims carefully to remove any fat. Adjust lids.

Pressure–process at 10 pounds (240 F/116 C)—pints for 75 minutes, quarts for 90 minutes. Remove jars; complete seals if necessary.

In Plain Cans

Pack cut-up meat, leaving *no* headroom. *Add no liquid.* Exhaust cans in a slow-boil bath to 170 F/77 C (*c.* 70 minutes). Remove from exhaust bath. (Optional: Add ½ teaspoon salt to No. 2 cans, ¾ teaspoon to No. 2½ cans.) Wipe can rims carefully to remove any fat. Seal.

Pressure–process at 10 pounds (240 F/116 C)—No. 2 cans for 65 minutes, No. 2½ cans for 90 minutes. Remove cans; cool quickly.

Preferred: Pack Hot (Precooked)

Follow Raw pack preparation. Put meat in a large, shallow pan, with just enough water to keep it from sticking; cover. Precook until Medium done. Stewing-size pieces take less tending if you do them in a 350 F/77 C oven; but you can also precook them to Medium on top of the stove, turning or stirring them from time to time.

If you want to brown the meat before canning it, do *not* dredge in flour first—just put it under a hot broiler long enough to brown it on all sides. Slosh a little water around the pan to pick up any juice, and save the water to use in precooking the meat, as above.

In Straight-sided Jars

Pack hot meat loosely, leaving 1 inch of headroom. (Optional: Add ½ teaspoon salt to pints, 1 teaspoon salt to quarts.) Add boiling meat juice (extended with boiling water if necessary), leaving 1 inch of headroom. Wipe jar rims carefully to remove any fat. Adjust lids.

Pressure–process at 10 pounds (240 F/116 C)—pints for 75 minutes, quarts for 90 minutes. Remove jars; complete seals if necessary.

In Plain Cans

Pack hot meat loosely, leaving ½ inch of headroom. (Optional: Add ½ teaspoon salt to No. 2 cans, ¾ teaspoon salt to No. 2½ cans.) Fill cans to the top with boiling meat juice (extended if necessary), leaving *no* headroom. Wipe can rims carefully to remove any fat. Seal.

Pressure–process at 10 pounds (240 F/116 C)—No. 2 cans for 65 minutes, No. 2½ cans for 90 minutes. Remove cans; cool quickly.

Canning Ground Meat, see Chapter 10.

Canning Pork Sausage, see Chapter 10.

Canning Bologna–Style Sausage, see Chapter 10.

Canning Corned Beef, see Chapter 10.

CANNING VARIETY MEATS

Most of the variety meats—liver, heart, tongue and sweetbreads and brains—are best cooked and eaten right away. Certainly sweetbreads and brains, the most delicate foods of the lot, should be served when they are fresh. For liver and kidneys, freezing is recommended. Tongue may be canned satisfactorily, as well as frozen.

Canning Beef Tongue

The following procedure of course may be used for smaller tongues.

Soak the tongue in cold water for several hours, scrubbing it thoroughly and changing the water twice. Put it in a deep kettle, cover with fresh water, and bring to boiling. Skim off the foam well, then salt the water lightly; cover, and cook slowly until Medium done—*not tender* in the thickest part. Remove from kettle and plunge into cold water for a moment; peel off skin and trim off remaining gristle, etc., from the root.

Cut in container-size pieces, and pack Hot as for "Large Pieces of Meat," or slice evenly and pack Hot as for "Small Pieces of Meat." Pressure–process at 10 pounds (240 F/116 C) for the times required (q.v.).

CANNING FROZEN MEAT

If you're ever faced with a freezing emergency, you may salvage frozen meat by canning it—provided it is good quality to start with, was correctly frozen and stored (see Freezing, and the table "Freezer Storage Life of Various Foods" in Chapter 11).

First, thaw it slowly in the refrigerator below 40 F/4 C. Then handle it as if it were fresh, using Pressure Canning only, Hot pack only, and the processing times that apply for Canning Large/Small Pieces of Meat, above.

Canning Soup Stock, see Chapter 10.

Canning Poultry and Small Game

The following instructions—which use chicken as the example for simplicity's sake—may be applied to canning domestic rabbits, wild birds and other small game, as well as canning other domestic poultry such as ducks, guinea hens, geese and turkeys, etc. *All these animals may be canned the same way:* general preparation (with specific exceptions as they come along), packing and processing are the same for all.

> • NOTE: Read the introduction to this chapter for "Warning about Game," necessary equipment, and the special care required in handling all meat for processing.

If you refrigerate adequately, prevent contamination during handling, work quickly, and don't try short cuts in packing and processing, poultry and small game may be canned satisfactorily.

Freezing of course is easier.

Use Pressure Canning only. Use Raw or the preferred Hot pack. Use straight-sided jars or plain cans.

WHERE CANNING OF POULTRY, ETC., IS DIFFERENT

Unlike the procedures given in the preceding section for packing meat, the methods that follow include canning with the bone left in.

Also, the skin on large pieces of birds—breast, thighs, drumsticks—is left on: processing at 240 F/116 C compacts the surface of meat next to the sides of the container (making a pressure mark), so the skin you leave on acts as a cushion. Breast meat is skinned if packed in the center of jars/cans (surrounded by skin-on pieces that touch the containers' sides); so skin as you pack.

TO DRESS POULTRY, ETC.

Dressing involves two steps: (1) removing feathers by plucking or removing the fur pelt by skinning, and (2) drawing, which is removing the internal organs in one intact mass. Domestic birds are plucked before being drawn because they are handled for food immediately after they're killed.

However, a hunter *field-dresses* his kill by removing the innards on the spot, since they spoil a great deal more quickly than muscle tissue does; and he waits to skin it until after he's home. Immediate drawing therefore reduces the chance of spoiling the rest of the meat en route home, and is especially necessary with mammals. Game birds may be held for several hours before being drawn; but if they cannot be taken home for handling within half a day, they too should be drawn in the field, and plucked later.

Plucking a Chicken

Pluck feathers from the still warm, fresh-killed and bled chicken, being careful to get all the pinfeathers. Hold the bird by its feet and pull the feathers toward the head, in the opposite direction to the way they lie naturally. Scalding the whole bird is not necessary, but if the feathers are resisting enough so you're afraid of tearing the skin, you can spot-scald: lift the chicken by the feet with its head dangling, and pour nearly boiling water into the base of the feathers, where it will be trapped momentarily against the skin.

Dry the bird and singe off the hairs. Wipe it clean.

Drawing a Chicken

Cut off the head of the fresh-killed and plucked bird if it is still on; remove feet at the "ankle" joint just below the drumstick. Cut out the oil sac at the top of the tail (it would flavor the meat unpleasantly, so don't break it).

Lay the chicken on its back, feet toward you. Using a sharp knife, cut a circle around the vent (anus), so it can be removed intact with the internal organs still attached. Cut deeply enough to free it, and be careful not to cut into the intestine that leads to it.

Insert the tip of the knife, with cutting edge upward, at the top of the circle around the vent, and cut throught the thin ventral wall toward the bottom of the breast bone, making the slit long enough so you can draw the innards out through it with vent attached.

Reach clear to the front of the body cavity and gently pull out the mass of organs. Separate and save the heart, liver and gizzard.

Next, turn the chicken over and slit the skin lengthwise at the back of the neck—if you slit down the *front* of the neck you may cut into the crop; push away the skin and remove the crop and windpipe.

Cut the neck bone off close to the body. Wash the whole bird. Look inside it, and remove any bits of lung, etc., that may remain in the cavity.

Return to the giblets. From the liver, cut away the green gall sac, roots and all; and be mighty careful not to break it, because gall ruins the flavor of any meat it touches. Split one side of the gizzard, cutting until you see the tough inner lining. Press the gizzard open and peel the lining away and discard it and its contents. Trim the heart.

Refrigerate each dressed chicken, either whole or cut up, until you are ready to can it.

Cutting Up Poultry

Lay the dressed, clean bird on its back and, using a sharp boning knife, disjoint the legs and wings from the body. Separate thighs from drumsticks at the "knee" joint. If the bird is very large—like a turkey or goose—separate the

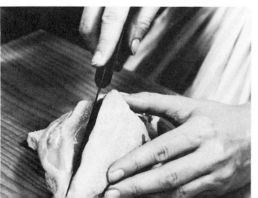
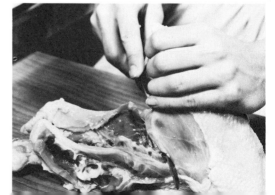

wing at its two joints, saving the two upper meaty sections for canning with bone in. (Very small birds, such as grouse, etc., may do best merely quartered with poultry shears.)

Turn the chicken crossways to you, hold the bottom of the breast section, and cut under it, through the ribs, until you reach the backbone; separate it from the backbone by cutting through the ribs. Poultry shears or heavy kitchen shears will be handy for use on the stronger bones at the shoulder joint.

Bone the breast meat by cutting down one side of the breast bone and easing the white meat off in a large piece; repeat on the other side.

Remove lumps of fat and any bits of broken bone from each piece of chicken and wipe it with a clean damp cloth.

Drawing, Skinning, Cutting Up Rabbits

Lay the fresh-killed rabbit on its back, and proceed to draw it as if it were a chicken: cut around the vent carefully; make a slit in the abdominal wall, reach in and pull out the innards with vent attached; save the liver and heart.

Cut off the feet. Working from the hind legs upward, work the rabbit out of its skin, easing the job with your knife where you need to. The head may be skinned, but chances are you'll prefer to remove it with the skin when you reach it. Cut away the gall sac from the liver; trim the heart. Wash the dressed rabbit and pat it dry. *Refrigerate each dressed rabbit until you are ready to can it.*

If you raise rabbits for the table you'll find it simpler to skin them as soon as they are killed and before drawing them.

Because of its anatomy, think of a rabbit as making two fore quarters, two hind quarters, and a saddle. Split the saddle down the backbone as you would split the breast of a chicken, boning it if you like. The size of the rabbit has a lot to do with whether you joint the quarters.

CANNING POULTRY, ETC., BONE IN

Prepare and Pack Raw

Pack meaty pieces loosely and more or less upright in the containers, putting breasts in the center (therefore skinned), surrounded by thighs and drumsticks (skin on) next to the sides of the jars/cans.

In Straight-sided Jars

Pack, leaving 1 inch of headroom. Exhaust to 170 F/77 C in a slow-boil bath (*c.* 75 minutes). (Optional: Add ½ teaspoon salt to pints, 1 teaspoon salt to quarts.) *Add no liquid:* there will be enough juice. Wipe jar rims carefully to remove any fat. Adjust lids.

Pressure–process at 10 pounds (240 F/116 C)—pints for 65 minutes, quarts for 75 minutes. Remove jars; complete seals if necessary.

(In *this instance alone*—Raw pack in jars with bone in—some cooks omit the exhaust-bath-to-170 F/77 C-step, and Pressure–process at 10 pounds (240 F/116 C) for longer time: pints for 70 minutes, quarts for 80 minutes.)

In Plain Cans

Pack, leaving *no* headroom. Exhaust to 170 F/77 C in a slow-boil bath (*c.* 50 minutes). (Optional: Add ½ teaspoon salt to No. 2 cans, ¾ teaspoon salt to No. 2½ cans.) *Add no liquid.* Wipe off rims carefully to remove any fat. Seal.

Pressure–process at 10 pounds (240 F/116 C)—No. 2 cans for 55 minutes, No. 2½ cans for 75 minutes. Remove cans; cool quickly.

Preferred: Pack Hot (Precooked), Bone In

Put raw meaty pieces in a large pan, cover with boiling water or boiling unseasoned (chicken) broth. Cover the pan and cook the meat slowly over moderate heat on top of the stove or in a 350 F/177 C oven until Medium done. Pack hot meat with breasts preferably in the center (so skin them), surrounded by legs and thighs (unskinned, because they touch the sides of the containers).

In Straight-sided Jars

Pack hot meat in loosely, leaving 1 inch of headroom. (Optional: Add ½ teaspoon salt to pints, 1 teaspoon salt to quarts.) Cover with boiling unseasoned cooking liquid, leaving 1 inch of headroom. Wipe jar rims carefully. Adjust lids.

Pressure–process at 10 pounds (240 F/116 C)—pints for 65 minutes, quarts for 75 minutes. Remove jars; complete seals if necessary.

In Plain Cans

Pack hot meat in loosely, unskinned if they touch the side of the can; leave ½ inch of headroom. (Optional: Add ½ teaspoon salt to No. 2 cans, ¾ teaspoon salt to No. 2½ cans.) Add boiling unseasoned cooking water to the top of the cans, leaving *no* headroom. Wipe can rims carefully to remove any fat. Seal.

Pressure–process at 10 pounds (240 F/116 C)—No. 2 cans for 55 minutes, No. 2½ cans for 75 minutes. Remove cans; cool quickly.

CANNING POULTRY, ETC., WITHOUT BONES

Whether you pack Raw or Hot, remove bones from good meaty pieces before you start. But leave skin on pieces of birds until you're actually filling the containers; then skin the pieces in the center of the pack (usually breast meat), and leave skin on the pieces that touch the side of the jar/can (usually legs).

Prepare and Pack Raw

In Straight-sided Jars

Fill with boned raw pieces, skin taken off the ones in the center, skin left on the ones touching the side of the jar. Leave 1 inch of headroom. Exhaust to 170 F/77 C in a slow-boil bath (*c.* 75 minutes). (Optional: Add ½ teaspoon salt to pints, 1 teaspoon salt to quarts.) *Add no liquid.* Wipe jar rims carefully. Adjust lids.

Pressure–process at 10 pounds (240 F/116 C)—pints for 75 minutes, quarts for 90 minutes. Remove jars; complete seals if necessary.

In Plain Cans

Pack, with skin on pieces that touch the side of the can, leaving *no* headroom. Exhaust to 170 F/77 C in a slow-boil bath (*c.* 50 minutes). (Optional: Add ½ teaspoon salt to No. 2 cans, ¾ teaspoon salt to No. 2½ cans.) *Add no liquid.* Wipe can rims carefully. Seal.

Pressure–process at 10 pounds (240 F/116 C)—No. 2 cans for 65 minutes, No. 2½ cans for 90 minutes. Remove cans; cool quickly.

Preferred: Pack Hot (Precooked), Without Bones

Remove bones from good meaty pieces, but leave skin on all pieces of poultry until you're filling the containers: then skin the ones in the center of the pack (usually breasts), leaving skin on the ones that touch the sides of jars/cans (usually legs).

Cover boned meat with boiling water or unseasoned broth and cook slowly on stove or in oven until Medium done as for Hot pack, Bone In, above.

In Straight-sided Jars

Pack hot boned meat loosely (with outside pieces unskinned). Leave 1 inch of headroom. (Optional: Add ½ teaspoon salt to pints, 1 teaspoon to quarts.) Add boiling unseasoned broth, leaving 1 inch of headroom. Wipe jar rims carefully. Adjust lids.

Pressure–process at 10 pounds (240 F/116 C)—pints for 75 minutes, quarts for 90 minutes. Remove jars; complete seals if necessary.

In Plain Cans

Pack hot boned meat loosely, with outside pieces unskinned. Leave ½ inch of headroom. (Optional: Add ½ teaspoon salt to No. 2 cans, ¾ teaspoon salt to No. 2½ cans.) Add boiling unseasoned broth to the top of the cans, leaving *no* headroom. Wipe can rims carefully. Seal.

Pressure–process at 10 pounds (240 F/116 C)—No. 2 cans for 65 minutes, No. 2½ cans for 90 minutes. Remove cans; cool quickly.

CANNING POULTRY GIBLETS

Giblets are more useful if they are canned together, rather than spread out among the cans of meat (use them chopped in gravies, meat sauces or spreads, as fillings for main-dish pies, on rice as a supper dish, etc.). Furthermore, the livers are better and handier if they are canned separately; and being so tender, they need much shorter precooking before Hot packing and processing.

Pressure Canning only. Use Hot pack only. Use straight-sided pint jars or No. 2 plain cans.

Prepare and Pack Hot (Precooked) Only

Cut clean gizzards in half, trimming off the gristle; cut smaller if necessary. Remove tops of hearts where the blood vessels come in; halve hearts if they're very large. Cover gizzards and hearts with hot water or hot unseasoned broth and cook until Medium done.

Remove all fat from the livers; cut away connecting tissue between the lobes. Cover livers with hot water or hot unseasoned broth and cook gently until firm and Medium done; stir occasionally to prevent sticking.

Pack gizzards and hearts together, pack livers separately.

IN STRAIGHT-SIDED PINT JARS

Fill with hot gizzards and hearts, or hot livers, leaving 1 inch of headroom. (Optional: Add ½ teaspoon salt.) Add boiling cooking liquid, leaving 1 inch of headroom. Wipe jar rims carefully. Adjust lids.

Pressure–process at 10 pounds (240 F/116 C)—pint jars of either livers, or gizzards and hearts for 75 minutes. Remove jars: complete seals if necessary.

IN NO. 2 PLAIN CANS

Fill with hot gizzards and hearts, or hot livers, leaving ½ inch of headroom. (Optional: Add ½ teaspoon salt.) Add boiling cooking liquid to the top of the cans, leaving *no* headroom. Wipe can rims carefully. Seal.

Pressure–process at 10 pounds (240 F/116 C)—No. 2 cans of either gizzards and hearts, or livers for 65 minutes. Remove cans; cool quickly.

CANNING FROZEN POULTRY, ETC.

In case your freezer conks out, or you have a windfall of frozen poultry, domestic rabbits or small game, you may can it—*if:*

1. It is good quality and was properly frozen (see the table "Freezer Storage Life of Various Foods" in Chapter 11), and
2. It is thawed slowly in the refrigerator below 40 F/4 C.

Then treat it as if it were fresh, using Pressure Canning only, Hot pack only, straight-sided jars or plain cans. Follow preparation and processing under "Bone In/Boned," above.

CANNING CHICKEN STOCK (BROTH)

Make broth from bony pieces of chicken (or other poultry, rabbits, wild birds, etc.) as you made it from meat, and pack and Pressure–process it the same way (see "Canning Soup Stock," in Chapter 10).

9 🌿

CANNING SEAFOOD

Among the most satisfying developments by the end of the 1970's in North America were the strides made in counteracting pollution in the Great Lakes. The measures were so effective that freshwater sport fishing once again became a major attraction in the north-central tier of States, and their land-grant colleges and universities were able to publish bulletins and pamphlets on preserving fish by a number of methods for the first time in several decades. At much the same time Maryland, Florida, Texas, California, Oregon, Washington and Alaska—among others—issued material on how to deal with ocean fish and shellfish. Where to inquire about many of these publications is given in Chapter 25, "Where to Find Things," under the subheading for this chapter you're reading.

WHY SEAFOOD IS TRICKY

Finned or shell-bearing creatures taken from salt or fresh water are right up among the front-runners in the botulism sweepstakes. Add to this that in general they are the most perishable of all fresh foods and have great density of texture, and you see why fish and shellfish require faultless handling and longer Pressure–processing than do other foods that are canned at home.

So why can them? Why indeed, when proper freezing (q.v.) is an all-round better, and safer, means of putting them by?—or when even salt-curing followed by drying (q.v. again) and cold storage is, in the regions that practice this twofold method, less of a hazard?

But maybe you're faced with a surfeit of fresh seafood, and either freezing or curing-and-drying the excess is impossible. If such a bonanza is a repeated occurrence, you could plan ahead and organize a community kitchen, complete with good equipment and a skilled director in charge, as described in Chapter 3. If it's a once-in-a-lifetime event, though, and comes without warning (like the beach full of lobsters cast up by a hurricane that hit the Maine coast)— well, go ahead and can what you and your neighbors aren't able to eat, or swap for staples, or give to a public-service group near by.

The following procedures are for canning, without frills, some representative varieties of fresh fish and shellfish. We do not include canning fish that's been smoked (described at the end of Chapter 20, on Curing), or seafood in sauces, or chowders. For further information we refer you to Chapter 25.

15 psi for Seafood at High Altitudes

These times are from the Presto pamphlet cited several times earlier (see Chapter 25 under entries for chapters on canning and altitude). Individual instructions that follow use only pint or ½-pint jars—nothing larger. The times here are the same for both ½-pints and pints.

IN LARGE PRESSURE CANNERS (12–QT OR MORE) AT 15 PSI			
Food	ALTITUDE UNDER 3000 FT/ 914 M MINUTES	BETWEEN 3000 FT/ 914 M 7000 FT/ 2134 M MINUTES	ALTITUDE OVER 7000 FT/ 2134 M MINUTES
Clams (Littleneck)	25	50	75
Crabmeat	25	50	75
Fish (except tuna)*	80	115	155
Lobster	35	65	95
Salmon	80	115	155
Shrimp	20	40	60
Tuna (& King Mackerel)*	80	115	155

*Parenthetical notes supplied.—ed.

Relevant Metrics for Canning Seafood

Full metric conversions, with the arithmetic for refining them, are given at the start of Chapter 17 ("Common Ingredients and How to Use Them"), but the following—rounded off—apply in this chapter.

If you live above the sea-level zone (i.e., *over* 1000 ft/305 m), consult the subsection "Correcting for Altitude" in Chapter 3. (And do pay attention to the need for extra headroom in jars at high altitudes.)

• • •

Temperatures (@ sea level): 170 F/77 C——185 F/85 C——212 F/100 C——240 F/116 C——250 F/121 C.

Volume: ¼ *teaspoon* = 1.25 mL———½ *teaspoon* = 2.5 mL———1 *teaspoon* = 5 mL———2 *teaspoons* = 10 mL———1 *tablespoon* = 15 mL———⅓ *cup* = 80 mL———¾ *cup* = 200 mL———½ *pint* = 250 mL———1 *pint* = 500 mL— —1 *quart* = 1 L———1 *gallon* = 4 L.

Length: ½ *inch* = 0.64 cm———½ *inch* = 1.27 cm———¾ *inch* = 1.9 cm— —2½ *to* 3 *inches* = 6.4 *to* 7.6 cm———4 *inches* = 10.1 cm.

Weight: 25 lbs = 11.34 kg.

EQUIPMENT FOR CANNING SEAFOOD

You cannot can fish or shellfish at home without an honest-to-goodness Pressure Canner. Not a pressure *saucepan:* the leading manufacturers do not recommend use of these small utensils for the extra long processing required for such low-acid food as fish (see under "Pressure Canners" in Chapter 3 for full details).

And, just as for canning meats and poultry, you'll need a pencil-shaped glass thermometer because you'll be exhausting your jars here too.

In addition to the standard kitchen furnishings and the sharp good knives and cutting-boards you used for preparing meat, and the wherewithal to keep everything properly sanitary, you need:

Modern straight-sided ½-pint and pint canning jars in perfect condition, their 2-piece screwband lids ditto
Inexpensive styrofoam chest(s) in which to hold fish on ice
Hose or sprayer connected to your sink's drinking-water tap, for washing fish or shellfish
Fish scaler
Small wire brush for scrubbing shells, etc.
Big crocks or enameled vessels for soaking fish in salted water to remove blood from the tissues (dishpans will do)
Large enameled kettle for boiling shellfish, treating crabmeat, etc., to a mild salt/acid "blanch," or steaming open clams (your B–W Bath kettle is fine)
Special blunt knife for opening clams (if you shuck them raw)
Wire basket or rack for steaming
Shallow pans with perforated bottoms that will fit inside your Pressure Canner (for the so-called "tuna pack")

GENERAL HANDLING—PLUS REASONS WHY

From the sources mentioned above, and others, we have compiled the following stipulations, which must be followed by everyone who undertakes to can fish or shellfish at home.

All seafoods must be processed in a regular Pressure Canner for the *full long time* required, and *at the pressure given* (which of course is corrected for altitudes higher than 1,000 feet; see in Chapter 3). If the pressure drops below the recommended level at any time during the processing period, for safety's sake you must raise the pressure to the correct number of pounds, and start re-timing as if you were starting the entire processing period from scratch.

Reason: The average natural acidity of seafood is so low that it flirts with Neutral on the *pH* scale (q.v. in Chapter 2). Therefore constant pressure for the full time is needed if enough heat is to penetrate the dense pack and sterilize the tissues, thus destroying dangerous bacteria.

Use only modern jars, manufactured for home-canning under pressure, that have 2-piece screwband lids. And use only ½-pint or pint jars (preferably straight-sided ones so the contents can slip out easily).

Reasons: For seafoods—or all home-canned products—it doesn't make sense to use makeshifts, or old-style jars and closures, or any other containers that have not been tested under the conditions required for safety by independent food scientists, and okayed. As for the 2-piece screwband lids, the flat metal discs indicate, by having snapped down to be concave, that you have obtained a proper seal. And finally, adequate processing cannot be assured for jars larger than 1 pint—or larger than ½-pint for certain fish or shellfish.

(We recommend *against cans* for home-processing of seafoods: (1) the correct sizes—like the commercial ones—are different from the cans used for other foods in this book; and (2) especially with the meat of lobsters and crabs, parchment-paper liners are usually needed to make an attractive product.)

All home-canned fish must be exhausted to a minimum of 170/77 C at the center of the packed jar before it is Pressure–processed.

Reason: Before actual processing begins, we must drive air from the tissues of raw fish as well as from the pack to help ensure the seal and to prevent unwanted shrinkage of the food during processing. Fish in the so-called "tuna pack"—i.e., fully precooked—are cooled completely before packing; these packs also must be exhausted. (The completely precooked, and picked, meat of lobsters, crab, shrimp and clams is not exhausted when packed in small jars.)

Exhausting jars of fish is done best in the Pressure Canner at Zero pounds. Place filled jars on the rack in the bottom of the canner and pour hot water around them until it comes halfway up their sides. *Lay* the cover on and *leave the vent open.* Turn the heat up high, and when you hear the water boiling hard inside the canner and steam flows strongly in a steady stream from the vent— indicating that the temperature has reached 212 F/100 C inside (see "Correcting for Altitude," in Chapter 3 if you're canning above 1,000 feet)—start counting the exhaust time. It will take 10 to 20 minutes for the center of the filled jars to reach the desired minimum of 170 F/77 C, depending on the size of the jar and the size of and solidness of the fish pieces; always insert your pencil thermometer deep in a test jar to make sure.

Water used in cleaning seafoods and preparing them for packing *must be of drinking quality*—whether it's the running water for washing them (which is always done under a tap, or with a spray or hose), or the water in a brine or anti-discoloration solution, or the canning liquid that goes in the jar.

Reason: It's easy to introduce dangerous bacteria, including *C. Botulinum* itself, into the flesh by using polluted or contaminated water at any stage. Do not rinse fish in stream or lake water. Do not precook shellfish in seawater. If your household drinking water contains a lot of minerals, use bottled water at least for the canning liquid (iron, especially, reacts with the sulfur in the meat of shellfish and causes the product to darken).

All seafoods to be canned must be as fresh as is humanly possible to have them. Fish must be gutted as they're caught, and refrigerated or packed in ice immediately, to be kept cold until they are recooked or packed. Head shrimp immediately as they come from the water: if the head section is removed within 30 minutes after the shrimp is caught, the black "sand vein" (colon) will come out easily, attached to it; refrigerate shrimp or hold on ice. Keep lobsters, crabs and clams alive and cool until you prepare them for packing.

Reason: It takes only a couple of hours at room temperature to make dead seafood unfit to can; and spoilage is hastened if intestines and body wastes are not removed.

The flesh of all dressed and cleaned fish and shelled shrimp is given a preliminary brining; lobsters and crabs are precooked in brine and well rinsed before shelling. (The picked meat of lobsters, crabs and clams is given a further anti-darkening treatment in a mild acid "blanch" before packing.)

Reason: Brining draws diffused blood from the tissues, and reduces the chance that white curds of coagulated protein will occur in the processed jars. (Brines must be made up just before use, and should be *used only once.*)

The day after the seafood has been canned, store the jars in a cool, dry, dark place.

Reason: Storage that lets the jars freeze can also break the seals; storage over 50 F/10 C courts spoilage; damp storage rusts metal closures and endangers the seals. During the 24 hours between processing and storing, check all seals, clean and label the jars.

CANNED SEAFOOD TROUBLES AND WHAT TO DO

Do *NOT reprocess* jars of seafood found to have poor seals during the 24 hours of grace between canning and storage. And even if the contents are decanted into fresh containers and done over from scratch, the result is likely to be unsatisfactory (all the more reason for taking care in the first place).

After jars are stored you must be super-critical in examining them for *external* signs of spoilage: broken seal (flat lid no longer concave)—seepage around the closure—gassiness in the contents—cloudy, yeasty liquid or sediment at the bottom of the jar—contents an unnatural color or texture. *If any of these signs are present, destroy the food so it cannot be eaten by people or animals, sterilize the container and closure by boiling, and discard the sterilized closure.*

Even when the seal seems good and none of the trouble symptoms just listed is apparent, these are the signs of spoilage when you open a *jar of seafood:* pressure inside the container (instead of a vacuum), or spurting contents—fermentation—sour, cheesy odor—soft, mushy contents. If any of these signs is present, *destroy the food and sterilize the container and closure, as above.*

• • BEFORE TASTING HOME-CANNED SEAFOOD: You must be unshakably certain that your Pressure Canner was operated correctly—pressure gauge accurate and dead-weight/weighted gauge signaling properly—and that requirements for times and corrections for altitude were followed.

Unless you are sure that these safeguards were observed, a margin of protection is added by boiling the food hard for 20 minutes to destroy possible hidden toxins, stirring to distribute the heat and adding water if necessary. If the food foams unduly or smells bad during boiling, destroy it completely so it cannot be eaten by people or animals.

A QUIET METHOD OF DESTROYING BOTULISM TOXIN

The instructions in the special warning above are standard—standard because they have been proved to be (1) capable of disclosing the presence of spoilers other than/in addition to the toxin of *C. botulinum*—which by itself is not certain to create undue foaming or an unpleasant smell; and (2) destroying the botulinum toxin if it is present. This vigorous boiling of from 10 to 20 minutes (depending on the density of the pieces of food), stirring all the while, does not do great harm to the texture of, say, mixed vegetables; but it does make a jar of canned fish into a fairly sad ingredient for salmon mayonnaise on a buffet supper table.

Therefore Dr. Margy Woodburn, microbiologist of the Department of Foods and Nutrition, Oregon State University, Corvallis, and Edward J. Schantz and Jennifer Rodriguez, both of the Food Research Institute, University of Wisconsin, Madison, performed a series of tests whereby toxins from several types of *C. botulinum* were introduced into glass jars of home-canned salmon; the jars were then incubated. Here is what the research team says to do to inactivate by heat the toxin(s) in home-canned fish:

Open the jar. If there are no signs of spoilage as noted in the warning above, insert the pencil (or meat) thermometer you used for exhausting jars in canning meat and will use in canning seafood, so the tip is as near the center of the contents as you can judge; cover the jar with foil. Put the jar in an oven at 350 F/177 C for 30 to 40 minutes for either ½-pint or 1-pint jars—*or until the thermometer registers 185 F/85 C* (the time taken to reach the required temperature is not the important factor: the 185 F/85 C is).

Do not speed the cooling. Let the hot jar stand at room temperature for 30 minutes to complete the heat treatment. At the end of the 30 minutes, serve hot (or reheated if necessary), or refrigerate for use later.

SPECIFIC SEAFOOD PRODUCTS

Salmon and Shad

Pressure Canning only. Use Raw pack and exhaust. Use pint jars (preferably straight-sided) with 2-piece screwband lids only.

Twenty-five pounds of round fish (i.e., whole and not dressed) will fill about 12 1-pint jars.

Dress, scale, scrub perfectly fresh fish; cut away the thin belly flap. Using a jar laid on its side as a measure, cut the fish across the grain in jar-length pieces—and *not one whit longer* lest they interfere with the seal (the fish will shrink in the jar to leave headroom). Prepare a cold brine of ¾ cup pure pickling salt dissolved in 1 gallon of water, an amount of brine that will do 25 pounds of prepared fish. Use enameled or non-metal tubs; use brine only once. Weight the fish pieces down in the brine for 60 minutes to draw out diffused blood and firm the flesh. Drain the pieces for 10 minutes; do not rinse.

Fill the jars solidly and in effect just to the top—this means no more than ¹⁄₁₆ inch below the sealing rim—packing the pieces upright, skin side next to the glass, and carefully inserting slimmer pieces to fill vertical gaps. Do not crush down on the pieces or they'll spring back up later and endanger the seal.

Next, *half*-close the filled jars. To do this, place the flat lid on the sealing rim of the jar, and screw the band down *just until the band cannot be pulled up off the threads.* (Practice on an empty jar to get the feel of this half-closure). Exhaust the jars in the Pressure Canner at Zero pounds (as described in "General Handling" above) until the center of the contents reaches a minimum of 170 F/77 C—about 15 minutes.

When jars are exhausted, lift the canner off heat and finish screwing the bands firmly tight as for any processing. Return the canner to heat, put on the lid and let steam vent in a strong, steady flow for 10 minutes before closing the petcock/vent and starting to time the processing period. The amount of very hot water remaining in the canner after exhausting the jars should be ample for Pressure–processing.

Pressure–process at 10 pounds (240 F/116 C) for 1 hour and 50 minutes. Remove jars; air-cool naturally.

Tunas, Large and King Mackerel

Pressure Canning only. Precook completely, cool, then exhaust. Use only ½-pint jars with 2-piece screwband lids.

Estimate 12 ½-pint jars for every 25 pounds of round fish. Dress, gut, scrub the fish; cut away the thin belly flap. Cut fish crossways in good-sized chunks (it will be cut for the jars after it's precooked).

For the precooking stage you will need several large round pans with perforated bottoms that can be stacked inside your Pressure Canner. Put 2½ to 3 inches of hot water in the canner; put a perforated support on the bottom of the canner—a wire cake rack, laid on some retired screwbands to help it take the weight of the fish; or an inverted metal pie pan with holes punched in its bottom; stack the pan-loads of fish in the canner. Put the lid on the canner; vent it (a strong, steady flow for 10 minutes); close the vent and Pressure-cook the fish at 10 pounds (240 F/116 C) for 2 hours.

Remove fish, cool on large beds of cracked ice for several hours to ensure firm texture and good flavor. Then scrape away the skin, lift out the bones, remove dark streaks of flesh along the sides. Cut the cold chunks of fish ¾ inch shorter than the height of the containers (½-pints are about 4 inches tall, so the steak rounds of fish would be about 3¼ inches thick). Put ½ teaspoon *optional* salt and 3 tablespoons fresh water (or salad oil) in the bottom of each jar. Pack solidly with fish, and leave ½ inch of headroom.

To exhaust, *half*-close the lids as for Salmon, and boil hard in the Pressure Canner at Zero pounds (q.v. Salmon again) for 10 minutes: check center of contents of a test jar to make sure it has reached 170 F/77 C. When jars are exhausted, finish screwing the bands down firmly tight.

Pressure–process at *15 pounds* (*250 F/121 C*) for 75 minutes. Remove jars; air-cool naturally.

Lake Trout, Whitefish, Small Mackerel, Florida Mullet

Pressure Canning only. Raw pack and exhaust. Use pint jars (preferably straight-sided) with 2-piece screwband lids only.

About 35 pounds of fish, round weight, will fill 12 pint jars.

Dress, clean, scale, scrub perfectly fresh fish. Split the fish, leaving in the backbone; cut away the thin belly strip. Cut in jar-length pieces (as for Salmon, above), and brine the pieces for 60 minutes in a cold solution of ¾ cup pure pickling salt dissolved in 1 gallon of water. Remove the fish pieces, drain, and pack solidly just to the top of the jars—not more than ¹⁄₁₆ inch below the sealing rim—alternating head and tail sections upright in the jars for a firm pack, with skin sides next to the glass.

Use the kettle of your big enameled Boiling–Water Bath for exhausting the jars, because they will be boiled in a weak brine that would mar the metal surface of your Pressure Canner. Do not cap the filled jars; put them, open, on the rack in the B–W Bath kettle; pour in a fresh hot brine of ⅓ cup pure pickling salt dissolved in 1 gallon of water, until the brine comes 1 inch above the top of the jars. Bring to boiling, and boil the jars briskly for 15 minutes, which should be enough to raise the temperature deep inside the jars to a minimum of 170 F/77 C (check with your thermometer to make sure).

Remove the jars and invert them to drain on a wire cake-cooling rack for about 3 minutes. (Clap the slotted blade of a metal spatula over the mouth of the jar before you up-end it, and you won't have to worry about bits of fish sliding out.) Right the jars, wipe their rims carefully to remove any speck of material that would interfere with the seal; put on the lids and screw the bands down firmly tight.

Pressure–process at 10 pounds (240 F/116 C) for 1 hour and 40 minutes. Remove jars; air-cool naturally.

Crab—Dungeness (Pacific) and Blue (Atlantic)

Pressure Canning only. Precook and exhaust. Use only ½-pint jars with 2-piece screwband lids.

To fill 12 ½-pint jars it will take about 25 pounds live weight of average-size Atlantic crabs, or 13 to 15 average Pacific crabs.

Use enameled or stainless-steel ware for boiling or acid-blanching shell-fish—*never use* copper or iron. And *never use* seawater: use fresh drinking water to which you've added salt, etc.

For canning use only fresh-caught, frisky crabs in prime condition (not recently molted, not feeble or sickly). To avoid needless contamination of the meat by visceral matter you should butcher and clean them before precooking. Stun the live crab by submerging it in ice water for several minutes, then quickly twist off the legs, take off the back, remove gills and "butter" and the rest of the innards; clean out the body cavity under a strong flow of fresh, cool drinking water. Save claws and bodies of Atlantic crabs, discarding their legs as too small to bother with; save legs as well as claws and bodies of Pacific crabs, which are larger.

Meanwhile prepare and have heating in your biggest enameled B–W Bath kettle enough brine to cover the broken crabs you're dealing with, made in the proportion of 1 cup pure pickling salt and ¼ cup lemon juice to each 1 gallon of fresh water. Dump crab pieces in the brine, bring back to boiling, and boil hard for 15 minutes by your timer. Quickly dip out the crab pieces and cool them quickly under cold running water *just until* they're cool enough to handle (the meat comes more easily from the shells if it's still warm). Pick out the meat, keeping body meat separate from leg and claw meat. Wash the meat piecemeal under a gentle spray to get rid of any curds of coagulated protein, etc., and press excess moisture out with your hands.

The following acid-blanch is designed to prevent natural—and harmless but unsightly—sulfur compounds present in shellfish from darkening the meat during processing. Therefore prepare beforehand and have ready a cold mixture in the proportions of 1 cup lemon juice (or of the citric-acid solution described in Chapter 17, or of distilled white vinegar in a pinch) to 1 cup salt dissolved in 1 gallon of water. This amount will treat 15 pounds of picked meat; make up fresh brine for each batch. Dealing with a colander-ful at a time, immerse leg meat for 2 minutes, body meat for 1 minute. Drain well, pressing out excess moisture with your hand.

Fill ½-pint jars firmly with meat, making a solid pack with attractive pieces next to the glass; leave ½ inch of headroom. Add boiling water to cover the meat—it won't take much—leaving ½ inch of headroom. Half-close jars and exhaust at Zero pounds (see Salmon, above) until the inside of the pack reaches a minimum of 170 F/77 C on your thermometer—about 10 minutes. Finish screwing down bands firmly tight.

Pressure–process ½-pint jars at 10 pounds (240 F/116 C) for 65 minutes. Remove jars; air-cool naturally.

Lobsters

Pressure Canning only. Precook and exhaust. Use only ½-pint jars with 2-piece screwband lids.

To fill 12 ½-pint jars, figure on 7 to 10 lobsters—depending on size and whether they're the huge-clawed Atlantic lobster of cold North American waters or the bigger-tailed spiny lobster without claws.

Can only fresh-caught, healthy, lively lobsters. Cook and then cool them in separate containers of brine made of 2 tablespoons pure pickling salt to each 1 gallon of fresh drinking water: *never cook or cool lobsters in seawater;* make up fresh cooking/cooling brines for each batch.

In your biggest B–W Bath kettle, bring to boiling 3 to 4 gallons of the brine just described. Plunge live lobsters head first into the boiling salted water and, when it returns to boiling, boil them until their entire shells are bright red—about 20 minutes on the average. Lift them from the kettle and immerse them immediately in a tub of very cold brine (also made as above) to cool as fast as possible. When well cooled, each lobster is split, cleaned under running water, and the meat picked from the shell. Quickly and gently spray the picked meat as necessary to remove curds of coagulated protein. Press out excess liquid. Dip the picked meat, a small amount at a time, in a fresh acid-blanch as for Crab (in the proportions of 1 cup lemon juice and 1 cup salt dissolved in 1 gallon of water). Press out extra liquid and pack attractively in ½-pint jars, fitting claw and tail meat carefully to get a firm, solid pack; leave ½ inch of headroom. Just cover the meat with boiling fresh brine made of 1¼ teaspoons salt to each 1 quart of water; leave ½ inch of headroom. Exhaust as for Crab, above. Finish screwing down bands firmly tight.

Pressure–process ½-pint jars at 10 pounds (240 F/116 C) for 70 minutes. Remove jars; air-cool naturally.

Shrimp

Pressure Canning only. Precook and exhaust. Use only ½-pint jars with 2-piece screwband lids.

About 10 pounds of fresh-caught headless shrimp will fill 12 ½-pint jars.

If shrimp are headed within 30 minutes after catching, the "sand vein" will come out with the head section. At any rate, pack raw shrimp immediately in crushed ice and hold them on ice to retard spoilage—and also to make peeling them easier. Remove heads, peel off shells, take out the sand vein; wash the meat quickly in fresh water and drain thoroughly.

In a large enameled kettle make enough cold brine to cover the meat, in the proportion of 2 cups of pure pickling salt dissolved in each 1 gallon of water. Hold the meat in the brine 20 to 30 minutes depending on the size of the shrimp, stirring from time to time to make this first brining uniform. Remove the meats and drain thoroughly.

Meanwhile prepare an acid-blanch of 1 cup lemon juice and 1 cup pure pickling salt for each 1 gallon of fresh water (the same as for Crab and Lobster, above); make enough to deal with all the shrimp you're working with, because you must use a fresh lot of the solution for each blanching-basket's worth of shrimp meat; otherwise the liquid will become ropy from diffused blood, etc. Bring to boiling enough of the acid-blanch to cover a household deep-frying basket *half*-filled with shrimp. Boil the meat 6 to 8 minutes (again depending on size of the shrimp) after the liquid returns to the boil. Lift out the shrimp, spread them on wire racks to air-dry and cool. An electric fan blowing across the shrimp will hurry the process: shrimp must be cool and surface-dry when packed.

Fill ½-pint jars with shrimp, fitting them in carefully to get a solid pack—but *don't crush them down;* leave ½ inch of headroom. Add boiling water just to cover the shrimp, leaving ½ inch of headroom. Half-close and exhaust as for Salmon, Crab and Lobster. Finish screwing down bands firmly tight.

Pressure–process ½-pint jars at 10 pounds (240 F/116 C) for 35 minutes. Remove jars; air-cool naturally.

Hard-Shell Clams (Littleneck, Butter, Razor, Quahaugs) Whole or Minced

Pressure Canning only. Blanch, pack and exhaust. Use only ½-pint jars with 2-piece screwband lids.

To fill 12 ½-pint jars with *whole* clam meats (including their juice), you'll need about 6 quarts of raw shucked meats; about 12 quarts of raw shucked meats will fill 12 ½-pint jars with *minced* clams.

The early steps for preparing clams for canning are the same for either whole or minced meats. We'll describe the complete procedure for canning whole clams, and give the variations for minced clams separately later.

Have ready some large vessels filled with clean salt water in which to hold your clams from 12 to 24 hours, so they'll have time to get rid of any sand in their stomachs. *Do not use seawater:* instead, approximate the necessary salinity by making a mild brine in the proportion of ¼ cup pure pickling salt for every 1 gallon of drinking water; and make enough to cover them by several inches.

Pick over the clams, choosing only those with tightly closed shells or ones that quickly retract their siphons (necks) when touched; discard any with broken or open shells. Scrub them with a stiff brush, rinse quickly, and put them in your mild holding brine. Sprinkle a few handfuls of cornmeal in the brine and swish it around; during the night the critters will eat the cornmeal and spit out sand.

Take the clams from their holding brine, throwing away any that don't have shells closed fiercely tight. Open the clams by steaming, or by shucking the live clams with a blunt knife as described in "Freezing Oysters, Clams, etc." in Chapter 15. If you open them live, work over a bowl to catch the juice (which you save, strain through cheesecloth, boil down to ⅔ its original volume, and use for canning liquid in the jars). *To steam open:* Take clams from their holding brine, spray-rinse, and pile them wet on a rack in the bottom of a big steel or enameled kettle with a tight lid; work with about ½ peck at a time, because their volume increases as they open. Cover the kettle, put it on high heat; reduce the heat to medium when the liquid from the clams starts to boil, and let them steam until their shells are part way open—up to 20 minutes.

From each opened clam, remove the dark gasket-like membrane that runs around the inside edge of the shell and encloses the siphon/neck; snip off the dark tip of the neck. Keep the dark stomach mass if you like: it's nutritious, but it also could give the canned product an unappetizing color or odor. Wash the dressed meats thoroughly in a fresh brine made in the proportion of 3 tablespoons pickling salt to each 1 gallon of water; make enough so you can change the washing-brine often.

Acid-blanch the meats in a boiling solution of 2 teaspoons pure citric acid powder dissolved in 1 gallon of water, making enough so you can change the blanch often. Half-fill a deep-frying basket with clam meats and hold them submerged in the acid-blanch for 2 minutes after the liquid returns to boiling. Lift out the basket of meats; drain.

Pack in ½-pint jars, leaving ¾ inch of headroom; do not add salt. Add boiling-hot, reduced clam juice to cover the meats, leaving ½ inch of headroom. Half-close the lids and exhaust as for Crab, Lobster, Shrimp, above. Finish screwing bands down firmly tight.

Pressure–process ½-pint jars at 10 pounds (240 F/116 C) for 1 hour and 10 minutes. Remove jars; air-cool naturally.

MINCED CLAMS

Remove the dark stomach mass as you dress the meats after the clams are opened. Proceed with washing the meats in brine and acid-blanching, as above. Drain. Put the meats through a food grinder, using a plate with ⅜-inch holes. Strain the clam broth through cheesecloth, bring to boiling. Pack minced clams in ½-pint jars, leaving ¾ inch of headroom; do not add salt. Add hot clam broth, leaving ½ inch of headroom.

Exhaust and Pressure–process as for whole meats.

10

CANNING CONVENIENCE FOODS

Canning convenience foods that may be taken off the pantry shelf, decanted, heated and eaten needs the exercise of forethoughtfulness and vigilance—more of both virtues than a beginner might think is necessary. Not that *PFB* is setting out to make the procedures mysterious: far from it, because we shall tie them in with the important points made in Chapter 2 on up until now. Then the newcomer to canning will understand that this way of producing almost-table-ready dishes courts more danger than any other way of putting by such foods.

> • **THE METRIC CONVERSIONS** that apply to canning by either Boiling–Water Bath or Pressure–processing have been given at the start of Chapters 5 through 9, and the conversions that apply to various cooking procedures are in Chapter 24: We refer you to such special notes at the start of the chapters cited.

Comparing this chapter with 16, "Freezing Egg, Dairy and Convenience Foods," shows the much narrower selection for canned dishes. And with good reason. Whereas leftovers may be frozen with slapdash wrappings, barring a long power failure or bad mishandling after the package is taken out to be thawed, the food is likely to be poor in quality *but it is not likely to contain much greater numbers of bad micro-organisms than when it was popped into the freezer.*

Such is not the case with canned food, especially canned low-acid food. So we underscore these points again:

1. The acidity of the ingredients must be balanced in such a manner that each component remains palatable and safe *after* the food is taken from the canner and stored on the shelf.
2. Pressure Canning is required, and *for the full length of time needed for the lowest-acid ingredient in a combination* unless it is a mixture whose processing has been researched, and published, by food scientists who give step-by-step procedure and time.

170

There are no single vegetables given in the following recipes, because there are canned vegetables aplenty in Chapter 7. And there are canned meats ready to serve in Chapter 8, and seafood in Chapter 9. However, we have included several recipes-plus-procedures for using tomatoes in combination with a variety of vegetables; these are intended as bases for pasta sauces, or for whatever your own recipe file indicates, and are included under "Meats and the Makings of Main Dishes."

Where flavorings usually included in such recipes are omitted, it is because some herbs and spices produce an unwanted taste after Pressure–processing. This is especially true of artificial sweeteners and salt substitutes: add these at the time the food is to be served. And note that salt may be left out, since it is optional.

Finally, the amounts canned are limited to pint-size jars, with only a couple of exceptions. We followed Miss Gertrude Russell's example for many foods here, and geared amounts to very small families.

• **NOTE:** Cans are omitted from most of the specific instructions for individual foods even though they are included throughout Chapters 5 to 8 on canning. However, it is unlikely that a householder cooking for just one or two people would crank up for using cans. So: jars are preferred. And pint jars or smaller (except for some of the Meat Broth/Stocks in quarts).

For ½-pint jars leave the same headroom as for pints. Process ½-pints the same length of time as is given for pints.

Remember that you will need more headroom at altitudes above 3000 ft/914 m. See Chapter 3, under the section "Correcting for Altitude" to save trouble and loss of liquid (or eventual loss of seal).

• • **BEFORE TASTING ANY CANNED FOOD WITH LOW-ACID IN-GREDIENTS:** You must be unshakably certain that your Pressure Canner was operated correctly—pressure gauge accurate and dead-weight gauge signaling properly—and that requirements for times and corrections for altitude were followed.

Unless you are sure that these safeguards were observed, a margin of protection is added by boiling the canned low-acid food hard for 15 minutes to destroy any hidden toxins (corn, greens, meat and seafood require 20 minutes), stirring to distribute the heat and adding water as necessary. If the food foams unduly or smells bad during boiling, destroy it completely so it cannot be eaten by people or animals.

Canning Soup Stock and Broth

Good broth or soup stock, whether all-vegetable or all-meat or a savory combination, is one of the most valuable staples to have on hand—partly because of its versatility, partly because of its cost at the supermarket, and a great deal because you are the monitor for the amount of salt that goes into it.

The following are the simplest of broths to make. We wish there were room to include delicious variations and some of the consommés, etc., but you will find recipes for Fish Stock and Brown Bone Stock in Chapter 24, "Cooking"; and there's always your own inventiveness or the fun of hunting for specialties in gourmet cookbooks. Another reason for keeping the seasonings simple here: their flavors change too much in Pressure–processing (and you probably like to add your own touches, anyway, when you use the broth).

BROTH/STOCK FROM MEAT OR POULTRY

Meaty bones from beef, veal or lamb and from turkey, chicken or duck all make good soup bases; beef, veal and chicken are especially good all-purpose broths for such pleasures as Greek Egg Lemon Soup (below) or adding your own homemade noodles. Stocks with more pronounced flavors of their own are excellent for sauces or combination main-dish soups.

Freezing also is satisfactory for putting by these broths or stocks, but they really should be boiled down to more concentrated form to save valuable freezer space.

Pressure Canning only. Use Hot pack only. Use pint or quart jars.

Prepare

Cover the meaty bones with water, and salt only very lightly *if you use salt at all:* there's no certain way to remove too much salt after the broth has reduced to the strength you want. You could add a whole peeled onion, a few ribs of celery; some dill if for chicken—all optional. Bring to a slow boil over medium heat, and skim carefully to remove the grey protein froth that will collect: this will take only a couple of minutes. Then reduce the heat to low, and *simmer* until meat falls from the bones, because simmering is the main way to obtain clear broth.

Lift out the bones and onion, celery, etc.; and when the bones are cool enough, remove any good little bits of meat. Meanwhile let the pot simmer a while longer until the broth is nearly the strength you want it. Pour the broth through a sieve into another large kettle or large bowl; save any meat residues in the colander, discarding gristle, skin, bits of bone, etc.

If there is an accumulation of sediment and little edible pieces, do not throw it away: instead, strain the broth again, and reserve the sedimentary things for a special container that will be used for gravies or casseroles or the like. The simplest way to clarify small batches of stock is to heat it again, and pour it by limited amounts through a good coffee filter into a large ceramic or glass coffee pot (which can be emptied as needed into another bowl for defatting).

If there is not much fat, you can get it by laying absorbent paper towels gently and briefly on the surface of the stock; change the towels each time they absorb the fat. If there is a good deal of fat, chill the bowls of broth until the fat can be lifted off in a hard sheet; chicken fat may be saved and used for the pastry or biscuit toppings for meat pies or for meat tarts, but the other fats would be welcome treats for birds in cold weather.

When fat is removed, from broth strained and unstrained, heat the two broths separately, and can them separately.

PACK HOT IN JARS

Pour boiling hot stock into jars, leaving 1 inch of headroom. Wipe jar rims carefully. Adjust lids.

Pressure–process at 10 pounds (240 F/116 C)—pints for 20 minutes, quarts for 25 minutes. Remove jars; complete seals if necessary.

ALL–VEGETABLE BROTH/STOCK

Useful, light, with a bouquet that should never be smothered; what is often designated as vegetarian broth should be a staple for meat-eaters too. The main rule to follow—of course in addition to Pressure–processing—is that the vegetables and their trimmings that are used *must be impeccable—no blemishes, scars, cuts, spoiled spots, blossom or stem ends.*

A favorite broth is based on quite thick potato peelings and leeks. Scrub about 4 pounds of fresh baking potatoes (around 8), cut out all eyes and blemishes, then cut off quite thick peels. Put these in a good-sized enameled or stainless-steel kettle with 1 medium leek, split and cleaned, then cut in 4-inch chunks (or 2 medium onions, peeled and quartered); 2 ribs of celery and 1 large scraped carrot, both cut in chunks; about 1 cup of carefully cleaned mushroom trimmings (stems and peels); ½ teaspoon dried rosemary leaves. Cover the vegetables with 2 quarts of water (*½ teaspoon salt optional*), bring just to the boil, skim for a couple of minutes; reduce heat and simmer, *covered,* for 1 hour. Check the liquid level, add 1 cup water (or more) if needed. Put lid on again, and continue cooking gently for 1 hour more.

Strain off most of the broth, correct the salt as desired; put remaining broth and soft vegetables through a food mill to make a purée. Keep clear stock and puréed base separate in canning. Together they will yield about 4 pints.

Pressure Canning only. Use Hot pack only. Use pint jars.

Follow processing procedures and times for Broth/Stock from Meat or Poultry, above.

Shrimp Stock

Fresh raw shrimp, either peeled or in their shells, are just covered with cold water, brought to boiling; then the heat is reduced and they are cooked more gently only until they curl, turn pink, and the flesh is opaque. Lengthy, brisk boiling toughens them. *Salt*—¼ teaspoon for each 1 pound of shrimp—helps their flavor, but *is optional.*

Remove shrimp from water, cool and handle as desired. Meanwhile turn up heat, reduce the stock to ¾ or ½ its original volume. Strain through a sieve to remove coagulated material. Reheat and pack in clean, hot jars. This stock makes a superior base for seafood soufflés and sauces.

Pressure Canning only. Use Hot pack only. Use ½-pint jars with 2-piece screwband lids.

IN ½-PINT JARS

Pour hot stock into clean, hot jars, leaving ½ inch of headroom. Wipe jar rims carefully; adjust lids.

Pressure–process at 10 pounds, sea level (240 F/116 C) for 30 minutes. Remove jars to cool naturally.

Clam Broth

This is a tasty by-product of steamer clams, whether they are the soft-shell type of the New England and Maritime shores, or the hard-shell variety generally steamed on the Pacific Coast.

Scrub clams thoroughly, put them in a heavy enameled or stainless-steel kettle, or regular clam-steamer designed for large batches. If they're loose in a kettle, they'll need only about ¼ cup water per 1 pound in addition to the water clinging to their shells; you may add ¼ cup per 1 pound more water if you want extra broth to can, after cups of broth are served with the clams.

Over moderate heat, bring the covered pot to boiling; turn the clams over once with a large spoon to ensure that all are exposed to steam. Cook just until they are opened—5 to 10 minutes, depending on size and the shell. Remove clams and eat.

Reduce remaining broth to ¾ or ½ its volume. Pour through a good coffee filter into a ceramic or glass coffee pot to clarify and remove sediment. Return broth to heat, and pack in clean, hot ½-pint jars.

The broth can be diluted and heated to serve before a meal, or to combine with other juices for an appetizer. It is a great help in boosting the flavor of oyster stew or scalloped oysters—which can be a little shy on liquid. All these aside from its virtue in clam dishes—bisques, chowders, and bouillabaisses.

Pressure Canning only. Use Hot pack only. Use ½-pint jars with 2-piece screwband lids.

IN ½-PINT JARS

Pour hot broth into clean, hot jars, leaving ½ inch of headroom. Wipe jar rims carefully; adjust lids.

Pressure–process at 10 pounds, sea level (240 F/116 C) for 30 minutes. Remove jars and cool naturally.

Tennessee Vegetable Soup Base

In this and in any other vegetable combination, Pressure–process the length of time stipulated for the vegetable(s) *requiring the longest processing time.* In this case the critical vegetable is corn, which is lower-acid than fresh lima beans or okra. If you substitute lima beans for *all* the corn, the processing time would be 40 minutes for pints. But if some corn is used, the whole recipe must be processed for corn's 55 minutes for pints. Sounds more complicated than it is—just look up the individual vegetables. And *don't use short-cut processing.*

5 quarts peeled, cored and quarted unblemished ripe tomatoes
2 quarts corn kernels OR 2 quarts fresh lima beans
2 quarts prepared okra
(optional 2 tablespoons salt)

Save all the tomato juice possible while preparing the tomatoes. Blanch ears of corn to set the milk, then cut from the cob at ⅔ the depth of the kernel (this, to avoid the points of the hulls); shell fresh lima beans. Wash and trim tender pods of okra, boil for 1 minute; cut pods in 1-inch pieces. Combine the vegetables (and salt, if wanted) and cook to the consistency of thick soup.

Pressure Canning only. Use Hot pack only. Use pint jars.

In Pint Jars

Ladle bubbling-hot soup into clean, hot jars, leaving 1 inch of headroom; remove any trapped air and adjust lids. Process at 10 pounds, sea level (240 F/116 C) for 55 minutes. Remove jars; complete seals if necessary.

Country Tomato Soup
About 4½ quarts

This plain and good soup is not diluted for serving.

Pressure Canning only (onions and peppers are low-acid). Use Hot pack only. Use jars only; for a very small household pints are more useful.

Wash 1 peck (8 quarts) of ripe red tomatoes; remove blossom and stem ends and cores; cut in pieces. In a large kettle, cook and stir the tomatoes until soft—about 15 minutes. Push the pulp and juice through a wire strainer or food mill to remove skins and seeds; return the purée to the kettle but do not reheat yet.

Cook together until soft (in enough water just to cover) 3 large onions and 2 green peppers—all finely chopped. Sieve, and add to the puréed tomatoes in the kettle. Mix together ¾ cup of sugar, and 8 tablespoons cornstarch; blend in 3 tablespoons white vinegar and just enough more water or cool tomato juice to make a smooth paste. (Optional: Add 2 tablespoons salt to the paste.) Pour slowly into the sieved tomatoes, stirring all the while. Heat to boiling and stir until the liquid clears. Pack hot.

Hot pack only, in jars. Pour boiling-hot soup into clean, hot jars, leaving ¾ inch of headroom for pints, 1¼ inches for quarts. Adjust the lids. Pressure–process at 10 pounds (240 F/116 C)—pints for 20 minutes, quarts for 30 minutes. Remove jars; complete seals if necessary.

Beans (Dried) in Sauce

Only Pressure Canning. Only Hot pack. Use either pint jars or plain cans. Use clean beans—kidney, navy, pea or yellow-eye as you prefer—that are free of any musty odor (mustiness could indicate active mold spores—and the possibility of dangerous toxins). Cover with boiling water, boil 2 minutes. Remove from heat and let soak 1 hour in their cooking water. Yield: 1 cup dry beans will make about 2 or 2½ cups after soaking.

To pack, reheat to boiling, drain (saving water to use in the sauce), and put hot beans in containers.

To make about 4 cups of sauce, enough to do 4 to 5 pints of beans:

Tomato—4 cups tomato juice, 3 tablespoons sugar, 1 tablespoon onion pulp, a few grains of cayenne. (Optional: 2 teaspoons salt). Herbs and spices are better added when the canned beans are being heated for serving. Heat to boiling. (Blah but O.K. in a bind: 1 cup tomato catsup, 3 cups of the drained-off soaking water, and 1 teaspoon salt, or to taste; boil.)

Molasses—4 cups of drained-off soaking water, 3 tablespoons dark molasses, 1 tablespoon vinegar, ½ teaspoon dry mustard, ¼ teaspoon ginger; boil. (Optional: 2 teaspoons salt.) Maple syrup is great in beans; so is some onion pulp. Experiment!

Hot Pack Only

In pint jars. Fill only ¾ full with drained hot beans. Lay on top of the beans a 1-inch-square slice of salt pork or bacon end. Add boiling sauce, leaving 1 inch of headroom. Adjust lids. Pressure–process at 10 pounds (240 F/116 C) 65 minutes. Remove jars; complete seals if necessary.

Stewed Tomatoes with Added Vegetables

The addition of lower-acid vegetables to tomatoes means that you must Pressure–process the mixture *according to the specific rule for the lowest-acid vegetable in the combination.*

How much of which of the usual vegetables is added for interest of course depends on the family's taste. However, *density* of the pack is an important factor in any timetable for processing. Therefore we say that the total amount of several added vegetables *should not exceed one-fourth the volume of tomatoes in the mixture.* For example, to 8 cups of prepared cut tomatoes we would add no more than 1 cup chopped celery, ½ cup chopped onion and ½ cup chopped green pepper. Incidentally, this balance of added vegetables also makes for good flavor.

(Although tomatoes with zucchini squash are a popular side dish, the amount of squash added is generally so large that this mixture is better if you combine canned Squash (q.v.) with as much canned Stewed Tomatoes as you like, and the two are heated together just before serving.)

General Handling

Pressure Canning only. Use Hot pack only.

To avoid diluting acidity or flavor, it's a good idea to prepare 3 or 4 cups of Tomato Juice (see Chapter 6) to have ready in case you need extra hot liquid when filling the containers; or use canned juice, heated.

Wash, peel, core and cut the tomatoes in quarters or smaller, saving the juice; measure. Add the desired proportion of well-washed coarsely chopped celery, finely chopped onions, or chopped seeded green peppers. Combine the vegetables in a large enameled kettle and boil them gently in their own juice *without added water* for 10 minutes, stirring to prevent sticking.

Hot Pack Only, in Pint Jars

Ladle boiling hot into clean hot pint jars, leaving ½ inch of headroom. Add ¼ teaspoon citric acid (or 1 tablespoon white vinegar). (Optional: Add ½ teaspoon salt to pints.) If there is too little free liquid, make up the difference with boiling tomato juice, *not water*. Adjust lids; process. After processing, remove jars; complete seals if necessary.

With only onion added, Pressure–process at 10 pounds (240 F/116 C)—25 minutes for pints.

With celery added, Pressure–process at 10 pounds (240 F/116 C)—30 minutes for pints.

With green peppers added, Pressure–process at 10 pounds (240 F/116 C)—35 minutes for pints.

Minnesota Tomato Mixture
Seven Pints

This combination has been developed by the Agricultural Extension Service of the University of Minnesota to be in such accurate *pH* balance that, although the celery, onions and green pepper are all low-acid foods, the extremely large proportion of tomatoes guarantees that the over-all acidity remains intense enough to allow for processing in a Boiling–Water Bath.

But it cannot be stressed too strongly that the proportion of green pepper, onion and celery to tomatoes CANNOT BE INCREASED—unless the mixture is to be Pressure–processed for the full time required to deal with the vegetable with the lowest amount of acid.

12 cups peeled, cored and quartered tomatoes
 1 cup chopped celery
 ½ cup chopped onion
 ½ cup chopped pepper
   (optional 3 teaspoons salt)   *(Recipe continued on next page)*

Simmer the vegetables for 10 minutes, then ladle into clean, hot pint jars: the vegetables will have released their juices to provide canning liquid, so *do not add any water.* Leave ¾ inch of headroom; adjust lids.

Process in a B–W Bath for 40 minutes for the pints. Remove jars; complete seals if necessary.

Meats and the Makings for Main Dishes

With the exceptions of the recipes and procedures for Baked Beans, Beans in Sauce and the simplified Beef Stew with Vegetables—which invites titivating *after it is opened and is being prepared for serving*—there are no complete main dishes given here.

The reason is simple and has been stressed before: Varying degrees of acidity, as well as varying densities and textures, dictate Pressure–processing times that would subdue completely some ingredients in order to deal safely with another ingredient in the same combination. Therefore the components are canned in separate groups, to be put together for heating and serving.

Ground Meat

Freezing ground meat gives a much better result than canning does. But if circumstances oblige you to can it, *do not can it in bulk in a solid mass.* Make it up into meatballs by your favorite recipe (omitting herbs and spices that change character in canning); brown lightly under a medium broiler, because frying is a very poor way to precook meat for canning: the meat is case-hardened, and tastes overcooked. Or shape it in thin patties; these you can always break up and add to the Minnesota Tomato Mixture, say, or Tomatoes Stewed with Vegetables to use with pasta.

Pressure Canning only. Use Raw or Hot pack. Use straight-sided pint jars.

An exception: If you have a lot of meat to put by, use cans (plain, No. 2) if you like.

Prepare and Pack Hot (Precooked)

Trim and grind *lean* meat *adding no fat.* Make meatballs, browning their surface and draining well; or shape thin patties, slightly smaller in diameter than the containers. In a slow oven (325 F/163 C) precook meatballs or patties until Medium done. Skim off all fat from the drippings in the pan, saving the pan juices.

In Straight-sided Pint Jars

Pack hot patties (in layers) or hot precooked meatballs, leaving 1 inch of headroom. (Optional: Add ½ teaspoon salt to pints.) Cover with boiling *fat-free* pan juices (extended with boiling meat broth if necessary), leaving 1 inch of headroom. Wipe jar rims carefully to remove any fat. Adjust lids.

Pressure–process at 10 pounds (240 F/116 C)—pints for 75 minutes. Remove jars; complete seals if necessary.

THE EXCEPTION FOR PLAIN NO. 2 CANS

Pack hot patties (in layers) or hot precooked meatballs, leaving ½ inch of headroom. (Optional: Add ½ teaspoon salt to No. 2 cans.) Cover with boiling *fat-free* pan juices (extended with boiling meat broth if necessary), leaving *no* headroom. Wipe can rims carefully to remove any fat. Seal.

Pressure–process at 10 pounds (240 F/116 C)—No. 2 cans for 65 minutes. Remove cans; cool quickly.

Corned Beef

Corn the beef (see Chapter 20).
Pressure Canning only. Use Hot pack only (but in this case the meat is not precooked as for fresh meat: it is still raw, but some of the salt cure has been removed in freshening). Use straight-sided jars.

PREPARE AND PACK HOT (FRESHENED)

Wash the corned beef and cut it in chunks or thick strips to fit your containers, removing all fat. Put the pieces of meat in cold water and bring to boiling. Taste the broth in the kettle: if it's unpleasantly salty, drain the meat, cover it with fresh cold water, and bring again to boiling. This boiling merely freshens (removes salt), *it does not cook the corned beef.*

IN STRAIGHT-SIDED PINT JARS

Fit hot freshened meat in jars, leaving 1 inch of headroom. Add boiling broth in which the meat was freshened, leaving 1 inch of headroom. Wipe jar rims carefully to remove any fat. Adjust lids.

Pressure–process at 10 pounds (240 F/116 C) 75 minutes. Remove jars; complete seals if necessary.

Pork Sausage

Freezing is better for pork sausage, especially in view of the large amount of fat (but remember that fatty food has short freezer-storage life).
Make your sausage by any tested recipe (see how in Chapter 23), *but use your seasonings lightly* because such flavorings change during canning and storage; and *omit sage*—it makes canned pork sausage bitter. And note that precooking is done in the oven.
Pressure Canning only. Use Hot pack only. Use straight-sided pint jars.

PREPARE AND PACK HOT (PRECOOKED)

Shape raw sausage in thin patties, slightly smaller in diameter than the containers. In a slow oven (325 F/163 C) precook patties until Medium done. Skim off all fat from the drippings in the pan, saving pan juices.

IN STRAIGHT-SIDED PINT JARS

Pack hot sausage patties in layers, leaving 1 inch of headroom. Cover with boiling *fat-free* pan juices (extended with boiling meat broth if necessary), leaving 1 inch of headroom. Wipe jar rims carefully to remove any fat. Adjust lids.

Pressure–process at 10 pounds (240 F/116 C) for 75 minutes. Remove jars; complete seals if necessary.

Bologna–style Sausage

If you don't have adequate cold, dry storage for Bologna-style sausage (see Chapter 23 for recipe and storing), you may can it.
Pressure Canning only—*and at 15 pounds.* Use Hot pack only. Use straight-sided pint jars.

PREPARE AND PACK HOT (COOKED COMPLETELY)

When the sausage has been simmered until it is completely cooked and floats (see recipe under Smoking), remove it from the kettle, saving the cooking water. Cut the hot sausage in lengths the height of your containers for packing.
If the sausage is not fresh from cooking and therefore is cold, heat it through by simmering for 10 to 20 minutes, depending on thickness, in a bland broth (bland, so as not to change the flavor of the sausage). Save the broth, cut the hot sausage to length, and pack.

IN STRAIGHT-SIDED PINT JARS

Fit pieces of hot sausage lengthwise in the jars, leaving 1 inch of headroom. Add boiling broth, leaving 1 inch of headroom. Wipe the jar rims carefully to remove any fat. Adjust lids.

Pressure–process at 15 pounds (250 F/121 C) for 50 minutes. Remove jars; complete seals if necessary.

Vegetable–Beef Stew
Makes Seven or Eight Pints

Because of the long Pressure–processing and its effect on some of the seasonings that might be used if the stew were served from its pot, this is not a dish with gourmet touches. But this is a virtue, under the circumstances; and titivating touches can be added when the jars are opened and their contents are being heated for a meal. Being packed Raw, the ingredients provide a good deal of the canning liquid needed for convection as well as conduction heat through the contents.

4 cups lean beef (chuck is good) cut in 1-inch cubes
4 cups new potatoes cut in ½-inch cubes
4 cups carrots cut in ½-inch pieces
4 cups small whole onions, peeled
1½ cups coarsely chopped celery

Put prepared meat in a very large bowl; add vegetables and mix with the meat. Pack firmly into clean, hot pint jars, leaving 1 inch of headroom, and apportion juices collected in the bowl among the jars, adding ¼ cup boiling water if needed. (Add an optional ½ teaspoon salt to each pint jar.) Wipe sealing rims of jars. Adjust 2-piece screwband lids firmly tight.

Process in a Pressure Canner at 10 pounds, sea level (240 F/116 C) for 60 minutes. Remove jars; cool naturally.

Sweets and Beverages

Boiled Cider
Six ½-pint Jars

Boiled cider is an old-time sweetener—tart, full of character—and in specialty shops it costs a fortune. In the Fall you can make your own—and it is able to be canned well for future use as a delectable "mystery" ingredient in squash-pie fillings, in baked puddings, and as the base for several dessert sauces.

The casual old receipts indicated that boiled cider was fresh cider reduced to one-fourth its original volume—4 gallons of cider made 4 quarts of boiled cider. But with today's fresh unpasteurized cider bought from roadside stands well after Labor Day, it must be boiled down further: even to one-sixth or one-eighth, depending on how syrupy you want it. We started with 2 gallons and got 6 ½-pints to our liking.

On high heat, in a large enameled or stainless-steel kettle, bring the cider to a rolling boil, and cook hard for 30 minutes, stirring often. Reduce the heat, and continue boiling less frenziedly for another 15 minutes or so. Remove the kettle from heat, and pour the hot cider by quarts through a strong muslin jelly bag (or a lined maple-syrup felt strainer, as described in Chapter 18). This straining will remove sediment that has coagulated as the fresh juice cooked. Return the cider to the rinsed-out kettle, and—if you don't want to stand over it—put it in a 325 F/163 C oven, stirring occasionally and testing for desired consistency. It should coat a metal spoon thinly, and drip off *in separate droplets*—not nearly so stiff as jelly. It will have bite, and considerable personality.

Pour the finished cider into clean, hot ½-pint jars, leaving ¼ inch of headroom; adjust 2-piece screwband lids firmly tight. Process in a Boiling–Water Bath for 10 minutes. Remove jars, let cool naturally.

Boiled Cider Sauce
Makes 1 ¼ Cups

This is especially good with Steamed Carrot Pudding (q.v. in Chapter 24).

1 cup sugar
⅓ cup butter (or good margarine)
2 tablespoons cornstarch
½ cup very hot water
½ cup Boiled Cider

Rub butter, sugar and cornstarch to a cream. Put it in the top of a double boiler, add ½ cup hot water; smooth and stir, and cook over medium-low heat as the sauce thickens and clears—about 20 minutes, stirring to prevent globbiness. Remove from heat, blend in the Boiled Cider, serve hot in a sauce boat.

Apple Pie Filling
Five Quarts

7½ quarts of thinly sliced firm, ripe Fall apples (about 14 pounds)
3½ cups sugar
⅓ cup cornstarch
2 tablespoons ground cinnamon
½ teaspoon plain pickling salt
1½ cups light corn syrup
⅓ cup lemon juice

Wash, core, peel and slice apples. In a large enameled or stainless steel kettle combine the sugar, cornstarch, cinnamon and salt. Add the corn syrup and the lemon juice, mixing well. Bring to boiling over medium heat, stirring constantly, and boil for 2 minutes; the syrup mixture will clear. Increase the heat and add the apples; stirring all the while, bring to boiling and boil 3 minutes. Remove kettle from heat and lift hot apples out of the syrup and pack immediately in clean hot quart jars, leaving 1 inch of headroom. Return kettle to heat briefly to bring syrup back to boiling, immediately pour hot syrup into jars to cover fruit, leaving ¾ inch headroom. Remove any trapped air with a spatula or table knife; wipe sealing rim of jars and adjust lids. Process in a Boiling–Water Bath for 20 minutes. Remove jars, complete seals if necessary.

Each quart is enough filling for a 9-inch pie (see Chapter 24 for a rule for two-crust Pie Pastry.) Pour one quart of filling into a pastry-lined 9-inch pie pan; dot with 2 tablespoons good margarine. Top with crust, crimping with fingertips to seal. Brush with egg glaze (1 egg beaten lightly with 2 tablespoons cold water) or milk; slash top to let steam escape. Bake in the center of a 425 F/218 C oven for 35 minutes or until browned.

Susan Osgood's Melba Sauce
Six ½-pint Jars

This beautiful sauce, named for turn-of-the-century opera star Nellie Melba, traditionally is poured over poached/canned Peach halves, q.v., filled with vanilla ice cream. And try it on cold soufflés . . .

Pick over and rinse in cold water 8 pints of fresh raspberries; whirl in a blender at Purée setting, 3 cups of berries at a time. To remove seeds, press each batch through a sieve into a large enameled saucepan before dealing with the next 3 cups. Add 1 cup sugar to the finished berry purée, and ¼ cup crème de cassis (black-currant liqueur). Over medium heat stir until sugar is dissolved; reduce to low heat and simmer for 45 minutes to 1 hour, or until sauce has thickened.

Pour hot sauce into clean, hot ½-pint jars, leaving ¼ inch of headroom; cap firmly tight with 2-piece screwband lids whose discs have been held in simmering water. Process in a finishing Boiling–Water Bath for 10 minutes. Remove jars; complete seals if necessary.

Indian Pudding

In Chapter 24 are two recipes for this good cornmeal-molasses dessert: Yankee Indian Pudding, and Pueblo Indian Pudding. Both are good at Thanksgiving, or as the finish for a midwinter meal. They can be canned successfully— better than freezing them, actually—which is a help when "make-aheads" can ease the work before a holiday.

They should be canned bubbling hot from their original long baking.

Come the time for serving, if they show any sign of separation or graininess, just turn the contents of the jar into the blender or the bowl of an electric beater and beat at high speed for a minute or so; then put the smooth pudding in a well-buttered baking dish in a 350 F/177 C oven for 20 minutes, or until thoroughly heated through; then just turn the oven off and let the pudding relax: it doesn't need to be boiling hot when served. Vanilla ice cream is good as a topping.

In Jars

Ladle pudding bubbling-hot from baking directly into clean, hot pint or quart jars, leaving ¾ inch of headroom for pints, 1¼ inches of headroom for quarts. Remove any air bubbles with a spatula or the blade of a table knife. Adjust lids.

Pressure–process at 10 pounds, sea level (240 F/116 C)—20 minutes for pints, 30 minutes for quarts. Remove jars; complete seals if necessary.

Raspberry Vinegar
About Six Pints

This makes a Summer quencher beautiful to see and charming to taste.

5 quarts fresh ripe raspberries
1 quart cider vinegar
  sugar

Pick half the berries over, removing blemished or damaged ones; refrigerate the rest. Put the cleaned berries in a large ceramic or enameled bowl or very large jar, pour the vinegar over the berries, and let stand overnight in a cool, protected place. In the morning, pick over the remaining half of the berries, put them in the ceramic bowl. Hang over this new bowlful of berries a muslin jelly bag wetted with vinegar; pour into the bag the vinegared berries from the preceding day. When all the juice has drained onto the remaining berries, cover the bowl and let stand 24 hours in a cool, safe place.

At the end of the second 24 hours, strain the contents of the bowl through the vinegar-wet jelly bag until all the juice has been collected. Measure the juice into a large enameled kettle and add an equal amount of sugar. Put over high heat and bring to a full rolling boil, stirring constantly, for 3 minutes. Remove from heat, skim, and ladle immediately into clean, hot pint jars, leaving ½ inch of headroom; adjust 2-piece screwband lids firmly tight. Process in a Boiling–Water Bath for 15 minutes to ensure the seal. Remove jars and let cool naturally.

For each serving pour ¼ cup Raspberry Vinegar over ice cubes, add ¾ cup water or seltzer water.

Annette Pestle's Tomato Cocktail
About Seven Quarts

This is delicious as an appetizer or for aspic. The herb seasonings may be varied, and *of course the salt is optional,* but NEVER decrease the proportion of tomato-juice-plus-added-acid to the total amount of vegetables. Annette says she has never had this cocktail separate after it sits in properly cool storage; but in case yours does, just give it a good shake.

Quart jars are worthwhile to have on hand with this, even for a small family.

Remember: *Never* process different sizes of container in the same canner batch, except where specifically O.K.'d.

Use a Boiling–Water Bath. Use Hot pack only.

To make about 7 quarts of cocktail, you'll need 8 quarts of cut-up tomatoes. Wash thoroughly the firm-ripe unblemished tomatoes; remove stems, blossom ends and cores; cut in small pieces. In a large enameled kettle simmer the tomatoes over low heat until soft; put through a fine sieve or food mill to remove skins and seeds, and set the strained juice aside. Rinse the kettle, and into it measure 2 cups of the tomato juice, add 2 diced medium onions, 1¼ cups diced celery (including a few leaves), 1 large seeded and chopped green pepper, 3 bay leaves, 8 or 10 fresh basil leaves (or 2 teaspoons dried basil), ½ teaspoon ground pepper, 3 tablespoons sugar, and 2 teaspoons Worcestershire sauce. (Optional: Add 4 teaspoons salt.) Boil over medium heat—stirring, and adding extra juice as needed to keep the mixture from sticking—until soft, about 30 minutes. Pick out the bay leaves, then press the vegetables through a fine sieve or food mill. Add 3½ teaspoons crystalline citric acid (or ⅔ cup bottled lemon juice OR ¾ cup white vinegar) and the rest of the tomato juice. Bring to simmering. Pack hot.

Hot pack only, in jars. Fill jars with hot juice, leaving ½ inch of headroom; adjust lids. Process in a Boiling–Water Bath (212 F/100 C)—15 minutes for pints, 20 minutes for quarts. Remove jars; complete seals if necessary.

11

GETTING AND USING A FREEZER

Freezing is the most versatile means of preserving safely, because it can store all manner of foods—liquid or porous or dense, strong- or low-acid, raw or precooked or sometimes even table ready.

It is also the quickest method to prepare food *for*—although in many cases, and compared with the few minutes spent on initial handling and packaging, it's the most time-consuming method to finish preparing food *from*.

Proper freezing lets more foods keep more of their original flavor and texture, and generally more of their nutrients, than any other way of putting by.

And proper freezing is far and away the most expensive method of preservation.

We'll qualify that a bit: It is relatively very expensive, but it can be worth the cost if (1) the right type and size of freezer was bought to answer the family's needs; (2) good quality food in good variety and at realistic prices goes into it; (3) its stock is managed well—it is kept at least ¾ full, with the contents rotated and none left to languish in frosty corners long after the food's quality has suffered; and (4) the freezer itself is maintained in optimal condition for efficiency and mechanical safety.

WHAT FREEZING DOES

Freezing does NOT destroy the organisms that cause spoilage, as canning does—it merely stops their growth temporarily. When they become suitably warm again, they multiply as quickly as ever. This matter will come up repeatedly.

Freezing correctly means subjecting each sealed-from-the-air parcel/container of food to the sharpest cold we can manage to give it—ideally −20 F/−29 C—for 24 hours, and then storing it at a sustained Zero F/−18 C for as long as its quality holds well; thereafter it is wasting expensive storage space, even though it has not become dangerous to eat.

Food does carry a startling bacterial load, a load that increases geometrically

186

if it is held too long at thawing (usually when it is allowed to thaw at room temperature, especially if it's low-acid, and occasionally if an unrecognized power failure has ruined whatever was stored in the freezer).

It is only fair to note that some food scientists feel that the *sharp* freeze need no longer be standard practice. Instead, they say, it is all right to freeze food at the freezer's regular storage temperature *but* limit the amount of food being frozen at any one time, and make sure that the to-be-frozen food has good air circulation around it.

In this vein, they add that one should limit the load of new food being introduced for freezing to ⅟₁₅ of the listed capacity of the freezer. (This can be an annoying problem in arithmetic, since the listed capacities are usually less than the brochures say.)

The freezers that *PFB* knows best are held at Sharp Freeze, with the result that the temperature in the chest model in the cellar registers −10 F/−23 C near the top, and the upright freezer in the pantry is Zero to 5 F/−18 C to −15 C depending on how much more often the door is opened.

CONSIDERATIONS IN GETTING A FREEZER

Decent freezing requires a mechanical freezer. It used to be that one could rent space, if just a drawer, in a freezer locker plant, and this was a good start for young families on a strict budget. Nowadays, though, such lockers are few and far between (but try under "Warehouses—Cold Storage" in the Yellow Pages, or ask your County Agent if there's a slaughterhouse with locker space near you. Instead, one can learn a good deal about freezer management through using well the separate freezer compartment in the usual modern refrigerator/freezer. From this can be developed a workable food-storage program and an idea of what size and kind of freezer is feasible.

Those Frozen–Food/Freezer Plans

There are a number of companies that sell, on time payments, a package deal of freezer and food supply replenished over a period of several years. Some of these plans involve a membership fee of several hundred dollars to join, payable either as a lump sum or by installments; in addition, the buyer contracts in advance to purchase food at stated intervals. Still other plans offer only a food-purchase contract without the freezer.

All such plans undoubtedly are convenient: the householder orders ahead of time, and therefore has always on hand a certain quantity and type of food.

We recommend that everyone who is considering joining any such food/freezer plan check the company's offer with the local Better Business Bureau or other consumer protection group. Any contract which the householder is tempted to sign deserves careful investigation as to quality of product, be it freezer or food; terms of purchase, including carrying charges; and reliability of the firm, including what recourse either the company or the buyer may have if the contract appears to have been violated.

This recommendation is not to be construed as a blanket condemnation, even implied, of group-purchasing agreements. Prior investigation simply makes sense if the family is to get a suitable plan sponsored by a reliable organization.

Relevant Metrics for Freezing

Full metric conversions, with the arithmetic for refining them, are given at the start of Chapter 17 ("Common Ingredients and How to Use Them"), but the following—rounded off—apply in this chapter.

If you live above the sea-level zone (i.e., *over* 1000 ft/305 m), consult the subsection "Correcting for Altitude" in Chapter 3 for help in figuring blanching times (viz. variable boiling points for water at lower atmospheric (pressure), and see metrics note at start of Chapter 13, "Freezing Vegetables."

• • •

Temperatures (@ sea level): −20 F/−29 C——— −10 F/−23 C———Zero F/−18 C———10 F/−12 C———20 F/−7 C———212 F/100 C.

Cubic measures: 1 cubic foot = 0.028 cubic meters———10 cubic feet = 0.28 cubic meters———15 cubic feet = 0.43 cubic meters———20 cubic feet = 0.57 cubic meters.

Length: ½ inch = 1.27 cm———1 inch = 2.54 cm———1¼ inches = 3.18 cm———1½ inches = 3.75 cm———2 inches = 5.1 cm———3 inches = 7.6 cm.

How Big a Freezer?

Some advisers recommend 6 cubic feet of freezer space for each person in the family. A cubic foot holds about 35 pounds of food ideally, but actually a good deal less because some foods are more dense than others (pork loin roast takes only a little more space than a loaf of Italian bread, which of course weighs less).

• **NOTE:** Manufacturers' sales brochures describing cubic-foot sizes in freezers are sometimes approximate, so check the specifications and measurements to determine the actual usable interior space. See the entries in Chapter 25, mentioned a minute ago.

Of all the ways to put food by, freezing limits storage room most severely, so what you freeze should be given careful thinking-through beforehand. If your freezer is to be more than a place to stash random things you're not going to use right away, figure out a system of priorities. A good rule-of-thumb is to assign freezer space first to the more expensive and heavier foods, and to ones that can't be preserved so well any other way. Therefore, plan to freeze meats and seafood; and plan to freeze certain vegetables (prime example, broccoli) and certain fruits (prime example, strawberries—assuming you don't want all of them in jam), and mentally allot room for some favorite main-dish combinations or desserts.

What Type of Freezer?

To do its job, the freezer must have adequate controls, no warm spots ("warm" being a constant temperature higher than the rest of the recommended Zero F/−18 C storage area), and the ability to provide the initial Sharp-Freeze for 24 hours at −20 F/−29 C.

The small enclosed space for ice cubes or below 32 F/Zero C storage in some refrigerators is not adequate unless it has its own controls for Sharp Freeze and proper storage, and has its own outside door.

CHEST

The chest type with a top opening offers the best use of the space within it, and it holds its temperature better than do the uprights. Cold air sinks downward, so you don't spill cold air when you lift the lid of a chest freezer, but cold air tumbles out from an upright whenever the door is opened.

A chest should be set up on 2-by-4's or some other supports at the corners to make it easier to draw off water when defrosting. It must be in a dry and cool place.

Chest freezers are not built to have automatic defrosting features. Chests are more of a chore to keep reasonably clear of frost than upright models; however, frost builds up in them less readily than in uprights.

Also, more planning-ahead is needed in filling the chest freezer, because you must bend over the freezer to paw through contents that were piled in any which way. Separate dessert materials from vegetables, meats, convenience foods and oddments, and keep track of the more perishable foods in each category.

Chest freezers are less expensive to buy, and less expensive to run, than uprights are. Of two freezers of *c.* 15-cubic-foot capacity, the upright is likely to cost as much as 30 percent more with the self-defrost feature. As for operation, a manually defrosting upright costs about 14 percent more to run than its chest counterpart, and sometimes even up to 60 percent more to operate if it has automatic defrosting.

UPRIGHT

The upright ones with a refrigerator-type door of course take up less space in the room, but plenty of room must be allowed for the side-opening door: the angle between front of shelves and fully opened door must be *at least* 90 degrees. Uprights are easier to load and unload than the chests, and the little shelves on the door are handy for temporary storage of dabs and snippets.

More cold spills out when the door is opened than is lost with opening a chest; and irregular-shaped packages may tumble out at the same time.

TWO-DOOR COMBINATIONS

Side-by-side or stacked (one above the other) freezer-refrigerator combinations save floor space, and the freezer section is an adequate, though usually smaller, variation of the upright type with its own controls.

To think about: The freezer space is usually too limited to accommodate more than a quite modest freezing program and storage for bargains from markets' sales. With care, though, it could hold a balanced supply of food types and varieties for a very small family.

Where to Put It?

Locate the freezer near the kitchen: you'll use it more (which means using it better) than if it's in the cellar or other remote spot.

If you have a choice of convenient locations, choose the cooler one—so long as the place isn't actually freezing.

Put it in a relatively dry room, because moisture rusts the mechanism and can build up frost inside non-defrosting models, particularly upright ones.

And *please* place it away from a back wall, so there's adequate air circulation and you can get under and around it to get out the fluff. Lack of air and a build-up of dust can make the motor overheat and even cause fire. Mounting it on small rollers is a help in cleaning.

USING A FREEZER

Operating costs per pound of food are less if the freezer is kept at least ¾ full at all times.

For the initial sharp freeze, set the control at the lowest possible point: at or below −20 F/−29 C, the temperature that makes smaller ice crystals in the food and gives a better finished product.

Place packages in single layers in contact with the parts of the box which cover the freezing coils—these would be certain shelves or walls or parts of the floor—and leave the food spread there for 24 hours before stacking the packages compactly for storage. For best results, don't try to sharp-freeze, at one time, more than 2 to 3 pounds of food for each 1 cubic foot of available freezer space. Later, when you're not sharp-freezing but simply storing, turn the controls back to no higher than Zero F/−18 C.

For storing food after it's sharp-frozen, stack packages close together, and keep the storage section temperature at Zero F/−18 C or lower.

How Long in the Freezer?

Frozen foods lose quality when subjected to freezer temperatures above Zero F/−18 C. While the storage life of different products varies, it can be stated generally that each rise of 10 degrees Fahrenheit cuts the storage life in half. (Thus if a food has a storage life of 8 months maintained at Zero F/−18 C, its safe storage life will be only 4 months maintained at 10 F/−23 C, and only 2 months if maintained at 20 F/−7 C.) Foods maintained at −10 F/−23 C (10 degrees below Zero Fahrenheit/−23 C) *in general* will keep their quality longer—although keeping an item more than 12 months is uneconomical use of freezer space. The table on page 196 is a workable guide to quality.

Keeping an Inventory

Running a freezer is like running a small store—you have to know what you have on hand and how long you've had it.

First, label and date each package of frozen food so you know how much of what is in each parcel; and when it was put by.

Store similar foods together, and you won't end up with a hodgepodge you have to paw through to find what you're looking for.

Devise some sort of inventory sheet or board that lets you keep track of food going in and coming out of your freezer. Some cooks make a sort of pegboard arrangement by driving part way into a board one nail for each type of food, labeling the nail, and slipping on it some sort of marker (a plastic ring, a washer, even a paper clip) for each package of that food when it is put in the freezer. As a package is taken out, a marker from the corresponding nail is removed.

Check the contents of your freezer every so often, and put maverick or to-be-used-soon items in places where you can't overlook them.

CARING FOR A FREEZER

Freezers need little care—just respect.

Treat the outside the same way that you do your refrigerator. Keep the surface and the door gaskets wiped clean—taking care to clean the condenser coils—and keep the protective grid over the motor free of dust.

Many are self-defrosting, but it is easy to do the defrosting yourself. Do it once or twice a year at times when the food supply is low. Disconnect the freezer, remove the food and wrap it in newspapers and blankets to keep it frozen. Use a wooden paddle—or similar tool that won't scratch the finish—to scrape the condensation (frost) from the walls of the cabinet onto papers or towels. Wipe the box with a clean cloth wrung out in water and baking soda. Dry the box before restarting the motor. About once a year, really wash the inside of the freezer.

By the way, have you read the manufacturer's instruction book lately?

WHEN THE FREEZER STOPS FREEZING

Now and again everybody's electricity fails for a time. Or, Heaven forbid, someone accidentally disconnects the freezer. Or the motor isn't working properly. Resist the impulse to open the door to check everything: make a plan of action first.

Find out, if you can, how long your freezer has been, or is likely to be, stopped. If it can be running in a few hours, don't worry. Food in a fully loaded, closed freezer will keep for two days; if it's less than half loaded, the food won't keep longer than one day.

A freezer full of meat does not warm up as fast as a freezer full of baked foods. Reason: the meat is denser, and so is more like a block of solid ice.

The colder the food, the longer it will keep.

The larger a well-stacked freezer, the longer the food will stay frozen.

But you must not open the door.

Emergency Measures for a Long Stoppage

If you foresee that your freezer will be out of running order for more than 48 hours, try to locate a freezer-locker plant (near metropolitan areas, the Yellow Pages may have listings under "Warehouses—Cold Storage" or under "Butchering") to see if they can take care of your food while your emergency lasts. Then take out all the food, wrap it in many layers of newspapers and blankets, or pack it closely in insulated cartons, and hurry it down to the locker.

If your good friends have extra space, ask their help, and divvy your food among their freezers—writing your name on each package beforehand, and insulating it well for the trip to your neighbors'.

If you can't parcel your food out for storage, arrange for a supply of dry ice—which is carbon dioxide (CO_2 and we'll meet it again in Chapter 21, "Drying"); in its solid state it is *107 degrees below Zero Fahrenheit*. It has no liquid state, but becomes a gas when it is in the presence of oxygen, and hence evaporates into nothing after several days in the freezer. Look under "Dry Ice" or "Ice and Fuel" in the Yellow Pages; and try places that sell welders' supplies too: in some machine shops, the welders use CO_2 to freeze—and thereby shrink—metal that they are working on. A 50-pound cake of dry ice is $10 \times 10 \times 10$ inches. A 10-pound piece of dry ice will hold 20 pounds of food frozen for around 24 hours, so do your arithmetic and order accordingly.

When you get your dry ice, wrap it in many layers of newspaper (that great insulator) *and use lineman's gloves to handle it, because just touching the stuff can cause severe frostbite.*

Consolidate the food packages into a compact pile. Put heavy cardboard directly on the food packages and lay the dry ice on the cardboard. Then cover the entire freezer with blankets, but leave the air-vent openings free so the motor won't overheat in case the current comes on unexpectedly.

But If All That Food Thaws . . .

If, despite your emergency measures, the food in your freezer thawed, there are several things you can do. You can refreeze some of it, you can cook up some of it and freeze the cooked dishes from scratch; some of it you may can. And some you may have to destroy.

WHEN TO REFREEZE

This calls for good judgment, and a definition of terms.

When food has *thawed,* it still contains many ice crystals; individual pieces may be able to be separated, but they still contain ice in their tissues; and dense foods, or ones that pack solidly, might have a firm-to-hard core of ice in the middle of the package, in addition to the crystals in the tissues. Many thawed foods may be refrozen. Be sure to re-label them for limited storage.

When food has *defrosted,* all the ice crystals in its tissues have warmed to liquid. *No foods that have warmed above refrigeration temperature—except very strong-acid fruits—should be refrozen.* Reason: Defrosted low-acid foods, if refrozen, are possible sources of food poisoning. (Technically, if the foods have just reached refrigeration temperature, they are still safe to refreeze. But the problem is, how can we know for sure what their temperature is, and how long it has held at an acceptable level? We can't.)

If the foods are still icy—see below—they may still be safe.

Remember, however, that defrosted low-acid foods, vegetables, shellfish and precooked dishes all may be spoiled although they have no telltale odor, and could be downright dangerous if cooked up and served.

WHAT CAN BE SAFELY REFROZEN

The first check of thawed food in a package or a non-rigid container is to squeeze it. *Don't open it.* Squeeze it: if you can feel good, firm crystals inside, the package is O.K. to refreeze—provided that the food is *not highly perishable in the first place,* and of course that its quality is appealing.

Of course food in rigid containers must be opened to be inspected for adequate ice crystals.

Even though they're defrosted, strong-acid fruits may be refrozen if they're still cold; there will be definite loss in quality, however.

Refreeze thawed vegetables only if they contain plenty of ice crystals.

Give wrapped meat packages the squeeze test. Beef, pork, veal, lamb and poultry that are firm with ice crystals may be refrozen, but you can always cook them up in convenience dishes and freeze them from scratch. The salt in merely thawed short-storage cured pork helps the ice crystals, and it can be refrozen, but with a noticeable loss in quality. Thawed seafoods, being extremely perishable, should be cooked and served instead of being refrozen, because they lose quality so quickly.

Never refreeze melted ice cream. Never refreeze cream pies, eclairs, or similar foods. But you can refreeze unfrosted cakes, uncooked fruit pies, bread, rolls, etc.

FREEZER–PACKAGING MATERIALS

There is no simple definition we can give homemakers that will enable them to recognize whether the wrappings and bags and rigid containers are truly moisture/vapor-proof or moisture/vapor-resistant. But although a manufacturer might not say on the label that his product is *not* for the freezer, he surely will announce, loud and clear, that it *is* "ideal for freezing."

The prime purpose of freezer packaging is to keep frozen food from drying out ("freezer-burning"), and to preserve nutritive value, flavor, texture and color. To do this, packaging should be moisture/vapor-*proof*—or at least *-resistant*—and be easy to seal. And the seal should do its own job too.

And Don't Be Sad If. . .

Don't expect perfect results from all your work if you package the food for your freezer in household waxed paper or regular aluminum foil or wrappings that are intended for short-term storage in the refrigerator.

And don't expect perfect results if you make-do with those coated-paper cartons that cottage cheese or milk or ice cream came from the store in.

And don't expect perfect results if you seal your good food with the sticky tape you use on Christmas parcels. The adhesive used on made-for-the-freezer tape remains effective at temperatures way below Zero Fahrenheit/−18 C—and the stuff on regular household tapes does not.

Rigid Containers

As the name implies, these hold their shape and may be stood upright, and are suitable for all foods except those with irregular shape (a whole chicken, say); and they are the best packaging for liquids.

Made of aluminum, glass, plastic, or plastic-coated cardboard, these boxes, tubs, jars and pans come fitted with tight-sealing covers. If the rims and lids remain smooth they often may be re-used; however, the aluminum ones have a tendency to bend as the packages are opened.

A leading maker of home-canning jars has come out with a very sturdy plastic freezer box which, with proper care, stands re-use remarkably well.

Some modern glass canning jars may also be used for freezing most fruits and vegetables. The wide-top jars with tapered sides are advised for liquid packs: the contents will slide out easily without having to be fully defrosted.

Importance of "Food Grade"

In Chapter 4 there is a section called "Those Space-age Plastics," and it's about whether certain chemicals in plastic materials are proven to be acceptable for use with food. The operative words here are "proven" and "acceptable," because the U.S. Food and Drug Administration must be satisfied that proper testing qualifies products to be designated as *food grade* before the agency accepts them as safe for contact with food. Sometimes a product contains some chemical that has not met the criteria for such acceptance, so the FDA forbids the maker to market it as food grade. Often—as with some giants of the petrochemical industry—the maker has never intended to market such products as suitable for use with food. Rather, it is members of the general public who think anything plastic for use in the home is O.K. to store food in (like using a small wastebasket liner to wrap a roast for the freezer—which is *not* good).

Non–Rigid Containers

Non-rigid containers are the moisture/vapor-resistant bags and sheet materials used for Dry pack fruits and vegetables, meats and poultry, fish, and sometimes liquids. They are made of cellophane, heavy aluminum foil, plio-film, polyethylene or laminates of paper, metal foil, glassine, cellophane and rubber latex.

The best ways of using sheet wrapping are the *butcher wrap* and the *drugstore fold*—both shown in the "Freezing Roasts" subsection of Chapter 14.

Usually food in bags, and sometimes sheet-wrapped foods, are stored in a cardboard carton (re-usable) for protection and easier stacking in the freezer.

And then there are the so-called "cook-in" or "boil-in" pouches or bags, which are not as readily available as the regular non-boilable ones. Made of a tougher plastic to withstand hard boiling for up to 30 minutes, they are a good deal more expensive than conventional freezer bags; in addition, they come only in relatively small sizes. Also, because they're too stiff to twist and tie tight like the regular bags, they must be heat-sealed with a special appliance. Cook-in-pouch foods are described at the end of Chapter 16, "Freezing Eggs, Dairy and Convenience Foods."

Coming on the market around 1980 was a self-locking heavyweight plastic freezer bag in two sizes, the larger one being 1 quart. The "lock" occurs when a tongue-in-groove formation near the edge of the lips is pressed together. The bags are a good deal more expensive than thinner ones that seal with a twist-tie.

Sealing and Labeling

The packaging is no better than the sealing that closes it.

SEALING RIGID CONTAINERS

Some rigid freezing containers are automatically sealed by their lids, or by screw-type bands, or by flanged snap-on plastic covers.

Then there's the waxed-cardboard freezer box with a tuck-in top that is sealed tight shut with freezer tape. If the contents are already sealed in an inner bag, though, you don't have to seal the box top.

There is also the re-usable container like a coffee can with an extra plastic lid: for your seal, tape the lid to the can all around.

The lids for glass jars must have an attached rubber-composition ring or a separate rubber ring to make a seal.

The lids for cans are put on with their own special sealing machine, as effectively for the freezer as for the Pressure Canner.

SEALING NON–RIGID CONTAINERS

Freezing bags are best sealed by twisting and folding the top, and fastening them with string, a rubber band, or a strip of coated wire.

Heat-sealing is possible—but it's tricky unless you have the special equipment for doing it. (Again, see Chapter 16.)

Non-rigid sheet wrappings sometimes can be heat-sealed, but people more often seal all the edges with freezer tape.

Labeling

Use a wide, indelible marking pen to label each package with the name of the contents, the amount, and the date packaged.

Maximum Freezer Storage for Best Quality Maintained at Zero Fahrenheit/(–18 Celsius)

Food	Months at 0°F.	Food	Months at 0°F.
Fruits		*Fish and Shellfish*	
Apricots	12	Fatty Fish (Mackerel, Salmon, Swordfish, etc.)	3
Peaches	12		
Raspberries	12	Lean fish (Haddock, Cod, Flounder, Trout, etc.)	6
Strawberries	12		
Vegetables		Lobster, Crabs	2
Asparagus	8 to 12	Shrimp	6
Beans, green	8 to 12	Oysters	3 to 4
Beans, Lima	12	Scallops	3 to 4
Broccoli	12	Clams	3 to 4
Cauliflower	12	*Bakery Goods (Precooked)*	
Corn on the cob	8 to 10	Bread:	
Corn, cut	12	Quick	2 to 4
Carrots	12	Yeast	6 to 12
Mushrooms	8 to 10	Rolls	2 to 4
Peas	12	Cakes:	
Spinach	12	Angel	4 to 6
Squash	12	Gingerbread	4 to 6
Meats		Sponge	4 to 6
Beef:		Chiffon	4 to 6
Roasts, Steaks	12	Cheese	4 to 6
Ground	8	Fruit	12
Cubed, Pies	10 to 12	Cookies	4 to 6
Veal:		Pies:	
Roasts, Chops	10 to 12	Fruit	12
Cutlets, Cubes	8 to 10	Mince	4 to 8
Lamb:		Chiffon	1
Roasts, Chops	12	Pumpkin	1
Pork:		*Other Precooked Foods*	
Roasts, Chops	6 to 8	Combination dishes (Stews, Casseroles, etc.)	4 to 8
Ground, Sausage	4		
Pork or Ham, smoked	5 to 7	Potatoes:	
Bacon	3	French-fried	4 to 8
Variety meats (Liver, Kidneys, Brains, etc.)	Up to 4	Scalloped	1
		Soups	4 to 6
Poultry	6 to 12	Sandwiches	2

12

FREEZING FRUITS

With families increasingly concerned about good nutrition—and surely about the need to cut down drastically on our national per capita consumption of sugar—fruits frozen at home will grow ever more popular as staple desserts in themselves. Not that midwinter strawberry shortcakes or peach pies or berry cobblers will be forgotten: just that a greater variety of fruits will be served in their own juices, and a compôte of frozen fresh fruit will be considered the perfect ending to a party dinner.

GENERAL PREPARATION

Use only perfect fruit, and treat it with respect. You've invested a good deal of money in a freezer, your packaging materials cost a bit if they're good quality food grade re-usable containers; add your time, your freezer's portion of the monthly bill for electricity, and all these items require that your raw materials be top quality to start with.

Handle only a small quantity at a time—2 or 3 quarts. A good way to wash fruits: Put them in a wire basket and dunk it up and down several times in deep, cold water. After peeling, trimming, pitting and such, fix fruits much as you would for serving. Cut large fruits to convenient size, or crush. Small ones, such as berries, usually are left whole, or just crushed.

Crush soft fruits with a wire potato masher or pastry blender, firm ones in a food chopper. To make purée, press fruits through a colander, food mill or strainer. (Blenders can liquify too much; food processors liquify even more unless you're careful—the directions for your processor are reliable here.)

Headroom for Fruits

If you use rigid containers—as against bags alone or inside protective paper boxes—you must leave ample headroom so that the expansion of the food during freezing doesn't force off the closures.

The wide-top containers referred to are tall, with sides either straight or slightly flared. The narrow-top containers include canning jars, which may be used for freezing most fruits that are *not packed in liquid*.

TYPE OF PACK	WIDE-TOP CONTAINER		NARROW-TOP CONTAINER	
	PINT	QUART	PINT	QUART
Liquid pack:				
(Fruit in juice, sugar, syrup or water; or crushed or puréed)	½ inch	1 inch	¾ inch	1½ inches
Fruit juice	½ inch	1 inch	1½ inches	1½ inches
Dry pack:				
(Fruit packed without added sugar or liquid)	½ inch	½ inch	½ inch	½ inch

Relevant Metrics for Freezing Fruits

Full metric conversions, with the arithmetic for refining them, are given at the start of Chapter 17 ("Common Ingredients and How to Use Them"), but the following—rounded off—apply in this chapter.

• • •

Volume: ¼ teaspoon = 1.25 mL——½ teaspoon = 2.5 mL——1 teaspoon = 5 mL——1 tablespoon = 15 mL——⅓ cup = 80 mL——¼ cup = 60 mL——½ cup = 125 mL——1 cup = 250 mL.

Length: ½ inch = 1.27 cm——¾ inch = 1.9 cm——1 inch = 2.54 cm——1½ inches = 3.75 cm.

Press air out of bags, then twist and tie the tops.

Yields in Frozen Fruit

Since the legal weight of a bushel of fruits differs between States, the weights given below are average; the yields are approximate.

FRUITS	FRESH	PINTS FROZEN
Apples	1 bu (48 lbs)	32–40
	2½–3 lbs	2
Applesauce	1 bu (48 lbs)	30–36
	2½–3½ lbs	2
Apricots	1 bu (50 lbs)	60–72
	2–2½ lbs	2–3
Berries (excluding strawberries)	24-qt crate	32–36
	5–8 cups	2
Cherries, as picked	1 bu (56 lbs)	36–44
	2–2½ lbs	2
Cranberries	1 peck (8 lbs)	16
Figs	2–2½ lbs	2
Grapes	28-lb lug	14–16
	4 lbs	2
Grapefruit	4–6 fruit	2
Nectarines	18-lb flat	12–18
	2–3 lbs	2
Peaches	1 bu (48 lbs)	32–48
	2–2½ lbs	2
Pears	1 bu (50 lbs)	40–50
	2–2½ lbs	2
Pineapple	2 average	2
	5 lbs	4
Plums and Prunes	1 bu (56 lbs)	38–56
	2–2½ lbs	2
Rhubarb	15 lbs	15–22
	2 lbs	2
Strawberries	24-qt crate	38
	6–8 cups	2

To Prevent Darkening

Apples, apricots, peaches, nectarines, pears and other oxidizing foods are kept from darkening by the addition of ascorbic acid (Vitamin C) either crystalline or tablets; commercial mixtures with an ascorbic acid base; crystalline citric acid, or plain lemon juice. Or steam-blanching for 3 to 5 minutes, depending on size of the pieces, may be used (see the directions for blanching Mushrooms in Chapter 13, "Freezing Vegetables").

Fruit has a tendency to float to the top, where it changes color when exposed to the trapped air; so crumple some moisture-resistant food-grade sheet wrapping and put it on the top of the packaged fruit to hold it below the syrup. Seal and freeze.

ASCORBIC ACID, CRYSTALLINE

Usually available from drugstores, or from some freezer-locker plants. If bought in ounces, figure that 1 ounce will give roughly 40 ¼-teaspoons or 20 b½-teaspoons (these being the most common amounts called for in freezing). Less expensive are Vitamin C tablets of 500 or 1000 mg; more on these later.

There is no record of known undesirable side effects from using ascorbic acid to hold the color of processed foods. It is Vitamin C. (There's more about it in Chapter 17, "Common Ingredients and How to Use Them," and in Chapter 21, "Drying.")

It is the most effective of the agents employed in freezing to prevent darkening, because it will not change the flavor of the food, as the larger amounts needed of citric acid or lemon juice will do.

It dissolves easily in cold water or juices. Figure how much you'll need for one session at a time (see individual instructions), and prepare enough.

For wet pack with syrup. Add dissolved ascorbic acid to cold syrup and stir.

For wet pack with sugar. Just before packing, sprinkle the needed amount of ascorbic acid—dissolved in 2 or 3 tablespoons of cold water—over the fruit before you add the sugar.

For wet pack in crushed fruits and purées. Add dissolved ascorbic acid to the prepared fruit; stir well.

In fruit juices. Add dry ascorbic acid to the juice and stir to dissolve.

In dry pack (no sugar). Just before packing, sprinkle dissolved ascorbic acid over the fruit; mix gently but thoroughly to coat each piece.

ASCORBIC ACID TABLETS

It takes 3,000 milligrams (mg) worth of ascorbic acid to equal 1 teaspoon of the crystalline form. Crush the tablets and dissolve in a little water.

COMMERCIAL ASCORBIC ACID MIXTURES

These mixtures of crystalline ascorbic acid and sugar—or ascorbic acid, sugar and citric acid—are sold under trade names. They are not quite as effective, volume for volume, as plain ascorbic acid, but are readily available and easy to use. Follow the manufacturer's instructions.

CITRIC ACID

Drugstores carry citric acid in pure crystalline form—but again, it is expensive bought this way. National and ethnic grocery stores (and what treasures they offer!) sell it in bulk, chunked like chopped nuts, as "sour salt" for kosher cooking, or as "lemon salt" for Greek cooking. See Chapter 17, "Acids to Add," and "Anti-discoloration Treatments."

You need three times more of this than ascorbic acid to help prevent discoloration.

Dissolve the required amount in 2 or 3 tablespoons of cold water. Following directions for the individual fruits, add it as for dissolved ascorbic acid, above.

LEMON JUICE

A long-time favorite, it contains both citric and ascorbic acids. An equal amount of crystalline ascorbic acid is six times more effective than lemon juice—which also imparts its own flavor to the food.

STEAMING

Steaming in a single layer over boiling water is enough to retard darkening in some fruits (for example, apples). The treatments described above are easier, though.

> • • IMPORTANT NOTE ABOUT SUGAR: It is too cumbersome to indicate in every individual instance later on that sweetening with sugar—or with any other natural or non-nutritive sweetener—is OPTIONAL. But it is. The amounts and types of sweet syrups and sugar are intended as maximum indications only, and are given for the use of people who are used to added sweetening for a special purpose, and want to include it in the pack. Alternatives to sugar are discussed in detail in Chapter 17, "Common Ingredients, etc."

THE VARIOUS PACKS

A few fruits freeze well without sweetening, but most have a better texture and flavor when packed in sugar or a sugar syrup.

Unlike *canning* fruits, the size and texture influence the form in which you pack them for freezing. The intended future use is your final deciding factor.

Fruit to freeze whole, in pieces, juiced, crushed or puréed, is packed Dry or Wet.

DRY PACK (ALWAYS SUGARLESS)

The simplest way is just to put whole or cut-up firm fruits in containers (do not add a thing), seal and freeze. This is especially good for blueberries, cranberries, currants, figs, gooseberries and rhubarb.

If you have the space, spread raspberries, blueberries, currants or other similar berries one layer deep on a tray or cookie sheet and set in the freezer. When berries are frozen hard, pour them into polyethylene bags and seal. They won't stick together. Later the bag may be opened; the needed amount taken out, the bag reclosed and returned to the freezer.

Versatile Dry pack lets you use the fruits as if they were fresh.

WET PACKS

This means adding some liquid—such as its own natural juice, sugar syrup, crushed fruit, or water.

Wet pack with sugar. Plain sugar is sprinkled over and gently mixed with the prepared fruit until juice is drawn out and sugar is dissolved. Then you pack and freeze. Fruit fixed this way is especially good for cooked dishes and fruit cocktails. This has less liquid than the Wet pack with Syrup.

Wet pack with syrup. Fruit, whole or in pieces, is packed in containers and covered with cold sugar syrup to improve their flavor and make a delightful sauce around the fruit. Generally best for dessert dishes.

Plan on using ⅓ to ½ cup of syrup for each pint package of fruit.

A 40 Percent Syrup (see "Sugar Syrups for Freezing Fruit") is used for most fruits, but to keep the delicate flavor of the milder ones, use a thinner syrup. A 50 to 60 Percent Syrup is best for sour fruits such as pie cherries.

Wet pack with fruit juice. The fruit—whole, crushed, or in pieces—is packed in the container and covered with juice extracted from good parts of less perfect fruit, and treated with ascorbic acid to prevent darkening. Pack with a piece of crumpled moisture-resistant sheet wrapping on top to hold fruit below the liquid. Seal and freeze. People on sugar-restricted diets can enjoy this unsweetened fruit. Or artificial sweeteners may be added at serving time: see "Sweeteners" in Chapter 17.

Sugar Syrups for Freezing Fruits

DESIGNATION	SUGAR	WATER	YIELD
30 percent (thin)	2 cups	4 cups	5 cups
35 percent	2½ cups	4 cups	5⅓ cups
40 percent (medium)	3 cups	4 cups	5½ cups
50 percent	4¾ cups	4 cups	6½ cups
60 percent (very heavy)	7 cups	4 cups	7¾ cups
65 percent	8¾ cups	4 cups	8⅔ cups

Dissolve the sugar thoroughly in cold or hot water (if hot, chill it thoroughly before packing). Syrup can be made the day before and stored in the refrigerator: it must be kept quite cold.

Roughly, estimate ½ to ⅔ cup of syrup for each pint container of fruit.

Substitutions: Generally, ¼ of the sugar may be replaced by light corn syrup without affecting the flavor of the fruit; indeed, the additional blandness is often desirable for delicately flavored fruits, and some cooks prefer substituting even more corn syrup.

Honey or maple syrup may also replace ¼ of the sugar—if the family likes the different flavor either imparts. Brown sugar of course affects the color and, to some degree, the flavor.

For general use, sugar may be dissolved in the juice in the same proportion used in making a sugar syrup suitable for the particular fruit.

A greater degree of natural flavor is kept in the Juice pack, either sweetened or unsweetened, than in the Syrup pack.

Wet pack, purée. Fruit is puréed by forcing it through a food mill, strainer or colander. Dissolved ascorbic acid or lemon juice is mixed with the purée before packing to prevent darkening. Sweetening may or may not be added.

Wet pack with water. This is similar to the Juice and Syrup packs, except that the added liquid is cold water in which ascorbic acid has been dissolved. The flavor is not as satisfactory as it is in Juice or Syrup packs.

Apples

Apples, more so than most produce, store well by several methods: fresh in a root cellar, or dried, or as canned applesauce or dessert slices (all q.v.). But you may want to freeze a few for late-season cooked dishes—especially in a package shaped for a pie.

SLICES

Prepare. Peel, core and slice. As you go, treat against darkening by coating the slices with ½ teaspoon pure ascorbic acid dissolved in each 3 tablespoons of cold water. Or steam-blanch. Less satisfactory but easier: drop slices in a solution of 2 tablespoons salt to each 1 gallon of water (no vinegar) for no longer than 20 minutes; rinse well and drain before packing.

Dry pack, no sugar (for pies). Arrange in a pie plate as for a pie, slip the filled plate into a plastic bag and freeze. Remove the solid chunk of slices from the plate as soon as frozen and overwrap it tightly in moisture-vapor-proof material—as if it were a piece of meat (q.v.)—and return to the freezer. (Handy at pie-making time because you lay the pie-shaped chunk of slices right in your pastry, put on the sugar and seasonings, top with a crust and bake.)

Wet pack, sugar. Sprinkle ¼ cup sugar over each 1 quart of slices for pie-making. Leave appropriate headroom.

Seal; freeze.

Wet pack, syrup. Cover with 40 Percent Syrup for use in fruit cocktail or serving uncooked. Leave appropriate headroom.

Seal; freeze.

SAUCE

Prepare. Make applesauce as you like it—strained, chunky, sweetened or unsweetened.

Wet pack, puréed. Fill containers. Leave ½ inch of headroom.

Seal; freeze.

Apricots

HALVES AND SLICES

Prepare. If apricots do not need peeling, heat them for 30 seconds in boiling water to keep their skins from toughening. Cool immediately in cold water. Cut up as you like.

Wet pack, syrup. Pack in container, cover with 40 Percent Syrup to which has been added ¾ teaspoon ascorbic acid to each 1 quart of syrup. Leave appropriate headroom.

Seal; freeze.

Wet pack, sugar. Sprinkle ¼ teaspoon ascorbic acid dissolved in ¼ cup water over each 1 quart of apricots. Mix ½ cup of sugar with each 1 quart of fruit, stir until sugar dissolves. Pack in containers with appropriate headroom.

Seal; freeze.

CRUSHED OR PURÉED

Prepare. Wash and treat skins as for whole fruit. Crush or put through a sieve or food mill.

Wet pack, sugar. Mix 1 cup sugar with each 1 quart of crushed or sieved fruit. Add anti-darkening agent. Pack, leaving ½ inch of headroom.

Seal; freeze.

Avocados

Most versatile if frozen plain but with some anti-discoloration protection. Sweetening for milk shakes or ice cream, etc., may be added when you make them up. And for Guacamole, the further seasonings—minced onion, tomatoes, peppers, etc.—are also better added shortly before serving this delicious dip/spread.

Prepare. Peel and mash. If intended for future sweet dishes, add ⅛ teaspoon crystalline ascorbic acid to each 1 quart of purée to prevent darkening. If for Guacamole, add 1 tablespoon lemon juice (anti-darkening plus flavoring) and a dash of salt for each 2 avocados as you mash them.

Wet pack, puréed. Leave ½ inch of headroom.

Seal; freeze.

Most Soft Berries

WHOLE

Prepare. Sort, wash gently and drain: blackberries, boysenberries, dewberries, loganberries, youngberries.

Dry pack, no sugar. Pack in containers, leaving ½ inch of headroom. Or see the alternate Dry method in "The Various Packs."

Seal; freeze.

Wet pack, syrup. (For berries to be served uncooked.) Pack and cover with 40 to 50 Percent Syrup. Leave ½ inch of headroom.

Seal; freeze.

Wet pack, sugar. (For berries to be used in cooked dishes.) In a bowl mix ¾ cup sugar with each 1 quart of berries. Mix until sugar dissolves. Pack; leave ½ inch of headroom.

Seal; freeze.

CRUSHED OR PURÉED

Wet pack, puréed. Add 1 cup sugar to each 1 quart crushed or puréed berries. Mix well. Pack; leave ½ inch of headroom.

Seal; freeze.

Most Firm Berries

Prepare. Sort and wash blueberries, elderberries, huckleberries. Optional: steam berries for 1 minute to tenderize skins.

WHOLE

Dry pack, no sugar. (For berries to be used in cooked dishes.) Pack; leave ½ inch of headroom.

Seal; freeze.

Wet pack, syrup. (For berries to be served uncooked.) Pack; cover with 40 Percent Syrup, leaving ½ inch of headroom.

Seal; freeze.

CRUSHED OR PURÉED

Wet pack, puréed. Add 1 to 1½ cups sugar to each 1 quart of crushed or puréed berries; stir to dissolve. Leave appropriate headroom.

Seal; freeze.

Cranberries

WHOLE

Prepare. Wash and drain.

Dry pack, no sugar. Fill containers with clean berries. Leave ½ inch of headroom.

Seal; freeze.

Wet pack, syrup. Cover with 50 Percent Syrup. Leave appropriate headroom.

Seal; freeze.

PURÉED

Prepare. Wash and drain berries. Add 2 cups water to each 1 quart (1 pound) berries and boil until skins burst. Press through a sieve and add 2 cups sugar to each 1 quart purée. Mix.

Wet pack, puréed. Pack; leave appropriate headroom.

Seal; freeze.

Currants

Prepare. Wash; remove stems.

WHOLE

Dry pack, no sugar. Treat like Cranberries.

Seal; freeze.

Wet pack, sugar. Add ¾ cup sugar to each 1 quart of fruit; stir gently to dissolve. Pack; leave appropriate headroom.

Seal; freeze.

Wet pack, syrup. Treat like Cranberries.

Seal; freeze.

CRUSHED

Wet pack, crushed. Add 1⅛ cups sugar to each 1 quart crushed currants; stir to dissolve sugar. Pack; leave appropriate headroom.

Seal; freeze.

JUICE

For beverages, use ripe currants. For future jellies, mix in some slightly underripe currants for added pectin.

Prepare. Crush currants and warm to 165 F/74 C over low heat. Drain through a jelly bag. Cool.

Wet pack, juice. Sweeten with ¾ to 1 cup sugar to each 1 quart of juice, or pack unsweetened. Leave appropriate headroom.

Seal; freeze.

Gooseberries

Prepare. Wash; remove stems and tails.

Dry pack, no sugar. (Best for future pies and preserves.) Pack whole berries; leave ½ inch of headroom.

Seal; freeze.

Wet pack, syrup. Cover whole berries with 50 Percent Syrup. Leave appropriate headroom.

Seal; freeze.

Raspberries

The versatile and very tender raspberries freeze even better than strawberries do. The wild ones, though small, have fine flavor. Real seedy berries are best used in purée or as juice.

WHOLE

Prepare. Sort; wash very carefully in cold water and drain thoroughly.

Dry pack, no sugar. Fill containers gently, leaving ½ inch of headroom.

Seal; freeze.

Wet pack, sugar. In a shallow pan, carefully mix ¾ cup sugar with each 1 quart of berries so as to avoid crushing. Pack; leave ½ inch of headroom.

Seal; freeze.

Wet pack, syrup. Cover with 40 Percent Syrup. Leave appropriate headroom.

Seal; freeze.

CRUSHED OR PURÉED

Prepare. Crush or sieve washed berries.

Wet pack, juice. Add ¾ to 1 cup sugar to each 1 quart of berry pulp; mix to dissolve sugar. Pack; leave appropriate headroom.

Seal; freeze.

JUICE

Prepare. Select fully ripe raspberries. Crush and slightly heat berries to start juice flowing. Strain through a jelly bag.

Wet pack, juice. For beverage, sweeten with ½ to 1 cup sugar to each 1 quart of juice. (For future jelly, do not sweeten.) Pour into containers; leave appropriate headroom.

Seal; freeze.

Strawberries

Choose slightly tart firm berries with solid red centers. Plan to slice or crush the very large ones. Sweetened strawberries hold better than unsweetened.

WHOLE

Prepare. Sort; wash in cold water; drain. Remove hulls.

Wet pack, sugar. In a shallow pan, add ¾ cup sugar to each 1 quart of berries and mix thoroughly. Pack; leave ½ inch of headroom.

Seal; freeze.

Wet pack, syrup. Cover berries with cold 50 Percent Syrup. Leave appropriate headroom.

Seal; freeze.

Wet pack, water (unsweetened). To protect the color of the berries, cover them with water in which 1 teaspoon crystalline ascorbic acid to each 1 quart of water has been dissolved. Leave appropriate headroom.

Seal; freeze.

SLICED OR CRUSHED

Prepare. Wash and hull as for whole berries, then slice or crush partially or completely.

Wet pack, sugar. Add ¾ cup sugar to each 1 quart of berries in a shallow pan. Mix thoroughly. Pack; leave appropriate headroom.

Seal; freeze.

JUICE

Prepare. Crush berries; drain juice through a jelly bag.

Wet pack, juice. Add ⅔ to 1 cup sugar to each 1 quart of juice—or omit sugar if you wish. Pour into containers; leave appropriate headroom.

Seal; freeze.

Cherries, Sour (for Pie)

As pie timber these are better canned; but if you want to freeze them, here's how.

WHOLE

Prepare. Use only tree-ripened cherries. Stem, wash, drain and pit. (The rounded end of a clean paper clip makes a good cherry-pitter.)

Wet pack, sugar. Add ¾ cup sugar to 1 quart of pitted cherries; stir until dissolved. Pack, leaving appropriate headroom.

Seal; freeze.

Wet pack, syrup. Cover pitted cherries with cold 60 to 65 Percent Syrup. Leave appropriate headroom.

Seal; freeze.

CRUSHED

Wet pack, juice. Add 1 to 1½ cups sugar to each 1 quart of crushed cherries. Mix well. Pack; leave appropriate headroom.

Seal; freeze.

PURÉED

Wet pack, juice. Crush cherries; heat just to boiling and press through a sieve or food mill. Add ¾ cup sugar to each 1 quart of purée. Pack; leave appropriate headroom.

Seal; freeze.

JUICE

Home-made cherry juice in a party punch makes it exceptional!

Wet pack, juice. Crush cherries, heat slightly (*do not boil*) to start juice flowing. Strain through a jelly bag. Add 1½ to 2 cups sugar to each 1 quart of juice; or pack unsweetened. Pour into containers; leave appropriate headroom.

Seal; freeze.

Cherries, Sweet

The dark and "black" varieties are best for freezing—but do handle them quickly to prevent color and flavor changes. Use only tree-ripened fruit and remove the pits: they give an almond flavor to cherries when frozen.

Whole

Wet pack, syrup. Cover pitted cherries with 40 Percent Syrup in which you've dissolved ½ teaspoon crystalline ascorbic acid to each 1 quart of syrup. Leave appropriate headroom.

Seal; freeze.

Crushed

Wet pack, juice. To each 1 quart of crushed cherries add 1½ cups sugar and ¼ teaspoon crystalline ascorbic acid; mix well. Pack; leave appropriate headroom.

Seal; freeze.

Juice

Sweet red cherries and sweet white cherries are handled differently for juice.

Prepare. Heat sweet *red* cherries slightly (to 165 F/74 C) to start the juice. Strain through a jelly bag.
  Crush sweet *white* cherries *without heating.* Strain through a jelly bag. Then warm this juice in a double boiler or over low heat to 165 F/74 C. Cool the red or white juice and let it stand covered overnight.

Wet pack, juice. Pour off the clear juice into containers, being careful not to include any sediment from the bottom of the kettle. Add 1 cup sugar to each 1 quart of juice; or leave unsweetened if you prefer. Leave appropriate headroom.

Seal; freeze. (Sweet cherry juice by itself is pretty blah. So mix some *sour* cherry juice with the sweet to make a better beverage.)

Coconut

If you have a windfall, freeze some simply for fun—you may want to have a Mainland luau!

Prepare. Puncture the "eye" of the coconut; drain out and save the milk. Remove the meat from the broken-open shell. Shred it, or put it through a food chopper.

Wet pack, juice. Cover shredded meat with coconut milk. Leave appropriate headroom.

Seal; freeze.

Dates

Prepare. Wash, if necessary, and dry on paper toweling; remove pits.

Dry pack, no sugar. Pack in containers with no headroom.

Seal; freeze.

Figs

WHOLE OR SLICED

Prepare. Only tree-ripened, soft-ripe fruit, please; and check a sample for good flavor clear through the flesh. Sort, wash and cut off stems. Peeling is optional.

Dry pack, no sugar. Fill containers with the prepared figs; leave appropriate headroom.

Seal; freeze.

Wet pack, syrup. Cover with 35 Percent Syrup to which you have added ¾ teaspoon crystalline ascorbic acid—or ½ cup lemon juice—to each 1 quart of syrup.

Seal; freeze.

Wet pack, water. Pack figs; cover with water to which you have added ¾ teaspoon crystalline ascorbic acid to each 1 quart of water. Leave appropriate headroom.

Seal; freeze.

CRUSHED

Wet pack, juice. Crush prepared figs. Mix ⅔ cup sugar and ¼ teaspoon crystalline ascorbic acid with each 1 quart of crushed fruit. Leave appropriate headroom.

Seal; freeze.

Fruit Cocktail (or Compôte)

Freezing is excellent for your favorite combinations of fruit to serve either as an appetizer or dessert. A few added blueberries or dark sweet cherries make a nice color contrast.

Prepare. Use any combination of fruits peeled, cored, etc., and cut to suitable size.

Wet pack, syrup. Pack. Cover with cold 30 to 40 Percent Syrup in which ¾ teaspoon crystalline ascorbic acid to each 1 quart of syrup has been dissolved. If cut-up oranges are in the mixture, the ascorbic acid may be omitted. Leave appropriate headroom.

Seal; freeze.

Grapefruit (and Oranges)

Commercial processors do a fine job with citrus fruits. It's hardly worthwhile to compete unless you've a surplus of grapefruit and/or oranges.
Use heavy, blemish-free, tree-ripened fruits.

SECTIONS OR SLICES

Prepare. Wash; peel, cutting off the outside membranes. Cut a thin slice from each end. With a sharp, thin-bladed knife, cut down each side of the membranes and lift out the whole sections. Work over a large bowl to catch the juice. Remove seeds. Oranges may be sliced.

Wet pack, syrup. Cover fruit with 40 Percent Syrup made with excess fruit juice, and water if needed. (For better quality, add ½ teaspoon crystalline ascorbic acid to each 1 quart of syrup before packing.) Leave appropriate headroom.

Seal; freeze.

JUICE

Prepare. Use good tree-ripened fruits. Squeeze, using a squeezer that does not press oil from the rind.

Wet pack, juice. Either sweetened with 2 tablespoons sugar to each 1 quart of juice, or pack unsweetened. (For best quality, add ¾ teaspoon crystalline ascorbic acid to each 1 gallon of juice before packing.) Pour into glass freezing jars. Leave appropriate headroom.

Seal; freeze.

Grapes

Canning is probably smarter for these—but you may want to freeze some for gelatine salads and desserts. Juice is likely to be the best frozen use of grapes.

WHOLE OR HALVES

Prepare. Use firm-ripe grapes with tender skins and nice color and flavor. Wash and stem. Leave seedless grapes whole; cut other varieties in half and remove their seeds.

Dry pack, no sugar. Leave appropriate headroom.

Seal; freeze.

Wet pack, syrup. Cover grapes with cold 40 Percent Syrup. Leave appropriate headroom.

Seal; freeze.

JUICE

For a beverage or future jelly-making, use firm-ripe grapes.

Prepare. Wash, stem, crush. Do *not* heat. Strain through a jelly bag. Allow juice to stand overnight in the refrigerator while sediment settles to the bottom. Carefully pour off the clear juice.

Wet pack, juice. Pour into containers; leave appropriate headroom.

Seal; freeze.

(If tartrate crystals—the basis for cream of tartar—form in frozen juice, strain them out after the juice thaws.)

Melons

SLICES, CUBES OR BALLS

Prepare. Cut firm-ripe melons in half; remove seeds and soft tissues holding them. If for slices or cubes, cut off all rind; cut to shape. If for balls, do not cut off rind, but scoop out with a baller, taking care not to include any rind.

Wet pack, syrup. Cover with 30 Percent Syrup. Leave appropriate headroom.

Seal; freeze.

CRUSHED (NOT FOR WATERMELON)

Prepare. Halve, cut off rind; remove seeds and their soft tissue. Crush or put through the food chopper, using a coarse knife.

Wet pack, juice. Add 1 tablespoon sugar to each 1 quart of crushed melon, if you wish (and an added 1 teaspoon lemon juice points up the flavor). Stir to dissolve. Pack; leave appropriate headroom.

Seal; freeze.

Nectarines

These are not as satisfactory frozen as most other fruits are.

HALVES, QUARTERS OR SLICES

Choose only firm, fully ripe nectarines—avoiding overripe ones, which often develop a disagreeable flavor in the freezer.

Prepare. Wash and pit. Peeling is optional.

Wet pack, syrup. Put ½ cup of 40 Percent Syrup in each container and cut fruit directly into it. (For a better product add ½ teaspoon crystalline ascor-

Crumpled wrap keeps peaches from floating up to the headroom and darkening.

bic acid to each 1 quart of syrup before packing.) Gently press fruit down and add extra syrup to cover. Top with crumpled moisture-resistant wrap to hold fruit in place. Leave appropriate headroom.

Seal; freeze.

PURÉED

Treat like Peach Purée.

Peaches

Peaches are excellent canned; they freeze well.

HALVES AND SLICES

Prepare. Use firm, ripe peaches without any green color on their skins. Wash, pit, and peel. (They are less ragged if peeled without the boiling-water dip.)

Wet pack, sugar. Coat cut peaches with a solution of ¼ teaspoon crystalline ascorbic acid dissolved in each ¼ cup of water to prevent darkening. Add ⅔ cup of sugar to each 1 quart of fruit, and mix gently. Pack, leaving appropriate headroom.

Wet pack, syrup. Put ½ cup 40 Percent Syrup in the bottom of each container. Cut peaches directly into it. (For better product add ½ teaspoon crystalline ascorbic acid to each 1 quart of the syrup before packing.) Gently press fruit down and add extra syrup to cover. Top with crumpled moisture-resistant wrap to hold fruit in place. Leave appropriate headroom.

Seal; freeze.

Wet pack, water. Cover cut peaches with water in which 1 teaspoon crystalline ascorbic acid has been dissolved in each 1 quart of water. Leave appropriate headroom.

Seal; freeze.

CRUSHED OR PURÉED

Prepare. Loosen skins by dipping peaches in boiling water for 30 to 60 seconds. Cool immediately in cold water; peel and pit.

Crush coarsely. For purée, press through a sieve or food mill; it's easier to make the purée if you heat the peaches in a very little water for 4 minutes before you sieve them.

Wet pack, juice. Mix 1 cup sugar and ⅛ teaspoon crystalline ascorbic acid with each 1 quart of peaches. Pack; leave appropriate headroom.

Seal; freeze.

Pears

Use Bartlett or a similar variety—not any of the so-called winter pears, which keep in cold storage (see "Root-Cellaring," Chapter 22).

HALVES OR QUARTERS

Prepare. Choose well-ripened pears, firm but not hard. Wash, cut in halves and quarters; core. Cover them with cold water to prevent their oxidizing during preparation (leaching is negligible because immersion time is so short).

Wet pack, syrup. Handling no more than 3 pints at a time in a deep-fry basket, lower cut-up pears into boiling 40 Percent Syrup for 1 to 2 minutes. Drain; cool. (Save the hot syrup for another load of fruit.) To pack, cover cooled pears with cold 40 Percent Syrup to which has been added ¾ teaspoon crystalline ascorbic acid to each 1 quart of syrup. Leave appropriate headroom.

Seal; freeze.

PURÉED

Prepare. Wash well-ripened pears that are not hard or gritty. Peeling is optional. Proceed as for Peach Purée.

Persimmons

PURÉED

Purée made from late-ripening native ones needs no sweetening, but nursery varieties may be packed with or without sugar.

Prepare. Choose orange-colored, soft-ripe persimmons. Sort, wash, peel and cut in sections. Press through a sieve or food mill. Mix ⅛ teaspoon crystalline ascorbic acid—or 1½ teaspoons crystalline citric acid—with each 1 quart of purée.

Wet pack, juice (unsweetened). Pack unsweetened purée. Leave appropriate headroom.

Seal; freeze.

Wet pack, juice (sweetened). Mix 1 cup sugar with each 1 quart of purée. Pack; leave appropriate headroom.

Seal; freeze.

Pineapple

Prepare. Use firm, ripe pineapple with full flavor and aroma. Pare, removing eyes, and core. Slice, dice, crush or cut in wedges or sticks.

Wet pack, syrup. Pack fruit tightly. Cover with 30 Percent Syrup made with pineapple juice, if available, or water. Leave appropriate headroom.

Seal; freeze.

Wet pack, juice (unsweetened). Pack fruit tightly without sugar: enough juice will squeeze out to fill the crevices. Leave appropriate headroom.

Seal; freeze.

Plums (and Prunes)

Frozen plums and prunes are good in pies and jams, salads and desserts. Use the unsweetened pack for future jams. To serve unsweetened whole plums raw, see below.

WHOLE, HALVES OR QUARTERS

Prepare. Choose tree-ripened fruit with deep color. Wash. Cut as desired. Leave pits in fruits you freeze whole.

Wet pack, syrup. Cover with cold 40 to 50 Percent Syrup in which is dissolved ½ teaspoon crystalline ascorbic acid to each 1 quart of syrup. Leave appropriate headroom.

Seal; freeze.

Wet pack, juice (unsweetened). Pack plums tightly. Leave appropriate headroom.

Seal; freeze. (To serve whole plums uncooked, dip them in cold water for 5 to 10 seconds; remove skins, and cover with 40 Percent Syrup to thaw. Serve in the syrup.)

PURÉED

Purée may be made from heated or unheated fruit, depending on its softness.

Prepare. Wash plums, cut in half and pit. *Unheated fruit:* press raw through a sieve or food mill. Add ¼ teaspoon crystalline ascorbic acid—or ½ teaspoon crystalline citric acid—to each 1 quart of purée. *Heated fruit* (the firm ones): add 1 cup water to each 4 quarts of plums; boil for 2 minutes; cool, and press through a sieve or food mill.

Wet pack, juice. Mix ½ to 1 cup sugar with each 1 quart of purée. Pack; leave appropriate headroom.

Seal; freeze.

JUICE

Prepare. Wash plums, simmer until soft in enough water barely to cover. Strain through a jelly bag and cool the juice.

Wet pack, juice. Add 1 to 2 cups sugar to each 1 quart of juice. Pour into containers; leave appropriate headroom.

Seal; freeze.

Rhubarb

Freeze only firm, young, well-colored stalks with good flavor and few fibers. (See also "Canning Fruits," Chapter 5.)

PIECES

Prepare. Wash, trim and cut in 1- to 2-inch pieces, or longer to fit the package. Heating rhubarb in boiling water for 1 minute and cooling immediately in cold water helps to set the color and flavor.

Dry pack, no sugar. Pack either raw or preheated (and now cold) rhubarb tightly in containers. Leave appropriate headroom.

Seal; freeze.

Wet pack, syrup. Pack either raw or preheated (and now cold) rhubarb tightly. Cover with cold 40 Percent Syrup. Leave appropriate headroom.

Seal; freeze.

PURÉED

Prepare. Prepare as pieces. Add 1 cup water to each 6 cups of rhubarb and boil 2 minutes. Cool immediately; press through a sieve or food mill.

Wet pack, juice. Add ⅔ cup sugar to each 1 quart of purée. Pack; leave appropriate headroom.

Seal; freeze.

JUICE

Prepare. Select as for pieces. Wash, trim, and cut in 4- or 5-inch lengths. Add 4 cups water to each 4 quarts of rhubarb, and bring just to a boil. Strain through a jelly bag.

Wet pack, juice. Pour into containers. Leave appropriate headroom.

Seal; freeze.

Tomatoes, see Chapter 13, "Freezing Vegetables"; also Chapter 6 for canning them.

13

FREEZING VEGETABLES

Vegetables could be regarded as the original—and usually the most satisfactory—frozen "convenience" foods. They are easy to prepare for the freezer; they do not need to accumulate to make a batch worth a long morning's work; and they generally retain more nutrients, color and texture than can be promised by any other method of putting food by.

With a very few exceptions, any vegetable that cans well freezes equally well at home, if not better. The exceptions at this writing (all raw) are whole tomatoes, greens for salads, white (Irish) potatoes and cabbage. Because they have a high water content, formation of ice crystals ruptures their flesh, and the result is loss of texture or shape when defrosted. The extremely low temperature now being used by some frozen-food companies bypasses the crystal stage in freezing, so commercially frozen white potatoes or whole tomatoes are infinitely superior than those done at home.

Certain vegetable varieties are better for freezing than others, so read your seed catalogs carefully to see which ones you'll have the most luck with. Or ask your County Agent for a listing in your area. Or a truck gardener can tell you (but sometimes the person tending his roadside stand can't).

Because of the investment in nutrition and money that freezing entails, you'll want to freeze only prime vegetables that are garden-fresh and tender-young (younger, usually, than for canning). If you can't freeze them the day they're picked, refrigerate them overnight.

GENERAL PREPARATION

The first step, after you've gathered your packaging, etc., is to wash the vegetables. Use cold water and lift the vegetables out of it to leave any grit in the bottom of the pan.

You may need to take a further step to draw out possible insects in broccoli, Brussels sprouts and cauliflower: simply soak them for ½ hour in a solution of 1

218

tablespoon salt to each 1 quart of cold water; insects will float to the surface, to be skimmed off and discarded. Wash vegetables again in fresh cold water to get rid of the salt.

Sort the vegetables according to size, or cut them to uniform pieces. Peel, trim and cut as needed.

Yields in Frozen Vegetables

Since the legal weight of a bushel of vegetables differs between States, the weights given below are average; the yields are approximate.

VEGETABLES	FRESH	PINTS FROZEN
Asparagus	1 bu (45 lbs)	8–11
	3–4 lbs	3–4
Beans, Lima, in pods	1 bu (32 lbs)	12–16
	4–5 lbs	2
Beans, snap/green/wax	1 bu (30 lbs)	30–45
	1½–2 lbs	2
Beets, without tops	1 bu (52 lbs)	35–42
	2½–3 lbs	2
Broccoli	25-lb crate	24
	2–3 lbs	2
Brussels sprouts	4 qts	6
	1 lb	1
Carrots, without tops	1 bu (50 lbs)	32–40
	2½–3 lbs	2
Cauliflower	2 medium heads	3
	1 bu (12 lbs)	8–12
Corn, in husks	1 bu (35 lbs)	14–17
	4–5 lbs	2
Eggplant	2 average	2
Kale	1 bu (18 lbs)	12–18
	2–3 lbs	2
Okra	1 bu (26 lbs)	34–40
	1½ lbs	2
Peas, green, in pods	1 bu (30 lbs)	12–15
	2–2½ lbs	1
Peppers, sweet	⅔ lb (3 peppers)	1
Pumpkin	50 lbs	30
	3 lbs	2
Spinach (most greens)	1 bu (18 lbs)	12–18
	2–3 lbs	2
Squash, summer	1 bu (40 lbs)	32–40
	2–2½ lbs	2
Squash, winter (strained)	3 lbs	2

Blanching

Even after vegetables are picked, the enzymes in them make them lose flavor and color and sometimes make them tough—*even at freezer temperatures.* Therefore the enzymes must be stopped in their tracks by being heated for a few minutes (how many minutes depends on the size and texture of the vegetable) before the vegetables are cooled quickly and packed. This preheating is necessary for virtually all vegetables: green (sweet) peppers are the notable exception.

IN BOILING WATER

Practically all vegetables are safely blanched in boiling water. Use a large kettle which has a wire basket that fits down in it. Put in at least 4 quarts of water and bring it to a boil. Lower the basket of prepared vegetables (no more than 1 pound) into 4 quarts briskly boiling water: these proportions allow water to keep boiling. Start counting. Shake the basket to let heat reach all parts of its load. When the specified time is up, lift out the basket and immediately dunk the vegetables in ice-cold water to cool them fast.

> • **ALTITUDE NOTE:** If you live more than 4000 feet/1219 meters above sea level, preheat vegetables one minute longer than the time called for. And see the discussion on blanching in "Correcting for Altitude" in Chapter 3.

BLANCHING IN STEAM

A few vegetables are better if heated in steam, and some may be done in either steam or boiling water.

For steaming, use a large kettle with a tight lid and a rack that holds a steaming basket at least 3 inches above the bottom of the kettle. Put in 1 or 2 inches of water and bring it to a boil.

Cool food as soon as possible after it's blanched.

Put your prepared vegetables in the basket in only a single layer, so the steam can reach all parts quickly. Cover the kettle and keep heat high. Start counting the time as soon as the cover is on.

As in the altitude note added to the boiling–water blanch, add 1 minute to steaming time if you live 4000 feet/1219 meters above sea level.

A Blanch for Vegetables in a Microwave Oven

Follow the instructions that accompany your oven. This is good sense, not laziness on our part, because, aside from their increasing and varied sophistication, ovens differ in capacity and in the wattage to run them, and both factors affect the way each oven treats food.

You can't go badly wrong with microwave blanching, though, and the color is superior to that retained in other blanching methods. Your container of course is suitable for such an oven. Deal with *only 1 pound* of prepared food—peeled, split or cubed—*at a time,* and in very little water. Re-arrange the food once, to ensure even heating (this is especially needed for food that tends to mat); depending on the density of the food, blanching will take from 2½ to 6 minutes, as described in the individual instructions. The moment that the blanching time is up, remove the food and submerge it in ice water for the same amount of time you precooked it. Test a piece for chill: bite it to see if it is cold clear through. If it is, lift the rest from the ice water, drain, pat off clinging water, package and freeze.

OTHER WAYS TO PREHEAT

Pumpkins, squash and sweet potatoes are best fully cooked in a pressure *cooker* (if you use one) or baked in an oven; when done, they are scooped out, mashed/strained, cooled and frozen. Cleaned, trimmed, whole or sliced mushrooms may be pan-broiled in a nonstick skillet, or in a little butter/margarine (a little, because fat acts as an insulator and generous amounts of it can reduce storage life of a food); sautéed this way, they produce some juice, which is frozen with them.

COOL AFTER BLANCHING

Cool all vegetables as quickly as possible after they've been preheated. Use plenty of ice water, and change it often to keep it cold. It takes as much time to cool vegetables properly as it did to blanch them.

When they are completely cooled, drain them well on clean, absorbent toweling: you want as few crystals as possible in the pack.

THE PACKS

Vegetables for freezing may be packed either dry or in brine. The Dry pack is easier and lets you use the vegetables as you would if they were fresh, so Dry pack is the method we'll use the most.

Incidentally, a trick borrowed from commercial processors will make your packaging of dry-packed vegetables (and some fruits) easier. Just place a single layer of any freezer-ready small vegetable on a tray and sharp-freeze it fast (near −20 F/−29 C). Then pour the frozen vegetable into a freezer-type container and seal. Because the pieces are not stuck to each other, you can pour out the amount needed, reclose and seal the container, and return it and its partial contents to the freezer.

COOKING FROZEN VEGETABLES

The secret of cooking frozen vegetables well (if it is a secret), is to cook them in a small amount of liquid, and only until they are tender. When you blanched them for the freezer, you already did a small part of the cooking.

So treat your frozen vegetables like fresh ones—except for a shorter cooking time. This way you'll keep more of the nutrients, as well as more of the natural color, flavor and texture.

To Thaw or Not to Thaw

Most are best cooked *without* thawing.

Defrost the leafy ones just enough to separate the leaves.

Fully defrost corn-on-the-cob, or else the cob will not be heated through and the cooked kernels will cool too soon at the table. Open only the amount needed of any style corn and cook and serve it at once. (P.S. See "Letter from North Dakota" in Corn.)

Boiling

Generally you bring to the boil ½ cup water for each 1 pint of frozen vegetables. Add the vegetables, cover, and begin to count cooking time when water returns to the boil.

Exceptions: 1 cup water to each 1 pint of lima beans; water to cover for corn-on-the-cob.

Cooking times. Spinach—3 minutes; turnip greens—15 to 20 minutes; all other greens—8 to 12 minutes.

Depending on size of pieces: large lima beans, cut green/snap/wax beans, broccoli, carrots, cauliflower, corn in all forms, green peas—all from 3 to 10 minutes.

Kohlrabi (and similar-textured vegetables)—8 to 10 minutes.

Summer squash—up to 12 minutes.

At high altitudes, boil a bit longer—water boils at about an average 2 degrees *lower* than 212 F/100 C for each 1,000 feet above sea level.

Pressure–cooking

The best guide is the manufacturer's instructions which come with the pressure saucepan.

BAKING

Most frozen vegetables can be cooked well by baking in a covered casserole. (It takes longer than boiling, but if your oven is running anyway, why not.)

Partially defrost the vegetable to separate the pieces; put it in a buttered casserole. Add the seasonings you like. Cover and bake at about 350 F/177 C. Most thawed vegetables cook in about 45 minutes.

For corn-on-the-cob, brush the completely defrosted ears with butter or margarine (and optional salt), then roast at 400 F/205 C about 20 minutes.

PAN-FRYING

Use a heavy skillet with a cover. Put in about 1 tablespoon of table fat for each 1 pint of the frozen vegetable (which has thawed enough to separate in pieces). Cook tightly covered over moderate heat, stirring occasionally, until tender. Season to taste, and serve right away.

Asparagus, broccoli and peas will cook tender in about 10 minutes. Mushrooms will be done in 15 minutes. Green/snap/wax beans pan-fry to tenderness in 15 to 20 minutes.

REHEATING

Those vegetables fully cooked before freezing—usually leftovers—just need gentle reheating to serving temperature.

Frozen vegetables used in made dishes are treated like fresh ones. They're good creamed or scalloped, served au gratin or added to soufflés, cream soups and salads.

Relevant Metrics for Freezing Vegetables

Full metric conversions, with the arithmetic for refining them, are given at the start of Chapter 17 ("Common Ingredients and How to Use Them"), but the following—rounded off—apply in this chapter.

If you live above the sea-level zone (i.e., *over* 1000 ft/305 m), consult the subsection "Correcting for Altitude" in Chapter 3 to help in figuring blanching times at lowered atmospheric pressures. (A rule-of-thumb: For every additional 1000 ft/305 meters above sea-level zone, water boils at about 2 degrees F *lower*—e.g., @ 5000 ft/1524 m water boils at 202.6 F/94.8 C.)

• • •

Temperatures (@ sea level): −20 F/−29 C—— Zero F/−18 C——212 F/100 C.

Volume: 2 tablespoons = 30 mL——4 tablespoons = 60 mL——½ cup = 125 mL——1 cup = 250 mL——1 pint = 500 mL——1 quart = 1 L——1 gallon = 4 L.

Length: ½ inch = 1.27 cm——1 inch = 2.54 cm——1¼ inches = 3.18 cm——1½ inches = 3.75 cm——2 inches = 5.1 cm——3 inches = 7.6 cm.

BLANCHING VEGETABLES AT HIGH ALTITUDES

The following procedures are based on information compiled at New Mexico State University, and were given us by the Home Economics agent of Santa Fe County (where most of the terrain is more than 7000 feet/2134 meters above the sea). Any deviations from standard NMSU material are *PFB's* as we worked for rules-of-thumb that could be applied to a wide variety of produce, and differences in altitude.

The most important recommendation we make is to *blanch by boiling* in very high country—rather than by steaming. (See also "A Blanch for Vegetables in a Microwave Oven.") Follow the usual system of gathering loosely not more than 1 pound of the prepared vegetable and immersing it in 4 quarts of water that is at a full, thrashing boil; hold for the time required after the water has returned to a rolling boil. Remove the vegetables, chill in ice water, etc., etc.

Add 1 minute of blanching time for every 1000-foot/305-meter increment above 7000 feet/2134 meters.

Cauliflower, broccoli and Brussels sprouts may be soaked in a solution of 2 tablespoons/30.6 mL salt to each 1 gallon/4 L fresh water for 20 minutes to drive out from their folds and crannies any insects lurking inside. Cut cauliflower and broccoli in pieces no larger than 1 inch in diameter.

BLANCHING SPECIFIC VEGETABLES

Asparagus: large 5 minutes, small 4.

Beans (snap/green/wax): frenched or split 3 minutes, whole 4.

Beans, Lima: small 3 minutes, large 4.

Beets: Leaving on stems and roots—small 30 minutes, large 50; then trim, slip off skins, cut/dice/whatever.

Broccoli: Splitting to no more than 1 inch in diameter after soaking to de-bug—small 4, large 6.

Brussels sprouts: After salt-soak if it's needed, and removing outer leaves—small 3 minutes, medium 5 minutes, large 6 minutes.

Carrots: Marginal for freezing, as a rule, but trimmed, scraped, very small tender ones, whole 7 minutes.

Cauliflower: Soak for insects if needed, then flowerets 1 inch maximum in diameter—5 minutes.

Corn, Whole-kernel: After husking and de-silking—small ears 5, medium 6, large 7. Cut ⅔ kernels deep off the cob after thoroughly cooled: the milk will have set well.

Corn on-the-cob: After husking and de-silking—small ears 8 minutes, medium 10, large 12. (Be sure to see "Letter from North Dakota" under the specific handling of Corn-on-the-Cob later on.)

Greens: Only young, tender, green leaves, with stems and heavy veins removed; washed—3 minutes.

Peppers, sweet: Well-formed, crisp, red or green color; after removing skin (by searing), stem, remove seeds, slice—slices 3 minutes, halves 4.

Squash, summer: Small, tender, with soft rinds, small seeds; after peeling and slicing—¼-inch slices 4 minutes, ½-inch 5.

GETTING DOWN TO FREEZING

Asparagus

Prepare. Sort for size, wash well. Peel slightly tough ends *c.* 2 inches back from the bottom, cut off the really tough ends. Leave spears in lengths to fit the package, or cut in 2-inch pieces.

Blanch. In boiling water—small-diameter stalks for 2 minutes, medium stalks for 3 minutes, thick ones for 4 minutes. Cool immediately; drain.

Pack. Leave no headroom. With spears, alternate tips and stem ends; if it's a wide-top container, pack tips down.

Seal; freeze.

Beans, Lima

These are handier canned: but freeze the tenderest ones, if you can afford the space.

Prepare. Shell and sort for size.

Blanch. In boiling water—small beans for 2 minutes, medium for 3 minutes, large for 4 minutes. Cool immediately and drain.

Pack. Leave ½ inch of headroom.

Seal; freeze.

Beans, Fresh Shell

Prepare. Shell and wash.

Blanch. In boiling water—1 minute. Cool immediately and drain.

Pack. Leave ½ inch of headroom.

Seal; freeze.

Beans—Snap/String/Green/Italian

These also can well. Fancy young tender ones are better frozen.

Prepare. Cut in 1- or 2-inch pieces, or in lengthwise strips (frenching), or leave whole if they're very young and tender.

Blanch. In *soft* boiling water—for 3 minutes. Cool immediately, drain.

Pack. Leave ½ inch of headroom.

Seal; freeze.

Beets

Baby ones are worth freezer space. (Why not can larger ones plain or pickled?)

Prepare. Wash and sort for size—maximum 3 inches, small are best. Leave on tails and ½ inch of stem so their juice won't bleed out while boiling.

Boil. Until tender—25 to 30 minutes for small beets, 45 to 50 for medium. Cool quickly. Slip off skins; trim and cut in slices or cubes.

Pack. Leave ½ inch of headroom for cubes; no headroom for whole or sliced.

Seal; freeze.

Broccoli

Prepare. Peel coarse stalks, trimming off leaves and blemishes; split if necessary. Salt-soak for ½ hour (1 tablespoon salt for each 1 quart cold water) to drive out bugs; wash well. Sort for uniform spears, or cut up.

Blanch. In steam—5 minutes for stalks; in boiling water—3 minutes for stalks. (Reduce blanching time for cut-up or chopped.) Cool immediately; drain.

Pack. Leave no headroom for spears or large chunks; arrange stalks so blossom ends are divided between either end of the container. Leave ½ inch of headroom for cut-up or chopped (they have less air space).

Seal; freeze.

Brussels Sprouts

Give freezer space only to the best heads.

Prepare. Salt-soak as for Broccoli if necessary. Wash well. Trim off outer leaves. Sort for size.

Blanch. In boiling water—small heads for 3 minutes, medium heads for 4 minutes, large heads for 5 minutes. Cool immediately, drain well.

Pack. Leave no headroom.

Seal; freeze.

Cabbage (and Chinese Cabbage)

Plan to use these only in cooked dishes: after being frozen they aren't crisp enough for salads.

Prepare. Trim off coarse outer leaves; cut heads in medium or coarse shreds or thin wedges, or separate the leaves.

Blanch. In boiling water—1½ minutes. Cool immediately and drain.

Pack. Leave ½ inch of headroom.

Seal; freeze.

Carrots

These cold-store and can well, so freeze only the fancy young ones (preferably whole).

Prepare. Remove tops, wash and peel. Leave baby ones whole; cut others into ¼-inch cubes, thin slices or lengthwise strips.

Blanch. In boiling water—tiny whole ones for 5 minutes; dice, slices, or lengthwise strips for 2 minutes. Cool immediately; drain.

Pack. Leave ½ inch of headroom.

Seal; freeze.

Cauliflower

Infinitely better frozen than canned.

Prepare. Break or cut flowerets apart in pieces *c.* 1 inch across. Salt-soak as for Broccoli for ½ hour to get rid of bugs, etc. Wash thoroughly; drain.

Blanch. In boiling salted water (1 teaspoon salt to each 1 quart of water)—3 minutes. Cool immediately; drain.

Pack. Leave no headroom.

Seal; freeze.

Celery

Usable only in cooked dishes, so assign it freezer space accordingly. Tender leaves may be cut small and frozen in small packets for flavoring soups and stews; finely minced, it is a basic for ragú sauces or braising mixtures. A number of condiments use celery: see Corn Relish in Chapter 19, and freeze it accordingly in recipe-size amounts.

Prepare. Strip any coarse strings from any young stalks; wash well, trim, and cut in 1-inch pieces.

Blanch. In boiling water—3 minutes. Cool immediately; drain.

Pack. Leave ½ inch of headroom.

Seal; freeze.

Corn

Feasibility for freezing sweet corn: whole-kernel, Yes (it's better than canning); cream-style, Maybe (it's certainly handier canned, and there's not much difference in the product); on-the-cob, No—unless you've got loads of freezer space and don't mind thawing it before cooking it for the table (it shouldn't be popped frozen into the pot because the kernels will be cooked to death by the time the core of the cob is hot through.)

WHOLE-KERNEL

Prepare. Choose ears with thin, sweet milk; husk, de-silk and wash. (Cut from cob *after* blanching.)

Blanch. In boiling water—4 minutes. Cool ears immediately; drain.

Pack. Cut from cob about ⅔ the depth of the kernels, and don't scrape in any milk. Leave ½ inch of headroom.

Seal; freeze.

CREAM-STYLE

Prepare. Choose ears with thick and starchy milk. Husk, de-silk and wash. (Cut from cob *after* blanching.)

Blanch. In boiling water—4 minutes. Cool immediately; drain.

Pack. Cut from the cob at about the center of the kernels, then scrape the cobs with the back of the knife to force out the hearts of the kernels and the juice (milk); mix with cut corn. Pack, leaving ½ inch of headroom.

Seal; freeze.

ON-THE-COB

Prepare. Choose ears with thin, sweet milk (as for whole-kernel). Husk, de-silk, wash; sort for size.

Blanch. In boiling water—small ears (1¼ inches or less in diameter) for 7 minutes, medium ears (to 1½ inches) for 9 minutes, large ears (over 1½ inches) for 11 minutes. Drain on terrycloth, and refrigerate immediately on dry toweling, in a single layer.

Pack. In containers, or wrap in moisture/vapor-resistant material.

Seal; freeze.

Letter from North Dakota

Our less than enraptured comments on the feasibility of freezing corn-on-the cob brought us a kind letter from Mary Stephens of Necedah, Wisconsin, who brings the frozen ears out "an hour or two ahead of time," butters them, and "bake [them] for 30 minutes in a preheated 350 F/177 C oven"—and she reports that it is delicious.

More detailed is Jeanne Stinnett's description from Grand Forks, North Dakota; her letter is amplified by our notations in italics made when we telephoned our thanks to her: "... For the 6th summer I just told myself I must write you about CORN, the only vegetable to which you have done an injustice. ... Hank and I put away 100 ears of corn per year, and we eat garden-fresh ears out of the freezer all year: the secret's in the cooking.

"Pick *tender, mild yellow, very sweet ears, slightly younger than table-ready* and then strip, husk and silk immediately, wash, then trim if necessary *and pat dry.* DO NOT BLANCH! Put individual ears in small freezer bags, then bag a meal's worth—double-bagging.

"When ready to use, place FROZEN ears in fresh tap water to cover in a large pot, put pan on high heat; bring to a boil, and after water boils start the timer for how long you would normally cook fresh corn (we like 4 minutes). Drain, serve hot with butter. A sensation at Christmas!

"Remember: do not blanch, and do not thaw!"

MAVERICK FREEZING IN THE HUSK

People who know the *Why's* and the *How's* of freezing say: "Never freeze corn without blanching it first to stop enzymatic action." But one hears of corn frozen successfully in its husk (though de-silked), without blanching.

• NOTE: "Successfully" doesn't mean much unless you make the comparison by using identical ears from the same crop, picked and treated and frozen at the same time and for the same period, and cooked the same way for the same meal. Prepare it as described below.

Prepare and pack. Without husking, pull out the silk; and, to save freezer space, remove a little of the outer husk. Do not blanch. Pack in freezer bags; freeze.

Eggplant

Choose glossy, rather small fruits whose seeds are tender. Because most people are watching their sodium intake, we opt for steam-blanching without any salting to draw out juice (blanching also reduces oxidation).

Prepare and pack. Very young eggplant need not be peeled. If to be fried, cut in ¾-inch slices; for casseroles or in mixed vegetables, dice or cut in strips. Steam-blanch 2 minutes for small dice/thin slices, up to 5 minutes for thick slices. Chill in cold water to which 4 teaspoons of lemon juice have been added to each 1 gallon of water. Drain, pat dry.

Pack. Leave ½ inch of headroom.

Seal; freeze.

Greens, Garden

Prepare. Remove imperfect leaves, trim away tough midribs and tough stems; cut large leaves (like chard) in pieces. Wash carefully, lifting the leaves from the water to let silt settle.

Blanch. In boiling water, and shake the pot to keep the leaves separated—spinach, New Zealand spinach, kale, chard, mustard and beet and turnip greens: all for 2 minutes; collards for 3 minutes. (Steam-blanching causes leaf vegetables to mat, and thus prevents correct blanching.) Cool immediately; drain.

Pack. Leave ½ inch of headroom.

Seal; freeze.

Greens, Wild

Prepare and blanch in boiling water. Collect and clean fiddleheads (ostrich fern) according to directions given in Chapter 24, blanch for 2 minutes. Cool and drain.

Collect and clean dandelions according to directions given in Chapter 24. If you like the slightly bitter taste, merely blanch the very tenderest leaves for 1½ minutes; otherwise boil in two or more waters. Cool and drain.

Collect milkweed and boil in several waters according to directions given in Chapter 24. Cool and drain.

Collect American cowslips (the marsh-marigold) and bring to boiling in several waters, cooking thoroughly to get rid of toxin. Cool and drain.

Pack. Leave ½ inch of headroom.

Seal; freeze.

Jerusalem Artichokes

Treat like Kohlrabi or small Turnips (q.v.).

Kohlrabi

Prepare. Cut off the tops and roots of small to medium kohlrabi. Wash, peel; leave whole or dice in ½-inch cubes.

Blanch. In boiling water—whole for 3 minutes, cubes 1 minute. Cool immediately and drain.

Pack. Whole in containers or wrap in moisture/vapor-resistant material. Cubes in containers, leaving ½ inch of headroom.

Seal; freeze.

Mushrooms

Prepare. Wash carefully in cold water. Cut off ends of stems. Leave stems on fancy small buttons if you like; if mushrooms are larger than 1 inch across the caps, slice or quarter them. If serving cold (in salads, etc.), blanch in steam; if serving hot (as garnish for meats, or in combination dishes), precook.

Blanch. In one layer, over steam—whole for 5 minutes, quarters or small caps for 3½ minutes, slices for 3 minutes. (This also prevents darkening; see "To Prevent Darkening" early in Chapter 12.) Cool immediately; drain.

Precooking. In table fat—sauté in a skillet until nearly done. Air-cool, or set the skillet in cold water (you'll freeze them in the good buttery juice from the pan).

Pack. Leave ½ inch of headroom.

Seal; freeze.

Okra (Gumbo)

Use in soups and stews.

Prepare. Wash. Cut off stems, being careful not to open the seed cells.

Blanch. In boiling water—small pods 3 minutes, large pods 4 minutes. Cool immediately; drain. Leave whole, or cut in crosswise slices.

Pack. Leave ½ inch of headroom.

Seal; freeze.

Parsnips

Really best left in the ground over winter for the first fresh treat of spring—freezing is only a second choice.
Treat like Carrots.

Peas, Black-eyed (Cowpeas, Black-eyed Beans)

Prepare. Shell; save only the tender peas (see "Sorting Trick" next page).

Blanch. In boiling water—for 2 minutes. Cool immediately, drain well.

Pack. Leave ½ inch of headroom.

Seal; freeze.

Peas, Green

Prepare. Shell; use only sweet, tender peas (see "Sorting" next page). For Edible-pod/Snow types, see "Peas, Green," Chapter 7; continue as below for freezing.

Blanch. In boiling water—for 1½ minutes. Cool immediately; drain.

Pack. Leave ½ inch of headroom.

Seal; freeze.

> • • SORTING TRICK FOR PEAS: It's fun to pass on an idea
> new to us, and interesting—especially if its source is as
> impeccable as Ohio State University's Co-operative Ex-
> tension Service (see Chapter 25 for the bulletin title). To
> size peas as a guide to their tenderness or maturity, make
> a solution in the proportions of 1½ cups regular canning-
> pickling salt to 1 gallon of cool water, and put the peas in
> it: floating peas are likely to be the very tender ones,
> while peas that sink are usually older or more mature. Lift
> out the floaters in a strainer, rinse well in cold water to get
> rid of the salt; collect the sinkers by pouring off the salt
> solution, and rinse in cold water.
>   Ohio recommends that shelled peas be washed in
> shallow pans before sorting, by the way, because un-
> formed peas and bits of skin will float, and may be
> skimmed off and discarded.

Peppers, Green (Bell, Sweet)

Here is a vegetable that *does not require* blanching: the brief precooking described below is designed to make them more limp, so you can pack more peppers in the container—and it's for large-ish pieces you plan to use in cooked
dishes, at that.

If you plan to serve them raw (for instance in thin rings as a garnish, or diced
in a salad), don't bother to blanch.

Prepare. Wash; cut out stems, remove seeds and white "partitioning" material. Cut in halves, or cut in slices, strips, rings or dice (depending on future
use).

If blanched. In boiling water—halves for 3 minutes, slices for 2 minutes.
Cool immediately; drain.

Pack. Blanched, leave ½ inch of headroom. Raw, leave no headroom.

Seal; freeze.

Peppers, Hot

Prepare. Wash and stem.

Blanch. No.

Pack. Leave no headroom.

Seal; freeze.

Pimientos

Prepare. Wash and dry crisp, thick-walled pimientos.

Roast. In a 400 F/205 C oven—for 3 to 4 minutes. Rinse and rub off charred skins in cold water. Drain.

Pack. Leave ½ inch of headroom.

Seal; freeze.

Pumpkin

Pumpkin makes fine pies and breads (see recipes in Chapter 24), but is seldom used as a table vegetable. Why not can it *cubed* instead?

Prepare. Wash whole pumpkin; cut or break in pieces. Remove seeds. Do not peel.

Precook. Until soft—in boiling water, steam, a pressure cooker or in the oven. Scrape pulp from rind; mash through a sieve. Cool immediately.

Pack. Leave ½ inch of headroom.

Seal; freeze.

Rutabagas

Prepare. Cut off tops of young, medium-sized rutabagas; wash and peel. Cut in cubes to freeze merely blanched, or in large chunks to cook and mash before freezing.

Blanch (for cubes). In boiling water—for 2 minutes. Cool immediately; drain.

Cook (chunks to mash). In boiling water until tender. Drain; mash or sieve. Cool immediately.

Pack. Leave ½ inch of headroom for either cubed or mashed.

Seal; freeze.

Soybeans

Prepare. To serve as a vegetable, wash firm, well-filled, bright-green pods (shell *after* blanching).

Blanch. In boiling water—5 minutes. Cool quickly. Squeeze beans out of pods.

Pack. Leave ½ inch of headroom.

Seal; freeze.

Sprouts, see Chapter 23.

Squash, Summer (and Zucchini)

Only young squash with small seeds and tender rinds are suitable for freezing.

Prepare. Cut off blossom and stem ends; wash and cut in slices.

Blanch. In boiling water—for 3 minutes. Cool immediately in ice water; drain well.

Pack. Leave ½ inch of headroom.

Seal; freeze.

Squash, Winter

Root-cellar mature squash with hard rinds. Treat it like Pumpkin if you do freeze it, though.

Sweet Potatoes (and Yams)

Use medium to large sweet potatoes that have air-dried (to cure) after being dug. Pack whole, sliced or mashed.

Prepare. Sort for size; wash. Leave skins on.

Precook. Cook, until almost tender, in water, steam, a pressure cooker or an oven. Cool at room temperature. Peel; cut in halves, slices or mash.

Prevent darkening. Dip whole peeled sweet potatoes or slices for 5 seconds in a solution of 1 tablespoon citric acid or ½ cup lemon juice to 1 quart of water. For mashed sweet potatoes mix 2 tablespoons orange or lemon juice with each quart.

Pack. Leave ½ inch of headroom.

Pack variations. Roll slices in sugar. Or cover whole or sliced with a cold 50 Percent Syrup. In either case, leave appropriate headroom.

Seal; freeze.

Tomatoes

Tomatoes are so easy to can—and are so handy in several table-ready forms—that we question the feasibility of freezing them. And aside from taking up a good deal of freezer space, a frozen whole tomato has limited appeal: its tender flesh is ruptured by ice crystals, and you have a deflated mush when you defrost it.

STEWED TOMATOES

Prepare. Remove stem ends and cores of ripe tomatoes; peel and quarter.

Cook. In a covered enameled or stainless-steel kettle, cook gently in their own juice until tender—10 to 20 minutes. Set the kettle bodily in cold water to cool the contents.

Pack. Leave appropriate headroom.

Seal; freeze.

TOMATO JUICE

Prepare. Cut vine-ripened tomatoes in quarters or smaller. In an enameled or stainless-steel kettle simmer them in their own juice for 5 to 10 minutes— or until tender with a good deal of liquid. Put through a sieve or food mill. Season with ½ teaspoon salt to each pint of juice, or 1 teaspoon to each quart if liked.

Pack. Leave appropriate headroom.

Seal; freeze.

Turnips, White

Turnips are similar to rutabagas, but they mature more quickly. Freeze them in cubes or fully cooked and mashed. They also keep well in the root cellar.
Cubes: treat like Rutabagas.
Mashed: treat like Winter Squash or Pumpkin.

14

FREEZING MEATS

One of the world's disappointed people is the householder who invests, with such high hopes of economy and good eating, in a quarter, a half—even a whole—big food animal, only to discover that almost 25 percent of it is waste, and that so many of the dreamed-of chops and roasts and steaks have turned into stew or ground meat for patties. For the newcomer to putting by rather large amounts of food, it is far better to watch for supermarket sales of individual cuts of meat.

Meanwhile, for those who are handling the meat of large animals virtually from scratch, we refer to the detailed discussion of sanitation, refrigeration, cutting up and preparing for storage early on in "Canning Meats," Chapter 8. The same kitchen equipment, methods and safeguards apply as well to meat that is to be frozen.

And descriptions of freezer supplies and wraps are given in detail in Chapter 11, "Getting and Using a Freezer."

Relevant Metrics for Freezing Meat

Full metric conversions, with the arithmetic for refining them, are given at the start of Chapter 17 ("Common Ingredients and How to Use Them"), but the following—rounded—apply in this chapter.

● ● ●

Temperatures (@ sea level): −20 F/−29 C——Zero F/−18 C——170 F/77 C——200 F/93 C——212 F/100 C——300 F/149 C.

Length: ½ inch = 1.27 cm——5 inches = 12.64 cm——6 inches = 15.2 cm.

COOKING FROZEN MEAT

Generally, any cut of meat may be cooked either frozen or thawed—which leaves the decision up to you. How do you plan to serve it?

THAW THESE:

- Meat to be coated with crumbs before cooking.
- Meat to be browned as the first step in cooking.
- Ground meat that must be shaped for cooking.
- Large roasts: they can overcook on the outside before the inner part is done, if they're not defrosted first.

APPROXIMATE THAWING TIMES FOR MEAT

In the refrigerator: large roasts—4 to 5 hours per pound; small roasts—3 hours per pound.

At room temperature NOT recommended.

Under cold running water: small pieces of meat overwrapped in plastic bags and sealed. Quickest safe method.

THESE MAY BE COOKED FROZEN:

- Preshaped ground meat patties.
- Meat loaves.
- Thin steaks or chops.
- Meatballs in their own gravy or broth.

APPROXIMATE TIMES FOR COOKING FROZEN MEAT

Juices rich in B vitamins seep out of all frozen meat and poultry as they defrost. Therefore, if possible thaw meat completely before cooking it, and save the dripped-out juice for the pan gravy. However, juice can be kept in chops or ground-meat patties if they are cooked as soon as ice crystals have disappeared from their *surfaces*. Also, large pieces (roasts) may be put in a preheated oven when the surface yields to the pressure of your hand.

Roasting. If you're caught short of time and must roast a big piece of frozen meat, do it in a preheated oven *about 25 degrees lower* than generally used for roasting unfrozen meat (that is, do it in an oven not more than 300 F/149 C), and *increase the roasting time by one-half.*

Broiling. Broil frozen meat of any thickness *at least 5 to 6 inches below* the heat source, and *increase broiling time by one-half.*

Pan-broiling. Cook frozen *thin* hamburgers, chops and steaks in a *very hot skillet* with a small amount of fat swished around to keep meat from sticking.

Start to cook frozen *thicker* patties, chops and steaks in a *warm skillet* with 1 tablespoon of fat. Heat the meat slowly and turn it until thawed. Then *increase the heat* and pan-broil the meat as for unfrozen thin cuts.

Freezing Roasts

Prepare. Trim away excess fat. Wipe with a clean damp cloth. Pad protruding sharp bones with rescued pieces of clean though crinkled aluminum foil or with extra wrapping, so they can't pierce the package.

Pack and seal. Package individual roasts tightly in sheet wrapping, using either the butcher wrap or drugstore fold.

Label; freeze.

Freezing Chops and Steaks

Prepare. Trim away excess fat. Wipe with a clean damp cloth.

Pack and seal. Package, in sheet wrapping, the number needed for one meal. Put a double layer of wrapping between individual chops/steaks or layers of chops/steaks. Press outer sheet wrapping closely to the bundle of meat to exclude air. Use either the butcher wrap or drugstore fold.

Label; freeze.

Freezing Ground Meat

Use only freshly ground meat to freeze as patties, loaves or in bulk. Freshly made Pork Sausage (see recipe in Chapter 23) also may be frozen; but its freezer life is short because of its high fat content (see Loaves, Uncooked).

PATTIES

Prepare. Make up ready to cook—but omit seasonings noted in Loaves, Uncooked, below; and see "These Don't Freeze Well" in Chapter 16.

Pack and seal. Put double layers of lightweight freezer wrap between patties for easy separation when you are ready to cook them. In each bundle, tightly wrap enough patties for one meal, using either the butcher wrap or drugstore fold.

Label; freeze.

LOAVES, COOKED

Prepare. Cool cooked loaves, remove from baking pan.

Pan and seal. Wrap tightly, using either the butcher wrap or drugstore fold.

Label; freeze.

LOAVES, UNCOOKED

Prepare. Because the onions lose strength and some herbs—especially sage—get bitter when held in the freezer, raw loaves should be stored only for several weeks, to avoid disappointment. Mix loaves as for baking. Line loaf pans with foil; fill with meat-loaf mixture and fold ends of foil over meat. *Freeze.*

Pack and seal. Remove loaves from pans when frozen, and overwrap tightly, using either the butcher wrap or drugstore fold.

Label; store in freezer for only a short time.

THE DRUGSTORE FOLD

THE BUTCHER WRAP

Roll folded edge down, turn over

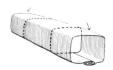

Fold ends of roll down

Ends up and over, tuck tight

Sides over end

Tuck sides in

Fold tip of point over

Fold up and tape

Roll to end of paper—
seal open edges with tape

BULK

Pack and seal. Put meal-size quantities in freezer boxes or bags, excluding air. Seal tightly.

Label; freeze.

Freezing Stew Meat

Prepare. Cut in cubes. They may be packed without browning, but for easier use later, sear them under a hot broiler; when the surfaces of the meat are browned nicely, rinse the pan juices out with a small amount of boiling water (which you'll reduce, cool, and add to the pack). *Frying* meat is usually *not* a good browning treatment for meat to be frozen or canned.

Pack and seal. Fill rigid containers with meal-size portions of browned cubes. Cover with pan liquid or broth, leaving ½ inch of headroom. Seal.

Pack unbrowned cubes in rigid containers, freezer bags or sheet wrapping, excluding air. Seal tightly.

Label; freeze.

Freezing Cooked Meat

Prepare. It's better to freeze cooked meat or poultry in large pieces (so less surface may be exposed to air). Slices of meat or poultry keep best if covered with broth or gravy. Do read about the best thickener for frozen gravy—*mochiko*—in Chapter 16, "Freezing Convenience Foods."

Pack and seal. Large pieces are wrapped tightly, using either the butcher wrap or drugstore fold. Slices are stored in rigid containers of suitable size and covered with broth or gravy, then closely covered and sealed.

Label; freeze.

Freezing Store-bought Cuts

(Meaning those prepackaged fresh meats from the market's display case.)

Pack and seal. Remove the store wrapping—even though it is well sealed; discard the tray, and rewrap and seal the meat closely in your own freezing materials. This will close out air and give the meat a more durable cover. (There's too much air held in store packages—and this causes freezer burn; also, the clear film that's O.K. to sell it in is not strong enough for freezer storage.)

Label; freeze.

FREEZING POULTRY AND SMALL GAME

Once more it is necessary to start off a new section with a warning against allowing the food to become contaminated by micro-organisms that cause illness, but we shall keep it mercifully brief and point out that certain game is likely to carry tularemia, and that some of the commonest "food poisoning" bacteria are the Salmonellae—which dearly loves poultry.

Freezing does not destroy bacteria; it merely slows down or temporarily halts their growth. They are able to grow and multiply at a stunning rate once they start getting warm again. Read the "Bacterial Load" section in Chapter 4. The best way to keep it down is to handle food with scrupulous care.

And here again, "poultry" applies to domestic and wild birds, domestic rabbits, and small game.

COOKING FROZEN POULTRY

All freshly killed and dressed birds are better if stored in the refrigerator for 12 hours to develop their greatest tenderness before freezing.

For best results, thaw before cooking (unless you're boiling it to use in a fricassee or such): roasting or broiling is more uniform if the poultry is thawed first, and the meat is less likely to be dry or rubbery. Pieces to be coated before frying, or browned before stewing, should always be thawed beforehand. It's easier to stuff a thawed bird than one that's still frozen.

Cook all poultry soon after thawing, for best quality.

APPROXIMATE THAWING TIMES FOR FROZEN POULTRY

Thaw it in its freezer wrappings.

In the refrigerator: 2 hours per pound.

At room temperature NOT recommended.

Under cold running water: small individually frozen birds, or large joints, etc., may be bagged and sealed in waterproof plastic so they do not get waterlogged.

Stuff It Later

Even if the cook is careful at every step, dangerous bacteria causing food spoilage can develop in poultry stuffed at home and then frozen: *the slow cooling as it freezes in the center of a densely packed cavity will produce spoilers in the stuffing, and normal roasting will not destroy such products.* Prestuffed frozen birds sold by big commercial processors are prepared under controlled conditions of temperature and humidity, etc., that cannot be duplicated in the home.

Freezing Birds Whole

Any bird may be frozen whole for future stuffing and roasting.

Prepare. Tie legs of dressed, washed birds together with thighs close to body; press wings snugly against breast.

Pack and seal. Put bird in a heavy-duty food-grade plastic freezer bag, press out air and tightly close the bag top. Or wrap the bird in moisure/vapor-resistant material (see wrapping illustrations); seal tightly. Pack and freeze giblets separately.

Label; freeze.

Freezing Birds in Halves

Prepare. Split dressed, washed birds lengthwise and cut off the backbone (use it in soup stock).

Pack and seal. Put a double layer of freezer paper between the halves. Pack and seal in a freezer bag or wrap as for Whole.

Label; freeze.

Freezing Birds in Smaller Pieces

Prepare. Cut in pieces suitable for intended use (see "Canning Poultry," Chapter 8).

Pack and seal. Put a double layer of lightweight wrap between meaty pieces and pack them snugly together in freezer bag or carton; wrap tightly in sheet material. Seal.

Label; freeze.

FREEZING SEAFOOD

Properly handled at every stage, frozen seafood can be nearly as delightful in taste and texture as if it were freshly caught. The operative words here are "properly handled," because fish and shellfish are the most perishable of all fresh foods, and therefore are the most vulnerable to careless treatment. Therefore fish must be cleaned immediately and washed in fresh, running water; ocean fish may be kept alive in sea water, but neither fish nor shellfish should be cleaned or cooked in sea water. Ice-pack refrigeration or an accepted substitute method of chilling is a must, especially if you catch your own. You will be meticulous about sanitation and sterilizing surfaces. The packaging materials will be adequate for preventing ice crystals or freezer burn. The seafood will be sharply frozen, stored at minimum temperature, and used relatively soon (compared with a frozen beefsteak).

But it's all worth the trouble. And compared with canning, drying and curing, the actual freezing procedure is simplicity itself.

Detailed instructions for preparing seafood for processing are given in Chapter 9, "Canning Seafood": do read them.

All fish and shellfish must be stored at ZERO FAHRENHEIT (−18 Celsius) *after initial sharp freezing at c. −20 F/−29 C.*

PRELIMINARIES TO FREEZING FISH

For handling, fish may be divided into two categories: Lean and Fat.

The Fat—mackerel, pink and chum salmon, ocean perch, smelt, herring, lake trout, flounder, shad and tuna—are more perishable than the leaner varieties; plan to freezer-store these not more than 3 months.

The Lean fish—cod, haddock, halibut, yellow pike, yellow perch, freshwater herring, Coho and King and red salmon—all keep well in frozen storage up to 6 months.

DRESSING (CLEANING)

Scale the fish (or skin it, depending on the variety); remove fins and tail. Slit the belly with a thin-bladed sharp knife and remove the entrails, saving any roe; remove head (optional). Wash fish in cold, drinkable *running water.*

Relevant Metrics for Freezing Fish and Shellfish

Full metric conversions, with the arithmetic for refining them, are given at the start of Chapter 17 ("Common Ingredients and How to Use Them"), but the following—rounded off—apply in this chapter.

If you live above the sea-level zone (i.e., *over* 1000 ft/305 m), consult the subsection "Correcting for Altitude" in Chapter 3, for considerations in precooking.

• • •

Temperatures (@ sea level): −20 F/−29 C——Zero F/−18 C——36 F/2 C——400 F/205 C.

Volume: 1 teaspoon = 5 mL——2 teaspoons = 10 mL——1 tablespoon = 15 mL——1 cup = 250 mL——3 cups = 750 mL——1 quart = 1 L——1 gallon = 4 L.

Length: ½ inch = 1.27 cm——1 inch = 2.54 cm.

Weight: ½ lb = 0.23 kg——2 lbs = 0.91 kg——4 lbs = 1.82 kg.

FLAVOR-PROTECTING DIPS

The Fat fish (and roe) are given a 20-second dip in an *ascorbic-acid* solution—2 teaspoons crystalline ascorbic acid dissolved in 1 quart of cold water—to lessen the chance of rancidity and flavor change during storage.

The Lean fish are dipped for 20 seconds in a *brine* of 1 cup salt to 1 gallon of cold water; this firms the flesh and reduces leakage when the fish thaws.

GLAZING WITH ICE

Sometimes whole fish or pieces of fish are ice-glazed before wrapping. This helps keep the air away, thus saving the flavor. The fish is frozen until solid, then dipped quickly in and out of ice-cold water, whereupon a thin coat of ice will form on the fish. Repeat several times to thicken the ice, then wrap the fish for storage.

CUTTING TO SIZE

Fish are frozen whole if they are small enough (under 2 pounds); or are cut in steaks—crosswise slices about 1 inch thick, or are filleted. Exception: large-ish fish you expect to bake whole, you freeze whole.

Fillets are made usually from fish weighing 2 to 4 pounds. Lay the cleaned fish on its side on a clean cutting-board. Run a thin-bladed sharp knife the length of the backbone and slightly above it, and continue cutting to separate the side of the fish from the backbone and ribs; repeat on the opposite side. (This works on most fish; but not on shad—whose build is so complicated that it takes special skill to fillet them.)

COOKING FROZEN FISH AND SHELLFISH

With two exceptions, frozen seafood may be cooked when still frozen—the exceptions being a large whole fish you're baking and pieces that are to be crumbed or coated with batter before cooking.

Small whole fish—under ½ pound—may be defrosted just enough to separate them before they're fried (without crumbs or batter coating) or broiled on a greased broiler.

Fish fillets and steaks are baked or poached from the frozen state; they're partially defrosted before boiling or frying (without crumbs or batter coating).

Shellfish and fish for stews, chowders and Newburgs are cooked still frozen.

Freezing Large Whole Fish

Prepare. Dress (clean) as above, removing the head if you wish.

Pack and seal. Freeze-glaze with ice (q.v. above). Wrap snugly with moisture/vapor-proof covering, using the butcher wrap or drugstore fold—then overwrap for security. Seal.

Label; store in freezer.

Freezing Small Whole Fish

Prepare. Dress as for large whole fish, leaving on heads if you like.

Pack and seal. Small whole fish are most often packed in rigid containers with added cold water to fill crevices between the fish. Hold the lid tightly on the container with freezer tape wrapped around the rim, and overwrap with moisture/vapor-proof freezer paper, using the butcher wrap or drugstore fold. Seal.

For easy separation in thawing, individual small fish may be enclosed in a household plastic bag or other clear wrapping before going into the rigid freezer containers. Proceed with overwrap, and seal.

Sport fishermen often freeze their catch covered with water in large bread pans or the like, the whole thing sealed in a freezer bag, and frozen. When solid, the block of fish-in-ice is removed from the pan and tightly wrapped in moisture/vapor-proof material, closed with the butcher wrap or drugstore fold, then sealed.

Label; store in freezer.

Freezing Fish Fillets and Steaks

Prepare. Dress and cut up strictly fresh fish. Treat Fat fish pieces with the ascorbic-acid dip, or Lean fish pieces with the brine dip (q.v.). Fillets may also be glazed with ice before wrapping.

Pack and seal. Fill rigid containers with layers of fillets or steaks, dividing layers with double sheets of freezer wrap for easy separation when frozen. Cover and seal.

For even greater odor prevention, overwrap the container with sheet freezer material, using the butcher wrap or drugstore fold.

Layers of fillets and steaks may also be wrapped in bundles and sealed instead of going into rigid containers; the bundles are then overwrapped and sealed.

Label; freeze.

Freezing Fish Roe

Roe is more perishable than the rest of the fish, so it should be frozen and stored separately from the fish.

Prepare. Carefully wash each set of roe from strictly fresh fish and prick the covering membrane in several places with a sterilized fine needle. Treat the roe with an ascorbic-acid dip (q.v.), even though it may come from a Lean fish.

Pack and seal. Wrap each set of roe closely in lightweight plastic for easy separation when frozen, smoothing out all air. Pack in flat layers in rigid containers and seal; then overwrap the containers in moisture/vapor-proof material, using the butcher wrap or drugstore fold. Seal.

Label; freeze. (Sharp-freeze at −20 F/−29 C; store at Zero F/−18 C or below for not more than 3 months before using.)

Poaching Shad Roe for Freezing

Shad roe is, to some people, a treasure to be shared only with true believers in its charm, and for them *PFB* offers the following procedure for freezing—provided that there is any shad roe left uncooked and uneaten.

Prepare a court bouillon in a large enameled skillet: enough water estimated to cover the pair of roe, and for every 2 cups of water add 1 peppercorn, ½ teaspoon salt (optional), 1 teaspoon lemon juice, ¼ teaspoon crystalline ascorbic acid, and either a pinch of savory *or* rosemary, *or* 1 bay leaf to the total amount of water. (These herbs are up to you; as is adding ¼ cup dry white table wine to the total water.) Wash the roe, gently remove as much of the center engorged membrane as you can without tearing the egg case, then gently slide into the court bouillon one pair of roe at a time. Let it putter along until poached through: it will be hard to the touch when cooked. Cool quickly by laying it on foil over a bed of ice. Thoroughly chilled, it may be wrapped closely in several rollovers of freezer film, then packed in a freezer bag for subsequent boxing and storage. An alternative idea: with a pastry brush paint a sheet of aluminum foil (a piece large enough to make a good drugstore-fold wrap for the pair of roe) with bacon fat leaving 3 inches of foil all around un-oiled. Lay the roe on the bacon fat, complete the drugstore fold; slide each foil-wrapped packet in its own freezer bag; store and freeze.

To serve, heat unthawed and still wrapped in foil in a 350 F/177 C oven; open foil after 20 minutes, and lay crossways on top of the pair of roe 2 pieces of partially cooked bacon. When bacon is fully cooked, and roe is heated through, serve.

Freezing Eels

Prepare. Skin the eel. Tie a stout cord tightly around the fish below the head and secure the end of the cord to a strong, fixed support (a post or whatever). About 3 inches behind the head, cut completely through the skin around the body of the eel, necklace fashion. Grip the cut edge of the skin and pull it downward, removing the entire skin inside out.

Remove the entrails; wash the eel.

Cut in fillets or in the more usual steak-type rounds.

Because eel is a Fat fish, treat the pieces with an ascorbic-acid dip. Pack as for fillets or steaks of other fish, above. Seal.

Label; freeze.

Freezing Crab and Lobster Meat

Prepare. Scrub frisky live crabs and lobsters, butcher; cook the meat as described fully in "Canning Seafood," Chapter 9. Rinse and cool under drinkable running water; pick the meat carefully, removing all bits of shell and tendon.

Pack and seal. Fill rigid containers solidly with meal-size amounts; add no liquid, but leave ½ inch of headroom. Seal.

Label; freeze.

Freezing Shrimp

As with other shellfish, shrimp you freeze must be absolutely fresh. They are best frozen raw, though they may be precooked as for the table before you freeze them.

Raw Shrimp

Prepare. Wash, cut off the heads and take out the sand vein. Shelling is optional. Wash again in a mild salt solution of 1 teaspoon salt to each 1 quart of water. Drain well.

Pack and seal. Pack snugly in rigid freezer containers without any headroom. Seal tightly.

Label; freeze.

COOKED SHRIMP

Prepare. Wash in a mild salt solution of 1 teaspoon salt to each 1 quart of water; remove heads. Boil *gently* in lightly salted water until pink and curled tight—average sized for 5 minutes, up to 10 minutes for large to jumbo sizes. Cool. Slit the shell and remove the sand vein (for table-ready use remove shells and vein). Rinse quickly. Drain.

Pack and seal. Pack snugly in rigid freezer containers, without any headroom. Seal tightly.

Label: freeze.

Freezing Oysters, Clams, Mussels and Scallops

Probably the most perishable of the shellfish, these should be frozen within hours of the time they leave the sea and *held at refrigerator temperature* (c. *36 F/2 C*) during any waiting period.

Cooked oysters, clams and mussels toughen in the freezer: freeze them raw.

Prepare. Wash in cold water while still in their shells to rid them of sand. Shuck them over a bowl to catch the natural liquid. Wash them quickly again in a brine of 4 tablespoons salt to 1 gallon of water.

Shucking is removing the shells. Since shucking bivalves (oysters, clams, etc.) involves severing the two strong muscles that close the two halves of the shell, you can cut yourself badly if you go about it wrong. *DO NOT USE a sharp or pointed knife.* Instead, use a dull blade with a rounded tip; insert it between the lips of the shell just beyond one end of the hinge, twist to cut the muscle at that point, and repeat at the other end of the hinge. A good shucker does it in one continuous *safe* motion: get someone who knows how, to show you.

Pack and seal. Put in rigid containers and cover with their own juice, extended with a weak brine of 1 teaspoon salt to 1 cup of water. Scallops are packed tightly, then covered with the brine (they have little juice). Leave ½ inch of headroom—unless the container is larger than 3-cup size (more than 3-cup is not advised: it takes too long to defrost; see the table "Headroom for Fruits" in Chapter 12.) Seal tightly.

Label; freeze.

16

FREEZING CONVENIENCE FOODS, EGGS AND DAIRY PRODUCTS

Store-bought frozen convenience foods turn up in greater variety all the time, and they're costing more money. Chances are they will cost even more, proportionately, if they are made with less sodium, or less cane and beet sugars, and labeled "dietetic"; and as for carefully hypoallergenic combinations . . .

But if you have the freezer space to stow any of these foods at home, you have the means of putting them by yourself—at great saving and of course adapted entirely to your own needs and purposes. You can make particular favorites; choose your components and use your own preferred measurements; package for one, two, or a crowd; work ahead for a party or a holiday; accommodate special dietary requirements. You can double a recipe and serve half and freeze half. You can pick up luxury ingredients when they're on sale, or spot uncommon ones that re-appear after an absence: these may be divided in portions and pretreated for quick use later in building main dishes.

In comparison with freezing convenience foods, the four preceding chapters could be thought of as dealing with staple raw materials, some in greater bulk than others. Here, although some items will be raw, except for Eggs and Dairy Foods they will be pared/chopped/minced/grated; others are partly precooked.

PREPARING TO FREEZE SPECIALTIES

A well-managed freezer need not be the symbol of only a big self-reliant family that figures on a side of beef and half a pig and tiers of neat boxes filled with all manner of produce from the nearby garden. Nor, if it is the special freezer section of a modern refrigerator in a city apartment, need it be mainly the cache for ice cream, several TV dinners, anonymous leftovers and an emergency supply of ice cubes.

If you already use freezing, generally the larger your family the more likely you are to have a 15- or 20-cubic-foot freezer, and to have in it a greater proportion of raw materials than if your household is small. On the other hand, one or two people, or an older couple, can get along fine with a 2½-cubic-foot freezing compartment. But the interesting difference is how these freezers are handled, not their sizes. If it also is managed well, the little one will concentrate more on short-storage items like precooked heat-and-serve foods, or the prepared components of main dishes. And in both freezers will be a special place for those small packets of extras that can make a stolid combination sparkle.

EQUIPMENT

If you already have a freezer of some sort, you are sure to have at hand the basic utensils for using it (see Chapter 11). An important item you should have are scales that weigh grams/ounces as well as larger fractions of kilograms/pounds—certainly up to 4.54 kg/10 lbs. You will need these as well as volume measures when you are adapting a favorite rule, increasing or decreasing it. If you have the room, you'll be likely to prepare, measure and package separately the raw materials for a late-January session of making jelly, jam or relishes.

Investigate the feasibility of buying the simple heat-sealing machine for cook-in-pouch freezing. We'll talk about the procedures for such preserving and cooking at the end of this chapter.

Relevant Metrics for Freezing Convenience Foods, etc.

Full metric conversions, with the arithmetic for refining them, are given at the start of Chapter 17 ("Common Ingredients and How to Use Them"), but the following—rounded off—apply in this chapter.

If you live above the sea-level zone (i.e., *over* 1000 ft/305 m), consult the subsection "Correcting for Altitude" in Chapter 3 for considerations in precooking, especially boiling.

• • •

Temperatures (@ sea level): Zero F/−18 C———32 F/Zero C———40 F/4 C———350 F/177 C———375 F/191 C———450 F/232 C.

Volume: ¼ teaspoon = 1.25 mL———½ teaspoon = 2.5 mL———1 teaspoon = 5.0 mL———1½ teaspoons = 7.5 mL———1 tablespoon = 15 mL———2 tablespoons/1 fl oz = 30 mL———¼ cup = 60 mL———½ cup = 125 mL———1 cup = 250 mL———1 pint = 500 mL.

Length: ⅛ inch = 0.32 cm———¼ inch = 0.64 cm———½ inch = 1.27 cm———1 inch = 2.54 cm———2 inches = 5.1 cm———8 inches = 20.3 cm.

CONTAINERS

With microwave ovens so popular, and convection ovens increasing in use, householders are often likely to freeze in the container they will be reheating and cooking in. It depends, really, on how formal you want to be. You can always freeze the prepared makings of a casserole or stew or hash in the well-lined and straight-sided dish in which you plan to serve it. When it's rock hard, remove and overwrap it, label and stack it. Come the time you want to cook it, remove all wrappings, put it in its chosen container, and carry on with thawing or cooking or whatever must be done to serve it.

Meanwhile there is in any supermarket an almost endless variety of aluminum-foil pans in all shapes and sizes; they are re-usable if you clean them carefully and make sure that they don't get punctured the first time you serve from them.

BUT such metal pans are not for microwave ovens. Instead, shape-freeze in ceramic ramekins or dishes designed to be used for microwave cookery, and follow the wrapping-to-shape idea above. And you can always thaw or reheat in plastic in these ovens, a thing that could mean disaster in a conventional or convection oven.

Foil is ideal for convection ovens, though. Because of the drying effect of the moving hot air, it's a good safeguard to cover the food in the cooking pan with foil crimped around the rim for part of the reheating or cooking time.

It goes without saying that your wrappings and containers should be just as moisture/vaporproof as for regular freezing. Still, if you must make-do in a hurry, you can always use the best food-grade clinging plastic film, patting and smoothing it to the newly frozen shape, and using several layers; then put it into a plastic food-storage bag of suitable strength (tucking a written label inside with it), remove as much air as possible from the bag, and seal it. This system is particularly good with an odd-shaped piece of food (small unfrozen but precooked poultry, for example—which of course does *not* contain stuffing); and it helps to prevent the freezer-burn that comes from moist air held inside with the contents.

- **NOTE:** One of the most valuable containers/shapes for freezing a 6-serving main dish is the 8-×-8-inch square cake pan. Its 2 inches is deep enough, it can be divided evenly in thirds by two cuts vertically, and then divided further by one horizontal cut across the center. Generous helpings.

One of the beauties of doing your own convenience foods is the leeway you have in freezing very small portions, collecting them in a fairly large bag, and taking out what you want—instead of taking an ice pick to one end of a quart brick of, say, spaghetti sauce. So freeze it in muffin tins: a large muffin's-worth of sauce should be generous for a normal serving of pasta; if not, make it two.

If the consistency is stiff-ish, freeze any such thing in dollops on a cookie sheet. Whatever its shape when it is frozen hard, first wrap each bit separately (either in clinging plastic food film, or in a flimsy little plastic storage bag), then collect the pieces in best-quality true freezer containers. Tuck a label inside the large freezer bag, or stick a label on the box with clear plastic tape you can read through. Be sure to say what the measurement is.

". . . Tuck a Label Inside"

It's workmanlike, sensible and worthy to keep a good log of what goes into your freezer when, and the date it's removed. But given the choice of a proper log *or* fail-safe labeling, *PFB* opts for labels. We'll hedge a bit,

though, and hold out for one section of a large freezer used for miscellaneous convenience foods; the size of the section depends on how much
prebaked goods you have, and whether main-dish packages will feed
more than six. The 2½- to 3+-cubic-foot freezer in today's refrigerator,
being used as a back-up rather than as a long-term storage unit, is likely
to have a bargain pork roast or small turkey and an overwrapped half-
gallon carton of ice cream as the bulkiest items. We would expect the
foods here to be packed mostly in servings for 2 or 3 people, with many
collections of individual packets.

So labeling is the important thing. And it must be durable. The most
permanent is a slip of paper inscribed in wax crayon with name, treatment, amount, date, and (1) slipped *face outward* between the inner individually wrapped contents and the stronger outer bag before the latter is
sealed; (2) or the same slip is attached flat to the outer wrap or carton with
the toughest of wide transparent tapes covering all the legend. (Example:
¼ # sautéed mushroom stems 8/11/80—no need to add "fresh &
chopped.") Once there was a ½-pint jar with an unreadable label: it
looked for the world like clarified chicken broth until, in the saucepan, it
became coagulating egg whites.

These Don't Freeze Well

Rather than note crankiness or poor behavior in freezing as some ingredients
come along, we think it's sensible to deal with them in a bunch. So:

These suffer flavor changes:

Garlic, especially if uncooked, gets stronger.
Onion, though, tends to lose its flavor (although being sautéed before its
   being added to the other ingredients will help it hold).
Sweet green (or the ripe red stage) bell peppers get stronger.
Sage gets bitter; so does some pepper.
Cloves get both stronger and sharp. (A number of spices either give up or
   over-do when frozen, but short storage will be O.K.) You can always
   add apple-pie spices before cooking, etc.
Artificial vanilla essence gets truly unpleasant in freezing.
Artificial sweeteners should wait until actual serving time to be added.
Artificial table salt—substituting for a sodium compound—should wait to
   be added until the food is being served.
Table salt (sodium chloride) fades, and has the added drawback of inhib-
   iting good freezing if used in pronounced quantities (ham, bacon, etc.,
   don't hold long in the freezer, although part of this failure is their fat
   content).
Fried, especially deep-fried, foods taste stale: not rancid, just tired.

These suffer texture changes:

Hard-cooked egg whites get rubbery and tough. (So don't freeze dishes garnished with chopped egg or egg slices; or chopped-egg sandwich fillings; or stuffed eggs.)

Cooked soft meringue toppings get tough and shrink.

Mayonnaise separates and boiled dressings separate when frozen alone.

Cream sauces or wheat-flour-thickened gravies separate—*but there's a whole section on frozen sauces coming under "Sauces for Main Dishes" in a minute.*

Lettuce, tomatoes, celery, cucumbers and similar salad vegetables get limp and watery. (But they hold in gelatin salad, also coming.)

Raw apples and grapes get mushy. Raw apples, bananas, avocados, peaches and pears get dark without an anti-oxidant treatment (see Chapter 12, "Freezing Fruits," and Chapter 17, "Common Ingredients, etc.")

Old potatoes get grainy and soft in a frozen stew; new ones freeze better. But why not add potatoes when you're reheating the stew?

Green peas are better frozen separately and added to a combination during reheating.

Cooked pasta loses texture, but cooked rice does not: try substituting the rice from time to time.

Cheese-and-crumb toppings get soggy and dull: add when you're preheating the food for serving.

Custards—stirred (also called "boiled" though it's not), or baked or used as fillings—separate or weep.

Soft cake frostings and boiled icings get tacky (butter-and-sugar ones freeze well, however).

FREEZING EGGS

There's a giant *IF* with using frozen eggs and it has several parts.

You may use a frozen egg raw or nearly raw or quick-cooked just enough to set it if you can vouch for its having been (1) taken newly laid from the nest, (2) perfectly sound and unblemished, (3) properly refrigerated immediately, and kept in this careful cold storage only a short time before use, (4) thoroughly washed and dried before being cracked open, and thereafter (5) handled with scrupulous cleanliness and dispatch.

Otherwise frozen eggs should be used only in long-cooked or long-baked foods. The reason is simple. Uncooked eggs are possibly the favorite growing medium of Salmonellae, which cause severe but usually short-term gastrointestinal illness in the person who eats them. And freezing does not destroy bacteria, it merely slows their growth to a halt. So if they have entered a nest-cracked egg or have been transferred inside from an uncleansed shell when the egg was opened, they will multiply if the eggs are thawed at room temperature or warmer; and they will not be destroyed by heat low and brief enough merely to set eggs delicately.

Be cautious, therefore, of using defrosted eggs in mayonnaise, Hollandaise sauce and its cousins, stirred (or so-called "boiled" custard that of course is not really boiled), quick-scrambled eggs or omelets. You must satisfy all the safeguards above before you make chocolate mousse or the old-fashioned "snow" puddings.

Instead, think of thawing your eggs to use for fancy cakes or breads, or for any dessert like Indian Pudding or rice pudding.

How Much in a Batch?

As you prepare to freeze your eggs, examine each one before adding it to the others in the freezer container. For eggs to be frozen whole—i.e., yolks and white combined gently by stirring—break each egg into a saucer, and look for desirable firm whites and plump, high-standing yolks. For freezing separated eggs, put each white and each yolk in its own saucer before adding either to the batch being frozen.

Eggs to be frozen must be stirred gently in the freezing container after they are counted and added. For whole eggs, combine by stirring. Do the same for whites, taking care lest any bubbles get incorporated (air will dry the whites). Do the same for yolks—*with this added treatment to help prevent them from coagulating during storage:* gently stir in ½ teaspoon salt OR 1 teaspoon granulated sugar, or other natural sweetener, into 6 yolks. And note the sugar/salt on the label.

If you are dealing with many eggs at once, and want to prepare them in bulk even though they will be packaged in small amounts, stir in the total anticoagulant needed for however many times you have multiplied the per-6-yolks proportion, then fill individual freezing molds according to the equivalents given below.

Surely you don't want to whack off a chunk of frozen egg and guess at the resulting measurement: much simpler to have in mind several basic recipes you use a good deal, and package the eggs according to the amounts you'll want. For the rest, freeze in small quantities—bring out the muffin tins and the ice-cube trays again—and use the following measurements:

Equivalent measurements in large fresh eggs

1 tablespoon stirred egg yolk	= 1 egg yolk
2 tablespoons stirred egg white	= 1 egg white
3 tablespoons mixed whites and yolks	= 1 whole egg
1 cup whole mixed eggs	= 5 whole eggs
1 pint mixed whole eggs	= 10 whole eggs
1 pint stirred whites	= 16 whites
1 pint stirred yolks	= 24 yolks

Thawing Eggs

Frozen eggs must never be thawed by warming of any kind (viz. the increased bacterial load of Salmonellae, for one example, if the fresh eggs were mishandled). Therefore a 1-pint container may take up to 10 hours to thaw properly in a refrigerator. An alternative would be to thaw the container under *cold running water:* this would cut thawing time to about 3 hours.

It's much simpler to package in smaller amounts, and thaw correctly in correspondingly less time.

Thawed eggs may NEVER be refrozen.

FREEZING DAIRY FOODS

Homogenized Milk

As an emergency ration, sealed 1-quart cartons of homogenized milk may be held for up to 3 months in a freezer; or the milk may be decanted into straight-sided freezer jars or rigid plastic containers, with 1 inch of headroom for pints, 1½ inches of headroom for quarts.

Usually the milk thaws smoothly enough to drink; certainly it does well for sauces or soups or custards.

The fat in milk *not* homogenized separates out as flakes that will not blend again when the milk thaws. It may be used for some cooking purposes, however.

Freezing Cream

Cream must be heavy, with at least 40 percent butterfat, to freeze successfully. It sends an oily film over hot coffee, although this drawback may be minimized if the cream is heated to 175 F/80 C for 10 to 15 minutes, and 3 tablespoons of sugar is added to each 1 pint of cream. Cool quickly, pour into straight-sided freezer jars or rigid plastic containers with tight covers, leaving 1 inch of headroom for each pint.

Thaw in the refrigerator.

Frozen cream whips well.

Cream rosettes: Whip heavy cream, as above, with ¼ cup confectioner's sugar for each 1 pint of cream. When it peaks, drop it in rosettes onto freezer film laid over a cookie sheet, and freeze on the coldest shelf at Sharp Freeze setting. Check after 8 hours (they should be solid); when they can be handled without losing shape, remove and wrap each separately in several folds of fresh film (which helps to cushion as well as to prevent freezer burn); pack in rigid boxes or between two paper or foil pie plates taped together to form a hollow container.

Little thawing is necessary: just lay rosettes atop individual servings of pudding, parfait, etc., before carrying to the table.

Sour cream separates when frozen, perhaps because of the butterfat content or because of the commercial souring method. It may be combined with other ingredients (see "Sauces," later) and frozen. Spread as a topping, it may be sweetened slightly and "set" by a few minutes in a Hot oven (*c.* 450 F/232 C).

Freezing Butter

For best and safest results, freeze it freshly made from sweet pasteurized cream, salted or unsalted (salted has shorter ideal storage, 2 to 3 months). If it's store-bought and in ¼-pound portions, overwrap the carton.

If it's in bulk, devise your own portions as to volume/weight; roll each piece like a small cylinder of cookie dough, wrap with plastic film, then store several pieces together in freezer bags. Be sure to label according to the amount in each portion.

Thaw in the refrigerator.

Freezing Cheese

Cheeses that freeze well are Camembert, Port du Salut, Mozarella, Liederkrantz and their cousins, and Parmesan.

Cheeses with a high fat content (such as Cheddar, Swiss, and American brick, etc.), are best kept at refrigerator temperatures (32 to 40 F/Zero to 4 C). If you have more than you can use soon, though, cut it in ½-pound (or less) pieces, wrap each piece tightly, label and freeze.

Plain cream cheese (fatty) mixed with cream for dips, etc., will freeze satisfactorily.

If the curds of cottage cheese are *not washed,* it keeps quite well. This means you can freeze homemade cottage cheese, but not the commercial kind. But it, too, may be combined with other ingredients in a gelatin salad for freezing.

Freezing Ice Cream

Either purchased or homemade ice cream keeps its quality up to 2 months in the freezer—although your own recipe, using a rich custard or gelatin base, holds the better of the two. Neither will keep well unless it is carefully wrapped and sealed after every time it is opened.

Store homemade ice cream in good plastic freezer tubs with tight covers; allow 1½ inches of headroom for each 1 pint because of its expansion. Either repack commercial ice cream in good plastic freezer containers, or put the carton/tub in a freezer bag and seal with a tie.

Press a layer of plastic freezer film down on the ice cream in a partially used container to prevent crystals from forming; leave headroom, cover securely.

FREEZING MAIN DISHES

It may seem to be putting the cart before the horse to talk about main dishes now instead of soup and salad, but we offer just one all-important recipe in this section—plus a worthwhile procedure for changing an entrée into an hors d'oeuvre or a dessert: they both have bearing on auxiliary foods that you are likely to freeze. Let's deal with some necessary general things first, though.

ROUNDUP OF POINTS THAT MAKE A DIFFERENCE

See Chapter 24, "Cooking," for metric conversions that apply to main dishes particularly and for correcting temperatures/times if you cook at high altitudes (these latter are in Chapter 3 as well).

The TV dinner pitfall is an ordinary hazard: we all start out wanting to create platter meals like the ones in the supermarket, only better. However, the bought ones usually have at least one part that is undercooked deliberately, while its sidebars can stand long reheating. The makers have established why to leave some parts sealed, others partly covered, and one wholly uncovered during the platter's time in the oven. And we haven't.

So cook and package your own favorite things in separate reheating containers or decant them into a saucepan over low heat; deal with each part of your meal on its own merits when you're putting it together—and stand back for the compliments.

Re-cooking Times

These can be tricky. Some authorities murmur to undercook any dish that must be reheated. This is easy for, say "brown and serve" Parker House rolls; it's not so easy for a multi-component casserole. Probably the best solution to the problem is to start by cooking fully any dish you plan to freeze and reheat, leaving off the cheese-crumb topping until it goes into the oven for the last time; then *thaw the food in the refrigerator,* and rely on oven time only for decent reheating.

Later, with experience (and jotting notes on your recipe card) you can figure on the time required for cooking the dish as it comes frozen from the freezer. There is no absolute rule-of-thumb for the time required to cook still-frozen main dishes like casseroles, layered pasta combinations, pot pies, etc., these ideas may help:

1. *Temperature.* Use the oven-setting at which the dish was originally cooked; or, if it's a pot pie whose filling is precooked, use the oven-setting required to cook the top crust perfectly.
2. *Time.* Start with *less than double* the original cooking time: if it took 30 minutes to bake your pasta-plus-sauce-plus-cheese dish for serving, think first of baking it frozen for 50 minutes. Then check: it should be bubbling around the edges, and the center must be hot—and neither of these is happening. Check in another 15 minutes: nearly ready; add a few minutes more. *And use your pencil thermometer* (the good one you got when you were canning in cans, or were exhausting seafood in jars);

or *use your roasting thermometer,* by golly. They'll tell you if the center is hot enough when the sides are bubbling just right.

In the back of your mind will be the feeling that you will end up by using double the original cooking time, but there's no need to be rigid about it. Use the appearance around the edges of the dish, and the color of a topping or a crust—AND a thin and reliable thermometer.

Microwave ovens have their own instructions for dealing with hard-frozen foods. Convection ovens generally will ask you to rely more on appearance and internal temperature.

And then there are the foods to be heated loose—dumped from their containers into an ovenproof serving dish (and heated in a Medium oven, with minimum stirring; and perhaps a crumb topping added in the last few minutes). Or heated over simmering water in a double boiler. No problems here: you can tell when they're ready to serve.

Length of Freezer Storage

The maximum storage times for convenience foods given by experts is 6 months for cookie dough (more, if they're baked) down to 2 weeks for gelatin salads (which break down over longer hauls). These and the times for more robust dishes mean the length of time that the food is still at its peak and retains best texture, flavor, etc.; it does *not* mean that, if stored longer than for the stated recommendation, the foods have become spoiled or dangerous to eat.

Dairy products' best storage ranges from up to 6 months for butter, down to 3 months for cream, 6 weeks for ice cream, and about 1 month for whipped cream. These spans are approximate, but they're a good yardstick.

Pastries have a longer freezer life than the creams. Hearty soups and stews are good for from 2 to 4 months; their relatively short life comes from the fact that they often contain seasonings that do not stand up well for long freezing (see "These Don't Freeze Well," earlier).

Roasted meats are frozen usually cut off the bone, or in serving-size slices, etc. It is important to remove fatty skin and fatty tissue to prolong freezer life (fat impairs freezing). Small game birds, rabbit or poultry may be precooked as the start of becoming a fricassee or being served in a chafing dish with a special brown sauce; if their cooking is arrested so it can be finished later, the storage time is less than for fully cooked meat dishes, which can hold well up to 4 months.

Large pieces of meat may be packed in a large container, but it is best to separate the pieces by double folds of freezer film, or to wrap each piece in foil or film before adding it to the pack. Such dividers allow you to remove easily only part of what's in a large container, or to spread all the contents out for quicker thawing or reheating.

All small pieces of meat, or sliced meats, keep much better if they are covered with a gravy or a cream sauce to help keep out the air. These sauces are the most difficult aspect of preparing homemade convenience main dishes, and they are worth a separate main section all their own which follows.

Mochiko: "Sweet" Rice Flour for Frozen Sauces

Gravies and sauces thickened with all-purpose wheat flour, with potato flour—even with that old standy-by, cornstarch—are likely to separate in freezing; wheat-flour sauces require thinning after mere refrigeration. But there is an almost magic ingredient that prevents curdling in the freezer: *mochiko* (mo'-chi-ko), a special rice flour that is often termed "waxy" by occidentals and is known as "sweet" rice flour by the Japanese (it's not sweet in itself, but gets its name from being used in cakes and other confections). Its virtue for our purposes is that it "stretches," resulting in a sauce notable for smoothness and elasticity, as the makers of brand-name frozen convenience foods have known for a long time.

WHERE TO GET IT

PFB is pleased to know how householders can get it. Which is at any oriental food store in fairly large cities, and routinely in supermarkets that serve communities with Indonesian or Japanese heritage.

If there is no such store handy to you, ask your favorite neighborhood market to stock it. The brand we've seen most often in the United States is "Blue Star," from Koda Farms, Inc., Dos Palos, California 93665. Your local merchant can get it from them; and make clear at the outset that you don't expect to pay an exorbitant price for it. (Needing potato flour for gnocchi, reluctantly we paid $2.54 for 2 pounds of potato starch at a health-food store; perhaps its being labeled hypoallergenic explains the price. The recipes on the bag used it as a thickener for puddings and in place of wheat flour in baked goods.) In 1981 the range of prices on our 1-pound boxes of mochiko were $1.29 in uptown Manhattan in New York City, 79 cents in Boston, 75 cents in Orange County, California.

ALTERNATIVES TO MOCHIKO

If you do not have this sweet rice flour, here are some things you can do to hinder curdling:

1. At high speed you beat the dickens out of the cooked sauce before you combine it/pour it over the food that's to be frozen; or you can wait to do it when the food is being heated for serving (which means that the sauce must be removed from the food, and the job could be messy).
2. You can substitute ½ the milk called for in a cream sauce with a not-too-vigorous meat/chicken/seafood stock if the food lends itself to the flavors of these broths.
3. You can add an egg to the cream sauce this way: In a tall mixing bowl, or in your blender at low speed, beat together 1 egg yolk with 2 tablespoons heavy cream; pour slowly onto this beaten-egg mixture—stirring all the while so the egg doesn't get a chance to start cooking—1 cup of hot freshly made white sauce (or call it cream sauce, or Béchamel

sauce without the onion). When thoroughly mixed, the sauce is poured back into the heavy pot in which you made the original white sauce and, over low heat and stirring gently, you cook it till it thickens. Be wary of correcting the seasoning before you freeze the food: wait until it's being heated for serving to add salt, which fades, or pepper, which can get bitter in freezing; see "These Don't Freeze Well," earlier.

Parenthetically, as substitutes for mochiko we prefer these procedures to using tapioca flour, which lengthens the time needed to prepare the sauce, and which must be prevented from coming inadvertently to a boil lest it get stringy—and there goes your texture.

BASIC FREEZER SAUCE WITH MOCHIKO

To adapt a favorite recipe for mochiko, start with the fact that you use it measure-for-measure like white all-purpose flour as a thickening agent. This is simplified, but workable. With the 1-to-1 proportion, you can translate by using the following comparisons with white all-purpose wheat flour: the liquid is 1 cup/8 oz/250 mL, which should yield 1 cup of White Sauce (see Chapter 24). Potato starch and regular cornstarch have twice the thickening power as the wheat flour above. With tapioca flour and delicate arrowroot, 1 tablespoon does the work of 2½ tablespoons of the wheat flour. However, even more important than ratios in dealing with mochiko is that it *does not behave like white wheat flour* if it is heated with butter before the hot liquid is added: under such treatment it gets gummy and clumps.

The recipe below makes a good 1½ cups of fairly thick, rich white sauce for creamed or scalloped dishes. Chicken, poultry or seafood broths may be substituted for part or all of the milk.

>   4 tablespoons butter or margarine
> 1½ cups milk
>   pinch (⅛ teaspoon) ground white pepper
>   (optional ¼ teaspoon salt)
> 2½ tablespoons mochiko
>   ¼ cup cold milk

Over low heat combine in an enameled heavy saucepan, or in the top of a double boiler over simmering water, the 1½ cups of milk and the butter and seasonings. When the liquid is hot but not scalding, add a well-blended paste of the mochiko and the ¼ cup of milk. Stir gently and constantly as the sauce cooks and for a few minutes after it thickens.

Variations with Mochiko Sauces

1. Use mochiko for brown gravies, where the pan juices are eked out with meat stock, and such additions as minced sautéed mushrooms, small julienned vegetables, minced ham, or wine or special herbs give the dish its special character. Make the sauce in the manner described above—adding mochiko paste to heated liquid, etc. The sliced or

chunked meat is packed in a freezer container, and the cooled sauce is poured over it in such a way that it gets into every cranny and covers the food completely. Leave appropriate headroom.

2. Use mochiko to thicken the sauces for stews, oriental dishes that call for cornstarch, "deviled" fillings, à la king mixtures (remembering that some of the ingredients for these last dishes change flavor: see "These Don't Freeze Well").

3. Use mochiko to thicken the juices of berry or fruit pies that are frozen unbaked. Make a thin paste of mochiko, add it to simmering fruit until it is incorporated; cool the fruit filling quickly, pour it into the pastry shell and proceed according to the description later for dessert pies.

4. For scalloped dishes that are built in part from raw ingredients, to be frozen uncooked, use light mochiko cream sauce instead of cream; this is particularly good for oysters in a scallop; it also helps fish fillets smothered in a flavored sauce otherwise made with wheat flour (which is likely to separate). By the way, cheese added to sauces can make them stringy from freezing and reheating: best to add cheese to such sauces when the food is being prepared for serving.

Other Main Dishes

You have your own favorite recipes, and some from Chapter 24 adapt well to freezing. For extremely large batches—the usual amount of ingredients given will serve 24—we recommend USDA *H&G Bulletin No. 40* (1973), *Freezing Combination Main Dishes.* There are other publications dealing in part with convenience dishes listed in Chapter 25, under the subsection referring to this present chapter.

THE BEAUTY OF FILO PASTRY SHEETS

The freezers *PFB* knows best always contain a supply of *filo* (also *phylo,* which is closer to the Greek) pastry sheets, bought sealed in boxes by the pound from Antonio Recchia's Milano Importing Company in Springfield, Massachusetts. We make a point of asking Mr. Recchia for them, because he notifies us when a fresh supply is coming in; then it is up to us to freeze them for the first time. The filo comes in two widths (we use them both) and the sheets are so parchment-thin that they're translucent. They can be used as pastry for meat-and-rice pies, for the famous Spinach Pie (*Spanakopitta*) below, as "thousand-layer" cases for tiny dessert tarts or for canapes or for main-dish piroshkis.

Basically, each sheet is laid out on a board or in a pan, then dribbled/painted with melted butter and oil, and another sheet is placed on it, treated the same way. By using half the sheets as a bottom crust, as it were, and putting a filling in the middle, and topping the whole thing with more buttered layers of filo, you have achieved a dish that freezes well, heats splendidly, and always brings pleasure.

The trouble in working with filo is that the sheets dry extremely quickly and start to crumble at the edges even while you are spreading the bottom layers and preparing to deal with the top. So work fast. And take a scrupulously clean tea towel, wring it out in warm water, and lay it on the sheets that are waiting to be oiled/buttered. If you have unused sheets, let them dampen ever so little from the towel, then fold them over and over with waxed paper between the folds; wrap the baton of filo in freezer film, using several thicknesses, then return the filo to its own moisture/vapor-proof envelope; slide it back into the box; seal the box. Remember to label the box with how much filo remains before you freeze it.

If you have bought fresh filo and frozen it in its unopened box, let it thaw for 2 hours before trying to use it: the folds will break unless they're limber—and, though it's all edible and you can use scraps in the layers—the sheets will tear.

Greek Spinach Pie
About Ten Servings, or Two 8-by-8-inch Pans' Worth

---

about 20 ounces frozen spinach (weigh your packets, or buy 2 10-ounce
  boxes from the supermarket)
½ pound feta cheese
½ pound small-curd cottage cheese, preferably uncreamed
½ teaspoon freshly grated nutmeg
½ teaspoon dried mint rubbed fine
1 tablespoon scraped onion pulp
6 large eggs, beaten
  (optional: ½ teaspoon salt)
1 pound of fresh, or freshly thawed, filo
½ cup light oil
½ pound butter or margarine, melted

Cook the spinach, drain it thoroughly, and put it in a blender or food processor (steel blade), or in a mixing bowl for an electric beater. Add eggs, cheeses, seasonings, and beat at high speed until the spinach is in particles, the eggs have frothed, and the cheese is combined well with the other ingredients. Let the filling rest while you prepare the filo.

Use a 9-×-13-×-2-inch pan, or two 8-×-8-inch cake pans (these latter will cut to serve 6 portions).

Unfold filo and lay it out under the damp tea towel at the top of your bread board. Think of it as being divided half for the bottom of the large pan, the other half for the top; if you are using the two smaller pans, you will have to trim your sheets to fit—don't worry, they'll work out fine. Work with one sheet at a time.

With a soft pastry brush (a stiff one will tear the filo when it is oiled) paint the bottom of your pan with a mixture of oil and melted margarine/butter.

Drape a trimmed sheet of filo so that it will tuck well in at the corners on the bottom, and rise up over the rim of the pan all round; paint it with oil; continue layering the pan until you have used all the filo allotted for the bottom. Spoon in the filling, taking it to each corner. Lay the first top sheet over the filling, oil it, repeat; when the last sheet is used, fold—*never trim off*—the raw edges of filo over themselves several times until they make a roll all the way around below the rim of the pan. Brush the top and the roll with remaining oil mixture, and bake in a 350 F/177 C oven for 45 minutes to 1 hour, or until the top is golden and crisp.

Chill in the refrigerator before freezing. To protect the fragile top crust, put gently crumpled freezer film over the top, and devise a box lid to prevent the pie's being crushed. Use special freezer wrap in a drugstore fold (see Chapter 11); label with a wax crayon, and put the wrapped pie in a freezer bag; seal.

Often it is better to freeze pastries uncooked, but the filling has often made our unfrozen Spinach Pie tough on the bottom, so we prefer to freeze it fully cooked. Thaw in the refrigerator, heat at 350 F/177 C for 35 to 40 minutes with the top covered with foil for the first 15 minutes.

Greek Cheese Tarts

How large you make these crisp, plump triangles depends on how wide you cut the strips of filo from which you make them, so we can't give you a definite yield from the proportions below. Still, the filling freezes well, and you can always wait to build some tarts until you have extra filo thawed. Cutting strips smaller than 2 inches wide makes folding too finicky; as wide as 4 inches means that the pastries are large piroshki or sandwich size.

These tarts do well prebaked to a brown-and-serve stage just short of crispness, and they're small enough to go frozen into the oven and get finished in fairly short time (how long depends upon how big). Cooked completely and merely to be reheated, they need extra cushioning in the freezer. They should not be served merely thawed: heat them through before serving.

½ pound feta cheese
½ pound dry cottage cheese
4 eggs, beaten
¼ teaspoon freshly grated nutmeg
   (optional: ¼ teaspoon salt if feta is used; ½ teaspoon if all cottage cheese)
½ pound margarine or butter, melted
¼ cup light cooking oil
½ pound filo pastry sheets, thawed

Combine the cheeses, eggs, nutmeg and optional salt in a mixing bowl or blender, and beat at high speed until the mixture becomes silky and peaks. Lay the unfolded filo sheets at the top of your pastry board so as to leave free working space near you; cover the waiting sheets with a slightly dampened towel. Combine oil and melted butter in a saucepan; have ready a soft pastry brush. Lift off the top sheet of filo and lay it as a horizontal rectangle near you;

lightly oil it with the pastry brush. Starting at the left and going right (if you're right-handed) quickly cut 2- or 3-inch strips crossways—but of course use whatever width will divide the pastry sheet evenly without waste.

Folding Filo

The next step is rather like the ceremonial folding of the Flag.

Starting with the strip nearest you, dab 1 rounded teaspoon of filling 1 inch from the left end of the strip if the strip is 2 inches, and still assuming that you are right-handed; it would be about 1½ inches from the end if the strip is 3 inches—*and* midway between top and bottom. Bring the upper left corner of the strip down over the filling until it touches the lower edge of the strip: this will make a right triangle. Next, bend the triangle over so the new fold is vertical, and the edges of the pastry are aligned at the bottom. Then fold toward the right again, this time bringing the lower left corner up to the *top* edge of the still-unfolded pastry.

Keep folding down-to-right, then across, then up-to-right until the strip is all used. The filling now is sealed inside the pastry; lay it on a baking pan with the last raw edge underneath.

The triangles may be placed fairly close together, because the pastry does not rise, although the filling will make the finished tart plump when it bakes. To serve, bake in a 350 F/177 C oven for 30 to 35 minutes or until the pastry is flaky and golden. Serve warm.

To freeze, bake 20 minutes, then check to see if the tarts are plump, cooked on the bottom, but have not yet begun to brown. Remove; cool completely on a rack. Wrap closely in one thickness of paper toweling, overwrap with freezer film, pack gently in freezer boxes or between facing foil pie pans; seal, label, freeze.

Side-dish variations. Make the strips wider, and use Basic Sautéed Cabbage (Chapter 24) to make vegetarian piroshkis. (When you make large triangles, though, work with two sheets, each oiled; otherwise the casing is too fragile to contain the filling.) Minced turkey or chicken, with a little stuffing, and all moistened with gravy; or ground lamb and rice combined with a little cottage cheese and bound with an egg—any imaginative leftover becomes important in filo cases.

Sweet variations. There are many readily at hand, like: Mincemeat; or an apple chopped with raisins and some walnuts and moistened further with apricot jam for paraphrased strudel; dry cottage cheese, sweetened and flavored and bound with an egg.

FREEZING AUXILIARY PARTS OF A MEAL

SOUPS

Concentrate soups to save space. The Dutch Green Pea Soup in "Cooking," Chapter 24, does very well as a concentrated base: just add hot water to let it down.

From this same chapter—and also some broths/stocks canned in Chapter 10—take other soups to freeze, *except for* the onion soup. The flavors in French Onion Soup will suffer from freezing.

The base for New England Fish Chowder also freezes well, although it does not store so long as stocks or clear soups do. Thaw it in the refrigerator, then stir in hot milk before putting it over heat in a heavy pot.

BAKED GOODS

BREADS AND ROLLS

Generally, homemade doughs for yeast breads and rolls do not bake as well as frozen dough from the supermarket does; and they hold well in the freezer only for several weeks.

Unless you must have loaves of sandwich bread on hand for emergencies, save your space for already baked yeast breads made with extra shortening and sugar: party or sweet rolls or holiday breads or individual breakfast pastries.

It is possible to freeze quick-bread dough packaged in the form of rolled-and-cut biscuits, or muffins in baking cups. However, they take much longer to bake when put directly from the freezer into the oven (no thawing here), that the results are often disappointing. They hold well only for several weeks in the freezer. Best for these reasons to whip up batches as needed.

CAKES

Angelfood, sponge and butter cakes freeze well; fruit cake is the longest freezer without suffering loss of quality.

Icings made from butter and confectioner's sugar freeze well; boiled and soft frostings do not freeze well. Custard fillings do not freeze well.

Wrap closely in freezer film, then put in a freezer bag and seal; it is often good to hold them in pastry boxes to protect them from heavier foods.

Avoid artificial vanilla.

Ideal storage time: up to 2 months.

COOKIES

Baked cookies freeze well, but why bother to wrap against breakage when raw cookie doughs are such a godsend when rolled and frozen in cylinders from which thin slices may be cut off and put in the oven?

Ruth Hertzberg's Stand-by Cookies (Chapter 24) are ideal. Avoid artificial vanilla; also, strong spices can get bitter. Baked or unbaked, they hold well up to 9 or 10 months.

TWO-CRUST PIES

Do not skimp on the shortening used in your pastry if you intend to freeze your pies.

Freeze pies with pastry *uncooked* for best texture. Use thoroughly chilled cooked fillings for best results. Starch-or-egg-yolk-thickened pies lose texture, unless instead of wheat flour you use mochiko—see earlier in this chapter— measure for measure instead wheat flour, or twice the called-for measure of mochiko if you'd use cornstarch.

Thicken cooked fruit fillings more for pies to be frozen than if they are to be cooked and served without freezing.

For freezing uncooked pies, treat them to "Help for the Bottom Crust," which follows the general rule for Pie Pastry in Chapter 24: this helps to prevent sogginess.

Freeze pies and pie shells completely *before* wrapping them for freezer storage; this prevents breaking the crust. Line the pie pan with freezer film, shape the rolled pastry to fit and crimp the edge, etc., as you like. When the pastry is fully frozen, lift it carefully from the molding container, wrap carefully, label; store in flat boxes if you have them, to protect the pastry from blows during storage.

Do not slit the tops of pies that are to be frozen before baking. And wait to glaze with milk or beaten egg until you put them in the oven.

Come the time for baking, frozen pastry cooks better in oven-proof glass or in dull tin or darkened aluminum. Preheat the oven to 450 F/232 C, bake the frozen pie for 20 minutes; reduce heat to the normal baking temperature and continue until it is done (about 350 to 375 F/177 to 191 C). It will take longer to finish cooking than if it were thawed before baking.

Pies frozen *after being baked* should be thawed in a Slow oven (about 325 F/163 C).

Pies with gelatin-based fillings should be thawed in the refrigerator. (Soft meringue toppings do not freeze well; add and bake them before cooling to serve.)

Freezing fruits for pie fillings are mentioned in Chapter 12; there's also a recipe for canning Apple Pie Filling in Chapter 10. If you plan to freeze specially prepared pie fillings, allow a good 2 cups of the mixture for an 8-inch pie, and 3½ cups for a 10-inch pie. Results are usually better, though, if the berries are frozen loose and stored in rigid containers, to be seasoned and sweetened, etc., just before baking. Remember that custard-based fillings do not freeze satisfactorily.

SANDWICHES

Filled sandwiches hold only for a week or so in the freezer; but, frozen, they beat last-minute hassles before a crowd arrives, or the chance of curled edges if stored ahead in the refrigerator.

These fillings *do not freeze well:* any "salad"-type combination that contains chopped egg whites (leathery), mayonnaise or cooked salad dressing (they separate), lettuce or tomato or celery or cucumber (flabby and watery), jam and jelly (weepy).

These fillings are *good for freezing:* cooked egg yolk, peanut butter, minced meat, poultry or fish with chopped pickle and just enough salad dressing to hold things together; sliced luncheon meat or meat loaf; slivered cheese and chopped olives.

Use bread at least one day old (a bite of thawed perfectly fresh bread can be a wodge), and spread both slices with butter or margarine to prevent the filling from soaking in. Mayonnaise and the like can make frozen bread soggy.

Wrap each cut sandwich closely in plastic freezer film, then package or overwrap in moisture/vapor-proof material. Label and freeze.

Freezing Gelatin Salads

Experiment to arrive at your best combinations before trying these out on guests. Here are some basics to keep in mind:

Use only ¾ of the TOTAL liquid called for in your recipe, whether the salad calls for a dessert gelatin as the vehicle for fruit, minced celery, cucumbers—yes! these fresh salad vegetables keep crisp in a gelatin salad—or you are using unflavored gelatin and say, Tomato Cocktail (in Chapter 10, "Canning Convenience Foods") to carry a medley of cooked vegetables or cooked fish like tuna. This means dissolving gelatin in ½ cup of liquid, and adding only 1 cup more (hot) liquid, to make 1½ cups—when the recipe calls for ½ cup to dissolve, plus 1½ cups added.

Dessert gelatins tend to lose color and get uneven in texture, but they are fine if they are used merely as layers to hold the other ingredients in shape.

Fresh pineapple contains an enzyme that prevents a gel, so it *may not* be one of the fruits used in a fruit-salad mold.

Frozen gelatin salads keep for only 2 weeks in the freezer; then they start to lose quality.

They may be served still nearly frozen on a bed of lettuce. Or they can start thawing for 1 hour before being served.

Whipped cream, whipped softened cream cheese, whipped cottage cheese, a little mayonnaise, sour cream—these all combine well in a gelatin salad to be frozen.

Canned fruit salad, mixed cooked vegetables, flaked fish, even minced leftover chicken or turkey make tasty salads.

General Preparation for Freezing Gelatin Salads

Save woe by freezing in the old stand-by square metal 8-x-8-inch cake pan. Line it with freezer film if you are using it only for the frozen mold, and plan to package it merely wrapped (you will unwrap and return it to its original pan for brief thawing and cutting in 6 generous serving portions). This size may be cut smaller, to serve 9, if the salad is to be a fruit dish on the side, rather than a hot-weather mainstay of aspic, vegetables and meat/fish, etc. You can always use a ring mold after your technique is perfected.

Prepare your gelatin base, refrigerate until it becomes syrupy. Meanwhile prepare the fillings: with lime or lemon or raspberry dessert gelatin, use chopped apples, minced celery, raisins; with dessert gelatins use fresh fruit (except for pineapples, and some varieties of grapes can get soft); treat apples with ascorbic acid (see "Anti-discoloration Treatments" in Chapters 12 and 17). Add whipped cream cheese, etc., and perhaps some chopped celery for more texture. Pour some of the nearly set gelatin in the pan, and put it in the freezer for a few minutes to thicken further. Remove it; fold together the solid ingredients and any cream, cream cheese, etc., with the remaining gelatin mixture, and pour all gently into the pan. Refrigerate or freeze until well set, then complete the wrapping in freezer film or moisture/vapor-proof materials. Seal and freeze.

Freezing Dabs and Snippets

The simplest way to deal with this section is to tell what's in the packets stashed in the door shelves of an upright freezer in a kitchen *PFB* knows well, and say what the ingredients were meant for. (There's another freezer, a husky chest affair, down cellar; here are stored the makings for batches of Corn Relish, q.v., and a specialty condiment or two, plus the usual large cuts of meat and related staples.) Each packet is labeled with name of the food, the measurement involved, the date, and sometimes the purpose.

You'll note that most of the items are prepared to the point needed for combining them with other ingredients to build a particular dish.

FOR SOUPS

Two-serving portions of the base for Irenja's Borscht, Dutch Green Pea Soup, and Fish Chowder. Sautéed sorrel, chopped in ½-inch strips, in ½-cup amounts; each little bag will be added to clarified Chicken Broth, to become a serving of *shav* (with sour cream and chopped dill leaves, the latter also on the door-shelf). In summer the shav is chilled in the refrigerator and poured over a cold boiled new potato in its jacket for a hottest-evening-of-the-year supper. There's also sorrel essence to enliven vegetable stews.

The ½-pint freezer jars of Clam Broth (this also was canned, in Chapter 10) will strengthen the character of scalloped oysters (which will be made with a cream sauce using mochiko), or perhaps go into oyster stew (if not clam chowder; or be served hot in its own right as an appetizer). Reduced further, it will help stretch the white clam sauce that goes well on homemade spinach linguini.

HELP FOR MAIN DISHES

There's concentrated Shrimp Stock (again, it was canned as well) to use in a jambalaya or paella, or a deviled seafood filling for filo tarts. Pan juices of chicken, lamb, pork—perhaps for fried rice; or, combined with some of the peeled roasted chestnuts, as a special stuffing for something.

There's enough roast chicken taken off the bone to combine with some chicken broth, and thicken, and drop dumplings in for a chicken fricassee for two plus two. Slices of roast lamb in gravy, each slice in its own flat little bag for easy separating, and all stacked in a box, well labeled. Slices of Baked Liver Loaf (which is so good that one forgives a graininess from freezing); several ramekins of smooth-as-satin chicken liver pâté with wine.

Two divided pairs of shad roe, poached in a court bouillon, and each now wrapped in foil with bacon fat inside for lubrication; come the time to eat them—better soon—they'll be put still wrapped in a 400 F/205 C oven for 15 minutes, then opened and partly cooked strip of bacon laid on each, to finish heating and cooking.

Some minced Italian capicola, to be used sparingly in a brown-sauce-with-wine for fresh veal kidneys when they're a good buy.

For pasta there's pesto sauce (basil-garlic-pignolias-Parmesan cheese-olive oil), frozen in patties dolloped onto a cookie sheet; then each wrapped separately, and all bagged together. The dab in the small rigid box is stuffing for tortellini pasta. Tucked behind is a chunk of Parmesan cheese.

VEGETABLES

Trimmed kale, blanched with a bit of bacon in the boiling water: this will be served with lemon. So will the several asparagus stalks; but the nearly cooked green beans will be thawed and served cold with a little olive oil.

Every fresh herb from the garden, minced and packed small. But large containers of minced fresh parsley to make taboulleh salad from. The cooked green peppers with stuffing are truly emergency food, as are the grilled tomatoes that have plenty of flavor but little presence.

A whole stuffed cabbage (sausage), cut in wedges and each wrapped in foil for quick heating. Two containers of peas bonne femme, really a vegetable stew of peas and lettuce cooked in a brown sauce. Endive, bought on sale, split and half finished for braising.

DESSERTS

Wedges of cheesecake, each wrapped separately. A handful of small cream-puff shells. Two 1-quart tubs of special boysenberry sherbert; a roll of good cookie dough to slice thin and bake and serve with it.

Fresh lemon juice frozen as ice cubes, each in its flimsy envelope and all gathered in a big freezer bag—well labeled, too, as equaling 1 or 2 lemons. Many twists of microtome-thin strips of lemon peel: start the steel blade of the food processor, put in sugar, then add the lemon zest—and you have grated lemon peel for sponge cake or buttermilk soup or a cold pudding.

That sort of thing . . .

COOK–IN–POUCH FREEZING

Microwave ovens have stolen the thunder from what was, in the late 1960's and early '70's, a novel way to serve special foods in small portions at odd hours. This was the home model of the sealer for extra-strong and boilable plastic freezer bags, in which a good planner could store all manner of emergency rations instead of spending a good deal more for them at the supermarket.

Still, a lot of us don't have microwave ovens with their magic ability to thaw and heat in a few minutes, and a heat-sealer and pouches can be wonderfully husband- and teenager-proof.

Most householders know the advantages of having handy packets of diet or wholesome snack foods on hand for family members working odd shifts, or a crowd of guests needing staggered meals. Anyone who can read the directions for cooking (certain to be part of the label in a well-run kitchen) can make part of a meal in a pot of boiling water.

THE SEALER AND HOW IT WORKS

Because a hot flatiron cannot be guaranteed to make an adequate seal even when wielded with care, you should have a special electric heat-sealer. This costs about as much as a very good automatic toaster; the price is high for just one more fun gadget that takes up space, but it's fair for a sturdy appliance you plan to use often. The leading mail-order firms offer sealers under proprietary names; you should also be able to get them in well-stocked housewares departments of large stores.

The special pouches/bags are included with the sealer, and they can be ordered separately from the outfits that sell the sealers. Usually listed in a range of small sizes, they cost roughly four times as much as conventional freezer bags—which regularly come in much larger sizes to boot.

The preparation and packaging is more complicated than for conventional freezing. Cook-in-pouch foods are either fully cooked (to be reheated), or are at least half-cooked (to be finished), before they are sealed and frozen in relatively small portions. Therefore you should get organized for a fairly concentrated session, and this means more planning ahead.

Filling Pouches and Sealing

Three hands are better than two here. And the sealer can be mounted on a wall or the side of a cupboard; or, as shown in the picture, it can rest on a chopping block to allow the weight of the food to pull the pouch down and help to expel air.

Our sealer came with an elliptical plastic collar that fits inside the pouches (all of which are the same width—it's their height that varies for the different capacities) and holds the bag open wide for filling. The collar also prevents dribbles from reaching the inside sealing surfaces, which must be entirely free of food particles in order to seal right.

If you don't have the collar, make some by cutting the bottoms from small-size aluminum-foil bread pans, then pinching little tucks in the foil to reduce the circumference of the pan to the right size. These handy makeshifts let you or your helper keep several propped-open bags ready for filling.

Rest the bottom of the collared bag on a pie dish; put in the food, *leaving 2 inches of headroom.* Remove the collar and, holding the bag by the sides near the top, snap it shut, thus forcing air out of the headroom.

Many sealers have pegs to help hold bags steady for sealing, and many pouches have perforations high on their sides to catch on the pegs (see photo). So, holding the bag upright and stretched between your hands, place its closed top in the sealer—being careful to maintain the 2-inch headroom at the sealing point—and operate the heat/pressure according to the manufacturer's directions.

Cool the sealed pouches in the refrigerator. Then label and lay them flat in the freezer, preferably only one layer deep until they're frozen; pat each bag to distribute the contents to be *uniformly about 1 inch thick.* This even thickness is important: boil-in times are based on it.

What to Freeze in Cook-in Pouches

Unless you have particular needs in mind, your likeliest foods for cook-in-pouch freezing would be programmed extras, sealed in 1-pint bags (about 3 average servings) or 1½-pint bags (5 servings). The mail-order sealer we're most familiar with offers extra 1-quart bags, but a casual consensus from house-holders who actually go in for this type of freezing is that amounts larger than 4 to 5 servings are probably handled more easily over-all if they're packaged conventionally for freezing, and are decanted for regular reheating on the stove-top or in the oven.

These extras can be grouped roughly as main dishes (fully precooked, just to be reheated); side-dish vegetables (partly precooked, to be finished in the boil-in bag); and dessert fruits (raw, to be defrosted by putting the sealed pouch in a bowl of warm water). The manufacturers' pamphlets include many more dishes, but a number of them seem like too much fuss for the benefit, frankly; you'll judge for yourself.

Main Dishes

Thin slices of meat in its gravy, stews, chicken à la king, fillets of fish in a favorite sauce, creamed things—the list goes on. Prepare as for the table: all are fully precooked. Remember that any thickened sauces are best made with mo-

Heat-sealing the special cook-in pouch; note headroom flattened, below.

chiko (special rice flour), as described at length under its own main heading, a short while ago.

Cool the food slightly—just enough so you can handle the filled pouches—and pack it immediately, leaving 2 inches of headroom for both 1-pint and 1½-pint bags (this air-space will flatten away as the bag is held to the sealer).

Boneless meats and fish take 18 minutes' boil-in time for 1-pint bags, 20 minutes for 1½-pint bags.

Casseroles and pastas take 13 minutes' boil-in time for pints, 15 minutes for 1½-pint pouches.

SIDE-DISH VEGETABLES

Of course all your vegetables will be perfectly fresh, and young and tender-crisp; carefully washed and cut/trimmed, etc., as for serving.

Precooking times given below are average for *half*-cooking the individual vegetables—which will then be finished during the boil-in time of 15 minutes for pints, 18 minutes for 1½-pint pouches.

Use only enough water to cover. Don't salt it now because salt and onion flavors tend to disappear in freezing while some herbs get strong or bitter.

When it's half-cooked, the vegetable should be cooled only enough to allow you to handle the filled pouches comfortably. Leave 2 inches of headroom as for Main Dishes. Refrigerate the sealed bags for an hour before freezing them.

Unless you use stick butter or margarine that's easily sliced, slowly melt your butter or whatever, pour it ⅛ to ¼ inch deep in a bread tin; chill quickly until it's solid, and cut squares to insert in the pouches when you fill them.

Asparagus. Choose uniformly slender spears; trim to length to fit your pouches with 2 inches of headroom, or cut small. Cook gently in your usual manner for 5–8 minutes, depending on length of the pieces. Drain, cool slightly; pack and seal.

Beans—green/Italian/snap/string/wax. Cook gently for 10 minutes. Drain, cool slightly; pack and seal.

Broccoli. Cook split young spears gently for 5 minutes. Drain, cool slightly; pack and seal.

Carrots. Cook slices gently for 15 minutes. Drain, cool slightly; pack and seal.

Cauliflower. Cook prepared flowerets gently for 5 minutes. Drain, cool slightly; pack and seal.

Corn, whole-kernel. Husk, remove silk, wash. Cut from the cob over a bowl to catch the milk. In its milk—plus only enough water to keep from sticking—cook gently for 3 minutes. Drain, cool slightly; pack and seal.

Peas, green. Cook shelled peas gently for 10 minutes. Drain, cool slightly; pack and seal.

Spinach, etc. Remove stems and any tough midribs, cut large leaves in several pieces. Boil gently for 15 minutes. (Or, for very tender leaves, shake off extra water and steam-sauté in a little oil, covered, for half the full cooking time you use for this method—about 4 minutes.) Drain, cool slightly; pack and seal.

COMMON INGREDIENTS
AND HOW TO USE THEM

What should be universal—and therefore the most common—thing in North American households is metrics, but in the United States they are far from being the accepted means of measurement. A pity, because they were adopted years ago by the government of Canada and the Canadians are well along to being completely metric. The Americans may come to them sooner or later if only as a matter of domestic convenience. Motives aside, though, we start this roundup chapter with how to translate customary measurements to metric equivalents that apply to the various ways of preserving food. By doing so we get them out of the way, enable ourselves to use equivalent measures from most of the rest of the world, and provide what truly will, in time, turn out to be a valuable service to our readers.

Metrics dealt with, we turn to ingredients we take for granted. They are everyday things, but their idiosyncrasies can make a vital difference in the safety of the food we put by.

METRIC CONVERSIONS

Seldom has any logical, ultimately beneficial, program been met with such bland mulishness as the American public has shown toward having the United States join the rest of the world's major countries in "going metric." Spurred by the smooth start made in Canada, the Congress passed the Metric Conversion Act of 1975: not to enforce change but simply to co-ordinate and plan the increasing use of the metric system in the United States. The movement would need quite a selling-job, sure; but for openers there's already the snob appeal used in citing economy cars' engine displacement in cubic centimeters or liters, as if they were racing machines in international competition.

At this writing (1982) the Dominion has virtually completed "going metric," while—aside from internal progress made by our industrial giants—supportive data for progress in the U.S.A. could note 2-liter beverage bottles, signs flashing outside banks to tell air temperature in Celsius and Fahrenheit, kilometers and miles on interstate highway markers near the Canadian border, cost-per-liter for a few brands of gasoline, and rounded equivalents in metric volume molded on the newer canning jars. Supermarket labels, however, do carry grams and milliliters on processed foods.

Hardly a landslide vote for metrics. Yet the area where it could win great popular support is in the average cook's home: here measurements of some sort are a three-meals-a-day business. Although *PFB* has 1 pound 12 ounces (0.7938 kilogram) of federal publications designed to woo us to metrics, we have been able to gather only a few crude devices—crude compared with equipment used in the test kitchens where most American recipes using grams/milliliters/Celsius originate.

So try your own hand at converting. Start with temperatures, as easiest. Unless you're a scientist, or a technician involved in the physical sciences, mainly you *feel* temperature, or turn a switch or a knob. You just recognize; you don't have to do much of anything else.

METRIC CONVERSIONS FOR TEMPERATURE

In 1714 Gabriel Daniel Fahrenheit proposed a thermometer that fixed Zero at the lowest temperature reached by a freezing mixture of ice and salt. He divided the interval between Zero and the temperature of the human body into 96 parts. Using this scale, pure water at sea level freezes at 32 degrees Fahrenheit and boils at 212 F.

Nearly three decades later, Anders Celsius invented the Centigrade thermometer, using the freezing and boiling points of water at sea level as its fixed points and putting 100 degrees between them. Thus in the Fahrenheit scale there are 180 degrees between freezing and boiling temperatures of water, compared with the 100-degree interval in the Celsius scale, where water freezes at Zero C and boils at 100 C. The two scales intersect only at −40 degrees F and C.

THE ARITHMETIC

The list of equivalents includes the temperatures cited frequently in this book. To convert other temperatures, you can use the following formulas.

If you know *Fahrenheit,* you can find *Celsius* (Centigrade) by subtracting 32, then multiplying by 5/9 (i.e., multiply by 5 and divide by 9). For example, 200 F = (200−32) × 5 ÷ 9 = 93 C.

If you know *Celsius* (Centigrade), you can find *Fahrenheit* by multiplying by 9/5 then adding 32. For example, 93 C = 93 × 9 ÷ 5 + 32 = 200 F.

Because the usual American householder's measuring equipment is not precise enough to reflect the mathematical computations in the temperatures that follow, we indicate *in italics* the rounded-off figure that offers a reasonable equivalent for everyday use.

FAHRENHEIT AND CELSIUS (CENTIGRADE)
(AT SEA LEVEL TO 1000 FEET/305 METERS ALTITUDE)

F	C (ROUNDED)	F	C (ROUNDED)	F	C (ROUNDED)
-35	*-37*	80	*27*	220	*104*
-30	*-34*	85	*29*	225	*107*
-25	*-32*	90	*32*	228	*109*
-20	*-29*	100	*38*	230	*110*
-15	*-26*	110	*43*	235	*113*
-10	*-23*	120	*49*	240	*116*
-5	*-21*	130	*54*	245	*118*
0	*-18*	140	*60*	250	*121*
5	*-15*	142	*61*	255	*124*
10	*-12*	145	*63*	260	*127*
15	*-9*	150	*66*	265	*130*
20	*-7*	160	*71*	270	*132*
25	*-4*	165	*74*	275	*135*
30	*-1*	170	*77*	280	*138*
32	*0*	175	*80*	285	*141*
35	*2*	180	*82*	290	*143*
36	*2*	185	*85*	295	*146*
37	*3*	190	*88*	300	*149*
38	*3*	195	*91*	325	*163*
39	*4*	198	*92*	350	*177*
40	*4*	200	*93*	375	*191*
45	*7*	203	*95*	400	*205*
50	*10*	205	*96*	425	*218*
60	*16*	208	*98*	450	*232*
65	*18*	210	*99*	475	*246*
70	*21*	212	*100*	500	*260*

METRIC CONVERSIONS FOR VOLUME

Perhaps two reasons why initial enthusiasm for metrics hasn't dragged American kitchens along with it are (1) no two items of our collection of tables/manuals agree at every point we think is relevant, and (2) makers of kitchen tools seem to be slacking off from marketing dual-measurement gadgets. For ready reference *PFB* uses ovenproof glass volume measures, one side marked for fluid ounces and cups, the other in milliliters (also in *deciliters,* or ¹⁄₁₀-liter steps—which so far haven't cropped up much; but not in *gills,* a rarely used amount that equals ¼ pint, or ½ U.S. cup). The comparison set of spoons offers double ends, one side going from ¼ teaspoon, to ½, to 1 teaspoon, to 1 tablespoon, and the other side giving the workable metric equivalent. Their drawback is that the measuring ends are not shaped like spoons, but rather are straight-sided, fairly deep, round wells; the contents therefore can't be divided in the old-fashioned way of cutting lengthwise down the center from handle to tip and sliding the unwanted half off the side. Designed by a designer, not by a cook.

The terms *teaspoon, tablespoon, gill, cup, pint, quart* and gallon in the list that follows—and indeed throughout the book—are U.S. measurements. Although their volumes differ in some cases from those of similar British or European designations, their metric equivalents provide the means for translating recipes from around the world. Further (but marginal): Americans are used to seeing the term *cubic centimeter* for volume in pharmaceutical prescriptions and solutions, etc., so note that *1 cubic centimeter (cc) = 1 milliliter (mL)*.

The first list below—"The (Fairly Pure) Arithmetic"—shows how to figure back and forth between units of current standard volume and metrics, because it's important to know the method, and you can always fall back on it. Because the householders' means for measuring volume metrically are so much less precise than are the available thermometers, diet scales and foot/centimeter rules, we must round off volume measurements quite roughly ("Now Rounded Off"). They're workable for now, though; and they often come on measuring cups and canning jars.

The (Fairly Pure) Arithmetic

Start with the U.S. fluid ounce, and work back for spoonfuls:

One fluid ounce (fl oz) = 29.574 milliliters (mL).
There are 2 tablespoons in 1 fl oz, so 1 tablespoon = 14.787 mL.
There are 3 teaspoons in 1 tablespoon, so 1 teaspoon = 4.929 mL.
To get ½ teaspoon, divide 4.929 by 2 = 2.465 mL.
To get ¼ teaspoon, divide 4.929 by 4 = 1.232 mL.
To get ⅛ teaspoon (usually "a pinch"), divide 4.929 by 8 = 0.6161 mL.

Now work with cups:

If you know fluid ounces (fl oz), you find milliliters (mL) by multiplying by 29.574.
There are 8 fl oz in 1 cup (c), so multiply 29.574 by 8 and get 1 c = 236.59 mL.
To get ¼ cup, multiply 29.574 by 2 (oz) = 59.148 mL.
To get ⅓ cup multiply 29.574 by 2.67 (oz) = 78.96 mL.
To get ½ cup (1 gill) multiply 29.574 by 4 (oz) = 118.30 mL.
To get ⅔ cup, multiply 29.574 by 5.33 (oz) = 157.74 mL.
To get ¾ cup, multiply 29.574 by 6 (oz) = 177.44 mL.
To get 1 pint (16 fl oz) multiply 29.574 by 16 = 473.18 mL.
To get 1 quart (32 fl oz) multiply 29.574 by 32 = 946.36 mL.
To get 1 gallon (128 fl oz) multiply 29.574 by 128 = 3785.4 mL.

NOW ROUNDED OFF

⅛ teaspoon = *0.62 mL*	⅛ cup = 1 fl oz = *30 mL*
¼ teaspoon = *1.25 mL*	¼ cup = 2 fl oz = *60 mL*
½ teaspoon = *2.5 mL*	⅓ cup = 2⅔ fl oz = *80 mL*
¾ teaspoon = *3.75 mL*	½ cup = 4 fl oz = *125 mL*
1 teaspoon = *5 mL*	¾ cup = 6 fl oz = *200 mL*
1¼ teaspoons = *6.25 mL*	1 cup = 8 fl oz = *250 mL*
1½ teaspoons = *7.5 mL*	2 cups = 16 fl oz = *500 mL*
1¾ teaspoons = *8.75 mL*	1 (U.S.) pint = 16 fl oz = *500 mL*
2 teaspoons = *10 mL*	1 quart = 32 fl oz = *1000 mL/1 liter (L)*
2½ teaspoons = *12.5 mL*	4 quarts = 128 fl oz = *4 L*
3 teaspoons = ½ fl oz = *15 mL*	1 gallon = 128 fl oz = *4 L*
1 tablespoon = ½ fl oz = *15 mL*	(1 dec*i*liter = *0.10 L*)
2 tablespoons = 1 fl oz = *30 mL*	(1 dec*a*liter = *10 L*)

METRIC CONVERSIONS FOR WEIGHT

If you know ounces avoirdupois (oz av), you can find grams (g) by multiplying by 28.35.

If you know pounds (lb: 16 oz av), you can find kilograms (kg: 1000 g) by muliplying by 0.4536.

If you know grams, you can find ounces avoirdupois by multiplying by 0.0353.

If you know kilograms (kg), you can find pounds by multiplying by 2.205.

Because even our good spring-type scales (see Chapter 25) are not refined enough to reflect the mathematical computations in the amounts below, we show *in italics* at the end of the line a *rounded-off* figure that offers a reasonable equivalent for everyday use.

1 oz (¹⁄₁₆ lb) = *28 g*	2 lbs = *0.91 kg*
2 oz (⅛ lb) = *57 g*	5 lbs = *2.27 kg*
4 oz (¼ lb) = *113 g*	10 lbs = *4.54 kg*
8 oz (½ lb) = *227 g*	15 lbs = *6.80 kg*
12 oz (¾ lb) = *340 g*	20 lbs = *9.07 kg*
16 oz (1 lb) = *454 g/0.454 kg*	25 lbs = *11.34 kg*

METRIC CONVERSIONS FOR LENGTH

Automobile mechanics and machinists are luckier than homebodies when it comes to metrics, because so much of their equipment has meticulous conversions that allow workers to deal with the measurements of foreign supplies and specifications.

If you know inches (in) you can find centimeters (cm: 1/100 metre) by multiplying by 2.54.

(*PFB* doesn't deal with millimeters—mm: 1/1000 metre—but if you know inches, you find millimeters by multiplying by 25.40.)

If you know centimeters, you can find inches by multiplying by 0.394.

If you know millimeters, you can find inches by multiplying by 0.0394.

Because the usual American householder's measuring equipment is not precise enough to reflect the mathematical computations in the amounts below, we show *in italics* a rounded-off figure that offers, as best it can for the time being, a reasonable equivalent for everyday use.

⅛ in =	*0.32 cm*	2 in =	*5.1 cm*
¼ in =	*0.64 cm*	3 in =	*7.6 cm*
½ in =	*1.27 cm*	4 in =	*10.1 cm*
¾ in =	*1.90 cm*	6 in =	*15.2 cm*
1 in =	*2.54 cm*	8 in =	*20.3 cm*
1½ in =	*3.75 cm*	12 in =	*30.5 cm*

COMMON INGREDIENTS

WATER

There's hardly any method of putting food by that does not involve water somewhere along the line, beginning with the first washing of raw materials, continuing to the various water-based solutions used in canning and freezing and curing—which includes brining of all sorts, to ferment or to preserve—and even extending to some steps in drying.

The most important single thing about water used in any process for preserving food is this:

The water must be fresh and at least *of drinking quality.*

A staggering number of spoilage micro-organisms are added to food by impure water. Therefore:

Don't assume that "it's-going-to-be-cooked-anyway" will counteract *all* the extra contamination. Remember that an excessive bacterial load can tax your preserving method beyond the point where it is effective. (Nor is there any sure-fire, non-toxic sterilizing substance that you can tuck into a container of food before you process it—never mind what folkloric compounds keep surfacing in descriptions of ye olde-tyme methods.)

In any step of preserving food, don't use any water that you cannot vouch for as safe to drink. In the late 1970's an outbreak of botulism from home-canned food was traced to the soil-borne bacteria in a family's water supply; the canning procedures were not able to deal with it.

And change wash-water often, or wash under running tap water you would drink.

DEALING WITH MINERALS IN WATER

"Hard" water has above-average mineral content (calcium is often an offender here). Hard water can shrivel pickles or toughen vegetables.

You can check for hardness by shaking a small amount of soap—*not* detergent—in a jar of water: if it makes a good head of suds in your water, hardness is not a problem.

Or ask your municipal water department to tell you the composition of the water that comes from your tap. In rural areas, your health officer can tell you how to have your private water supply tested for mineral content as well as for bacterial count.

Where there's *no dangerous air pollution* ("acid rain," etc): If your water is hard, and you can't get distilled water, collect rainwater *in the open*—not as run-off from dusty roofs—and strain it through layers of cheesecloth.

Or if you know that hardness is caused by calcium or magnesium carbonates, boil the water for 20 to 30 minutes to settle out the mineral salts; then pour off and save the relatively soft water, taking care not to disturb the sediment.

If you plan to make pickles with whole small cucumbers, another means of dealing with very hard water is to boil it for 15 minutes, then let it stand carefully covered for 24 hours; remove the expectable light film of scum from the top, and do not disturb the sediment. Pour off the water carefully into a clean, large container, again not disturbing the sediment; add 1 tablespoon white vinegar for each gallon of boiled water before you use it.

Or add ½ cup vinegar to each 1 gallon of water, so the acid will cause precipitation of calcium and other minerals; then pour off the treated water, as above.

Iron compounds in your water will darken the foods you put by.

In preparing fish or shellfish for processing or freezing, do not wash in sea water or use sea water for precooking, etc.

Don't use water that contains sulfur if you can avoid doing so. The sulfates in water do settle out with boiling, but become more concentrated as the water evaporates. Sulfur will darken foods.

SALT

Only about 2 percent of all the salt—the common salt all of us know, which is sodium chloride (Na Cl)—used in the United States is used for food, a statistic indicating that great amounts of available salt are not food-grade. In this book we refer often to salt, and always mean either table salt or a pickling salt that is fit to put in our food. We offer a quick description of the various kinds of salt that are offered at retail to householders in order to clear up some misunderstandings that probably stem from simple misnaming.

• • USE OF ANY SALT IS OPTIONAL: Added salt to canned foods is only a flavoring, because it is included in amounts so small that it has no effect as a preservative. It is up to individual choice to avoid foods that need a good deal of salt as a preservative (certain pickles, cured meats, fish, vegetables—Chapters 19, 20 and 21).

Table salt is finely ground; is either plain or with an added iodine compound (if it is iodized the legend on the box will say so); and it has a non-caking agent as a filler. This "free-running" additive that prevents caking is not soluble, and therefore gives a cloudiness to a canning or pickling liquid. The very small optional amounts in canning are not enough to produce noticeable cloudiness, but this effect would be quite apparent in pickling liquids that contain much greater amounts of salt.

Any iodine in the table salt would discolor or darken pickled foods; this is why we specify plain pickling salt for such food.

Characteristically, table salt is in the form of tiny cubes. Its density is such that 1 pound of this salt will equal as near to 1⅓ cups as makes no difference in household use.

Cooking and canning salt usually comes in 5-pound containers. It is pure sodium chloride with nothing added to it—no agent to prevent caking, no iodine compound. Its density equals that of the table salt above, so 1 pound of it will also be about 1⅓ cups.

Kosher salt is so named because it is used in the ritual cleansing of food in the Jewish religion, and it can come in granules coarser than table salt, or as "gourmet" *flaked* salt (i.e., made by rolling out granulated salt). The density of this particular flaked salt from the Morton company and sold in the blue, rectangular, 3-pound box is such that 1 pound makes *c.* 1½ cups. Another kosher salt, this one from the Diamond Crystal company (orange carton) and made by the Alberger process, is even fluffier: it takes *c.* 1⅔ cups to equal 1 pound.

There are still other kosher salts sold in the specialty sections of supermarkets; some have large, square crystals that are sprinkled on the tops of breads and rolls to enhance the crusts. Their densities vary.

Dairy salt, though it is mentioned in many cookbooks as an acceptable food-grade salt sold at retail, it is not sold under this name by Farm Bureau outlets or by the large regional and national seed-and-feed suppliers in *PFB*'s area. Instead, the salt used in making butter, etc., by farm households is table/pickling salt sold in 25-pound bags, and is clearly designated as *food-grade* and containing no anti-caking or iodine compounds. (NOT TO BE USED with food for human beings are the trace-mineral salts designed to be, and sold as, supplements for animal feed.)

Sea salt comes in many grades. One is sold in gourmet and natural-food stores and is considered to be purified enough for use with food; it is quite expensive compared with regular table/canning/pickling salt, but is used presumably because it contains minerals from sea water (the minerals can affect the color of preserved foods). It often is coarse, and is ground in a hand-mill at the table. Its cost and its mineral content are likely to discourage its use as a preservative for food.

Solar salt sometimes is referred to as "sea salt," but it is a far cry from the gourmet variety just mentioned, and is *not food-grade,* is *not labeled food-grade,* and has never been promoted by its manufacturer as food-grade. Instead, this salt is produced mainly for use in water-purifying systems, and its coarse, rather soft pellets are discolored by the organic residues of dead aquatic life. It is called "solar" because it is evaporated in open ponds; among the sources of it in North America are the Great Salt Lake, San Francisco Bay, Baja California around the Sea of Cortez, Great Anagua in the Bahamas (legendary Turks Island salt comes from this chain of islands in the Caribbean).

The 50-pound bag *PFB* bought on our comparison-shopping spree cost less than 10 cents per pound, an attractive price for a bad ingredient.

(Apropos Turks Island salt, which was a favorite several generations ago, we bought some at 25 cents per pound, and 1 pound made 1¾ cups. The salt was bought in bulk by the store, which did not guarantee its being food-grade, but just said that "the older folks used to use it a lot, but we seldom have a call for it.")

• TRIPLE WARNING: Never use (1) solar sea-salt in curing, *especially* in curing meat and similar low-acid foods—not food-grade, it contains substances that interact with protein to cause spoilage. Never use (2) halite salt, the sort used to clear ice from walkways—it is not food-grade, and therefore could contaminate the food it was supposed to protect. Finally (3), never use a salt substitute as a seasoning in preparing food that is going to be heat-processed—it can have an unpleasant aftertaste from canning or even just cooking.

BRINING

Brine is salt dissolved in liquid, and for the purposes of this book there are two kinds of brine. One is the result of adding pure pickling salt to water by volume of proportion. The other is the solution that results when dry salt is added to plant or animal material to draw out the juices from the tissues, and the salt combines with the juices.

When we describe brine as being of a certain *percent,* we are referring to the proportion of weight of salt to the volume of liquid—*NOT* to the sophisticated salinometer/salometer reading used in laboratories or in industry (and occasionally confused in some bulletins with the simple weight/volume rule-of-thumb that is adequate for use in putting food by at home). Which is: 1 part of salt to 19 parts of water (totaling 20 parts) = 5 percent, allows some benign fermentation; 1 part of salt to 9 parts of water (totaling 10) = 10 percent, the strongest solution generally used in pickling at home, prevents the growth of most bacteria.

Brine of 2½ percent actually encourages benign fermentation; brine of 20 percent controls the growth of even salt-tolerant bacteria (see Chapter 20).

These percentages are offered for your ready reference, but are not really needed here: At every stage in every procedure involving brine, we tell you how much salt and how much liquid you need to achieve the result desired (Chapters 9, 15, 19 and 20). Above, we gave volume-per-pound equivalents for the main types of salt used in pickling and preserving just as a help in figuring these proportions.

SWEETENERS

The relatively small amount of sugar (sucrose) or alternative natural sweetener used in canning or freezing fruit helps keep the color, texture and flavor of the food, *but it is optional* (Chapters 5 and 12).

The sugar in jams and jellies (Chapter 18) *helps the gel to form,* points up the flavor, and, in the large amount called for, acts as a preservative. As a preservative and for the gel sugar is *not* optional. (The so-called sugarless or "diet" confections rely on gelatin, not pectin; are made with artificial non-nutritive sweeteners; and must be refrigerated or frozen.)

A sweetener is also an ingredient in some vinegar solutions used for vegetable pickles, where it enhances the flavor (also Chapter 19).

In curing meats like ham, bacon, etc., a relatively small amount of sugar (perhaps brown) is combined with the salt; but the sweetener is added more to feed flavor-producing bacteria than to provide flavor on its own (Chapter 20).

In canning, freezing and drying fruits, sweetening is in the form of a syrup of varying concentrations of sugar; in addition, dry sugar is used for some types of packs of fruit for freezing.

THE "NATURAL" CHOICES

The usual granulated table *sugar* (sucrose) is white and refined from cane or beets. It is the sweetening implied in almost all the instructions that do not specify another type of sweetener. Other sweeteners may be substituted for it; where the volume ratio of the substitution will make a difference in the product this fact is noted below. One teaspoon (5 mL) granulated white sugar contains 18 Calories.

Brown sugar, semi-refined and more moist than white—is called for in some directions for curing meats or cooking (Chapters 20 and 24). It also may be used in place of white sugar where its color and flavor will not affect the looks and taste of the put-by food in a way you might dislike (it would impart its characteristic taste to canned or frozen fruit, for example). Substituting it for white sugar: measure for measure, but pack it down well; 1 teaspoon (5 mL) has 16 Calories.

Corn syrup comes in light and dark forms; use light only in substituting for sugar—and then replace only up to 25 percent of the sugar with the corn syrup. Corn syrup increases the gloss and jewel-like color of jellies and jams, and helps canning syrups to cling to the fruits. One teaspoon (5 mL) has about 20 Calories.

Fructose was the glamour sweetener of the end of the 1970's, but by 1982 it began suffering backlash from being over-promoted as natural (the process for extracting it is no more natural than the means of refining table sugar), and as a boon to diabetics and to those wanting to lose weight. Fructose occurs naturally in fruit, but most of what is used in supermarket products comes from corn. Industry uses high-fructose syrup (HFS), a substance far from easily available to the householder looking for a substitute for sucrose (sugar); fructose sold in tablet and liquid form as a sweetening agent is not the concentrated sweetener HFS.

Granulated 100 percent fructose is sold in specialty food stores; *PFB*'s sample 8 ounces cost $2.38. Fructose has the same Calories per teaspoon as white table sugar but, because on the average it's ½ *again* as sweet (150 percent) as sugar, 10 Calories' worth will do the job of 15 Calories of sucrose.

Fructose is notably sweeter on cold foods, and especially on fresh fruit; its sweetening power seems noticeably less on hot foods. In cooking with fructose it is a good idea to lower the temperatures slightly, because it tends to caramelize more quickly than sucrose.

Honey has nearly twice the sweetening power of white sugar. Because of a distinctive taste, use mild-flavored honey. You will get best results by replacing only part (no more than ½) of called-for sugar with honey.

Maple syrup—which is usually too hard to come by for routine use in the kitchen—should replace only about ¼ of the required sugar, because of its pronounced flavor and color.

Sorghum and *molasses* are not recommended for most food-preservation because of their strong flavors.

ARTIFICIAL SWEETENERS

Also called "non-nutritive" sweeteners, these are available in liquid or tablets in the United States.

Although amounts of artificial sweetener to use are given in the recipes, it is sensible also to read carefully the equivalent-to-sugar measurements on the label of the sweetener. Sweetening power may vary from one brand name to another, and between liquid and tablet and granulated forms. What you want is the effect, not volume, in the non-nutritive sweetener you use.

Aspartame won final approval from the U.S. Food and Drug Administration in July of 1981 (approval had been withdrawn pending studies about a side-effect that resembled a problem with some glutamates), and thereby gave the American public an alternative to saccharin. Aspartame is *180 times* sweeter than sugar and does not have the bitter aftertaste of saccharin.

Cyclamates—banned in 1970—are under continued investigation by the FDA and therefore are not on the market.

Saccharin is *10 times sweeter than aspartame*—which makes it 1800 times sweeter than sugar. Saccharin is prohibited as a sweetener in commercial food products in Canada, and home economists in the Dominion recommend strongly against its use in food prepared and served at home. The thorough and highly regarded Canadian studies helped to prompt FDA action against saccharin in the food supply of America. Following a general outcry against the U.S. action, saccharin is used in foods sold commercially, but the products are obliged to carry on their labels this legend: "Use of this product may be hazardous to your health. This product contains saccharin which has been determined to cause cancer in laboratory animals."

ANTI–DISCOLORATION TREATMENTS

Special treatments are given the cut surface of certain fruits to prevent oxidizing in the air and turning brown when they are canned, frozen or dried. Vegetables are treated to prevent discoloration from enzymatic action when they are frozen or dried. Some cured meats may be treated to retard the inevitable loss of their appetizing pink color during storage. Canned shellfish are given a pre-canning treatment to prevent discoloration from the natural sulfur in their flesh. Fatty fish are given a special treatment to forestall some of the oxidation that causes them to turn rancid in the freezer after awhile.

C-enamel and R-enamel tin cans (see Chapter 3) have special linings that prevent naturally sulfur-y or bright-colored foods from changing color in contact with the metal. If glass jars of red or bright fruits are not stored in the dark or wrapped in paper, the light will bleach the contents. Fruit canned with too much headroom or too little liquid is likely to darken at the top of the jar; for the same reason, keep fruit submerged in its juice or syrup during freezer storage.

Specifically for Fruits

Ascorbic acid is Vitamin C, and volume for volume it is the most effective of the anti-oxidants. You should be able to get pure crystalline ascorbic acid at any drugstore and perhaps at any natural-food store; certainly either is likely to have Vitamin C in tablet form. There are about 3,000 milligrams of ascorbic acid in 1 teaspoon of the fine, pure crystals, so buy 400-mg or 500-mg tablets to get the maximum amount of Vitamin C with the minimum of filler, then crush them between the nested bowls of two spoons. Ascorbic acid dissolves readily in water or juice (both of which should be boiled and cooled before the solution is made).

It is used most often with apples, apricots, nectarines, peaches and pears; in a strong solution, it is a coating for cut fruit waiting to be processed or packed.

Generally speaking, the ascorbic-acid solution is strongest for drying fruits (Chapter 21), less for freezing them (Chapter 12), and least strong when they're canned (Chapter 5).

The crystals also may be added to the canning syrup or to the Wet packs of frozen fruit.

Citric acid is known to Kosher cooks as "sour salt" and to Greek cooks as "lemon salt": so designated, it is sold in specialty or ethnic food stores—or occasionally in gourmet sections of a metropolitan super-market—as coarse crystals. *PFB* is still working with some lemon salt bought at Ratto's in Oakland, California, and with some sour salt bought at Zabar's on Manhattan's West Side. It is much more expensive from your drugstore, where it is finely granulated; special-order it in advance if you have to. The large crystals are easily pulverized between the nested bowls of two spoons or in a mortar and pestle. (See also "Acid to Add for Safety" later.)

Volume for volume, it's about ⅓ as effective as ascorbic acid for controlling oxidation (darkening), and therefore enough to achieve the same result could mask delicate flavors of some fruits.

Lemon juice contains both ascorbic and citric acids. Average acid-strength of fresh lemons is about 5 percent (also usually the strength of reconstituted bottled lemon juice; some strains of California lemons are less strongly acid, however).

Being in solution naturally, it's about ⅙ as effective volume for volume as ascorbic acid for preventing darkening. Even more of a flavor-masker than citric acid, it also adds a distinctive lemony taste to the food.

Commercial color-preservers are gettable at supermarkets alongside paraffin wax and commercial pectins; most often comes in 5-ounce tins. The best-known brand has a sugar base, with ascorbic acid and an anti-caking agent. Expensive to use because of the relatively small proportion of ascorbic acid in the mixture. The label tells how much to use for canning or freezing.

Another brand contains sugar and citric acid, plus several other ingredients, but no ascorbic acid. Moral: Read labels to learn what you're paying for.

Both preparations, and similar ones, also have directions for using with fresh fruit cocktail, etc., that is made well in advance and chilled.

Mild acid-brine holding bath. In Chapter 5 this is one of the choices for treating apples particularly, but also apricots, nectarines, peaches and pears while they wait to be packed in containers and processed. It's a solution in the proportions of 2 tablespoons salt and 2 tablespoons white (distilled) vinegar to each 1 gallon of water. Cut fruit is held for no longer than 20 minutes in the acid-brine (which does leach nutrients), then is well rinsed (to remove salt taste), drained and packed.

A similar treatment before freezing these fruits, particularly apples, omits the vinegar (Chapter 12). We recommend against using any such holding bath before drying (Chapter 21) because it adds some liquid to fruit you're trying to take the moisture out of.

Never use the regular cider vinegar or a wine vinegar. Either could add its own color and, perhaps, sediment to the fruit.

Steam-blanching. Used sometimes before freezing fruits (especially apples) likely to darken when cut, and always before drying (even though sulfuring is recommended standard treatment in addition to blanching for fruit that is to be open-air/sun dried). Blanch in a single layer held in strong steam over briskly boiling water, 3 to 5 minutes depending on size of pieces. (See Chapters 12 and 21.)

Microwave-oven blanching. Each make or model comes with particular instructions for its use, so do read the directions that came with your oven. A rule-of-thumb would be, however: (1) of course use only an appropriate vessel to hold the food in the oven; (2) blanch only in 1-pound batches, with very little water; (3) re-arrange the food once during the blanching process; and (4) depending on the density of the food's tissues, blanch for 2½ to 6 minutes.

If the food is to be frozen, dunk it immediately in ice water to stop the cooking action and to chill it; pat it dry; package and freeze.

Syrup-blanching. Again a pre-drying treatment to hold color (Chapter 21), but the syrup is so heavy—1 cup sugar or equivalent natural substitute to each 1 cup water—and the fruit is in it so long (about 30 minutes all told) that you end up with a crystallized (or "candied") confection.

Syrup holding bath is simply dropping each piece of cut fruit into the syrup it will be canned or frozen in, and to which you may have added ascorbic acid (Chapters 5 and 12). Fruit held this way before canning is usually packed Hot (precooked); if Raw pack, the fruit must be fished out, put in the containers, and covered with the syrup after it has been brought to boiling.

Sulfuring before drying. In addition to steam-blanching most fruits in order to slow enzymatic action, all fruits and berries (except grapes) that are to be dried in open-air/sun are the better for exposure to sulfur dioxide (SO_2), which is the fumes from burning pure sulfur. "Better" means protection of Vitamins A and C (both hurt by air), protection against molds and yeasts, possibly some protection against insects (though pasteurizing is called for to kill insect eggs laid on the fruit during long exposure); and sulfuring also protects color. Sulfur is a natural substance, long used in many "spring tonics" and mineral waters.

Get "sublimed" sulfur (also called "sulfur blossoms") from the drugstore; it's pure, is a soft-yellow powder, and a 2-ounce box will sulfur 16 to 18 pounds of prepared fruit. Chapter 21 tells how to burn it. (*Don't use fumigating compounds* even though they contain some sulfur.)

Sulfur-compound solutions we dislike because they tend to distribute the sulfur unevenly in the tissues, they leach nutrients, and, if the fruit is left in too long, it gets waterlogged.

Specifically for Vegetables

Blanching. All vegetables to be frozen (except for sliced onions or sweet green bell peppers) or dried are blanched beforehand in order to slow down enzymatic action and produce the side-effect of helping to protect natural color and some texture. Blanching may be done in boiling water, in steam, or in a microwave oven (as in treating fruits, earlier). Specific times are given in instructions for individual foods later.

Before canning, white potatoes are held in a mild salt solution; salsify (oyster plant) is held in the mild acid-brine bath we mentioned earlier for certain cut fruits.

Specifically for Meats: The Nitrates/Nitrites

Potassium nitrate and *sodium nitrate* have been called *saltpeter* for generations, and for even longer have been used in the salt-curing of meats. Most simply, nitr*ates* are changed into nitr*ites* by metabolism when we eat them, or by the action with the protein of raw meat being cured. The nitrites, in turn, help to make nitrosamines—and these latter substances have been found to cause cancer in laboratory animals. It is this fear of carcinogens in human beings that has caused a continuing controversy about the use of nitrites in preservation of food, and they are under scrutiny by the FDA and the USDA.

Meanwhile it has been established that nitrites do help prevent the formation of the dreaded *C. botulinum* toxin—aside from stabilizing the appetizing pink color of ham, cured meats, frankfurters, etc., that may or may not be smoked following their cure in salt and nitrates/nitrites. Because they are considered able to help reduce the possibility of botulism poisoning, nitrites currently are tolerated in small amounts by food scientists.

The answer to their use is continued vigilance and restriction to minimum proportions in commercially prepared foods. The amounts of saltpeter given in the directions in Chapter 20 are currently (1982) acceptable to the agencies guarding the safety of our food supplies. It is important not to add more nitrates/nitrites than are given in these recipes, or to increase the amounts of commercially prepared cures containing these substances and which are sold in hardware and farm supply stores, and some supermarkets.

It is interesting that most Americans ingest at least as much nitrite-forming substances in leafy and green vegetables and other highly approved foods as they get in the cured meats.

Ascorbic acid. Good old Vitamin C again. It will hold the color of cured meat—not so brightly and certainly more briefly than saltpeter does. *It will not prevent botulism.* Use ¼ teaspoon pure crystalline ascorbic acid for every 5 pounds of dressed meat to be cured; add it to the salt mixture or to the brine.

Nitrates/nitrites are also discussed in Chapter 20, in the section "Salting Meat."

Specifically for Seafood

Citric acid (and lemon juice). For canning: the picked meat of crabs, lobsters, shrimp and clams is given a brief dunk in a fairly tart solution of citric acid or lemon juice as a way to offset the darkening action of minerals naturally present in such foods (otherwise the meats would be likely to discolor during processing and storage). The dip lasts about 1 minute, and the meat is pressed gently to remove excess solution. (See Chapter 9).

White (distilled) vinegar may be used too, but it might contribute a slight flavor of its own.

Ascorbic acid. For freezing fatty fish, a 20-second dip in a cold solution of 2 teaspoons crystalline ascorbic acid dissolved in 1 quart of water will lessen the chance of rancidity during freezer storage. The fish to be treated include mackerel, pink and chum salmon, lake trout, tuna and eel, plus all fish roe.

ACID TO ADD FOR SAFETY

Three acid substances—citric acid, lemon juice and vinegar—are added to foods in this book for reasons that have little to do with the cosmetic purpose of helping to control oxidation or color changes in put-by food (see "Anti-discoloration Treatments," above).

ADDING ACIDS TO PRESERVES AND PICKLES

We add acid to enhance flavor, making it brighter or more tangy, in condiments like ketchup or chili sauce or chutney. We add it to help create the balance that makes a gel in combination with pectin and sugar, in cooked jellies and jams. And we *add it much more lavishly* to aid preservation of a number of pickles served as garnishes. How much of which particular acid is added to all these foods is given in the specific instructions in Chapters 18 and 19.

ADDING ACID TO NATURAL FOODS

The relationship between a food's natural acidity (*pH* rating) and its ability to provide hospitable growing conditions for spoilage micro-organisms is discussed at some length in the first part of Chapter 2. In Chapters 5 and 7, small amounts of acid are added for canning specific foods: figs, berry juices, the nectars and purées of apricots, peaches and pears; sweet green bell peppers and pimientos; and only sparingly—if at all—in canning tomatoes (Chapter 6).

> • • ADDED ACID IS NOT A CRUTCH. Acid is added *only* to the foods cited immediately above before canning them by the method specified and for the specified processing time. The added acid does *not allow any short cut* for any step in safe canning procedure, and it does *not permit any fiddling* with canning methods.

The Three Acids

Citric acid. Pure crystalline citric acid, U.S.P. (meaning "United States Pharmacopoeia" and therefore of uniform stability and quality) is the acid that USDA Extension Service nutrionists allowed (in April 1975) added in canning tomatoes. It is sold by weight, is gettable at most drugstores, is not expensive—especially when you consider that 4 ounces (the consistency is like finely granulated sugar) will do about 45 quarts or slightly more than 90 pints of tomatoes. (As an anti-oxidant it is cheaper than ascorbic acid, though less effective.)

For where to buy citric acid, see under "Anti-discoloration Treatments—Specifically for Fruits," earlier.

Citric acid is preferred for increasing acid-strength of foods because it does not contribute flavor of its own to food (unlike lemon juice and vinegars, which can alter flavor if used in large enough amounts).

Fine citric acid may be substituted for a 5-percent acid solution (the average for store-bought vinegar or for the juice of most lemons) *whenever the called-for measurements of the solutions are by the spoonful,* in this general proportion: ¼ teaspoon citric acid powder = a generous 1 tablespoon of 5-percent lemon juice/vinegar; ½ teaspoon citric acid powder = a generous 2 tablespoons of the vinegar or lemon juice. (The equivalents actually are ¼ = 4 teaspoons, and ½ = 8 teaspoons, but 1 and 2 tablespoons are easier measurements to make in the usual household's kitchen.)

To reverse the coin and make a 5-percent solution of citric acid, use the rule-of-thumb for making salt brines: dissolve 1 part fine citric acid in 19 parts of boiled (and cooled) water. Translated into measurements used in the average kitchen, this means dissolving 2 tablespoons fine citric acid in 1 pint (2 cups) of boiled water; or, if you want to be metric, dissolving 30 mL of fine citric acid crystals in ½ liter (500 mL) of boiled water. Either translation will produce a solution around 6 percent instead of 5—but the result will serve the purpose we're after.

Lemon juice. This is recommended over the other acids for use in canning fruit juice in Chapter 5, and for increasing the acidity of fruit juices to ensure a good gel for jellies and jams in Chapter 18.

The people who live in citrus-growing regions are likely to know the virtues and relative acidities of the different strains of lemons; the rest of us buy anonymous lemons at the market and assume that their average acidity equals a 5-percent solution.

If you squeeze lemons ahead of time to have the juice handy, don't hold the strained juice in its sterilized, tightly capped jar in the refrigerator for more than a couple of days: its flavor tends to change as it sits around.

Even just-squeezed juice can alter the flavor of foods, especially when used in fairly large amounts. Therefore rank it below citric acid on this score—but above vinegar.

Vinegar. Vinegar is acetic acid, and all vinegars corrode metal, so when you use them in larger-than-spoonful amounts—in making pickles and relishes (Chapter 19)—make sure your kettle or holding vessel is enameled, stainless steel, ceramic or glass. Acetic acid reacts badly with iron, copper and brass, and with galvanized metal (which we don't like to use with *any* food because of the possibility of contamination from cadmium in connection with the zinc used in galvanizing; and zinc itself can be toxic). Vinegared foods corrode aluminum.

The cider vinegar bought in supermarkets usually runs about 5 to 6 percent acid. Its pronounced flavor can be an asset with spicy condiments and pickles, but a drawback elsewhere. Its color is unimportant for dark relishes, but hurts the looks of light-colored pickles. Because of its flavor and color, it should not be used with fruits or bland foods. The minerals present in any vinegar that has not been distilled can react with compounds in the water or the foods' tissues to produce undesirable color changes. All of which boils down to: *do not use* cider (or malt) vinegar to reduce the *pH* rating of the specific fruits and vegetables cited above—unless it's a last resort, and unless you're prepared for changes in color and flavor.

Use *white (distilled) vinegar* for decreasing *pH* rating of foods mentioned above if you don't have citric acid or lemon juice—though it is close to interchangeable with lemon juice. White vinegar sometimes is slightly less acid than cider vinegar, but not enough to oblige you to alter measurements. Certain pickle recipes call for white vinegar specifically. See "Citric Acid" above for translating.

Avoid using "raw" or "country" vinegar for the purposes cited here—it's likely to have sediment, and its flavor is pronounced. And save wine and special herbed vinegars for dressing salads or vegetable dishes.

FIRMING AGENTS

Having raw materials in prime condition and perfectly fresh, plus handling them promptly and carefully add up to the best *natural* means of ensuring that your put-by foods are firm and appetizing.

> *Salt.* In canning, freezing or curing fish for smoking, a short stay in a mild brine (proportions vary, and are given in Chapters 5, 9, 12, 15 and 20, respectively) that is kept ice-cold will not only draw diffused blood from the tissues but also will firm the flesh and result in a better product.
>
> In drying fish (Chapter 21), a larger concentration of salt is generally used to draw moisture from the tissues and make the flesh firm.
>
> In pickles, the original "short-brine" (q.v. Chapter 19) firms the vegetables. It also helps to shave off the vestigial remains of the blossoms of pickling cucumbers, because this is where enzymes concentrate; and unless enzymatic action is halted, such foods will soften.
>
> *Cold.* Refrigerating meats, poultry and produce, and holding seafoods on ice until they are prepared for processing, will do much to ensure food with good, firm texture.
>
> *Calcium hydroxide*—$Ca(OH)_2$—is also called *slaked lime* (slaked, because liquid has been added to it, whereby it became heated, and the residue remains) and *pickling lime*. It is sold in drugstores as a firming agent for pickles; it also is gettable as one of the products of a line of preservatives

and jelly-making products whose manufacturing headquarters is in Tupelo, Mississippi (see Chapter 25). Calcium hydroxide is preferred by nutritionists over alum and calcium chloride (both below).

Pectin, a starch found in large amounts in green apples and the white spongy layer under the thin skin of citrus fruits, swells to form a clear, thick substance when heated with sugar (usually sucrose) and acid. There is more about pectin in Chapter 18, "Jellies, Jams and Other Sweet Things"; plus a discussion of low-methoxyl pectin, which creates a gel with less-than-standard amounts of sugar, but which requires a calcium compound as an aid to firming.

Alum is any of several allied compounds, and was called for in old cookery books to make pickles crisp—usually watermelon or cucumber chips. If you see it in a responsible modern cookbook, follow the directions for its use carefully: when a fairly large amount is eaten, it often produces nausea and even severe gastro-intestinal trouble. Alum is not an ingredient in any of the pickle recipes in this book.

Calcium chloride. Some people find this more acceptable than alum, but we do not include it in any pickle recipe or canning instruction in this book. It is an ingredient often used by commercial canners, especially in tomatoes.

If you feel impelled to use it, get it from a drugstore in a food-pure form—*not* as sold at farm and garden supply centers for settling dust on roads or for dehumidifying closets, etc., or for fireproofing. And, because too much of it could leave a bitter aftertaste, never substitute it measure-for-measure for regular salt (sodium chloride, $NaCl$). Instead, figure how much salt you'll need for a batch of, say, tomatoes, and in advance mix *not more than 1 part calcium chloride* with 2 parts regular salt. Then add the mixture in the amount of optional salt seasoning that the canning instructions call for.

JELLIES, JAMS AND
OTHER SWEET THINGS

Aside from heavenly rich desserts, there is probably no food group that's easier to take sugar from than the sweet fruit spreads. And luckily there are ways to cut down on the sugar used in our jellies and jams without sacrificing unduly on flavor.

It is with the statistic in mind that Americans consume 100 pounds of white sugar per capita each year, that we have reorganized this chapter from our old, and the standard, presentation. Now, instead of presenting together all the jellies, with subsections for ones made with reduced sugar or with no sugar, and then repeating the same arrangement for jams, we offer the jellies, jams and their cousins according to the procedures used for making them. We think that the householder interested mainly in reduced- or no-sugar spreads wants first to know *how* to make them, and is happy to flip a couple of pages to find a particular fruit or a texture.

The general mechanics of cooking fruits with sweeteners, and what makes the ingredients do what they do, come next. Then will come the major section that uses old-time amounts of sugar, with subdivisions dealing with variations; and the third major section will deal with the reduced-sugar and no-sugar products, including the use of low-methoxyl pectin.

A full list of recommended sources for products and recipes and procedures will be found in Chapter 25.

The Finishing B–W Bath

Preserves (including jams and marmalades) and pickles can suffer from mold and other spoilage micro-organisms when storage is not the ideal 32 to 50 F/Zero to 10 C and dark and dry—conditions not always possible in warm, humid climates or in modern centrally heated homes. Therefore we recommend that all such foods from the preserving kettle *except jellies and the so-called Diet or Freezer jams* be packed in conventional ½-pint or pint canning jars with ½ inch of headroom. Then adjust the lids and process in a short Boiling–Water Bath (212 F/100 C); complete seals if necessary, cool and store.

Relevant Metrics for Jellies, Jams and Other Sweet Things

Full metric conversions, with the arithmetic for refining them, are given at the start of Chapter 17 ("Common Ingredients and How to Use Them"), but the following—rounded off—apply in this chapter.

If you live above the sea-level zone (i.e., *over* 1000 ft/305 m), consult the subsection "Correcting for Altitude" in Chapter 3 for help in figuring boiling points (viz. the variations for water at lowered atmospheric pressure).

• • •

Temperatures (@ sea level): 212 F/100 C———220 F/104.4 C.

Volume: ⅛ teaspoon = 0.62 mL———¼ teaspoon = 1.25 mL———½ teaspoon = 2.5 mL———1 teaspoon = 5.0 mL———1 tablespoon = 15 mL———¼ cup = 2 fl oz = 60 mL———½ cup = 4 fl oz = 125 mL———1 cup = 8 fl oz = 250 mL———1 pint = 2 cups = 500 mL———1 qt = 1 L.

Weight: 1 oz = 28 g———2 oz = 57 g———1 lb = 454 g.

EQUIPMENT FOR JELLIES, JAMS, ETC.

For starters, your regular kitchen utensils will be adequate. Roughly in order of importance, you will need:

6- to 8-quart enameled or stainless steel kettle with a good lid (so it can double as a B–W Bath canner if you do not have one)

A jelly bag for straining juice. You can make a good one from ½ yard of 36-inch wide top grade unbleached muslin, folded so selvage edges are together. Machine-stitch with durable thread down the side seam and across the bottom, leaving top open for filling. Make a stout hem around the opening, through which you'll run a strong cord to tie the bag shut; the cord will hold the filled bag above a wide container to catch the juice. Wash before using to remove any filler in the fabric.

Boiling–Water Bath canner.

Jars/glasses in prime condition, with lids/sealers/gaskets ditto

Paraffin for sealing (with lids to cover the wax after it has set; *and* an expendable spouted metal pot for melting and pouring the wax)

Household scales

Clock with sweep second hand for close timing

Minute-timer with warning bell for longer processing periods

Sieve or food mill for puréeing (better is a food blender and the ultimate is
   a food processor)
Jelly (syrup) thermometer
Shallow pans (dishpans are fine)
Ladle
Long-handled wooden spoon for stirring
Wide-mouth funnel for filling containers
Jar-lifter
Sieve or strainer for de-seeding blackberries or other large-seeded fruits
Colander, for draining
Large measuring cups, and measuring spoons
Plenty of clean dry potholders, dishcloths and towels
Large trays

GENERAL PROCEDURES FOR JELLIES, JAMS AND SWEET PRESERVES

Jellies, jams, preserves, conserves, marmalades and butters are the six cousins of the fruit world. All have fruit and sugar in common, but differences in texture and fruit-form distinguish one from another.

Jelly. Made from fruit juice, it is clear and tenderly firm. Quiveringly, it holds its shape when turned out of the jar.
Jam. Made from crushed or ground fruit, it almost holds its shape, but is not jelly-firm.
Preserves. These are whole fruits or large pieces of fruit in a thick syrup that sometimes is slightly jellied.
Conserves. These glorified jams are made from a mixture of fruits, usually including citrus. Raisins and nuts also are frequent additions.
Marmalade. This is a tender jelly with small pieces of citrus fruit distributed evenly throughout.
Butters. These are fruit pulps cooked with sugar until thick.

THE FOUR ESSENTIAL INGREDIENTS

Fruit

This gives each product its special flavor, and provides at least a part of the pectin and acid that combine with added sugar to make successful gels.

Full-flavored, just-ripe fruits are preferred, because their flavor is diluted by the large proportion of sugar that is added for good consistency and keeping quality. Never use overripe fruit.

Unsweetened frozen fruit makes good jelly and jam.

PECTIN

This substance, which combines with added sugar—or other sweeteners, *except* artificial ones—and natural or added acid to produce a gel, is found naturally in most fruits. (See "Pectin/Acid Content of Common Fruits," coming in a minute.) Pectin content is highest in lightly underripe fruit, and diminishes as the fruit becomes fully ripe; overripe fruit, lacking adequate pectin of its own, is responsible for a good deal of runny jam and jelly. Pectin is concentrated in the skins and cores of the various fruits: this is why many recipes say to use skins and cores in preparing fruit for juicing or pulping.

Most commercial pectin is made from the white pulp under the skin of citrus fruits; only one major brand that we know of—although of course there may be more—is made from apples, and the label on the packet announces the fact. Again with one exception that we know of, pectin marketed widely for home use comes in powdered/granular form in 1¾-ounce packages. The exception is the liquid that used to be marketed in 6-ounce bottles, and since 1980 or so has come in dual 3-ounce foil pouches.

(The low-methoxyl pectin used in reduced-Calorie jellies and jams—discussed in the introduction to the second major subsection of this chapter, "Low-sugar/No-sugar Jelly and Jam," is also made from citrus, though by a method different from that used in widely sold commercial varieties.)

This natural pectin in the fruit can be activated only by cooking—but *cooking quickly,* both in heating the fruit to help start the juice, and later when juice or pulp is boiled together with the sugar. And *too-slow cooking,* or *boiling too long,* can reduce the gelling property of the pectin, whether natural or added.

In the old days apple juice was added to less pectin-rich juices to make them gel, and this combination still works. Today, though, the readily available commercial pectins take the guesswork out of jellies, jams, and the like.

Testing for pectin content. There are several tests, but the simplest one uses ready-to-hand materials. In a cup, stir together 1 teaspoon cooked fruit juice with 1 tablespoon rubbing alcohol (everyday 70 percent kind). No extra pectin is needed if the juice forms one big clot that can be picked up with a fork. If the fruit juice is too low in pectin, it will make several small dabs that do not clump together. DON'T EVER TASTE THE SAMPLES—rubbing alcohol must never be taken by mouth.

HOMEMADE PECTIN

Apple pectin can be made at home to add to the non-gelling juices of strawberries, cherries, rhubarb or pineapple to set a perfect jelly.

For about a pint of pectin you will need 10 pounds of apples, a 10- to 12-quart preserving kettle, and a good strong jelly bag.

Wash apples, cut in quarters *without peeling or coring,* but remove stems and blossom ends. Put the apples in the kettle, barely cover with cold water, and set over moderate heat; cover and cook slowly for about 30 minutes, or until the fruit is quite soft. Turn the cooked apples into the dampened jelly bag, letting it hang overnight to extract as much juice as possible without squeezing. This will produce around 3 quarts of juice, which you boil down to about ⅙ or ⅛ its original volume to make 1½ to 2 cups of heavy, almost ropy, syrup. Strain before using.

To store for later use. Pour the hot, strained pectin into hot ½-pint canning jars; adjust the lids and process in a Boiling–Water Bath for 5 minutes. Remove jars; complete seals if necessary. Store in a cool, dry, dark place.

To use homemade pectin. Add ½ to ¾ cup apple pectin to 4 cups low-pectin fruit juice in a large kettle and bring to a boil; after 2 or 3 minutes of boiling add 2 to 3 cups of sugar for the amount of fruit juice used (4 cups, above) and boil rapidly until the jelly stage is reached (see "Testing for Doneness"). Skim, ladle into hot glasses; seal.

There has been a publication issued by Louisiana State University on how to make pectin at home from citrus fruit. See Chapter 25, this chapter's subsection, for where to write for it.

Acid

None of the fruits will gel or thicken without acid. The acid content of fruits varies, and is *higher in underripe* than in the fully ripe fruit.

Taste-test for acid content. This is a comparison. If the prepared fruit juice is not so tart as a mixture of 1 teaspoon lemon juice, 3 tablespoons water and ½ teaspoon sugar, your juice needs extra acid to form a successful gel. A rule-of-thumb addition would be 1 tablespoon lemon juice or homemade citric acid solution (for how to make it, see "Acids to Add" in Chapter 17) to each 1 cup prepared juice.

Sweeteners

Sugar. This helps the gel to form, is a preserving aid and increases flavor in the final product. The sugar called for in the recipes for jellies, jams, and other preserves is, unless otherwise specified, refined white cane or beet sugar.

The semi-refined brown sugars (sometimes called "raw") differ in sweetening power from white sugar—a difference that could upset the balance needed for a successful gel in recipes calling for added pectin. The color and pronounced flavor of brown sugars will affect the looks and taste of jellies and jams, etc.

Corn syrup (light only). As a general rule, in recipes *without added pectin* you may substitute light corn syrup for ¼ the sugar called for in jellies, and up to ½ the sugar used in jams and preserves. Add it when you add the sugar. And be prepared to boil the mixture longer than usual to evaporate the extra moisture contained in the corn syrup.

In recipes using *powdered pectin,* light corn syrup may replace ½ the sugar needed in either jellies or jams. Where *liquid pectin* is used, light corn syrup may replace up to 2 cups of the sugar.

Honey (light-colored and mild-flavored seems to work best). Although some groups promoting the use of honey recommend substituting it measure-for-measure for sugar in making jellies and jams, we have not been satisfied with our results when we did so. Honey generally has *nearly twice the sweetening power* of the same amount of white sugar; this property, coupled with the distinctive flavor imparted by even mild honey in such quantity, was enough to eclipse the delicate fruit taste we like in jellies and jams. However, we were more successful when we replaced only part of the called-for sugar with honey, adding it when we added the sugar, and cooking the jelly/jam a bit longer to get rid of the extra moisture in the honey.

In recipes *without added pectin,* we suggest substituting no more than ½ the sugar with a mild-flavored honey. In recipes *with added pectin,* we replace no more than 2 cups of the required sugar with an equal measure of honey. *Caution:* In small batches (5- or 6-glass yield), no more than 1 cup of the sugar should be replaced by honey.

Sorghum and *molasses* are not recommended for making preserves because their flavors are so strong, and their relative sweetening powers are varied.

Artificial sweeteners require fairly detailed specific treatment when used in preserves, and are dealt with in "Sugarless Jams and Jellies with Gelatin" later. Meanwhile, do read the label on the artificial sweetener you may be using to see if its virtue is affected by processing or storage. A detailed discussion of the various non-nutritive/artificial, as well as natural, sweeteners is given in the preceding chapter, "Common Ingredients and How to Use Them."

Pectin/Acid Content of Common Fruits

Group I. These fruits if not overripe usually contain enough natural pectin and acid to gel with only added sugar: apples (sour), blackberries (sour), crabapples, cranberries, currants, gooseberries, grapes (Eastern Concord), lemons, loganberries, plums (except Italian), quinces.

Group II. These fruits usually are low in natural acid or pectin, and *may* need added acid or pectin: apples (ripe), blackberries (ripe), cherries (sour), chokecherries, elderberries, grapefruit, bottled grape juice (Eastern Concord), grapes (California), loquats, oranges.

Group III. These fruits *always* need added acid or pectin, or both: apricots, figs, grapes (Western Concord), guavas, peaches, pears, prunes (Italian), raspberries, strawberries.

Steps in Making Cooked Jelly

The recipes that follow are for cooked jellies—that is, ones boiled with sugar and pectin as indicated. (Uncooked jellies are discussed later.)

Always work with the recommended batch. The quantities given are tailored for success: the longer boiling needed for larger amounts can prevent desired flavor and texture in the finished product.

Preparing Fruit and Extracting Juice

A rough, very rough, rule-of-thumb for estimating how much fruit will be needed to make a particular batch of jelly is: 1 pound of prepared fruit (i.e., washed, stemmed/trimmed/cut as the recipe says to) will make 1 cup of juice.

Plan to process the fruit as soon as possible after it's picked or bought; refrigerate, for no more than 1 day, soft fruits and berries if you can't handle them right away. When you do start, keep at it and work right along.

Pick over the fruit carefully, discarding any that is overripe or has rotten spots. For a successful gel from recipes that have no pectin added, make up the amount called for with ¼ the total in underripe and ¾ in just-ripe fruit.

Wash the fruit quickly but thoroughly. Don't let it soak; lift it out of the basin of fresh water, don't pour it with the water into a strainer. The lighter and quicker you are in handling berries, the better. And always use good, clean drinking water for washing your fruit.

Remove the stems and blossom ends of apples and quinces and guavas, but retain their skins and cores. The skins of plums and grapes also contain a good deal of pectin, so keep them too. The stems and pits of cherries and berries need not be removed: the jelly bag will take care of them when the pulp is strained.

To Extract Juice

Sparkling clear, firm jelly calls for carefully strained juice. Modern recipes describe the way the juice is to be extracted—simply by crushing; or by short heating, with or without "enough water to keep from sticking"; or by longer cooking with more water added—and these instructions should be followed.

Sometimes, though, you will like the sound of an older recipe that's not explicit about method, so we offer the following rules-of-thumb as a help in figuring out what to do.

Always start heating the fruit at a fairly high temperature.

To heat ripe soft berries without any water, crush a layer in the bottom of the kettle to start the juice (mashing them with the bottom of a drinking glass, or with a pastry-blender); pile on the remainder and put the kettle on fairly high heat, stirring to mix the contents; reduce heat to moderate and boil gently and stir until all the fruit is soft—5 to 10 minutes.

To heat soft berries that are slightly underripe, Concord and wild grapes, currants, add no more than ¼ cup water to each 1 cup of prepared fruit. With currants, cook until they are translucent and faded. Add ½ cup of water to chokecherries and wild cherries; add a scant ¼ cup to juicy sour cherries.

To cut-up (but unpitted) plums, add water to *just below the top layer* in the kettle, and cook until soft—about 15 minutes.

To prepared apples, crabapples, quinces and guavas, add water *just to cover,* and cook until soft—20 to 25 minutes.

Strain all crushed raw or cooked fruit through a jelly bag. Dampen the bag to encourage the juice to start dripping through it; bunch the top together and tie it with strong string. Hang it high enough over a big mixing bowl so the tip of the bag cannot touch the strained juice (a broomstick laid across the tops of two kitchen chairs makes a good height).

Squeezing the jelly bag forces through bits of pulp that will cloud the jelly, but pressing the back of a wooden spoon against the bag will often quicken the flow without clouding the juice.

If there is traffic through the room, with attendant insects and dust, drape a clean sheet over the whole business.

Be fussy about washing the jelly bag after each use and rinsing it well; even a little diluted juice left in the fabric will spoil, and a musty, winey bag will hurt the next juice that's strained in it.

Refrigerate, in a tightly covered sterilized container, any juice left over from measuring for the batch of jelly.

Sugar and Pectin

When you add the sugar depends on the type of commercial pectin you use. Each recipe stipulates the type—*and they are not interchangeable.* Always follow the recipe exactly, because time and quantity variations almost always bring failure.

> *Powdered pectin* is added to the strained juice *before* heating. Heat rapidly, bringing to a full rolling boil—i.e., a boil which cannot be stirred down; *then add the sugar,* bring again to a full rolling boil, and boil for 1 minute.
>
> *Liquid pectin* (except for homemade pectin, above) is added to the strained juice and sugar *after* the mixture is brought to a full boil. Stir constantly during heating. Add pectin, bring again to a full rolling boil, boil for 1 minute.

WITHOUT ADDED COMMERCIAL PECTIN

Jellies with enough natural pectin (like Basic Apple Jelly) require less sugar per cup of juice than jellies with added *store-bought* pectin do. The longer cooking needed to reach the jelly stage produces the right proportion of sweetness, acid and pectin.

Testing for Doneness

Because barometric pressure as well as altitude affects the boiling point, make necessary adjustments for heights above 1,000 feet/305 meters above sea level, and for whether the day is close and damp, or clear and dry.

220 F/104.4 C and a full rolling boil in all its glory: the jelly is done.

Jelly with added pectin will be done if boiled as the individual instructions for time and quantity specify.

Jelly without added pectin is done when it reaches 8 degrees Fahrenheit (the Celsius comparison is meaningless here) above boiling; usually, under good conditions at 1,000 feet/305 meters or less, this is 220 F/104.4 C.

If you have no jelly thermometer, use the Sheet Test. Dip a cold metal spoon in the boiling jelly and, holding it 12 to 18 inches above the kettle and out of the steam, turn it so the liquid runs off the side. If a couple of drops form and run together and then tear off the edge of the spoon in a sheet, the jelly is done.

BUT this test is not for jam: sheeting in the same manner means that the jam has cooked too long, and will be stiffer than the soft texture one is accustomed to.

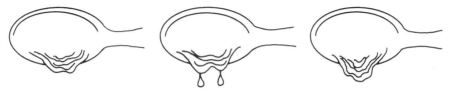

Progress of sheeting test, left to right.

Or use the Refrigerator Test. Remove the kettle from the heat (so it won't raise Cain while your back's turned) and pour a tablespoon of jelly into a saucer. Put the saucer in the ice-cube compartment of your refrigerator for a minute or two: if it has become tender-firm, your jelly is ready to pour and seal.

Jelly at High Altitude

First, the sheeting test is likely to be more helpful to you if you live at 3500 feet/1067 meters, because you must compensate for the excessive evaporation, and you do this by cooking the jelly to a lower temperature than sea level would require to make it sheet. (It doesn't matter if it is commercial powdered or liquid pectin or natural pectin in the juice.)

Thus, if the gelling point would be 8 F/4.4. C above the boiling point of water at sea level, you would be at 220 F/104.4 C. But if you live in Denver, say, one mile high, the final cooking temperature would be decreased by the difference in boiling-water temperature in Denver (203 F/95 C) and that of sea level—or 212 F minus 203 F = 9 F; and 100 C minus 95 C = 5 C. So you'll expect the temperature reading for finished jelly in Denver to be 211 F/99.4 C.

These figures work out to an approximate *decrease* of 2 F/1.1 C for each increase of 1000 ft/305 m in altitude.

Quickly, some other equivalents in Fahrenheit and feet because of space (see Chapter 17 for your own Celsius): 218 F @ 2000 ft; 216 F @ 3000 ft; 214 F @ 4000 ft; 212 F @ 5000 ft; 210 F @ 6000 ft; 208 F @ 7000 ft; 206 F @ 8000 ft.

Pouring & Sealing, Labeling & Storing

The moment your jelly tests done, remove the kettle from heat and skim off the foam, working deftly so as not to stir any fluff down into the jelly. Ladle boiling-hot jelly immediately into clean sterilized glasses (see how to sterilize them and their caps in "About Jars and Cans" in Chapter 3). With a clean cloth wrung out in boiling water, wipe any dribbles from the rim of the container and from the inside above the level of the jelly. Seal each jar at once.

SEALING WITH PARAFFIN

If you seal with wax, leave ¼ inch of headroom, wipe the inside lip of the glass, and cover the jelly with a ⅛-inch layer of hot paraffin. Melt the wax in a double boiler arrangement (you can have a scary fire on top of your stove if you melt paraffin in a saucepan over high heat); or melt it in an old metal teapot or pitcher set in a larger pan of simmering water, and you have a good pourer for the liquid wax.

Use only fresh, clean paraffin, because re-used or dusty wax has acquired impurities that can cause spoilage. Wax that's too hot—a haze will rise from the surface if it is—can have little breaks in it after it cools. With a sterilized darning needle prick any air bubbles on the surface of the paraffin, because these are likely to cause holes in the wax as it cools, and there goes your seal.

A too-thick layer of wax usually will fail to seal, so stick to the ⅛-inch rule; and don't try to cover a faulty thin layer by topping it with more wax: seal again from scratch.

When the paraffin is cold, protect it with a metal cap or snap-on plastic lid.

SEALING WITH MODERN LIDS

If you are using the modern jelly jars that have 2-piece screwband lids, leave only ⅛ inch of headroom. Wipe dribbled jelly from the rim of the jar, put on the sterilized caps and screw the bands tight. Soon after each jar is tightly capped, a perfect vacuum seal will form as the hot jelly cools.

Some older manuals tell you to invert the capped jar the moment the lid is tightly on. Sometimes this is a good way to get a spurt of near-boiling jelly over your hand.

Labeling & Storing

During the 24 hours before you store your jelly, check it for loose texture and faulty seals (see "Jelly, etc., Failures and What to Do" in this chapter). Carefully clean away any stickiness from the glasses/jars, giving extra attention to the tops around the closures where outside mold can attack the seal. Label each container with the kind and the date; it's a good idea to indicate the batch number if you made more than one lot of the same sort that day. And if you used a method or recipe different from your usual one, note this fact too: it could help to pinpoint reasons for trouble, as well as for outstanding successes.

Storage in a "cool, dark, dry place" is the same as for canned goods: ideally between 32 and 50 degrees Fahrenheit (Zero and 10 degrees Celsius)—certainly not where the contents will freeze (which can break seals), certainly not at normal room temperature (which encourages growth of spoilers). Dark, because the pretty colors can turn brown or fade in the light; otherwise you put them in cartons or wrap them in paper or cover the whole shebang with an old blanket or the like. And dry because humidity can corrode metal caps and lids and lead to broken seals.

Steps for Cooked Jams and Marmalades

Jams and marmalades call for the same care in selecting and preparing fruit that jellies do (q.v.) However, in several important ways their cooking and sealing differs from the handling of jellies. The most notable of these differences is that they all—*except for the so-called Diet and Freezer (Uncooked) jams*—are given a finishing Boiling–Water Bath as insurance against spoilage. This means that they are packed in regular canning jars—usually ½-pints or pints, with the right caps/lids—and are given ½ inch of headroom.

Sugar and Pectin

The general proportions for substituting other *non-artificial* sweeteners for called-for sugar are the same for jams and marmalades as for jelly (q.v.).

With added pectin, the crystalline type is mixed with the unheated prepared fruit. Liquid pectin is added to the cooked fruit-and-sugar mixture after the kettle is removed from heat. With either form of pectin the cooking time is the same: 1 minute at a full boil.

Without added pectin, the cooking time is increased to a range of from 15 to 40 minutes, depending on the character of the fruit. Jam is more likely to scorch than jelly is, so stir it often during cooking.

For *diet jam,* etc., see jelly, above.

Testing for Doneness

Jams, etc., with added pectin will be done when they are boiled according to the individual instructions for time and quantity.

Without added pectin, jam is done when it reaches 9 degrees F above the boiling point of water, usually 221 F at 1,000 feet of altitude or below.

No thermometer? Jam is ready when it begins to hold shape in the spoon. Or use the Refrigerator Test for jelly, above.

Pouring, Sealing, Processing, Storing

Remove the kettle from heat, skim carefully, and then stir the jam gently for 5 minutes to cool it slightly and thus prevent floating fruit.

Ladle the still-hot jam or marmalade carefully into hot sterile canning jars, leaving ½ inch of headroom; wipe the mouths carefully with a clean cloth wrung out in boiling water, cap, and process in a B–W Bath 212 F/100 C) for 10 minutes. Complete seals if necessary. Cool, clean the containers, label and store.

- **SPECIAL NOTE:** Because the general methods for making Preserves, etc., and Butters are described as part of the recipes, and are quite brief, the procedures for them are given with the specific instructions at the end of the next major section, "Old-style Use of Sugar."

Steps for Freezer (Uncooked) Jelly and Jam

The fresh-picked flavor of summer fruits can be retained virtually intact in jellies and jams that are made to be stored in the freezer, and therefore are not cooked. The same basics must be present along with the fruit juice for a satisfactory result: the fruit's natural acid (eked out with lemon juice or a citric-acid solution if necessary, as described earlier), pectin and sugar.

The general handling of these jellies differs from that for conventional ones in several ways. Not being sterilized through boiling, they must be stored in the freezer to prevent spoilage—although freshly made or defrosted jelly will keep well for up to 3 weeks in the refrigerator. Also, because their natural pectin is not activated by boiling, pectin must be added; and it is added after the sugar, regardless of whether it is liquid or powdered. And finally, the jellies must be packed in sterilized freezer-proof jars, with headroom to allow for expansion; and must be sealed with sterilized tight-fitting lids, *not* with paraffin.

Filled and capped, the containers must stand at room temperature until the jelly is set—which can take up to 24 hours—before going into the freezer.

The juice for this jelly is made from *unheated* fresh fruit. However, it can be made with frozen juice *not heat-extracted or sweetened;* or with juice from berries that have been frozen, *without added sugar,* for making jelly later on. It *cannot be made successfully from canned fruit juices,* because there the natural pectin has been impaired by the heat of processing.

People seem to make more freezer jams than jellies perhaps because there is more leeway to a jam's consistency than there is for jelly. Certainly the lovely garden-fresh flavor of berries and fruits is more pronounced in jams. Like their jelly counterparts, opened freezer jams must be refrigerated.

The folders that come with the containers of commercial powdered or liquid pectin have a number of good jams and jellies; and the proportions have been worked out after much testing. We recommend them.

Failures and What to Do

In theory, we'd all have perfect jellies, jams, marmalades, preserves, conserves and fruit butters if we used prime ingredients, if we measured carefully, and if we followed procedures conscientiously. But things can go wrong, even when we mean to be careful. Therefore here is a rundown of the symptoms and causes of common failures, listed now (rather than at the end of all the recipes, as other publications do), so you can keep them in mind as you work along.

We'll start by saying that you shouldn't stash away any of these Preserving Kettle products until they have stood handy by for 24 hours. Aside from allowing you a wonderful gloat, this day of grace before storing them will let you check the seals in time to do them over again if you find any poor ones. With paraffin it is not enough merely to add another layer of melted wax: you must remove the wafer of old wax, wipe the inside lip of the glass with a scrupulously clean cloth wrung out in boiling water, and pour on ⅛ inch of fresh hot wax.

Now for the problems that can be dealt with *safely*—provided that the seal is intact, and that there is no mold or fermentation in the contents.

> *Too stiff, tough.* Too much pectin in proportion, or cooking no-added-pectin products too long; sliced citrus rinds in marmalades not precooked before added to syrup. Nothing can be done for pectin-added things, and it's not feasible to do the others over with more liquid. They're still probably tastier than store-bought.
>
> *Too-soft jelly.* Tilt the containers: if you can see the contents shift, the jelly is too soft. This condition can be caused by cooking too long (as when the batch was too big and so was boiled beyond the ideal time limit); or by cooking too slowly; or by too much sugar; or by too little sugar or pectin or acid; or by not cooking long enough. Sometimes you can sal-

vage such jelly by cooking it over; not always—but it's worth a try. Work with only 4 cups of jelly at one time.

Without added pectin. Bring 4 cups of the jelly to boiling and boil it hard for 2 minutes, then test it for signs of gelling. Let it try to sheet from a cold spoon, or (having removed the kettle from heat) chill a dab of it; if it shows signs of improving, boil a minute or so longer until it tests done. Then take it off the heat, skim, pour into hot sterilized containers, and seal.

With added powdered pectin. For each 4-cup batch of jelly, measure 4 teaspoons of powdered pectin and ¼ cup water into the bottom of the kettle; heat the pectin and water to boiling, stirring to keep it from scorching. Add the jelly and ¼ cup of sugar, bring quickly to a full rolling boil for 30 seconds, stirring constantly. Remove from heat, skim, pour into hot sterilized containers, seal.

With added liquid pectin. Bring 4 cups of jelly to a boil quickly. Immediately stir in 2 tablespoons of lemon juice, ¾ cup of sugar and 2 tablespoons of liquid pectin. Bring it back to a full rolling boil, and boil it hard for 1 minute, stirring constantly. Remove the kettle from heat, skim, pour into hot sterilized containers, and seal.

Runny jam. Jam isn't supposed to be as firm as jelly, so if it's only a little bit looser than you'd like it to be, don't bother to remake it. If it's really thin, though, try one of the remedies for too-soft jelly. If a test batch won't turn out right, make sure all the seals are intact and that storage is good—cool, dark and dry—and mark the remaining jars to be used as a sweet topping for ice creams, puddings, pancakes, etc.

Runny conserves and butters. Often simply cooking them over again will help; try a small batch. Is your storage too warm?

"Weeping" jelly. This is the partial separation of liquid from the other ingredients, and it can come from too much acid or from gelling too fast—or from storage that's warm. So check the seals, make sure there's no mold or fermentation, and move it to a cool, dark, dry place; this should help keep it from getting worse. Such jelly is still usable: decant it just before serving and mop up the juice with clean paper towels.

Mold. Imperfect seals, unsterilized containers and lids, letting the product stand uncovered before sealing, re-used wax, storage in a warm, damp place—take your choice. We don't believe in "a-little-mold-won't-hurt-you" (see Chapter 4, "On Guard"). *Destroy all jellies, jams, marmalades, preserves, conserves and fruit butter THAT HAVE MOLD IN THEM.*

Once in a while you'll find that a glass of your paraffin-sealed jelly has mold outside on the top of the wax, and it could be growing not on seepage from the contents, but on a little smear of jelly that had not been wiped from the rim or the neck of the jar. Even if the wax seems to be tight, lift it off and look critically for mold on the underside or on the surface of the jelly. If there is no sign of mold, wipe the rim and the inside (lip or neck, whichever) of the container with a clean cloth wrung out in boiling water, and seal the contents again with fresh hot paraffin.

Fermentation. The stuff has spoiled. Heave it.

WITH OLD–STYLE USE OF SUGAR

These recipes start with the jellies and jams that take no added pectin, thereby reducing almost by half, generally, the sugar called for in the more generous result when pectin is an added ingredient. The temptation indeed was great to include these rules, in a body, in the later section called "With Low Sugar/No Sugar." But they *are* old-style. What could be more so than proportions or methods followed since sugar became a staple for the common man as well as for the rich?

Then, for tastes more hurried, there will be the confections made with that relatively new thing: store-bought pectin, which increased the size of the batches by asking for so much more sweetening.

Some of the following "receipts," to use the pleasant old term, are translated into today's methods. Ingredients for all are given for small, easy-to-work-with batches; especially with jellies, you get best results if you handle no more than 3 to 6 cups of juice at a time.

- **Random and handy:** 1 cup juice + 1 cup sugar = 1¼ cups jelly. Overboiling will reduce the jelling ability of the natural gel in the juice.

I.   With No Added Pectin

Apple (or Quince) Jelly with No Added Pectin
Four ½-pint jars or five 6-ounce glasses

3 pounds tart red apples
3 cups water
3 cups sugar
2 tablespoons lemon juice (optional)

Four cups of prepared juice are needed.

To prepare juice, use ¼ *underripe* and ¾ fully ripe apples. Wash, remove blemishes, stems and blossom ends; do not peel or core. Cut apples in small pieces, add water; cover and bring to boiling over high heat. Reduce heat and simmer for 20 to 25 minutes, or until apples are soft. Put apples through a moistened jelly bag. Measure 4 cups of juice into an enameled or stainless-steel kettle. Add sugar; strain lemon juice, and add, stirring well. Bring to boiling over high heat to 8 F/4.4 C above the boiling point of water, or until two drops of jelly merge and tear from a spoon. Remove the kettle from heat, skim the jelly quickly, and immediately pour it into hot sterilized ½-pint jars, leaving ⅛ inch headroom. Cap with 2-piece screwband lids. (With 6-ounce jelly glasses, leave ¼ inch of headroom, and quickly pour on ⅛ inch melted paraffin; cover when paraffin is cool.) Makes about 4 ½-pint jars, or 5 6-ounce glasses.

Minted variation: At midpoint in the boiling, wash about 6 8-inch sprigs of fresh-picked mint and, holding the bunch by the cut ends, swish the mint around in the boiling jelly for 10 seconds; remove and proceed as above. It's just a hint of mint that adds a delightful bright flavor to the jelly.

Crabapple Jelly with No Added Pectin
Five ½-pint Jars

   3¼ pounds sound fruit, ¼ underripe and ¾ just ripe
   3 cups water
   4 cups sugar

Four cups of prepared juice are needed.

Sort, wash, remove blemishes and stem and blossom ends—*don't pare,* because you want the pectin lying near the skin. Do not core (pulp will be strained). Cut apples small, add water, cover the kettle, and bring to boiling on high heat, reduce heat and simmer for 25 minutes until fruit is soft. Put pulp through a moistened jelly bag. Measure juice into a large enamelware kettle, add sugar, stirring to dissolve. Boil over high heat to 8 F/4.4 C above boiling point of water, or until two drops of jelly merge and tear off the edge of a spoon. Remove from heat, skim, and pour into sterilized ½-pint jars; leave ⅛ inch headroom, cap with 2-piece screwband lids. Makes 5 ½-pint jars.

Red Currant Jelly Without Added Pectin
Five to Six Medium Glasses

---

   4 cups currant juice (about 2½ quarts currants)
   3½ cups sugar

Pick over the currants, discarding overripe or spoiled ones; wash quickly but carefully, and drain off excess water. Measure the washed currents into a large kettle, and *add no more than ¼ as much water as currants.* Over moderate heat, cook the currants until they are soft and translucent, stirring as needed to ensure that they cook evenly—about 10 minutes. Strain the currants with their juice through a damp jelly bag; do not squeeze, lest the juice become cloudy (this classic jelly should always be sparkling clear and jewel-like). Measure 4 cups of juice into a large kettle, bring to boiling, and boil briskly for 5 minutes. Add the sugar, stirring to dissolve it, and boil rapidly until the jelly sheets from a cold spoon or the temperature reaches 8 degrees F/4.4 C above the boiling

(Recipe continued on next page)

point of water in your kitchen. Remove from heat and skim off the foam; pour immediately into hot sterilized glasses, leaving about ½ inch of headroom, and seal at once with ⅛ inch of hot melted paraffin. (Or fill hot sterilized ½-pint jars, leaving ⅛ inch of headroom, and cap with 2-piece screwband lids.)

An alternate method for preparing the juice is to crush first a shallow layer of currants in the bottom of the kettle to start the juice, then pile on the rest of the currants. Heat slowly over low temperature setting for 5 minutes, then boil gently until currants are soft and translucent; strain.

Beach Plum Jelly
About Five ½-pints

Traditionally this jelly is made without added pectin, so the yield is smaller than in the rule for Sand Plum Jelly, later in this chapter.

3½ pounds beach/wild plums, about 1 pound with some green color and
     2½ pounds ripe red
1½ cups water
 3 cups sugar

Wash and pick over the fruit, but do *not* pit or peel. Crush in the bottom of a large enameled kettle with the water; bring to a boil over medium heat, reduce to a strong simmer, and cook for 20 minutes, stirring. Put through a jelly bag to get 4 cups of juice. Return juice to the kettle, stir in the sugar, and boil until the jelly stage is reached: 220 F/104.4 C at sea level, or until jelly sheets from the spoon in testing (q.v.). Remove from heat, skim quickly, and pour immediately into sterilized ½-pint jars, leaving ⅛ inch of headroom. Cap tightly with 2-piece screwband lids.

Concord (or Wild) Grape Jelly with No Added Pectin
Five to Six Medium Glasses

For best results use Eastern Concord or wild grapes (the latter have a flavor especially good with meats and game), and they should be *slightly underripe* for a natural pectin content higher than in fully ripe fruit. Holding the juice overnight in a cool place, and then straining again, will remove the crunchy little slivers of tartrate crystals that form in grape juice.

4 cups grape juice (3½ to 4 pounds of grapes)
1 firm apple
3 cups sugar

Wash and stem the grapes, put them in a large kettle and crush. Wash the apple and cut it in eighths *without peeling or coring,* and add it with ½ cup of water (to prevent sticking). Bring all quickly to a boil, stirring, then reduce the heat and let the fruit cook gently until it is soft—about 10 minutes. Turn the pulp and juice into a damp jelly bag and drain well without squeezing. Refrigerate the bowl of juice overnight, and in the morning strain again through a damp jelly bag to remove the tartrate crystals. Measure 4 cups of juice into a large kettle, stir in the sugar, and boil quickly until the jelly sheets from a cold spoon or its temperature reaches 8 degrees F/4.4 C above the boiling point of water in your kitchen. Remove from heat, quickly skim off the foam, and pour immediately into hot sterilized glasses, leaving about ½ inch of headroom; seal at once with ⅛ inch of hot melted paraffin. (Or pour it into hot sterilized ½ pint jars, leaving ⅛ inch of headroom, cap tightly with 2-piece screwband lids.)

Strawberry Jam with No Added Pectin
Four to Five ½-pint Jars

4 cups prepared crushed berries (about 2¼ to 2½ quarts)
4 cups sugar

Sort and wash berries, removing stems and caps. Crush berries. If you plan to seed the berries, add ¼ cup water to berries in an enameled kettle, bring to boiling over medium-high heat, stirring. Put berries through a food mill to remove some seeds; if you want *all* seeds out, press the pulp through a fine-meshed wire sieve. Measure strained pulp into the rinsed-out kettle, add an equal amount of sugar; over medium-high heat bring to boiling and, stirring constantly, cook until jam begins to thicken (but not so much as jelly does at this stage). Remove from heat, skim and stir a couple of minutes, then ladle into clean, hot ½-pint jars, leaving ¼ inch of headroom. Cap with 2-piece screwband lids turned firmly tight. Process in a Boiling–Water Bath for 10 minutes after the canner returns to a full boil. Remove jars. Cool.

Sun-cooked Strawberry* Jam

You need a blistering hot, still day to do this. Have a table set up in the full sun, its legs set in cans or small pans of water to keep crawling insects from the jam. To protect it from flying insects, have handy a large sheet of clean window glass, the means to prop it at a slant over the platters, and cheesecloth or mosquito netting to tape like a curtain around the three sides left open to the air. And work in *small* batches.

Wash and hull berries, and measure them to determine how much sugar you need. Put a layer of berries in the bottom of a big kettle, cover with an equal number of cups of sugar; repeat a layer of berries and cover it with sugar. Set aside for about 30 minutes to let the berries "weep" and the juice start drawing. Place over very low heat and bring slowly to simmering, stirring occasionally to prevent scorching until the sugar is dissolved.

* Or cherries. Or raspberries—but *not washed* before layering.

Pour syrupy berries ½ inch deep into large plates or platters. Set platters on the table in strong sun. Prop the glass over them with one edge on the table, the opposite edge raised 4 to 6 inches high (this allows any condensation to run harmlessly down the glass onto the table, instead of dripping back on the jam to slow the jelling process). Arrange netting around the open sides.

As the fruit cooks in the sun, turn it over with a spatula—2 or 3 times during the day. When it has obviously jelled enough, pour it into hot sterilized *½-pint* jars, leaving ¼ inch of headroom. Adjust lids, and process in a Boiling–Water Bath (212 F/100 C) for *15 minutes* after the water boils. Complete seals if necessary. (If pint jars are used, increase the headroom to ½ inch, and process in the B–W Bath for 25 minutes.)

If the sun is not strong or if there's wind, jelling can take 2 or 3 days. In that case bring the platters indoors each night.

Blackberry Jam with No Added Pectin
About Four ½-pint Jars

---

    4 cups crushed blackberries (3 quarts if to be seeded)
    4 cups sugar

You may need only about 2½ quarts if you are not going to remove seeds. But the exact amount is not vital, because you will be adding an amount of sugar equal to the measurement of prepared berry pulp.

Sort and wash berries, remove stems and caps; crush well. Put berries into an enameled or stainless-steel kettle. If you will seed the berries, add ½ cup water; stir, place over high heat, and bring to boiling, stirring well. When berries are soft, put them through a food mill, and—if you want absolutely *no seeds*—press again through a fine-meshed wire sieve. Measure purée into the rinsed-out kettle, add an equal amount of sugar, stirring to dissolve. Bring to boiling, stirring as the mixture thickens (test on a cold saucer in the refrigerator). Remove from heat, skim, stir for a minute or two. Ladle into clean, hot ½-pint jars, leaving ½ inch of headroom; cap with 2-piece screwband lids, turning until firmly tight. Process in a Boiling–Water Bath for 10 minutes, after water has returned to a full boil. Remove jars; cool. Makes 4 to 5 ½-pint jars.

II.   With Added Pectin

Grape Jelly
Eight to Nine 8-ounce Glasses

---

    4 cups grape juice (3½ to 4 pounds grapes)
    7 cups sugar
    1 3-ounce pouch liquid pectin

Sort, wash and stem ripe Concord (or wild) grapes; crush, add ½ cup of water, and bring to a boil. Reduce heat and simmer for about 10 minutes. Turn into a damp jelly bag and drain well; do not squeeze. Hold the juice overnight in a cool place, then strain through 2 thicknesses of damp cheesecloth to remove the tartrate crystals that form in grape products. Measure 4 cups of juice into a large kettle, add the sugar and mix well; bring quickly to a full boil that cannot be stirred down. Add the pouch of pectin, bring again to a full rolling boil and boil hard for 1 minute. Remove from the heat, quickly skim off the foam, and pour the jelly into hot sterilized glasses, leaving about ½ inch of headroom; seal immediately with ⅛ inch of hot melted paraffin. (Or seal in ½ pint jars with 2-piece screwband lids, leaving ⅛ inch of headroom.)

Helen Ruth's Sand Plum Jelly
With Pectin, Nine ½-pint Jars

The cherry-sized sand plum of the American Southwest is kin to the beach plum, that favorite for preserves from the sandy coasts of the Northeast up into the Canadian Maritimes. The sand plum is ripe in early June; the season for beach plums starts around the middle of August; the sand plum is a lovely pink when ripe, the beach plum is purple for conserve later in the month but is picked red for jelly. Both varieties gel better if at least one-fourth the amount of fruit is not quite ripe, thus having more natural pectin.

4 pounds sand plums, 3 pounds ripe and 1 pound underripe
1 cup water
1 package powdered pectin (1¾ ounces)
7 cups sugar

Wash and pick over the plums; do *not* pit or peel. Crush them in the bottom of a large enameled kettle with the 1 cup water, bring to a boil, and simmer for 15 minutes. Crush again with a vegetable masher as the fruit softens. Strain through a jelly bag: add a little water to bring the measure up to 5 cups of juice. Return juice to the kettle, reserving 1 cup in which to mix the pectin; combine pectin mixture with juice and bring to a full boil, stirring constantly. Add the sugar, continue stirring, and boil hard for 2 minutes. Remove from heat, skim, and immediately pour into sterilized ½-pint canning jars, leaving ⅛ inch of headroom. Cap tightly with 2-piece screwband lids. Makes 9 ½-pints of a pretty, pink jelly.

For 6-ounce jelly glasses: Fill sterilized glasses, leaving ¼ inch of headroom; quickly top with a thin layer of melted paraffin. When paraffin has cooled and set, cover with a protective cap. Makes 12 glasses.

Pyracantha (Firethorn) Jelly

Five ½-pint Jars

The red-orange pomes of this spiky hedge plant are a favorite for jelly-making in the American Southwest.

    3 generous quarts Pyracantha berries
    3 cups water
      juice of 1 grapefruit
      juice of 1 lemon
    1 box powdered pectin (1¾ ounces)
   4½ cups sugar
    ¼ teaspoon salt

Sort, pick over the berries and put them in a large enameled kettle with the 3 cups of water. Boil for 20 minutes, add the citrus juices, bring briefly to boiling again and pour all into a dampened jelly bag to strain slowly into a crockery bowl. The result should be 3½ cups of juice. In a bowl, combine the pectin and 1 cup of the juice, then pour the mixture into the preserving kettle with the remaining 2½ cups of juice. Bring to a hard boil, add the sugar and the salt and bring to a full rolling boil; stir and boil 3 minutes. Remove from heat, skim quickly, and pour into sterilized ½-pint jars, leaving ⅛ inch of headroom. Cap immediately with sterilized two-piece screwband lids, twisted tight.

If using paraffin, leave ¼ inch of headroom and quickly pour on enough melted wax to form an ⅛-inch thickness when cool.

Pueblo Wild Rose Hip Jelly

Five ½-pint jars

   4½ pounds wild rose hips, gathered in the autumn when they are ripe and
        softened
    4 cups water
    1 box powdered pectin (1¾ ounces)
   5½ cups sugar

Wash the fruit, spread on clean tea towels and roll gently between the towels to remove water and any fuzz. Cut off stems and blossom ends; split hips and remove the balls of seeds. Crush fruits thoroughly, add water, bring to boil and simmer covered for 10 minutes. Put through a jelly bag: there should be 4 cups of juice; add water if needed.

Mix pectin with juice in large enameled kettle and bring to hard boil over high heat. Add sugar and bring to rolling boil for 1 minute, stirring constantly. Remove from heat, skim, pour into clean hot ½-pint jars, leaving ⅛ inch of headroom. Cap tightly with 2-piece screwband lids. Makes about 5 ½-pint jars.

This recipe is updated from an old Pueblo Indian method.

Fresh Mint Jelly
Two Pints

   1 cup fresh mint leaves and stems, firmly packed
   ½ cup apple cider vinegar
   1 cup water
 3½ cups sugar
   4 drops green food coloring
   1 3-ounce pouch liquid pectin

Do *not* remove leaves from the stems. Wash the mint, drain and place in a saucepan. Bruise well with the bottom of a heavy glass tumbler. Add vinegar, water and sugar. Bring to a full, rolling boil over high heat, stirring until sugar melts. Add coloring and pectin and bring again to a full, rolling boil, stirring constantly. Boil hard for 30 seconds. Remove from heat and skim. Pour through a fine sieve into hot sterilized glasses; seal. Makes about 2 pints.

Lemon-Honey Jelly
Two Pints

 2½ cups honey
   ¾ cup fresh lemon juice, strained of all pulp
   1 tablespoon grated lemon rind
   1 3-ounce pouch liquid pectin

Combine honey, lemon juice and grated rind. Stir over moderate heat until mixture reaches a full boil. Add pectin and bring again to a full, rolling boil, stirring constantly. Boil hard 1 minute. Remove from heat and stir 3 minutes. Seal in hot sterilized glasses. Makes about 2 pints.

Tomato Jelly
Six Medium Glasses

 1¾ cups canned tomato juice
   ½ cup strained fresh lemon juice
   2 teaspoons Tabasco sauce
   4 cups sugar
   1 3-ounce pouch liquid pectin

Combine all ingredients except pectin. Stir over high heat until mixture reaches a full, rolling boil. Stir in pectin and bring again to a full, rolling boil. Boil 1 minute, stirring constantly. Remove from heat. Stir and skim for about 3 minutes. Seal in hot sterilized glasses. Lively flavor, good with meats.

Wine Jelly
Five 3-ounce Glasses

This jelly is good with meats; and, in small pretty containers, makes an attractive present. It is *not boiled,* lest the alcohol be cooked away. Work only with small batches.

2 cups white wine (Chablis is good)
3 cups sugar
1 3-ounce pouch liquid pectin

Mix wine and sugar in the top of a double boiler; put over boiling water, stirring constantly until sugar is dissolved—about 3 minutes. Remove and, off heat, stir in the pectin, mixing well. Pour quickly into hot sterilized glasses; as each jar is filled, promptly seal it with ⅛ inch of paraffin (delaying with the paraffin allows a white skin to form on the exposed surface as the mixture gels).

Variations: Substitute ½ cup sherry for ½ cup of the white wine for more emphatic wine flavor; or use all sherry if you can afford it.

Red wines of comparable sweetness to the white wine may be used, and of course Port wine jelly is a classic. Very dry red table wines, however, have not always produced a satisfactory gel for us—perhaps because their acid-to-sweetness ratio is out of kilter for the pectin. Experiment.

Freezer (Uncooked) Berry Jellies with Powdered Pectin
Six 8-ounce Jars

3 cups prepared juice (about 2 to 2½ quarts of fresh strawberries, blackberries or red raspberries)
6 cups sugar
1 package powdered pectin (1¾ ounces)
¾ cup water

Crush the berries and strain them through a damp jelly bag or four layers of damp cheesecloth; squeeze gently if necessary. Add the sugar to the measured 3 cups of juice; stir well and let stand for 10 minutes (a few sugar crystals may remain, but they will dissolve in the time it takes the jelly to set). In a small saucepan stir together the ¾ cup water and the pectin; bring the mixture to the boil and boil hard for 1 minute, stirring constantly. Remove from heat and add it to the sweetened juice; continue stirring for 3 minutes. Then pour into sterilized jars that are freezable and have tight-fitting lids or 2-piece screwband lids, leaving ½ inch of headroom; seal. Let stand at room temperature until set—up to 24 hours—then freeze. Makes 6 8-ounce jars.

No Claim to "Diet" Status

With the rising interest in curtailing the amount of sugar we eat, it's natural to hope that we're cutting down if we treat an old stand-by recipe to different ingredients or a new method. We shouldn't. Not automatically. As witness this warning from General Foods, bending over backward to *deny* special benefits attributed to using its fruit-flavored dessert gelatins in home-made jams: "The analysis performed does not indicate a sufficient difference between the two end products [homemade jams], one prepared with gelatin and the other with pectin, to substantiate a claim that the sugar content is lower in the jam prepared with gelatin. Thus, we cannot give approval to this claim."

So the cooks can have fun, and the spread is tasty—but there's nothing "diet" about such confections as this, made with a dessert gelatin.

Rhubarb-Berry Jam
Four ½-pint Jars or Five 6-ounce Glasses

This is an elusive recipe *PFB* has been asked about a good deal—elusive because the older ladies who referred to it as a "diet" jam had always had it from a friend, but never themselves had seen it in print. Its main features are that it uses dessert gelatin rather than added pectin, and its storage life depends upon refrigeration. And please take to heart the "No Claim to 'Diet' Status" statement at the beginning of this subsection on gelatin-based jellies and jams: *its sugar content is NOT lower than in a jam prepared with pectin.*

6 cups diced fresh rhubarb (about 1½ pounds)
3½ cups sugar (1½ pounds)
¼ cup water
    3-ounce package of strawberry OR raspberry-flavored dessert gelatin (Jell–O*)

In a large enameled or stainless-steel kettle, mix together thoroughly the rhubarb, sugar and water. Cook and stir over high heat until sugar is dissolved—about 2 minutes. Cover, reduce to medium heat, and cook—stirring as needed—until rhubarb is tender. Uncover and boil 12 to 15 minutes longer, or until the fruit mixture has begun to thicken, stirring to prevent scorching. Remove from heat, sprinkle in gelatin, stir well until completely dissolved, then skim off any foam, if necessary, and ladle into sterilized ½-pint jars or 6-ounce jelly glasses. Leave ⅛ inch of headroom for jars, cap with 2-piece screwband lid, tightened. Leave ¼ inch of headroom with the smaller glasses, top quickly with ⅛ inch of melted paraffin; cover to protect paraffin. When cool, store in the refrigerator and use within 1 month (thereafter it becomes extremely thick, according to the manufacturer).

*NOTE: This recipe was given us by the makers of Jell–O brand desserts.

"Best-Ever" (Frozen) Strawberry Jam

Five to Six 8-ounce Jars

---

2 cups prepared fruit (about 1 quart ripe strawberries)
4 cups (1¾ lbs sugar)
¾ cup water
1 box powdered fruit pectin (1¾ ounces)

Thoroughly crush, one layer at a time, about 1 quart of fully ripe strawberries. Measure 2 cups of crushed berries into a large bowl. Add the sugar to the fruit, mix well, and let stand for 10 minutes; a few sugar crystals may remain but they'll dissolve as the jam sets. Mix water and pectin in a small saucepan, bring the mixture to a boil and boil for 1 minute, stirring constantly. Remove from heat and stir the pectin into the fruit; continue stirring for 3 minutes. Ladle quickly into sterilized freezable jars, leaving ½ inch of headroom. Seal immediately with sterilized tight-fitting lids, *not with paraffin*. Let jars stand at room temperature until the jam is set—which may take up to 24 hours—then freeze. Makes 5 to 6 8-ounce jars.

III.   Marmalades, Butters & Preserves

Ginger Squash Marmalade

About Four Pint Jars

---

4 pounds prepared winter squash (or pumpkin)
4 pounds sugar
2 lemons, grated and juiced
2 ounces crystallized ginger
½ teaspoon ground ginger
3 cups water

Peel the squash, scrape out the strings and seeds from the center; save the seeds. Slice and cut the peeled squash to make 4 pounds of ¼-inch cubes. Put the squash in a crockery bowl with the sugar, gingers, grated peel and juice of the lemons. Meanwhile break the seeds, put them in a pan with the water, and boil gently for 30 minutes; strain, and add 2½ cups of the liquid to the squash mixture. Cover and refrigerate overnight. Put into an enameled kettle, and over medium heat, bring to a slow boil, stirring constantly. (Here you can finish it in a 325 F/163 C oven, or let it putter along with a heat-reducing pad under the kettle.) Cook and stir until the squash is clear and will set—45 to 60 minutes. Ladle immediately into clean hot jars, leaving ½ inch of headroom for pints, ¼ inch for ½-pints. Adjust lids; process in a Boiling–Water Bath for 15 minutes for pints, 10 minutes for ½-pints. Remove; complete seals if necessary.
This is a paraphrase of a very old Scottish rule.

Spicy Carrot Marmalade for Game
Four to Five ½-pint Jars

4½ cups coarsely ground raw carrots
3¼ cups sugar
    about ¼ cup fresh lemon juice
¾ teaspoon finely grated zest of lemon
½ teaspoon ground ginger
½ teaspoon ground cloves
½ teaspoon ground cinnamon
½ teaspoon salt

Trim and scrape carrots, run them through the coarse knife of a food grinder. Put them in a heavy enameled kettle, add the sugar, spices and salt. Warm or roll on a hard surface two lemons (to make them easier to juice), but do *not* cut: the next step is to grate off the thin yellow skin of the rind, taking care not to get any of the bitter white portion. Add the grated zest to the ingredients in the kettle. Halve and juice the lemons, add the juice to the kettle. Over low heat, and stirring, bring the mixture to a very slow boil, and cook for about 30 minutes or until it is thick. Pour into hot ½-pint jars, leaving ¼ inch of headroom; cap with clean hot lids. Process in a Boiling–Water Bath for 10 minutes. Remove; complete seals if necessary. Makes 4 to 5 ½-pint jars.

With a food processor: Either quarter the carrots lengthwise and stand them upright in the feed tube against the grating disc, or cut them in pieces and chop—a small amount at a time—with the steel blade. Remove carrot pieces and dry the processing bowl. Peel the lemons very thinly; start the steel blade, drop in the curls of zest and immediately add 1 cup of the sugar on the whirring blade; pulse on and off, add the remaining sugar, process for 15 seconds, and combine with the carrots.

Green Tomato Marmalade
Two Pints

2 quarts sliced, small, green tomatoes
½ teaspoon salt
4 lemons, peeled (save the rind)
4 cups sugar

Combine tomatoes and salt. Chop lemon rind fine and add. Cover with water and boil 10 minutes. Drain well. Slice the peeled lemons very thin, discarding seeds but reserving all juice. Add lemon slices and juice and the sugar to the tomato mixture. Stir over moderate heat until sugar melts. Bring to boiling, reduce heat and simmer until thick—about 45 minutes. Stir frequently. Pack in hot sterilized jars and process. Makes about 2 pints.

This classic from long ago is especially good served with meat to add a "company dinner" touch.

Classic Orange Marmalade
Five to Six ½-pint Jars

The Scots make highly prized marmalades, among them this one from Mildred Wallace, which is characterized by a darker color and slightly bitter flavor compared with the most popular supermarket brands in the United States. The precooking prevents the peel from becoming tough when it is boiled with the sugar.

> 2 pounds Seville oranges (or other bitter variety, like Calamondin), left whole
> 2 large lemons, whole
> 8 cups water (about)
> 8 cups (4 pounds) sugar

Wash the oranges and lemons well, removing any stem "buttons," and put the clean washed whole oranges and lemons in a large kettle with enough water to cover them; put the lid on the kettle and bring to a boil, then simmer until a slender fork will easily pierce the fruit—about 1½ hours. Remove the fruit to cool, saving the liquid; when they are cool, cut them in half the long way, then cut the halves in *very thin* slices (your knife must be sharp!), and take out and save the pips. Return the pips to the juice in the kettle and boil for about 10 minutes (this contributes to the bitter flavor). Strain the juice and return it to the kettle. Add the fruit slices and heat to boiling. Add the sugar, stirring until it dissolves, and continue cooking at a fast boil—stirring only enough to prevent scorching—until it starts to thicken and its temperature reaches *9 degrees F* (1 degree more than for jelly) above the boiling point of water in your kitchen. Remove from heat, skim off any foam, pour at once into hot sterilized ½-pint jars with 2-piece screwband lids, leaving ½ inch of headroom. Adjust lids; process in a Boiling–Water Bath (212 F/100 C) for 10 minutes.

Yellow Tomato Marmalade
1 ½ pints

> 3¼ cups coarsely chopped, peeled, ripe, yellow plum-type tomatoes
> ¼ cup fresh lemon juice
>   grated rind of 1 large lemon
> 6 cups sugar
> 1 bottle liquid fruit pectin (6 ounces)

Place chopped tomatoes in small pan and set over low heat and cover. *Do not add any water.* Bring to boiling, reduce heat and simmer about 10 minutes, stirring frequently. Remove from heat and measure out 3 cups of the tomatoes and liquid. In a large kettle, combine the 3 cups tomatoes with the lemon juice, grated rind and sugar. Stir over moderate heat until boiling. Boil hard 1 minute. Turn off heat and add pectin. Stir for 5 minutes. Skim as needed. Pack in hot sterilized glasses and process. About 1½ pints.

Steps in Making Butters

Butters are nice old-fashioned spreads and they're good with meats. Their virtues are that they take about ½ as much sugar as jams from the same fruits (½ cup sugar to each 1 cup of fruit pulp), and they can be made with the sound portions of windfall and cull fruits that you'd probably not bother with for jelly or jam. Their one drawback is that they require very long cooking—and careful cooking at that, because they stick and scorch if you turn your back.

Butters are made from most fruits or fruit mixtures. Probably apple is the best-known ingredient, but apricots, crabapples, grapes, peaches, pears, plums and quinces also make good butters.

To Prepare The Fruits

Use prime ripe fruit or good parts of windfalls or culls. Wash thoroughly and prepare as follows:

Apples: Quarter and add ½ as much water or cider (or part water and part cider) as fruit.

Apricots: Pit, crush, add ¼ as much water as fruit.

Crabapples: Quarter, cut out stems and blossom ends, and add ½ as much water as fruit.

Grapes: Remove stems, crush grapes and cook in own juice.

Peaches: Dip in boiling water to loosen skins; peel, pit, crush and cook in their own juice.

Pears: Remove stems and blossom ends. Quarter and add ½ as much water as fruit.

Plums: Crush and cook in their own juice. The pits will strain out.

Quinces: Remove stems and blossom ends. They're hard, so cut in small pieces and add ½ as much water as fruit.

Making The Pulp

Cook the fruits prepared as above until their pulp is soft. Watch it—it may stick on.

Put the cooked fruit through a colander to rid it of the skins and pits, then press the pulp through a food mill or sieve to get out all fibers.

Sugar and Cooking

Usually ½ cup of sugar to each 1 cup of fruit pulp makes a fine butter. It's easiest to use at one time not more than 4 cups of fruit pulp, plus the added sugar.

Let the sugar dissolve in the pulp over low heat, then bring the mixture to a boil and cook until thick, stirring often to prevent scorching.

When the butter is thick enough to round slightly in a spoon and shows a glossiness or sheen, pack while still hot into hot, sterilized ½ pint or pint canning jars, leaving ½ inch of headroom. Adjust lids and process the jars in a Boiling–Water Bath (212 F/100 C) for 10 minutes. Remove jars, complete seals if necessary. Cool and store.

Alternative cooking method: Butters stick so easily when they are cooking on the stove top that it's a real chore to keep them from scorching. Some cooks put about ¾ of the hot uncooked purée in a large, uncovered, heatproof crockery dish or enameled roasting pan and cook it in a 275 to 300 F/135 to 149 C oven until it thickens. As the volume shrinks and there is room in the dish, add the other ¼ of the purée. When the butter is thick but still moist on top, ladle it quickly into containers and process.

Optional Spices

Any spices are added as the butter begins to thicken. For 1 gallon of pulp use 1 teaspoon ground cinnamon, ½ teaspoon ground allspice, and ½ teaspoon cloves. Ginger is nice in pear butter—1 to 2 teaspoons to 1 gallon of pulp. For smaller quantities of pulp reduce measures of spices proportionately. If the butter is to be light in color, tie whole (not ground) spices loosely in a cloth bag and remove the bag at the end of the cooking.

Apple Butter
About Six Pints

---

5 pounds juicy tart apples, 12 to 15 (Winesap, Northern Spy, Jonathan)
1 cup apple cider (or water)
    about 2½ cups sugar,* or to taste
½ teaspoon ground cinnamon
¼ teaspoon ground cloves
¼ teaspoon ground nutmeg

Remove blemishes, core and cut apples in eighths. Put apples and cider in a heavy enameled kettle and cook over medium heat until soft; stir to prevent sticking. Remove from heat, and when the pulp is cool enough to handle, put it through a food mill or sieve. For every 1 cup pulp add ¼ cup white or brown sugar. Return to the heavy kettle and bring it to a low boil until sugar is melted.

Now choose: (1) Cook quickly over medium-high heat to a brisk boil, stirring constantly. Or (2) put the kettle in a preheated 300 F/149 C oven, where you need stir only occasionally to keep a caramelized skin from forming on top. The quick stove-top boil produces brighter color, but scorches the purée if you turn your back; the oven makes darker color and takes longer, but doesn't scorch (any caramelized skin can be rolled off easily).

* If you sweeten with honey, use ⅘ as much honey as sugar (see metrics, which are easier here). If you use fructose, use ⅔ as much granulated fructose as sugar. If you use an artificial (non-nutritive) sweetener, wait to sweeten to taste until after the purée is cooked down enough to be ready to put in jars: remember that, like substitutes for sodium chloride (table salt), these sweeteners can produce an unwanted aftertaste if cooked for a long time, or processed at high heat.

By either method, cook the purée until it mounds slightly on the spoon and has a sheen to it. On a jelly thermometer it will register 220 F/104 C at sea level. Ladle into clean hot jars, leaving ¼ inch of headroom for ½-pint jars, ½ inch for pints. Adjust lids, process in a Boiling–Water Bath for 10 minutes. Remove jars, complete seals if necessary.

Variation: Omit cinnamon and cloves; instead use ½ teaspoon scraped zest of lemon and ½ teaspoon freshly grated nutmeg.

Blender/food processor: Instead of putting cooked fruit through a food mill or sieve to remove skins before adding sweetener, purée in small amounts at the highest speed of the blender, then strain the sauce into the heavy kettle, adding sweetener and seasonings as liked.

In a food processor with the steel blade in place, purée the cooked apples and their skins, small amounts at a time; the result will be smoother—and runnier—than with the blender, but you may want to sieve the purée. (Also using the steel blade, you can save time by whirring thin shavings of fresh lemon peel with 1 cup of the sugar.)

Steps in Making Preserves

Wash the fruit and remove stem and blossom parts. Peel peaches, pears, pineapples, quinces and tomatoes. Shred pineapple, less the core. Cut slits in tomatoes and gently squeeze out the seeds, cut large tomatoes in quarters, leave small ones whole. Pears and quinces are thinly sliced after halving and coring. Take the pits from sour cherries. Of course strawberries and raspberries are left whole.

To cook, carefully follow the specific recipe. Generally, dry sugar is added to the soft fruits to start the juice flowing. There should be enough juice to cook the fruit. Hard fruits are cooked in a sugar-and-water syrup. The recipe will tell you how long to cook each of the preserves.

Ladle hot preserves into hot sterilized canning jars, leaving ½ inch of headroom; wipe the mouths of the containers carefully with a clean cloth wrung out in boiling water; adjust lids, and process in a Boiling–Water Bath (212 F/100 C) for 10 minutes; complete seals if necessary. Cool, clean the jars, label and store.

Strawberry Preserves
About Four ½-pint Jars

---

     generous 6 cups prepared strawberries (a good 1½ quarts)
4½ cups sugar
¼ cup fresh lemon juice, strained (optional)

(Recipe continued on next page)

Perfect preserves and fine jam are not intended to be interchangeable (unless your jam is runny or your preserves are too stiff): preserves are intended to be the perfect topping to good ice cream or other delicacies.

Use only tart, firm, uniform pretty strawberries; wash and drain them, then remove caps. Discard any hollow berries. In a china bowl, make alternate single layers of berries and sugar, and let stand over night to "weep" in the refrigerator. The next day, heat the berries and their juice—and optional lemon juice—in an enameled kettle over medium-high heat until boiling. Boil quickly, stirring to prevent sticking, but being gentle so as not to break fruit. When syrup has thickened—but not so much as for jam: about 15 minutes—remove the preserves from heat and skim. Ladle into clean, hot ½-pint jars, cover with 2-piece screwband lids, turned firmly tight. Process in a Boiling–Water Bath 10 minutes. Remove jars; cool. Makes 4 ½-pint jars.

Sweet Cherry (or other) Preserves
Two Pints

---

4 cups pitted sweet cherries, tightly packed
3 cups sugar

In a 4-quart saucepan crush the cherries lightly to start the juice flow. Boil cherries and their juice about 10 minutes—or until fruit is tender. Add sugar to the cherries, stir well, and boil for 5 minutes more. Now cover the kettle and let the cherries stand for 2 minutes while they absorb more of the sugar. Stir the hot preserves to prevent floating fruit, then pour into hot sterilized jars, leaving ½ inch of headroom; process for 10 minutes in a B–W Bath (212 F/100 C). Makes about 2 pints.

This is a basic rule for similar fruit preserves, and offers scope for variations of your own devising. Be individual!

Blueberry Conserve
Six ½-pint Jars

---

1 orange
1 lemon
3 cups water
5 cups sugar
½ cup dark seedless raisins
6 cups blueberries, stemmed and washed

With vegetable peeler, remove each outer rind of the orange and the lemon—cutting so thinly that none of the white underlayer comes with it; chop fine. Remove and chop the pulp, discarding any seeds. Bring the water and sugar to a boil in large stainless-steel kettle, and add orange, lemon and raisins; simmer for about 5 minutes. Add the blueberries, and cook over moderate heat until the mixture thickens—about 30 minutes—stirring often to prevent sticking. Pour boiling hot into hot ½-pint jars leaving ¼ inch of headroom. Adjust the lids and process in a Boiling–Water Bath for 10 minutes. Remove and complete seals if necessary. Makes about 6 ½-pints.

This is especially good as topping for ice cream or plain white or yellow cake.

Sweet-and-Sour Spiced Crabapples

Five Pints

---

   3 pounds firm ripe crabapples (about)
   3 cups cider vinegar
   3 cups water
2¼ cups sugar
   3 dozen whole cloves
   4 to 6 3-inch sticks of cinnamon
   6 short blades of mace*

To prepare the crabapples, wipe the fuzz from the blossom ends, but leave stems on; wash well, then prick the skins with a large darning needle to keep the fruit from bursting while cooking. Tie the spices loosely in a square of muslin or double thickness of cheesecloth, and put the bag in a large enameled kettle with the vinegar, water and sugar; bring to boiling and boil together for 3 minutes. Add the crabapples and simmer until just tender—not mushy. (Test after 15 minutes by poking one deeply with a darning needle: there should be a little resistance.) Discard the spice bag, and pack the crabapples immediately in hot pint jars and cover them with the very hot syrup in which they were cooked, leaving ½ inch of headroom. Adjust the lids and process the jars in a Boiling–Water Bath (212 F/100 C) for 10 minutes. Remove; complete seals if necessary. Makes about 5 pints.

* Or use 1 teaspoon ground mace or nutmeg, although it could come through the bag and make the liquid cloudy.

WITH LOW SUGAR/NO SUGAR

Many things are called "diet" these days: it depends, really, on what one is trying to stay away from—sucrose, sodium, cholesterol, the list can go on. In general, though—and certainly in context here—the word indicates that the amount of white cane or beet sugar has been reduced, by using low-methoxyl pectin, even below the amounts used in proportion to fruit juice/pulp when no pectin was added at all. Then from L–M pectin they continue down till the end is Zero sugar in the spreads using artificial sweeteners.

Time Out for Low-methoxyl Pectin

The question *PFB* has been asked most by readers—next to how to find a Boiling–Water Bath canner that will do its job right—is where to get low-methoxyl pectin. This substance must be accompanied by added calcium, but it can make cooked fruit juice or pulp gel with only a fraction of the sugar called for by the universally available pectins. And, unlike some proprietary brands that rely on vegetable gums or gelatin as firming agents, this one *is* a pectin, extracted from citrus by a method different from the one used for virtually all the conventional store-bought pectins, liquid or granular/powdered.

In Chapter 25 we tell the places we know of, at this writing, where you can get it. Two are the major retail sources on the East Coast that sell the powdered pure L–M (low-methoxyl) pectin along with the calcium compound they prefer (plus some folksy-loose instructions). A company in the South has marketed it in a traditional 1¾-ounce box; ready-mixed, according to the label, with corn sugar, citric acid and a preservative, the package makes no mention of either the L–M pectin or the calcium compound that *PFB* was assured were contained in it—a reticence that's considered a defect by many consumer groups. Dr. Margy Woodburn of Oregon State University, Corvallis indicated that West Coast supermarkets carry their own proprietary brands of L–M pectin; we assume they are made up and easily ready to use.

As background, the giant Sunkist combine in southern California pioneered in standardizing citrus-type pectin; for years it made L–M pectin, and was to resume production in the early 1980's. Sunkist has never stopped making regular pectin. Meanwhile Hercules, Inc., in Delaware, has been importing the special pectin from Italy, and sells it mainly to the food industry for lowered-Calorie jams and jellies, and for thickening the fruit mixtures in yogurt, etc.

HOW TO USE IT, GENERALLY

The following procedures are a meld of the instructions that accompanied bulk L–M pectin *PFB* bought, along with the di-calcium phosphate to boost its power to gel, from two Northeast suppliers; to the directions are added what could be called side comments from the company that distributes pectin of all types to the conglomerates that put it eventually in shopping carts in grocery stores across North America.

The operative ingredient in low-methoxyl confections is calcium. It doesn't matter technically what kind of calcium it is so long as it is food-grade—monocalcium, di-calcium or tri-calcium phosphate—or a calcium compounded with the less-pleasing chloride—*and* that the amount of free calcium in each of the compounds has been taken into account. Actually, though, we found that di-calcium phosphate made jelly more nearly like the old thing we were used to. And it had the added benefit of being the compound most generally recommended by the distributors we dealt with.

IDIOSYNCRASIES TO WATCH FOR

First: L–M pectin will form globs like half-cooked tapioca if you give it the slightest chance. So, if you are using it with a granulated nutritive sweetener of some sort (as against an *artificial* sweetener, either liquid or granular), mix the pectin with the sugar, which then acts as a wetting agent. Be mighty careful that the utensils you mix the pectin and sugar in, and with, are perfectly dry, or you'll have the start of a mess.

Then, di-calcium phosphate is put into what is termed a solution. But it really doesn't dissolve at all—it just hangs there in suspension; and, though it can be made ahead and kept in the refrigerator, its storage jar must be shaken hard each time you put the measuring spoon into it. This is how to ensure that you're getting enough calcium to do the job.

And add the calcium at the end: *do not add it too early and cook it.* This is the warning of Dianne Leipold of Hercules, Inc., who supplies the people who in turn supplied us. One of the main causes for L–M jelly/jam to go wrong, Dr. Leipold said, is allowing the calcium to cook, and cooking it results in grainy jelly that releases its water. Calcium can be added even when the kettle is taken from the stove, and be stirred into the sweetened fruit-and-pectin just before the boiling mixture is ladled into ½-pint jars.

• • IN BOILING WATER BATH.   By now the B–W Bath is an established safeguard for shelf storage, and especially so for jams and even jellies like these. However, the B–W Bath treatment for 10 minutes for ½-pint jars just might undo the care you took *not* to cook the calcium after it was added: despite your carefulness, the boil could give you grainy, runny jam or jelly. Here's the beauty of working with 1-cup trial batches: test a jar or two in the B–W Bath. And if your jelly/jam suffers . . . well, make only a small amount at a time, perhaps with frozen prepared juice/pulp.

PROPORTIONS FOR USING L–M PECTIN WITH SOME SUGAR

You can increase this batch to 4 cups of juice, or even more. However, we recommend that you start with 1-cup batches until you get the consistency you like. After all, your water may be hard (contain calcium): this will affect the stiffness of your jelly/jam. The day may be muggy. All the things that could go awry with other jelly-making could play hob here. The proportions:

1 cup prepared fruit juice (prepare it as for any jelly)
OR
1 cup fruit pulp (seeded, skins removed, etc., as for any jam)
¼ cup (4 tablespoons) sugar OR 3 tablespoons fructose
½ teaspoon granular low-methoxyl pectin
1 teaspoon di-calcium phosphate *solution*

And you make the solution by adding ¼ teaspoon granular di-calcium phosphate to ½ cup boiled and cooled water, and storing it in a sterilized, tightly closed container in the refrigerator. This amount of solution will "do" 24 cups of prepared juice or prepared fruit pulp, because at the end of cooking you add 1 teaspoon of the solution for each 1 cup of fruit.

PROCEDURE

Prepare fruit; boil jars and hold them and their 2-piece screwband lids in the hot water. In a completely dry container, and with a dry spoon, add ½ teaspoon granular L–M pectin to the ¼ cup sugar and mix thoroughly. Bring the fruit to boiling over moderate heat, add the sugar-pectin in one swoop and stir well to dissolve it.

(Here Dr. Leipold says to boil the whole thing hard for 1 minute, just as is done with conventional jelly. If you're doing trial batches, follow her advice.)

At any rate, when the sugar and pectin are dissolved in the hot fruit, add the 1 teaspoon of (well-shaken) calcium solution, stir, and fill hot jars to within ⅛ inch of the top. Wipe rims, adjust lids and screw them down tightly. Stand the jars upright out of drafts and let them cool naturally. Jars may be stored in the pantry until opened; then they go in the refrigerator.

With the next 1-cup batch, you can test a spoonful of jelly/jam on a dish in the coldest part of your refrigerator to see if it sets to your liking. Again, this is what you do in making standard jellies and jams. No one mentioned a sheeting test or a thermometer reading to us, so here again you'll have to experiment a bit. But with 1 cup of juice at a time, and only ¼ cup of sugar, you can't go far wrong by trial and error until you get your results down pat.

PROPORTIONS FOR USING ARTIFICIAL SWEETENER

Because you will be making a solution of L–M pectin in advance and storing it in the refrigerator, you will be dealing with a firm measurement of unflavored gel (containing the equivalent of ¾ teaspoon pectin for each 1 cup of fruit, rather than ½ teaspoon as used with the sugar—but the actual amount of dry pectin is academic).

Make the L–M pectin *solution* by whirring 2 tablespoons of granulated pectin in 2 cups of hot water at high speed in a blender. When completely dissolved, it is decanted into a sterilized wide-mouth pint jar, and stored, well capped, in the refrigerator. It will form a gel on its own, and from this you will measure the amount required for each batch of jelly/jam.

For each 1 cup of prepared juice/pulp, brought to the boil, add ¼ cup of the pectin solution (it's a gel now, if it has been cooled in the refrigerator, remember: but it can be heated gently in a heavy pot over low heat, or in a double boiler; or—best of all—in a heatproof glass measuring cup set on a trivet in a pan of hot water). Bring to boiling, add the equivalent in artificial sweetener of ¼ cup white sugar (or 3 tablespoons of fructose); restore the boil, and remove from heat, stirring in 1 teaspoon of the (shaken) calcium solution. Pour immediately into hot sterilized jars, leaving ⅛ inch of headroom; cap tightly with sterilized lids; cool upright; store. Refrigerate immediately upon opening.

• **WARNING ABOUT KEEPING QUALITIES:** Because there is no added sugar or acid to help prevent spoilage, the contents must be kept most carefully refrigerated after opening. Even so, the jelly/jam will not keep so long as the product made with some sugar.

Sugarless Jellies and Jams with Gelatin

Ruth Hertzberg's comments about these confections should introduce the following recipes. First, she says, it is just possible that the amount of gelatin used for a dessert may be "just a whisker" too stiff for smooth spreadability. And stirring finished jam may break it up too much to be spreadable the next time you want it.

It's possible to freeze these, *but*—might not freezing make them tough?

Without the usual sugar as a preservative, these are perishable, so there is little use in making much at a time (but the temptation is great for a sweet-starved diabetic).

Finally, Ruth recommends that next to no headroom be left: ⅛ inch is plenty for refrigeration. For freezing, though, allow ½ inch for expansion.

Sugarless Apple Jelly
Two 8-ounce Jars

---

    2   cups unsweetened apple juice
    4   teaspoons unflavored gelatin
 1½   tablespoons lemon juice
    2   tablespoons liquid artificial sweetener, to equal 1 cup sugar (read the
         label, especially if substituting a dry artificial sweetening agent)
    1 or 2 drops red food coloring if you like

Soften the gelatin in ½ cup of the apple juice. Meanwhile heat the remaining 1½ cups juice to boiling; remove from heat and stir in the softened gelatin until it is dissolved. Add the artificial sweetener, the lemon juice, the food coloring if you like it. Return to heat and bring to the boil, then pour into hot sterilized ½-pint jars that have 2-piece screwband lids, leaving ⅛ inch of headroom; seal. Store in the refrigerator when cool, and use within 3 to 4 weeks.

Sugarless Grape Jelly
Two 8-ounce Jars

 1½   cups unsweetened grape juice
    4   teaspoons unflavored gelatin
 ½   cup water
    2   tablespoons liquid artificial sweetener, to equal 1 cup sugar (read the
         label, especially if substituting a dry artificial sweetening agent)

(*Recipe continued on next page*)

Soften the gelatin in the ½ cup water. Meanwhile heat the grape juice to boiling; remove from heat and add the softened gelatin, stirring until it dissolves. Add the liquid artificial sweetener, and bring again to the boil. Remove, pour into hot sterilized ½-pint jars that have 2-piece screwband lids; seal. Store in the refrigerator when cool, and use within 3 to 4 weeks.

Diet Grape Jam
Four ½-pint Jars

4 teaspoons unflavored gelatin
¼ cup water
3 pounds Concord or other juicy grapes
2 tablespoons liquid artificial sweetener

In a small bowl soften the gelatin in the cold water. Wash and stem the grapes, then press them through a food mill or coarse sieve to remove skins and seeds. Measure the pulp and add enough water to make 4 cups, then put it into a 4-quart kettle and add softened gelatin; stir well to dissolve it. Over medium heat, bring to a boil and boil for 1 minute, stirring all the while to prevent scorching. Remove from heat, skim off any foam, and stir in well the liquid artificial sweetener. Pour into hot sterilized ½-pint jars, leaving ⅛ inch of headroom if to be refrigerated, ½ inch if to be frozen. Cap tightly with sterile 2-piece screwband lids. Makes about 4 ½-pint jars.

When cool and set, store in the refrigerator for use within one month. Each 1 tablespoon of jam has 12 Calories.

Diet Peach Jam
Four ½-pint Jars

2 tablespoons unflavored gelatin
¼ cup cold water
3½ pounds ripe peaches
8 teaspoons lemon juice
4 tablespoons liquid artificial sweetener

In a small bowl soften the gelatin in the ¼ cup of water. Wash and peel peaches, remove pits and cut in chunks. In a 4-quart enameled or stainless-steel kettle over medium heat, bring the cut peaches to a simmer until soft. Remove from heat and crush lightly. Measure and add enough water to make 4 cups of pulp. Return to the kettle and add softened gelatin and lemon juice, stirring well to dissolve the gelatin. Over medium heat, bring to a boil and boil 1 minute, stirring all the while. Remove from heat, skim, and stir in well the liquid artificial sweetener, and pour immediately into hot sterilized ½-pint jars, leaving ⅛ inch of headroom (½ inch if to be frozen, to allow for expansion). Cap tightly with 2-piece screwband lids. Makes about 4 ½-pint jars.

When cool and set, store the jars of jam in the refrigerator for use within one month. Each 1 tablespoon of jam has 10 Calories.

Frozen Diet Raspberry Jam

Two to Three ½-pint Jars

1 quart fresh red raspberries
1 tablespoon lemon juice
1 package powdered fruit pectin (1¾ ounces)
3 to 4 teaspoons liquid artificial sweetener

Crush raspberries thoroughly; put half (or more) through a food mill to remove some seeds, if you like. Crush the berries directly into a large stainless-steel or enameled kettle. Add the lemon juice and the powdered pectin, stirring until the pectin is thoroughly dissolved. Over medium heat, bring the mixture to boiling, and boil hard for 1 minute. Remove from heat, add the sweetener and stir for 2 minutes. Ladle into hot sterilized ½-pint glass freezer jars, leaving ⅛ inch of headroom if to be refrigerated, ½ inch if to be frozen. Cap at once with sterilized two-piece screwband lids; *do not use paraffin.* Let the jars stand at room temperature for a day or so, until the jam is set. Freeze.

Store in the refrigerator after opening and thawing. Each 1 tablespoon of jam has 7 Calories.

Sugarless Strawberry Jam

Two 8-ounce Jars

2 cups crushed strawberries (about 1 quart whole berries)
4 teaspoons unflavored gelatin
1½ tablespoons lemon juice (particularly if blackberries are substituted)
2 tablespoons liquid artificial sweetener, to equal 1 cup sugar (read the label, especially if substituting a dry artificial sweetening agent)

Soften the gelatin in ½ cup of the juice from crushed berries. Meanwhile heat the remaining 1½ cups of crushed berries to boiling; remove from heat and add the softened gelatin, stirring until it is dissolved. Add the lemon juice and the artificial sweetener. Return to heat and bring to the boil, then pour into hot sterilized jars that have 2-piece screwband lids, leaving ⅛ inch of headroom; seal. Store in the refrigerator when cool, and use within 3 to 4 weeks.

Diet Damson Plum Jam
Four ½-pint Jars

---

   1 tablespoon unflavored gelatin
  ¼ cup cold water for softening gelatin
 2½ pounds Damson or other firm-bodied plums
  ½ cup water
   3 to 4 tablespoons liquid artificial sweetener

In a small bowl soften the gelatin in the ¼ cup of cold water. Wash, stem, halve and stone the plums. In a 4-quart enameled or stainless-steel kettle, boil the plums with ½ cup water over medium heat until just soft. Remove from heat and crush lightly. Measure and add just enough water to make 4 cups of pulp, then return it to the kettle and add the softened gelatin, stirring well to dissolve. Bring to a boil and boil 1 minute, stirring all the while. Remove the kettle from heat, skim, stir in well the artificial sweetener, and pour the jam immediately into hot sterilized ½-pint jars, leaving ⅛ inch of headroom. Cap tightly with 2-piece screwband lids. Make 4 ½-pint jars.

When cool and set, store jars of jam in the refrigerator and use within a month. Each 1 tablespoon of jam has 9 Calories.

19

PICKLES, RELISHES AND OTHER SPICY THINGS

Just as jellies and their cousins can be prime sources of sugar that we probably could do without, so some pickles are vehicles for sodium chloride that no doubt we should do without. In Chapter 17, "Common Ingredients and How to Use Them," there is a fairly long section on salt: we refer you to this discussion to save space because it tells how the difference in density can account for seemingly contradictory measurements for brining, etc. (To be on the safe side, go by *weight* of salt per *volume* of liquid.)

Pickles and relishes are first cousins. Their major difference is that vegetables and/or fruits for relishes are chopped before being put with the vinegar mixture, and those for pickles are left whole or cut to size for the recipe.

Any firm-fleshed vegetable or fruit may be used. There are some that hold their shape and texture particularly well in pickles, such as the black-spine type of cucumber and the Seckel pear.

Pickle products and relishes are packed in regular canning jars, trapped air is removed (see "Leaving Headroom in Jars" and "Filling, Bubbling & Capping" in Chapter 3, which describes general canning procedures). Then the jars are capped *and processed in a Boiling-Water Bath (212 F/100 C) for a specified time to ensure a good seal,* and are stored as any other canned food is—in a cool, dry, dark place.

ESSENTIAL INGREDIENTS

THE PRODUCE ITSELF

Fresh, prime ingredients are basic. Move them quickly from garden or orchard to pickling solution. They lose moisture so quickly that even one day at room temperature may lead to hollow-centered or shriveled pickles.

Perfect pickles need perfect fruits or vegetables to start with. The *blossom ends* of cucumbers must be removed (since any enzymes located there can cause pickles to soften while brining), but do leave ¼ inch or so of *stem.*

331

Equipment for Pickles and Relishes

If your pickle-making is modest in amount, you will need only a Boiling–Water Bath canner and a deep enameled kettle in addition to your regular kitchen utensils. The one pickle characteristic to keep in mind is the interaction of the vinegar and salt with metals: use enameled, earthenware or glass containers to hold or cook these mixtures—*never use* anything that's galvanized, or copper, brass, iron or aluminum. A stoneware crock is best for brining (but often they're hard to come by); glass 1-gallon, or larger, jars or straight-sided containers are a good substitute.

Boiling–Water Bath canner
6- to 8-quart enameled kettle for short brining and cooking pickles
Jars in prime condition, with lids/sealers/gaskets ditto
Minute-timer with warning bell to time processing periods
Shallow pans (dishpans are fine)
Ladle or dipper
Long-handled wooden or stainless spoon for stirring
Wide-mouth funnel for filling containers
Jar-lifter
Colander for draining
Large measuring cups, and measuring spoons
Squares of cheesecloth to hold spices
Plenty of clean dry potholders, dish cloths and towels
Household scales
Stoneware crocks

SALT

Use only plain, pure salt, either coarsely or finely ground, without additives. The 5-pound bags of canning/pickling salt from the supermarket are ideal. (See Chapter 17 for a discussion of "sea" and "solar" salts.)

Do not use table salt. Although pure, the additives in it to keep it free-running in damp weather make the pickling liquids cloudy; the iodine in iodized salt darkens the pickles.

Do not use the so-called rock salt or other salts that are used to clear ice from roads and sidewalks: they are not food grade.

Salt, as used in brining pickles, is a preservative. A 10-percent brine, about the strongest used in food preservations, is 1 pound/*c*. 1½ cups salt dissolved in each 1 gallon of liquid. Old-time recipes often call for a brine "that will float an egg"; translate this to "10-percent brine."

Brine draws the moisture and natural sugars from foods and forms lactic acid to keep them from spoiling.

Juices drawn from the food dilute the brine, weakening the original salt solution.

VINEGAR

Use a high-grade cider or white distilled vinegar of 4 to 6 percent acidity (40 to 60 grain). Avoid vinegars of unknown acidity or your own homemade wine vinegar. The latter develops "mother" that clouds the pickling liquid. Use white vinegar if you want really light pickles.

And *never reduce the vinegar* if the solution is too tart: instead, add more sugar.

SWEETENERS

Use white sugar unless the recipe calls for brown. Brown makes a darker pickle. Sometimes a cook in the northern United States or in Canada may use maple sugar or syrup in her pickles for its flavor—but this is feasible only if she has lots of it to spare. (See "Sweeteners" in Chapter 17.)

SPICES

Buy fresh spices for each pickling season. Spices deteriorate and lose their pungency in heat and humidity, so they should be kept in airtight containers in a cool place.

ADDITIVES FOR CRISPING PICKLES

To enhance the crispness of various cucumber and rind pickles, old cookbooks sometimes called for a relatively short treatment with *slaked lime* (calcium hydroxide) or *alum* (see also "Firming Agents" in Chapter 17). Such chemicals are *not necessary* for good-textured products if the ingredients are perfect—well grown, unblemished and perfectly fresh—and are handled carefully according to directions.

However, a crisper-upper also mentioned in heirloom recipes is a natural one that, so far as we can discover, is safe to use without restriction. One bygone rule we've seen says to cover the bottom of the crock with washed grape leaves and put a layer of them on top of the pickles; and a Southern homemaker says scuppernong leaves are best. Another uses cherry leaves.

WATER

Water used in making pickles should of course be of drinking quality (because otherwise contaminants can increase the bacterial load that leads to spoilage). Also, water with above-average calcium content can shrivel pickles, and iron compounds can make them darker than we like.

See "Water" in Chapter 17 for ways to rid water of some excess minerals, and for a discussion of how "hard" or "soft" water affects texture.

METHODS

LONG–BRINE

Vegetables such as cucumbers are washed and dropped into a heavy salt solution (plus sometimes vinegar and spice) and left in a cool place to cure for 2 to 4 weeks. Scum *must be removed* from the brine each day. Following this the pickles are packed loosely in clean jars and covered with the same or freshly made brine and processed in a Boiling–Water Bath.

SHORT-BRINE

Vegetables are left overnight in a brine to crisp up. The next day they are packed in jars, covered with a pickling solution and processed in a Boiling-Water Bath (212 F/100 C) for a suitable time.

COMPLETE PRECOOKING

Complete precooking is the rule for relishes and similar cut-up pickle mixtures in a sweet-sour liquid. Packed hot in regular canning jars, these products then have a short Boiling-Water Bath.

Pickle, etc., Troubles and What to Do

If you find any imperfect seals during the 24 hours between processing and storing your pickles, relishes and sauces, you can dump the contents into the preserving kettle, bring to boiling, pack into hot canning jars, and process again in the Boiling-Water Bath (212 F/100 C) for the required time. (Of course if only one seal is imperfect, it's easier to pop that jar in the refrigerator and eat the food within the next week).

The interim day before storing in a cool, dry, dark place is the only time that these foods can be salvaged by repacking in sterilized containers and processing over again from scratch.

If, after these foods are checked and put in the storage area, you find any of the following, DESTROY THE CONTENTS SO THAT THEY CANNOT BE EATEN BY PEOPLE OR ANIMALS; then deal with the containers as described in Chapter 3, "The Canning Methods."

- Broken seal.
- Seepage around the seal, even though it seems firmly seated.
- Mold, even a fleck, in the contents or around the seal or on the underside of the lid.
- Gassiness (small bubbles) in the contents.
- Spurting liquid, pressure from inside as the jar is opened.
- Mushy or slippery pickles.
- Cloudy or yeasty liquid.
- Off-odor, disagreeable smell, mustiness.

If this sounds strict, it's meant to. Our most shiver-producing bedside reading is not the latest Janwillem van der Wettering, but the cumulative statistics on outbreaks of botulism in the United States, published regularly by the Center for Disease Control of the U.S. Public Health Service. Surprisingly to a layman, condiments—including home-canned tomato relish, chili sauce and pickles—have been found to contain *C. botulinum* toxin. Maybe the product was not truly pickled, because the recipe was altered—perhaps by cutting down on the vinegar to reduce tartness (*which is wrong*), rather than by increasing the sweetener to achieve a result more bland. Or, as has been described in Chapter 6, "Canning Tomatoes," unclean handling or faulty processing allowed spoilage that reduced the acidity of the food, and thus in turn the botulinum spores could grow.

In addition to the sloppy treatment noted above, warm storage conditions contribute to such spoilage. As does the old "open-kettle" canning method now in disrepute.

Often, low-acid vegetables are spoiled by the scum that naturally forms on top of the fermentation brine; the scum should be removed faithfully. And it is not only the top layer of pickles that is affected, for the scum (which contains wild yeasts, molds and bacteria) can weaken the acidity of the brine.

Also, hard water that contains a great deal of calcium salts can counteract some of the acid, or keep acid from forming well enough during brining, and thus interfere with the process that is meant to make certain pickles safe with an otherwise adequate Boiling–Water Bath.

And of course "knife out" air bubbles before capping.

• WARNING ABOUT MEASUREMENTS: The critical ingredient is the vinegar in pickled products or tart relishes, and this is easy to measure. But proportions can be thrown off by how chunky ingredients are measured: for example, ¾-inch cubes of vegetables should be measured by the quart—not by 4 separate level cupfuls—and be rounded: this rounding compensates for the wasted space in the container. On the other hand, shredded cabbage is pressed down to the rim of the measuring cup (but not down to the 1-cup mark slightly below the rim).

NOT PERFECT, BUT EDIBLE

If jars have good seals, if there are none of the signs of spoilage noted above, and if the storage has been properly cool, you can have less-than-perfect pickles that arc still O.K. to eat.

Hollow pickles. The cucumbers just developed queerly on the vine; you can spot these odd ones when you wash them: usually they float. So use them chopped in relishes. Or they stood around more than 24 hours after being picked. If you can't get around to doing them the day you get them, refrigerate.

Shriveled pickles. This can come from plunging the cucumbers into a solution of salt, vinegar or sugar that's too strong for them to absorb gradually (here's the reason why some recipes handle pickles in stages). Or they've cooked too fast in a sugar-vinegar solution. Or the water used was too hard (see also "Water," in Chapter 17).

Darkened pickles. Iron in hard water, or loose ground spices.

Bleached-looking pickles. With no signs of spoilage present, this could mean that jars were exposed to light during storage. Wrap the jars in paper or put them in closed cartons if the place they're stored is not dark.

Relevant Metrics for Pickles, Relishes and Other Spicy Things

Full metric conversions, with the arithmetic for refining them, are given at the start of Chapter 17 ("Common Ingredients and How to Use Them"), but the following—rounded off—apply in this chapter.

If you live above the sea-level zone (i.e., *over* 1000 ft/305 m), consult the subsection "Correcting for Altitude" in Chapter 3 for help in figuring boiling points (viz. the variations for water at lowered atmospheric pressure).

• • •

Temperatures (@ sea level): *212 F/100 C——220 F/105 C——240 F/116 C——325 F/163 C.*

Volume: ⅛ *teaspoon = 0.62 mL——¼ teaspoon = 1.25 mL——½ teaspoon = 2.5 mL——1 teaspoon = 5.0 mL——1 tablespoon = 15 mL——¼ cup = 2 fl oz = 60 mL——⅓ cup = 2.7 fl oz = 80 mL——½ cup = 4 fl oz = 125 mL——1 cup = 8 fl oz = 250 mL——1 pint = 2 cups = 500 mL——1 qt = 1 L——1 gallon = 4 L——1 decaliter = 10 L.*

Length: ⅛ *in = 0.32 cm——¼ in = 0.64 cm——½ in = 1.27 cm——¾ in = 1.9 cm——1 in = 2.54 cm.*

Pickles and Relishes

Sweet Pickle Chips
Four to Five Pints

These are so delicious and so easy that you'll want to make several separate batches as the cucumbers come along.

4 pounds pickling cucumbers (3 to 4 inches long)

BRINING SOLUTION
1 quart distilled white vinegar
3 tablespoons salt
1 tablespoon mustard seed
½ cup sugar

CANNING SYRUP

1⅔ cups distilled white vinegar
3 cups sugar
1 tablespoon whole allspice
2¼ teaspoons celery seed

Wash the cucumbers, remove any blemishes, nip off the stems and blossom ends and cut them crossways in ¼-inch-thick slices. In a large enameled or stainless steel kettle, mix together the ingredients for the *brining solution;* add the cut cucumbers. Cover and simmer until the cucumbers change color from bright to dull green (about 5 to 7 minutes).

Meanwhile have ready the *canning syrup* ingredients heated to the boil in an enameled kettle. Drain the cucumber slices and pack them, while still piping hot, in hot 1-pint canning jars, and cover them with very hot syrup, leaving ½ inch of headroom. Remove air bubbles, and adjust lids. Pack and add the hot syrup to one jar at a time, returning the syrup kettle to low heat between filling and capping each jar, so the syrup doesn't cool. Process filled and capped jars in a Boiling–Water Bath (212 F/100 C) for 10 minutes. Remove jars and complete seals if necessary. Makes 4 to 5 pints.

Mustard Pickles

Twelve Pints

---

1 bunch of celery
2 rounded quarts green tomatoes cut in bite-size chunks
4 sweet red bell peppers
1 quart tiny white onions, not larger than ¾ inch diameter
3 cauliflowers, about 6 to 7 inches in diameter
4 large green cucumbers
1 cup pickling salt
4 quarts cold water

Refrigerate each prepared vegetable as it's completed, until all are ready for salting—an extra pair of hands will shorten the chore. And this is another pickle that benefits from being divided into half-batches for the final cooking (simultaneous boiling in two kettles for a short time), as being quicker and therefore more likely to retain crispness.

Wash, trim and cut each celery rib in ½-inch lengths. Slice stem and blossom ends from green tomatoes and cut in small bite-size pieces. Wash peppers, remove stems and seeds and cut in ¾-inch chunks. Peel and wash onions. Peel cucumbers, cut into quarters and remove seeds with a spoon and cut in ¾-inch squares. Wash cauliflowers, remove heavy center stems, break into small flowerettes and heat to boiling for 3 minutes in a small amount of water; drain and cover immediately with very cold water to stop the cooking.

(*Recipe continued on next page*)

Now, put all the prepared vegetables in a large enameled or stainless-steel kettle and mix the cup of pickling salt throughout the whole. Pour over the vegetables 4 quarts of cold water and let stand overnight. In the morning bring all to a boil, then quickly drain thoroughly, and put into one large 12-quart or two smaller 6-quart preserving kettles to hold while you make the mustard sauce.

MUSTARD SAUCE

1 cup flour
6 tablespoons dry mustard
7 cups sugar
1½ tablespoons turmeric dissolved in a bit of cold vinegar
1 quart of boiling-hot vinegar

Combine in the order given and mix very well, over the still-hot vegetables—dividing the sauce if you're using two kettles. Over medium heat, bring to a boil, and boil gently for 5 minutes, stirring well to prevent the flour from lumping. Ladle into hot pint jars, leaving ½ inch of headroom. Adjust lids, and process in a Boiling–Water Bath (212 F/100 C) for 15 minutes. Remove and complete seals if necessary. Makes 12 pints.

Bread-and-Butter Pickles
Seven Pints

This recipe is an especially good one, from Isabelle Downey's *Food Preservation in Alabama*.

6 pounds medium cucumbers
1½ cups sliced onions
2 large garlic cloves, left whole
⅓ cup salt
2 trays of ice cubes or crushed ice
4½ cups sugar
1½ teaspoons turmeric
1½ teaspoons celery seed
2 tablespoons mustard seed
3 cups white vinegar

Wash the cucumbers thoroughly; drain; cut unpeeled cucumbers into ¼-inch slices. In a large bowl, combine the cucumber slices, onions, garlic and salt; cover with the crushed ice or ice cubes, mix thoroughly and let stand for 3 hours. Drain off the liquid and remove the garlic. Combine the sugar, spices and vinegar and heat just to a boil. Add the cucumber and onion slices; simmer together 10 minutes. Pack loosely in clean, hot pint jars, leaving ½ inch of headroom; remove air bubbles. Adjust lids; process in a Boiling–Water Bath (212 F/100 C) for 10 minutes. Remove, complete seals if necessary.

Sally Stott's ("Short-form") Bread-and-Butter Pickles
Twelve Pints

---

  6 quarts of thinly sliced pickling cucumbers (about 15 6-inch)
  6 medium onions, thinly sliced
  ½ cup pickling salt
 1½ quarts white vinegar
 4½ cups sugar
  ½ cup whole mustard seed
  1 tablespoon celery seed

Wash cucumbers, remove stem and blossom ends, slice thin on the broad blade of a food grater, or on the thin-slicing disc of a food processor. Peel onions, slice thin. Put sliced vegetables in an enameled, crockery or stainless-steel bowl, combine them with the ½ cup of pickling salt; let stand 3 hours, then drain well but do not rinse. Meanwhile combine the vinegar, sugar, mustard and celery seed in a large stainless-steel or enameled kettle and bring to a boil. When boiling, add the cucumber and onion slices; over medium heat, bring up to a low boil, and pack immediately in clean, hot 1-pint jars, leaving a good ½ inch of headroom. Adjust clean, hot lids, and process in a Boiling–Water Bath for 10 minutes. Remove; complete seals if necessary. Makes 12 pints.

Good because they're simple. The slicing disc of a food processor is grand help here. Allow several weeks for the flavor to develop.

Sweet Pumpkin Pickle
Three Pints

---

  6 cups prepared pumpkin
  2 cups vinegar
  2 cups sugar
  2 large sticks whole cinnamon

Prepare pumpkin by peeling and cubing flesh, discarding seeds and inner pulp. Place pumpkin cubes in a colander and set over boiling water: make sure water does *not* touch the pumpkin. Cover and steam until just tender. Drain. Simmer vinegar, sugar and cinnamon for 15 minutes. Add pumpkin cubes and simmer 3 minutes. Set aside for 24 hours. Heat and simmer 5 minutes more. Remove cinnamon. Pack boiling hot in hot canning jars leaving ½ inch of headroom, adjust lids and process in a Boiling–Water Bath (212 F/100 C) for 10 minutes. This pickle compares favorably with that made of cantaloupe.

Little Cucumber Crock Pickles

This is an old-time rule, producing small, crisp, whole pickles with good flavor. They take 4 to 5 weeks to make; and if they're put in brine as they come along in season, and kept in a cool place, they should last well into winter.

(*Recipe continued on next page*)

1 gallon cider vinegar (regular 5 percent)
½ cup sugar (or 1 teaspoon powdered straight saccharin)
1 cup whole mustard seed
1 cup pickling salt (pure, no fillers) + salt to add later
  optional: 4 fresh dill heads; or more, if you like stronger dill
  3- 4-inch pickling cucumbers (about 10 pounds total, or a scant peck)

Thoroughly scrub a 5-gallon earthenware crock with hot water and soap, rinse well, then scald with boiling water; be energetic about it, because any residue of fat or milk from a previous use will ruin the pickles. In the crock mix together the vinegar, sweetening, mustard seed and salt; lay dill heads on the bottom if you like them. Keep the crock in a constantly cool place (40 to maximum 50 F/4 to maximum 10 C).

As they're gathered, wash the little cucumbers well, rub off the blossom ends (where enzymes are concentrated), and drop the cucumbers into the brine. Push newly harvested ones toward the bottom of the container as it fills, so the last ones in will not be the first ones out. Hold the pickles beneath the brine with a weighted plate (a pint jar filled with water weighs enough), and cover the crock with a layer of clean cheesecloth or muslin.

If you put all the cucumbers in at the same time, after three days add 1 cup more pickling salt, laid on the plate where it will dissolve slowly downward (the extra salt counteracts weakening of the brine as the natural juice is drawn from the cucumbers). One week later, put ¼ cup more salt on the submerged plate; and continue adding ¼ cup salt in this manner each week until the pickles are ready. At the end of a month, test by cutting a pickle crossways: if it is firm, and clear throughout with no white center, the pickles are ready to eat.

If you harvest your cucumbers piecemeal over a period of, say, two weeks, lay ½ cup pickling salt on the plate when the crock is half full, and add another ½ cup salt when the crock is filled; thereafter add ¼ cup salt each week until the pickles are ready.

A gray-white film will appear on the surface of the brine after the cucumbers have been in the pickling solution a few days: skim it off, and keep removing it as it forms. The film is to be expected as a natural part of the brining process, but if allowed to stay on the pickles it will hurt the acidity of the pickling solution, and your pickles will spoil.

When there's no more film, and your pickles test evenly clear to the center, start enjoying them. Always replace the weighted plate after taking any out, and cover the crock to keep the contents clean.

CANNING

If the conditions for storing your crock of pickles are not good, or if you foresee that you can't eat them all within their storage life of several months—can them.

Take all the pickles from the brine, and fit them vertically in clean pint or quart jars, leaving ½ inch of headroom. From the pickling solution remove any dill heads (and the mustard seed, if you like); bring the solution to boiling and pour it over the pickles, leaving ½ inch of headroom. Remove trapped air with the blade of a table knife, adjust lids with their clean fresh rubbers or sealers, and process in a Boiling–Water Bath—10 minutes for pints, 15 minutes for quarts. Remove jars; complete seals if necessary.

Quick Dill Pickles

Seven Pints

30 to 40 medium pickling-type cucumbers, 5 inches long
¾ cup sugar
¾ cup pickling salt
1 quart vinegar
1 quart water
7 fresh dill heads
   (optional: 7 garlic cloves)
   (optional: 3 tablespoons mixed whole pickling spices)

Mix together the sugar, salt, vinegar and water and bring to a boil. Tie optional pickling spices loosely in a thin white cloth and boil in the vinegar mixture for about 10 minutes; remove and discard. Scrub cucumbers, remove stems and blossom ends; cut lengthwise in halves or quarters, not longer than the shoulder-height of the jar. Put 1 whole head of fresh dill in each clean hot jar. Pack the jars with cut cucumbers upright, then tuck in a clove of garlic if you like it. Pour in the boiling vinegar mixture, leaving ½ inch of headroom. Adjust lids. Process in a Boiling–Water Bath (212 F/100 C) for 10 minutes. Remove jars; complete seals if necessary. Yield: about 7 pints.

Small-batch Freezer Pickles

Three Pints

2 rounded quarts of thinly sliced pickling cucumbers, *not* peeled
2 large yellow onions, peeled and thinly sliced
2 tablespoons pickling salt
1 cup white vinegar
1½ cups white sugar

Scrub cucumbers, remove stem and blossom ends, slice thin on the broad blade of a vegetable grater, or with the slicing disc of a food processor. Peel onions, slice like the cucumbers. Put cucumbers and onions in a large crockery bowl, sprinkle with the salt, let stand for 2 to 3 hours. Meanwhile combine vinegar and sugar, bring to a boil. Drain the vegetables but do *not* rinse, and pack into 1-pint freezer containers (either plastic or straight-sided can/freeze jars), leaving ¾ inch of headroom. Pour in the hot syrup, leaving ½ inch of headroom. Seal, cool, freeze. Yields about 3 pints.
Use within one week after thawing.

(Recipe continued on next page)

Note that pickling spices are not used here, because freezing reduces the flavor of spices.

These pickles are a fine way to use up cucumbers that aren't enough for a batch of canned pickles—provided you have a special spot in your freezer for oddments.

Watermelon Pickles
Four Pints

8 cups prepared watermelon rind
½ cup pickling salt
4 cups cold water
4 teaspoons whole cloves
4 cups sugar
2 cups white vinegar
2 cups water

Choose thick rind. Trim from it all dark skin and remains of pink flesh; cut in 1-inch cubes. Dissolve salt in cold water, pour it over rind cubes to cover (add more water if needed); let stand 5 to 6 hours. Drain, rinse well. Cover with fresh water and cook until barely tender—no more than 10 minutes (err on the side of crispness); drain. Combine sugar, vinegar and water, add cloves tied in a cloth bag, and bring to boiling; reduce heat and simmer for 5 minutes. Pour over rind cubes, let stand overnight. Bring all to boiling and cook until rind is translucent *but not at all mushy*—about 10 minutes. Remove spice bag, pack cubes in hot sterilized pint jars; add boiling syrup, leaving ½ inch of headroom; adjust lids. Process in a Boiling–Water Bath for 10 minutes. Remove jars and complete seals if necessary. Makes about 4 pints.

Gertrude Russell's Ripe Cucumber Pickles
About Eleven Pint Jars

about 15 large ripe (yellow) cucumbers
salt for mild soaking brine
3 cups vinegar (local or native)
1 cup water
2 cups white sugar
5 cups brown sugar
2 tablespoons mixed pickling spice
½ teaspoon cinnamon
½ teaspoon cloves

Peel, quarter lengthwise, scrape out seeds. Soak overnight in salted water (to taste, not heavily salted) in a 12-quart crockery or stainless-steel bowl. Cut in

1½-inch pieces, drain in a colander; do not rinse. Mix syrup and spices, leaving spices loose (you may want to remove some of the red chili pieces). Add cucumbers, and over medium heat cook them until they are transparent, but not mushy. Pack boiling hot into hot pint jars, leave ½ inch of headroom, adjust lids, and process in a Boiling–Water Bath for 15 minutes. Remove; complete seals if necessary. Makes 10 to 12 pints.

Dot Robbins's Christmas Pickle
Seven Pints

---

   8 or 9 large *ripe* cucumbers
   7 cups white sugar
   2 cups white vinegar
  ½ teaspoon oil of cloves
  ½ teaspoon oil of cinnamon
   3 10-ounce jars of maraschino cherries

First day: Peel cucumbers, remove seeds, cut in 1-inch pieces and put them in a large enameled or stainless-steel kettle. Add water to cover and boil gently until barely tender (about 10 minutes). Remove, drain well, and put in a large glass or crockery bowl. Combine sugar, vinegar and oils of clove and cinnamon in the empty kettle, bring to a boil, and then pour over the cucumber pieces in the bowl. Cover and let stand overnight at room temperature.

Second day: Drain off syrup and bring it to a boil. Pour over the cucumbers and again let stand overnight.

Third day: Put cucumber pieces, with syrup, in the kettle, bring all to a boil, and add three jars marashino cherries and their juice. Return to heat, and when it is boiling again ladle into hot pint jars, leaving ½ inch of headroom. Adjust lids and process in a Boiling–Water Bath (212 F/100 C) for 10 minutes after the canner has returned to a full boil. Remove and complete seals if necessary.

    The spice essences are usually carried in natural-food stores.

Zucchini Pickle
Four Pints

---

   2 quarts thin slices of unpeeled, *small* zucchini squash
   2 medium onions, peeled and thinly sliced
  ¼ cup salt
   2 cups vinegar
   2 cups sugar
   1 teaspoon celery seed
   2 teaspoons mustard seed
   1 teaspoon turmeric
  ½ teaspoon dry mustard

(Recipe continued on next page)

Combine zucchini and onions. Sprinkle with the salt, cover with cold water and let stand 2 hours. Drain; rinse with fresh water, and drain again. Combine remaining ingredients in an enamelware kettle and bring to boiling. Cook 2 minutes. Add zucchini and onions, remove from heat, and let stand 2 hours. Bring again to boiling and cook 5 minutes. Ladle hot into hot pint jars, leaving ½ inch of headroom, and process in a Boiling–Water Bath (212 F/100 C) for 10 minutes. Makes about 4 pints.

Sweet Mustard Pickle

Four Quarts

---

    1 quart small green tomatoes, quartered
    1 quart *small* unpeeled cucumbers (about 2 inches)
    1 quart unpeeled *medium* cucumbers
    1 quart tiny pickling onions
    1 small head cauliflower, broken into flowerets
    3 green peppers, seeded and diced
    2 cups green beans, cut in 1-inch slices
    1 cup salt
    1 cup flour
    ⅓ cup dry mustard
    2 teaspoons turmeric
    2 cups sugar
    2 quarts vinegar

Combine vegetables and sprinkle with salt. Cover with cold water and let stand overnight. Place over moderate heat and bring just to boiling point, then drain thoroughly. Combine remaining ingredients smoothly. Stir over moderate heat until smooth and thick. Add well-drained vegetables and bring *just to boiling point*: they should never be overcooked and mushy. Ladle hot into hot canning jars, allow ½ inch of headroom, and process in a Boiling–Water Bath (212 F/100 C) for 10 minutes for pints or quarts. Makes about 4 quarts.

Dill Cucumber Pickles (Short-brine)

Seven Quarts

---

    17 to 18 pounds of pickling cucumbers (3 to 5 inches)
    2 gallons of 5 percent brine (¾ cup pickling salt to each 1 gallon of
        water)
    6 cups vinegar
    ¾ cup salt
    ¼ cup sugar
    9 cups water

(*Recipe continued on next page*)

  2 tablespoons whole mixed pickling spices
 14 teaspoons whole mustard seed (2 teaspoons go in each quart jar)
  7 to 14 cloves garlic (1 to 2 cloves go in each quart jar)
 21 dill heads (3 heads go in each quart jar)
    OR
  7 tablespoons dill seed (1 tablespoon to each quart jar)

Put washed and brush-scrubbed cucumbers in a noncorroding crock or kettle and cover with the 5 percent brine. Let stand overnight, then drain and pack cucumbers in clean, hot quart jars. Add the mustard seed, dill and garlic to each jar.

Combine vinegar, salt, sugar and water; tie pickling spices loosely in a clean, thin, white cloth and drop it into the mixture. Bring to a boil. Take out the spice bag and pour boiling liquid over cucumbers in jars, leaving ½ inch of headroom. Adjust the lids and process in a Boiling–Water Bath (212 F/100 C) for 20 minutes. Makes about 7 quarts.

"Dilly" Green Beans
Seven Pint Jars

---

  4 pounds table-perfect whole green beans
 1¾ teaspoons crushed dried *hot* red pepper
 3½ teaspoons dried dill seed, *or* 7 fresh dill heads
  7 cloves of fresh garlic, peeled
  5 cups vinegar
  5 cups water
  ½ cup less 1 tablespoon pickling (non-iodized) salt

Wash beans thoroughly, remove stems and tips, and cut them as much as possible in uniform lengths to allow them to stand upright in 1-pint canning jars, coming to the shoulder of the jar. Have jars clean and very hot, and lids and sealers ready in scalding water. In each jar place 1 dill head *or* ½ teaspoon dill seed, add 1 garlic clove and ¼ teaspoon crushed hot red pepper. Pack beans upright in jars, leaving 1 inch of headroom. Heat together the water, vinegar and salt; when the mixture boils, pour it over the beans, filling each jar to ½ inch from the top. Run a table knife down and around to remove trapped air, adjust lids, and process in a Boiling–Water Bath (212 F/100 C) for 10 minutes after the water in the canner returns to boiling. Remove jars, complete seals if necessary. Makes 7 pints.

The beans are almost garden-crisp, but the high acidity of the vinegar allows this B–W Bath processing to be safe for a low-acid food.

If you substitute ground cayenne pepper for the crushed hot red pepper, *halve the amount of cayenne:* use only ⅛ teaspoon cayenne to each jar.

Wait at least two weeks for these beans to develop their flavor.

Green Tomato Pickles
Six Pints

  7½ pounds green tomatoes (about 30 medium)
   6 good-sized onions
  ¾ cup pickling salt
   1 tablespoon celery seed
   1 tablespoon whole allspice
   1 tablespoon mustard seed
   1 tablesoon whole cloves
   1 tablespoon dry mustard
   1 tablespoon peppercorns
  ½ lemon
   2 sweet red peppers
  2½ cups brown sugar
   3 cups vinegar (*c.* 5 percent acidity)

Wash tomatoes well, cut off blossom ends, blemishes and stems. Slice thin crossways. Peel and slice onions in thin rings. Sprinkle salt over alternate layers of sliced tomatoes and onions in an earthenware dish, and let stand in a cool place overnight. Drain off the brine, rinse the vegetables thoroughly in cold water and drain well. Slice the lemon thinly and remove the seeds; wash the peppers well, remove stems and seeds, slice thinly crossways. Tie all the spices loosely in muslin or a double layer of cheesecloth, add the spice bag and the sugar to the vinegar in a large enamelware kettle; bring to a boil. Add the tomatoes, onions, lemon and peppers. Cook for 30 minutes after the mixture returns to a boil, stirring gently to prevent scorching. Remove the spice bag, pack the pickles in hot jars and cover with boiling–hot liquid, leaving ½ inch of headroom. Adjust lids. Process in a Boiling–Water Bath (212 F/100 C) for 10 minutes. Remove jars; complete seals if necessary. Makes about 6 pints.

RELISHES AND SAUCES

Piccalilli
Four Pints

---

   6 medium-size green tomatoes
   6 sweet red peppers, seeded
   6 medium onions, peeled
   1 small cabbage
  ¼ cup salt
   2 cups vinegar
  2½ cups light brown sugar (or raw)
   2 tablespoons mixed pickling spices

(Recipe continued on next page)

Put vegetables through the food grinder, using a coarse knife. Sprinkle with the salt, cover and let stand overnight. Drain; then cover with fresh water, and drain again. When thoroughly drained, put into a large kettle and add vinegar and sugar. Tie spices in a small cloth bag and add. Bring to boiling, then reduce heat and simmer about 20 minutes, stirring frequently. Remove the spice bag and turn the hot piccalilli into hot jars, leaving ½ inch of headroom; adjust lids and process in a Boiling–Water Bath for 10 minutes. Makes about 4 pints.

Beet Relish
About Five Pints

Unusual, because it's made from raw, not precooked, beets. And it's a handy way to use large beets that are on the woody side. A food processor makes quick work of what would otherwise be a fairly splashy preparation.

4 cups coarsely ground fresh beets—about 2 pounds before peeled
6 cups coarsely ground green cabbage—3-pound head before coring
2 cups coarsely ground onions—about 1 pound
2 cups cider vinegar
2 cups sugar
2 teaspoons salt
2 tablespoons freshly grated horseradish (or bottled)

Peel and cut beets lengthwise in eighths or finer, feed them upright onto the grating disc of a food processor. Empty processor bowl, grate slender wedges of cabbage; grate quartered onions. Combine vegetables in an enameled or stainless-steel kettle, add vinegar, sugar, salt and horseradish. Bring to a boil over medium heat, cook and stir until thick—about 25 minutes. Remove from heat, ladle into clean hot 1-pint jars, leaving ½ inch of headroom. Adjust lids and process in a Boiling–Water Bath for 20 minutes. Remove, complete seals if necessary. Makes 4 to 5 pints.

Green Tomato Relish
Eight Pints

3 pounds green tomatoes (about 12)
1½ pounds onions
4 sweet red bell peppers
3 pounds ripe tomatoes (about 10)
½ cup pickling salt
2 medium bunches of celery, each rib cut in ⅛-inch slices
1 quart vinegar
3 pounds light brown sugar
½ teaspoon ground cloves
½ teaspoon ground cinnamon
½ cup mustard seeds

(Recipe continued on next page)

Wash green tomatoes, remove stems and blossom ends; peel onions; wash peppers, remove stems and seeds—and put all three through the coarse blade of a food-chopper. Scald and peel the ripe tomatoes, cut in chunks and add to the chopped vegetables. Put the vegetables in a large enameled bowl, stir in the salt, and let stand overnight. Next morning drain very well and put the mixture into a large enameled or stainless-steel kettle and add the thinly sliced celery, brown sugar, vinegar and spices. Bring to a boil and cook on medium heat for 1 hour, stirring now and then to prevent sticking. Fill clean, hot pint jars, leaving ½ inch of headroom. Adjust lids, and process in a Boiling–Water Bath (212 F/100 C) for 10 minutes. Remove, complete seals if necessary. 8 pints.

Margaret Hawes's Zucchini Relish

Five to Six Pints

---

     10 cups finely chopped zucchini (if small, leave in the seeds; if over 8
          inches, remove seeds)
      4 large onions
      4 green bell peppers, seeded
      4 red bell peppers, seeded
      ½ cup salt
     2½ cups white vinegar
      4 cups white sugar
      2 tablespoons cornstarch
      1 teaspoon ground nutmeg
      1 teaspoon turmeric
      2 teaspoons celery seed
      ½ teaspoon ground black pepper

Wash, peel zucchini, removing stems and blossom ends; remove seeds if squash is cut in large chunks for grinding. Peel and quarter onions; seed and quarter the bell peppers. Put vegetables through the food grinder, using a coarse knife. (With a food processor, use the shredding disc: the steel blade can make these ingredients lose too much texture.) Put ground vegetables in a crockery or stainless-steel bowl, stir in the salt; keep the vegetables in the resulting brine by holding them down with a weighted plate. Let vegetables stand overnight. The next day, drain off the brine and rinse vegetables with cold water; drain again, and squeeze well by hand. Mix cornstarch with the sugar and four other dry seasonings, add all to the cold vinegar, blending well. Over medium heat, bring to boiling, stirring well to prevent lumping. When sugar is melted and the syrup is clear, add the vegetables; simmer 30 minutes, stirring often. Pour into clean very hot jars, leaving ½ inch of headroom; adjust sterilized lids, and process in a Boiling–Water Bath for 10 minutes after the water has returned to a full boil. Remove, complete seals if necessary.

Corn Relish
Three Pints

---

   4 cups corn kernels (about 9 ears' worth)*
   1 cup diced sweet green peppers
   1 cup diced sweet red peppers
   1 cup finely chopped celery
   ½ cup minced onion
1½ cups vinegar
   ¾ cup sugar
   2 teaspoons salt
1½ teaspoons dry mustard
   1 teaspoon celery seed
   ¼ teaspoon Tabasco sauce
   ½ teaspoon turmeric, for color (optional)
   2 tablespoons flour, for thickening (optional)

Prepare corn by boiling husked ears for 5 minutes, cooling, and cutting from cob (do not scrape). In an enameled kettle combine peppers, celery, onion, vinegar, sugar, salt, celery seed and Tabasco sauce; boil 5 minutes, stirring occasionally. Dip out ½ cup hot liquid, mix it with dry mustard and turmeric, and return it to the kettle. Add the corn. (If you want the relish slightly thickened, blend the 2 tablespoons flour with ¼ cup cold water and add to the kettle when you put in the corn.) Boil for 5 minutes, stirring extra well if the relish has been thickened, so it won't stick or scorch. Immediately fill clean hot pint jars within ½ inch of the top, adjust lids, and process in a Boiling–Water Bath for 15 minutes. Complete seal if necessary; cool and store. Makes 3 pints.

* You can use frozen whole-kernel corn that's been thawed slowly: 3 10-ounce packages will equal 4 cups of fresh kernels.

Pickled Pears
Four Pints

---

4 to 5 pounds underripe pears*
3 cups granulated sugar
1 cup water
2 cups white vinegar
2 teaspoons chopped fresh ginger root (1 teaspoon dried)
2 sticks cinnamon
1 teaspoon whole allspice
1 teaspoon whole cloves

* Bartletts are good. So are large Kieffers that have been picked before field maturity and held for a couple of weeks in a dry place at 60 to 65 F/16 to 18 C to develop flavor and texture.

(*Recipe continued on next page*)

Make an anti-discoloration solution of 2 tablespoons vinegar in 2 quarts of water. Pare and core, halve or quarter, pears, dropping the pieces in the holding solution as you work. Combine sugar, 2 cups white vinegar and the water in a large enameled or stainless-steel kettle. Tie the four spices in muslin and add; boil 10 minutes. Reduce heat, spoon the pears one layer deep in the kettle, and simmer for 5 minutes or until just tender. Hold pears in the kettle, covered, in a cool place overnight to allow them to absorb syrup. Next morning, carefully lift pears out of syrup and pack in clean hot 1-pint jars. Bring the syrup to a boil, pour over pears, leaving ½ inch of headroom; add a little boiling water if needed. Adjust lids, process in a Boiling–Water Bath for 15 minutes. Remove; complete seals if necessary. Makes 4 pints.

Spiced Pears, see under Canning.

Indian Chutney
Three Pints

The rule for this fine Calcutta-style chutney was given us by Frances Bond, who lived twenty years in India before moving to Vermont, and she has tailored it for ingredients easy for the North American housewife to come by. It's ideal with budget-stretching curries or pilau, with hot or cold meats, and it makes a delightful present packed in decorative ½-pint canning jars.

For best results, the fruit—whether apples, peaches or pears—should be firm varieties, or slightly underripe. The fruit, raisins and crystallized ginger are added after the syrup ingredients have cooked together for 30 minutes, to let them keep their identity in the finished product: they should be tender but recognizable in the syrup, which is thick and a rich brown in color. The chutney improves after a couple of months in sealed jars.

       juice, pulp and peel of 1 lemon, finely chopped
    2 cups cider vinegar
   2½ cups dark brown sugar (1 pound)
    1 clove garlic, minced
       pinch of cayenne pepper (⅛ teaspoon)
       pinch of chili powder (⅛ teaspoon)
   1½ teaspoons salt
   5½ cups coarsely chopped firm apples, peeled and cored (about 3
          pounds), or peaches or pears*
    ¾ cup crystallized ginger**—cut small but not minced (about 3
          ounces)
   1½ cups raisins, preferably seeded (½ pound)

* Caught without fresh fruit in a chutney-making mood, Mrs. Bond substituted 5½ cups of coarsely chopped canned, drained pears, but adding them in the last 10 minutes of cooking. Results: heavenly.
** Ground ginger contributes only flavor without texture, and reconstituted dry cracked ginger is usually woody, so don't substitute with either of them. Minced, peeled fresh ginger root is a logical substitute, but ¼ cup, prepared this way, should do.

Chop the lemon, removing seeds and saving the juice (a blender is good here), and put it in an open, heavy enameled kettle with the sugar, vinegar, minced garlic, salt, cayenne pepper and chili powder. Boil the mixture over medium heat for 30 minutes, stirring occasionally. Meanwhile prepare the apples (or peaches or pears), and add them to the syrup with the raisins and ginger. Boil all slowly, stirring to prevent sticking and scorching, until the fruit is tender but not mushy and the syrup is thick—about 30 to 45 minutes longer. Ladle the boiling-hot chutney into sterilized pint or ½-pint jars, filling to ⅛ inch of the top, and cap each jar immediately with a sterilized 2-piece screw band lid. Cool topside up and store. Makes 3 pints, or 6 ½-pints.

Tomato Ketchup

Six Pints

Because of the extra acidity from the vinegar, this good ketchup can be processed safely in a 10-minute B–W Bath. Some cooks add the sugar later with the vinegar to reduce the chance of scorching, but we think that adding the sugar earlier—with the spices—enables the flavors of the spices to develop in a pleasant way.

1 peck ripe tomatoes (8 quarts, or *c.* 50 medium tomatoes)
2 cups finely chopped onions (*c.* 3 large)
1 cup chopped sweet red peppers (*c.* 2 large)
1 clove garlic, finely chopped
1 tablespoon salt
1 tablespoon celery seed
1 tablespoon whole allspice
1 tablespoon whole cloves
1 tablespoon peppercorns
2 teaspoons mustard seed
1 bay leaf
¾ cup brown sugar
2 cups cider vinegar

Wash the tomatoes, but don't bother to peel; cut them small, saving all the juice. In a heavy kettle combine the tomatoes, onions, peppers, garlic and salt, and simmer the mixture until soft—about 25 minutes. Press through a sieve or food mill to remove seeds and skins. Tie the spices and bay leaf in muslin or double-thick cheesecloth and add the bag and the brown sugar to the mixture. Cook quickly at medium boil, stirring frequently, until the mixture is reduced to ½ its original volume—about 1 hour. Remove the spice bag. Add the vinegar; simmer 10 to 15 minutes longer, stirring often, until the mixture thickens again. Pour while boiling into hot ½ pint or pint jars, leaving ½ inch of headroom. Run the blade of a table knife around the inner side of the jar to release any trapped air; adjust lids. Process ½ pints and pints in a Boiling–Water Bath (212 F/100 C) for 10 minutes. Remove, complete seals if necessary. Makes 6 pints.

Chili Sauce
Five to Six Pints

Because of extra acid from the vinegar, this can be finished safely in a B–W Bath.

  4 quarts chopped ripe tomatoes (about 9 to 10 pounds)
  5 large onions, peeled and chopped small
  4 sweet red peppers, seeded and chopped
  2 cups cider vinegar
  1 cup brown sugar, packed firmly
  2½ tablespoons salt
  1 stick of cinnamon 3 inches long, broken in pieces
  1 tablespoon mustard seed
  2 teaspoons celery seed
  1½ teaspoons ground ginger
  1 teaspoon ground nutmeg
  1 teaspoon peppercorns*

Peel, core and chop tomatoes; peel and chop onions; seed and chop peppers. Put them in a heavy enameled kettle, add the vinegar, sugar, salt; tie the spices in a double thickness of muslin or four thicknesses of cheesecloth (extra density of cloth will hold the ground spices better) and add the bag to the ingredients in the pot. Bring the mixture quickly to boiling, stirring so it won't scorch, then reduce the heat and cook at a slow boil until the sauce is thick—from 3 to 4 hours. It wants to be a little thicker than ketchup but not so thick as jam; and it will scorch if it's not watched and stirred, especially toward the end. Remove the spice bag and pack hot in hot canning jars, leaving ½ inch of headroom. Adjust lids and process in a Boiling–Water Bath (212 F/100 C) for 15 minutes. Remove, complete seals if necessary. Makes about 5 to 6 pints.

* For "hotter" sauce, substitute 1 teaspoon crushed dried *hot* red pepper pods. This is one of those recipes whose seasonings can be tinkered with according to the family's taste.

MINCEMEAT

Mincemeat
Five Pints

  1 pound boiled lean beef
  ½ pound beef suet
  2½ cups seeded raisins
  ¼ pound chopped citron

(*Recipe continued on next page*)

3 cups coarsely chopped apples
2 cups dried currants
2¼ cups light brown sugar
3 tablespoons light molasses
2 cups sweet cider
¾ teaspoon ground cinnamon
¾ teaspoon ground mace
¾ teaspoon ground cloves
¼ teaspoon ground nutmeg
¼ teaspoon ground allspice
¼ teaspoon salt
1 cup brandy

Put beef, suet and raisins through the food grinder, using a coarse knife. Put citron and apples through the grinder. Combine all in a heavy kettle and add remaining ingredients in order, *except the brandy*. Bring to boiling, stirring constantly. Reduce heat and simmer about 1 hour, stirring frequently. *The mixture will scorch easily, so use a heatproof pad under the kettle.* Remove from heat and stir in brandy. Ladle hot into hot pint canning jars, allowing ½ inch headroom, and process at 10 pounds pressure (240 F/116 C) for 20 minutes. Makes 5 pints, enough for 5 nine-inch pies.

Green Tomato Mincemeat
Eight Pints

3 quarts prepared green tomatoes
3 quarts prepared apples
1 cup ground suet
1 pound seedless raisins
2 tablespoons grated orange rind
2 tablespoons grated lemon rind
5 cups well-packed light brown sugar
¾ cup vinegar
½ cup fresh lemon juice
½ cup water
1 tablespoon ground cinnamon
¼ teaspoon ground cloves
¼ teaspoon ground allspice
2 teaspoons salt

Wash the tomatoes, remove stem and blossom ends, and chop fine with a chef's knife or with the coarse blade of a food grinder; wash, peel and core the apples, chop like the tomatoes. (For a food processor, cut tomatoes and apples in fairly small chunks to drop through the feed tube, and use the shredding disc.) Put suet through a finer blade of the food grinder or mince it by hand

(*Recipe continued on next page*)

somewhat smaller than the tomatoes. Combine tomatoes, apples and suet with all the other ingredients in a large enameled or stainless-steel kettle over medium heat and bring just to a boil, stirring frequently. Turn down heat and simmer until dark and thick, stirring occasionally—about 2½ hours. A heat-reducing pad under the kettle will help prevent scorching.

Toward the end of the cooking time, wash and scald at least eight 1-pint canning jars, and prepare their lids; hold in scalding water. Quickly ladle boiling-hot mincemeat into jars, leaving a good ½ inch of headroom, and cap; process in a finishing B–W Bath (212 F/100 C) for 25 minutes. Remove jars from the canner and complete seals if necessary. Makes 8 pints, enough for eight 9-inch pies.

Like the Fruit Butters described earlier in the section on jams, this mincemeat can be cooked in a 325 F/163 C oven as insurance agaoinst scorching. But do stir it.

Vegetarian note: Instead of the suet, cut in small pieces 1 tablespoon of butter or margarine for each 1 pint of mincemeat, and press the pieces into the filling when you build your pies.

This mincemeat is excellent used for small holiday tarts: fold inside Filo Pastry (for folding, see Chapter 16, "Freezing Convenience Foods").

20

CURING: SALT & SMOKE

Curing always calls for salting, and only sometimes involves smoking, even though for many people "cured" evokes bacon sizzling in a black iron skillet or kosher sausages grilling over the coals of an outdoor barbecue.

Salting may be mild, done with a light hand to induce fermentation—in which case the food tastes bright and tart rather than salty, and it must be given further treatment to be held very long in storage.

Or salting may be done in concentrations so heavy that it is the major part of preserving certain high-protein foods. An example is *bacalao,* the slabs of salt cod so hard they're like billets of firewood; they can be found lying uncovered in their wooden packing crates in old-time markets.

In the preceding chapter we dealt with one type of salting: brining cucumbers to "pickle" them by fermentation. Here we'll start the first—and longer—of our two main sections with "Salting," breaking it down into treating vegetables and then meats. The other major section, "Smoking," will give the *Why/How* of smoking meats, and, as an example of the treatment for fish, coho salmon from the Great Lakes.

Relevant Metrics for Curing

Full metric conversions, with the arithmetic for refining them, are given at the start of Chapter 17 ("Common Ingredients and How to Use Them"), but the following—rounded off—apply in this chapter.

If you live above the sea-level zone (i.e., *over* 1000 ft/305 m), consult the subsection "Correcting for Altitude" in Chapter 3.

• • •

Temperatures (@ sea level): Zero F/−18 C——32 F/Zero C——38 F/3.3 C——50 F/10 C——70 F/21 C——90 F/32 C——100 F/38 C——120 F/49 C——180 F/82 C.

Volume: ¼ teaspoon = 1.25 mL——½ teaspoon = 2.5 mL——1 teaspoon = 5.0 mL——1 tablespoon = 15 mL——¼ cup = 60 mL——½ cup = 125

mL——1 cup = 250 mL——1 pint = 500 mL——1 quart = 1 L——1 gallon = 4 L——5 gallons = c. 19 L——10 gallons = c. 38 L.

Weight: 1 oz = 28 g——2 oz = 57 g——4 oz = 113 g——10 oz = 284
g——1 pound = 0.454 kg——25 pounds = 11.34 kg——30 pounds =
13.61 kg——100 pounds = 45.4 kg.

Length: ⅛ inch = 0.32 cm——¼ inch = 0.64 cm——½ inch = 1.27 cm
——1 inch = 2.54 cm——2 inches = 5.1 cm——4 inches = 10.1 cm.

SALTING

We don't discuss curing two sorts of food: (1) the kind that cannot stand up
to the taste of salt—fruit is obvious in this case; and (2) extremely perishable
high-protein foods whose flavor, even though enhanced by a little salt, would
be ruined by the process of heavy salting—organ meats are an example. (So is
fish roe; but what, then, about caviar? Best leave this to the experts . . .)

Still, there are many cured foods that must have most of their salt washed
out before they can be cooked and eaten. Or they were salted so lightly that
they must be refrigerated; or, if they really are to be put by, they must be
canned or frozen. In Chapter 21, "Drying," there are instructions for meat
(Jerky) and for cod.

WHAT SALTING DOES

A concentrated brine—which is salt + juice drawn from the food by the salt
(called "dry-salting"), or salt + water if juice is limited or not easily extracted
(called "brining")—cuts down the activity of spoilage micro-organisms in direct relation to the strength of the solution. The following general proportions
give the idea, with percentages reflecting ratios by weight of salt to water, not
sophisticated salinometer readings. (For more about salt, see Chapter 17.)

- **NOTE:** The salt used in the instructions is granulated, food-grade, regular pickling and canning salt—don't use gourmet sea-salt and never use
"solar" salt evaporated in open basins and unrefined, and never salt with
iodine or "free-flowing" additives.

A 5 percent solution (1 pound, or about 1½ cups, of salt to 19 pints of
juice/water) *reduces* the growth of most bacteria.

A 10 percent solution (1 pound, or about 1½ cups, of salt to 9 pints of
juice/water) *prevents* the growth of *most bacteria.*

A solution from 15 percent (1 pound, or about 1½ cups, of salt to 5½ pints of juice/water) to 20 percent (1 pound, or about 1½ cups, of salt to 4 pints of juice/water) *prevents* the growth of *salt-tolerant bacteria.*

The amounts of salt given in the individual instructions are designed to give the necessary protection to the food being cured, provided that any further safeguards are followed as well. Sometimes a brine is added to make sure that enough liquid is present to carry out the curing process, because you can't add plain water without diluting the strength of the salt required to treat the particular food satisfactorily.

Because salt draws moisture from plant and animal tissues in proportion to its concentration, heavy salting is often a preliminary step in drying or smoking high-protein foods.

EQUIPMENT FOR CURING WITH SALT

Especially for vegetables:

Large stoneware crocks or jars (5-gallon size is good here)
  OR
The biggest wide-mouth canning jars you can get—or ask the high-school cafeteria or your friendly neighborhood snack bar for empty gallon jars (wide-top) that their mayonnaise or pickles came in
  OR
Sound, unchipped enamelware canner (if you can spare it) with lid
Vegetable grater with a coarse blade; large old-style wooden potato-masher
Safe storage area at *c.* 65 to 70 F/18 to 21 C for fermenting vegetables; plus cooler—*c.* 38 F/3 C—storage for longer term

Especially for meats and fish:

Large stoneware crocks (10-gallon or larger)
  OR
Wooden kegs or small barrels—new, or thoroughly scrubbed and scalded used ones (before curing in them, though, fill them with water to swell the staves tight together, so the containers won't leak when they're holding food)
Moisture/vapor-proof wrappings; plus stockinet—tubular cotton-knit—for holding the wrap tight to the meat after it's packaged
Safe, cold storage area (ideally 36 to 38 F/2 to 3 C) for curing meats and fish—and for longer-term storage of meats and vegetables in their curing solutions

For both vegetables and meats, etc.:

Cutting-boards and stainless-steel knives (see Canning Meats)
Large enameled or glass/pottery pans or bowls for preparing the curing mixtures
Big wooden spoons, etc., for mixing and stirring
China or untreated hardwood covers that fit down inside each curing container: an expendable plate, a sawed round, etc.

Weights for these covers, to hold the food under the curing brine—a canning jar filled with sand is good; but nothing of limestone or iron, which mess up the curing solutions

Plenty of clean muslin (old sheets do beautifully) or double-weight cheese-cloth

Glass measuring cups in 1-cup and 4-cup sizes

Scale in pounds (up to 25 is plenty, with ¼- and ½-pound gradations)

Good-sized working space, particularly for dealing with meats

Salting Vegetables

Unless you're fermenting vegetables—as for sour cabbage (Sauerkraut), etc., below—there's only one reason for salting them: you have no other way to put them by, so you either salt your vegetables now or do without vegetables later.

Vegetables are brined whenever they don't release enough natural juice to form adequate liquid during their cure, i.e., when they are not cut small or when they have little natural juice to start with.

Juicy or finely cut vegetables are dry-salted. If a relatively small amount of salt—2½ percent by weight—is added to certain vegetables, they ferment to make a "sour" product (Sauerkraut again); but if 25 percent salt by weight is added to these or other prepared vegetables, the high concentration of salt prevents the growth of the yeasts and bacteria that cause fermentation, and thereby preserves them.

DRY–SALTING TO PRESERVE VEGETABLES

Corn, green/snap/string/wax beans, greens, even cabbage and Chinese cabbage and a number of root vegetables may be dry-salted, but some are more interesting—and certainly more nutritious, since freshening isn't necessary before cooking—if they are fermented instead.

It's not good to add newly prepared vegetables to any already curing, so use a container that will hold the batch you're working with. Just be sure to allow enough headroom to keep the food submerged under the weight: 4 inches should be enough for a 5-gallon crock, less for a smaller one; and the weight can rise above the rim of the container.

Salted Sweet Corn

Select sweet corn in the milk stage as you'd choose it for serving in season as corn-on-the-cob. Husk, remove the silk, and steam it for 10 to 15 minutes over rapidly boiling water or until the milk is set. Cut it from the cob about ⅔ the depth of the kernels (as for whole-kernel processing); weigh it. Mix 4 parts of cut corn with 1 part salt—1 pound of pure pickling salt for each 4 pounds of corn; or 1 cup of salt to 4 cups of cut corn if you don't have a scale.

Pack the corn-salt mixture in a crock to within about 4 inches of the top, cover with muslin sheeting or a double thickness of cheesecloth, and hold the whole business down with a clean plate or board on which you place a weight. If there isn't enough juice in 24 hours to cover the corn, add a salt solution in the proportions of 3 tablespoons salt to each 1 cup of cold water; replace the weighted plate to submerge the corn.

Store the crock in a safe, cool place (about 38 F/3 C). The corn will be cured in from 3 to 5 weeks. Remove meal-sized amounts by dipping out corn and juice with a glass or china cup (don't use metal). Change the cloth as it becomes soiled, and always replace the weighted plate. Keep the crock in cool storage.

To cook the corn, freshen it (soak in cold water a short time, drain, and repeat) until a kernel tastes sweet. Simmer until tender in just enough water to prevent scorching; serve with butter or cream and seasoning to taste.

Salted Green/Snap/String/Wax Beans

Use only young, tender, crisp beans. Wash, remove tips and tails; cut in 2-inch pieces, or french them. Steam-blanch 10 minutes and cool. Weigh the beans, and measure 1 pound (1½ cups) of pure pickling salt for every 4 pounds of beans. Sprinkle a layer of salt in the bottom of a crock, add a layer of beans; repeat until the crock is filled to within 4 inches of the top or until the beans are used; top with a layer of salt. Cover with clean muslin sheeting or doubled cheesecloth and hold down with a weighted plate. If not enough brine has formed in 24 hours to cover the beans, eke it out with a solution in the proportions of 3 tablespoons of salt to each 1 cup of cold water.

Proceed as for Salted Sweet Corn, above.

Salted Dandelion (or other) Greens

Green salads were a rarity with New England hill folk in the early nineteenth century; nor did they go in for leaf vegetables much, except for dandelions in early spring and beet or turnip tops from their gardens in late summer.

Sometimes they salted their greens according to the 1-to-4 rule. Nowadays we'd go them one better, though, and steam-blanch the washed, tender leaves until they wilt—from 6 to 10 minutes, depending on the size of the leaves. Cool the greens, weigh them, and layer them in a crock with 1 pound (1½ cups) of pure pickling salt for every 4 pounds of greens. Proceed as for Salted Sweet Corn and Salted Green Beans, above.

To cook, rinse well and freshen in cold water for several hours, rinse again, drain, and simmer gently in the water adhering to them. Season with small dice of salt pork cooked with them, or serve with vinegar.

Salted Rutabagas (or White Turnips)

Use young, crisp vegetables without any woodiness. Peel; cut in ½-inch cubes. Steam-blanch from 8 to 12 minutes, depending on size of the pieces; cool. Weigh the prepared turnips and proceed with the 1-to-4 rule—1 pound

(1½ cups) of pure pickling salt for each 4 pounds of turnips—and handle thereafter like Salted Sweet Corn, above.

To cook, rinse and freshen for several hours in cold water, rinse again; then simmer until tender in just enough water to keep from scorching. Mash if you like and serve with butter and seasoning to taste.

Salted Cabbage

Remove bruised outer leaves; quarter, cut out the core. Shred as you would for cole slaw. Steam-blanch for 6 to 10 minutes until wilted. Cool, weigh; follow the 1-to-4 rule for Salted Greens above, and continue with the cure.

To cook, rinse and freshen for several hours, rinse again; then simmer until tender in just enough water to prevent scorching. Season during cooking with 2 teaspoons of vinegar and ¼ teaspoon caraway; or drain and return to low heat for 3 minutes with crumbled precooked sausage or small dice of salt pork; or serve with butter and seasoning to taste.

BRINING TO PRESERVE VEGETABLES

This is not the same thing as the preparation for making pickles, which is designed either to crisp the ingredients or to season them as a base for adding vinegar, sugar, spices, etc.

What you're doing here is to reproduce the 25 percent, 1-to-4, rule in "Dry-salting to Preserve Vegetables," above—but you're making up for the insufficiency of natural juice by using water with a heavy concentration of salt. Therefore you will begin by making a strong brine—either about 15 percent, or 20 percent (see the rules-of-thumb for the solutions in "What Salting Does" at the start of this chapter); then, over the 4 to 5 weeks needed to effect the cure, you will add a little salt each week. Always you will keep the vegetables well under the surface of the brine by weighting them down. If you hold to the 1-to-4 rule, for 10 pounds of vegetables you would use 2½ pounds of salt (which would equal around 3¼ to perhaps a little more than 3¾ cups, depending on the density of the salt).

It's easier to gauge the amounts of brine and salt needed if you think in terms of 10 pounds of whole vegetables (or large pieces of cut ones) held in a 5-gallon container: there'll be extra room, but that doesn't matter—you'll weight the vegetables to keep them under the surface of the cure. If you'd rather work in 5-pound lots, use a 2-gallon container and halve the given amounts of brine and salt.

Weigh out 10 pounds of fresh, perfect vegetables, and to them add 2 gallons of brine of the strength given for the individual vegetable; this much brine should cover them, but make a bit more if it doesn't. Cover the brined vegetables with clean muslin or doubled cheesecloth, and on it lay a weighted plate to keep them submerged.

The next day you start gradually to increase the salt in the solution, thus compensating for the natural juice that's drawn out to weaken the brine.

First, for each 10 pounds of vegetable, pour 1 pound (1½ cups) of pickling salt on the wet cloth where it will dissolve slowly into the brine; replace the weight on the mound of salt.

One week later, put 4 ounces in weight (about 6 tablespoons in volume) more salt on the cloth to absorb. Repeat once a week for 3 or 4 weeks more—making a *total* of 1 to 1¼ pounds of salt added in the weekly doses.

The vegetable is cured in 4 to 5 weeks. Take away the cloth, cover the container with a close-fitting lid, and store at an ideal 38 F/3 C.

To cook, freshen the vegetable in several cold waters, and simmer in a very little water until tender, seasoning to taste.

Brined Green Peppers

Halve firm, crisp peppers, remove their seeds; weigh. For 10 pounds of peppers make 2 gallons of strong brine—around a *15 percent solution*— by dissolving 2¾ pounds (about 4⅓ cups) of pure pickling salt in 8 quarts of water. Pour it over the peppers in a 5-gallon crock (it should cover them, but make a bit more if it doesn't). Cover with cloth and weight down. About 24 hours later, put your first addition of salt on the cloth, carrying on with the general method described above.

Brined Cauliflower

Wash heads of fresh young cauliflower, remove leaves and core, and break apart the flowerets in *c.* 1-inch pieces. Continue with a solution of *about 15 percent* as for Brined Green Peppers, above.

Brined Onions

Peel whole, fresh onions, not large ones—and not grown from sets (these can have an inner core wrapped in brown "paper"). Weigh. For every 10 pounds of onions prepare 2 gallons of very strong brine—*around a 20 percent solution*—by dissolving 4 pounds (6 cups) of pure pickling salt in 8 quarts of water.

From here on, follow the method for Brined Green Peppers, above.

DRY-SALTING TO FERMENT VEGETABLES

This edition of *PFB* is coming out too early to be able to quote from the long-awaited *Fermentation of Foods* by Von Mendenhall and Gary Richardson of Utah State University, Logan. What we know of it we recommend to anyone interested in this field of food preservation.

Meanwhile: Most often fermented are cabbage (Sauerkraut) and Chinese cabbage, and rutabagas or white turnips.

Generally speaking, the sweeter vegetables make a more flavorful product, while firmer ones provide better texture. Don't relegate tough, old, woody vegetables to the souring crock—use the best young, juicy ones you can get.

If you feel like experimenting with a small batch (5 pounds, say, in a 1-gallon jar, or less in a smaller container) you could add with the salt the traditional German touches of caraway or dill; or try a bay leaf or two, or some favorite whole pickling spice, or some onion rings, or even a few garlic cloves, peeled (but whole, so you can fish them out before serving).

Some rules advocate starting fermentation with a weak brine, but this procedure offers a loophole for too low a concentration of salt, and the likelihood of mushy food or even of spoilage instead of the desired acidity. Unless you're an old hand with sauerkraut and its relatives, you'll do well to stick to dry salting here.

As with vegetables preserved with salt earlier, you should never mix a fresh batch with one already fermenting.

Produce to be soured *is not blanched:* you want to encourage the micro-organisms that cause fermentation.

For fermenting you use 1/10 the amount of salt you needed for the preserving just described. This means 2½ percent of pure pickling salt by weight of the prepared food: 10 ounces (15 tablespoons or a scant 1 cup) of salt to 25 pounds of vegetables; 4 ounces (6 level tablespoons) of salt for 10 pounds of vegetables; 2 ounces (3 level tablespoons) of salt for 5 pounds of prepared food. This ratio of salt turns the sugar in the vegetables to lactic acid, and the desired souring occurs.

The vegetables should be kept between 68 to 72 F/20 to 22 C during the fermenting period, which takes from 10 days to 4 weeks, depending on the vegetable being processed. Temperatures below 68 F/20 C will slow down fermentation; above 72 F/22 C, and you court spoilage.

As a rough estimate, allow 5 pounds of prepared vegetables for each 1 gallon of container capacity, with the crock/jar holding a slightly greater weight of dense food that's cut fine. The instructions below use 10-pound batches, but you may want to deal with 25 or 30 pounds of cabbage or turnips at a time, using a 5-gallon crock.

Keep all souring vegetables covered with a clean cloth and weighted below the brine during fermentation. A top-quality vegetable should release enough juice to form a covering brine in around 24 hours; if it hasn't, bring the level above the food by adding a weak brine in the proportions of 1½ teaspoons of pickling salt for each 1 cup of cold water.

By the second day a scum will form on the top of the brine. Remove it by skimming carefully; then replace the scummy cloth with a sterile one, and wash and scald the plate/board before putting it back and weighting it.

Take care of this scum every day, and provide a sterile cloth and plate every day; otherwise the scum will weaken the acid you want, and the food will turn mushy and dark. If the brine gets slimy from too much warmth it's best not to tinker with it: do the simplest thing and decant the batch on the compost pile—and wait until cooler weather to start over again.

Fermentation will be continuing as long as bubbles rise to the top of the brine. When they stop, remove the cloth and weighted plate, wipe around the inside of the headroom; cover the vegetable with a freshly scalded plate/board, and put a close-fitting lid on the container. Then store the whole thing in a cool place at *c.* 38 F/3 C.

Dip out with a glass or china cup what you need for a meal, making sure that enough brine remains to cover the vegetable so it won't discolor or dry when exposed to air. Always keep the container well closed.

Fermented vegetables may be canned. See individual instructions below.

Sauerkraut (Fermented Cabbage)

Quarter each cabbage, cut out the core; shred fine and weigh. Using 2½ percent of pickling salt by weight—6 tablespoons to each 10 pounds of shredded cabbage (or see other amounts in the general method above)—pack the container with alternate layers of salt and cabbage, tamping every two layers of cabbage to get rid of trapped air and to start the juice flow—you don't need to get tough with it: just tap it gently with a clean wooden potato-masher or the bottom of a small jar. Top with a layer of salt. Cover with a sterile cloth and weight it down with a plate, etc.; hold at 68 to 72 F/20 to 22 C while it ferments.

Follow the daily skimming procedure given above. When fermenting has stopped in about 2 weeks or so, the sauerkraut will be a clear, pale gold in color and pleasantly tart in flavor. It's a good idea to lay a clean plate on it to keep it below the brine's surface; at any rate cover the container with a close-fitting lid. Store in a cool place and use as needed.

If your storage isn't around 38 F/3 C, you'd better can it (q.v.).

Chinese Cabbage Sauerkraut

Follow the method for Sauerkraut. The result usually has more flavor than regular fermented cabbage does, thanks to more, and sweeter, natural juice.

Sour White Turnip (Sauer Rüben)

Peel and quarter young rutabagas or white turnips (rutabagas are usually firmer and juicier than turnips). Shred find or chop with medium knife of a food grinder, catching stray juice in a bowl placed underneath. Pack with layers of salt as for Sauerkraut, but do not tamp down—there should be juice aplenty without tamping, and it's enough to press down on the topmost layer to settle the pack.

Proceed in every way as for Sauerkraut.

Sour Rutabagas, handle like White Turnips

Souring Other Lower-acid Vegetables

Even though correct fermentation raises the acidity (or lowers the *pH* rating) of lower-acid raw vegetables, *unless they are heat-processed for storage* they cannot be regarded as safe from spoilage or from growth of certain dangerous heat-sensitive bacteria.

So, because you should can them anyway for safe storage, it doesn't make much sense to go through the business of fermenting them as a preamble to putting them by for serving later as accompaniments to meat or whatever.

Especially when there are recipes for relishes and pickles made from corn, pumpkin, zucchini and beets in Chapter 19.

Especially when, if you're strapped for canning jars, the chances are that you can rig up some kind of heat to dry them with (see Chapter 21).

Salting Meat

The four keys to successful salt-curing of any meat are (1) strictly fresh meat to start with, properly handled and chilled; (2) sanitation; (3) temperature control; and (4) salt content. The same quality, cleanliness and care required for canning or freezing meat (q.v.) obtain in the procedures described below, and we give in the specific instructions the exact proportions of salt required to do each job.

However, temperature control demands special emphasis here. The meat must be kept chilled—held as constantly as possible at 38 degrees Fahrenheit—before curing; this is why country-dwellers wait for winter weather to slaughter hogs and beeves for their own tables. Once in the cure, meat should be held between 36 and 38 F/2 and 3 C; for the largest pieces this means a thermometer inserted to the center of the meatiest part.

Below 36 F/2 C, salt penetrates the tissues too slowly. If the temperature of the storage area drops below freezing and stays there for several days, *increase the days of salting time by the number of freezing days.*

Above 38 F/3 C, the chances of spoilage increase geometrically with each degree of rise in temperature, and the cure changes from a clear, fresh liquid to a stringy-textured goo. It is the rare modern home that has natural storage constantly cool enough for curing meat right. Indeed, failure to ensure good temperature control is the main cause of unsuccessful curing in town and country alike.

In general, home-frozen meats do not cure well: even when defrosted completely, their texture has been changed too much to allow the cure to penetrate the tissues uniformly.

The term "pickle" is used in some manuals to designate a sweetened brine that contains some sugar as well as salt; it is *not* the solution with added vinegar that is described for pickles in Chapter 19. "Sugar cure" usually means adding ¼ as much sweetener as there is salt in the mixture; this amount of sugar is important as food for benign flavor-producing bacteria during long cures.

Salt-curing of meats is almost always followed by exposure to smoke in order to dry the surface of the meat, to add flavor, and to discourage attacks by insects. Smoking procedures are described in detail in the section following this one.

Some valuable references and pictures about cutting meat can be found in Chapter 8 under "Cuts of Meat from Large Animals."

"SALTPETER" AND NITRATES/NITRITES

Throughout most of the decade of the 1970's there was worry over the use of nitrate compounds added to our food supply. In Chapter 17, "Common Ingredients and How to Use Them," we went into the history of the concern and why the compounds were feared. It is enough here, therefore, to say that for generations householders—and, back in less technologically sophisticated times, commercial processors too—used saltpeter in the cures for many meats and meat products. What is still called saltpeter is either potassium nitrate or sodium nitrate (this latter often termed "Chilean" nitrate). If you buy the substance at a drugstore you are likely to get the compound with potassium, and note that it is labeled as a diuretic. If you buy it at a farm-supply store, it will probably be sodium nitrate.

Many store-bought curing mixtures already made up—some even containing spices and simulated hickory-smoke flavoring—contain both a nitrate *and* sodium nitr*ite*. The nitrites are the result of nitrates' being metabolized by microorganisms on the meat; the same change occurs in human stomachs when we eat foods treated with nitrates. It is the nitrites that cause the most uneasiness, and they still are under intense scrutiny by the FDA and the USDA, which have set up a government/industry task force to evaluate their use. The problem is that nitrites may combine with products from protein hydrolysis and form new compounds (in animal tests, carcinogens); this reaction may also occur in human beings. However, our foods provide other sources of nitrite in addition to that in cured meats—which actually furnish only 10 to 20 percent of the nitrite ingested in the usual American diet.

Saltpeter has been used for centuries as a means of intensifying and holding the red color considered so appetizing in ham and allied pork products, and in corned beef, etc. It also has an anti-microbial action along with the large amounts of salt used in the cures: at the levels used, nitrites help to prevent the growth of *C. botulinum*. (Refrigerating the meat for storage is a further help.)

STORING CURED MEAT

Their heavy concentration of salt protects Corned Beef and Salt Pork for several months if the brine in which they're held is kept below 38 F/3 C.

Freezer storage of sausage and cured meats is relatively limited: after more than 2 to 4 months at Zero F/−18 C, the salt in the fat causes it to become rancid.

• **NOTE OF WARNING:** A home-cured ham is not the same as a commercially processed one that has been "tenderized," etc. *Home-cured pork is still RAW.*

SALTING BEEF

Because they lack what producers and butchers call "finish," veal or calf meat shouldn't be used to make corned or dried beef. The product is disappointing.

Corned Beef

Use the tougher cuts and those with considerable fat. Bone, and cut them to uniform thickness and size.

To cure 25 pounds of beef, pack it first in pickling salt, allowing 2 to 3 pounds of salt (3 to 4½ cups) for the 25 pounds of meat. Spread a generous layer of coarse pickling salt in the bottom of a clean, sterilized crock or barrel. Pack in it a layer of meat that you've rubbed well with the salt; sprinkle more salt over the meat. Repeat the layers of meat and salt until all the meat is used or the crock is filled to within a couple of inches below the top.

Let the packed meat stand in the salt for 24 hours, then cover it with a solution of 1 gallon of water in which you've dissolved 1 pound (2 cups) of sugar, ½ ounce (*c.* 1 tablespoon) of baking soda, and 1 ounce (*c.* 2 tablespoons) of saltpeter.

Put a weighted plate on the meat to hold every speck of it below the surface of the brine; cover the crock/barrel; and in a cool place—not more than 38 F/3 C—let the meat cure in the brine from 4 to 6 weeks.

The brine can become stringy and gummy ("ropy," in some descriptions) if the temperature rises above 38 F/3 C and the sugar ferments. The baking soda helps retard the fermentation. But watch it: if the brine starts to get ropy, take out the meat and wash it well in warm water. Clean and sterilize the container. Repack the meat with a fresh sugar-water-etc. solution (above), to which you now add 1½ pounds (2¼ cups) of pickling salt; this salt replaces the original 2 pounds of dry salt used to pack the meat.

To store it, keep it refrigerated in the brine; or remove it from the brine, wash away the salt from the surface, and can or freeze it (q.v.).

Dried (Chipped) Beef

Dried beef—which has about 48 percent water when produced commercially—is made from whole muscles or muscles cut lengthwise. Select boneless, heavy, lean-muscled cuts—rounds are best—and cure as for Corned Beef (above) *except* that you add an extra ¼ pound of sugar (½ cup) for each 25 pounds of meat.

The curing is completed in 4 to 6 weeks, depending on size of the pieces and the flavor desired. After it has cured satisfactorily, remove the meat, wash it, and hang it in a cool place to air-dry for 24 hours.

Then it is smoked at 100 to 120 F/38 to 49 C for 70 to 80 hours (see "Smoking")—or until it is quite dry.

To store, wrap large pieces in paper and stockinette (tubular, small-mesh material, which holds the wrap close to the meat) and hang them in a cool (below 50 F/10 C), dry, dark, insect-free room; certainly refrigerate small pieces. Plan to use all the dried beef before spring.

- **NOTE:** And see Jerky in Chapter 21, "Drying."

SALTING PORK

All parts of the pig may be cured by salting. Some—such as the fat salt pork for baked beans, chowders, etc.—are used as they come from the salting process. The choice hams, bacon and, perhaps, loins are carried one step further and are smoked (q.v.) after being cured.

Have the meat thoroughly chilled, and hold it as closely as possible to 38 F/3 C during the process of curing: salt penetrates less well in tissues below 36 F/2 C, and spoilage occurs with increasing speed in meat at temperatures above 38 F/3.3 C.

"Pumping"—i.e., forcibly injecting a strong curing solution into certain parts of a large piece of meat—is not included in the instructions below because we're leery of it: Much safer to allow safe curing time than to try to speed the process by localized "spot" applications of the cure.

Allow 25 days as the minimum curing time for Dry-Salted pork, with some of the larger pieces with bone taking longer. Allow at least 28 days for Sweet Pickled (Brined) pork, and more for the larger pieces. The days-per-pound are given for each cut cured by each method.

Before smoking or storing large pieces containing bone, run a skewer up through the meat along the bone, withdraw the skewer and sniff it. If the odor is sweet and wholesome, fine—proceed with the smoking or storing; but if there's any "off" taint, any whiff of spoilage, destroy the entire piece of meat, because it is unsafe to eat.

Dry–Salting Large Pieces (Hams and Shoulders)

For each 25 pounds of hams and shoulders mix together thoroughly 2 pounds (*c.* 3 cups) of coarse-fine pickling salt, ½ pound (*c.* 1 cup) sugar—and ½

Parts of a pig: A—ham; B—loin and backfat; C—bacon strip with leaf fat; D—shoulder butt and plate; E—picnic shoulder; F—head; G—feet.

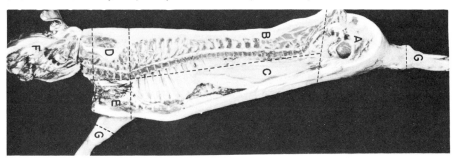

ounce (*c.* 1 tablespoon) of saltpeter. Rub ½ the mixture in well on all surfaces of the meat. Poke it generously into the shank ends along the bone (you can even make a fairly long internal slit with a slender boning knife inserted at the shank, and push the mixture up into it: this is better than relying on "pumping" a strong solution to such areas where the salt must penetrate deeply). Plan to leave an ⅛-inch layer of the mixture on the ham face (the big cut end), with a thinner coating on the rest of the ham and on the shoulders.

Fit the salt-coated meat into a clean sterilized barrel or crock, taking care lest the coating fall off. Cover with a loose-fitting lid or cheesecloth and let cure in a cold place, 36 to 38 F/2 to 3 C.

One week later, remove the meat, re-coat it with the remaining half of the curing mixture, and pack it again in the barrel/crock.

Curing time: At least 25 days. Allow 2 to 3 days for each 1 pound of ham or shoulder, being sure to leave them in the curing container even after all surface salt is absorbed.

Then smoke them (q.v.).

Dry-Salting Thin Cuts (Bacon, "Fat Back," Loin, etc.)

For each 25 pounds of thin cuts of pork, mix together thoroughly 1 pound (*c.* 1½ cups) of pickling salt, ¼ pound (½ cup) of brown or white sugar, and 1½ teaspoons of saltpeter.

Coat the cuts, using all the mixture. Pack the meat carefully in a sterilized crock or barrel, and cover it with a loose-fitting lid or layer of cheesecloth, and let it stand at 36 to 38 F/2 to 3 C for the *minimum* total curing time of 25 days; allowing 1½ days per pound. Thin cuts do not require an interim salting— that's why you used all the mixture in the first place. And leave them in the crock even after the surface salt has been absorbed.

All but the "fat back" (Salt Pork) is then smoked (q.v.). Wrap the Salt Pork in moisture/vapor-proof material; refrigerate what is intended for immediate use, and freeze the rest.

Heavy salting for heavy cuts, left; then into the barrel/crock to cure.

"Sweet Pickle" Salting Large Pieces (Brining Hams, etc.)

Curing hams and shoulders in brine is slower than the Dry Salting treatment just described, and therefore is well suited to colder regions of the country.

Pack the well-chilled (38 F/3 C) hams and shoulders in a sterilized crock or barrel. For every 25 pounds of meat, prepare a solution of 2 pounds (c. 3 cups) of pickling salt, ½ pound (1 cup) of sugar, ½ ounce (c. 1 tablespoon) of saltpeter and 4½ quarts of water. Dissolve all thoroughly, and pour over the meat, covering every bit of it: even a small piece that rises above the solution can carry spoilage down into meat submerged. Put a weighted plate or board over the meat to keep it below the brine, and cover the barrel/crock. Hold the storage temperature to 38 F/3 C.

After 1 week, remove the meat, stir the curing mixture, and return the meat to the crock/barrel, making sure that every bit of it is weighted down below the surface of the brine.

Remove, repack, and cover with the stirred brine at the end of the second and fourth weeks.

If at any time during the cure you find that the brine has soured or become ropy and syrupy, remove the meat, scrub it well, and clean and scald the barrel/crock. Chill the container thoroughly, and return the meat, covering it with a fresh, cold curing solution made like your original brine, except that you *increase the water to 5½ quarts*.

Curing time: A minimum of 28 days; allow 3½ to 4 days for each 1 pound of ham or shoulder.

Cover with cold brine, then weight it all down below the surface.

"Sweet Pickle" Salting Small Pieces (Bacon, Loin, "Fat Back")

Pack the pieces in a sterilized crock or barrel, and cover with a brine like that for large pieces, except in a milder form: use 6 quarts of water, rather than 4½ quarts.

Proceed as for hams and shoulders, keeping the pieces well submerged, and overhauling the contents as above at the end of the first, second, and third weeks.

Curing time: A minimum of 15 days for a 10-pound piece of bacon, allowing 1½ days per pound; but 21 days for heavier pieces of bacon, or for the thicker loins.

Pork that is not to be smoked may be left in the brine until it is to be used—but it will be quite salty.

Smoking

Without intending either to pun or to discuss the pro/con of this traditional finishing process for many cured meats and a few cured fish, we feel duty bound to note that smoking any food is under fire nowadays from some critics.

However, as we indicated in the individual salting instructions above, meats may be left in brine or dry salt until they're ready to be used. Or remove them from the cure, scrub them well to remove surface salt, and hang them in a cool dry, well-ventilated place for from several days to a week to let them dry out a bit before storage.

We do not recommend using so-called "liquid smoke" or "smoke salt" in place of bona fide smoking. Either smoke your meat or call it a day at the end of the salt cure.

WHAT "COLD SMOKING" DOES

We're not concerned here with what is known as "hot smoking"—which in effect is cooking in a slow, smoky barbecue for several hours, thus making the food partially or wholly table-ready at the end of the smoking period.

What we'll do is hold the food in a mild smoke at never more than 120 F/49 C, and usually from around 70 to 90 F/21 to 32 C, for several days to color and flavor the tissues, help retard rancidity and, in many cases, increase dryness—the actual length of time depending on the type of food.

The food is then stored in a cool, dry place, or is frozen, to await future preparation for the table.

MAKING THE SMOKE

Use only hardwood chips for the fire—never one of the evergreen conifers, whose resinous smoke can give a creosote-y taste, or other softwoods. Among the most popular woods are maple, apple and hickory.

Or use corncobs. These should be the thoroughly dried cobs from popcorn or flint corn that has dried on the ear: cobs saved from a feast of sweet corn-on-the-cob aren't the same thing at all. If you don't have your own cobs or can't get them from a neighboring farmer, look in the Yellow Pages for a handler of hardwood sawdust or shavings; such a dealer often has chopped cobs to use as a tumbling medium for polishing. Merrill Lawrence of Newfane, Vermont—whose family has been curing and smoking meat for generations—says 2 bushels of cut corncobs can produce 72 hours of smoke, or enough to do a whole ham in a small smoke-box.

Avoid chemical kindlers, either fluids or small bricks impregnated with flammable mixtures, because their fumes can take a long time to dissipate (you don't want your meat to taste of them). Small, dry hardwood laid tepee-fashion over crumpled pieces of milk cartons catch well, and form a good base for the fire. Get your fire well established and burning clean, but do not have it hot; keep it slow, just puttering along evenly so the meat is in no danger of cooking. Hang a thermometer beside the food closet to the fire: fish, which is so highly perishable (even when lightly salted for smoking), should be smoked at 40 to 60 F/4 to 16 C, and then for a relatively short time compared to the temperature for meats.

The fire can be made and held in any sort of iron or tin brazier suitable for the size of the smokehouse or box.

If you use sawdust or fine chips or chopped corncobs, the smoke might also be maintained well enough by using an electric hot plate to fire a tin pie pan that's filled with the smoke-making material. Set the hot plate on High to start the pan of stuff smoldering, then reduce the heat to Medium or Low. Experiment.

No matter which smoke-making fuel you use, it's important to know how it burns, and how much air intake you need to keep it going or to quiet it down for the type of smoker you have, before you commit a batch of cured meat to the smoking process.

Smoking Meat

Because bacteria in meat grow faster between 70 and 100 F/21 to 38 C, you should smoke meat in fairly cold weather, in late fall or early spring, when temperatures are between 30 and 50 F/−1 and 10 C during the day. However, really cold weather, down to Zero, is not for the beginner who's using the highly simplified smoke-boxes described below.

Smoking should be as sustained as is reasonably possible, simply because you want to get it over with and get the meat cooled and wrapped in moisture/vapor-proof material and stored in a cool, dry place (or frozen). But it won't suffer from the hiatus if you can't smoke at night: the weather will probably keep it cold enough without freezing so you can leave it in the smokehouse and just start your smoke-maker again in the morning.

If you have a sudden sharp drop in temperature, though, you had better bring inside to cool storage any meat that shows danger of freezing without the warmth of the smoke. Resume counting the total smoking time when the smokehouse is operating again.

PREPARING THE MEAT FOR THE SMOKEHOUSE

Remove the meat from the salting crock, scrub off surface salt, using a brush and fresh lukewarm water. Then hang the meat in a cool, airy place for long enough to get the outside of it truly dry—up to 24 hours.

Run several thicknesses of bailing twine or a strong stainless-steel wire through each piece of meat several inches below one end; tie the string or double-twist the wire to form a loop that will hold the weight of the meat. Hams are hung from the shank (small) end. It's a nuisance to have the meat fall to the bottom of the smoke-box because either the loop or the meat has given way.

SMALL HOMEMADE SMOKE–BOXES

The USDA bulletin on processing pork, cited earlier, contains plans for a full-fledged smokehouse, and also a description of a barrel smoke-box. Here are our variations of the barrel.

A Barrel

You can get the smoking parts of half a 200-pound pig in a 55-gallon steel barrel that you make into a "smokehouse." This means that one ham, one shoulder, and one side of bacon cut in pieces can be smoked at the same time (assuming that you've put a jowl and two feet into Head Cheese, q.v.).

Wooden barrels large enough to do the job are (1) hard to come by these days, and (2) their staves shrink when dried out (as they'd be after several days' worth of warm smoke) and open. So use a metal barrel with one head removed. If it's had oil in it, set the residue of oil on fire and let it burn out; then scour the drum thoroughly inside and out with plenty of detergent and water; rinse; scald the inside, and let it dry in the air.

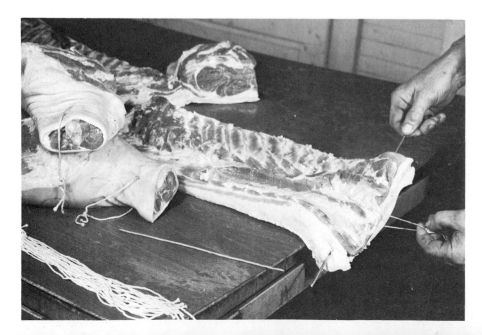

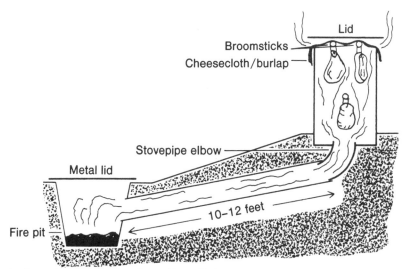

Smoke barrel made from a 55-gallon oil drum.

OUTSIDE ON THE GROUND

In the bottom of the barrel cut a hole large enough to take the end of an elbow for whatever size of stovepipe you want to use (see the sketch). Set the barrel on a mound of earth—with earth banked high enough around it to hold it firm and steady—and dig a trench from it down to a fire-pit at least 10 feet away, and inclining at an angle of something like 30 degrees. Via the trench either connect the barrel to the pit with stovepipe, or build a box-like conduit (stovepiping is easier to remove and clean). You should have the length in order to cool the smoke on its way to the meat, and the pitch to encourage the draft.

Put a cover of close-fitted boards over the fire-pit, arranged so it can be tilted to increase the draft when necessary.

ON THE PORCH, OR IN A GARAGE

The electric-plate/pan-of-sawdust arrangement should be used only in a dry place with fire-retardant material underneath it. This can be sheet metal, or a concrete floor.

Set your barrel on supports—cinder-blocks or trestles of some sort—to hold the elbow well away from the floor. Connect the stovepipe, and lead it from the barrel to the electric smoke-making unit. Make a wooden box, lined with fire-retardant material, to house the hot plate and the pan of sawdust, cut adequate slits for regulating air intake; and merely lift off the box when you want to add more fuel for making smoke.

SMOKING IN THE BARREL

Get the fire or smoke-maker well established and producing evenly before hanging the meat to smoke. There should be good ventilation from the top in order to carry off moisture the first day (to keep the fire from getting too hot, though, reduce the air intake at the bottom of the fire-pit as much as you can without letting the fire go out).

Hang the ham, shoulder and chunks of bacon (or comparable sizes of beef pieces) from broom-handles or stainless-steel rods—not galvanized, not brass, not copper—laid across the top of the barrel. Stagger the meat so that none of it touches other pieces or the side of the barrel; suspend smaller pieces on longer loops of strong steel wire so they drop below the large pieces. Hang your thermometer.

Over the whole business lay a flat, round wooden cover slightly bigger than the barrel's top. It will be held up from the rim by the thickness of the supporting rods. If this isn't enough clearance at the beginning, or if the draft seems to be faltering, prop the lid higher with several cross-pieces of wood laid parallel to the supporting rods.

Close down the ventilation on the second day by draping a piece of clean burlap or several thicknesses of cheesecloth over the supporting rods *under* the lid. The cloth will also protect the meat inside from debris, or from insects attracted to it if the smoke stops. Weight the lid down over the cloth with a good-sized rock to keep it in place.

How Long?

Smokiness—color and flavor of the meat—is a matter for individual taste. If it's oversmoked, the meat is likely to be too pungent, especially on the outside. And you can always put the meat back for more smoking if the flavor isn't enough for you.

So try out your system in a small way. Give a shoulder of cured pork, say, 45 to 55 hours of smoking; take it out and slice into it—you may want to give it a few hours more: 60 hours is about average for a smoked shoulder.

The average ham takes about 72 hours of total smoking time.

Bacon, being a thinner piece of meat, is usually smoked enough in a total of 48 hours.

BUT ALL THESE TIMES ARE APPROXIMATE—they're mentioned merely as guides.

Smoking Fish

Perhaps nowhere in North America has interest in smoking fish grown so fast as in the Great Lakes region, thanks to increasingly effective pollution control and to stocking these waters with the coho salmon. Therefore the following procedure deals with this salmon and related species.

Before we go further, however, we say frankly that the product is not likely to equal the world-famous smoked Nova Scotian salmon—which is most often cured and smoked by specialists attached to private fishing clubs. Nor will it have the keeping qualities of the storied smoked salmon of the Northwest Indians: to be stored for any length of time at 40 to 50 F/4 to 10 C, the moisture in the fish must be reduced to 20 percent, and about the best that can be done with home-smoking equipment is a reduction to about 40 percent. And meticulous handling and sanitation are vital, as we explained at length in "Canning Fish," Chapter 9.

Pre-smoking Preparation

Dress, scrub and fillet your salmon, taking special care to remove the dark lateral line of flesh that is capable of harboring unusually large numbers of spoilers; hold the pieces as close to 32 F/Zero C as possible. In your largest kettle or tub—enameled, ceramic or wooden, *never* one that can corrode—prepare enough ice-cold brine to cover your fish, made in the proportion of 3 cups pure pickling salt dissolved in each 1 gallon of fresh drinking water. Depending on the thickness of the fillets, hold the fish in this 30-to-40-degree-F/−1-to-4 C brine for 1 to 2 hours, during which time diffused blood will be drawn out, the oil in the tissues will be sealed in to a large extent, and the flesh will be chilled so much that the following dry-salt cure will not penetrate too rapidly.

Remove the fillets, drain, and scrub away debris. Using pickling salt in the proportion of 3½ pounds (5¼ cups) for each 10 pounds of fish, dredge the pieces completely in salt and pack them in a large non-corrodible container with plenty of salt between the layers. Put the pieces skin-side down, except for the top layer; cover the top layer with salt. Keep the container as cool as possible, and hold the fish in it for 3 hours.

Remove fish, rinse well. Air-dry in single layers away from sun or heat for 1 to 3 hours until a thin shiny "skin," or pellicle, forms on the surface. The fish is now ready to smoke.

Cold-smoking the Fish

Many beginners are confused by the term "hot-smoking," which is a sort of long-distance barbecue in which the flesh reaches an internal temperature of up to 180 F/82 C after which it is eaten within a couple of days—as with any cooked food—or is frozen. We are not speaking here of this type of smoke-cooking.

Build your regular hardwood fire; after it is burning well, smother it with fine hardwood chips or sawdust to produce a very dense smoke with little heat—the temperature inside the smoke chamber ideally should never exceed 70 F/21 C in order to inhibit growth of bacteria in this highly perishable food. Tend the fire night and day: smoking fish is a continuous process.

After the end of 4 full days of smoking, sample a piece of fish to see if its color, flavor and texture are what you want. If not, smoke it 24 hours more, and test again. When it is smoked to your satisfaction, air-dry the pieces in a cool place for several hours. Then package the fillets individually in plastic wrap and store between 32 and 40 F/Zero and 4 C for up to 3 months.

Freezing will cause salt in the tissues to deposit on the surface of the fillets. We do *not* recommend that smoked fish be canned at home.

21 🌿

DRYING

Of all methods of preserving food, by the start of the 1980's drying was getting the most publicity. A decade earlier, though, the average North American living away from "sun country" gave it very little thought. Which was interesting, because quietly a lot of people were drying a good deal of food, and relying on their stored supplies to help get them through to the next harvest. And to some, like the Mormons, dried food has been automatically a part of their life for generations.

Partly this unawareness was caused by there being so little in print, for the general public, on how to dry food. Horace Kephart's *Camping & Woodcraft* told about concentrated food for the trail; other woodsmen's manuals gave cursory how-to that seemed to rely on folkways reported by Kit Carson or Jim Bridger. It was necessary for *PFB* to start almost from scratch.

We were lucky to have two good out-of-print publications. One, a long and thorough exposition by the USDA around the end of World War I, required a dryer so big that it could handle the harvests from a farmstead kitchen garden as they came along; a good deal of its pre-drying treatments would not be followed strictly today because they used substances no longer in good repute. The other, and smaller, pamphlet is still one of our favorites. Our copy was issued in 1958, and was compiled by experts in the Philippines, Greece and the Southwest United States, and dealt entirely with sun-drying. It is explicit and careful to point out where the pitfalls are. After all, the people being taught from the booklet were often desperately poor, and their lives depended on drying their skimpy crops without chance of spoilage—either during the process or later in storage.

The mid-'70's saw an impetus toward drying, much of the new thrust coming from the commune families and the young homesteaders who were looking for an alternative life-style. They seldom had freezers, often lacked Pressure Canners; they wanted to return to basics, and they did. Some had the sun, but others needed safe and reasonably prompt indoor drying and the techniques for using it. The answer came in books devoted to the procedure, and marked the beginning of a big market for mail-order dryers to use at home.

At this writing the spotlight on drying has been switched to such high beam that it's a commonplace advertisement that cites the fun of serving one's own

376

jerky as cocktail tidbits, or morsels made in a counter-top dryer from fruit flown in from the tropics. Perhaps the peak of "in-ness" came in a 1981 pre-Christmas television commercial for a versatile appliance that made either delicious fruit snacks or delicious yogurt. This play-food image of drying seemed to us as belittling to an ancient and worthy procedure as were the scare ads that offered dehydrated "gourmet" dishes as a means of preventing famine. But when the promoters began claiming that the dryer's products were lower in Calories than fresh fruit, *PFB* decided that such a flat misstatement of fact demands energetic rebuttal. Dried fruit, weight for weight, is *not* lower in Calories: 100 grams of fresh apricots have 51 Calories, the same weight of dried apricots has 260 (and, if truly dehydrated—more on this distinction in a minute—332 Calories). These proportions hold roughly for all fruits.

WHAT DRYING DOES

The purpose of drying is to take out enough water from the material so that spoilage organisms are not able to grow and multiply during storage (see "Why Put-by Foods Spoil" in Chapter 2). The amount of remaining moisture that is tolerable for safety varies according to whether the food is strong-acid or low-acid raw material, or whether it has been treated with a high concentration of salt—and, to some degree, with the type of storage.

In addition, properly home-dried fruits and vegetables, uncooked, have roughly ⅙ to ⅓ the bulk and only around 10 to 20 percent of the water of their original fresh state.

• LANGUAGE NOTE: Although "drying," "dehydrating" and "evaporating" are often used casually as meaning the same thing, the USDA Research Service's fine multivolume *Agriculture Handbook No. 8,* which tells the composition of raw, processed and prepared foods of all sorts, lists as dehydrated those foods containing only 2.5 to 4 percent water—the other 96+ percent having been removed by highly sophisticated processes that we can't hope to equal at home. It lists as dried those foods still containing roughly 10 to 20 percent water (the amount depending on whether they're vegetables or fruits). We can take out all but this much moisture with the equipment and methods described in this section—and we'll call it *drying.*

GENERAL PROCEDURES IN DRYING

Dry only food that is in prime condition and perfectly fresh, just as you choose it for any method of putting by; and handle it quickly.

Be scrupulously clean at every step. A number of the micro-organisms that cause food poisoning, ranging from the Salmonellae to *C. botulinum* and including molds and fungi, contaminate the food because they are in the soil or on the surfaces of our workplaces or even in the air around us.

The procedures described hereafter do not undertake to *sterilize* food. There is nothing about dryness, in itself, that kills the spores of molds or the worst bacteria, although a moisture content of less than 35 percent can greatly slow their growth. The temperatures at which food is dried are much lower than those used for cooking, and there are bad actors among the contaminators that don't mind long exposure to drying heat.

Before drying starts and after the food is pared/cored/sliced or whatever, much of it will be given some sort of treatment to preserve color, prevent decomposition and safeguard nutrients (in general, though, drying is hard on some of the vitamins). Depending on the type of food, these treatments are: for fruit, coating with an anti-oxidant or sulfuring; for vegetables, blanching in boiling water or steam to stop enzymatic action; and, in the case of meat or fish, salting.

Throughout the drying process the food must be protected from airborne spoilers and from vermin—and simply from poor handling. Regardless of where it is being dried, it will lie on only food-grade materials and it will be shielded from insects. After it tests dry, any unevenness in moisture content will be equalized by conditioning; insect eggs, if there are any, will be destroyed by pasteurizing the food; it will be stored in food-grade containers, safe from infestations or dampness or temperatures too warm.

EQUIPMENT FOR DRYING

Keep everything simple, even rudimentary, in the beginning: aside from saving money it's a lot more fun in this hypertechnical age to return to elementals. You can always branch out with more sophisticated gear when you get your technique down pat for one type of food and start with a new one that requires a different treatment. Try for as much uniformity in size as possible, though, so you can swap equipment from one system to another.

Trays First

Shallow *wooden* trays are necessary whether you dry outdoors in sun or shade, or indoors in a dryer or an oven. *Never* use aluminum, copper or galvanized metal, or wire with a plastic coating that is not food-grade. The trays should have slatted, perforated or woven bottoms to let the air get at the underside of the food. Don't make them of green wood—which weeps and warps; and don't use pine, which imparts a resinous taste to the food; and don't use oak or redwood, which can stain the food. Ingenuity will turn up many suitable materials; the following ideas are just a sampling.

The simplest frames to make would be those cut from wooden crates that produce comes in: saw the crates in several sections horizontally, rather as you'd split a biscuit.

If you're making frames from scratch, you can use 1-inch × 1-inch material of the kind you're likely to be using anyway for vertical cleats at the corners of a dryer or for bracing. It will give your trays only 1 inch of depth for holding food; this could be a disadvantage for open-air sun-drying—which requires that food be protected by netting of some sort stretched over the top of the tray—but this extreme shallowness doesn't matter much in a dryer.

Tempered hardboard (this is not underlayment) would be good. It is strong despite its thinness and comes in 4-foot × 8-foot sheets that is fine material for making dryers and sulfuring boxes. One sheet will give you a dryer 14 inches wide, 24 inches deep and 36 inches high, plus frames for 6 trays to fit inside, and some usable trimmings left over. For each tray with sides 2 inches high, cut two sides and two ends and fasten them together in a rectangle by nailing them, not to each other, but to 1-inch × 1-inch cleats; fourpenny box nails will do the job well. Diagonal cross-bracing of the cleat material to form an X, with the end of each arm nailed to the corner cleat, will strengthen the frame, and will also provide valuable extra air space when trays are stacked; put it on after the bottom of the tray is attached.

How Big?

Each 1 square foot of tray space will dry around 1½ to 2½ pounds of prepared food.

Loaded trays shouldn't be too large to handle easily, and they should be uniform in size so they stack evenly. The flimsier the construction, the smaller they should be; but even well-built ones for sun-drying are better if they're not more than 2 feet by 2 feet.

However, since you can have an emergency that means you will need to finish off in an oven or dryer a batch you've started outdoors, it makes sense to have the trays smaller, and rectangular. Make the trays narrow enough for clearance when you slide them inside, and 3 to 4 inches shorter than the oven or dryer is from front to back: you'll want to stagger the trays to allow air to zigzag its drying way up and over each tray as it rises from the intake at the bottom to the venting at the top.

Consider having the trays 1 to 2 inches deep, 12 to 16 inches wide, 16 to 20 inches long—but first having found the inner dimensions of the oven or dryer (less the fore-and-aft leeway for staggering the trays).

No Metal for the Bottoms Either

Don't use metal screening for the bottom. Aluminum discolors and, more important, it corrodes easily. Copper destroys Vitamin C. And galvanized screen has been treated with zinc and cadmium—and cadmium is dangerous stuff indeed to mix with food. (When old-time instructions called for "hardware cloth" they meant galvanized screen, so ask a knowledgeable dealer what his screening is made from; if he knows his stuff he can tell you.) If you have little choice, however, protect the food with clean muslin, or the like, between it and the screen.

Steer clear of fiberglass mesh: minute splinters of fiberglass can be freed easily and impregnate the food.

Vinyl-coated screen in beguiling ¼-inch and ½-inch mesh looks like the answer at first glance, *BUT is it food-grade?* And what will it do at 140 F/60 C, the average heat in a dryer—melt? peel?

Any cloth netting will do if its mesh isn't larger than ½-inch. Two layers of cheesecloth work, as does mosquito net, etc.—but they're hard to clean without getting frazzled. Old clean sheets let less air up through, but they're stouter. (In a pinch you can dry food on sheets laid flat in the direct sun.) When cutting cloth for tray bottoms, allow 2 inches more all around so you can fold it over itself on the outside of the frame; then staple it in place.

We've seen good trays with bottoms of twine or strong cord strung back and forth and then cross-hatched the other way. Draw the twine tight and flat, staple each loop to the outside of the frame-strip before you turn around and go back, keeping the strands ½ inch apart. *Do not use hay-baler twine,* a conscientious reader pointed out to us: this is now treated with a pesticide, so it's bad for food.

Strong, serviceable bottoms are made by nailing ½-inch wood strips to the bottom of the frame ½ inch apart; the strips run in only one direction. More finished—but worth it, because they're smooth and easy to clean—are ¼- or ½-inch hardwood dowels; these are nailed inside the frame with small box nails driven through from the outside, and they also go in only in one direction.

One thickness of cheesecloth laid over bottoms will keep sugar-rich food from sticking to them while it dries; so will a thin coating of oil. Even a few recent publications suggest mineral oil for lubricating the trays—it doesn't impart flavor and doesn't get rancid—but use any fresh, low-flavored vegetable oil. You'll be scrubbing your trays anyway, regardless of what oil you use.

Relevant Metrics for Drying

Full metric conversions, with the arithmetic for refining them, are given at the start of Chapter 17 ("Common Ingredients and How to Use Them"), but the following—rounded off—apply in this chapter.

If you live above the sea-level zone (i.e., *over* 1000 ft/305 m), consult the subsection "Correcting for Altitude" in Chapter 3 to help in figuring blanching times at lowered atmospheric pressures.

• • •

Temperatures (@ sea level): 32 F/Zero C——40 F/4 C——80 F/27 C——90 F/32 C——100 F/38 C——110 F/43 C——120 F/49 C—— 130 F/54 C——135 F/57 C——140 F/60 C——145 F/63 C——150 F/66 C——155 F/68 C——175 F/80 C——212 F/100 C——240 F/116 C.

Volume: ½ teaspoon = 2.5 mL——1 teaspoon = 5 mL——1½ teaspoons = 7.5 mL——3 teaspoons/1 tablespoon = 15 mL——½ cup = 125 mL——1 cup = 250 mL——½ pint = 250 mL——1 pint = 500 mL——1 quart = 1 L.

Length: ¼ inch = 0.64 cm——½ inch = 1.27 cm——1 inch = 2.54 cm——6 inches = 15.2 cm.

Weight: ½ pound = 0.23 kg——1 pound = 0.45 kg——2 pounds = 910 g/0.91 kg.

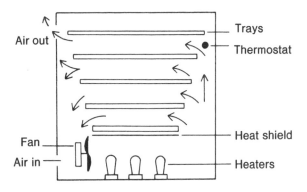

OREGON'S GOOD HOMEMADE DRYER

Buy a dryer if you can, but if you are at all handy and enjoy doing for yourself, *PFB* recommends a make-it-yourself dryer to set on a table. It is described in full in Circular 855, *How to Build a Portable Electric Food Dehydrator,* by Dale E. Kirk, Agricultural Engineer, Oregon State University, Corvallis; but directions—and diagrams—for building it are also contained in USDA *H&G Bulletin 217, Drying Foods at Home* (1977), and in material abridged and issued by New Mexico State University, Las Cruces. More fun to get it from its originator in Corvallis, we'd think; see Chapter 25, under the subsection for this chapter.

The dryer offers around 8½ square feet of tray surface, and thereby will handle around 18 pounds of fresh fruit or vegetables. Basically, it is a plywood box that holds five screen trays above the heat source, which is nine 75-watt light bulbs; the heat is dispersed by a shield and forced upward through the trays of food by an 8-inch household fan.

This Oregon dryer is quicker than the passive solar dryer that resembles a coldframe, coming in a moment; and quicker than the large air-draft, and therefore more efficient, solar dryer sketched by Alex Wilson. It is not so fast as a convection oven, or as the speediest of all: a box with vertical heating element and air blown horizontally across the trays of food.

SOLAR DRYERS

With the proven value of solar energy channeled to heat water and homes even in New England's wait-a-minute weather, it is to be expected that solar food dryers would be designed for use virtually everywhere in the Temperate Zone of North America.

And they have been developed. Alex Wilson, formerly associate director of the New Mexico Solar Energy Association and at this writing executive director of the New England counterpart association, has sketched the prototype large solar food dryer. It is a high box on legs, with an apron slanting downward from the front below the tray area. Facing south, the apron's collector

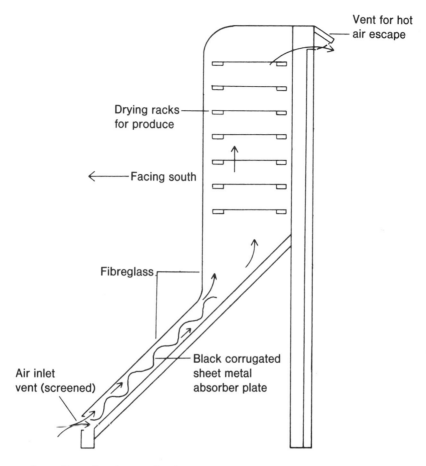

draws air up from intakes at the front feet, heats it; and, because the warm/hot air rises naturally, it rises through the food on the trays, to escape through a wide vent across the top of the dryer in back of the trays. This dryer is being modified with a draft-booster—also natural—for use in the Northeast's chancy climate.

A smaller, simpler and more passive version is for small-scale drying outdoors with plenty of sunshine. You can put together a dryer that looks, and acts, much as a coldframe does (see sketch).

The tilted glass panel—one or more pieces of storm sash are fine—intensifies the heat from the sun, and this rise in temperature inside lowers the relative humidity correspondingly, so that drying occurs faster than is possible outside the dryer. The ample screened venting allows circulation of air.

This dryer is not effective on overcast days.

PROTECTIVE COVERINGS

Food dried in the open, whether outdoors or in a warm room, needs protection from insects and airborne gurry. If the trays have high enough sides (*c.* 2

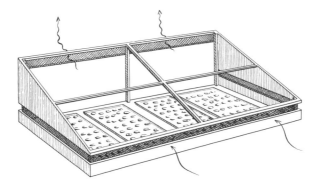

inches) so the metal can't touch the food, fine-mesh non-galvanized screen does the job. If the trays are so shallow that the covering is likely to sag on to the food, a layer of cloth netting, stretched tight, is better. The problem is not so much what to use, as how to fasten it adequately and still have it easy to re-move and replace at the times when the food is stirred or turned over to hasten drying.

Many people cut the covering 2 inches larger all around than the tray it's in-tended for, bend it over, and thumbtack the overlap to the sides of the tray. Or sometimes it's easier to stretch cheesecloth, etc., over several trays laid side by side, and fasten the cloth to the surface the trays rest on. Or you can use the framed screen from a window: it's weight is usually adequate to keep it lying on top of a drying tray. And there's always simply laying a cloth net over the trays and weighting it down all around outside the trays.

• **WARNING:** Be wary of any such plastic as shower curtains, weather-proofing (e.g., for temporary storm sashing), painter's dropcloths, etc.: these are not food-grade, and your food would be subjected to the volatiles of non-approved chemicals. (See "Those Space-age Plastics," Chapter 4.)

Food that's drying outdoors must be protected from dew at night—unless it is brought inside outright. So stack the trays under a shelter and cover the stack with a big carton found at a supermarket or a store that sells large household appliances. Or drape the stack with a clean old sheet. If there's chance of rain, use a light tarpaulin if you have one (putting a clean sheet between the food and the tarp); a plastic shower curtain or tablecloth; or a painter's dropcloth, plastic or not, but certainly without paint or turpentine on it.

MISCELLANEOUS FURNISHINGS

Trestles, racks, benches. No set sizes or types for these, so just know where you can get bricks or wood blocks for raising the first course of trays off the ground; scrap lumber for building rough benches or racks to hang drying food from; smaller stuff to use as spacers. And not all at once and none of it fancy.

Sulfuring box. We're going to suggest sulfuring in certain instances, and we'll tell how to make and use a sulfuring box in a minute.

Auxiliary heaters. Easier to list what *not* to use: No small stove burning flammable material—wood, oil, coal, etc.—that sits inside any portion of the dryer-box. Never any sort of front-blowing electric heater laid on its back to blow hot air upward. Avoid electric hot plates.

Drying Over a Floor Register—NO

Drying food over a floor register leading from the furnace is not recommended: too much dust—even with clean air filters.

And there are usually fumes from the combustion, even though they're unnoticeable in the room.

However, a cluster of 150- or 200-watt light bulbs (totaling 750 watts for the "Oregon" dryer described earlier) gives good, even heat—sometimes *too* even: unless there's an automatic control, you must unplug the whole thing or unscrew some of the bulbs to reduce the heat when you need to. Because the bulbs overheat themselves in a cluster, especially in such a confined space, they should be in porcelain sockets; and get extended-service bulbs with a heavy-duty element for longer bulb life.

The wiring of all electrical heating and blowing units must meet all safety criteria.

Electric fan. To boost the natural draft in an indoor dryer or to augment a cross-draft when drying in an open room or outdoors. It needn't be large; it should be directable, and *it must have a safety grill covering the blades.*

Thermometers. Even with a dryer or oven having a thermostat, you'll need a food thermometer—a roasting, candy or dairy type will do—to check on the heat of food being processed; plus the most inexpensive kind of oven thermometer to move around between the top and bottom trays to keep track of the varying temperatures.

Scales. Not vital but a great help is scales that go up to 25 pounds/11.34 kilograms, with quarter- and half-pound gradations; use it for judging water-loss by weight, per-pound treatments before drying.

Blanching kettle. Your preserving kettle or Boiling–Water Bath canner will do. Enamelware is best; and with a close-fitting cover. Plus a rack or basket—or even a cheesecloth bag—to hold the food above the steam.

Assorted kitchen utensils. Dishpan, colander, crockery or enameled bowls; stainless sharp knives for cutting and paring; apple-corer and a melon-ball scoop; cutting-board; vegetable slicer or a coarse shredder; spoons—some wooden, at least one slotted; also plenty of clean towels and paper toweling, and an extra packet of cheesecloth.

Materials for storing. Several large covered crocks for conditioning dried food before storing—or strong cartons, moisture-proofed with a lining of plastic sheeting; plastic or paper bags (not big) for packaging dried food in small quantities; mouse-proof, sealable containers for the packages. And cool, dark, dry storage when you're done.

THE DRYING METHODS

Basically, drying food at home combines sustained mild heat with moving air to accomplish its purpose. This means (1) heat adequate to extract moisture, but moderate enough so that it doesn't cook the material; and (2) currents of air dry enough to absorb the released moisture and carry it off. These conditions can occur outdoors naturally, or they can be reproduced indoors in dryers.

Open-air/Sun

Successful outdoor drying is possible only in sun-drenched regions with prolonged low humidity, where foods are exposed for perhaps only a minor portion of their total drying time to direct sun, and are partially shaded by a roof of some sort from the fierce rays at midday. An open, south-facing veranda is a favorite place for drying in many parts of the American Southwest; an alternative is a mat of leaves or branches held over the food by poles at each corner. There are also the passive and air-flow solar dryers just discussed. Because the food is covered or brought inside after dark if nighttime condensation might undo the sun's work, drying most foods in open-air/sun takes a minimum of several days, and generally longer.

Where to Sun-dry

Hereout, "sun-drying" will mean outdoors in open air, the food exposed to sun but not in full sun at all times of the day, lest it "case-harden"—that is, cook the outside to form a crust that prevents the inside from drying well.

In North America, the interior of California and the high country of Southwestern states possess the ideal climate for sun-drying: predictably long periods of hot sun and low humidity. Next come the wide Plains east of the Rockies in the United States and Canada, where occasional showers are not a great problem if the food hasn't got wet and if drying can be resumed in open air the next day. Sun-drying can be done in parts of the Northwest east of the Cascade range, and in the Appalachians. Despite their heat, the humid areas of the South are not so good. It is worth noting that Cornell University's excellent 1977 bulletin (again, see Chapter 25) does not include drying outdoors or in the sun. The authors' tacit instruction is *not* to try sun-drying in the Northeast.

Locate the drying area near enough to the house so that you can tend the food several times during the day and put it under cover easily at night—but keep away from places where dust can be stirred up or where animals are quartered or pastured.

Don't dry food outdoors IF: you're in a smog belt; you're in urban sprawl with superhighways surrounding your community; or even if you're rural but have a well-traveled secondary road within a thousand yards of your home. (The late Dr. Henry A. Schroeder cited the case of a cow that aborted her calf after eating hay cut from a vacant lot in a small New England town. The hay was heavily polluted with lead from the exhausts of cars using the street, which is a numbered highway.)

What to Dry in Open-air/Sun

• **BEFORE WE START, A WARNING THAT WILL BE REPEATED SEVERAL TIMES:** Eggs, poultry and meat—except for very lean beef, young lamb or venison made into jerky—are not good for home drying; nor is fish, unless it is heavily salted cod, etc., that is more likely to be dried as a commercial venture. Reason: Salmonella and staphylococcus bacteria thrive on these foods.

There are also some vegetables whose storage life is comparatively short, but we'll cite these when we come to the section that deals with them. They are not dangerous, like the foods above; they just may not be worth a lot of bother.

The following list of sun-dryable produce is taken from the out-of-print booklet mentioned in the introduction to this chapter as a favorite of ours because of its explicitness and the way it explains the *Why* of pitfalls. We note that the list is based on completely ideal conditions of continued sunshine, high temperatures and low humidity.

It is also important to mention that most of the fruits were exposed to extensive sulfuring before drying—the length of the sulfur dioxide treatment presumably compensating for the long time required for total drying in the sun. Full *Why* and *How* of sulfuring has a section of its own later on in "Pre-drying Treatments for Produce."

Fruits easier to sun-dry—Apples, apricots, cherries, coconut, dates, figs, guavas, nectarines, peaches, pear, plums and prunes.
Fruits harder to sun-dry—Avocados, blackberries, bananas, breadfruit, dewberries, Loganberries, mameys (tropical apricots), and grapes.
Vegetables easier to sun-dry—Mature shell beans and peas, lentils and soybeans in the green state, chili (hot) peppers, sweet corn, sweet potatoes, cassava root, onion flakes, and soup mixture (shredded vegetables, and leaves and herbs for seasoning).
Vegetables harder to sun-dry—Asparagus, beets, broccoli, carrots, celery, greens (spinach, collards, beet and turnip tops, etc.), green/string/snap beans ("leather britches" to old-timers), green (immature) peas, okra, green/sweet peppers, pimientos, pumpkin, squash, and tomatoes.

UNDER MORE TEMPERATE CONDITIONS

Because micro-climates and facilities vary from one sun-drying area to another, it's worth noting that authorities who speak only for conditions in the

North Temperate Zone agree that vegetables dried in the sun are often inferior in quality to sun-dried fruits and are more likely to spoil during processing. Furthermore, even with some of the "easier" fruits, consensus seems to be that color and flavor are better when they finish drying in stacks in the shade—if humidity is low enough—or are brought indoors to a dryer if it isn't.

In general, then, you might start with sun-drying herbs and flavoring leaves, slices of apples and large-stone fruits, kernel corn and slivers of pumpkin and squash and peppers, before undertaking more.

Drying Produce in Open-air/Sun

Wash, peel, core, etc., and pre-treat according to individual instructions. Because vegetables must have more of their water removed than fruits do for safe drying, cut vegetables smaller than you cut fruits so they won't take too long to dry (being low-acid, vegetables are more likely to spoil during drying).

Spread prepared food on drying trays one layer deep (½ inch, or depending on size of the pieces); put over it a protective covering as described above; place trays in direct sun on a platform, trestles, or merely raised from the ground on stones or wood blocks—on any sort of arrangement that allows air to circulate underneath them. The trays may be laid flat or tilted by means of an extra support under one end; often a slanting low roof is a good place.

If you use clean sheets or the like to hold the food, a table, bench or shed roof is a good place, but you lose the benefit of air circulating *under* the food.

Stir the food gently several times each day to let it dry evenly.

Before the dew rises after sundown, bring the trays indoors or stack them in a sheltered spot outdoors. If the night air is likely to remain very dry, the outdoor stack need not be covered; otherwise wait a little until the warmth of the sun has left the food, then drape a protecting sheet over the stack. Return the food to the direct sun the next morning.

At the end of the second day, start testing the food for dryness after it has cooled. If it doesn't test dry (See "Tests for Dryness in Produce" and "Postdrying Treatments" later on) put it out again until it does. Then it's ready for conditioning and packaging and storing.

Stack-drying Produce in Shade

This variation of sun-drying relies on extremely dry air having considerable movement, and therefore shouldn't be attempted in muggy areas even though the sun is hot. But where you have hot, dry breezes this method gives a more even drying with less darkening than if the food was done entirely in direct sun; apricots, particularly, retain more of their natural color when shade-dried.

Prepare the food, cutting it in small pieces; put the trays in direct sun for one day or more—until the food is ⅔ dry. Then stack the trays out of the sun but where they'll have the benefit of a full cross-draft, spacing them at least 6 inches apart with chocks of wood or bricks, etc. After several days the dried food is conditioned and packaged for storing.

You can also stack-dry small quantities of food on an open porch by using an electric fan to boost the movement of the air and thus increase its evaporating power. Separate the trays of partly dried food with 6-inch blocks and set the fan at one end of the stack, directing its blast across the trays (which you'll have to shift around a good deal, since the food nearest the fan dries first). Condition and store.

Using a Solar Dryer

Because of the conditions it is designed to overcome, a solar dryer (sketched earlier) accommodates only a relatively small amount of material at one drying session, and the food "started" in it usually cannot be finished off by stack-drying. On the plus side, however, are the fact that it dries faster than would be possible in the open air, and it costs nothing to operate.

Prepare the food as for sun-drying and spread it one layer deep on the trays. Check the material every hour or so, stirring it gently so it dries evenly; if convenient, turn the dryer several times so it faces direct sunshine. As soon as the interior has cooled when the sun gets low, cover all the ventilators. Remove the covering the next morning and set the dryer to get the full benefit of the sun's heat.

If the sun is hot enough and there is no exposure to humidity from the outside, the food should be dried in about two days. Condition and store.

INDOOR DRYING

Almost every food that sun-dries well can make a better product if it is dried more quickly, either in a solar dryer with good air draft or in a dryer with separate heat source and blown air. For some foods, especially the low-acid vegetables, processing in an indoor dryer is recommended even though outdoor drying conditions are reliable during the harvest months. But for Heaven's sake don't forgo drying your produce if you don't have a dryer and do have sun: just take care.

Herbs dry best in the natural heat and draft of a well-ventilated room, or hung in large kraft-paper bags (from the supermarket), tied by their stems and the whole thing slung from a beam.

Depending on the water content and size of the prepared food, and whether the dryer is loaded heavily or skimpily, good drying is possible within 12 hours in an indoor dryer.

On a smaller scale, the conventional oven of a cookstove can be made to perform as a dryer; the processing time is rather longer.

Jerky meats, fresh or lightly salted, dry well in an oven (which is an indoor dryer of sorts)—often better than they do on trays in a regular drying box.

Salt fish is best done in open air, since a breeze outdoors on a sunny day is preferable to the limited ventilation afforded by a dryer or an oven. But if the weather turns poor, and you don't mind the aroma indoors, you can finish off a batch in the dryer, or do a small amount in the oven.

USING A DRYER

Here you're increasing the speed of drying by use of temperatures higher than those reached outdoors in the sun, so be prepared to regulate heaters and shift trays around if you want the best results.

Rules-of-Thumb for Indoor Dryer Times

With so many new types of indoor food dryers on the market, and each—we trust—with its own adequate set of directions for using it to prepare wholesome and safe food, there is considerable leeway in how much time is needed for drying various foods. Beginning with the slowest times, we expect that drying in (1) a conventional oven without benefit of air moving inside the oven takes longer than doing food in (2) the home-built "Oregon" dryer, which has a small fan in its base; that less tedious is using (3) a convection oven, and quickest of all would be the (4) ready-made (and relatively expensive) dryer with vertical heat elements and warm/hot air blown horizontally across each tray of food.

The specifics for individual foods will say to start at a relatively lower temperature (this, to avoid case-hardening), then raising the heat after an hour or so, and lowering it again during the last one-third of drying time to prevent any "cooked" flavor, caramelizing or scorching. However, one manual that bases its directions on a particular dryer with horizontal forced air pleads for a temperature of not more than 120 F/49 C for as long as all day plus perhaps all night—and with no pre-drying treatments. (The products from this treatment and dryer are apparently an abundance of extra-dry snack foods, rather than small crops.)

For drying purposes a conventional oven fluctuates in such swoops that it's simpler to set its thermostat at 140 F/60 C, and not change the heat unless the food may be tending to caramelize or cook toward the end of the drying time; then of course the temperature is lowered by 10 degrees F/5.6 C. The convection oven may also be set initially at 140 F/60 C and let to carry on; with its fan, its times will be shorter than for the regular range oven.

This 140 F/60 C is the best across-the-board temperature if your dryer cannot be fine-tuned to changes, because it results in a safe product if not always a thrilling one. Aside from this, there is no workable way of taking temperatures/times from one kind of dryer and coming up with the precise number of hours that would be needed for the whole process in a different dryer: you'll just have to rely on the tests for doneness, and be prepared to make periodic checks. (As an example out of doors, Alex Wilson estimates the times required in a tiered solar dryer like the one he rough-sketched to be "about 70 percent of sun-time.")

• • DRYING IN MICROWAVE OVENS: Drying successfully is not possible in a microwave oven, except for herbs and some leaf vegetables. Reason: Foods seem *overcooked*, rather than dried, and they taste like it.

The *How* of drying by artificial heat is simple if you keep in mind a few *Why's*.

1. In the usual home dryer—which has the heat source directly under the box, and relies on natural draft sometimes augmented by a small fan— the temperature at the top of the stack is less than the temperature at the bottom, near the heater.

   So always keep track of the temperature at the lowest tray, so you can use this heat as the base for judging the temperature higher up.

   And rotate the trays up or down every ½ hour to correct this difference and ensure even drying.

2. Fresh food won't dry well if it is exposed to too much heat too soon: either it will case-harden—its exterior being seared and toughened, so natural moisture can't exude and be evaporated—or it will cook, with the cells rupturing and creating an unattractive product. (As a general thing, the juicier the food, the more likely it is to rupture, and the lower is the temperature at which it should be started in the dryer.)

   So if you add fresh food to a batch already drying, always put it in at the top of the dryer.

   If the whole load is fresh, have the heat inside the cabinet 20 or so degrees below the maximum temperature you'll hold it at later. After probably not much more than 1 hour, start increasing the heat by 10 degrees each ½ hour till you reach the recommended maximum.

3. But for the majority of its total drying time the food must have enough heat to kill the growth cells of some spoilers, as well as to remove moisture that lets other ones thrive. This means that, no matter how low the temperature at which you start food in order to prevent case-hardening, etc., you have to raise the heat to a killing level and hold it there long enough to make it effective.

When the food has reached the ⅔-dry stage, tend it with extra care to make sure it won't scorch. Keep rotating trays away from the heat source. If you need to, during the last 1 hour reduce the heat by 10 degrees or so, but stick to the 140-F/60-C rule just above.

Handling Food in a Dryer

Line or oil the trays—see the comments on tray bottoms under "Equipment for Drying"; spread prepared food on them one layer deep if it's in large pieces, not more than ½ inch deep if it's small. Place halved, pitted fruit with the cut side up (rich juice will have collected in the hollows if it was sulfured).

At this point newcomers to drying by artificial heat may want to weigh a sample tray of food for comparison with the weight of the same trayful after it's been in the dryer for a while, as a help in judging how much moisture has been lost.

Stagger the trays on the slides: one pushed as far back as possible, the next one as far forward as possible, etc. (as in the sketch earlier).

Check the food every ½ hour, stirring it with your fingers, separating bits that are stuck together. Turn over large pieces halfway through the drying time—but wait until any juice in the hollows has disappeared before turning apricots, peaches, pears, etc. Pieces near the front and back ends of the trays usually start to dry first: move them to the center of the trays.

If you add fresh food to a load already in progress, put the new tray at the top of the stack.

Make needed room for fresh food by combining nearly dry material in deeper layers on trays in the center of the dryer; it can be finished here without worry, but keep stirring it.

Using an Oven

As far as you can, use an oven as you would a dryer, following general procedures and the specific instructions for each food.

Leave the upper (broiling) element of an electric oven turned off, and use only a low-temperature Bake setting for drying. With some electric ranges this broiling element stays partially on even with a Bake setting: if yours does this, simply put a cookie sheet on a rack in the uppermost shelf position to deflect the direct heat from the food being dried.

Most gas ovens have only one burner (at the bottom) for both baking and broiling. If your gas oven has an upper burner, don't turn it on.

Gas ovens are always vented, but electrics may not be. If your electric oven isn't vented, during drying time leave the door ajar at its first stop position.

If your oven isn't thermostatically controlled, hang an oven thermometer where you can see it on the shelf nearest the source of heat, leave the door ajar—and be prepared to hover more than usual over the food that's drying.

Preheat the oven to 140 F/60 C. *If the oven cannot be set this low, skip the lowest slide you would otherwise be using: keep the bottom tray at least 8 inches from the heat source.*

Don't overload the oven: with limited ventilation (even with a fan aimed toward the partly opened door) it can take as much fuel to dry a batch too big as might be used to dry two fairly modest batches.

Room-drying

Also done indoors is what can be called, for simplicity, room-drying. By this method food is hung in a warm room—the kitchen or the attic—for the days required to dry the material. Old-timers would suspend racks of drying food above the big wood-burning range, finish off a flitch of beef near by, and festoon strings of apple or pumpkin rings near the ceilings. Herbs are still usually dried in attics or the kitchens of country houses, hung either in the open or in paper bags to protect them from dust.

In extremely dry areas it may be feasible to stack-dry certain fruits and vegetables indoors, following enough time in sun or dryer to get them better than halfway along. Stack the trays with 6 inches of space between them, open windows to allow a free circulation of air, and force a draft across the trays with an electric fan. Shift the trays end for end occasionally and turn the food to ensure even drying.

Pre-drying Treatments for Produce

Before being dried at home by any method, fruits make a better product if they undergo one or more of the treatments given hereafter, while all vegetables are treated to stop the organic action that allows low-acid foods to spoil.

And, still speaking generally, a pre-drying treatment for fruits is optional, but the pre-drying treatment for vegetables is a must.

The optional treatments for fruit involve (1) temporary anti-oxidants, to hold their color while they're peeled/pitted/sliced; (2) blanching in steam or in syrup as a longer-range means of helping to save color and nutrients; (3) very quick blanching—either in boiling water or steam (lye is not recommended)— to remove or crack the skins; (4) sulfuring as longest-range protection for some nutrients and for color. We'll sum up for or against these fruit treatments as best we can after we describe them. Then it's up to you to use them or not.

The treatment for vegetables is steam-blanching. The quick dunk in boiling water that's used in freezing is not adequate to protect them against spoilage in drying; and the much longer boiling time needed here would waterlog the material, in addition to leaching away a number of its nutrients.

The following descriptions are given in the order that the treatments are likely to occur in handling produce for drying: they're not necessarily in order of importance.

Temporary Anti-oxidant Treatment

Even though you intend to blanch or sulfur certain fruits to protect them during the long haul of drying and storage, chances are that you'll want to do something to prevent their darkening piecemeal while you're actually cutting a batch up.

The Good Ascorbic-Acid Coat

Pure ascorbic acid is our best safe anti-oxidant, and is used a lot in preparing fruits for freezing (q.v.). Use it here too. But with the difference that the solution will be somewhat stronger, and thus food coated with it can hold its color in transit in the open air for a longer time.

One cup of the solution will treat around 5 quarts of cut fruit, so prepare your amount accordingly. Sprinkle it over the fruit as you proceed with peeling, pitting, coring, slicing, etc., turning the pieces over and over gently to make sure each is coated thoroughly.

For apples: dissolve 3 teaspoons of pure crystalline ascorbic acid in each 1 cup of cold water.

For peaches, apricots, pears, nectarines: dissolve 1½ teaspoons of pure crystalline ascorbic acid in each 1 cup of cold water.

If the variety of fruit you're working with is likely to become especially rusty-looking when the flesh is exposed to air, it's O.K. to increase the concentration of ascorbic acid as needed. The proportions above usually do the job.

The commercial anti-oxidant mixtures containing ascorbic acid don't work as effectively, volume for volume, as the pure Vitamin C does, but they're often easier to come by. Follow the directions for Cut Fruits on the package.

Blanching Fruits in Heavy Syrup

It seems excessive to precook fruit in heavy syrup in order to help prevent discoloration while drying—particularly when we have better ways to do the job. But if you want to turn fruit into an extra-sweet confection, here is the syrup-blanch most often described for apples, apricots, figs, nectarines, peaches, pears, plums and prunes.

Make a syrup of roughly 1 part sweetener to 1 part water, using refined or raw sugar, or part corn syrup or honey (and see "Sugar Syrups for Canning Fruits," Chapter 5); heat it to 212 F/100 C, and in it simmer the fruits for 10 to 15 minutes, depending on the size of the pieces. Remove the kettle from the heat and let the fruit stand in the hot syrup for about 15 minutes more. Then lift the fruit out and drain it well on paper toweling to remove as much surface moisture as you can. Save the syrup for the next batch.

Dry the fruit by whichever method you like. Take extra care that it doesn't stick to the trays, or scorch during the last stage of drying in artificial heat. Fruit treated this way is more attractive than usual to insects, so cover it well during sun-drying. And package it well for storage in a really cool, dry place.

Treating Fruit Skins Without Lye

Not only is lye tricky to work with in its own right (do see especially "Warnings About Lye" in Chapter 23, describing making Hominy and Soap), but the alkali in soda compounds hurts many B vitamins and Vitamin C.

A very quick dip in boiling water, *quite apart from the steam-blanching that helps keep the color and nutrients of certain cut fruits,* works well instead of the lye treatment. And it's safer for you and for your food.

FOR CHECKING THE SKINS

Nature provides a wax-like coating on the skins of cherries, figs, grapes, prunes and small dark plums, and certain firm berries like blueberries and huckleberries, and they all dry better if this waterproofing substance is removed beforehand.

The chances of case-hardening and rupturing (q.v.) are also reduced if the relatively tough skins of such fruits and berries are cracked minutely in many places; this is called "checking," and it allows internal moisture to be drawn through to the surface and there to be evaporated.

Because the 30 to 60 seconds required for the de-waxing and checking operation is often too short to let live steam be effective for the contents of the blanching basket, the answer is to gather not more than 1 pound of berries loosely in cheesecloth and hold them in 1 gallon of briskly boiling water for 30 seconds; lift out, dunk in plenty of fresh cold water to stop any further cooking action; shake off water, and carry on with the drying. If the amount of food—

small in size or cut small—is kept to a maximum of 1 pound, and the water is at least 1 gallon and boiling its head off, there is virtually no lag between immersing the food and the return to a full rolling boil; so 30 seconds is feasible. At altitudes higher than 3500 feet/1067 meters, add boiling time to total 30 seconds for each additional 1000 feet/305 meters.

Some people use food-grade pickling lime—calcium hydroxide (see Chapter 17, under "Firming Agents")—in boiling water to check the skins. Use 1 gallon of water, have only 1 pound of food; make up the solution according to the instructions on the package for firming pickles.

Length of the dip depends on the relative toughness of the fruits' skins (cranberries are tougher-skinned than currants, for instance). Lay absorbent toweling on the fruit to remove excess moisture from their surface, and continue with the next step in handling the specific fruits.

For Peeling

Routine peeling of any fruit except apples isn't necessary for making a good dried product (see "When to Peel" for fruits), but if you feel that you must remove the skins from peaches, and even from apricots and nectarines, simply dip them, a few at a time, in boiling water for 30 to 60 seconds—ample time for firm-ripe fruit—cool them quickly in cold water, and pull their skins off by hand.

Steam-blanching Before Drying

On the whole, vegetables to be dried are blanched in full steam at 212 degrees F/100 C for longer time than they are blanched, either in steam or boiling water, before being frozen. The length of blanching time is given for each vegetable in the individual instructions, *as is a recommendation for high-altitude blanching.*

Steam-blanching also is suggested for certain fruits as an aid to discouraging oxidation, and for softening berries, as well as for checking (cracking) the skins of grapes, prunes and figs instead of treating them with lye. In addition to stopping the decomposing action of the enzymes and helping to fix the color of the food, steam-blanching protects some of the nutrients and loosens the tissues so drying is actually quicker.

Put several inches of water in a large kettle that has a close-fitting lid; heat the water to boiling, and set over it—high enough to keep clear of the water—a rack or wire basket holding a layer of cut food not more than 2 inches deep. Cover, and let the food steam for half the time required; then test it to make sure that each piece is reached by steam. A sample from the center of the layer should be wilted and feel soft and heated through when it has been blanched enough.

In a pinch you can use a cheesecloth bag, skimpily loaded with food, and placed on the rack to steam. Be careful not to bunch the food so much that steam can't get at all of it easily.

Remove the food and spread it on paper toweling or clean cloths to remove the excess moisture while you steam the next load; lay toweling over it while it waits for further treatment or to go on the drying trays.

A Basic Pre-drying Blanch in a Microwave Oven

Each microwave oven comes with its own explicit directions for use, and you should follow the instructions for your particular oven. This is just sense, not a way for us to sidestep a bit of research: aside from their increasing sophistication, ovens differ in capacity and wattage required to run them, and both these factors affect the ovens' treatment of food.

You can't go badly wrong in blanching in a microwave, though, and we offer a rule-of-thumb that is effective—even notably effective at altitudes of 3500 feet/1067 meters or more. Treat *only 1 pound* of prepared—peeled/split/shredded—*food at a time,* and in very little water; of course the container must be suitable for a microwave oven. Re-arrange the food once, to ensure even heating. The blanching will take from around 2½ to 6 minutes (see individual instructions under "Prepare") depending on the density of the food or if it tends to mat. The moment the blanching time is up, remove the food and stop any further cooking action by cooling it quickly in ice water; drain, pat off water with paper towels, and proceed to dry it.

Sulfur, Spoilage and Nutrients

For many years sulfur has been used to preserve the color of drying fruits whose flesh darkens when exposed to air. The fruits generally treated with sulfur have been apples, apricots, nectarines, peaches and pears; light-fleshed varieties of cherries, figs, plums and prunes have also been treated with sulfur to prevent oxidation, though not so routinely. Meanwhile it was noted that unsulfured fruits appear more likely to sour, get moldy or be attacked by insects during prolonged drying or in storage than is the case with the sulfur-treated dried fruits.

Further, sulfur is a mineral essential for life, and therefore is not harmful *per se* in the quantities used in home-drying (which allow plenty of leeway). The sulfur forms sulfurous acid when it unites with the water in the fruits' tissues, and the sulfurous acid evaporates during prolonged sun-drying, during storage, and from cooking; the residue that is eaten is turned into an innocuous compound that is then excreted. The more strongly acid the food, the greater is the power of sulfurous acid to inhibit the growth of molds and the bacteria that cause souring.

Further, nutritionists have published the results of research showing that, among others, Vitamins A (carotene), B_1 (thiamine) and C (ascorbic acid) are destroyed by exposure to air, but that sulfur aids in retention of A and C when they're hit by air, but helps to destroy what's left of B_1 (which often is present in negligible amounts anyway, compared with A and C).

• SUMMARIZING: These points seem to be adequate support for the consensus of the country's leading authorities on home-drying—to sulfur certain cut fruits to ensure better storage, less darkening, and less loss of Vitamins A and C. Sulfuring is optional: the results of drying without sulfur may be disappointing as to color, flavor and some aspects of nutrition, but food safety relies mainly on how competently these fruits are dried.

A Poor Way to Sulfur (Soaking)

There are two ways generally given for sulfuring at home, and we'll mention the quicker but unsatisfactory method first, to get it out of the way.

As in all soaks, cut fruits held in a sulfite solution lose some of their water-soluble nutrients and tend to get waterlogged; in addition, the sulfur compound may often penetrate the tissues unevenly.

Further, for us the available instructions offered too wide a spread for comfort. The substances were given variously as sodium sulfite, sodium bisulfite and potassium metabilsufite, with the amount to use in each 1 gallon of water ranging from 1½ teaspoons on up to 3½ tablespoons. And soaking times, seemingly not geared closely enough to the strength of the solutions, were from 15 to 30 minutes.

How to Sulfur Well (Fumes, in a Box)

We'll describe this at some length because, having decided that *sulfuring is O.K. in certain cases,* we experimented with the mechanics of the procedure in order to amplify the sketchy instructions found so far.

The main bother in burning pure sulfur for the dioxide treatment is that the raw fumes irritate eyes and breathing passages, and therefore the business must be done outdoors in the open air. (All to the good, though, is the fact that they are so irritating: one whiff and you duck away—as you do from ammonia or activated lye, though perhaps not as fast—so you're not likely to keep on breathing them unknowingly.)

Otherwise, it's very simple and direct. And fun, if you relax and think of sulfur as something the ancients knew well, for it's the brimstone of the Bible. Anyway, sulfur first melts—at around 240 F/116 C—becoming a brown goo before it ignites and burns with a clear blue flame that produces the acrid sulfur dioxide that penetrates evenly and is easy to judge the effect of. The usual amount to use is 1 level teaspoon burned for each 1 pound of prepared fruit.

Local drugstores had several kinds of dry sulfur, but we chose the "sublimed" variety—99½ percent pure, to be taken internally mixed with molasses (the classic folk tonic); it's a soft yellow powder with no taste and the faintest of scents that's nothing like the rotten-egg odor of hydrogen sulfide. The 2-ounce box was enough to do 16 to 18 pounds of prepared fruit. Also, from the hardware store we got a 4-ounce cake of 100 percent refined sulfur (with a short wick to start it melting and burning, because it's a fumigating candle to use in sealed rooms to get rid of bugs in the woodwork). This cake we found much harder than the powder to gauge the dose of: its weight figured in teaspoons, the amount of sulfur needed for a batch of fruit took longer to burn than the time required for exposure to the fumes.

Loading and stacking the trays. You'll be weighing your prepared fruit to determine how much sulfur to use in the treatment, and thus you can keep the batch within limits of what your sulfuring box will handle effectively. Nor should you sulfur more food in one session than your drying arrangements will accommodate as soon as the sulfuring is done—6 trays' worth, for example, if you use an indoor dryer the size of the one described earlier. Spread the fruit one layer in thickness on the trays (which *don't* have metal bottoms), placing any convex pieces with their hollow side up in order to prevent loss of the rich juice that collects during treatment (or press the halves inside out, as in Fermenia's Apricots, later). Limit each sulfuring batch to food of the same type and size: you won't be able to shuffle the food around to compensate for different exposure times, as you do in a dryer. And don't overload the trays or crowd the sulfuring box, because it's easier in the long run to deal with two short stacks, widely spaced, than with one stack too tall and inadequately spaced.

Put the bottom tray on blocks of some kind to raise it at least 4 inches above ground. Separate the trays above it with wooden spacers to hold them 3 inches or so apart. Allow for 6 inches of clearance between the top of the stack and the sulfuring box that will be inverted over it.

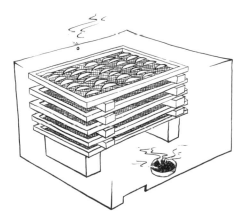

The sulfuring box. This you can make from the same materials used for the indoor dryer (q.v.); or you can cover a slatted crate snugly with building paper; or you can use a stout, large carton of the sort that household appliances are shipped in. The box should be tall enough to cover an adequately spaced stack of up to 6 trays, and be about 12 inches longer than the trays from front to back so there'll be room for the sulfuring dish *beside* the stack.

At the bottom near one corner, cut out a slot 6 inches wide by 1 inch high if the box is large, 3 × 1 inch if it's just the average supermarket carton; this will be the only air intake needed to keep the sulfur burning, and you'll cover the slot after the sulfur is consumed. Near the top of the side opposite the intake slot, make a hole the diameter of a pencil; this also will be covered when the sulfur has burned. (The need for this tiny upper hole is Norman Rogers's discovery: it wasn't mentioned in the various directions we started out with, but he found that, without it, the sulfur stopped burning prematurely and required relighting; and the escape of fumes through it was negligible.)

Lighting and burning. Loose sulfur powder burns better than the same amount in a paper spill.

Also, the sulfur burned best—i.e., steadily, without relighting, quickly and completely—when the powder was in a smooth layer *not more than ½ inch deep,* settled by tunking the bottom of the burning dish. And the depth, not the total amount, apparently determines the rate of burning.

Norman said he wasn't bothered by the little sulfur dioxide that escaped when he tilted the box to snake out the sulfuring dish to check on the burning. And the brimstone smell had evanesced from his hands within an hour after he was through with his experiments.

The sulfuring container should be set at the side or in front of the stack: if it were underneath, the food on the bottom tray directly above it would discolor from concentrated exposure to even the small amount of smoke involved in the combustion.

Whatever you have for a burning dish, it should be perfectly clean before each use. Heavy crockery dishes are easiest to clean, and do not corrode. Make sure that the dish is not too deep, because if the sides are too high in proportion to the burning surface of the powder, the flame can smother for lack of air. A flat round dish 3 inches in diameter takes about 12 teaspoons of powdered sublimed sulfur smoothed ½ inch deep; a 4-inch one takes about 18, and a 5-incher about 24 teaspoons.

How much sulfur? Weigh the prepared fruit before spreading it in a single layer on the treatment trays, and use 1 teaspoon of powdered pure sulfur for each 1 pound of fruit. This 1-for-1 ratio is conservative but, so far as we can find out, it's adequate for the average small-family operation; much better to adjust sulfuring *time* to your method than to increase the sulfur you burn per pound.

How long to sulfur? Sulfuring time varies according to the texture of the fruit, whether it's peeled, how big the pieces are, and whether it's exposed for a long time in air—as in sun- and shade-drying outdoors—or has a relatively short exposure, as in a drying box or an oven. Specific times are given in the instructions for individual fruits.

Start to count sulfuring time *after* the sulfur has finished burning, which will take about 15 minutes (see above), and you have tightly closed off the air-intake slot at the bottom of the box and the tiny breathing hole at the top. The reason: the necessary amount of sulfur dioxide must first be created by total combustion of the sulfur which has been measured for the weight of the batch being treated; then the fumes must be given time to reach and penetrate the surfaces of the fruit on the stacked trays. With the sulfuring box made airtight, you simply leave it inverted over the stacked trays for the required period.

In general, apples, apricots, peaches and pears are sulfured twice as long for sun-drying as they are for an indoor dryer. And a practical rule-of-thumb is to sulfur small slices of these fruits for the box dryer for a minimum of 20 to 30 minutes, and larger pieces for comparatively longer. Therefore, since we *recommend sulfuring for sun-drying* because of the extended time in vitamin-destructive open air, these fruits would be sulfured for about 60 minutes if they're to be sun-dried as slices, with double that sulfuring when they're quartered, and more than two hours when they're halved.

On the other hand, home-drying done in an indoor box or an oven is often a small-batch affair—and in such cases it's not always feasible to get cranked up to for the sulfuring operation. Though not as effective over-all as sulfuring, there are other measures that can be substituted for all or part of the sulfur treatment for fruit to be dried by artificial heat in small batches; they're correlated in the "Pre-drying Treatments for Produce" earlier in this chapter.

Unloading the sulfur box. Stand to windward of the box so the fumes won't come your way, reach across the top, and tilt the whole thing toward you until the box rests on its side or end: it's like lifting the lid of a Pressure canner to let the steam escape away from your direction.

Remove the trays from the top, being careful not to spill any juice that has collected in the hollows of the fruit. If sulfuring was done on trays that fit a dryer, just slide them as is into the preheated drying box or oven; otherwise lift the fruit on to trays all ready for going immediately out in the sun or in artificial heat.

Tests for Dryness in Produce

According to *Composition of Foods,* none of the fruits we'll be telling how to home-dry has less than 80 percent water in its fresh raw state, and the average comparable water content of the vegetables is not less than 85 percent.

The safe maximum percentages of water to leave in home-dried produce are: no more than 10 percent for vegetables, and no more than 20 percent for fruits. Commercially dried fruits often contain more water—especially when they're "tenderized"—but also they may contain additives other than simple sulfur dioxide to protect against spoilage from the higher content of moisture. But we don't have the food industry's highly refined means of testing for and controlling moisture, so we rely on appearance and feel to judge dryness.

Fruits generally can be considered adequately dry when no wetness can be squeezed from a piece of it when cut; and when it has become rather tough and pliable; and when a few pieces squeezed together fall apart when the pressure is released. "Leathery"—"suède-like"—"springy"—these are descriptions you'll see in the individual instructions. Several, such as figs and cherries, also are slightly "sticky."

Vegetables are generally "brittle" or "tough to brittle" when they're dry enough; an occasional one is "crisp." Again, instructions for specific vegetables will tell you what to look for.

When they are very nearly dry, some foods will rattle on the trays; this is another thing to check on when they're in natural heat/draft or in a dryer.

And then there's the ⅔ *dry* judgment. Without using refined correlations of drying rate against percentage of natural water and weight of solids before drying, we offer this rough rule-of-thumb: Compare the weight of a fresh sample of produce with its weight at some point during the total drying period—if it has lost ½ of its original weight, consider it ⅔ dry for your purposes.

Finally, foods still warm from the sun or hot from the dryer will seem softer, more pliable, more moist than they actually are. *So cool a test handful a few minutes before deciding it's done.*

Post–drying Treatments for Produce

Even after a sample from each tray of food has shown no moisture when cut and pressed, and feels the way its test says it should, you can't take for granted that the whole batch is uniformly dry. And especially if it's been dried outdoors do you need to get rid of any spoilers—airborne micro-organisms or bugs you can see—that may have got to it somewhere along the line.

Conditioning

This makes sense particularly for food done in a dryer because there's often more chance of spotty results than in sun-drying, and you'll want moisture content equalized between under- and overdried pieces.

Cool the food on the trays, then pour it all into a large, open, nonporous container *that's not aluminum*—a big crock, enamel- or graniteware canner, even a washtub lined first with food-grade plastic and then with clean sheeting (washtubs are generally galvanized). Have the containers raised on trestles or tables, and in a warm, dry, airy, well-screened, animal-proof room.

Stir the food once a day—twice if you can manage to—for 10 days or 2 weeks, depending on the size of the pieces. It's O.K. to add freshly dried food to the conditioning batch, but naturally not if the food in a container is almost ready to store.

Fruits, usually being in larger pieces (and therefore more likely to need finishing off) than vegetables, need more conditioning time.

Pasteurizing

Pasteurizing is recommended strongly for killing insect eggs deposited on foods that have been dried in open-air/sun. It is effective as well for re-treating vegetables held in storage, although *if the vegetables show ANY SIGNS OF MOLD they should be destroyed.* Some molds on vegetables produce aflatoxin, a dreaded food poisoning.

Don't bother cranking up the dryer for this, and don't do large amounts at a time: use an oven with a thermometer in it, and time the process.

Preheat the oven to 175 F/80 C. Spread the food loosely not more than 1 inch deep on the trays; don't do more than two trays' worth at the same time. Heat brittle-dried vegetables, cut small, for 10 minutes at 175 F/80 C; treat fruits—cut larger and therefore needing more time—for 15 minutes at 175 F/80 C.

Remove each pasteurized batch and spread it out to cool on clean toweling, etc. Cover lightly with cheesecloth to keep dried food clean. Package one batch while other batches are pasteurizing.

STORAGE

The seizure actions and notices of judgments are among the fascinating contents of the *FDA Consumer,* telling, as they do, of food condemned and destroyed by authorities because it contained rodent or insect filth or, actually worse, mold—and the deadly aflatoxin is a by-product of a mold. On a small scale, the householder who stores the family's supplies of dried food can face the same hazards. Here are some ways to avoid loss through spoilage or contamination.

First, hold your food in small quantities: 1-gallon glass jars with screwtop lids; or in 5-gallon *food-grade* freezer bags that are then stored in a metal container with a close-fitting lid. *Do not use heavy plastic trash or garbage bags,* or *plastic barrels,* or *galvanized metal barrels/trash cans* unless they are well lined with food-grade material that will not let any acid in the food come into contact with the metal. And remember that galvanized metal contains zinc, and this usually means cadmium: and cadmium is bad stuff to store food in. (See "Those Space-age Plastics" in Chapter 4, "On Guard!")

Check your supplies on a frequent schedule, to make sure that no part of your food has become damp or contaminated. (The conditioning treatment is a great safeguard here; as is pasteurizing to destroy any insect eggs.)

When the dry food—conditioned well, and pasteurized if necessary—is thoroughly cool, it will go into its safe and critter-proof containers; if it is still warm, it is likely to sweat and cause trouble. Then the containers will be labeled and go to storage in a cool, dry place.

Three temperatures are pivotal in the storing of food: freezing; 48 F/9 C, when insects start to become active; and when fats melt, about 95 F/35 C. The lowest temperature short of freezing is hard to maintain, so it makes sense to consider 40 F/4 C a low easily held, and 60 F/16 C a reasonable top. Temperatures more than 70 F/21 C should be avoided.

DESSICANTS

Assuming that your plastics are food-grade—and therefore do not contain any chemicals that would not be good for you to eat—your next problem could be how to keep large amounts of food, like grains, dry.

For the average householder, the best way is to examine the food, re-pasteurizing it if necessary. Or you could use carbon dioxide (CO_2)—which is the "dry ice" that reduces oxygen in the stored contents and hence retards rancidity or spoilage in a container of food. See Chapter 25 for how to locate this chemical (which you can also use to keep frozen food ice cold in an emergency); and when you handle it, take care lest you suffer frostbite. The Co_2 is placed near the top of the contents, because, its gas being heavier than air, the fumes sink down through the food.

For controlling moisture in grain or grain products stored in large containers, a natural dessicant of proven worth is "diatomaceous earth," also known as *Kieselguhr,* which absorbs up to 4 times its weight in water (moisture) without becoming fluid itself.

Silica gel is often recommended as a dessicant; it's gettable at craft-supply stores where it is bought by people who dry flowers. It seems quite expensive to us, but perhaps the cost is offset by the fact that it can be dried out in a slow oven and re-used often.

Simple, and cheaper, is to put in the bottom of a small glass storage jar a shallow layer of clean crushed concrete that has no added coloring or deodorizers: that's right, we're talking about catbox litter. It's not food-grade, so protect the food with coffee-filter paper trimmed enough larger than the circumference of the (small) jar to allow it to bend up the sides of the container for an inch or so. This paper will allow transfer of any moisture from the food down to the crushed concrete.

FUMIGANTS

Some experts in home-storage of quite large amounts of grains, especially, use carbon tetrachloride (CCl_4)—which we saw around in the old days to be used as a fabric cleaner and spot-remover. A few drops of this substance on a small wad of cotton is placed in the barrel of grain, etc. BE WARY OF THIS SUBSTANCE: In some States it is banned from sale to the general public. We mention it only because it was brought to *PFB*'s attention, and we cannot recommend it.

DRYING FRUITS

The following instructions are merely individual applications of the principles, methods and treatments described up till now in this section, and newcomers to drying are likely to have better results if they look at the introductory *Why-How* (and sometimes pro/con) before they tackle specific fruits.

In general below, sulfuring is strongly recommended for all cut fruits that are *sun-dried,* in order to help save important vitamins, prevent insect infestations and hold color; steam-blanching is recommended for fruits processed in a *dryer;* a temporary ascorbic-acid coating is suggested for certain fruits that oxidize readily, whether dried in the sun or in artificial heat outdoors; some whole fruits are "checked" with boiling water to crack their skins; pasteurizing is recommended for sun-dried fruits, to kill off any bugs that have got to them. All these treatments are optional: they are included because they result in a more nutritious and attractive product.

It is assumed that all the fruits are firm-ripe, without blemishes, and have been washed carefully in cold water as a preliminary to preparation.

See "Tests for Dryness in Produce," earlier.

COOKING DRIED FRUITS

Pour boiling water over them in a saucepan *just to cover*—no more now: they shouldn't be drowned, and you can always add more if you need to—and simmer the fruit, covered, for 10 to 15 minutes, depending on the size of the pieces. Remove from heat and let cool, still covered. Sweeten to taste at the very end of cooking, or when removed from heat (sugar tends to toughen fruit fibers in cooking). For best flavor, chill the fruit overnight before serving.

If the fruit is to be "reconstituted" to use in a cooked dish (a pie or a cream dessert, say), put it in a bowl, add boiling water just to the top of the fruit; cover; and let it soak up the water for several hours, or until tender. Add water sparingly and only if the pieces seem still to be tough, because the liquid is full of good things and should be included in the recipe as if it were natural juice.

APPLES

Best for drying are late-autumn or early-winter varieties, including: Baldwin, Ben Davis, Northern Spy, Spitzenburg; then Winesap, Jonathan, Greening, Rome Beauty, both Delicious, the Russets.

Prepare. Peel, core, slice in ⅛-inch rings. As you go, coat slices with strong ascorbic-acid solution to hold color temporarily.

Dryer. Steam-blanch 5 minutes; remove excess moisture. Begin them at 130 F/54 C; raise gradually to 150 F/66 C after the first hour; when nearly dry, reduce to 140 F/60 C. Test dry. Condition. Package; store. Average total drying time: up to 6 hours, depending on size of slices.

Open-air/sun. Prepare as above, using ascorbic-acid coating. If not steam-blanched for 5 minutes, sulfur for 60 minutes; if blanched, sulfur for 30 minutes. Proceed with drying. Test dry. Pasteurize. Package; store. *Solar dryer:* about 70 percent of open-air/sun time.

Room-drying. Prepare as above. Steam-blanch 5 minutes *and* sulfur 30 minutes; or sulfur only for 60 minutes. Thread on clean string, and festoon near the ceiling of a warm, dry, well-ventilated room (attic), or above the cookstove (kitchen). Test dry. Pasteurize.

The slices may also be dried on stacked trays with an electric fan blowing across them.

DRY TEST: Leathery, suède-like; no moisture when cut and squeezed.

Apricots

Pick before they are so ripe they drop from the tree.

Prepare. Halve and stone. Hold against oxidizing with ascorbic-acid coating.

Dryer. Steam-blanch halves 15 minutes, slices 5 minutes. Remove excess moisture and start in the dryer at 130 F/54 C, raise gradually after the first hour to 150 F/66 C. Reduce to 140 F/60 C for last hour or when nearly dry. Test dry. Condition; store. Average total drying time: up to 14 hours for halves, up to 6 hours for slices.

Open-air/sun. Prepare as above with ascorbic-acid coat. If steam-blanching (above, as for a dryer) sulfur slices 30 minutes, halves 90 minutes. If not blanched, sulfur slices 1 hour, halves 2 hours. Remove halves carefully to drying trays so as not to spill juice in the hollows, and place cut-side up in the drying trays. Turn when all visible juice has disappeared. Test dry. Pasteurize; store. *Solar dryer:* about 70 percent of open-air/sun time.

DRY TEST. Leathery, pieces fall apart after squeezing; no moisture when cut.

Fermenia's Apricots

This description of how the Indians of Las Trampas, New Mexico—around 8000 feet/2438 meters high—prepare and dry apricots is included in the Self Reliance Foundation film *Sun Dried Foods* (see Chapter 25). *PFB* visited a number of pueblos, and found that this method is general at high-country subsistence farms in the Rockies of the Southwest.

Prepare. Wash apricots and dunk them, whole, in a bath of warm salt water—about 2 tablespoons pickling salt to each 1 gallon of water—for a few minutes to preserve color, Fermenia says. Then she tears them in half, removes the pit and—as the photograph shows—presses against the skin-side of each half to make the cut side open out to expose maximum inner surface to the drying sun and air.

Open-air/sun. No blanching or sulfuring; halves are placed on racks in full sun for several hours—but not so long that they case-harden; then the racks are moved to a south-facing patio shaded overhead. (Fruit dried on cloths on a table, Fermenia said, must be turned over; turning is not necessary on the racks.) When it tests dry, she does not pasteurize the fruit, but does let it condition for several days in the dry air of her *dispensa* (pantry); it is then stored in air-tight containers and held in a cool place.

Fermenia said that the fruit is soaked in water to cover, then simmered (water is added if needed to prevent scorching) until it's reconstituted. Sweetening, spices, even other fruits, are added to be dessert, or the fruit can become filling for sweet tarts and pies.

BERRIES, FIRM

Prepare. Check (crack) the skins of blueberries, huckleberries, currants and cranberries, etc. by dipping for 15 to 30 seconds (depending on toughness of skin) in rapidly boiling water. Plunge into cold water. Remove excess moisture.

Dryer. Start at 120 F/49 C, increase to 130 F/54 C after one hour, then to 140 F/60 C; they will rattle on the trays when nearly dry. Keep at 140 F/60 C until dry. Test dry. Condition; store. Average total drying time: up to 4 hours.

Open-air/sun. Check the skins as above for the dryer. Remove excess moisture and put on trays one layer deep in the sun. Test dry. Pasteurize; store. *Solar dryer:* about 70 percent of open-air/sun time.

DRY TEST. Hard. No moisture when crushed.

BERRIES, SOFT

There are so many better ways to use these—canned, frozen, in preserves—that there's not much use in drying them. Strawberries are especially blah and unrecognizable when dried.

CHERRIES

If not pitting cherries, check their skins with a 15 to 30-second dunk in boiling water; cool immediately. Some people syrup-blanch (q.v.) before drying cherries.

Dryer. Remove excess moisture from checking treatment. Start at 120 F/49 C for one hour, increase gradually to 145 F/63 C and hold there until nearly dry. Reduce to 135 F/57 C the last hour if danger of scorching. Test dry. Pasteurize. Cool and store. Total drying time: up to 6 hours.

Open-air/sun. Pit. Sulfur for 20 minutes. Dry. Test dry. Pasteurize. Cool and store. *Solar dryer:* about 70 percent of open-air/sun time.

DRY TEST. Leathery and sticky.

FIGS

Prepare. Small figs or ones that are partly dry on the tree may be dried whole. Large juicy figs are halved.

Dryer. Check skins by a quick dunk in boiling water for 30 to 45 seconds. Cool quickly. If cut in half, steam-blanch for 20 minutes. Some people syrup-blanch (q.v.) whole figs before drying. To dry, start at 120 F., increase temperature after the first hour to 145 F/63 C. When nearly dry, reduce to 130 F/54 C. Test dry. Condition. Cool and store. Total average drying time: up to 5 hours for halves.

Open-air/sun. Check the skins as above if drying whole. Sulfur light-colored varieties (like Kadota) for 1 hour before drying. If figs are to be halved, do not check the skins—instead, steam-blanch the halves for 20 minutes and then sulfur for 30 minutes. Test dry. Pasteurize. Cool and store. *Solar dryer:* about 70 percent of open-air/sun time.

DRY TEST. Leathery, with flesh pliable; slightly sticky to the touch, but they don't cling together after squeezing.

GRAPES

Use only Thompson or other seedless varieties for drying.

Prepare. Check the skins by dipping 15 to 30 seconds in boiling water and cooling immediately. Proceed as for whole Cherries.

Dryer. Proceed as for Cherries. Total average drying time: up to 8 hours.

Open-air/sun. Handle like Cherries, but don't sulfur. *Solar dryer:* about 70 percent of open-air/sun time.

LEATHERS (PEACH, ETC.)

These sheets of pliable dried pulp may be made from virtually all fruits and berries, with peaches, apples and wild blackberries leading the field. Tomatoes, especially the meaty, pear-shaped varieties, also make good leather. The following is a general rule, so experiment with only small batches until you get the fresh, tart flavor you like. Three to 3½ cups of prepared fresh fruit will make approximately two good-sized leathers on cookie sheets—depending on the type of fruit and the size of the pieces.

Added sweetening is not necessary, but helps bind the texture. This increases the chance of scorching, so add a little water as needed, and stir often (the amount of sweetener suggested may not be enough for very tart plums). The pectin in apple skins helps texture: remove bits of cooked skin by straining.

Prepare. Use fully ripe fruit. Peel or not, core/stone, cut small; coat with an anti-oxidant (q.v.) if you like, but the brief precooking should prevent some darkening. Measure prepared fruit, and add 1½ tablespoons sugar or honey for each 1 cup of cut fruit; an alternative is 1 tablespoon granulated fructose for each 1 cup of puréed fruit. Bring just to boiling, cook gently until tender. Remove from heat and, when the fruit is cool enough to handle, put it through a fine sieve or food mill. Or purée in a food processor with the steel blade in place (work with only ½ cup of prepared fruit at a time, emptying the bowl after each bit is processed; trying to do much more at once will make the purée too runny). Or use a blender (work with only one-third of the fruit at a time and add 1 tablespoon of water or apple juice if necessary to get the fruit started, then add remaining fruit).

Lay long sheets of foil or plastic *freezer*-wrap on wet cookie sheets—wet, so the foil/plastic will cling—allowing extra at ends and sides, and oil it well. Pour enough fruit pulp in the center of each sheet, tilting it to spread ¼ inch deep (it will dry much thinner), and to within 2 inches of the rims.

Dryer. Start at 130 F/54 C; raise to 145 F/63 C after the first hour and hold there until the surface is no longer tacky to the touch, or for 45 minutes. When nearly dry, reduce heat to 135 F/57 C. Test dry. Cool.

Drying time depends on juiciness of the fruit—usually about 2 to 3 hours. To make heavier leather, spread fresh pulp thinly on a layer that has lost all tackiness: building up on a nearly dry layer is better than working with a too-thick original layer.

To store, leave each sheet of leather on the plastic wrap on which it was dried and roll it up, tucking in the sides of the wrap as you go along. Overwrap each roll for further protection against moisture. Refrigerate until used, up to a couple of months; freeze for long-term storage.

Open-air/sun. Cover from dust and insects with cheesecloth held several inches away from the fresh fruit pulp, and place in direct sun. Bring inside at night. Protective cover can be left off when the leather is no longer tacky to the touch. Finish with a pasteurizing treatment at 145 F/63 C for 30 minutes. Total sun-drying time about 24 hours.

DRY TEST. Pliable and leathery, stretches slightly when torn; surface slick, with no drag when rubbed lightly with the fingertips.

NECTARINES

Prepare as for Apricots.

Dryer. Steam-blanch halves 15 to 18 minutes, slices for 5 minutes. Dry with the same heat sequence as for Apricots. Test dry. Condition; store. Drying time will be roughly the same as for Apricots.

Open-air/sun. Prepare and handle like Apricots. Test dry. Pasteurize. Cool and store. *Solar dryer:* about 70 percent of open-air/sun time.

DRY TEST. Pliable, leathery.

PEACHES

Yellow-fleshed freestone varieties are the best for home-drying.

Prepare. Commercially dried peaches are dried in halves, and next to never peeled. For home-drying in slices, however, peel either by a knife as you are working along, or dip whole fruit in boiling water for 30 seconds, cool quickly and strip off skins.

Halve and stone the fruit; leave in halves or cut in slices. Scoop out any red pigment in the cavity (it darkens greatly during drying). Treat slices or halves with ascorbic-acid coat as you go along to hold color temporarily.

Dryer. Steam-blanch slices 8 minutes, unpeeled halves 15 to 20 minutes. Start drying at 130 F/54 C, increase gradually to 155 F/68 C after the first hour. Turn over halves when all visible juice has disappeared. Reduce to 140 F/60 C when nearly dry to prevent scorching. Average total drying time: up to 15 hours for halves and up to 6 hours for slices.

Open-air/sun. Prepare as for the dryer. If steam-blanching slices and halves as above, sulfur slices 30 minutes, halves for 90 minutes. If not blanched, sulfur 60 minutes and 2 hours, respectively. Be careful not to spill the juice in the hollows when transferring the halves to drying trays, where they're placed cut-side up. Proceed as for Apricots. Test dry. Pasteurize. Cool and store. *Solar dryer:* about 70 percent of open-air/sun time.

DRY TEST. Leathery, rather tough.

PEARS

Best for drying is the Bartlett. (Kieffer is better used in preserves.) For drying, pears are picked quite firm and before they are ripe. They are then held at not more than 70 F/21 C in boxes in a dry, airy place for about 1 week—when they are usually ripe enough for drying.

Prepare. Split lengthwise, remove core with a melon-ball scoop, take out the woody vein. Leave in halves or slice (pare off skin if slicing); coat cut fruit with ascorbic acid as you work, to prevent oxidizing.

Dryer. Steam-blanch slices 5 minutes, halves 20 minutes. Start at 130 F/54 C, gradually increasing after the first hour to 150 F/66 C. Reduce to 140 F/60 C for last hour or when nearly dry. Test dry. Condition; cool and store. Average total drying time: up to 6 hours for slices, 15 hours for halves.

Open-air/sun. Sulfur as for Peaches; dry like Peaches. Test dry. Pasteurize; cool and store. *Solar dryer:* about 70 percent of open-air/sun time.

DRY TEST. Suède-like and springy. No moisture when cut and squeezed.

PLUMS AND PRUNES

Joe Carcione, network television's "Green Grocer," has pointed out that the Italian prune-plums have so much more natural sugar than other varieties that they dry well *whole* without fermenting; nor need they be pitted beforehand— even though they're freestone, so pitting is easiness itself. Other kinds of plums should be pitted, then sliced or quartered in order to dry without spoiling in the process.

Prepare. Check the skins with a 30–45-second dunk in boiling water. Cool immediately.

Dryer. Steam-blanch 15 minutes if halved and stoned, 5 minutes if sliced. Start *slices* and *halves* at 130 F/54 C, gradually increase to 150 F/66 C after the first hour; reduce to 140 F/60 C when nearly dry.

Start *whole,* checked fruit at 120 F/49 C, increase to 150 F/66 C gradually after the first hour; reduce to 140 F/60 C when nearly dry. Test dry. Condition; cool and store. Average total drying time for slices: up to 6 hours; halves, up to 8 hours; whole, up to 14.

Open-air/sun. Check the skins of whole fruit. Sulfur whole fruit for 2 hours. Sulfur slices and halves for 1 hour. Test dry. Pasteurize. Cool and store. *Solar dryer:* about 70 percent of open-air/sun time.

DRY TEST. Pliable, leathery. A handful will spring apart after squeezing.

DRYING VEGETABLES AND HERBS

See the over-all introduction to this Chapter for a description of the techniques involved in the directions given below.

Vegetables are precooked by blanching before being dried. At low altitudes—below 3500 feet/1067 meters—vigorous steam-blanching is preferred. At high altitudes, the steam-blanching time is either increased according to the recommendations in "Correcting for Altitude" in Chapter 3, or the blanching is done for a longer time in boiling water than is given for sea-level-zone directions. And there is always blanching in a microwave oven, as described earlier in this chapter.

Whatever blanching method you choose, remember that *precooking is NOT optional:* it helps to stop enzymatic action that would lead to poor quality.

Except for corn dried on the cob, all vegetables are pasteurized if their processing heat has not been high enough, or prolonged enough, to destroy spoilage organisms. Pasteurizing is particularly important for sun-dried vegetables.

Vegetables are cut smaller than fruits are, in order to shorten the drying process—for the faster the drying, the better the product (so long as the food isn't *cooked*). The approximate total drying times in a dryer are not given below, but they range from around 4 to 12 hours, depending on the texture and size of the pieces.

See "Tests for Dryness in Produce" preceding Fruits section.

COOKING DRIED VEGETABLES

Before being cooked, all vegetables except greens are soaked in cold water just to cover until they are nearly restored to their original texture. Never give them any more water than they can take up, and always cook them in the water they've soaked in.

Cover greens with enough boiling water to cover and simmer until tender.

Beans—Green/Snap/String/Wax (Leather Britches)

Prepare. String if necessary. Split pods of larger varieties lengthwise, so they dry faster. Steam for 15 to 20 minutes.

Dryer. Start *whole* at 120 F/49 C and increase to 150 F/66 C after the first hour; reduce to 130 F/54 C when nearly dry. For *split beans,* start at 130 F/54 C, increase to 150 F/66 C after first hour, and decrease to 130 F/54 C when nearly dry. Test. Condition; pasteurize. Cool and store.

Open-air/sun. Handle exactly as for the dryer. Test dry. Pasteurize certainly. Cool and store. *Solar dryer:* about 70 percent of open-air sun time.

Room-drying. Prepare as above but do not split. String through the upper ⅓ with clean string, keeping the beans about ½ inch apart. Hang in warm, dry, well-aired room. Test. Pasteurize certainly. Cool and store. (Old-timers would drape strings near the ceiling over the wood cookstove; they gave the name "leather britches" to these dried beans—probably because they take so long to cook tender.)

DRY TEST. Brittle.

Beans, Lima (and Shell)

Allow to become full-grown—beyond the stage you would when picking them for the table, or for freezing or canning—but before the pods are dry. Shell. Put in very shallow layers in the steaming basket and steam for 10 minutes. Spread thinly on trays.

Dryer. Start at 140 F/60 C, gradually increase to 160 F/71 C after the first hour; reduce to 130 F/54 C when nearly dry. Test dry. Condition; pasteurize. Cool and store.

Open-air/sun. Not as satisfactory for such a dense, low-acid vegetable as processing in a dryer is. However, follow preparation as for a dryer. Test dry. Condition if necessary; pasteurize certainly. Cool and store. *Solar dryer:* about 70 percent of open-air/sun time.

DRY TEST. Hard, brittle; break clean when broken.

Beets

Prepare. Choose beets small enough so they have no woodiness. Leave ½ inch of the tops (they will bleed during precooking if the crown is cut). Steam until cooked through, 30 to 45 minutes. Cool. Trim roots and crowns. Peel.

Slice crosswise no more than ⅛ inch thick; OR shred them with the coarse blade of a vegetable grater: the smaller, thinner pieces dry more quickly, but of course their use in cooking is more limited.

Dryer. Put slices in at 120 F/49 C and increase to 150 F/66 C after first hour; reduce to 130 F/54 C when nearly dry.

Put finer shreds in at 130 F/54 C. Increase gradually to 150 F/66 C after first hour; turn down to 140 F/60 C when nearly dry. Test dry. Condition; pasteurize. Cool and store.

Open-air/sun. Prepare as for dryer, but shreds are recommended here instead of slices because they dry more quickly. Condition if necessary; pasteurize certainly. Cool and store. *Solar dryer:* about 70 percent of open-air/sun time.

DRY TEST. Slices very tough, but can be bent; shreds are brittle.

BROCCOLI

Prepare. Trim and cut as for serving. Cut thin stalks lengthwise in quarters; split thicker stalks in eighths. Steam 8 minutes for thin pieces, 12 minutes for thicker pieces.

Dryer. Start at 120 F/49 C, gradually increasing to 150 F/66 C after the first hour; reduce to 140 F/60 C when nearly dry. Test dry. Condition; pasteurize. Cool and store.

Open-air/sun. Prepare as for dryer. Test dry. Condition if necessary; pasteurize certainly. Cool and store. *Solar dryer:* about 70 percent of open-air/sun time.

DRY TEST. Brittle.

CABBAGE

Most people put it by in a root cellar (q.v.) or as Sauerkraut (see under "Salting," Chapter 20); but some of it dried can be handy for soup. Its storage life is relatively short, however.

Prepare. Remove outer leaves. Quarter; cut out core, and shred with the coarse blade of a vegetable grater, about the size for cole slaw. Steam 8 to 10 minutes. Cabbage—as do all leaf vegetables—packs on the trays during drying, so spread it evenly and not more than ½ inch deep. At a time, you'll dry only about half as much by weight of leaf vegetables as you do with other types of food, because they need more room to prevent matting.

Dryer. Start at 120 F/49 C, increase gradually to 140 F/60 C after the first hour; reduce to 130 F/54 C when nearly dry: the thin part of the leaves dries more quickly than the rib, and therefore is more likely to scorch and turn brown. Keep lifting and stirring the food on the trays to keep it from matting. Test dry. Condition if necessary; pasteurize. Cool and store.

Open-air/sun. Follow procedure for dryer. Test dry. Pasteurize certainly. Cool and store. *Solar dryer:* about 70 percent of open-air/sun time.

DRY TEST. Extremely tough ribs; the thin edges crumble.

Carrots

Like beets, above, they keep so well in a root cellar (q.v.) that it seems a shame to dry them—unless it's a choice between dried carrots or no carrots at all. Like cabbage, they do not hold long in storage.

Choose crisp, tender carrots with no woodiness. Leave on ½ inch of the tops.

Prepare. There's no need to peel good young carrots: just remove whiskers along with the tails and crowns—which is done *after* they're steamed. Steam until cooked through but not mushy—about 20 to 30 minutes, depending on the size. Trim off tails, crowns with tops, and any whiskers. Cut in ⅛-inch rings, or shred.

Dryer. Proceed as for Beets, either sliced or shredded. Test dry. Condition; pasteurize. Cool and store.

Open-air/sun. Proceed as for Beets, either sliced or shredded. Test dry. Condition if necessary; pasteurize certainly. Cool and store. *Solar dryer:* about 70 percent of open-air/sun time.

DRY TEST. Slices very tough and leathery, but will bend; shreds are brittle.

Celery

For drying *leaves,* see Herbs.

Prepare stalks. Split outer stalks lengthwise, leave small center ones whole; trim off leaves to dry as herb seasoning. Cut all stalks across in no larger than ¼-inch pieces. Steam for 4 minutes.

Dryer. Start at 130 F/54 C, increase to 150 F/66 C after the first hour; reduce to 130 F/54 C when nearly dry. Test dry. Condition; pasteurize, because the maximum heat may not be long enough to stop spoilers. Cool and store.

Open-air/sun. Prepare as for the dryer. Test dry. Pasteurize certainly. Cool and store. *Solar dryer:* about 70 percent of open-air/sun time.

DRY TEST. Brittle chips.

Corn-on-the-Cob

Use popcorn and flint varieties for this. (Flint corn was the food-grain of the Colonists, who were taught by the Indians to use it. It is different from "dent" corn, which shrinks as it dries.) The kernels of both flint and popcorn remain plump when hard and dry.

These varieties are allowed to mature in the field and become partly dry in the husk on the stalks. Both are usually air-dried in the husk. However, in some hot countries the husks are peeled back from the partly dried ears and braided together or tied together. In northern Italy, in the fall, whole sides of brick-lattice buildings are golden with corn being finished in the sun. Both popcorn and flint corn (which is ground into meal) rub easily from the cob when the kernels are dry. Save the cobs for smoking home-cured meats (q.v.).

DRY TEST for popcorn: rub off a little and pop it. If the result's satisfactory, then immediately put it into moisture–vapor-proof containers with tight closures, to prevent it from getting too dry to pop (the remaining moisture in the kernel is what makes it explode in heat).

DRY TEST for flint corn: brittle—it cracks when you whack it. Store in sound air- and moisture-proof barrels; but if you must hold it in large cloth bags, invert the bags every few weeks: this prevents any moisture from collecting on the bag where it touches the floor.

CORN, PARCHED

Correctly dried sweet corn is more than a stop-gap for the many people who consider it superior in flavor to canned corn. Any variety of sweet corn will do.

Prepare. Gather in the milk stage as if it were going straight to the table. Husk. Steam it on the cob for 15 minutes for more mature ears, 20 minutes for quite immature ears (the younger it is, the longer it takes to set the milk). It's a good idea to separate the corn into lots with older/larger and younger/smaller kernels so you can handle them uniformly. When cool enough to handle, cut it from the cob as for canning or freezing whole-kernel corn (q.v.). Don't worry about the glumes and bits of silk: these are easily sifted out after the kernels are dry.

Dryer. Spread shallow on the trays. Start at 140 F/60 C; raise to 165 F/74 C gradually after the first hour; reduce to 140 F/60 C when nearly dry, or for the last hour. Stir frequently to keep it from lumping together as it dries. Test dry. Condition. (Pasteurizing is not necessary following processing in a dryer *if the temperature has been held as high as 165 F/74 C for an hour.*) The silk and glumes will separate to the bottom of the conditioning container; but if you don't condition, shake several cupfuls at a time in a colander whose holes are large enough to let glumes and silk through. Best stored in moisture–vapor-proof containers in small amounts.

Open-air/sun. Prepare exactly as for the dryer. Stir frequently to avoid lumping. Pasteurize certainly. Shake free of glumes and silk. Package and store. *Solar dryer:* about 70 percent of open-air/sun time.

To cook. Rinse in cold water, drain; cover with fresh cold water and let stand overnight. Add water to cover, salt to taste, and boil gently until kernels are tender—about 30 minutes—stirring often and adding a bit more water as needed to keep from scorching. Drain off excess water, season with cream, butter, pepper.

DRY TEST. Brittle, glassy and semi-transparent; a piece cracks clean when broken.

GARLIC

It keeps so well when it's conditioned after harvesting that it's seldom dried at home. If you do want to dry it, though, treat it like Onions.

HERBS

This category includes celery leaves as well as the greenery from all aromatic herbs—basil, parsley, sage, tarragon: whatever you like.

All such seasonings are *air-dried* at temperatures never more than 100 F/38 C (higher, and they lose the oils we value for flavor); and as much light as possible should be excluded during the process.

For the best product, dry only the tender and most flavorful leaves from the upper 6 inches of stalk. Especially with bag-drying, check after the first week and every few days thereafter: the stalks should not be brittle-dry, lest you have trouble separating tiny pieces of stick from the fully dried leaves.

Gather and prepare. Cut them on a sunny morning after the dew has dried, and choose plants that have only just started to bloom; cut them with plenty of stem, then strip off tougher leaves growing lower than 6 inches on the stalk, and remove blossom heads. Hold in small bunches by the stems and swish the leaves through cold water to remove any dust, or soil thrown up from a rain. Shake off the water and lay on absorbent toweling to let all surface moisture evaporate.

Bag-drying. Collect 6 to 12 stems loosely together, and over the bunched leaves put a commodius brown-paper bag—one large enough so the herbs will not touch the sides. Tie the mouth of the bag loosely around the stems 2 inches from their ends, and hang the whole business high up in a warm, dry, airy room. When the leaves have become brittle, knock them from the stems and package them in air-tight containers and store away from light. You can pulverize the leaves by rubbing them between your hands; then store.

Tray-drying. Prepare as for drying in bags. Cut off the handle-stems, spread the leafed stalks one layer deep on drying trays. Put the trays in a warm, dark room that is extra well ventilated (if you use a fan, don't aim it *on* the trays—the herbs could blow around—instead, "bounce" the forced draft off a wall, so it will be gentler). Turn the herbs several times to ensure even drying. Test dry. Remove from stems, and package as above.

Celery leaves. Cut out the coarsest midribs. Tray-dry as for any leaf herb.

DRY TEST. Readily crumbled.

MIXED VEGETABLES

These are never dried in combination: drying times and temperatures vary too much between types of vegetables. Dry vegetables and seasoning separately, *then* combine them in small packets to suit your taste and future use.

MUSHROOMS

Only young, unbruised, absolutely fresh mushrooms should be dried.

Prepare. Wash quickly in cold water if necessary; otherwise wipe with a damp cloth. Remove stems (they're denser than the caps as a rule, so shouldn't be dried in the same batch with the tops). Slice the caps in ⅛-inch strips—cut stems across in ⅛-inch rings—and treat them with the ascorbic-acid coating if it's important to you to keep them from darkening as you work. Steam for 12 to 15 minutes.

Dryer. Start at 130 F/54 C, increase gradually to 150 F/66 C after the first hour; reduce to 140 F/60 C when nearly dry. Test dry. Condition; pasteurize. Cool and store.

Sliced caps and stems process at the same temperature sequences, but stem pieces usually take longer.

Open-air/sun. Prepare as for the dryer. Test dry. Condition if necessary; pasteurize certainly. Cool and store. *Solar dryer:* about 70 percent of open-air/sun time.

DRY TEST. Brittle.

ONIONS

Dried onions do not hold so long as other vegetables do in storage (they are like carrots and cabbage, above).

Prepare. Peel; slice in rings about ⅛-inch thick. Uniformity is important here, because slices too thin can brown and scorch; it's better to have evenly thicker pieces than some ⅛ inch and other paper-thin. No steaming is necessary.

Dryer. Put them in at 140 F/60 C and keep them there until nearly dry, watching carefully that thinner pieces are not browning. Reduce to 130 F/54 C for the last hour if necessary. Test dry. Condition. Cool and store.

Open-air/sun. Prepare as for the dryer. Test dry. Pasteurize. Cool and store. *Solar dryer:* about 70 percent of open-air/sun time.

DRY TEST. Light-colored, but brittle.

PEAS, BLACK-EYED, treat like Beans (Shell), above.

PEAS, GREEN

Choose young, tender peas as you'd serve them fresh from the garden. From there on, treat them like Shell Beans, above.

DRY TEST. Shriveled and hard; shatter when hit with a hammer.

PEPPERS, HOT (CHILI)

Choose mature, dark-red pods. Thread them on a string through the stalks, and hang them in the sun on a south wall. When dry, the pods will be shrunken, dark, and may be bent without snapping.

PEPPERS, SWEET (GREEN OR BELL)

Prepare. Split, core, remove seeds; quarter. Steam 10 to 12 minutes.

Dryer. Start at 120 F/49 C, gradually increase to 150 F/66 C after the first hour; reduce to 140 F/60 C when nearly dry (if any are thin-walled, reduce to 130 F/54 C toward the end, and keep stirring them well). Test dry. Condition. Cool and store.

Open-air/sun. Prepare as for the dryer. Test dry. Condition if necessary; pasteurize certainly. Cool and store. *Solar dryer:* about 70 percent of open-air sun time.

DRY TEST. Crisp and brittle.

POTATOES, SWEET (AND YAMS)

Only firm, smooth sweet potatoes or yams should be used.

Prepare. Steam whole and unpeeled until cooked through but not mushy, about 30 to 40 minutes. Trim, peel; cut in ⅛-inch slices, or shred.

Dryer. Proceed as for sliced or shredded Beets. Test dry. Condition; pasteurize. Cool and store.

Open-air/sun. Prepare as for dryer. Test dry. Condition if necessary; pasteurize certainly. Cool and store. *Solar dryer:* about 70 percent of open-air/sun time.

DRY TEST. Slices extremely leathery, not pliable; shreds, brittle.

POTATOES, WHITE (IRISH)

These root-cellar too well to bother drying. But dry like Turnips, below.

PUMPKIN

Deep-orange varieties with thick, solid flesh make the best product. There's not much use in drying in chunks, because they're to be mashed after cooking.

Prepare. Take them directly from the garden (they shouldn't be conditioned as for root-cellaring). Split in half, then cut in manageable pieces for peeling and removing seeds and all pith. Shred with the coarse blade of a vegetable grater (less than ⅛ inch thick). In shallow layers in the basket, steam for 6 minutes.

Dryer. Proceed as for shredded Beets, above. Test dry. Condition; pasteurize if length of maximum processing heat isn't enough to stop spoilers. Cool and store.

Open-air/sun drying. Prepare as for the dryer. Test dry. Pasteurize certainly. Cool and store. *Solar dryer:* about 70 percent of open-air/sun time.

DRY TEST. Brittle chips.

Historical note. In olden days, pumpkins were often halved at their equators, then cut in rings about 1 inch thick; rind and seeds and pith were removed from each ring. The rings were hung on a long stick and dried slowly in front of a fire until they were like tough leather.

SPINACH (AND OTHER GREENS)

Prepare. Use only young, tender, crisp leaves. Place loosely in the steaming basket and steam for 4 to 6 minutes, or until well wilted. Remove coarse midribs; cut larger leaves in half. Spread sparsely on drying trays, keeping overlaps to a minimum (leaves tend to mat).

Dryer. Start at 140 F/60 C, increase to 150 F/66 C after the first hour; if necessary, reduce to 140 F/60 C when nearly dry, to avoid browning. Test dry. Condition. Cool and store.

Open-air/sun drying. Prepare as for the dryer. Test dry. Pasteurize certainly. Cool and store. *Solar dryer:* about 70 percent of open-air/sun time.

DRY TEST. Easily crumbled.

SQUASH (ALL VARIETIES), treat like Pumpkin.

TURNIPS AND RUTABAGAS

Like white (irish) potatoes, which root-cellar extremely well if handled right (q.v.), turnips and rutabagas are seldom dried.

If you're compelled to dry them, though, quarter and peel them, then shred—and steam and dry as for shredded Carrots.

DRY TEST. Brittle chips.

Drying Meat and Fish

We shan't give blow-by-blow instructions for making jerky as the Mountain Men did, or drying codfish with the expertise of a Newfoundland native. Here are the basic steps. Work in small batches, with complete sanitation; don't cut corners. Refrigerate or freeze the finished product: high-protein foods like these invite spoilage.

USING DRIED MEAT AND DRIED FISH

Jerky traditionally was shaved off (or gnawed off) and eaten as is, because it was a staple for overland wanderers who were traveling light and far from assured supplies of fresh meat. (Helpful ins-and-outs of concentrated journey food are to be found in Horace Kephart's *Camping & Woodcraft;* see "pemmican" especially.) Today several versions of it appear in stick form as snacks, for either the Long Trail or a cocktail party.

Dried salt fish—the type described below—is always freshened by soaking beforehand, either in cold water or fresh milk; the soaking liquid is discarded here, because of the extremely high salt content.

Such fish were standard fare even in the hinterlands far from salt water. A small roadway in our wooded Green Mountains is still called by old-timers "Codfish Alley"—so named by homesteaders who went down to the flatboats coming up the Connecticut River to buy salt codfish, which they carried home in armloads like billets of stovewood. See Chapter 24.

DRYING MEAT (JERKY)

Jerked meat is roughly ¼ the weight of its fresh raw state.

Preferred meats for jerking are mature beef and venison (elk is too fatty), and only the lean muscle is used. Partially freeze meat if possible to make slicing easier. Cut lengthwise of the grain in strips as long as possible, 1 inch wide and ½ inch thick.

DRY TEST. Brittle, as a green stick: it won't snap clean, as a dry stick does. Be sure to test it *after* it cools, because it's pliable when still warm, even though enough moisture is out of it.

Unsalted Jerky

This does not mean unseasoned—there's a bit of salt for flavor—but the meat is not salted heavily to draw out moisture or to act mildly as a preservative.

Lay cut strips on a cutting-board, and with a blunt-rimmed saucer or a meat mallet, pound the following seasonings (or your own variations thereof) into both sides of the meat: salt, pepper, garlic powder, your favorite herb. Use not more than 1 teaspoon salt for each 1 pound of fresh meat, and the other seasonings according to your taste.

Arrange seasoned strips ½ inch apart on wire racks—cake-cooling ones, or the racks from the oven; put them in a preheated 150 F/66 C oven, and immediately turn the heat back to 120 F/49 C. Spread aluminum foil on the bottom of the oven to catch drippings. If your oven is not vented, leave its door ajar at the first stop position. After 5 or 6 hours turn the strips over; continue drying at the same temperature for 4 hours more, when you check for dryness. When dry enough, jerky is shriveled and black, and is brittle when cooled.

Wrap the sticks of jerky in moisture–vapor-proof material, put the packages in a stout container with a close-fitting lid, and store below 40 F/4 C in the refrigerator (or freeze it). Reconstitute by simmering in water to cover.

Salted Jerky

Dry this in the sun; or, if you're emulating the frontiersmen, over a very slow, non-smoking fire that's not much more than a bed of coals.

Prepare a brine of 2½ cups of pickling salt for 3 quarts of water, and in it soak the cut strips of meat for 1 or 2 days. Remove and wipe dry.

OVER COALS

Arrange a rectangular fire-bed and drive forked poles into the ground at each corner; the forks should come about 4 feet above the ground. Two hours before you're ready to begin drying the salted meat, start a fire of hardwood and let it burn down to coals.

Cut two fairly heavy poles to go from fork to fork on the long sides, and sticks as thick as a finger—and sharpened at one end—to lay at right angles over the side-poles. The salted strips may be draped over the cross-sticks; or they may be suspended from the sticks (pass the sharpened stick through the meat about 3 inches from one end) and spaced several inches apart.

Feed the fire with small hardwood so carefully that juice does not ooze out from the excess heat, or the meat start to cook.

Depending on conditions, drying could take 24 hours. Test for dryness; package and store in refrigerator or freezer.

In Open Air

This is nothing to try in a back yard—or indeed in any place near civilization. It needs clear, pure air, uncontaminated by animals or human beings: after all, it is a method used on old-time hunting trips deep into the High Plains.

Choose a time when you'll have good—but not roasting—sun, dry air day and night, and a gentle breeze. Hang the salted strips from a drying frame such as described above (of course with no fire), and leave them there until they become brittle-dry.

A BASIC PROCEDURE FOR DRYING FISH

Drying fish at home is not something to be undertaken lightly. The fish must be fresh-caught and handled scrupulously at every stage; it must undergo a long dry-salting period before it is put out to dry; and, since home-drying is best done outdoors in the shade, the procedure requires a trustworthy breeze,

Well Split Fish   Badly Split Fish

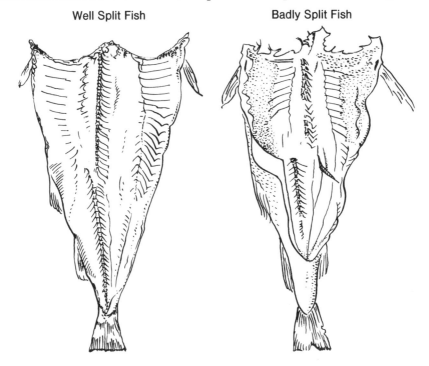

fairly low humidity, and critter-proof holding tubs and racks.

Dry any *lean* fish (cod of course is the classic), because fatty fish don't keep as well. It should be abundant, to make drying worth the bother.

Coat all surfaces of each fish liberally with pure pickling salt, using 1 pound of salt for 2 pounds of fish, and stack the opened fish flesh-side up on a slatted wooden rack outdoors. Don't make the stacks more than 12 layers deep, with the top layer skin-side up. Leave them stacked from 1 to 2 weeks, depending on the height of fish and the dryness of the air. Brine made by the salt and fish juices will drain away. Move the pile inside each night and weight it down to press out more brine.

Scrub the fish again to remove the salt, and put them on wooden frames outdoors to complete the necessary removal of moisture from their tissues. Hang or spread the fish on cross-pieces in an open shed with good ventilation; direct sun on the fish can start it to sunburn (cook) at only 75 degrees F/24 degrees C. Bring fish in at night, re-piling to ensure even drying; re-spread on the racks more often with skin-side up.

To store, cut in manageable chunks if the fish are large; wrap in moisture–vapor-proof plastic; pack in tight wooden boxes, and store in a dry, cool place between 32 and 40 F (Zero and 4 C).

DRY TEST. No imprint is left when the fleshy part of a fish is pinched between thumb and forefinger.

22 🌱

ROOT-CELLARING

When we turned "root cellar" into a homemade verb in the very early 1970's we simply forgot that the term might seem foreign to a great many North Americans who live above the sunbelt. So here is a translation:

To root-cellar is to store for the winter a variety of fresh, whole, raw vegetables and fruits that have not been processed in any way to increase their keeping qualities. This means that such foods must be held for use during the winter—and some even longer, into the next growing season—without being subjected to an unnatural amount of heat or of cold or of dryness.

And of all the time-tested ways of putting food by, only wintering-over in cold storage at home is less satisfactory today than it was a century or more ago. The reason is simple. All the technological advances we're so pleased with in construction and heating have given us cozy, dry basements instead of cool, damp cellars, and the chilly shed off the pantry has given way to a warm passageway between carport and kitchen. Therefore this section is telling how to re-create conditions that several generations of North Americans have devoted themselves to improving. It includes some indoor areas that are warmer and drier than the traditional outbuilding or cellar with stone walls and a packed earthen floor, and it also includes some arrangements outdoors that are a good deal more rough-and-ready.

Several of the ones described may require outlays of money or effort or hardihood beyond the expectations of the usual householder. In addition, most of them need more maintenance than does any other type of storage discussed up till now. This means constantly watching the weather to forestall the effects of sudden extra cold/warmth/wetness, and constantly checking the food for signs of spoil—but it's maintenance just the same.

HOW IT WORKS

Used commonly, root-cellaring means to hold these foods for several months after their normal harvest in a cold, rather moist atmosphere that will not allow them to freeze or to complete their natural cycle to decomposition.

The freezing points and warmth tolerances of produce vary. The range to shoot for generally, though, is 32 to 40 F/Zero to 4 C—the effective span for refrigeration—with only a couple of vegetables needing warmer storage to keep their texture over the months. In this range the growth of spoilage micro-organisms and the rate of enzymatic action (which causes overripening and eventual rotting) are slowed down a great deal.

Good home root-cellaring involves some control of the amount of air the produce is exposed to, since winter air is often let in to keep the temperature down. But fresh whole fruits and vegetables respire after they're harvested (some more than others: apples seem almost to *pant* in storage), so the breathing of many types is reduced by layering them with clean dry leaves, sand, moss, earth, etc., or even by wrapping each individually in paper. These measures of course aren't as effective as those of commercial refrigerated storage, which rely in part on drastic reduction of the oxygen in the air supply, but they work well enough for the more limited results expected from home methods.

We'll be describing a variety of storage arrangements in a minute, including a couple that are drier and sometimes warmer than the traditional ones (since we can't leave in limbo those foods that require something different from the classic old cellar treatment). But first a word about practicality.

The beauty of root-cellaring is that it deals only with whole vegetables and fruits and there are no hidden dangers: If it doesn't work, we know by looking and touching and smelling that the stuff has spoiled, and we don't eat it.

On the other hand it's something that sounds a lot more feasible than it may really turn out to be.

First, the householder must learn something about the idiosyncrasies of the fruits and vegetables he plans to store on a fairly large scale: for example, apples and potatoes—the most popular things to carry over through winter—can't be stored near each other, and the odor of turnips and cabbages in the basement can penetrate up into the living quarters, and squashes want to be warmer than carrots do.

Then he casts around for the right sort of storage. And the solution may cost more than its value to his over-all food program, especially if it's a structure more elaborate or permanent than the family's make-up warrants.

But aren't there the less pretentious outdoor pits, or the more casual barrels sunk in the face of a bank? Yes; and they're fun to use—except in deep-snow country when they can be a worry to get at.

Samuel Ogden of Landgrove, Vermont, organic gardener and noted Green Mountain countryman, warns the newcomer to cold-climate root-cellaring to avoid three things: (1) counting too heavily on cold storage; (2) having too much diversity; (3) and having the food inaccessible in bad weather. But for the family with a serious, long-term food program that depends in great degree on its own efforts, though, he recommends the Vermont experience of Helen and Scott Nearing described in *Living the Good Life:* the Nearings' recent root cellars are well-thought-out and substantial affairs—and represent total dedication to a way of life.

Equipment for Root–Cellaring

Storage place, indoor or outdoor (see below)
Clean wooden boxes/lugs/crates or barrels; or stout large cardboard cartons (for produce that wants to be dry, not damp)
Plenty of clean paper for wrapping individually, or shredding
Plenty of clean dry leaves, sphagnum, peat moss or sand
A tub of sand to keep moistened to provide extra humidity if needed
Simple wall thermometer certainly; humidity gauge (optional)

INDOOR STORAGE

The Classic Root Cellar Downstairs

There are fewer of these to be found as the years go by, even in the old houses in our part of the country. Usually in the corner of the original cellar-hole, they have two outside walls of masonry (part of the foundation), the floor is packed earth, and any partitions are designed more to support shelving than to keep out warmth from a nonexistent furnace. They incorporate at least one of the small windows that provide cross-ventilation for the whole cellar to keep overhead floor joists from rotting; propped open occasionally during the winter, it's the answer for regulating temperature and humidity.

Such a place can be ideal today, although the house is "restored" and now contains a furnace (protected from seepage in the springtime by a surrounding pit and an automatic sump pump). Just complete boarding-off the two inside walls, cut and hang a door in one of them, and apply whatever is handiest for insulation against heat from the furnace.

To be perfect, it should have an inner partition to separate storage of fruits and vegetables; and its own electric light. For the rest, build stout shelves or put up trestles to hold boxes, crates and baskets off the floor on the sides away from the window. Reserve one well-drained corner for the vegetables that will be clumped upright with their roots set in soil or sand and moistened by hand to keep them fresh.

Darken the window(s)—potatoes turn green in light when they're stored, and this isn't good. If necessary, keep clearing snow from the areaway that's below ground leading to the window.

And check the whole thing for places where field mice can get in and feast on your crops during the lean winter months, and stop them up.

A Modern Basement Store Room

To some extent, in a closed-off corner of a modern basement you can copy the conditions of the old-time downstairs root cellar.

Choose a corner preferably on the north or east (where the temperature is likely to be most even); it should have no heating ducts or oil or water pipes running through it. And if it has a window you'll be saved having to figure out a system for governing temperature, ventilation and humidity.

The store room should be at least 6 x 6 feet if you're going to bother building it at all.

The existing right-angled outside walls of the basement will become the outside walls of the store room. Make two inner right-angled walls of fiberboard or

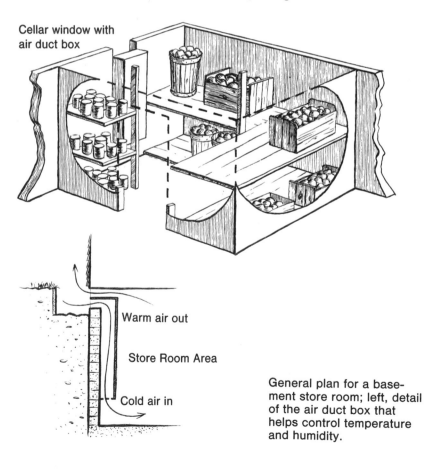

Cellar window with air duct box

Warm air out

Store Room Area

Cold air in

General plan for a basement store room; left, detail of the air duct box that helps control temperature and humidity.

½-inch lumber nailed to 2 x 4 studding spaced 2 feet apart and secured to a footing. Leave open space on one side to frame and hang a door.

Insulate the new room from the inside—glass batts that include a vapor barrier go easily between the studs. Finish the inside with wallboarding if you want to, covering the seams with common lath. Insulate the door and give it a simple latch. *Insulate the inside walls only.*

Make an air-duct box to cover at least the lower ⅔ of the window when it's opened, and carry the box part way down the side of the wall (see detail of the sketch). The duct brings cold incoming air to the lower part of the room and lets warm air from the upper part be drawn outdoors through the upper ⅓ of the opened window.

Ideally you should have a fruit-storage room too—or at least a part of the all-purpose store room blocked off for fruit. If you have a window in the fruit room too, build an air-duct box for it. Otherwise you'll regulate temperature/humidity by opening and closing the entrance to the fruit section.

Using a Bulkhead

Many middle-aged houses have an outside entrance to the cellar: a flight of concrete steps down to the cellar wall, in which a wide door is hung to give access to the cellar. The top entrance to the steps—the hatch—is a door laid at an angle 45 degrees to the ground.

On the stairway, which probably is closed from the outside during the coldest months anyway, you can store barrels/boxes of produce. You could put up rough temporary wooden side walls along the steps; but certainly lay planks on the steps to set your containers on. Insulate the door into the cellar proper with glass batts. If you need to, keep a pail of dampened sand on one of the steps to add humidity. You're likely to be propping the hatchway door open a few inches from time to time to help maintain proper temperature on the steps. This means shoveling snow from the bulkhead, and piling it back on when this outside door is closed again.

A Dry Shed

This takes the place of the garage advocated by some people—but not by us: too much oil and gasoline odor (some produce soaks stray odors up like a sponge), and far too great a quantity of lead-filled emissions from running motors. And anyway temperature is often uncontrollable.

Instead of using the garage, partition off storage space in the wood-floored shed leading into the kitchen, if you have an old house in the country. Or segregate a storage area in a cold, seldom used passageway.

Storage areas like these are usually not fit for such long-term storage as the basement root cellar or store room is.

Up Attic

An old-fashioned attic generally is the last place in the house to cool off naturally as cold weather sets in; and unless the roof is well insulated, the attic temperature rises on sunny winter days. This fluctuation doesn't matter much for some foods, however (see the chart), though it does for onions, say. The answer is to wall-off, and ceil, a northeast corner for anything that needs maintained low temperature and dryness. Then you can put pumpkins and such near the stairway leading to the attic—and leave the hall door downstairs open whenever you need to.

In Styrofoam Picnic Chests/Hampers

Harvest carrots, beets, turnips, etc., late in the fall. The handling described for carrots works well for the others too.

Cut tops off carrots, leaving about ½ inch of stem. Wash away garden soil, then wipe fairly dry—"fairly dry" because you want a little moisture; but not wet, lest the vegetables mold. Sack them 4 to 5 pounds at a crack in the largest *food-grade* freezer bags (see "Using Space–Age Plastics" in Chapter 4, for the warning against using trash or garbage bags in direct contact with food). Press out excess air from each filled bag, twist the top and tie it tight with string, rubber bands, coated wire.

Pack the bags in a styrofoam chest of the inexpensive sort you use to carry picnic food on ice, and store the chest in any cold spot, like an unheated roughly walled-off corner of the cellar or an enclosed sunless porch. Keep the lid tightly on the chest except when removing meal-size amounts from a bag.

Carleton Richardson of Brattleboro, Vermont, who taught us this type of storage, sometimes puts bags of beets directly on the cool cement floor of his cellar—and they keep beautifully for 6 months.

Late Apples in Milk Cans (or Small Metal Trash Cans)

High in Green Mountain ski country, Albert and Millie Dupell use four old 40-quart milk cans with tight-fitting lids to store two bushels each of Northern Spys and winter McIntoshes.

Wrap each perfect, fresh apple snugly in one standard-size page of clean newspaper, having balled and smoothed the paper beforehand so it will create tiny air pockets next to the fruit. Pack fruit in the cans firmly but without bruising, and store the cans anywhere that holds between 30 and 45 F/−1 and 7 C. Don't open too often—take out a couple of meal's worth at a time, refrigerating the extras—and seat the lid very firmly afterward.

To use small metal trash barrels, you'll need to provide some insulation so they will equal the efficiency of milk cans (which are becoming "collectibles" for nostalgia buffs, and so are fairly scarce). Put 3 inches of dry sawdust in the bottom of the barrel and pack 1 inch of sawdust between the outside apples and the metal sides. Electrician's tape or other heavy-duty plastic self-adhesive strips may be wound tightly around the upper edge of the barrel, just below the rim, to create friction with the cover and ensure that it fits as smoothly tight as a milk can's lid does.

SMALL–SCALE OUTDOOR STORAGE

There's a good deal of information around that contains ideas for full-dress outdoor buildings for root-cellaring. Of these we suggest the USDA *Home and Garden Bulletin No. 119, Storing Vegetables and Fruits in Basements, Cellars, Outbuildings, and Pits*—available from your County Agent. He can steer you to the most recent USDA and Commerce publications; don't forget your public library's catalog, or *Readers' Guide to Periodical Literature*. As the practicality of homesteading has been developed, so has grown the amount of material published on virtually every phase of preserving crops.

Some Mild-climate Pits, etc.

The USDA bulletin and the other sources describe several easy-to-make and cheap outdoor storage facilities, all either on well-drained ground or sunk only several inches below the surface. See the chart for which produce likes the conditions they provide.

However, such arrangements can be counted on *only in places with fairly mild winters* that have no great extremes in temperature. At any rate, make a number of small storage places, fill them with only one type of produce to each space, and be prepared to bring the entire contents of a store-place indoors for short storage once the space is opened.

MILD-CLIMATE CONE "PITS"

Most instructions call a storage place like this a pit, but it's really a conical mound above ground. To make it, lay down a bed of straw or leaves, etc.; pile the vegetables *or* fruits (don't mix them together) on the bedding; cover the pile well with a layer of the bedding material. With a shovel, pat earth on the straw/leaf layer to hold it down, extending a "chimney" of the straw to what

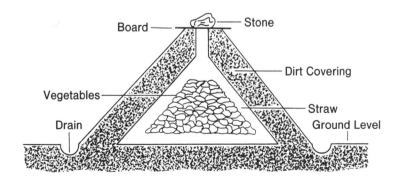

will be the top of the cone to help ventilate and control the humidity of the in-nards of the mound. Use a piece of board weighted by a stone to act as a cap for the ventilator. Surround the "pit" with a small ditch that drains away surface water.

As colder weather comes, add to the protective layer of earth, even finishing with a layer of coarse manure in January.

Mild-climate Cabbage "Pit"

This is quite like the cone above, except that it's longer and allows stored food to be removed piecemeal.

Lay the uprooted cabbages head-down on a bedding of straw, etc., pack in-sulating straw/leaves around them, and cover all with earth. Cut a drainage carry-off on each side of the pit.

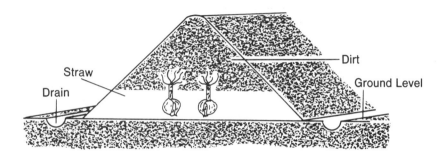

Mild-climate Covered Barrel

Still called a "pit" is a barrel laid on its side on an insulating bed of straw, chopped cornstalks, leaves, etc. Put only one type of produce in the barrel on bedding of straw/leaves. Prop a cover over the mouth of the barrel; cover all with a layer of straw, etc., and earth on top to hold it down.

Covered barrel and celery frame—both for a mild climate.

OUTDOOR FRAME FOR CELERY, ETC.

Dig a trench 1 foot deep and 2 feet wide, and long enough to hold all the celery you plan to store. Pull the celery, leaving soil on the roots, and promptly pack the clumps upright in ranks 3 to 5 plants wide. Water the roots as you range the plants in the trench. Leave the trench open until the tops dry out, then cover it with a slanted roof. This you make by setting on edge a 12-inch board along one side of the trench, to act as an upper support for the crosspiece of board, etc., that you lay athwart the trench. Cover this pitched roof with straw and earth.

Walter Needham's Cold-climate Pit

As he told in *A Book of Country Things,* he was raised in rural Vermont by a grandfather for whom a candle-mold was a labor-saving device. So whenever we want to learn about totally practical methods of pioneer living in the cold country, we turn to Walter Needham. He was the first to point out that the conical "pit" wouldn't do an adequate job in 20-below Zero Fahrenheit weather. This is his alternative:

Choose the place for your pit on a rise of ground to avoid seepage. There, shovel out a pit about 1½ to 2 feet deep and 4 feet wide at the bottom, throwing dirt up all around to build a rim that will turn water away; dig a V-shaped drainage ditch around it for extra protection (see sketches). Take out any stones near the sides of the pit because frost will carry from one stone to another in rocky ground. The pit needn't go below the deep frost-line if such frost conductors are removed. Pack the bottom of the pit with dry mortar sand 2 to 3 inches deep: the loam, having retained moisture, will freeze; the sand holds the food away from the loam.

On the layer of sand make a layer of vegetables not more than 1 foot deep; cover the vegetables with more fine sand, dribbling it in the crevices, to fill the pit nearly to ground level. Cover the sand with straw or Nature-dried hardwood leaves, or mulch hay (hay that got rained on before it cured), mounded to shed the weather. Hold down this cover with a thin layer of sod—or, nowadays, plastic sheeting weighted down with 1 to 2 inches of earth. Cover one end of the mound with a door laid on its side and slanted back almost like a bulkhead entrance. In winter you'll move the door away to dig in for the vegetables, and, as they're taken out, move the door back along the mound.

This root-pit is best for beets, carrots, turnips and potatoes.

Walter Needham's Sunken Barrels

Again, these are for cold-winter areas with uneven temperature.

Into the face of a bank dig space to hold several well-scrubbed metal barrels with their heads removed—one barrel for apples, say; one for potatoes, one for turnips. Take out any large stones that would touch the barrels and conduct frost to them, and provide a bedding of straw/dry leaves, etc., for the barrels to rest on. Slant the open end of the barrels slightly downward, so water will tend to run out.

RECOMMENDED CONDITIONS FOR OVER-THE-WINTER COLD STORAGE

PRODUCE	FOOD FREEZES AT (F)	TYPE OF STORAGE	IDEAL TEMPERATURE (F)	RELATIVE HUMIDITY (%)	AIR CIRCULATION	AVERAGE STORAGE LIFE
Fruits:						
Apples	29.0	RC-F	at 32	MM: 80–90	moderate	4–6 months
Grapefruit	29.8	RC-F	at 32	MM: 80–90	slight	1–1½ months
Grapes	28.1	RC-F	at 32	MM: 80–90	slight	1–2 months
Pears	29.2	RC-F	at 32	MM: 85–90	slight	2–7 months
Vegetables:						
Beans, dried	won't	DS; A	32–50	D: 70	moderate	12+ months
Beets	(c. 30)	BSR; P/B; RC	32–40	M: 90–95	slight	4–5 months
Cabbage	30.4	P/B; RC; DS	at 32	MM/M: 85–90	slight	late F–W
Carrots	(c. 30)	BSR; P/B; RC	32–40	M: 90–95	slight	6 months
Cauliflower	30.3	RC	at 32	MM: 80–90	slight	1½–2 months
Celery	31.6	BSR; frame; RC	at 32	MM/M: 85–90	slight	late F–W
Chinese cabbage	(c. 31.9)	BSR; frame; RC	32–34	VM: 95–98	slight	3–4 months
Dried seed, live	won't	A	32–40	D: 70	slight	12+ months
Endive	31.9	frame	at 32	MM/M: 85–90	moderate	2–3 months
Horseradish	(c. 30.4)	BSR; P/B; RC	at 32	M: 90–95	slight	4–6 months
Kale	(c. 31.9)	frame	at 32	VM: 95–98	moderate	1 month

Kohlrabi	(c. 30)	BSR; P/B; RC	32–40	M: 90–95	slight	2–3 months
Leeks	(c. 31.9)	BSR; P/B; RC	at 32	MM: 80–90	moderate	1–3 months
Onions	30.6	DS; A	at 32	D: 70	moderate	F–W
Parsnips	30.4	BSR; P/B; RC	at 32	M: 90–95	slight	F–W
Peas, dried	won't	DS;A	32–50	D: 70	moderate	12+ months
Peppers	30.7	BSR; RC; DS	45–50	MM: 80–90	slight	½–1 month
Popcorn	won't	A	to 75	D: 70	slight	12+ months
Potatoes	30.9	BSR; P/B; RC	35–40	MM: 80–90	slight	F–W
Pumpkins	30.5	BSR; A	at 55	MD/D: 70–75	moderate	F–W
Salsify	(c. 30.4)	BSR; P/B; RC	at 32	M: 90–95	slight	4–5 months
Squash	30.5	BSR; A; RC	at 55	VD: 50–70	moderate	F–W
Sweet potatoes	29.7	BSR; DS	55–60	MD/D: 70–75	moderate	F–W
Tomatoes, green	31.0	BSR; DS	55–70	MM: 80–90	moderate	1–1½ months
Turnips	(c. 30)	P/B; RC	at 32	M: 90–95	slight	2–4 months
Winter radishes	(c. 30)	BSR; P/B; RC	at 32	M: 90–95	slight	2–4 months

A = attic : BSR = basement store room : DS = dry shed : frame = coldframe : P = outdoor pit : B = buried barrel : P/B = pit or barrel : RC = root cellar : RC-F = root cellar for fruit : D = dry : VD = very dry : MD/D = moderately dry to dry : M = moist : MM = moderately moist : MM/M = moderately moist to moist : VM = very moist : F = fall : W = winter.

This tabular form could not accommodate metric conversions alongside Fahrenheit figures. Therefore we refer you to the relevant metric conversions in Chapter 17, as simpler for you.

FROM THE SIDE

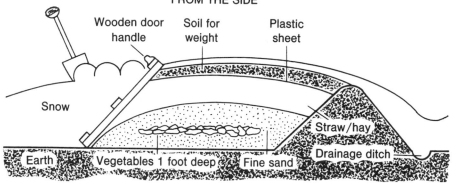

FROM THE FRONT

FROM THE TOP

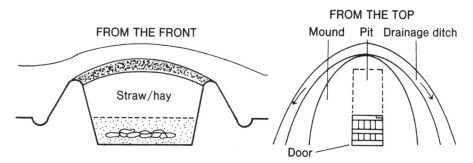

Cold-climate storage in a pit, above, and in sunken barrels.

FROM THE SIDE

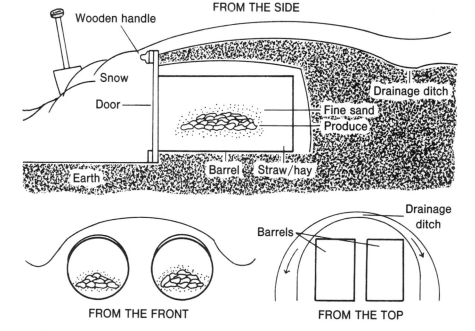

Put straw or whatever in the barrels for the produce to lie on, and fill the barrels from back to front, using dry leaves or similar material to pack casually around the individual vegetables or fruits if they need it.

Over the opening put a snug cover propped against it—a stout wooden "door" with a *wooden* handle (did you ever have the skin of your palm freeze on to metal in bitterly cold weather?). Dig a shallow V-shaped drainage ditch to carry surface water away from the barrels (as in the top-view sketch on the preceding page).

The snow will be added protection in the deepest cold of the winter. Shovel it back against the door after removing food from the barrels.

Root–Cellaring Fruits

Only several of the most popular fruits root-cellar well; and of these, apples retain their texture and flavor longest, with several varieties of pears next in storage life.

Like vegetables, fruits to be stored over the winter should be harvested as late as possible in the season, and be as chilled as you can get them before they're put in their storage containers (it will take even a properly cold root cellar a good deal of time to remove the field heat from a box of warm apples).

Because they absorb odors from potatoes, turnips and other "strong" vegetables, fruits should have their own special section partitioned off in the root cellar if they are stored in quantity; otherwise put them in another area where the conditions simulate those of a root cellar (see the chart), or keep them as far from the offending vegetables as possible.

We recommend clean, stout cartons, wooden boxes or splitwood fruit baskets over the classic apple barrels for storing fruits for a small family. Metal barrels are best used for fruits in underground storage, with the barrel well insulated from frost in the earth.

Some fruits are individually wrapped for best keeping, but all should be bedded on a layer of insulating—and protecting—straw, hay, clean dry leaves, with the straw, etc., between each layer of fruit, and several inches of bedding on top of the container.

All fruits need checking periodically for spoilage. If you're afraid your fruit will deteriorate faster than you can eat it fresh, have a midwinter preserve-making session. They're fun on cold lowery days.

How to Ripen Fruit

Apples keep longer if they don't touch each other, and apples and potatoes should never be stored close together. *Reason:* Apples respire more than most fruits do; they seem to give off extra amounts of the gas ethylene—along with other gases—and this peculiarity allows them to help pears, peaches and tomatoes to ripen. Use a heavy brown kraft-paper bag from the supermarket, punch about half a dozen small holes in it (to let some of the gases escape); put pears, peaches or tomatoes in the bag without crowding, *and include one sound ripe apple.* Bend over the top of the bag several times and hold it with a paperclip; set the bag on a shelf in the pantry where it will not be too warm. Check every day to make sure that no soft/rotten/mold spots are appearing, and that things are ripening well. It's amazing what two days will do for ripening these fruits.

Avocados ripen well in a brown paper bag; so do bananas; so do small melons. The brown paper is just porous enough to allow an exchange of fresh air and the gases from the fruit.

The popular plastic "ripening bowl" developed, if we remember right, by a scientist at the University of California, Davis department of agriculture, performs like a brown paper bag—but in a more deliberate, sophisticated and predictable fashion.

APPLES

Best keepers: *late* varieties, notably Winesap, Yellow Newton, Northern Spy; then Jonathan, McIntosh in New England, Cortland, Delicious. Pick when mature but still hard, and store only perfect fruit. Apples kept in quantity in home cold storage usually will be "aged" from Christmas on.

Apples breathe during storage, so put them in the fruit room of a root cellar so they don't give off their odor (or moisture) to vegetables. Wrap individually in paper (to cut down their oxygen intake); put them in stout cartons, boxes, barrels that can be covered, and have been insulated with straw, hay or clean dry leaves. If you use large food-grade plastic bags or liners for the boxes, etc., cut ¼-inch breathing holes in about 12 places in each bag.

They also may be stored in hay- or straw-lined pits or in buried barrels covered with straw and soil, etc.

Earlier, at the end of the "Indoor Storage" section, we described how the Dupells of Stratton, Vermont, store their late apples in old giant milk cans; as the fruit respires, it makes its own suitable humidity.

Check periodically and remove any apples that show signs of spoiling. See the chart for ideal conditions.

GRAPEFRUIT AND ORANGES

Store unwrapped in stout open cartons or boxes in the fruit room of a root cellar (see chart for conditions). Inspect often for spoilage, removing spoiled ones and wiping their mold off sound fruit they've touched.

GRAPES

Catawbas keep best, then Tokays and Concords. Pick mature but before fully ripe.

Grapes absorb odors from other produce, so give them their own corner of the root-cellar fruit room (see chart for conditions). Hold in stout cartons or boxes lined with a cushion of straw, etc., with straw between each layer; don't burden the bottom bunches with more than three layers above them, fitting the bunches in gently. Cover with a layer of straw. Check often for spoilage.

PEARS

Best keeper of the dessert varieties is Anjou, with Bosc and Comice popular among the shorter keepers. (Bartlett and Kieffer ripen more quickly and earlier: the former is especially good for canning, the latter for spicing whole or used in preserves; see Canning and The Preserving Kettle.)

Pick mature but still green and hard. Hold loosely in boxes in a dry, well-aired place at 50–70 F/10–21 C for a week before storing. Then store them like apples. See chart for conditions.

Warning: Pears that have started ripening above 75 F/24 C during the interim between picking and storage, or are root-cellared at too high a temperature, will spoil, often breaking down or rotting inside near the core while the outside looks sound.

Root–cellaring Vegetables

Root-cellared vegetables freeze sooner than fruits do, as a rule; and, if you store a variety beyond the commonest root crops—beets, carrots, potatoes, turnips and rutabagas—you need several different kinds of storage conditions. See the chart again, and the individual instructions below.

Wooden crates and movable bins, splitwood baskets, stout cartons—all make good containers for indoor storage. Insulating and layering materials are straw, hay, clean leaves, sphagnum and peat moss, and dry sand. The moist sand suggested for certain vegetables shouldn't be at all puddly-wet: if it's cold to the touch and falls apart when squeezed, leaving a few particles stuck to your hand, it should be the right degree of dampness.

Don't fill containers so deeply that the produce at the bottom is ignored in the periodic examinations for spoilage. And forgo building permanent bins that can't be moved outside for between-season scrubbing and sunning—stout shelving for the containers at convenient heights off the floor is a much better use of storage space.

BEANS (SHELL), DRIED

Cool the finished beans and package in plastic bags which you then put in large, covered, insect- and mouse-proof containers. See chart for conditions.

BEETS

Harvest in late fall after nights are 30 F/-1 C (they withstand frosts in the field) but when the soil is dry. Do not wash. Leave tails and ½ inch of crown when removing the tops. Pack in bins, boxes or crates between layers of moist sand, peat or moss; or bag like Carrots in the largest size of food-grade plastic freezer bags; cut ½-inch breathing holes in about 12 places. See chart.

Incidental intelligence: Miss Gertrude Russell always bakes her large beets (then takes off their tips and tails, peels them, cuts them for serving): she says they retain their juiciness and flavor best served this way. An old Shaker "manifesto" says much the same thing. Try it!

Cabbage, Late

Cabbage is not harmed by freezing in the field if it's thawed slowly in moist sand in the root cellar and not allowed to refreeze. Late cabbage can be stored effectively in several ways. (1) Roots and any damaged outer leaves are removed and the heads are wrapped closely in newspaper before being put in bins or boxes in an outdoor root cellar (the odor is more noticeable when they are wrapped than when covered with sand or soil). (2) With roots removed, the heads are covered with moist soil or sand in a bin in the root cellar. (3) In pit storage, stem and root are left on and they are placed head-side down. Straw, hay or clean, dry leaves may be packed between the heads for added protection and the whole business covered with soil. (4) The outer leaves are removed and cabbages are hung upside down in a dry place at normal room temperature for several days or until they "paper over." Then they are hung upside down in the root cellar.

- *Warning:* Cabbages have one of the strongest odors of all vegetables, so don't store them where the smell can waft through the house. See chart.

Carrots

Carrots may stay in the garden after the first frosts. After digging, handle like Beets. See chart for conditions.

Cauliflower

Another hardy vegetable that can withstand early frosts. Cut off the root and leave plenty of protecting outer leaves; store in boxes or baskets with loose moist sand around and covering the heads. See chart for conditions.

Celery

Celery should not be stored near turnips and cabbages, which taint its flavor.

Pull the plant, root and all; leave the tops on. Do not wash. Place the roots firmly in moist sand or soil, pressing it well around the roots. Water the covered roots to keep them moist *but do not water the leaves.*

The procedure for celery may be followed in a trench, a coldframe-bed, or in a corner of the root-cellar-floor that has been partitioned off to a height of six inches. The closer the celery is stood upright, wherever it's stored, the better. See chart for conditions.

Chinese Cabbage

Pull and treat like Celery. See chart for conditions.

Dried Seed (Live)

So long as it is kept quite dry, live seed won't germinate. Store in food-grade plastic bags that are then put in a large, mouse-proof covered container; or in canning jars that are wrapped in newspaper to keep out the light. It can't be hurt by natural low temperatures: see chart for conditions.

ENDIVE

Pull as for Celery. Do not trim, but tie all the leaves close together to keep out light and air so the inner leaves will bleach. Set upright and close together with moist soil around the roots, again as for Celery. See chart for conditions.

HORSERADISH

One of the three vegetables that winters-over beautifully in the garden *when kept frozen*. Mulch carefully until the weather is cold enough to freeze it, then uncover to permit freezing and, when it has frozen in the ground, mulch heavily to prevent thawing. For root-cellaring, prepare and handle like Beets. See chart for conditions.

KALE

Treat like Celery right on down the line. See chart for conditions.

KOHLRABI, handle like Beets; see chart.

LEEKS, see Celery and chart.

ONIONS

Pull onions after the tops have fallen over, turned yellow and have started to dry—but examine for thrips (which can cause premature wilting, etc.).

Bruised or thick-necked onions don't store well.

Onions grown from sets are stored in a cool, very dry place on trays made of chicken wire and the tops pointing down through the mesh.

Onions must be conditioned—allowed to "paper over"—in rows in the field; turn them several times so their outsides dry evenly. Smaller amounts may be surface-dried on racks in a dry, airy place under cover; or the tops may be braided and the bunches hung in a dry room. After they are conditioned, trim the tops and hang the onions in net bags or baskets in a dry, airy storage place. See chart for conditions.

PARSNIPS

Actually *improved* by wintering frozen in the garden (and not allowed to thaw), but may be root-cellared if necessary. Treat like Beets or Horseradish. See chart for conditions.

PEPPERS

Careful control of temperature and moisture is imperative in storing peppers (see chart): they decay if they get too damp or the temperature goes below 40 to 45 F/4 to 7 C.

Pick before the first frost; sort for firmness; wash and dry thoroughly—handling carefully because they bruise easily.

Put them one layer deep in shallow wooden boxes or cartons lined with food-grade plastic in which you cut about 12 ¼-inch holes; close the top of the plastic. Even under ideal conditions the storage life is limited.

Popcorn, see Beans (Shell), dried; see chart.

Potatoes, Early

Don't harvest after/during heavy rains, or on a hot day. Dig them carefully early in the morning when the temperature is no more than 70 F/21 C. Condition them for 2 weeks at 60–70 F/16–21 C in moist air to allow any injuries to heal: early potatoes will not heal if they are conditioned in windy or sunny places. After conditioning, store at 60 F/16 C for 4 to 6 weeks. These early varieties do not keep long, and spoil readily held at over 80 F/27 C.

Potatoes

Late potatoes are much better keepers than early varieties. Dig carefully. Hold them in moist air about 2 weeks between 60 to 75 F/16 to 24 C to condition: do *not* leave them out in the sun and wind. Put them, not too deep, in crates, boxes or bins stored in a dark indoor or outdoor root cellar; cover to keep away all light (to prevent their turning green, which could mean the presence of selenium, not good in large doses).

After several months' storage, potatoes held at 35 F/2 C may become sweet. If they do, remove them to storage at 70 F/21 C for a week or so before using them. Potato sprouts must be removed whenever they appear, especially toward the end of winter. Early sprouting indicates poor storage conditions. See chart for conditions.

- **Warning:** Potatoes make apples musty, so don't store these two near each other unless the apples are well covered.

Pumpkins

Harvest before frost, leaving on a few inches of stem. Condition at 80 F/27 C for about 2 weeks to harden the rind and heal surface injuries. Store them in fairly dry air at about 55 F/13 C (see chart). Watch the temperature carefully: too warm, and they get stringy; and pumpkins (and squashes) suffer chill damage in storage below 50 F/10 C—they're not for outdoor cellars or pits. Just because they are big and tough doesn't mean they can be handled roughly, so place them in rows on shelves, not dumped in a pile in a corner.

Salsify

The third vegetable (with parsnips and horseradish) that winters-over to advantage in the garden—so long as it remains frozen. If they must be stored, dig them when the soil is dry late in the season but before they freeze. Handle and root-cellar like Beets (and see chart).

Squashes, condition and store like Pumpkins—but drier (see chart).

Sweet Potatoes

If a killing frost comes before you can dig them, cut the plants off at soil level, so decay in the vines can't penetrate down into the tubers.

Sweet potatoes are really quite tender, so handle them gently: sort and crate them in the field. Condition at 80 to 85 F/27 to 29 C for 10 days to 2 weeks near a furnace or a warm chimney, maintaining high humidity by covering the stacked crates (which have wooden strips between for spacing) with plastic sheeting or a clean tarpaulin, etc. Then store in fairly dry and warm conditions (see chart). Like Pumpkins and Squashes, they damage from chill below 50 F/10 C.

TOMATOES, MATURE GREEN

For storing, harvest late but before the first hard frost, and only from vigorous plants. Wash gently, remove stems, dry; sort out all that show any reddening and store these separately.

Pack no more than two layers deep with dry leaves, hay, straw or shredded paper (plastic bags with air-holes are more likely to cause decay). Sort every week to separate faster-ripening tomatoes. See the chart.

TURNIPS

These and rutabagas withstand fall frosts better than most other root crops, but don't let them freeze/thaw/freeze. Storage odor can penetrate up from the basement, so store them by themselves outdoors (see chart for conditions).

Handle like Beets; pack in moist sand, peat, etc.

WINTER RADISHES, handle like Beets; see chart.

Waxing Turnips and Rutabagas

A number of readers have asked about the feasibility, and then the procedure, for waxing rutabagas and turnips the way commercial growers do, to prevent the vegetables' odor from spreading and to protect the skins. As to feasibility: not really practical for the usual householder. The vegetables must be dunked in the melted wax (it's plain old paraffin wax, the sort on hand to seal jellies and jams), and there must be enough of it in liquified form. And it must be just the right temperature—too cool and it globs, too hot and it scalds. And the air in the room must be just right as well, lest the wax break off before it penetrates the pores of the skins. (Remember, too, that rodents like paraffin wax.)

Better to use the most clinging of the food-grade plastic wraps, bought in extra-large rolls from your farm-supply/garden-and-seed store. Press the wrap tightly around each separate vegetable; you can bag several together, or put them in a large carton or bin.

If you do want to try waxing, though, be sure the rutabagas or turnips are clean and absolutely dry before you dunk them.

23

SPROUTS AND OTHER
GOOD THINGS

This chapter is a collection of ideas, foods, procedures that somehow did not fit easily into preceding chapters, usually because they required such a "side trip" from the theme being discussed. In addition, several of the methods or products were asked for over the years since the first *PFB* appeared in the early 1970's. So of course it's a catch-all. But it has been a pleasure to do.

> • • BECAUSE THE FOOD-HANDLING PROCESSES IN THIS CHAPTER ARE SO VARIED, we refer you to "Metric Conversions" (especially the rounded-off *italic* equivalents) in Chapter 17 for temperatures, volumes, weights, and lengths you may want to translate from the standard and old-style measurements used in the United States.

> • SPACE NOTE: In order to accommodate as many recipes as possible, we forgo the lengthy warning about de-toxifying home-canned food, and refer you instead to our standard warning as offered in Chapter 9, "Canning Seafood" and "A Quieter Method of Destroying Botulism Toxin."

Sprouting

Like so many new discoveries, sprouting had been practiced for centuries without fanfare as a means of having "live" food—and nutritious food—at hand during the nongrowing seasons. Then in the mid-'70's sprouting came into its own as do-it-at-home food that cost only pennies to produce, and was surely comparable to other green or not-yet-green vegetables in food value. And it will always be fun to do, whether you make-do with a canning jar, or have a tiered plastic container on your counter—of course made of sunproof green plastic, so it need not be shaded while the seeds do their thing.

440

Among the recent books we have, the most helpful is Esther Munroe's *Sprouts to Grow and Eat* (among other virtues it contains more than 150 recipes, ranging from appetizers to baby foods).

WHAT SPROUTING IS

Edible sprouts are the germinated seeds of an astonishingly wide variety of plants. You start with the dormant seed, give it the right combination of moisture, temperature, air and light to awaken it, and within a day the seed has swelled, and the coat has burst. Some species will produce cotyledons—the so-called "seed leaves"—and the finest possible hair-like roots by the third or fourth day. Some sprouts are eaten when they are about 1 inch long; others, from smaller seeds, will be ½ inch long when the crop is ready.

WHAT TO SPROUT

Some seeds are poisonous by nature and others have been made poisonous by people.

POISONOUS BY NATURE

Winston Way, who should know, includes in his list of poisonous species that "are definitely out" the castorbean, apple, stone fruits, sorghum, Sudan grass and potato (other writers add the tomato to this roster). He warns against sprouting seeds from any plant used for drugs.

MADE POISONOUS BY MAN

In order to prevent infestations and mold—even modern storage conditions can't always be guaranteed as ideal—virtually all seeds sold for planting have been treated with some chemical pesticide or fungicide that is highly toxic to human beings as well. Also, imported seeds are required by law to be stained with various colors, but their packets do not always contain the information that the seeds are dyed and therefore are taboo as human food. Therefore:

NEVER SPROUT SEEDS THAT HAVE BEEN TREATED CHEMICALLY, OR DYED. SPROUT ONLY THE SEEDS THAT HAVE BEEN CERTIFIED EXPLICITLY AS EDIBLE.

And we add a corollary: Never sprout for eating any certified-as-edible *seeds that have even the smallest amount of mold.* Reason: Mycotoxins, the poisons produced by growing molds, and they can mean bad trouble.

AND THEN THERE ARE DUDS

Even if you know they're safe, "hard seed" plants like birdsfoot trefoil don't always sprout satisfactorily for our eating purposes, and therefore too many seeds would be wasted.

You can sprout beans, lentils, chick-peas (the list is amplified in a minute), and of course these legumes are food-pure when sold in the supermarket. However, they've usually been dried so much and bashed around so hard that the yield in sprouts is disappointing. Cook them up instead.

And of course seeds must contain living embryos (even though dormant, they'll soak up their first moisture and burst into life). So make sure that the package label tells you the guaranteed percent of germination.

WHERE TO GET SPROUTING SEEDS

Health- and natural-food stores usually carry seeds for sprouting, plus information and equipment for the whole procedure.

A number of the large garden-seed companies list sprouting seeds and equipment in their catalogs: make sure the seeds you order are the ones they certify as edible.

And you can always grow your own—next year. Plant the varieties you want this coming growing season: use chemically treated seed for sowing. Raise your crop, harvest the seeds when fully mature. They are ready when the pods (using legumes as the illustration, because they are most commonly grown for sprouting) are dry, but just *before* they split open.

Dry the seeds in a warm, dry, airy place, preferably in the shade. If you must dry them indoors, *don't use the oven:* the seeds will get too hot and the embryo will be killed. If you use a dryer with a mild heat and fan, keep the temperature well below a killing range of 100 to 180 F/38 to 82 C; keep the seeds away from the heating element.

Check and store—*without pasteurizing*—in sterile, airtight containers. Here's a fine place to use the one-trip mayonnaise and pickle jars that you should not re-use for canning. Keep the containers in a cool, dry, dark place.

WHAT KIND TO GET

Sprouts have flavors as distinctive as the plants from which the seeds come. The following are popular, with the legumes leading the list. *Legumes:* alfalfa, clover, soybean, mung bean, adzuki bean, chick-pea (garbanzo). *Grains:* wheat, barley, millet, corn, buckwheat. *Vegetables:* radish, cress, celery, beet, pumpkin, squash. Herbs, wild greens and oil seeds are also sprouted.

Start small, though. First we'll try alfalfa. From there on it's up to you.

GENERAL PROCEDURE

There are many kinds of equipment and a great variety of seeds, but as a "starter set" we recommend this: certified-as-edible alfalfa seeds; clean, scalded 1-quart canning jar, preferably wide-mouth, with a screwband (no lid) or a stout rubber band; and a scrupulously clean nylon stocking. Time enough for deluxe fittings and dozens of different seeds after you become an expert in flavors and technique. Room temperature is usually best for all sprouting. Some seeds do well below the 65 to 70 F/18 to 21 C level; almost all seeds seem to grow faster at warmer temperatures, but anything above 70 F/21 C also helps to promote the growth of mold (see Chapter 2).

1. Put no more than 2 tablespoons of alfalfa seeds in your quart jar; fill half full of lukewarm water, and let stand overnight.
2. Make a strainer for the jar by stretching one layer of nylon stocking over the mouth, and fasten it snugly with the screwband or rubber.
3. In the morning, pour the water off the seeds (don't worry about browning). Rinse twice in lukewarm water, drain completely.
4. Hold the jar horizontally, tapping it to distribute the swollen seeds evenly; keep them away from the nylon: this is where the sprouts will get air to breathe. Lay the jar on its side in a dark cupboard that's not too warm (see above).
5. At midday and again at night take the jar from the cupboard and rinse the seeds (through the nylon) with lukewarm water, drain well. Rinsing is vital: the infant sprouts are undergoing metabolic change as they grow, and they throw off gases and substances that make the sprouts slimy if they're not drained. (Some sprouts also exude a mucilage as they develop.)
6. By the end of the second day in the cupboard—having been rinsed well and drained three times a day—little sprouts will appear, and in 12 hours more the sprouts will have roots ½ inch long.
7. After the morning rinse on the third or fourth day, place the jar in a sunny window. The cotyledons will turn green with amazing swiftness. By now most of the seed coats will come loose. Remove the netting and fill the jar with water to overflowing; shake it a little and many of the seed coats will float to the top and wash away: Let those in the bottom stay there. Seed coats, like popcorn hulls, are all right to eat but for appearance's sake you may want them removed.
8. Drain well. (You no longer need the nylon—the mass of sprouts will not fall out if you hold your fingers over the jar opening.) Store drained sprouts in the refrigerator in tightly covered containers. Like lettuce and celery, sprouts will stay sweet and fresh for four to six days.

RANDOM TIPS

For extra-delicious salads. Let the sprouts of alfalfa (and clover, rye, wheat, etc.) reach up to 2 inches in length; expose the sprouts to indirect sunlight for about 3 hours for the chlorophyll to do its work—and enjoy their sweet "green" taste in salads.

To freeze. For an unexpected surplus of sprouts, wash, remove husks, blanch in one layer at a time over vigorous steam for 3 minutes; cool quickly in ice water, drain, pack.

Babies on solid food thrive on sprouts cooked (with chicken or liver or whatever their diets allow), all whirled in a blender to the palatable consistency. Extra servings can be frozen in ice-cube trays, removed and wrapped separately for easy heating later; the packets are then bagged and stored in the deep freeze for use in a few weeks.

A Good Master Mix

Home economists at Purdue University developed this Master Mix, which is considerably cheaper than packaged mixes for specific items in the supermarket, and certainly it is more versatile. The recipes that follow are taken from *Brieflet 873, Homemade Mixes* (1963), by Anna M. Wilson, Extension Nutritionist, University of Vermont, with gratitude from *PFB*.

Proportions are given for 13-cup and 29-cup amounts, and individual recipes for using it are given in family-size and two-person quantities.

The Mix will keep for six weeks without refrigeration *if it is made with hydrogenated fat* (standard vegetable shortening that itself can be held without refrigeration after its container is opened). However, it should be held in a dry place that will not get above 60 to 65 F/16 to 18 C, or the texture will suffer.

Master Mix
Makes Thirteen Cups

---

  9 cups sifted all-purpose flour
        OR
10 cups sifted soft-wheat or cake flour
⅓ cup double-acting baking powder
  1 tablespoon salt
  1 teaspoon cream of tartar
¼ cup sugar
  2 cups shortening that *does not require refrigeration*

Stir baking powder, salt, cream of tartar and sugar into flour, then sift all together three times into a large mixing bowl (or onto a large square of plain paper). Cut in the shortening until the dry ingredients are the consistency of cornmeal. Store in covered containers at room temperature. To measure the Master Mix, pile it lightly into cup and level off with a spatula.

From this mix you can make cakes, breads, cookies and desserts.

BISCUITS
(Eighteen 2-inch biscuits)

3 cups mix
⅔ cups milk

Add milk to the mix all at once, stirring 25 strokes. Knead 15 strokes on lightly floured board. Roll ½ inch thick. Cut. Bake on baking sheet in hot oven 450 F/232 C for 10 minutes.

MUFFINS
(Twelve Medium)

3 cups mix
2 tablespoons sugar
1 cup milk
1 egg

Add sugar to the Mix. Combine milk and beaten egg. Add to the Mix. Stir until flour is moistened (about 25 strokes). Bake in greased muffin pans in hot oven 425 F/218 C about 20 minutes.

DUMPLINGS
(Twelve Medium)

3 cups mix
¾ cup milk

Add the milk to the mix all at once, stirring about 30 strokes. Drop by tablespoon on top of boiling stew. Cover and boil gently 12 minutes without removing cover.

These can be dropped as a topping on a meat or vegetable casserole and baked uncovered in a hot oven about 20 minutes.

YELLOW CAKE
(Two 8-inch Layers)

3 cups mix
1¼ cups sugar
1 cup milk
2 eggs
1 teaspoon vanilla

Stir sugar into the Mix. Combine milk, eggs, and vanilla. Stir half of the liquid into the Mix and beat 2 minutes or use electric mixer for 2 minutes at low speed. Scrape bowl occasionally. Add remaining liquid and beat 2 minutes. Bake in pans lined with waxed paper in a moderate oven 375 F/191 C for about 25 minutes.

Hominy: Dried Corn, Hulled and Cooked

Hominy is dried corn (see Corn, parched in "Drying Vegetables" in Chapter 21) with the hulls removed by a strong caustic solution. Coarsely ground as "grits," boiled hominy is a staple on Southern tables from breakfast through supper. As a canned vegetable from almost any supermarket in the Western

Hemisphere, the kernels are whole but swollen out of shape, rather like popped corn though more sedate and solid.

What is generally called an alkali—lye, potash (potassium carbonate) and, more refined, pearlash; slaked or pickling lime (calcium hydroxide), or the product of heating limestone or seashells (calcium carbonate); even gentle baking soda (sodium bicarbonate) and its harsher cousin, washing soda—is caustic in varying degrees, with commercial lye demanding the most care during use.

All the products above destroy Vitamin C and many of the B vitamins, a fault that has prompted nutritionists to warn against adding a touch of soda to vegetables to preserve their garden-bright color in the cooking pot.

Native Americans who start from scratch by growing their own corn and then drying it in the open-air/sun, if necessary will boil the kernels with sifted wood ashes, or use a solution of water leached through wood ashes, to skin the corn. They of course prefer using slaked, or pickling, lime (see "Firming Agents" in Chapter 17).

> *Hulling with lime.* Dissolve 4 tablespoons of "slaked" pickling lime in 2 quarts of water in an enameled kettle; add 1 quart dried corn. Bring to boiling, reduce to moderate heat and cook at a slow boil until hulls loosen—about 20 to 25 minutes. Remove from heat and drain; wash in fresh cold water, rubbing the kernels between the palms of your hands to get off the hulls; continue until the water comes clear. The hominy is now ready for boiling, to serve hot with a sauce, or in a stew.

- **NOTE:** Roughly, 1 quart of dried corn will make 4 quarts of hominy after it is cooked (see also Chapter 7, "Canning Vegetables," for how to can it). And the proportions of liquid to dried corn vary in the various procedures below because the concentration of alkali is different with lye, homemade potash water, and "slaked" pickling lime.

Warnings About Lye

The stuff called "lye" may be any one of several highly caustic alkaline compounds that, in the presence of only the moisture in the air on a muggy day, can become activated, burning and eating deeply into animal or other organic tissue—including human skin.

ANTIDOTE FOR SEARING CONTACT: slosh immediately with cold water, follow with boric-acid solution (eyes) or vinegar.

If you buy household lye/caustic soda for hulling corn, *make sure it's suitable for use with food,* and is designated as "lye" or "lycons" on the can and contains no aluminum, nitrates or stabilizers. Above all, avoid commercial drain-openers, either crystalline or liquid. (See "Soapmaking" for more details.)

Use only enameled- or granite-ware pots or kettles—*never use utensils of aluminum,* which react violently with lye in water.

Hulling with lye. In an enameled kettle, dissolve 4 tablespoons of suitable household lye in 8 quarts of water; add 8 cups of dried corn. Boil 30 minutes; let stand off heat 20 minutes more. Drain; wash off lye with several hot-water rinses; cool by rinsing in cold water. Work off the hulls and dark tips of the kernels by rubbing the hominy or washing it vigorously in a colander. When hulls and tips are removed, boil it in fresh water to cover for 5 minutes, drain; *repeat four times* (totaling 25 minutes of boiling in five fresh waters). After last repeat, cook in fresh water until kernels are soft—about 45 minutes. Drain and pack Hot for canning.

Hulling with homemade lye. When the liquid that has leached through a barrel of ashes (see "Soapmaking," coming soon) is strong enough to float an egg, put it in an enameled kettle with dried corn in the proportion of 4 parts liquid to 1 part corn. Boil until the hulls can be worked and rinsed off. Proceed with rinsing and cooking, as above.

Pickled Fish Fillets

Say "pickled fish" and we usually think of a crock-shaped glass container of fillets enlivened with onion rings and thin discs of carrot—all held in clear vinegar dotted with spices and everything cool as a fjord in March. Nor would we be far wrong: "pickled" to describe fish *always means vinegared,* following sojourns in brine or salt; it never means only salted or brined.

The following ingredients give the basic proportions required to keep 10 pounds of prepared fish or fish pieces for up to 6 weeks in the refrigerator at 38 to 40 F/3 to 4 C. As described in Chapter 9, the fish are given a quick preliminary treatment in a weak brine right after being dressed, to draw out diffused blood; next they are held overnight in an extremely strong brine. Then they're rinsed, poached briefly in a vinegar-spice mixture, chilled, put in glass containers, covered with their vinegar, and capped.

This précis emphasizes that these pickled fish are not canned, may not be kept on a shelf at room temperature; that they depend on salt *and* vinegar *and* refrigeration for what storage life they have. Small fish—alewives, smelt, small mackerel, small trout, perch, etc., take your choice; ideal is herring, which may be filleted. Plump fish may have slits scored lengthwise in their flesh to allow the brines and vinegar to penetrate more readily.

Longer treatment—and longer keeping, therefore—are described in PNW *Bulletin 183: Fish Pickling for Home Use* (Reprinted 1979), published by the Co-operative Extension Services of Oregon, Washington and Idaho (see Chapter 25).

Use only water of drinking quality in preparing the fish and making the solutions for curing and pickling it. As with any pickle, water containing calcium and iron will discolor fish; any magnesium will tend to make it bitter.

Vinegar should be distilled white, of 50 grain (5 percent); wine or cider vinegars will give the fish an unwanted flavor; vinegar of less than 5 percent acid strength will not ensure protection against botulism and less frightening spoilers. *Never reduce the proportion of vinegar if the solution seems too tart:* instead, add sugar—¼ cup white table sugar for each 1 quart vinegar to start with, and you may increase it.

Use only the best grade of food-grade canning salt, without added iodine or fillers. Do not use so-called sea salt, or solar salt. (Note that the amount of salt is given by weight: a sensible precaution in view of the different densities of granulated and flake salts.)

Spices should be whole, and fresh.

The Method

Dress fish and clean it thoroughly; keep well chilled. When it is cut in strips or split or whatever (depending upon its size), weigh it: the ingredients will take care of 10 pounds; more, and the proportions of vinegar, etc., will have to be increased suitably.

In a heavy enameled kettle or ceramic crock, cover the fish with a brine in proportions of 1 cup salt to 1 gallon of cold water and soak it for 1 hour. Drain the fish, pack it in another container of similar material and cover it with a very strong brine in the proportions of *2½ pounds of salt* (about 3 cups, but weigh it—don't go by volume with the salt here) to 1 gallon of water. Keep refrigerated at the temperatures noted above for 12 hours.

Remove from the brine, rinse, and poach in the spiced vinegar.

The Pickling Solution

   1½ quarts distilled white 5 percent vinegar
   2½ pints drinking water
    1 ounce (or less) whole allspice
    1 ounce (or less) whole mustard seed
    1 ounce whole white pepper
   ½ ounce bay leaves
   ½ ounce mixed whole pickling spice
     (optional sugar: ¼ cup for each 1 quart of vinegar)

Bring the pickling solution to a boil in an enameled kettle, add the fish, and poach at a simmer for 10 minutes or until the fish may be pierced with a fork. Lift out, drain, and chill quickly in a single layer in the refrigerator. Pack the cold fish in 1-quart or larger canning jars, add to each jar a bay leaf, 2 lemon slices, more thinly sliced onion, perhaps a couple of thin carrot discs. Strain the pickling vinegar, bring it to boiling, and pour it into the jars to cover the fish completely. Cap immediately with a clean, two-piece screwband lids. Refrigerate.

FARMERS' PORK SAUSAGE

See instructions for canning sausage in Chapter 10 or freezing ground meat in Chapter 14.

20 pounds of fresh pork trimmings—⅔ lean, ⅓ fat
½ cup pickling salt
6 tablespoons ground sage (omit if canning: it gets bitter)
3 tablespoons ground pepper
3 teaspoons ground ginger *or* ground nutmeg, if desired
2½ cups ice water (if you're freezing it in rolls like cookie dough)

Put the meat through the food grinder twice; add seasonings and put through a third time. Mix it all thoroughly on a large bread-board.

If you plan to freeze it—or just to refrigerate it—rolled in bulk, knead the ice water in gradually until the liquid is absorbed and the sausage is doughy. The water keeps the sausage from crumbling when it's sliced for frying.

BOLOGNA–STYLE SAUSAGE

This rule makes about 25 pounds of sausage. If canned, *it must be Pressure-processed at 15 pounds* (see Chapter 10).

Prepare. Using the coarse knife of a food chopper, grind 20 pounds of lean beef and 5 pounds of lean pork; add seasonings, and re-grind with the fine knife. Usually ½ pound of salt and 2½ ounces (a standard small box) or less of pepper are enough. To help hold the meat's color, mix 1¼ teaspoons pure crystalline ascorbic acid (Vitamin C) with the salt and pepper. Garlic juice may be added, or finely minced garlic; or coriander or mace.

For this quantity of seasoned meat, add 3 to 4 pints of very cold water, and, using your hands, mix it all thoroughly until all the water is absorbed into the meat. Stuff tightly, without air pockets, into beef casings or rounds that have been soaked in cold water (such casings are available from butcher-supply houses). Use short casings; or tie long ones at intervals short enough to allow you to cut sections suitable for family use. Tie ends with stout string. Smoke the sausage for 2 to 3 hours at 60 to 70 degrees Fahrenheit/16 to 21 degrees Celsius (see "Smoking").

Next, simmer the smoked bologna at about 200 F/93 C until it floats. A full-size sausage will take a whale of a kettle; if you don't have a pot big enough, cut the thing in sections where you've tied it off, and cook it piecemeal, holding any extra pieces at 30 to 38 F/−1 to 3 C until cooked.

Storage. Store in the refrigerator any sausage you'll use quite soon. Canning is best for longer-term storage at home (see above). Because of its fat content and seasonings, it doesn't hold flavor well when frozen.

FARM–WIFE'S PORK HEAD CHEESE

1 hog's head, thoroughly trimmed and then quartered
salt
pepper

Put the well-scrubbed quarters in a large kettle and cover with unsalted water. Simmer until meat falls from the bones—about 3 hours. Remove from heat and let cool until the meat can be handled, but don't let the broth get so cold that the fat congeals. Drain away the liquid, strain it well and return it to heat to reduce by ⅓ or ½.

Put the meat—which has been picked from the bones and gristle—in a wooden chopping bowl and chop it very fine. Add enough reduced broth to make a wet mixture and season all to taste with salt and pepper. Pack in several standard-size bread tins about ¾ full. Nest one pan on top of another with waxed paper in between and weight the top pan to press all the meat properly; if extra juice is pressed out it can be saved for stock if desired. Set the stack in the refrigerator overnight. In the morning slide each loaf from its pan and wrap it in moisture/vapor-resistant paper; freeze.

Of course you may add herb seasoning if you like; but do try this simple rule before you jazz it up. This head cheese is nothing like the commercial product. It's grand in a sandwich; and served with slices of cold Liver Loaf and home-made Bologna Sausage (both q.v.) it makes the best platter of cold cuts ever.

PASTEURIZING MILK

When you count the tests and immunizations a milch cow must have before she's shown at even a small accredited fair or her milk is offered for public sale, you see why pasteurizing is a mandatory safeguard for our store-bought milk. Even cows that pass all these tests and are healthy may contaminate milk with bacteria that can cause human illness. And pasteurization cannot guarantee that new spoilers will not attack the milk if it is handled carelessly later.

For pasteurizing milk you need a dairy thermometer, a sterilized large spoon for stirring, and an out-size double boiler (rig one up by setting a large pot/kettle in an old-fashioned enameled dishpan).

Put milk in the inner pot, which you set in the outer one (the dishpan). Pour water in the outer container until it reaches the level of milk in the inside pot.

Put the whole thing on the stove and heat it until the hot water in the dishpan raises the temperature of the milk to 145 degrees F/63 degrees C. Hold the milk there for 30 minutes, stirring to heat the milk evenly; check the thermometer in the milk pot to make sure you're maintaining a steady 145 F/63 C. Then take the milk from its hot-water bath and cool it by setting the milk pot in cold water. Get it down to 50 F/10 C as soon as possible, then refrigerate.

WATERGLASSING EGGS

From a Very Old Scottish Cookbook

Eggs can be tested in a number of ways to ascertain whether they are fresh. If the contents rattle, an egg is not fresh. A stale egg is likely to be shiny, while the shell of a fresh egg has a soft bloom. Another test is to place the egg in water. A fresh egg will go to the bottom and lie on its side; one slightly stale will lie with the large end partly lifted from the bottom; one that is altogether stale will either float or stand on end.

Refrigeration is the best temporary storage for fresh eggs, with freezing (q.v.) recommended for longer holding.

Waterglass is sodium silicate, and you buy it from building-supply places nowadays, to seal concrete floors or to stick insulation around heating pipes. It's already dissolved, rather syrupy, and tastes like washing soda. It fills the pores of the eggshells, thus preventing moisture loss from the inside or air damage from the outside. It does well enough for a *maximum of 3 months* if the eggs are kept in cold storage.

Select nest-fresh eggs with perfect shells; discard dirty ones. Wipe eggs with a clean dry cloth (washing would remove natural protective film) and put them in a crock. Cover them 2 or 3 inches above the topmost layer with diluted waterglass, using 1 part waterglass to 11 parts of cooled, boiled water (⅓ cup waterglass to each 1 quart of water). Cover the crock and hold it under 40 F/4 C.

Remove eggs as needed for cooking and wash them before breaking. The whites will have lost a good deal of viscosity (they'll be worthless for meringue, for example), but the eggs are O.K. for long-cooked dishes calling for whole eggs (see "Freezing Convenience Foods," Chapter 16). Examine each egg as it's broken before adding it to the food mixture.

Fertile eggs. Farmers, being experienced with hens and their proclivities, would isolate the rooster from the flock for at least 1 month before putting any new-laid eggs in waterglass.

DRYING PRODUCE IN A WOOD-STOVE OVEN

If you're familiar with the workings of an old wood-burning black iron cookstove, you know that the oven heats *from the top:* therefore you dry food below the center of the oven, rather than higher.

Dry with an old, banked fire—air intake at the bottom of the firebox closed, drafts up through the stack closed. Feed the fire only when absolutely necessary, and then with very large hardwood, one billet at a time. You may even have to tilt the stove lids to cool the top of the oven; open the cross-draft regulator at the top of the firebox to keep the fire as low as you can. Hang an oven thermometer on the *upper* rack of food to keep track of maximum temperature, and do your drying with the oven door halfway or fully open.

RE-CANNING MAPLE SYRUP

To deal with the haze of mold that can form on maple syrup in a large container that's been opened repeatedly, pour the syrup into a deep enameled kettle, bring it quickly to boiling over high heat. Remove from heat, immediately skim the surface clean, and pour the boiling-hot syrup into hot pint jars, leaving ½ inch of headroom; cap firmly with hot lids. Process in a Boiling–Water Bath (212 F/100 C) for 10 minutes to ensure the seal. Remove jars, cool naturally. Refrigerate opened syrup.

RENDERING LARD

Lard is in disrepute these days because of blanket indictments against animal fats as cholesterol-makers. This is a pity, because active, sensible eaters shouldn't automatically forgo the special flakiness and tenderness that good lard gives pastry and cakes—unless their doctor has advised them to do so.

Lard is fresh pork fat, rendered—i.e., melted—at no more than 255 F/124 C, and then congealed quickly and cold-stored for later use. The fine lard generally considered best by the purists comes from the "leaf" next to the bacon strip; backfat from along the loin and plate fat from the shoulder also are good (as in the photographs; and see also the labeled parts of a pig in "Salting Pork" in Chapter 20). The caul fat (attached at the stomach) and the ruffle fat (around the intestines) usually make darker lard than the other parts do, and so are rendered separately.

A live 225-pound hog will yield slightly more than 25 pounds of all fats usable for lard; obviously only a small part of the total can come from the leaf (but it gives up a higher percentage of its weight in lard than the other sections do). So stop now to decide how you want to use the fat: to render the leaf separately; to combine leaf, loin, plate and trimmed fat; to combine caul, ruffle and trimmed fat, rendering them for soapmaking later.

Cut the fat in small pieces. Put a little of it in a large kettle over *low* heat and stir. When melting starts, add the rest of the fat gradually—but don't fill the kettle more than to 3 inches from the top, lest the fat boil over. Stir often and keep the heat low; the cracklings—bits of tissue—can stick and scorch.

Cracklings that brown and float to the top will settle to the bottom later on when they lose fat and moisture. As the water in the tissues steams away, the temperature of the fat will rise slowly above 212 degrees Fahrenheit (100 degrees Celsius). Use a deep-frying thermometer to make sure the heat doesn't get above 255 F/124 C, which is the top temperature for thorough rendering.

Let the rendered lard cool a bit so all sediment and cracklings will settle to the bottom. Carefully dip the clear liquid from the top of the kettle into containers, filling them to the brim; cover tightly and seal. Label and store immediately at freezing or below to make a fine-grained product.

Strain the lard at the bottom of the kettle through several layers of cheesecloth to remove the settlings; pack and store as above.

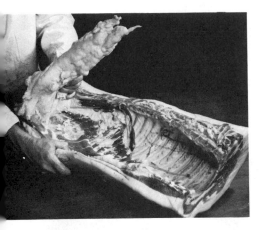
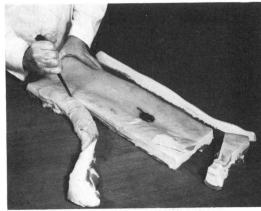

Main sources of lard: leaf fat, left above; trimming from bacon, right; plate fat from the shoulder, below left; back fat from the loin.

Air and light make stored lard rancid, and spoil it irrevocably for cooking purposes. Thorough rendering (to 255 F/124 C) eliminates the moisture that causes souring during storage.

Soapmaking

The Fundamental Rule

Never, *never*, *NEVER* make soap with young children around. Or pets.

Even a cold lye solution ⅙ as strong as the one below for soap-making may taste sweetish (much like a dose of baking soda in water to settle one's stomach) for a split second—but long enough for a child to swallow it; and then it burns painfully, with damage.

The heavy concentration of lye used in soap can strip off skin as easily as the peel is rubbed from a blanched peach.

Antidotes. Slosh eyes with cold water, follow immediately with cold boric-acid solution—which you'll do well to have handy by.

For hands, etc., wash immediately with cold water, followed by generous bathing with vinegar.

If taken internally, the sufferer should be made to drink salad oil (but don't pour a bit of it down the windpipe) AND TAKEN TO A DOCTOR AS FAST AS POSSIBLE.

Labels on containers give directions for other first-aid measures.

Lye can ruin a garbage disposal unit in the sink drain. Lye can raise Cain with the working of a septic tank.

Lye reacts violently with aluminum, so aluminum chips are used in commercial drain-openers for just this reaction.

Equipment for Soapmaking

First-aid supplies—cold water, boric-acid solution, vinegar, salad oil
An enameled or granite kettle for warming the fat (in a small batch)
(A big iron kettle and/or a wooden tub for larger batches)
A sturdy enameled kettle for dissolving the lye in water
Floating or dairy thermometer
Wooden paddles or long-handled wooden spoons for stirring
A shallow wooden box, large enough to hold about 2½–3 quarts of liquid;
   soak the box to make it tight, and line it with clean wet muslin that's big
   enough to drape generously over all the sides
A board to cover the box
A dripping pan big enough to hold the wooden box
An expendable rug or blanket to keep the new soap warm for a while
Tough string or fine wire (for cutting the soap in bars)
Glass measuring cups

What Lye Is (and Does for Soap)

Not This

Liquid or crystalline products that designate themselves as drain-openers contain nitrates, activating aids (like aluminum filings) and stabilizers. Such products are not remotely suitable for making soap.

O.K. Commercial Lyes

The several crystalline preparations sold simply as "lye" are sodium hydroxide; these also can double as drain-openers, but they don't have the additives that make bad soap. They come in 13-ounce cans. If you handle the lye immediately after the can is opened you may use ounces in weight and ounces in volume interchangeably when faced with instructions that call for lye either in pounds or in less than 13 ounces. The stuff readily absorbs moisture from the air, expanding in the process, so work quickly to get reasonably accurate measurements. Cap any remainder the minute you're through measuring.

This usable type of lye is mixed with cold water—whereupon it reacts and heats the water, giving off fumes that make ammonia seem bland in comparison. When the solution stops acting, it begins to cool; but its still frighteningly caustic.

When a solution of the right strength and temperature is poured into the right amount of clean warm fat at the right temperature, the fat saponifies—changes character and hardens.

Old-time "Potash Water"

Another kind of lye can be made by leaching cold water through pure hardwood ashes.

Remove the head from a water-tight wooden barrel and set it, open end up, on trestles high enough to allow a wooden pail to be set under it. Bore a small hole in the barrel's bottom near the front; make a tight-fitting plug for it and drive it in. Put several bricks in the bottom of the barrel, arranged to hold a protecting board over the hole, plus a layer of straw board and straw will prevent the ashes from packing too tightly on the bottom or fouling the hole.

Fill the barrel with firmly packed hardwood ashes. Make an opening in the center of the ashes, and in it pour all the cold water the barrel will hold. Cover the barrel and raise it at the rear so the liquid will run toward the front. Add more water the next day if the barrel will hold it.

After 3 weeks, remove the plug and draw off the lye into the wooden pail. The liquid will be, in the traditional saying, "strong enough to float an egg"—strong enough to make soap with. (Even if it's not, there's no worry: excess water can be boiled off when you make the soap.)

Fats Good for Soapmaking

Best for soap is tallow—rendered from beef or mutton fat as you rendered lard (q.v.); next best is lard, and a combination of lard and tallow; then comes olive oil, followed by other vegetable oils. Poultry fat doesn't do well alone. Mineral oil won't saponify at all.

All fats must be fresh, clean and salt-free to avoid disappointing results.

Master Recipe for Soap

Having the right temperature for both the lye solution and the fat is one way to ensure fine soap (the others are accurate measurement and fresh, clean, salt-free fat). Here are the temperatures:

Fresh, sweet lard at 80–85 F/27–29 C, lye solution at 70–75 F/21–24 C.

Half lard and half tallow at 100–110 F/38–43 C, with lye solution at 80–85 F/27–29 C.

All tallow at 120–130 F/49–54 C, with lye solution at 90–95 F/32–35 C.

Melt 6 pounds (c. 13½ cups) of clean rendered fat in a large enameled kettle until it's a clear liquid; cool it to the right temperature until it thickens; stir it occasionally to keep the fat from graining as it gets near room temperature.

Meanwhile, in a large enameled pot mix 1 just-opened can (13 ounces) of suitable crystalline household lye with 5 cups of cold water. Stir with a wooden paddle until it has dissolved—but stand clear of the fumes and avoid spatters of the caustic liquid: it will boil up like mad of its own accord. Let the solution cool to the proper temperature for the fat you're using.

When both fat and lye are the right heat, very carefully pour the warm lye into the fat in a *thin* steady stream, stirring the mixture very slowly and evenly (another pair of hands would be a great help here). If the combining temperatures are too cold or too hot, or if the fat and lye are combined too fast or stirred too hard, the soap will separate—and then you must boil the separated mixture with much extra water to make it get together again.

In 10 to 20 minutes of careful stirring the fat and lye will have blended thoroughly and become thick. Pour the saponified mixture at once into the soaked, cloth-lined box; set the box in the dripping pan to catch leaked soap. Lay the protecting board over the box and cover the whole shebang with a rug or blanket to hold the heat while the soap develops a good texture.

Don't disturb the soap for 24 hours. Then grasp the overhanging edges of the cloth liner and raise the soap block from the mold. Cut it by cinching strong twine or wire around the soap and pulling tight. Let the bars of young soap dry at room temperature in a draft-free place for 10 days or 2 weeks. Don't let the soap freeze during this time.

When the soap has conditioned, wrap each piece in paper and store it in a cool dry place. Aging improves soap.

Variations

Make floating soap by folding air into the thick saponified mixture before your pour it into the box-mold.

Make soap jelly by shaving 1 pound of soap into 1 gallon of fresh water; boil for 10 minutes; cool. Store in a closed container in a cool place. This is good for shampooing hair.

Make your own soap flakes by gently shaving 3-day-old soap against the medium holes of a vegetable grater. Stir the shavings gently as they air-dry. Store in closed containers.

COUNTRY–STYLE COTTAGE CHEESE

Cottage cheese is something you make at home only if you have considerable surplus fresh milk and more time than money. If you buy milk at supermarket prices to make cottage cheese, you'll be spending around 25 percent more for it per pound than you pay for the stuff ready made. However.

This type of cottage cheese has a small curd; it's well drained but not washed, so it's rather more soured-tasting than a cheese whose whey has been rinsed out; and the original rule has been translated from raw to pasteurized milk. The proportions are for 1 gallon of milk.

Bring the milk to 72 degrees F/22 degrees C—average room temperature in the kitchen anyway—and add ¼ to ⅓ cup fresh buttermilk. (Or add ⅛ to ¼ cup of lactic "starter"; and there's probably no reason why yogurt culture wouldn't work well too—experiment with proportions.)

Cover the kettle and keep the milk at 72 F/22 C overnight—at least 16 hours, or until the milk has curdled into a jelly-like substance, rather firm, with some watery whey on top.

In the kettle, cut the curd in ¼-inch pieces with a long-bladed knife. Slice the curd straight up and down in cuts about ¼ inch apart; then give the kettle a 90-degree turn and cross-hatch another series of up-and-down slices. Now the trick is to cut these square little columns of curd into something like cubes, and you can do a fair job by cutting through the curd again at a 45-degree slant, considering the bottom of the kettle as the base of the angle, then giving the kettle a quarter-turn and making another series of angled slashes.

Set the pot of cut curd in a larger container of water, and *slowly*—so slowly that it takes 30 minutes to raise the milk from 72 to 100 F/22 to 38 C—heat the milk over hot water, stirring gently every 5 minutes or so to distribute the heat. When the curd has reached 100 F/38 C you can raise its temperature more quickly to 115 F/46 C, and hold it there for about 15 minutes more. Test a curd: if it still breaks easily, bring the heat up to 120 F/49 C; if it's firm but not tough, remove it from the hot water so it starts to cool. The higher the temperature, the tougher the curd.

Dip off what whey you can, then pour the curd into a cloth-lined colander to drain for 5 minutes. The curd compacts if you let it drain a long time. People who want to wash the curd may do so now, by gathering the corners of the straining cloth to form a bag and dunking the bag of curd in fresh cold water, then letting it drain well.

Add salt to taste if you want to counteract the sourish-acid taste of the un-washed curd. Add 4 to 6 tablespoons of cream if you like.

Store in closed containers in the refrigerator.

24

COOKING

The recipes in this chapter do not try to reflect every category offered in a big cookbook, because *PFB*'s reason for being was to describe carefully the *procedures* that have proved safe for preserving all kinds of food at home. We wish we did have room to include more things that our readers, and we, like to eat.

There are, though, more of what dear Bea Vaughan called "receipts" in this edition than there were in earlier versions. They were chosen because they could be made from canned or frozen or dried or cured ingredients as well as from fresh materials, and because we think they have old-fashioned integrity.

But before we start cooking we must look hard at the need to compensate for high altitudes, and we should know how to translate our measurements into metric equivalents.

In Chapter 3 there is a fairly long discussion of the *Why* and *How* of dealing with lowered atmospheric pressure, and it's called "Correcting for Altitude." It would be a good idea to look at it again. Meanwhile there is a boiling chart, followed by conversions for a couple of other cooking methods.

• **NOTE:** Additional recipes are given in Chapter 10 ("Canning Convenience Foods") and in Chapter 16 ("Freezing Convenience Foods"). The latter describes the special requirements for adapting recipes for freezing and packaging; the ways to use mochiko—the special rice flour for thickening frozen foods—and Greek filo pastry are well worth considering along with food in this Chapter 24.

• • **BECAUSE THE FOOD-HANDLING PROCESSES IN THIS CHAPTER ARE SO VARIED,** we refer you to "Metric Conversions" (especially the rounded-off *italic* equivalents) in Chapter 17 for temperatures, volumes, weights and lengths you may want to translate from the standard and old-style measurements used in the United States.

• SPACE NOTE: In order to accommodate as many recipes as possible, we forgo the lengthy warning about de-toxifying home-canned food, and refer you instead to our standard warning as offered in Chapter 9, "Canning Seafood" and "A Quieter Method of Destroying Botulism Toxin."

Metric Equivalents for Boiling Points of Water

ALTITUDE FEET/*Meters*	WATER BOILS FAHRENHEIT/*Celsius*	ALTITUDE FEET/*Meters*	WATER BOILS FAHRENHEIT/*Celsius*
Sea Level: 0+/0+	212.0/*100*	5000/*1524*	202.6/*94.8*
1000/*305*	210.0/*98.9*	5500/*1677*	201.7/*94.3*
1500/*457*	209.1/*98.4*	6000/*1829*	200.7/*93.7*
2000/*610*	208.2/*97.9*	6500/*1981*	199.8/*93.2*
2500/*762*	207.1/*97.3*	7000/*2134*	198.7/*92.6*
3000/*914*	206.2/*96.8*	7500/*2286*	198.0/*92.2*
3500/*1067*	205.3/*96.3*	8000/*2438*	196.9/*91.6*
4000/*1219*	204.4/*95.8*	10,000/*3048*	194.0/*90.0*
4500/*1372*	203.4/*95.2*		

Metrics for Other Cooking Methods at Sea Level

Oven temperatures vary from one heat source to another, from one model to another—and often fluctuate within one oven during a baking. The following are metrics for conventional electric ovens, rounded off to the nearest sensible figure. The Gas Marks are found more often with European than with American ranges, but they may come in handy.

BAKING AND OVEN ROASTING

ELECTRIC	FAHRENHEIT	CELSIUS (ROUNDED)	GAS MARK
Very slow	250 to 275	121 to 135	¼ to ½
Slow	300 to 325	149 to 163	1 to 2
Moderate	325 to 350	163 to 177	3 to 5
Moderately hot	375 to 400	191 to 205	5 to 6
Hot	400 to 425	205 to 218	6 to 7
Very hot	450 to 500	232 to 260	7 to 9

CANDY–MAKING

DESCRIPTION	FAHRENHEIT	CELSIUS (ROUNDED)
Thread	230 to 234	110 to 112
Soft ball	234 to 240	112 to 116
Firm ball	244 to 248	118 to 120
Hard ball	250 to 266	121 to 130
Soft crack	270 to 290	132 to 143
Hard crack	300 to 310	149 to 154

About Microwave and Convection Ovens

In search of a rule-of-thumb for translating instructions for conventional ovens into usable directions for microwave and convection ovens, *PFB* logically turned to Jane Keely, from 1959 to 1979 Director of *Good Housekeeping* Magazine's Appliance and Home Care department of the Institute. In that position she supervised all product investigations of home equipment for the magazine's Seal, and produced editorial material on appliances and home management. Since 1979 Mrs. Keely has written a number of books in addition to her regular monthly contribution to the magazine, plus a variety of booklets for consumer education. So, when she told us the following, we took it as gospel, and we thank her:

"Regarding the addition of convection and microwave directions to conventional recipes, I really can't see any way of doing this: there are so many different versions of ovens ... [And], beyond the varying-power problem, moisture content of recipes might have to be reduced because of shorter cooking times and less evaporation.

"Convection ovens are less complicated, but they, too, vary in size—and special pans are needed in some. Full-size ranges that have convection baking in the regular oven are another matter entirely.

"With all of these ovens and ranges, cookbooks are available, and I don't feel that users expect a book like *Putting Food By* to attempt conversions for them."

SOUPS

Classic Brown Stock
Four to Six Pints

    3½ pounds shin bones of beef
     2 pounds veal knuckle bones
     2 large carrots, scraped and chopped
     1 large onion, chopped
     1 large parsnip, chopped OR 1 mild turnip
     2 large ribs of celery with a few leaves, chopped
     1 teaspoon dried parsley
     2 bay leaves
       (optional: 1 tablespoon salt)
    ½ teaspoon peppercorns
     4 quarts cold water

Preheat oven to 425 F/218 C. Saw the bones in small pieces, cracking them as needed to expose marrow. In a large shallow roasting pan, combine the bones with carrots, onions, parsnip/turnip. Bake in the hot oven until brown but not charred—about 35 minutes. Put baked vegetables and bones in a heavy large enameled or stainless-steel kettle with water, celery and parsley. Over medium heat bring to boiling, cook gently for 2 hours, skimming frequently: the best way to ensure clear stock is (1) skim, and (2) cook gently. At the end of 2 hours, add the peppercorns, bay leaves and optional salt; cook 3 hours longer.

Strain the stock through a colander, then a sieve, and let rest in the refrigerator overnight to settle any sediment and to allow fat to congeal and be lifted off. Be careful not to disturb sediment when pouring into containers for storage. Makes 4 to 6 pints of stock, depending on your patience with simmering.

If the stock is to be canned or frozen, reduce it further, strain it through a jelly bag or, piecemeal, through a good coffee filter. See Chapters 10 and 16— "Canning Convenience Foods" and "Freezing Convenience Foods."

Other Soups and Bases

In Chapter 10, "Canning Convenience Foods," will be found recipes (plus canning procedures) for Broth/Stock from Meat or Poultry; All-Vegetable Broth/Stock; Shrimp Stock and Clam Broth; Vegetable Soup Base; and Country Tomato Soup.

New England Fish Chowder
Six Servings

---

  2 pounds fillets of cod, turbot or ocean catfish
2½ cups water
  1 teaspoon salt
 ¼ cup finely chopped bacon ends, *or* salt pork
  1 large onion, chopped fine
  3 cups diced raw potatoes
     pinch of cayenne
  1 quart milk

Put water and salt in a very large skillet, bring to simmering, and lay fillets in the hot water, one layer deep, to poach. Baste tops of fish (rather than flop them over in the water). When fish can be broken apart, remove with a large slotted spoon to a dish to cool.

Meanwhile put chopped bacon/pork in a heavy enameled kettle over moderate heat, stir. When melted fat accumulates, add minced onion; turn down heat, cover; stir occasionally so no pieces get brown.

While onions are cooking, dice potatoes and cook them in the fish broth left in the skillet. Keep heat low, and turn them over often: there is little water, and it will become starchy—the potatoes could scorch easily.

(*Recipe continued on next page*)

When potatoes are cooked, add them to the onion mixture in the kettle. Reduce the potato water until it begins to thicken; add to kettle and remove kettle from heat. Remove bits of skin and bone from fish, break it up but let it keep its identity; add to kettle. Add a pinch of cayenne pepper, fold mixture to combine. The base can rest for several hours (it can even be frozen).

To serve, add 1 quart rich milk that has been heated separately but not boiled. Stir chowder as it heats well through to a simmer. Correct seasoning if necessary. Serve with pilot biscuit and sweet gherkin pickles. Serves 6 heartily

French Onion Soup

Six Generous Servings

---

6 cups thinly sliced yellow cooking onions, about 2 pounds
3 tablespoons butter
3 tablespoons good oil
2 tablespoons flour
1 good bay leaf
4 cups seasoned broth—chicken, meat or vegetarian
    salt and pepper to taste
6 thick slices from a large loaf of sourdough French bread, or 12 slices
    from a *baguette* loaf
1 tablespoon olive oil
1 clove garlic, cut
⅔ cup grated Parmesan cheese, *or* 1 cup grated Gruyère

Melt the butter in oil in a heavy enamelware kettle over low heat. Add the onions, the larger outer rings cut in half if preferred; cook uncovered slowly for 25 minutes, stirring occasionally, until the onions are a deep gold color. Remove from heat, sprinkle the flour over the onions to bind them, mixing together smoothly; add 1 cup of the broth, stir well, add the bay leaf, and return to heat. When the oils have been incorporated with the flour and the liquid has thickened slightly, add the rest of broth and simmer for 20 minutes. Add salt and pepper to taste, continue simmering for 20 minutes more.

Meanwhile paint both sides of each slice of bread with oil, toast in a slow oven, turning once, until both sides are crisp and golden. Rub with the cut garlic, cover each piece with grated cheese. The cheese can be melted under a slow broiler and the toast laid on top of each bowl of soup before serving; or classic ovenproof soup bowls can be filled, topped with the toast and uncooked cheese, and all put under the broiler until the cheese melts.

Serves 6 well.

Aunt Chat's Tomato Cream Soup
Five to Six Servings

4 cups canned tomatoes, undrained
1 medium onion, peeled and chopped
2 stalks celery, chopped fine
4 cups scalded milk
    about 1 tablespoon flour for thickening
    pinch of baking soda (⅛ teaspoon)
1 tablespoon butter or margarine
    salt and pepper to taste

Simmer tomatoes, onion and celery for 30 minutes. Thicken scalded milk with the flour, which has been mixed with a little cold water to make a paste. Stir over low heat until milk thickens slightly. Just before serving, add baking soda to the tomato mixture (to prevent curdling); as frothing subsides, pour all through a strainer into the hot milk, stirring constantly. Add butter and season to taste with salt and pepper. Serve at once. Serves 5 to 6.

The recipe may be doubled, but *never increase the amount of soda.*

Irenja's Borscht
Makes Six 8-ounce Cups

½ cup coarsely grated carrots
⅔ cup finely cut-up onions
2 cups shredded beets*
1½ cups shredded cabbage
2 tablespoons butter
1 teaspoon dry whole dillweed
½ teaspoon caraway seeds
4 cups of stock (beef, chicken or vegetable)
¼ teaspoon crushed Sour Salt (citric acid crystals) OR 1 tablespoon vinegar

Melt butter in heavy enameled kettle that has a close-fitting cover. Peel and shred carrots, chop onions, peel and shred beets, shred cabbage—Combine all with the melted butter in the pot. Add dillweed and caraway seeds and stir so all pieces of vegetables are coated with butter. Add 2 teaspoons water for safety's sake, and let vegetables steep, basically in own juice for 15 minutes (check mixture after 10 minutes as it may need another tablespoon of water). Add 4 cups of good stock with character—beef, vegetarian, chicken or turkey.

* NOTE: If you don't have fresh beets use 2 cups canned sliced beets, reserving liquid and cutting beets in fine slivers to make 2 cups of firmly packed beets. Reduce the amount of broth by the amount of juice to bring total liquid to 4 cups.

(*Recipe continued on next page*)

Cover and simmer for 15 minutes. If desired add ¼ teaspoon crystalline citric acid or 1 tablespoon vinegar—or more to taste. Serve in heated bowls and drop a dollop of sour cream on top. This will make 3 pints of a hearty soup of medium consistency.

Dutch Green Pea Soup
Ten Good Servings

A good Dutch housewife like Mikkie van de Graaf—who's also co-proprietor of the Hotel de la Poste in Amsterdam—wrote her way of making Erwtensoep this way:

"Pigsmeat, sausages, peas, potatoes, water, two leeks, winter carrot, onions, celeriac, parsley, some celery leaves, bay leaf, pepper, salt, meat stock."

For meat she likes smoked pork hocks, a pound or so of spareribs, perhaps a pig's foot, and—on the second day—some slices of good smoked sausage. She starts by simmering 2 pork hocks, the spareribs and the pig's foot in water to cover well, skimming often; at the end of an hour or so she adds salt, pepper, the bay leaf, and 1 pound ("half-kilo") of split green peas. Make sure there's water to cover well during the next hours of cooking.

Meanwhile clean the leeks, carrot, onions, celeriac, 2 large potatoes, celery leaves; cut in small pieces. When the meat has cooked off the bones, remove it and cut it in small pieces, discarding bones and gristle. Return meat to the pot with the carrot, leeks and celeriac; simmer an hour or so longer.

For many cooks this ends the first day. The second day, add the potatoes cut small, the parsley, onions, celery leaves, etc., and the slices of smoked sausage; and as needed, add 1 pint or more ("half-litre") of good meat stock. Simmer, stirring and defatting, until of desired thickness. Salt to taste.

Freezing note: This freezes extremely well as a soup base; freeze before adding extra stock or liquid for the table.

Cheese Chowder
Six Good Servings

A delightful soup to eat and to see, with smooth flavor and flecks of color from the carrot and green pepper. Do not use pasteurized processed sandwich-type cheese; use what earlier generations called "store" cheese—and known from its various places of origin as Tillamook (Oregon) Monterey "jack" (California), and as Cheddar in the Dominion and across the great dairy tier of the United States. Whether it is mild, medium or sharp is up to you.

Because good natural cheese gets stringy if it is cooked at too hot a temperature, never let this soup come to a boil after the hot milk is added.

1¼ cups shredded Cheddar cheese (about 5 to 6 ounces in weight)
3 medium ribs of celery, "unstrung" and grated
2 medium carrots, peeled and shredded small

(Recipe continued on next page)

1 large sweet green bell pepper, seeded and shredded small
1 medium onion, peeled and minced fine
2 cups chicken broth
3 tablespoons butter or margarine
2½ tablespoons flour
2¼ cups very hot milk
  pinch of cayenne pepper
  (optional: regular salt to taste; *add artificial salt at serving time*)

Break celery ribs backwards in several pieces and pull off the cords; grate. Peel and shred carrots to produce thin, short pieces (split them lengthwise if they're thick and draw the cut ends across the shredding holes of a hand-held grater). Seed the green pepper, slice it lengthwise, shred as you did the carrots. Shred the cheese, and set it aside. Simmer the celery, carrots, onion and pepper in the broth for 15 to 20 minutes, until tender. Melt butter, stir in the flour and allow to cook over low heat for 2 minutes; add a scant cup of the hot broth with vegetables to the butter and flour, stir until well combined, then pour the mixture back into the pot in which you cooked the vegetables. Cook gently, stirring, until the mixture is thickened and smooth. Remove from heat and immediately add the cheese, stirring until it is melted and incorporated. Add the very hot milk and the pinch of cayenne pepper; add optional salt. Return to heat but do *not let it come near a boil.* Serves 6.

VEGETABLE DISHES

Wild Fiddleheads

True fiddlehead greens, the young stalks of the Ostrich Fern (*Struthiopteris germanica*), appear in moist, fertile North Temperate woods in April and May, when American cowslips bloom in the marshes. Unlike most ferns, they are *not* fuzzy. Rather, their characteristic is a paper-dry, parchment-like sheath that is scaling off. Gather them when they're about 4 inches above ground—3 inches to stalk, 1 inch of tightcurled "fiddlehead" tip. Before they have a chance to wilt, rub the dry scales from tips and stalks and wash well. Sprinkle lightly with salt and cook covered in a small amount of water until tender. Drain and serve with melted butter, with seasoned hot cream as a dressing, or on toast.

They're almost as good up to 6 inches or so: strip off the uncurled leaflets when scaling them, and be prepared to cook them a little longer.

Stewed or Creamed Milkweed

Milkweed (*Asclepias syriaca*) comes along nearly a month after fiddleheads, and may be collected along any back-country road that's not been treated with

(*Recipe continued on next page*)

chemical de-icers—(and get far enough off the road so lead from car exhausts hasn't contaminated the vegetation). Gather the young stalks when they're about 5 inches high and the leaves are pressed closely together like praying hands. Rub the greens between your hands to remove the wool-like fuzz, then wash well. Because it is necessary to remove the bitter milk juice, several changes of cooking water are necessary. Cover milkweed with boiling water and boil five minutes; drain, boil for five minutes more in fresh water; repeat process again, this time adding salt to taste to the fresh water. Boil about 30 minutes in all—or until tender. Drain well and serve buttered and seasoned like fresh asparagus; or cover with hot seasoned cream or hot cream sauce and serve on toast as a main dish.

Plain Dandelion Greens

Early in the spring, even before the Ostrich Fern is producing its edible fiddleheads, come dandelion greens. Gather them when they are only a rosette of leaves without any blossom-stalk showing. Look for them in meadows, unkempt lawns, former barnyards that are growing up to grass, in pastures, and avoiding places frequented by dogs. Cut them off just below the surface of the soil—use a broad-bladed knife, or a piece of strap-iron with one end notched and the notch beveled to make a sharp cutting edge. Any tight little buds deep in the heart of the cluster are a dividend.

Wash well in deep water, and lift out, so grit and dirt sink to the bottom of the pan.

Handle like spinach for canning and freezing.

Only if you want to remove any bitter tang (delicious to many people) boil in two waters; cover with boiling water, cook 5 minutes, lift out greens and discard water; return greens to the pan with fresh water, salted, and cook until tender. Drain and serve hot, as is or garnished to taste.

Dandelion Greens, Potatoes and Cornmeal Dumplings
Six Servings

---

   3 pounds dandelion greens*
   1 teaspoon salt
  ¼-pound chunk of salt pork
   6 medium potatoes

Pick over and wash dandelions thoroughly in several changes of water. Place in a kettle, cover with unsalted boiling water and bring to boiling over medium heat. Cook 10 minutes, then drain to remove any lingering grains of sand (this also will take away a little of the bitter tang, if desired). Drain dandelions and half cover with fresh boiling water, adding the salt. Slice the salt pork down to

* Fresh greens are best for this good old one-dish meal. You can use salted greens (q.v.) after they've freshened overnight in cold water. If you use canned or frozen greens, adjust the cleaning/cooking accordingly.

the rind so that it will still be in one piece and add it to the dandelions. Cover the kettle and simmer 1 hour. Add potatoes and cook 30 minutes longer. Make Cornmeal Dumplings and drop by small spoonfuls on top of boiling greens and potatoes. Cover tightly and cook 15 minutes. Remove dandelions, potatoes and dumplings to a serving platter; finish cutting the slices of pork so they can be arranged around greens. Serves 6.

CORNMEAL DUMPLINGS

1 cup flour
1¼ teaspoons salt
2 teaspoons baking powder
1 cup cornmeal
1 beaten egg
about ¾ cup milk

Sift flour with salt and baking powder. Add the cornmeal and then the beaten egg, which has been combined with the milk. Stir well but do not beat. Drop by teaspoonfuls on top of boiling greens. Cover tightly and cook 15 minutes. Serve hot.

Saturday Night Baked Beans
Six Servings

1 pound yellow-eye or pea beans
½ teaspoon baking soda (optional)
½ cup maple syrup*
½ teaspoon dry mustard
½ pound salt pork
1 small onion (optional)
(optional: 1 teaspoon salt)

Cover beans with cold water and let stand overnight. In the morning, drain and cover with fresh water. Add the soda. Cover and simmer until beans are just tender: *don't overcook.* (A good test is to spoon out several beans and blow on them; if the skin cracks, the beans are ready.) Drain and put beans in a pot or casserole. Add salt, maple syrup and mustard. Some people like the flavor of onion in their baked beans; if you do, tuck the whole peeled onion well down into the center. Add boiling water just to the top of the beans. Score the salt pork and place on the surface of the beans. Cover the pot and bake slowly in a 275 F/135 C oven for at least 4 hours—you can scarcely bake beans too long, so don't worry about overcooking. But good baked beans should never be dry; inspect them occasionally and add a bit of boiling water if they appear dry.

* Substitute ½ cup sorghum; or ⅓ cup raw sugar and ⅓ cup water; or ⅓ cup of corn syrup and 3 tablespoons molasses—or whatever combination and amount of sweeteners you like.

Eggplant Party Casserole
Twelve to Fifteen Servings

This good main-dish vegetable casserole is a cousin to ratatouille, but the cheeses add an Italian touch and it is always served hot.

    1 quart (4 cups) frozen eggplant slices*
      (optional: about 2 tablespoons salt to draw out eggplant juice)
      about ¼ cup vegetable oil (olive is best here)
    2 medium onions, thinly sliced
    2 cloves garlic, chopped fine
    2 small unpeeled zucchini squash (about 7 inches), cut in ½-inch slices
    1 quart (4 cups) canned whole tomatoes,** drained, de-seeded and
      chopped
    2 good-sized ribs of celery, chopped small
    1 tablespoon fresh basil (or ½ teaspoon dried)
    ¼ cup chopped fresh parsley
      scant ½ cup grated Parmesan cheese (1½ to 2 ounces)
    1½ cups ½-inch fresh bread cubes (about 4 slices)
      about 2 tablespoons more oil (for pan-toasting bread cubes)
    1 cup (¼ pound) coarsely grated Mozarella cheese

Defrost eggplant slices (this is much easier if they've been frozen between double layers of plastic film), spread them in a large cookie pan and sprinkle them rather generously with salt. Let stand for 10 minutes to draw out excess moisture, then rinse away the salt and pat each slice very dry. Cut slices in ½-inch cubes and brown them lightly in hot oil in the bottom of a heavy pot over moderate heat. Add onions, garlic and zucchini, and cook them together for 2 to 3 minutes, stirring and adding a bit more oil as needed. Add celery, tomatoes and basil, cover and simmer until the squash is tender—about 7 to 10 minutes—stirring occasionally. Remove the pot from heat, stir in the Parmesan cheese and parsley; add salt and pepper to taste.

To bake the whole recipe (it makes about 10 cups), pour all the vegetable mixture into 3- to 4-quart casserole. Top with bread cubes, which have been lightly browned in about 2 tablespoons of hot oil in a heavy skillet, and sprinkle with the grated Mozarella cheese over all. Bake uncovered in a preheated 375 F/191 C oven until it's bubbly and browned—about 30 minutes.

To freeze: If the whole recipe is frozen in one big chunk, it would take ages to defrost at room temperature, or would need a too-long first baking to thaw and get hot enough for addition of the bread-and-cheese topping—so divide the batch in half and freeze it in two parts. Put each half of the thoroughly cooled vegetable mixture in a 1½- to 2-quart baking dish, and follow directions as

---

* Or peel and slice 2 fresh medium-sized eggplants, sprinkle with salt, let stand; rinse and pat dry, and cube as above.
** Or 4 cups peeled, seeded and coarsely chopped fresh tomatoes—about 3 pounds.

given for packaging in the introduction to "Freezing Convenience Foods," Chapter 16.

To bake the whole recipe, defrost both halves at room temperature, pour all into a 4-quart casserole, cover, and preheat in a 375 F/191 C oven until warm through before adding bread cubes and Mozarrela cheese.

To bake half the recipe without defrosting, drop the frozen chunk into its buttered casserole, and bake *covered* in a 375 F/191 C oven until the mixture is lukewarm—30 minutes or so. Remove the cover and top the vegetables with ¾ cup of pan-toasted bread cubes and ½ cup of coarsely grated Mozarella cheese. Return to the oven *uncovered* and continue baking until brown and bubbling—about 30 minutes more. Makes 6 good servings.

Mixed Vegetable Casserole

    3 strips bacon (or salt pork), diced
    1 cup thinly sliced onions
    1 clove garlic, minced
    2 small zucchini (about 7 inches), thinly sliced or cubed
    3 cups cut or frenched green beans (or a 1½-pint freezer container or 1
       pound fresh)
 1½ cups corn kernels, fresh, frozen or canned
    1 cup chopped tomatoes—canned and drained, or fresh
       (optional: 1 teaspoon salt)
  ¼ teaspoon ground black pepper
  ½ teaspoon sugar
    1 teaspoon lemon juice

Fry the bacon (or salt pork) in a skillet until lightly brown. Drain off all except 2 tablespoons of the fat. Add the onions and garlic and sauté until soft—about 5 minutes. Combine the remaining ingredients in a large bowl and stir in the onion-bacon mixture. Spoon into a greased casserole, cover and bake in a 350 F/177 C oven about 50 minutes. Stir occasionally and gently with a wooden spatula. If more convenient, cook in a heavy pan over low top-of-stove heat for about 45 mintues. In either case remove the cover for the last 5 minutes of cooking. Should the dish need more liquid during cooking, add a little water.

To freeze: The uncooked mixture may be frozen in its casserole for later cooking. Or a casserole may be lined with heavy foil, the mixture poured in and quick frozen; then removed from the dish. In either case tightly overwrap and seal with moisture–vapor-proof covering and return to the freezer.

To cook, defrost, wrapped, in the refrigerator. Bake as usual. Or put still frozen food in freezer-to-oven casserole and bake for about half again the usual time.

Basic Sautéed Cabbage
Six Servings

This vegetable and this recipe are so versatile that they can take any amount of titivating, as noted below; and do look at "Using Filo Pastry" in Chapter 16 for how to turn this cabbage into vegetarian *piroshkis.*

    2-pound head of fresh green cabbage, shredded fine
    4 tablespoons butter or margarine
    1 large sweet onion, minced
    1 clove garlic, pressed
    1 large rib of celery with several leaves, minced
    1 bay leaf
    ¼ teaspoon rubbed dried thyme
    ½ to 1 teaspoon caraway seed
    ¼ teaspoon freshly ground black pepper
    1 tart medium apple, peeled cored and grated
      salt to taste

A food processor, with shredding blade in place, comes into its own here. In a large, heavy enameled pot, heat the butter or margarine, prepare and stir in all the ingredients except for the black pepper, apple and salt. Turn the vegetables over several times until they're well coated; then put the lid on the pot, set the pot over low heat, and let the cabbage and its flavorings simmer in their own juice; check and stir occasionally, adding a tablespoonful of water from time to time if needed. After the half-hour, add pepper, the apple, and any salt you may want (it shouldn't need much, because the flavors are good in their own right, and compatible). Serves six.

Freezing note: As a frozen ingredient, this cabbage is handier if it's in rather flat form: it may be thawed and heated more quickly, and bits can be gouged off as filling for filo-wrapped piroshki; if it's frozen in a pie-shape (q.v. in Chapter 16, under "Pies") it can be put in a partly pre-cooked shell and baked for a fine vegetarian main dish.

Tomato-Corn Pudding
Six Servings

---

    2 cups canned cream-style corn
    1 cup canned tomatoes, undrained
    1 beaten egg
    ¼ cup saltine cracker crumbs
      (optional: ½ teaspoon seasoned salt)
      pinch of pepper
    1 tablespoon minced onion

(*Recipe continued on next page*)

1 tablespoon minced green pepper
1 tablespoon melted butter or margarine

Combine all ingredients in order, then turn into a buttered 1½-quart baking dish. Bake uncovered in a 400 F/205 C oven for about 30 minutes. Remove from oven and let stand 10 minutes before serving. Serves 6.

Salsify "Oyster" Patties

Four Servings

6 large salsify roots (2 cups mashed)
1 egg, beaten
  (optional: ½ teaspoon salt)
  pinch of pepper
1 tablespoon butter, melted
  flour for dusting
  fat for frying

Wash and scrape salsify; slice and boil until tender—about 30 minutes. Drain; mash well and mix with seasonings, beaten egg and melted butter. Shape in small cakes (about 2 tablespoonfuls to each cake), dust on both sides with flour, and fry in a small amount of hot fat, turning once, until brown. Serve hot. Serves 4.

Rinktum Tiddy

Six Servings

1 tablespoon butter
1 tablespoon chopped onion
1 quart canned stewed tomatoes, drained of their juice
2 well-beaten eggs to bind everything together
1 pound grated cheddar cheese (4 cups)
  salt, cayenne pepper and Worcestershire sauce to taste

In a 4-quart kettle simmer the onion in the butter until it is soft, add the drained tomatoes and continue to cook slowly for 10 minutes. Meanwhile beat the egg, stir a bit of the hot tomato mixture into it, then return it to the tomato mixture along with the grated cheese. Stir over medium heat until the cheese is melted. Add the salt, cayenne pepper and Worcestershire sauce in amounts to please your taste. To serve, ladle over toast squares, crackers or cooked noodles. Serves 6 easily.

Onions with Curry
Four Small Helpings

A pleasant change from deep-fried onion rings as a garnish for steak or the like.

4 medium onions sliced in ¼-inch rings
4 teaspoons margarine or butter
½ teaspoon mild curry powder
1 teaspoon lemon juice
¼ teaspoon sugar
  salt to taste

Melt margarine in a heavy skillet, add sliced onions and cook gently over moderate heat for 15 minutes, or until golden, stirring often. Add curry powder, lemon juice and sugar; sauté a few more minutes to bring out the curry flavor. Salt to taste, stir 3 or 4 minutes, and serve. Four small servings.

MAIN DISHES

Traditional Boiled Dinner
Eight Servings

4 pounds corned beef
1 pound salt pork, unsliced
¼ cup brown sugar*
1 large cabbage, quartered
10 large whole carrots, peeled
1 large turnip, peeled and cut in large chunks
8 large potatoes, peeled
8 parsnips, peeled
12 small beets, unpeeled

Simmer corned beef and salt pork for 1 hour in unsalted water to cover, to which you've added the ¼ cup of sugar. After an hour, add turnip, carrots and parsnips. Cook 1 more hour, then add potatoes and cabbage. Meanwhile cook beets separately in salted water until tender. When corned beef is very tender, remove to a platter with the salt pork. Drain vegetables and arrange around the meat. Drain beets, immerse briefly in cold water, and slip off skins; add to vegetables on platter. Serve at once. Serves 8.

* This boosts the flavor of corned beef, smoked shoulder or ham, but is not discernible in itself. Substitute ⅓ cup maple syrup or sorghum for the ¼ cup brown sugar.

Red Flannel Hash

4 cups corned beef (leftovers of Boiled Dinner)
4 cups cooked potatoes
  other leftover vegetables from Boiled Dinner
  salt to taste
  bacon fat for browning

The amounts given here are intended to show proportions rather than actual amounts, since leftovers seldom come out evenly. The rule-of-thumb is to have equal amounts of corned beef and potatotes, and enough beets to make the hash dark red. Put corned beef, potatoes and other vegetables through the meat grinder, using a coarse knife. Season to taste with salt and pepper, and brown in melted bacon fat in a large frying pan. Put on a low rack under the broiler for a few minutes to brown the top.

Corned Beef Hash
Four Good Servings

2 cups firmly packed minced or ground corned beef
4 medium potatoes, peeled and quartered (about 1¼ pounds)
½ medium onion, minced fine
2 tablespoons bacon fat
1 large egg
½ cup cream
1 teaspoon fresh or frozen parsley flakes
⅛ teaspoon black pepper
  salt to taste
  paprika for color
2 teaspoons more bacon fat for browning
2 teaspoons oil for the top

Boil potatoes in lightly salted water just until barely done; drain, then shake in the pot over low heat to dry. Sauté onion in bacon fat over low heat; add to potatoes and mix together by chopping and turning with a pastry blender (so potatoes retain some texture of their own). Beat together the egg and cream, pepper and parsley, combine with potatoes. Fold in the meat well, to blend. Add salt if wanted. In two 8-inch foil pie pans melt the extra bacon fat, swirling it so the bottoms of the pans are coated. Spoon hash evenly into pans, pressing it down. Cook on top of the stove for five minutes at Medium heat to set the hash. Bake in preheated 350 F/177 C oven for 15 minutes.
  This dish also freezes well.

Hearty Vegetable–Beef Stew
Eight Servings

---

about 2 pounds cubed stewing beef, dredged and browned
1½ quarts water
1 bay leaf
½ cup diced celery
¼ cup diced green pepper
4 medium carrots, peeled and sliced
1 large onion, peeled and diced
   (optional: 1 teaspoon salt)
¼ teaspoon pepper
4 medium potatoes, peeled and cubed
2 cups undrained canned tomatoes
¼ cup tomato catsup
1 cup canned tomato juice
¼ medium head of cabbage
1 teaspoon sugar

Combine first nine ingredients. Cover and simmer 2 hours. Add remaining ingredients and simmer 1 hour longer. Add additional salt and pepper, if needed. Serves 8.

General Notes on Game

Venison—which can be from deer, moose, elk or caribou—is finer-grained and much leaner than beef, and for these reasons dries out during cooking more quickly than beef does. Meat high on the upper hind legs and along the backbone is the most tender. Slice tender cuts from the loin quite thin—½ to ¾ inch—and pan-fry quickly in plenty of oil or fat (but *not* deer fat, which is gamey and acts like mutton tallow), searing both sides to hold the juices and then turning only once.

Roasts should be larded with strips of bacon or salt pork and cooked uncovered in a slow oven—325 F/163 C, Gas Mark 2—for 20 up to 25 minutes per pound, basting often. Make gravy from pan juices, and serve with herbed butter or Béarnaise Sauce (q.v.).

Bear chops from the loin are the best cut in general. They may be seared under a broiler on both sides, then wrapped in foil and baked until well done—the foil opened to revive browning during the last few minutes. Long-cooked stew is another way to use bear: treat it like beef. But in all its dishes, *bear must be cooked to the Well Done stage.* Reason: Bears often have trichinosis, the parisitic infestation that is so dreaded in pork (and is mainly responsible for a conscientious cook's refusal to serve underdone pork).

Rabbits have tender, pink meat that may be substituted for chicken in many recipes. Small rabbits are often fried; larger ones go into stews or pies. All rabbit meat should be cooked to the Well Done stage as a guard against tularemia, found in domestic as well as in wild animals.

See Chapter 25, under the subheading for this chapter, for a number of especially good regional bulletins about handling and cooking all types of game.

Roast Venison

In her classic *The Venison Book—How To Dress, Cut up and Cook Your Deer*, Audrey Alley Gorton points out that deer meat that has been properly dressed, skinned, trimmed and chilled should be treated like a prime cut of beef except for one difference. Which is: because venison fat is strong-tasting and acts like mutton fat, it must be trimmed away, and therefore the roast must be cooked with added lard, salt pork or bacon to prevent dryness. Otherwise, season it and cook it by your favorite method for roast beef, including degree of doneness.

However, if you have doubts about the flavor of your venison, marinate and cook it as follows:

   5-pound haunch roast
   ¼ pound salt pork, cut in strips
     (optional: 1 teaspoon salt)
   ⅛ teaspoon pepper
   8 cups buttermilk
   4 medium onions, peeled and chopped
   3 bay leaves

Add bay leaves, onions and salt to the buttermilk to make a marinade. Marinate the venison refrigerated for 48 hours, turning it night and morning. Discard marinade and lard venison well with the strips of salt pork tucked into deep slits cut in the meat. Place in a roasting pan and roast uncovered in a 350 F/177 C oven until tender, allowing 20 minutes to the pound.

Larry's "Any Chunk of Deer Meat"

This irresistible recipe is the work of Larry Torrance, District Agent, Agriculture and Natural Resources, Georgia. It is from *University of Georgia College of Agriculture Bulletin 648, Wild Game from Field to Table.*

   2 tablespoons Worcestershire sauce, just slosh it on
   ¼ cup wine (if you like it), just slosh it on
     salt, cover liberally
     black pepper, cover liberally
     tabasco, dash or two to taste
     garlic salt, sprinkle lightly
     meat tenderizer, sprinkle on

Arrange venison in a cooking pan with enough foil to wrap completely. Fold and crimp the foil all around to keep moisture in. Bake at 350 F/177 C until tender, or meat shrinks away from bones, about 45 minutes per pound.

De Luxe Venison Stew
Six to Eight Servings

---

    2 pounds venison stew meat, cut in 1½-inch cubes
    3 tablespoons fat
    4 cups boiling water
    1 tablespoon lemon juice
    1 teaspoon Worcestershire sauce
    1 clove garlic
    1 large onion, sliced
    2 bay leaves
       (optional: 2 teaspoons salt, or to taste)
    1 teaspoon sugar
    ½ teaspoon pepper
    ½ teaspoon paprika
       dash of ground allspice
    6 carrots, sliced
   12 small white onions, peeled
    3 potatoes, peeled and cut in large cubes

Sauté the meat on all sides in hot fat until brown. Add water, and all ingredients except the three vegetables. Cover, simmer 2 hours stirring occasionally to keep from sticking (or bake in a slow oven—300 to 325 F/149 to 163 C) for 2 hours. Remove bay leaves and garlic. Add carrots, onions, and potatoes. Cover. Continue cooking 30 more minutes or until vegetables are done. Thicken the liquid for gravy.

From Lewis Watson, Jr., Reynolds, Georgia. Also in *Wild Game from Field to Table* (see Chapter 25).

Alpine Stewed Venison (or Beef)
Ten to Twelve Servings

This is quite a large recipe, so half—or all of it, in 2 easy-to-handle amounts—can be frozen. If you do plan to freeze it, note the several small variations in handling below.

    3 pounds boned venison (or beef chuck), frozen or fresh
    ¼ cup flour*
       (optional: 2 teaspoons salt)
    ¼ teaspoon ground black pepper
    3 to 4 tablespoons vegetable oil

* If you plan to freeze this, use the same amount of mochiko (see Chapter 16) since wheat-thickened gravies and sauces tend to separate from freezing.

(*Recipe continued on next page*)

   1 cup chopped onions
   2 cloves garlic, minced
   1 tablespoon paprika
   1 cup water
   1 tablespoon tomato paste (or ½ cup drained, canned, stewed tomatoes,
      sieved)
1½ cups dry red wine
   1 cup sour cream, more or less according to taste

Cut the meat in 1½-inch cubes and dredge it well in a mixture of the flour, salt and pepper. In a heavy skillet or a Dutch oven, brown the meat in the oil. Add onions and garlic and continue cooking over moderate heat for 10 minutes, stirring often. Add paprika, water, wine and tomato paste (or sieved tomatoes). Bring to the boil, cover, reduce heat and cook slowly, stirring occasionally, until the meat is tender—about 2½ hours. Take care lest it cook dry: add a little hot water if needed. At serving time remove the meat to a warmed serving dish, and stir the sour cream into the gravy; heat to just below a simmer, and pour it over the meat. Serves 10 to 12.

To freeze: In addition to substituting for the wheat flour, as noted, *omit adding the sour cream.* Pack the well-cooled cooked meat and its gravy in an adequate freezer box (or, if you're freezing the whole recipe, in 2 boxes to cut down on defrosting time), seal, label and freeze.

To serve, defrost the meat overnight in the refrigerator, and heat it slowly in a casserole or Dutch oven. Remove the meat to a warm serving dish, *now add the sour cream* to the gravy; heat, and pour over the meat, as above.

Hamburger and Onion Shortcake
Four Hearty Servings

---

   1 tablespoon melted butter or margarine
   4 medium onions, sliced thin
 ½ pound lean hamburger
    (optional: 1 teaspoon salt)
 ¼ teaspoon pepper
   2 eggs, beaten
   1 cup sour cream
    paprika
 ½ batch Buttermilk Biscuits (1 cup flour)

Simmer butter and onions over low heat for about 10 minutes—until tender but not brown. Add hamburger, crumbling with a fork, and cook it for about 5 minutes until meat loses its red color. Beat eggs, sour cream and seasonings

(*Recipe continued on next page*)

well, and combine with meat mixture. Make half the rule for Buttermilk Biscuits (q.v.), roll out on a floured board to about ¼ inch thick. Press the pastry into a lightly greased 9-inch pie tin. Pour the meat mixture over the biscuit pastry, sprinkle with paprika, and bake in a 375 F/191 C oven for about 35 minutes. Serve hot, cut in wedges. Four hearty servings for hungry people.

Baked Liver Loaf
Six to Eight Servings

 1½ pounds beef liver, cut in strips
 ½ cup dry breadcrumbs
 1 large onion, ground
 ¾ pound sausage
   (optional: ½ teaspoon salt)
   pinch of pepper
   pinch each of marjoram, rosemary and basil
 ¼ teaspoon sage
 1 egg, slightly beaten
 ⅓ cup light cream
 4 large strips of bacon

Dredge liver strips in the breadcrumbs, then put them through the medium knife of a food grinder, with the onion. Mix with sausage and seasonings. Add cream to the egg and mix thoroughly in with the meat mixture. Pack firmly into a standard-size bread tin. Cut each bacon strip in half and lay it across the top, forming a solid layer of bacon. Bake in a 375 F/191 C oven for about 1 hour. Serves 6 to 8.

This tasty loaf is also good sliced cold, like a portion of pâté, or served cold with potato salad.

Fried Salt Pork and Gravy
Four to Five Servings

 ½ pound salt pork, sliced very thin
   flour and cornmeal for dredging
 2 tablespoons flour for thickening gravy
 2 cups milk (or sour cream)

Cover pork slices with boiling water and let stand 3 minutes: *do not allow to cook.* Remove slices and drain well. In a mixture of equal amounts of flour and cornmeal, dredge the slices. Fry in a heavy frying pan in their own fat until crisp and golden brown. Remove slices and drain on a paper towel: keep hot. Pour off enough fat from the pan to leave only 2 tablespoonfuls. Return the pan to heat and blend the flour into the fat. Add the milk. Stir and cook over low heat until smooth and thickened, making a creamy gravy speckled with tiny crumbs of pork. Serve pork slices with boiled potatoes, the gravy in a bowl on the side. Serves 4 to 5.

Olden cooks sometimes made the gravy with sour cream and omitted the flour, since the cream needs no additional thickening. The sour-cream gravy has an unusual and good flavor.

Ham and Dried Apples with Egg Dumplings
Six Servings

(This fine old Pennsylvania Dutch rule is based on using uncooked home-cured ham and dried apples: there's nothing "instant" about it, and it's wonderful eating.)

  end of ham with bone, about 3 pounds
2 cups dried apples
2 tablespoons light brown sugar (or raw)

Soak dried apples for several hours (or overnight if they're quite leathery) until they've softened a bit and begun to plump. Meanwhile cover ham with cold water and bring to a boil, covered. Simmer about 2 hours, then add drained apples; simmer about 1 hour longer. Remove ham to a platter, lift apples from the pot with a slotted spoon, and place them around the ham; keep all hot while the dumplings are cooking. Serves 6.

EGG DUMPLINGS

1½ cups sifted flour
  3 teaspoons baking powder
    (optional: ½ teaspoon salt)
  1 tablespoon butter or margarine
    about ¼ cup milk
  1 beaten egg

Sift flour with baking powder and salt. Rub in the butter with your fingertips and stir in enough milk to make a soft dough. Stir in the beaten egg. Drop from a spoon into the boiling ham broth. Cover tightly and simmer about 12 minutes. Arrange dumplings on the platter around the ham and apples, and serve.

Wonderful "Stretched" Chicken
Ten Servings

Delicious old-time food, and so easy on the budget!

1 fowl (*c.* 5 pounds), cut up (or 2 small cut-up chickens from the freezer)
at least 2½ quarts water (for broth)
1 small onion, peeled
salt to taste*
7 cups whole-wheat breadcrumbs
3 tablespoons soft butter or margarine
salt and pepper to taste
1 cup finely diced celery
5 eggs
4 tablespoons flour
1 chicken bouillon cube

Cover chicken with lightly salted water, add the onion and simmer until tender; save the broth. Remove the bones and skin and cut the chicken in small pieces (about 1-inch cubes). Season the crumbs with salt and pepper and blend in the butter; reserve 1 cup for the topping. Boil the celery for 10 minutes in 1½ cups of the broth, then add it, with its cooking liquid plus enough more broth to make 3 cups, to 6 cups of the seasoned crumbs; stir to mix, and add 2 of the eggs, slightly beaten. Set the mixture aside. Dissolve the bouillon cube in 3 cups of the broth and carefully blend in the flour; stir and cook gently until the broth is slightly thickened. Remove from the heat and quickly whisk in the remaining 3 eggs, well beaten; return to the heat and simmer and stir until thick; season to taste with salt and pepper; cool. In a large, oblong baking pan (about 10 × 13 inches) make alternate layers of crumb dressing, cut-up chicken, and the custard-like sauce; top with the reserved 1 cup of crumbs. Bake in a 375 F/191 C oven until slightly bubbly—about 30 minutes. Serves 10.

* If you're using cut-up fryers, add 2 bouillon cubes to the water to make a more flavorful broth, and reduce the amount of salt in the water.

Sausage Hash
Four Servings

2 cups chopped cooked potatoes (about 4 medium)
4 sausage patties, cooked (or 4 links)
½ teaspoon salt, or to taste
⅛ teaspoon pepper
1 tablespoon sausage fat, or margarine
¼ cup cream

Use boiled, peeled *cold* potatoes; cut ½-inch cubes, season with salt and pepper. Cook sausage in a small skillet with a little water until pink color is gone and water is evaporated; chop sausage in small pieces. Mix sausage and potatoes, pat down into a heavy skillet greased with sausage fat or margarine. Brown on top of stove, over low heat, for 15 minutes. Pour cream evenly over top, bake in a hot oven at 425 F/218 C until cream is absorbed and top is golden and crusty.

Salt Codfish Cakes
Four Servings

Whether you start with a small plank of salt cod, or with folds of it in a neat wooden box, you'll freshen it before cooking. First, cut it in fairly small chunks, and, if it's hard like a billet of wood, smack the chunks with your meat-tenderizing mallet. Then put it in an enamelware bowl with cold fresh water to cover, wrap plastic over the bowl, and hold it in the refrigerator for at least 24 hours, changing the water several times. Drain. (And here Bea Vaughan used to soak the fish for another 4 hours in cold fresh milk; drain, and rinse well.) In fresh water to cover, to which you've added 2 teaspoons of lemon juice or white vinegar for each 1 pound of fish, simmer for 30 minutes; drain, remove bones and bits of skin, and flake. You'll get a good 2 cups of flaked fish from 1 pound of meaty dried fillet.

1 cup freshened, flaked cod (½ pound dry salted)
6 medium potatoes (about 2 pounds), boiled*
2 tablespoons margarine or bacon fat
1 tablespoon grated fresh onion
2 eggs, well beaten
2 tablespoons cream
   salt to taste
   pinch of cayenne pepper
   fat/oil for pan-frying

Peel, quarter the potatoes, and cook just barely to doneness in lightly salted water to cover; drain well, and return to the stove for a minute, shaking the pot, so the potatoes will dry and not be soggy. Lightly sauté the grated onion in margarine or fat over low heat; add to potatoes in the pot, and mash all together with the cream. Add well-beaten eggs, stir flaked fish into the mixture; season to taste with salt, add a pinch of cayenne. Shape in patties, dust with flour and gently fry like pancakes, turning only once, until both sides are golden brown. Serve with Chili Sauce or Corn Relish on the side (see Chapter 19).

---

* Using boiled parsnips in place of half the potatoes is a wonderful touch, and said to have come down across the border from the Canadian Maritime Provinces.

Codfish Gravy

Allow 1 cup hot unsalted cream sauce to each 1 cup of freshened salt codfish. Freshen fish in cold water overnight, then drain. Cover with fresh water and simmer 5 minutes. Drain well and add to cream sauce. Serve hot with boiled potatoes.

Fish Hash

Five Servings

---

2 cups flaked cooked fish
2 cups diced cooked potatoes, cooled
2 tablespoons melted bacon fat
1 small onion, peeled and minced
2 hard-cooked eggs, peeled and chopped fine
1 teaspoon salt
   pinch of pepper
1 teaspoon Worcestershire sauce (optional)
⅔ cup milk

Sauté onion in the melted fat until light golden—about 5 minutes. Meanwhile stir gently together the fish, potatoes, chopped eggs, seasonings and milk. Mix lightly, then turn into the skillet with the onion and fat. Cover and cook over moderate heat until the bottom is crusty and brown (lift an edge to see). With a pancake turner, fold half the hash over the other half, as with a puffed omelet, and serve at once. Serves 5.

Kedgeree

Six Servings

A good way to use cooked fish as a supper dish, or as the mainstay of a winter brunch. Versatile, it can be made of lobster or shrimp or (canned) salmon, or it can use up fresh cod fillets, finnan haddock—even salt codfish, nicely freshened (see Salt Codfish Cakes). And it lends itself to light touches of seasoning: but keep them subtle.

2 cups cooked fish (1 pound)
2 cups cooked rice
4 hard-cooked eggs
⅓ cup butter or margarine
¼ cup cream
   salt to taste
   pinch of cayenne pepper
   pinch of freshly grated nutmeg, OR ½ teaspoon ground cumin

Flake or chop fish roughly; separate the cooked eggs, chop whites fine, rub the yolks through a wire sieve into a separate bowl. Heat butter or margarine in a heavy pot over medium heat; add fish, rice, chopped egg whites, seasonings. Stir as the mixture heats well through, then stir in the cream. Bring back to heat, pile on a hot serving dish, garnish with sieved egg yolks.

Baked Egg Cakes
Each 9-inch Pancake Serves Five

A favorite brunch or supper dish, easy for a crowd, and it lets the cook sit down and eat with the people. Pan-baked eggs, beaten with a little flour and milk, make these more like crustless quiches than breads. Two 9-inch enameled iron skillets, one with fresh apple in the batter and the other with cheese-bacon-onion, produce enough wedges to serve up to 10.

  5 extra-large eggs (7 large)
  ½ cup bread flour
  ⅓ cup milk
     (optional: ½ teaspoon salt)
  1 large tart apple, peeled, cored, quartered, shredded
  4 teaspoons sugar
  ¼ teaspoon ground cinnamon
  1 tablespoon butter or margarine
  3 strips good bacon, cooked
  1 tablespoon bacon fat
  1 tablespoon scraped onion (finely minced or grated)
  ½ cup shredded natural Cheddar cheese (about 2 ounces in weight)

With an electric beater set at Low, or in a blender, beat the eggs for 3 minutes. Then slowly add the flour alternately with the milk (and optional salt); continue beating for 4 to 5 minutes more, then let the batter rest while you prepare the apple, and the bacon-cheese-onion. Preheat oven to 425 F/218 C.

Peel, core, quarter and shred the apple; dredge in a mixture of the cinnamon and the sugar, and set it aside. Cook the bacon just until it will crumble, reserving 1 tablespoon of the fat separately; grate the onion and shred the cheese.

Put butter in one skillet, the reserved 1 tablespoon bacon fat in the other. Put both skillets in the oven and, when their fats are bubbling, remove; pour half the egg mixture into the buttered skillet, drop the sugared apple bits onto the batter (they will sink in slightly); return this skillet to the oven. Into the skillet with bacon fat, pour the other half of the batter, and top it with crumbled bacon, dot the grated onion around the top, sprinkle on the cheese; with the back of a fork, press these additions lightly until the batter covers them slightly: do not stir. Return the skillet to the oven.

(Recipe continued on next page)

Bake both for 8 minutes, then reduce heat to 350 F/177 C and put skillets back for 12 to 15 minutes more, or until the cakes are set and lightly browned. Serve hot from the skillets, cut in pie-shaped wedges. Maple syrup is good with the apple cake. The two serve 10.

Good Main–Dish Sauces

Greek Lemon Sauce
About 1 ½ Cups

This is a lovely sauce for fresh vegetables, meat loaf, lamb meatballs over rice pilaf—its versatility increases with your use of it. It can be made from thawed frozen materials—which have been measured, with fresh equivalents noted, and clearly labeled when put in the freezer: see Chapter 16.

    3 large eggs (OR 9 tablespoons' worth of frozen whole eggs, say ½ cup)
      juice of 2 fresh lemons, strained (say ½ cup)
    1 cup good, hot clear chicken broth (preferably your own, canned—see
      Chapter 10)
      salt and pepper to taste, if needed

In a blender or with a hand mixer, beat eggs at low speed until they are lemon-colored and thickened—about 4 minutes; add lemon juice slowly as you continue beating at low speed for another minute. In a small heavy pot, have 1 cup of chicken broth just before boiling, and, when the egg-lemon mixture is completely blended, boldly stir the egg evenly into the hot broth with a spatula or a spoon: the heat of the broth will cook the eggs without scrambling them, thus making a thick warm sauce. Serve immediately.

Béarnaise Sauce
About One Cup

There are many ways to make this heavenly accompaniment to steak or to broiled salmon from the Maritimes or British Columbia, because it's only classic Hollandaise with the addition of onion and tarragon. In a pinch we've used frozen egg yolks, which had been stirred with fresh lemon juice before going into the freezer. Some may do it in a blender, pouring melted butter into the seasoned beaten egg yolks (like making mayonnaise). This is the way the late Deisolina Desolata Roncarati of Bologna, Italy, made it. (A double boiler can get too hot; a bain-marie must sit in something. We've had best luck with a 1-pint pyrex measuring cup set on some canning-jar screwbands as a trivet, the whole business in a small stewpot set on low heat. The barely simmering— *never* boiling—water should come ⅔ of the way up the side of the container the egg yolks are in.)

   juice of 1 fresh lemon, strained
½ teaspoon minced fresh tarragon leaves
½ teaspoon freshly spoon-grated onion pulp
 2 large egg yolks
¼ pound butter, softened to room temperature
   (optional: ¼ teaspoon salt)
   pinch of white pepper

A serrated grapefruit spoon does a good job of scraping a cut onion across the grain to get the pulp. Combine onion, tarragon and lemon in a small heavy pot, and simmer for about 5 minutes; cool. Put egg yolks in a deep slender heat-proof bowl that is not too slender to take an egg-beater, add seasonings and stir briefly. Set the bowl on a trivet in a pot of hot water over low heat, add butter piecemeal, beating slowly. Do not let water boil; lift the bowl out of the water from time to time to prevent the eggs from scrambling. When the sauce is thick enough to mound gently, remove the bowl but stir to prevent further cooking. Makes about 1 cup, or 6 servings.

Tomato Sauce

1¾ cups fresh or canned stewed tomatoes
 1 generous slice of onion, chopped
 3 tablespoons butter
2½ tablespoons flour
   (optional: ¼ teaspoon salt)
¼ teaspoon pepper

Simmer onion with the tomatoes for 15 minutes, then rub through a sieve. Blend together the butter, flour and seasonings in a small saucepan and cook gently for 3 minutes, combine with sieved tomato mixture and cook until it thickens—about 5 minutes.

BREADS

Quick Pumpkin Bread
One Loaf

　1½　cups sugar
　½　cup vegetable oil
　2　eggs
　1⅔　cups flour
　¼　teaspoon baking powder
　1　teaspoon baking soda
　¾　teaspoon salt
　¼　teaspoon cinnamon
　½　teaspoon cloves
　½　teaspoon nutmeg
　1　cup mashed pumpkin (home-canned in cubes, drained & mashed
　　　smooth, OR strained store-bought; see in Chapter 7)
　½　cup chopped nuts
　1　cup raisins

Thoroughly mix together the first three ingredients. Sift together the dry ingredients and add to the sugar mixture. Mix well. Add pumpkin, nuts and raisins. Pour into a standard bread pan and bake in a 350 F/177 C oven for 1½ hours. Remove from the pan and cool on a rack.

Apple Bran Bread
One Loaf

　2　cups bran
　2　teaspoons salt
　½　cup sugar
　2　tablespoons melted butter or margarine
　1½　cups sweetened applesauce
　1½　cups boiling water
　1　yeast cake (or envelope dry yeast)
　⅓　cup lukewarm water
　　　about 8 cups sifted flour

Combine the first five ingredients, then stir in the boiling water. Let stand until lukewarm. Soften yeast in the lukewarm water and add to the first mixture when it has cooled to lukewarm. Add flour to make a smooth, easily handled dough. Knead slightly on a floured board, place in a large bowl; cover and let rise in a warm place until doubled. Knead again until smooth, then shape in 2 loaves. Place in lightly greased bread tins and cover with a towel; let rise until doubled. Bake in a 350 F/177 C oven for about 50 minutes or until bread tests done. Turn out on a wire rack and cool thoroughly before slicing.

Zucchini Tea Bread
Two Small Loaves

---

2 cups coarsely grated zucchini
3 eggs
2 cups sugar
1 cup vegetable oil
1 tablespoon vanilla
2 cups all-purpose flour
1 tablespoon cinnamon
2 teaspoons baking soda
    (optional: 1 teaspoon salt)
¼ teaspoon baking powder
1 cup chopped walnuts

Beat eggs until frothy, add sugar, vegetable oil and vanilla, beating all the while until thick and lemon-colored. Stir in grated zucchini, add flour that has been sifted together with cinnamon, baking powder, baking soda and salt. Dust chopped nuts with a little flour and pour into 2 small loaf pans, greased and floured. Bake at 350 F/177 C for 1 hour, or until a toothpick inserted in center comes out clean. Slices best the second day. This freezes well.

Country Buttermilk Biscuits
About 15 Biscuits

---

2 cups flour
    (optional: 1 teaspoon salt)
1 teaspoon any baking powder
½ teaspoon baking soda
4 tablespoons lard (or vegetable shortening)
    about ¾ cup buttermilk

Sift flour with baking powder, salt and soda. Quickly rub in lard, then add enough buttermilk to make a soft dough that yet can be handled. Turn out on a floured board and knead lightly a few strokes, then gently roll out to about ¾

(*Recipe continued on next page*)

inch thick. Cut in rounds, bake on a greased sheet in a 425 F/218 C oven for 15 minutes.

Substitute shortening: An equal amount of any solid vegetable shortening may be used instead of the lard. So may oil—but it does not give the same lightness and texture that solid shortening does.

Indian Fry Bread
One Dozen Flat Small Loaves

Something like the Middle Eastern *pita,* but certainly more interesting than the commercial bakeries' version of the Arab staple, "fry bread" can be bought from roadside cooks in the Southwest. Our best memories of it are from Jémez Pueblo, near Santa Fe, New Mexico, where it was cooked in a black iron "spider" (Vermont hill-country for "skillet") on a gridiron straddling a piñon-wood fire.

  3 cups unbleached all-purpose flour
1½ teaspoons baking powder
     (optional: ½ teaspoon salt)
1¼ to 1½ cups warm water
     shortening or cooking oil for shallow frying

Combine the three dry ingredients. Stir in the water a little at a time: you may need only 1¼ cups, or it could require a bit more; the dough does not want to be sticky and gluey, and it helps to knead it. Form into one large ball, cover and let it rest until the fat—1½ to 2 inches deep—is hot in the heavy skillet. Twist off pieces about the size of an egg, pat and pull and stretch it out flat— then poke a hole in the center with your finger, and drop the flattened dough into the hot fat. Blisters may appear soon; turn once when golden brown and still pliable. Drain and serve hot. Serves 12.

Mary "Tommie" Lopez's White Flour Tortillas
Sixteen Thick Tortillas

The Fry Bread of the various Southwest Indian pueblos is versatile and good, but Tommie's tortillas can't be surpassed for quickness and all-round usefulness. Fine sandwich timber (rather like *pita*), wonderful for sopping up sauce—and fewer Calories.

  5 cups all-purpose flour, unbleached
  3 teaspoons baking powder
     (optional: 1½ teaspoons salt)
  2 heaping tablespoons lard—⅓ cup
  2 cups warm water

In a large ceramic bowl combine flour, baking powder, salt. Rub in the shortening with your fingertips till the mixture is mealy. Rub hands with more lard, and mix and knead in the bowl until the dough leaves the sides clean and forms a ball. Make a cross on the dough, cover it and let it rest while you do other chores. To bake, twist off balls of dough the size of a lime, roll between your palms to finish making them round. With a rolling pin roll each ball out fairly thick, slapping and flapping the dough to make it lively. Bake on a hot griddle iron, like a pancake; when it has large warm freckles on the underside, turn it and cook the other side. The properly cooked tortilla will *tunk* like a loaf of bread when it is cooked right. Makes 16.

"TOMMIE'S" GUACAMOLE

Partly because it is the only dip recipe here, and partly because it comes so naturally now—reasons enough for the following dip.

Mary "Tommie" Lopez's Guacamole Dip
About 1½ Cups

2 medium avocados, fully ripe
1½ teaspoons fresh lemon juice
1 tablespoon finely chopped green chili, canned or fresh
2 tablespoons fresh tomatoes, chopped fine
1 tablespoon onion, chopped fine
½ small clove garlic, pressed (optional)

No blenders or processors here: texture requires fine chopping by hand, and a minimum of stirring.
Scoop the flesh of avocados into a ceramic bowl, mash it roughly with the lemon juice and then set it aside. If the chili is fresh, roast it on a skewer over high heat until the skin blisters, then peel and seed before chopping. Peel and seed a firm ripe tomato; chop. Slice onion in thin rings, chop fine. Press the garlic. Stir all chopped vegetables gently into the avocado mixture, add salt and pepper to taste. Serve as a dip for corn chips or tortillas. Makes 1½ cups.
This is best made within an hour or so before serving. It does not freeze well, and won't hold its charm long in the refrigerator. Dip with corn chips, corn tortillas, or pieces of Tommie's tortillas.
P.S. Out of respect for the fine native cooks of the Southwest, *PFB* originally spelled it "chile"—but we had to bow to standard dictionary usage. But anything Tommie makes with any chile is wonderful.

Sweet New England Blueberry Muffins
One Dozen

  ½ cup butter or margarine
1¼ cups sugar
  2 eggs
  2 cups all-purpose flour
  2 teaspoons baking powder
    pinch of salt
  ½ cup milk
  2 cups fresh or partially defrosted frozen blueberries

If necessary, pick over the berries to remove stems and shriveled bits, or remove from freezer container. Put them in a small bowl, mix with them 1 tablespoon of flour, and set aside.

Cream together the butter or margarine and sugar until fluffy. Add the eggs and beat until well blended. Sift together the flour, baking powder and salt; fold dry ingredients into the creamed mixture alternately with the milk. Do not overstir: doing so will toughen the muffins. Fold the flour-dusted blueberries into the batter, and pour into greased large-cup muffin pans, filling each cup about ¾ full. Sprinkle a bit of sugar over the tops and bake in a preheated 375 F/191 C oven for about 20 minutes. Makes 12 good-sized muffins. These freeze well.

DESSERTS AND SWEETS

Note: Boiled Cider (apple) and Susan Osgood's Melba Sauce (basically raspberry) are excellent—both are canned in Chapter 10.

Pueblo Indian Pudding
Eight Servings

---

  4 cups milk
  ½ cup yellow cornmeal
    (optional: ½ teaspoon salt)
  2 tablespoons honey
  6 tablespoons dark brown sugar, packed
  ½ teaspoon cinnamon
  ½ cup seedless raisins

Over gentle heat scald the milk, and slowly sprinkle into it the cornmeal and the salt, stirring constantly to keep it smooth while it begins to thicken. Stir sugar, honey and cinnamon into the pudding; add the raisins, continue stirring. Pour pudding into a greased baking dish and bake in a 300 F/149 C oven for 1 hour and 45 minutes. Stir twice during baking, once at 30 minutes, the second time at the 1-hour mark; do not stir toward the end of baking. Serve hot with cream. Serves 8.

Yankee Indian Pudding
Serves Ten

  ½ cup yellow cornmeal
  ½ cup cold milk, for moistening cornmeal
4½ cups milk, scalded
  3 tablespoons butter
  2 eggs, beaten
  ⅔ cup firmly packed light brown sugar
  ⅓ cup dark molasses
  1 teaspoon ground ginger
  1 teaspoon ground cinnamon
  ½ teaspoon nutmeg
    (optional: 1 teaspoon salt)

Combine ½ cup cold milk with the cornmeal, set it aside. In a heavy enameled kettle over low heat, scald the 4½ cups milk, stir in the wet cornmeal, and continue stirring as it thickens. Take care while the mixture is simmering on top of the stove before it goes in the oven; too thin to plop, it can scorch and thereby ruin the flavor of the finished pudding. When the pudding base is cooked to the consistency of heavy cream, take it off heat and, still stirring, add the butter, the beaten eggs combined with the spices and salt, and the sugar and molasses. Mix well and pour into a buttered baking dish and bake at 325 F/163 C for 1 hour; stir, reduce heat to 300 F/149 C and cook for one hour more. Serve warm with cream or vanilla ice cream. Serves 10 well.

Alternate sweetener: 1 cup maple syrup + 2 tablespoons dark molasses.

Frances Bond's Rhubarb–Berry Fool with Yogurt
Six Servings

This light and delicious dessert really gains from being made with frozen fruit. Mrs. Bond's only sweetening is in the rhubarb sauce, but a bit more sugar—or a touch of mild-flavored honey—may be folded into the mixture before it is chilled in the refrigerator if you like it sweeter.

2 cups frozen presweetened rhubarb sauce (1 pint container)
1 to 2 cups frozen unsweetened strawberries (or raspberries)
1 cup plain yogurt

Defrost the fruit completely at room temperature. Combine, and fold in the yogurt well—but do not mix so vigorously that the rhubarb loses its identity. Put it in a pretty serving dish and chill in the refrigerator for at least 1 hour before serving to allow flavors to blend. Serves 6.

• **NOTES:** In the true English tradition, a Fool is always sieved. You may press thawed raspberries through a food mill to remove most of the seeds, and follow with the rhubarb. Or remove as many raspberry seeds as is convenient, then put berries, rhubarb and yogurt (with optional extra sweetening) in a blender, and whirr at a Medium setting.

The color and texture are tantalizing if you add both raspberries *and* strawberries, sieved or not.

Whipped cream may be substituted for the yogurt—½ cup heavy cream makes 1 cup whipped—but this dessert loses lightness and tang when made with cream (and gains in Calories).

Mrs. Bond's yogurt is free from commercial stabilizers and preservatives. She does not hold her Fool more than a few hours before serving it. And she warns: "This lovely and light dessert freezes *disastrously!*"

Basic Rule for Fruit Cobblers
Six Servings

  around ¾ cup sugar
1 tablespoon cornstarch
1 cup boiling water
3 cups prepared fresh fruit
1 tablespoon butter or margarine
¼ teaspoon cinnamon (optional)
⅛ teaspoon nutmeg (optional)

TOPPING

1	cup sifted flour
1	tablespoon sugar
1½	teaspoons baking powder
½	teaspoon salt
¼	cup shortening
½	cup milk

Prepare fruit by washing, stemming, peeling and slicing as necessary. Combine sugar and cornstarch, blend with boiling water. Stir over moderate heat until it boils, then cook 1 minute more. Add prepared fruit, and pour all into a buttered 10 × 6-inch baking dish and dot with butter. Sprinkle with spices, if desired (cinnamon is especially good with fresh blueberries and blackberries). Put the dish in a 400 oven to keep hot while you make the topping. Combine sifted flour, sugar, baking powder and salt; sift together. Rub in shortening and stir in milk to make a soft dough. Drop by spoonfuls on to surface of the hot fruit. Bake at 400 for 30 minutes. Serve warm with plain cream. Serves 6.

Be sure the fruit mixture is bubbling hot when you add the dough, otherwise the topping will have raw spots underneath.

Steamed Carrot Pudding
Eight to Ten Servings

Even though this is less rich than the doggedly sumptuous plum pudding, it still comes at the end of what's usually a banquet and often is served with a hard sauce or drenched in spirits and topped with a cream—so we say that this much will serve up to 10 guests. To cut down on steaming time, it may be cooked in deep, individual baked-custard cups: how, will come below with the specifics of Steaming. It freezes well, and for this see Chapter 16, "Freezing Convenience Foods."

2 tablespoons melted butter or margarine for greasing the mold
1 cup grated raw carrots (about 3 medium)
1 cup grated raw potatoes (about 2 large)
1 teaspoon baking soda
½ cup butter or margarine, melted (1 ¼-pound stick)
1 cup brown sugar
1¼ cups all-purpose flour
   (optional: ½ teaspoon salt—which is half what the old rule asks for)
1 teaspoon ground cinnamon
½ teaspoon freshly grated nutmeg
½ teaspoon ground cloves
1 cup seeded raisins (OR 1 cup firmly packed chopped seedless raisins)
   (optional: 1 cup heavy cream for whipped topping)

(*Recipe continued on next page*)

First, grease your mold. Melt extra butter, and with a pastry brush paint the inside of the mold generously, paying special attention to any swirled designs in the bottom and to all surfaces of the center tube if it has one. (Older cooks had those squat 1-pound coffee tins for molds, but today's slender ridged jobs won't let the pudding slide out.) Best is the classic charlotte mold with a cover, or a straight-sided casserole or soufflé dish that can be covered with thick foil that's bound tight with wire. Put the mold in a cool place to let the butter congeal while you make the batter.

The steel blade of a food processor does a good job with the vegetables here, cutting them fine and freeing the juice well. In a bowl combine carrots and potatoes, dissolve the baking soda in the vegetables' juices. Stir in the sugar well, and add the ½ cup melted butter. Sift flour with spices and optional salt, and add; dust raisins with a bit of flour and stir in. Pour the batter into the greased mold to no more than ⅔ full; cover tightly and steam as directed below. When done, let sit in the mold for 5 to 10 minutes, then up-end on a rack if the pudding is to be cooled temporarily, or on a buttered salver if to be served warm (with flavored whipped cream or hard sauce if liked). Serves 8 to 10.

How to Steam Your Pudding

Here the Boiling–Water Bath *vs.* Pressure–processing has nothing whatever to do with *pH* ratings or safe preservation methods or a respectable shelf life. It's simply a *cooking* procedure, chosen by you because you have either lots of time or modern utensils that do things quicker. But regardless of your steaming method, fill your well-greased mold(s) no more than ⅔ full. If you do not have a clamped or friction lid, cover the mold with several folds of aluminum foil, which you hold stretched in place by tightly twisted fine wire, or by a heavy rubber band.

> *Steaming in boiling water:* Have a trivet or rack in the bottom of a good-sized kettle with a lid—your jelly-making kettle is fine. Have enough water boiling in the kettle to come *at least halfway* up the sides of the mold; you'll have to check fairly often, and have boiling water on hand to add, because the water must *never stop boiling*. If the mold tries to float, hold it down with a soup plate inverted over it, or with a heavier weight (if it floats, the batter slides and tilts, or perhaps water can enter the mold). Boil continuously for 3 hours. Remove from boiler; remove lid of mold, and let sit for 10 minutes for the pudding to collect iself. Then turn out upside down on a rack if it is to cool; or on a buttered salver if it is to be served warm. To serve, pour over it ¼ cup heated good brandy or other spirits, set aflame, and carry it in. Top with flavored whipped cream, or with a butter-sugar-rum sauce.
>
> *PFB* cannot offer a fail-safe way to translate the cooking time required for one full-size pudding into the minutes needed for steaming small individual puddings in a boiler. The rough rule-of-thumb for full-size cakes

down to cupcakes is to reduce baking time by half; you might develop your own rule by putting some batter in one small mold in a separate pot, and keeping track of how well it does at ½ the steaming time. (It may take even less, seeing that the diameter and depth is so much reduced.) At any rate, please write us what your success is.

Pressure-processing: Recommended by *PFB* even for the sea-level zone, because it cuts the time required down to about ⅓: a total of 80 minutes at 15 pounds (250 F/121 C) as against 3 hours. We use it because most of our cooking is well up in the Green Mountains. Here's the time: If you find a recipe that calls for steaming in a boiler for 30 minutes, Pressure–cook by venting for 5 minutes, then processing at 15 pounds for 10 minutes. If the conventional boiler's time calls for 45 minutes, pressure–cook by venting for 25 minutes, then processing at 15 pounds for 25 minutes. For this Carrot Pudding, which falls midway in the 2-to-4-hours of required boiling, we vent for 30 minutes, and process at 15 pounds for 50 minutes.

Now, About Altitude

You should Pressure–process any steamed pudding—even one that calls for a relatively short boiling time—if you live at or above 3000 feet/914 meters. Even if you have been lured into using a pressure *saucepan* (4 to 6, and for conservative operators, 8 quarts capacity) as a canner, remember that you CANNOT USE A SMALL PRESSURE COOKER AT 3000 feet/914 meters: YOU MUST USE A PRESSURE *CANNER*. Reason: Steaming a pudding at 15 pounds pressure can be like processing low-acid foods at the same psi—the smaller pressure cookers simply do not hold enough water to process foods for the relatively long times needed at high altitudes.

This is not *PFB* being independently stuffy about this: the warning came from Betty Wenstadt, Home Economist of Presto International, Inc., who make all sizes of pressure cookers and have no axe to grind.

Canned Fruit Cobblers

Following Basic Cobbler recipe, use 1 quart of your own canned fruit *but omit* the boiling water, and *cut down* the sugar to ½ cup, or to taste, if you have canned the fruit with sweetening.

Dried Apple Fruit Cake
Makes Two

---

  3 cups dried apples
  3 cups light molasses (right, 3: there's no other sweetening)
  1 cup seeded raisins
  3 cups flour
  1 cup softened shortening
  3 eggs, beaten
  1 teaspoon baking soda
  1 teaspoon salt
  1 teaspoon cinnamon
  ½ teaspoon nutmeg
  ¼ teaspoon cloves

Soak apples overnight in just enough water to cover. In the morning cut apples quite fine, add molasses, and cook until apples are very tender. Add raisins and cook 5 minutes more. Remove from heat; cool. Add shortening and eggs. Sift dry ingredients together and add. Blend well, then pour into 2 standard-size bread tins lined with waxed paper. Bake in a 350 F/177 C oven for 1 hour—or until a toothpick poked in the center comes out clean. Cool on a rack, remove from pans and peel off the paper. Wrap and store.

The bits of apple in this very old cake taste like citron.

Blueberry Buckle
Ten to Twelve Servings

  ¾ cup sugar
  ¼ cup soft vegetable shortening (or butter)
  1 egg
  ½ cup milk
  2 cups all-purpose flour
    (optional: ½ teaspoon salt)
  2 teaspoons double-acting baking powder
    (optional: ¾ teaspoon grated lemon rind)
  2 cups drained canned blueberries (or 1 pint defrosted frozen berries or 2
    cups fresh)

Preheat oven to 350 or 375 F/177 or 191 C.* Sift together the dry ingredients and set aside. In a large mixer bowl cream shortening with the sugar; when smooth beat in the egg and lemon rind. At low speed blend in the milk, then the sifted dry ingredients; when smooth stir in, by hand, the blueberries. Pour into a greased and floured 7½-×-12-inch baking pan and sprinkle topping (below) over the batter.

---

* If the pan is metal, bake this in a 375 F/191 C oven for 45 to 50 minutes; if the pan is glass, bake in a *350 F/191 C oven* for the same time. Cool, in the pan, on a wire rack. This is best served warm, but if time is a problem it does reheat quite well. Serves 10 to 12.

CRUMB TOPPING

½ cup sugar (or brown sugar, firmly packed)
⅓ cup flour
½ teaspoon cinnamon
¼ cup soft butter or margarine

Measure all ingredients into a small bowl and blend them with a fork or a pastry blender until the mixture is almost the consistency of cornmeal. Sprinkle it over the Blueberry Buckle batter before baking it. This is also a fine topping for a simple white or yellow cake instead of the usual icing.

Basic Pastry for Dessert Pies

Two-crust 9-inch

2 cups all-purpose flour
 (optional: 1 teaspoon salt)
½ cup chilled vegetable shorenting
¼ cup chilled butter or leaf lard
¼ cup ice water

Sift flour and salt together, put into a large, cool bowl and cut in the ½ cup of vegetable shortening with a pastry blender or with two knives. Cut lard/butter in small pieces, quickly rub into the flour mixture. Add ice water, tossing and lightly molding the dough with a fork, to make it gather. If needed, add cold water ½ teaspoon at a time to mold stray crumbs. Gently press together in two balls, one slightly larger than the other (this, for the bottom crust). Cover well with plastic wrap and chill well if time allows; let it reach room temperature before rolling, filling and baking. Handle lightly and sparingly; always roll from center outward.

Help for the bottom crust: To keep filling from sogging the bottom as a pie bakes—especially one with a custard-based filling—arrange your pastry in the pan as usual, then (1) brush the surface of the pastry well with barely beaten egg white, not yet frothy, and (2) bake the shell for just 1 minute in the pre-heated *hot* oven. Remove, fill, and pop the pie back into the oven to cook according to your recipe.

BAKING PIE SHELLS

Preheat oven to 450 F/232 C. Roll and lay carefully in pie pans: be careful not to stretch the pastry or it will pull back and shrink during baking. Pinch a stand-up edge, prick the dough generously with a fork on sides and bottom to prevent air pockets; fill with raw beans or pastry weights if desired (remove them toward the end of baking). Bake 12 minutes in a metal pan, 9 to 10 minutes in ovenproof glass, in either case until light golden. Cool before filling.

Basic Berry Pie
Eight Servings

---

3 cups fresh berries
about 1 cup sugar
¼ cup sifted flour
small dash of salt
2 tablespoons margarine or butter
¼ cup cold water
pastry for 2-crust pie

Turn the berries into a bowl. Sift sugar, flour and salt together and gently mix with the berries. Turn into a pastry-lined 9-inch pie pan. Dot with the margarine, then pour the cold water over all. Cover with the top crust, seal and crimp the edges and cut a vent in the top as usual. Bake in a 450 F/232 C oven for 10 minutes; reduce heat to 375 F/191 C and bake about 30 minutes longer. Cool before serving. Serves 8.

Unsweetened, whole frozen berries can be used in this good old rule. Blackberries and blueberries take kindly to ¼ teaspoon of cinnamon and 1 tablespoon of lemon juice. The amount of sugar depends on the tartness.

Cranberry Pie
One 9-inch Pie

This old-timer has welcome character in the midst of the usual Holiday sweets.

3 cups coarsely chopped cranberries (a good 1 pound of whole berries)
2¾ cups sugar
1 tablespoon flour
3 tablespoons dark molasses
½ teaspoon freshly grated orange peel (just the zest, no pith)
¼ cup hot orange juice
(optional: ¼ teaspoon salt)
pastry for a 2-crust Pie

Wash and pick over the berries, then cut them very coarsely—on a chopping board with a heavy knife, or even merely halving them with a paring knife. Put them in a bowl with the flour, sugar and salt. Heat the orange juice, add grated rind and molasses. Prepare bottom crust, then add the liquid to the berries and pour all into the pie. Cover with the top crust, wetting the bottom rim with milk to make the crimped edge hold tight and stand up. Cut vent holes, brush with more milk, and bake in a preheated 450 F/232 C oven for 15 minutes; reduce heat to 350 F/177 C, and cook about 30 minutes longer. Serves 6 nicely.

Old Newfane Inn Squash Pie
Serves Six to Eight

---

  1 cup mashed winter squash (canned in cubes)
1½ teaspoons flour
  1 cup sugar
  2 medium eggs
  1 pint (2 cups) milk
  1 tablespoon butter
 ⅛ teaspoon ground cinnamon
 ⅛ teaspoon ground nutmeg
 ⅛ teaspoon salt, if wanted
    pastry for a 1-crust pie (large)

In the large bowl of a mixer or in a blender combine the squash, flour, sugar, eggs and spices and beat until smooth. Scald the milk with the butter in it; add to the squash mixture and pour into a pastry-lined 9-inch pie plate. Bake in a 425 F/218 C oven for 15 minutes, reduce heat to 350 F/177 C and bake for 30 to 40 minutes longer or until a knife blade inserted about 2 inches from the center of the pie comes out clean. Remove to a wire rack to cool. Serves 6 to 8 depending on your generosity; you'll be tempted to hide the extra cut for yourself.

Applesauce Custard Pie
Serves Six to Eight

---

1 cup sweetened applesauce, very smooth
1 cup milk
2 beaten eggs
  pinch of salt
¼ teaspoon ground nutmeg
  pie pastry for 1 crust

Beat eggs well, and combine with applesauce, milk and seasoning. Continue beating together until thoroughly blended, then pour into a pastry-lined, 9-inch pie pan and bake in a 425 F/218 C oven for 10 minutes; reduce heat to 350 F/177 C and continue baking for 25 minutes longer—or until the custard filling is set. (Test by inserting a table-knife blade near the center of the filling: if it comes out clean, the custard is done.) Cool. Serves 6 to 8.

Mince Pie

Use 3 cups Mincemeat or Green Tomato Mincemeat (in Preserves) and your favorite 2-crust rule for a generous 9-inch pie. Bake 10 minutes at 425 F/218 C, reduce to 350 F/177 C and bake 25 minutes more. Serve with natural Cheddar. Serves 8.

Maple Syrup Pie
Serves Six to Eight

---

pastry for 2-crust 9-inch pie (*see* separate recipe)
1 cup maple syrup*
½ cup water
3 tablespoons cornstarch
2 tablespoons cold water
3 tablespoons butter
⅓ cup nuts, chopped

In a small enameled kettle, boil the maple syrup and ½ cup of water for 5 minutes. Blend the cornstarch with the 2 tablespoons of water, pour ½ cup hot syrup into the starch paste, return all to the kettle. Lower the heat and cook, stirring, until the mixture is smooth and transparent. Add the butter and chopped nuts. Remove from heat and let cool while rolling pastry. Bake between two crusts at 400 F/205 C for 25 to 30 minutes.

* The darker, late-run syrup called Grade B in Vermont will do well in this delicious pie.

Rhubarb Pie
Serves Eight

---

3 cups sliced uncooked rhubarb
1 cup sugar
2 tablespoons flour
few grains salt
1 beaten egg
pastry for 2-crust, 9-inch pie

Combine first five ingredients. Put the mixture in a pastry-lined pie pan. Cover with the top crust, seal around the edge and cut or prick vents in the center. Bake in a 400 F/205 C oven for about 50 minutes. Cool before cutting. Serves 8.

Ruth Hertzberg's Stand-by "Ice Box" Cookies
Around Seven Dozen

This antique, but still popular, recipe pre-dates electric refrigerators or freezers. The original rule suggests that the dough be "hardened in a winter-chilled spot."

¾ pound (3 sticks) butter or margarine, softened
1 cup white sugar

(*Recipe continued on next page*)

1 cup brown sugar
3 eggs
4 cups all-purpose flour
   (optional: 1 teaspoon salt)
1 teaspoon baking soda
1 teaspoon cinnamon
1 cup chopped nuts of your choice

Have your shortening at room temperature so it is soft. Combine it with the white and brown sugars, beating well; then beat in the eggs one at a time. Sift together the flour, optional salt, soda and cinnamon, and beat it into the egg-and-sugar until the resulting mixture is smooth. Add the chopped nuts. Line two 4½-by-8½-inch loaf pans with foil, allowing extra for folding over. Press half the dough evenly into each pan, cover the dough with foil, then fold and crimp the foil sides and tops to seal. Store in the freezer until firm. To bake, unwrap the resulting brick of dough, slice it thin (in shape each slice will be a rectangle that can be halved to make rather square cookies), bake on greased cookie sheets in preheated 375 F/191 C oven for 6 to 8 minutes. Cool on racks. Rewrap any unused dough and freeze again for later.

The yield is tricky to describe. You probably won't be cooking up this whole big batch at once (unless you've got the cookie detail for a party at school), but it could make at least 80 of the square cookies—depending on how thin the dough is sliced.—R.D.H.

Pumpkin Cookies
Makes Four Dozen

⅓ cup shortening
1 cup sugar
2 eggs
1 teaspoon vanilla
1 teaspoon lemon extract
1 cup mashed cooked pumpkin (or canned)
2½ cups flour
4 teaspoons baking powder
¼ teaspoon salt
½ teaspoon ginger
½ teaspoon nutmeg
1 cup seeded raisins
½ cup chopped nuts

Cream shortening and sugar, beat eggs in well. Stir in the vanilla and lemon extract. Put pumpkin through a sieve and add, mixing well. Sift dry ingredients and add with the raisins and nuts. Mix thoroughly. Drop by the teaspoonful onto a greased cookie pan and bake about 15 minutes in a 375 F/191 C oven. Makes 4 dozen.

Carrot-Orange Cookies
Makes Four Dozen

---

  1 cup mashed carrots (2 cups canned sliced, drained)
  1 cup sugar
  1 cup softened shortening
  1 tablespoon grated orange rind
  ½ teaspoon vanilla
  1 egg
  2 cups sifted flour
  2 teaspoons baking powder
  ½ teaspoon salt

Combine carrots, sugar, shortening, grated orange rind, vanilla and the egg and beat hard until thoroughly mixed. Sift flour with the baking powder and salt; stir into the batter. Mix well. Drop by heaping teaspoonfuls onto a greased cookie pan. Bake in a 375 F/191 C oven for about 20 minutes. Cool on a wire rack. Makes 4 dozen.

BEVERAGES

Oddments

See Chapter 10, "Canning Convenience Foods" for a recipe for Raspberry Vinegar.

Bea Vaughan's Spiced Blackberry Cordial

The pleasant old "company" refreshment makes a delightful Holiday present, especially for the older folks we love.

  4 cups home-canned blackberry juice*
  2 cups sugar, or its sweetening equivalent in honey**
  ½ stick of cinnamon
  2 tablespoons whole cloves
  ¼ ounce whole allspice
    about 1 pint unflavored brandy, or cognac

Tie the spices in a small double-layer cheesecloth bag, add to the juice and sugar, and bring all to boiling. Reduce heat, and simmer for about 20 minutes to get the benefit of the spices. Remove the spice bag and strain the hot juice into a hot sterilized pitcher, preferably enameled-ware. Stir in the brandy, and pour the cordial, still very warm, into sterilized bottles or small canning jars, leaving no headroom. Cap immediately with sterilized tops. Protect the join of cap and container with sealing wax or pressure-sensitive tape, unless you are using conventional 2-piece screwband lids for the jars.

Pretty slender-necked bottles that syrups or salad-dressings came in work well. If they have screw-tops, remove each lining disc before sterilizing the lids; put a small double fold of good-quality household plastic wrap over the rim of the bottle, and screw the cap on tight. Or buy appropriate corks from the hardware store, sterilize them, and push them down in the necks of the bottles (having left adequate headroom), and cover the seals with sealing wax.

* If the juice is presweetened, cut down on the added sweetening: the cordial doesn't want to be syrupy.

** How sweet you like the cordial is a matter of taste. Only mild-flavored honey should be used, and it should not be substituted measure-for-measure for sugar (see "Sweeteners" in Chapter 17).

Hay-time Switchel

About Six 7-ounce Glasses

1 cup light brown sugar
1 cup apple cider vinegar
½ cup light molasses
1 tablespoon ground ginger
1 quart cold water

Combine and stir well. Makes about 6 seven-ounce glasses.

This can be refrigerated, but old-timers made it with cold, cold spring water, and said nothing quenched a thirst or cooled a dusty throat in haying time so well as this homey drink. (It's a good energy-restorer without promoting "cotton mouth" in athletes; cross-country skiers or snowshoers should drink it during a tour race with the chill off, though.)

Rhubarb Punch

Makes About 3½ Quarts

8 cups diced uncooked rhubarb, not peeled
5 cups water
   about 2 cups honey or sugar
6 oranges
3 lemons
   a few drops of red food coloring, if needed
1 quart pale dry ginger ale, chilled

(*Recipe continued on next page*)

Simmer the rhubarb in the water until it's quite mushy. Strain (use a muslin jelly bag if you want it really clear), and measure the liquid into an enameled kettle. Add ⅓ cup sugar or honey for each 1 cup of rhubarb juice, stirring over low heat until the sweetening has dissolved. Cool. Add strained juice of oranges and lemons plus food coloring; chill. Just before serving, add ginger ale carefully. Serve over ice cubes. Makes about 3½ quarts of punch before icing.

In olden days, variations of this very good cooler were made for hill-country weddings where oranges and lemons were rare and ginger ale was virtually unheard of.

25 ✌︎

WHERE TO FIND THINGS

One of the good signs in this world aids the traveler who stops at the roadside maple-syrup stand of the Wheeler family on Route 100 north of Wilmington, Vermont: "Information offered," it says, "and accepted."

Such is the vein of this chapter. Over the years *PFB* has heard from readers and corresponded with food scientists and other experts, and studied sources and traveled around a bit, and some of the results are listed below. A few comments may repeat information given in the chapters cited; most of them amplify in a way not possible to include in the text. A virtue of handling the material this way is that changes and updates may be made here without casually disrupting earlier content or references.

IN GENERAL

The following people can help with a number of chapters in this book, and it's simpler to list them here than to repeat them or to bristle with cross-references.

From People

We say "ask your County Agent" at almost every turn in *PFB,* and for many people in the United States it is direction enough for finding a source of practical help cheerfully given. For other people, though, we offer some general background and some suggestions for finding a County Agent to ask.

Big, rich counties have many agents in their Extension Service offices, listing at least one agent each for Agriculture, Forestry, Youth (4–H) and Home Economics; this last department will have separate specialists in foods and nutrition, family economics, textiles and separate specialists in foods and nutrition, family economics, textiles and consumer education. Less well-endowed counties have one agent for each department. Really sparsely settled counties have only the Agriculture and Home Ec agents, but they will field all questions. Ably.

A huge metropolis may not have agents listed for every county it embraces geographically, but it is likely to have an Expanded Food and Nutrition Education Program (EFNEP) center, with branches in boroughs or settlement houses. Try them.

Telephone directories don't have an across-the-board system for indexing their entries; this is especially true for their Yellow Pages. Nevertheless look in your local telephone book under plain "Extension Service," or under "[Your county] Extension Service" or in the listings under your county government. The Yellow Pages may list County Agents under "Vocational and Educational Guidance."

Write to the information director of the Co-operative Extension Service at your land-grant college, which is usually the State University and often its branches as well. (Among the notable exceptions are Rutgers University in New Jersey and Cornell University in New York, both of which are land-grant colleges with thriving Extension Services; Massachusetts Institute of Technology is too, but has no Extension Service at this writing. The University of Massachusetts of course does, headquartered on the Amherst campus.)

Ask at your public library (a good reference librarian makes Sherlock Holmes look like a bunny when it comes to chasing down information).

Ask at your Chamber of Commerce.

Ask the Practical Arts department at your nearest vocational high school.

Ask local farm-supply dealers.

Ask any up-to-date honest-to-goodness farmer.

Ask your local newspaper if it's a big metropolitan daily, ask the Woman's-page editor or the Consumer Affairs editor or the Today's Living editor or the House and Garden editor.

Call radio stations that air farm-and-home programs, especially the ones that have shows very early in the morning (when they're likely to run taped interviews with area County Agents).

There's an annual *County Agents Directory* that a friend of yours in the country could ask his/her County Agent to look *your* County Agent up in—if you follow us.

From Those Good Government Agencies

In Canada visit or write your Provincial Agriculture Departments, which issue attractive materials that are notably to the point and well written. (Several of Ontario's slim pamphlets are mentioned under favorite source ideas for Chapter 24, "Cooking.")

Or write to Canada Department of Agriculture Information Division, Sir

John Carling Building, 930 Carling Avenue, Ottawa, Ontario K1A OC7.

You used to leave your County Agents' offices with handfuls of free booklets published by the USDA Co-operative Extension Service or by your own state university. Times change, so nowadays these materials are in limited supply; or you can expect to pay a small fee for them; or you must send away. And sending away can be a problem. Start with the Consumer Information Center, Department EE, Pueblo, Colorado 81009, and ask to be put on the mailing list for their *Consumer Information Catalog*—free, and it comes out quarterly. There are extensive catalog-lists of publications sold by the Superintendent of Documents, U.S. Government Printing Office, Washington, D.C. 20402. Send the correct amount of payment (money-order, check, stamps if they'll be accepted, but never coins or currency). Be prepared for backing-and-forthing for weeks if the material is temporarily unavailable or the price has gone up. Deal directly with the documents distribution people in Colorado, above, whenever you can.

In 1978 four USDA agencies—the Agricultural Research Service, the Co-operative Research Service, the Extension Service, and the National Agricultural Library—merged to become the Science and Education Administration (SEA), U.S. Department of Agriculture. A number of the resultant publications following this consolidation of agencies are still listed as prepared by the Agricultural Research Service. This is a nuisance for the consumer but perhaps a help to government computers. Anyway, look for the publications *by number* as well as by title; where the numbers have been changed, the familiar old one may appear either on the back cover with printing/edition information, or on the inside front cover (federal publications are not so picky as the book trade is about citing earlier publication data).

- **NOTE:** We'll try to give up-to-date numbers/publishers of the materials mentioned hereafter, but some of our favorites have not, so far as we know, been re-issued under new imprints. Where we're off, we apologize, and ask you to search a little harder. The information people at the various levels of the Extension Service are mighty good about helping.

The *FDA Consumer,* official magazine of the Food and Drug Administration, Rockville, Maryland 20857, is interesting for its articles, surely, but its sections on seizures and judgments, etc., make fascinating reading because they indicate the scope of food-handling problems.

The government bulletins published for the lay public in North America are, taken all in all, the best in the world. Probably this excellence comes from the fact that North Americans put by a larger number of different foods in a greater variety of ways than people of other hemispheres are able to do. Surely, too, it helps that we enjoy—even take for granted—climatic and agricultural bounty; nor does it hurt that we possess almost automatically such consumer goods as home freezers, Pressure Canners, food dryers, and packaging and storage materials in almost limitless quantity.

We must never forget to be grateful.

CHAPTER BY CHAPTER

The latter half of the 1970's saw not only the reprinting and revision of classic USDA bulletins—those stand-bys used without geographic limitation—but also the first appearance of many good regional bulletins and fact sheets. These and the Dominion reports are written from certainty and knowledge; even more, they reflect an interesting, and often delightful, personality of district or authorship.

This spurt of domestic material, much of it dealing with particular foods, was logical when you consider the impact of state and federal appropriations. Further, more land-grant colleges and universities began pooling their resources; the Pacific Northwest fish bulletins are an example, and so is joint publication of work done in the Northeast. Another aspect of this exchange has New Mexico distributing a pamphlet on the indoor food dryer developed at Oregon State and another bulletin describing conclusions reached by research teams at Minnesota. Good system.

To avoid duplicate listings as much as we can, we'll start with some general material that applies throughout this book, then move to individual chapters. Occasionally several chapters will be grouped under the over-all method if the publications straddle several foods. Remember that the material cited is only a small part of the literature available, nationally and regionally. The following are ones we use a lot.

GOOD GENERAL BOOKS OR BULLETINS

The Technology of Food Preservation (Third Edition), by Norman W. Desrosier, Ph.D., Avi Publishing Co., Inc., Westport, Connecticut 06880.

The multivolume USDA *Agriculture Handbook No. 8, The Composition of [Specific Foods]—Raw, Processed, Prepared* first came out in 1963 in one volume (later reprinted as a tradebook by Dover), but in 1976 began being separated and expanded as . . . *8-1—Dairy and Egg Products, etc.,* and since then the series has expanded to some ten volumes. It's a tricky series to collect through a catalog, because some of the titles are listed under "Foods" and some are under "Nutrition & Health"—but they are in the various listings/catalogs of government publications. Your best bet would be to inquire first from the Consumer Information Center, Department EE, Pueblo, Colorado 81009, as above; then try the U.S. Government Printing Office, etc., also above.

Because its authors are virtually a *Who's Who* among food scientists and nutritionists at the land-grant universities, do get the USDA *Agriculture Information Bulletin 410, Canning, Freezing, Storing Garden Produce.* It is reprints from the *1977 Yearbook of Agriculture.* (See also *Home Food Preservation, 534 K* from Consumer Information Center in Colorado, above.)

CHAPTER 1: IS IT WORTH IT?

Information Bulletin 158, The True Cost of Home Food Preservation (1979), by Ruth N. Klippstein, Co-operative Extension Programs, Cornell University. Orders: Mail Room, 7 Research Park, Cornell University, Ithaca, New York 14850.

CHAPTER 2: WHY PUT-BY FOODS SPOIL

A favorite, mentioned in the main text: *Morbidity and Mortality Weekly Report,* from the Center for Disease Control, Public Health Service, U.S. Department of Health and Human Services, Atlanta, Georgia 30333. Especially helpful about food poisoning— outbreaks of botulism (with Editorial Notes about likely causes), and the recurring appearance of salmonellosis from commercially sold "cold cuts."

USDA *H&G Bulletin No. 162, Keeping Food Safe to Eat.*

Food Safety for the Family, 533 K, from Pueblo, Colorado, above.

CHAPTER 3: CANNING METHODS

Starting with altitude: the Colorado State University pamphlets are especially good for their simplicity and quickness, among them: *Pamphlet 41, High Altitude Food Preparation (Revised 1977),* by Pat Kendall, Extension Specialist, Food Science and Nutrition, Colorado State University, Fort Collins 80523. (Inquire price from Bulletin Room.)

National Presto Industries, Inc., pamphlet AD78-3449B, *Canning at 15 Pounds Pressure* (1978), has, on its page 7, a detailed chart for high-temperature processing of vegetables, meats and seafood at altitudes ranging from under 3000 feet/914 metres to over 7000 ft/2134 m (but less tham 10,000 ft/3048 m). For copies write to Consumer Services division of this maker of pressure canners at simply Eau Claire, Wisconsin 54701. Mrs. Betty Wenstadt is Home Economist for Presto in charge of their test kitchens and is generous with information.

Mirro Corporation, maker of pressure canners, also has a very helpful consumer relations service, which provides information on high-altitude canning (as well as on using their canners at sea level). Write to P.O. Box 409, Manitowoc, Wisconsin 54220.

Also extremely valuable for their sensible recognition of the problems "out in the field" are the New Mexico State University, Las Cruces 88001, bulletins, especially *Guide E-313, Home Canning Pressures and Processing Times,* revised 1978 by Mae Martha Johnson, Extension Nutrition Specialist.

For setting up community canning kitchens: Dixie Canner Equipment Company, 786 East Broad Street, P.O. Box 1348, Athens, Georgia 30603, will send a catalog and information about equipment and management procedures for community canning kitchens *using "tin" cans.*

Food Preservation System, Brethren Service Center of World Ministry of Brethren Churches, 500 Main Street, Box 188, New Windsor, Maryland 21776. Joel M. Jackson in charge (1981) of the program that he headed at Ball Brothers, Muncie, Indiana, before it was given to the Brethren. The System designs, supplies and advises community canning kitchens, and uses *glass canning jars.*

For stockpots to use as B-W Bath canners, among others: Dura–Ware Company of America, Inc., 81 Spring Street, New York, New York 10012.

General Housewares, P.O. Box 4066, Terre Haute, Indiana 47804 (also B–W Bath canners *and check them for correct depth*).

Leyse Aluminum Company, Kewaunee, Wisconsin 54216.

Vollrath, 1236 North 18th Street, Sheboygan, Wisconsin 53081.

For buying Pressure Canners: Mirro Corporation and National Presto Industries, cited above about Altitude; also, the established mail-order houses, and of course any good kitchenware store.

A firm that has a range of 14 Western states is McGuckin Hardware, 2525 Arapahoe Avenue, Boulder, Colorado 80302. Ask for Mark McCrery in Housewares.

USDA *H&G Bulletin No. 30, Pressure Canners, Use and Care.*

CHAPTER 4: ON GUARD!

Because this is not a bibliography of *PFB*'s sources (long, dry and academic) we refer you to the *Readers' Guide to Periodical Literature* at your local public library, or the library of your high school. Much of our favorite material came from publications by long-established consumer groups, the government publications mentioned earlier, the files of newspapers and popular wide-circulation magazines.

• **SPACE NOTE:** The excellent publications cited for Chapters 5–10 all include careful instructions for every step of the procedures required for safe canning, so we do not duplicate the listing by including them here.

CHAPTERS 5–10: CANNING SPECIFIC FOODS

USDA *Home & Garden Bulletin No. 8, Home Canning of Fruits and Vegetables* (1975) is the enduring classic, and is sure to be the most widely used pamphlet on the subject in the United States. It has been slightly revised and issued regionally, as well. The material in recent printings remains the same good, straightforward stuff. (See same title, number *134K*, from Pueblo, Colorado.)

Extension Bulletin 413, Home Canning—Fruits, Vegetables, and Meats (Revised 1980), by Isabel D. Wolf and Edmund A. Zottola, Agricultural Extension Service, University of Minnesota, St. Paul 55108. Minnesota's reputation for excellence in research is fully deserved and this bulletin reports on increased pressures for processing foods canned at home. (It also elucidates an instruction for an innovative treatment in canning tomatoes, described in the next reference.)

Food Science and Nutrition *Fact Sheet No. 33—Home Canning Tomatoes* (1976), by Edmund A. Zottola and Isabel D. Wolf; Agricultural Extension Service, University of Minnesota, St. Paul 55108. Discusses the various methods of canning this most popular of home-preserved foods—and describes the momentary 15-pound-pressure treatment that depends on complete dependability of equipment and procedures (i.e., we would recommend a good deal of home-canning experience, a sweep second-hand for timing, and a dial gauge unimpeachably accurate before this method is undertaken).

Publication 789, Home Canning of Fruits and Vegetables (1972), Canada Department of Agriculture, Ottawa, K1A OC7.

Publication 468, Canning Ontario's Fruits and Vegetables, Ontario Department of Agriculture and Food, Parliament Buildings, Toronto.

Ball Blue Book: The Guide to Home Canning and Freezing (1979), Ball Corporation, Muncie, Indiana 47302.

We wish we had room to cite our regional favorites.

USDA *Farmers' Bulletin No. 2265, Pork Slaughtering, Cutting, Preserving, and Cooking on the Farm* (1978).

USDA *Farmers' Bulletin No. 2209 . . . Beef on the Farm* (1969).

USDA *Farmers' Bulletin No. 2152, . . . Lamb and Mutton,* etc. (1967).

USDA *H&G Bulletin No. 106, Home Canning of Meat and Poultry* (1970).

The Missouri, North Dakota and Georgia bulletins on dressing, cutting, preserving and cooking wild game are the most lively ones we've seen in a long time. Meanwhile Audrey Alley Gorton's *The Venison Book—How to Dress, Cut up and Cook Your Deer* (first published in 1957 and still going strong) is published by The Stephen Greene Press, P.O. Box 1000, Brattleboro, Vermont 05301.

Publication PNW 194, Canning Seafood (1979), A Pacific Northwest Extension Publication (Co-operative Extension Services of the Universities of Idaho, Oregon and Washington).

Publication P-128, Pressure Canning Alaskan Fish at Home (1979), Co-operative Extension Service, University of Alaska, Fairbanks 99701.

Leaflet 2425, Canning and Freezing Fish at Home (1977), Division of Agricultural Sciences, University of California, Berkeley 94720.

Public Information Report No. 120: Getting the Most from Your Great Lakes Salmon (1974), by C. E. Johnson, et al., University of Wisconsin Sea Grant College Program, Madison 53706.

Chapters 11–16: Freezers, and Freezing Specific Foods

Even the Yellow Pages of big-city telephone directories seldom list freezer lockers any more, but such rentals often can be found under *Butchering.* And look under *Livestock—Commission Sales:* the people there know what slaughtering, butchering, packaging, etc., services are good in surrounding areas.

Publication 892, Freezing Foods: Canada Department of Agriculture, Ottawa K1A OC7.

Several popular magazines have had particularly good surveys of freezers: *Consumer Reports* of August 1981, and *Changing Times* of March 1980.

Care for Your Frozen Foods, Ontario Ministry of Agriculture and Food, Parliament Buildings, Toronto, Canada.

USDA *H&G Bulletin No. 10, Home Freezing of Fruits and Vegetables* (1976). (University of Connecticut College of Agriculture and Natural Resources, Storrs 06268, has issued *Pamphlet 77-50,* an adaptation of the USDA classic.)

USDA *H&G Bulletin No. 93, Freezing Meat and Fish in the Home.*

USDA *H&G Bulletin No. 70, Home Freezing of Poultry.*

Again, there are a number of fine regional publications—Alabama's, North Dakota State at Fargo, and the Game bulletins mentioned in passing under the general Canning section.

Publication MP-1033, How to Freeze and Store Seafoods at Home, Texas A&M University, College Station, Texas 77840 is notable for dealing with Gulf seafood. Georgia and North Carolina have good publications. *Topics #15, Freezing Finfish,* University of Maryland Co-operative Extension Service, College Park 20742; also from this source: *Topics #16, Freezing Shellfish.*

SG 7, Home Freezing of Seafood (1976), Oregon State University, Extension Hall 118, Corvallis 97331, deals well with the excellent food from the Pacific.

Mochiko, the "sweet" rice flour gettable at oriental food stores, is the answer to nongluey frozen sauces. If you can't find it, write to Koda Farms, Inc., Dos Palos, California 93665 (Jeane Pate was a help to *PFB* here), or to Pacific National Rice Mills, Inc., 848 Kentucky Avenue, Woodland, California 95695.

One of the best books on its subject is *Deep Freeze Cookery,* by Norma McCulloch, Paul Hamlyn Pty Ltd., 176 South Creek Road, Dee Why West, New South Wales 2099, Australia.

Bulletin No. 369, Freezing and Using Vegetables, Fruits and Prepared Foods, Ohio Co-operative Extension Service, Ohio State University, Columbus 43210.

USDA *H&G Bulletin No. 40, Freezing Combination Main Dishes* (1973). (See also title, number *133K,* from Pueblo, Colorado, q.v.)

Chapter 17: Common Ingredients and How to Use Them

This is another chapter that relied mainly on up-to-date reporting in large-circulation publications rather than books or pamphlets. Consult *Readers' Guide to Periodical Literature* for updating. Meanwhile, for one of the best and briefest discussions of the notable Delaney Clause (responsible for the FDA's stand on saccharin—and many more deadly substances that were barred from public consumption in the U.S.A.) is the *Food Facts From Rutgers—Cancer: Laws and Chemistry,* Cook College, April–October 1981; P.O. Box 231, New Brunswick, New Jersey 08903.

USDA *H&G Bulletin No. 233, The Sodium Content of Your Food* (1980) is a handbook every householder should have.

The Morton Salt Company, 110 North Wacker Drive, Chicago, Illinois 60606, David Strietelmeier, Technical Director.

For Food-grade chemicals and other substances—plus information—Fisher Scientific Company, 461 Riverside Avenue, P.O. Box 379, Medford, Massachusetts 02155.

One source of metric kitchen scales is the Hanson company, Shubuta, Mississippi 39360. They're the makers of "dietetic" and "recipe" (their designations) scales, as well as larger metric ones for kitchen use.

Chapters 18 and 19: Jelly, etc., Pickles, etc.

USDA *H&G Bulletin No. 56, How to Make Jellies, Jams and Preserves at Home* (1971).

Publication 992, Jams, Jellies and Pickles (1973), Canada Department of Agriculture, Ottawa K1A OC7.

For low-methoxyl pectin, we got information from W. W. Nichols of Sunkist, Ontario, California, and main how-to and retailers from Dianne Leipold, Hercules, Inc., 910 Market Street, Wilmington, Delaware 19899. Dr. Leipold mentioned Walnut Acres, Penns Creek, Pennsylvania 17862, as an outlet. Another is Dacus, Inc., P.O. Drawer 528, Tupelo, Mississippi 38801; they distribute under a brand-name whose box tells none of the ingredients, and they also market under this brand a range of pickling mixtures. Whitney McDermut Co., Department 151, 474 Main Street, Fort Lee, New Jersey 07024, sells the pectin by mail, with the calcium compound and full instructions attached.

USDA *H&G Bulletin No. 92, Making Pickles and Relishes at Home* (1978).

Booklet HXT-90, Pickles, Relishes and Chutneys, University of California, Davis 95616.

And because we can't resist including it, *Food Preservation in Alabama,* by Isabelle Downey, Auburn University, Auburn, Alabama 36830.

Chapter 20: Curing

Fermentation of Foods (1982), by Von Mendenhall and Gary Richardson, Utah State University, Logan 84332. Write to the Department of Nutrition and Food Sciences for this long-awaited publication, which, coming out of Utah, is a fine contribution in this field.

A Complete Guide to Home Meat Curing, Morton Salt Company, 110 North Wacker Drive, Chicago, Illinois 60606.

USDA *Farmers' Bulletin No. 2265, Pork Slaughtering . . . Preserving . . .* (1978).

B-2259, Home Smoking and Pickling of Fish, University of Wisconsin, Agricultural Bulletin Building, 1535 Observatory Drive, Madison, Wisconsin 53706.

Publication P-325, Smoking Fish (1979), Co-operative Extension Service, University of Alaska and the USDA.

Again, inquire of your own State University Extension Service for bulletins dealing with food specialties in your region.

Chapter 21: Drying

USDA *H&G Bulletin No. 217, Drying Foods at Home* (1977), also has regional adaptations from University of California, Davis, and Cornell University. The California and USDA bulletins contain plans for the Oregon indoor dryer.

Circular 855, How to Build a Portable Electric Food Dehydrator, by Dale E. Kirk, Agricultural Engineer, Oregon State University, Corvallis 97331.

USDA *Sun Dry Your Fruits and Vegetables, A Guide for Home Economists Around the World.* Our favorite for sun techniques: out-of-print but worth hunting for.

For work done in the pueblos of New Mexico, the documentary film *Sun Drying Foods,* Self Reliance Foundation, Jeff Kline, Las Trampas, New Mexico 87120.

For possible purchase of bulk dried foods, especially grains, and for information about large storage containers and supplies, non-members of the Church of Jesus Christ of Latter-day Saints may call/write the head of the supply committee for the Stake in which you live. To locate the committee head, look up in the White Pages of the telephone book under *Mormon Elders* or *Church of Jesus Christ of Latter-day Saints,* and ask for the appropriate Bishop's committee; you will be told how to order as a member of the Church, or if orders from non-members are accepted. Some Stakes have begun a catalog service for such supplies; they stress, however, that the Church *does not want to compete with local non-member dealers in any way,* so requests the understanding and co-operation of non-members.

CHAPTER 22: ROOT CELLARING

USDA *H&G Bulletin No. 119, Storing Vegetables and Fruits in Basements, Cellars, Outbuildings and Pits* (1973).

CHAPTER 23: SPROUTS AND OTHER GOOD THINGS

Sprouts to Grow and Eat, by Esther Munroe (1976), The Stephen Greene Press, Box 1000, Brattleboro, Vermont 05301.

USDA *H&G Bulletin No. 129, Making Cottage Cheese at Home* (1967).

For using lye, write to Household Products Information, the Pennwalt Corporation, 3 Parkway, Philadelphia, Pennsylvania 19102.

Pamphlet No. PNW 183, Fish Pickling for Home Use (1979) Pacific Northwest Extension Service, Oregon State University, Corvallis 97331, et al.

CHAPTER 24: COOKING

Pamphlet 497 A (1978), High Altitude Baking, Co-operative Extension Service, Colorado State University, Fort Collins 80523. Also by Pat Kendall: *Pamphet 41, High Altitude Food Preparation* (1977); and other relevant titles. (Inquire prices from Bulletin Room.)

INDEX

A

Acetic acid, 289–90; *see* Vinegar
Acid, natural, in foods, 10–11
  canning methods, dictates, 14–15, 26, 32, 39, 103, 106, 114; *and see* Boiling–Water Bath; Pressure Canner(s)
  jelling aid, 288, 296
  mold reduces, 6, 65–66
  over-ripeness reduces, 73, 296, 297
  pH defined, 10–11
  R-enamel cans for, 49
  test for (fruit), 296
  ill. 7
  see also Fish; Fruit; Meat; Poultry; Shellfish; Vegetables
Acidity, food ratings (*pH*), 10–12
  anti-bacterial agent, 10
  5 percent solutions, 285, 289–90, 332
  offsetting tartness of, 103, 333, 448
Acid(s) to add, 93, 100
  anti-discoloration, 284–85, 287–88
  safety (against spoilers), 85, 104, 288–90
  jelling aid, 288, 296
Aflatoxin (poison from mold), 40; *see also* Botulism; Mycotoxin; Poisoning, food
Agriculture Handbook No. 8, Composition of [Specific Foods]—Raw, Processed, Prepared, 377, 399, 508
Altitude, cooking effects gen'l, 19–21, 25–26, 74–75, 299, 301
Altitude over 1000 ft/305 m, correcting for, 19–26, 159
  blanching, 26, 220–21
  boiling water, 20–21, 26
  B–W Bath (time increases), 21, 22
  pasteurizing, 21
  headroom (canning) increases, 25, 54, 74–75, 106, 115, 141, 159
  jelly & jam, 25, 299, 301
  pasteurizing, 21
  Pressure Canner (*psi* increases), 21, 22, 23–25, 34, 107, 141, 159

pressure *saucepans* (w/drawbacks), 32–33
  simmering, 21
Alum (firming pickles), 71, 291, 333
  alternative substances, 290–91, 333–34
Aluminum, poor w/acid food, 28, 379
  fish/shellfish, implied, 160
  jellies, etc., implied, 293 *ff*
  lye, bad reaction, 454
  pickles, etc., implied, 332–34 *ff*
  tomatoes, implied, 111 *ff*
Anti-discoloration @ foods
  canning fruit, 77
  canning shellfish, 162
  cans ("tin"), linings, 49–50
  drying, 392–95, 395–99 (sulfuring: SO_2)
  freezing, 199–201, 220–221
  headroom, canning jars, 54
  nitrates, nitrites @ meats, 287
  spices, ground @ pickles, 333, 335
  storage, 60, 196, 365, 401, 421–39 *passim*
  treatments, gen'l, 284–86
  water, 279
  ills. 87, 213
  see also Blanch; Brine; specific Fruits/Vegs
Anti-rancidity @ fish, 244, 246
Apple(s)
  anti-discoloration, 77, 199, 284, *ff*, 392–95 *passim; see also* Sulfuring (SO_2 treatment)
  baked (canned), 81
  butter, 319–21
  canning, 79–81
  chutney, 350–51
  cider, 99
  cider (boiled), 181–82
  drying, 403–04
  freezing, 203–04
  fruit cake (dried), 496
  jelly, 306–07
  juice, 100
  juice, from jelly, 299

Apple(s) (*continued*)
  pectin from, 18; *see also* Pectin, home-
    made
  pie filling, 10, 182
  purée, 92
  sauce (canned), 81
Apple Bran Bread, 486
Apple Butter (preserve), 319–21
Apple (Dried) Fruit Cake, 496
Apple Pie Filling (canned), 182
Apple (Quince) Jelly, no added pectin, 306
Applesauce Custard Pie, 499
Apricot(s)
  anti-discoloration, 119, 284–86, 394,
    398–99
  butter, 319
  canning, 81
  dried, Calories, 377
  drying, 404–05
  freezing, 204
  Leather, 406–07
  nectar (juice), canning, 100
  purée, canned, 93
  sulfuring, 398–99
  ill. 404
Artichokes, Jerusalem, freezing, 230
Artificial salt; *see* Salt substitutes
Artificial sweeteners, *see* Sweeteners, artifi-
  cial/non-nutritive
**Ascorbic acid (Vitamin C), 60, 128, 199, 200,
  286, 344, 393, 395, 446**
  anti-oxidant, most effective, 284
  rancidity, freezing fish, 244, 246, 288
  see also Anti-discoloration
Asparagus
  canning, 118–19
  freezing, 225
Aspartame
  (non-nutritive sweetener), 283
Aspirin, "canning pills," 71
"Atmospheric Steam" canner, 28, 62
  development of, 63
  using, 64–65
Avocados
  freezing, 204–05
  Guacamole Dip, 489

                    B

Bacteria
  disinfectants for, 12
  role in spoilage, 8
  ill. 7

  see also **Botulism; Poisoning, food; "Pto-
    maine"; Salmonella**
Bacterial load, 69–70
Beach Plum Jelly, no added pectin, 308
Beans, Baked, 467
  in sauce, canned, 176
Beans (Dried) in Sauce (canned), 176
Beans, Lima (fresh shell)
  canning, 121–22
  drying, 410
  freezing, 225
  swell (in canning), 54
  see also Peas, etc.
Beans (snap/string, green, Italian)
  acidity (*pH* rating), 10
  botulism, carriers, 114
  canning, 119–21
  drying, 410
  freezing, 225
  mushiness, avoiding, 119–20
  pickling, "Dilly," 345
  salt curing, 356–57
  ills. 198, 220
Bear
  canning, 144–45
  parasites in, 474
  see also Game
Beef
  butchering (cuts of), 144
  canning, 143–51 *passim*
  corned, 366, canned, 179
  curing, 355–74 *passim*
  dried (chipped), 366
  drying (jerky), 418–19
  freezing, 236–42
  hash, corned, canned, 473
  salting, 364–67 *passim*
  smoking, 371–74 *passim*
  tongue, canned, 151
  ills. 144, 145, 372, 373
Beet(s)
  baking, 3
  canning, 122
  drying, 410–11
  freezing, 226
  pickled, 122–23
  relish, 347
  root-cellaring, 435
Beet Relish, 347
Berries (firm and soft)
  canning, 93–98
  drying, 405–06
  firm "checking skins," 393–94
  freezing, 205–06

frozen, 84
juices, 100
ill. 97
see also under specific berries, jellies, jams
Berry Pie, Basic, 498; *and see* Cobblers
Beverages
  boiled cider, 181
  canning, 181–85
  concentrates, 98, 184
  fruit juices, 99–102
  nectars, 100, 102
  raspberry vinegar, 184
  rhubarb punch, 102, 503
  switchel, 24, 503
  tomato, 113, 184–85
Biscuits, 444
  Buttermilk, 487–88
  "Master Mix," 444
Blackberries
  canning, 95
  drying, 405–06
  freezing, 205
  jam, 310
Blackberry Jam with No Added Pectin, 310
**Blanch (partial precooking), usu. steam/
    water**
  altitude (high), correcting, 21, 26, 220–21,
    224
  anti-discoloration A fruits (steam), 119,
    394
  canning pre-treatment, 115, 120, 128
  crisper, canned green beans, 119
  drying pre-treatment, 26, 394–95, 409
  enzyme de-activation (vegs), 220–21, 224,
    286–87, 392, 394–95
  freezing pre-treatment, 26, 220 *ff*
  microwave oven in, 40, 68, 221, 286, 395
  syrup (fruits), 286, 393
  ill. 220
  see also Drying; Freezing Shellfish; Freez-
    ing Vegetables
Blueberries
  canning, 95
  "checking skins," 95
  drying, 405–06
  freezing, 205–06
Blueberry Buckle, 496–97
Boil-in bags
  equipment, 269–71
  freezing, 195
  what to freeze, 271–72
  see also Cook-in pouch; Freezing Conve-
    nience Foods

Boiling–Water Bath (B–W B), function/
    operation, 26–31
  altitude (high), processing increases, 20–
    22
  depth @ kettle problems, 27–28, 29
  dictated by *pH* rating (natural acid), 10,
    14, 26–27
  "finishing" for jellies, jams, pickles, etc.,
    13, 292–93
  headroom, jars/cans gen'l, 54–55
  Pressure Canner @ B–W B kettle, 29–30
  illus. 29
Book of Country Things, A, 429
Borscht, Irenja's, 463
**Botulism (poisoning from *C. botulinum*
    toxin), 9**
  **canning, bad methods, fostering, 58–59,
    103–04**
  symptoms, 9
  low-acid foods usu. sources of, 32
  **home-canned food source 90 + % reported
    cases, 114**
  see Clostridium botulinum, *toxin*
Boysenberries
  canning, 95
  drying, leathers, 405–6
  freezing, 205
Bread (*see* Tortillas, Wheat; Master Mix;
    zucchini, etc.)
  freezing, 265
**Brine (salt), percent salinity, 281–82, 344,
    356–57**
  anti-discoloration @ fruits, 77, 199, 203,
    285–87, 403
  anti-discoloration @ vegetables, 287
  blood extractor, fish, 162–66, 447
  curing meats, 366–69 *passim*
  curing vegetables (long-brine), 333,
    339–40
  fermenting vegs, 363–64
  firming fish, 162, 165, 244, 290, 374, 447
  firming vegs (short-brine), 334; *and see*
    pickle/relish recipes
  function, pickles, 332
  preserving vegs (strong), 360–61
  soak (weak), de-bug vegs, 123–24, 218–19
  ills. 367, 368, 369
  see also Blanch; Blanching, microwave
    oven
Broccoli
  canning, 123
  de-bugging, 123, 218–219
  drying, 411
  freezing, 226

Broth
  chicken, 172–74
  clam, 173–74
  meat, 172–74
  see also Stocks
Brown & Roberts (Brattleboro, Vt.), 36
Brown sugar, defined, 282
  in canning fruit, 76
  see also Cooking, desserts; Curing; Freezing; Meat (sweet pickle)
Brunton, Guy, 31
Brussels Sprouts
  canning, 123
  de-bugging, 123, 218–19
  freezing, 226
Butchering
  beef, large game, 143–45
  lamb (or goat), 147
  pork, 146
  poultry, small game, 153
  ills. 144–53 passim
Butter, freezing, 256
Buttermilk Biscuits, 487–88
Butter(s), preserves, described, 294
  steps in making, 319–21
  see also Jams; Preserves

C

Cabbage
  acidity (pH rating), 10
  canning, 123, 138
  dried, 411
  fermenting (sauerkraut), 10, 138
  freezing, 226–27
  Piccalilli (relish), 346–47
  root-cellared, 430
  sautéed, 470
Cabbage, Basic Sautéed, 470
Cadmium, danger of, 289–90, 379, 398
  see also Galvanizing; Zinc
Cakes, recipes for, 445–96 *passim*
  freezing, 265
Cake, Yellow, 445
Calcium hydroxide, firming agent @ pickles, 333
  see also Lime, slaked
Canner(s), B–W B
  altitude, high, corrections for use, 20
  anatomy, 27–28
  depth, importance of, 27–28
  fittings for, 27, 31
  Hot-Water Bath for, 21, 31

operation, gen'l, 30–31, 71
  substitutes, safe, 28, 29–30
  ill. 29
Canner(s), Pressure
  altitude, high *psi* increases, 21, 25, 33–34
  anatomy, 34, 35
  B–W Bath kettle, substituting for, 29–30
  "cooker," unhelpful, 32
  fittings for, 34
  gauge(s), dial, managing, 22, 23, 25, 35–38
  operation, gen'l, 36–39, 71
  saucepans, Pressure, advice against, 32–33, 115, 160
  ills. 37, 53, 125
  see also Canning: Meats; Seafood; Tomatoes; Vegetables
Canning, gen'l
  altitude affecting, 14, 19–25
  cans ("tin"), 49–51
  "community kitchens," 17–19
  equipment, 16–17
  filling, etc., containers, 55–56
  function, basic, 14
  headroom, 54–55
  heat penetration in, 14–16, 70
  Hot pack, 52–54
  jars for, 16, 42–48 *passim*
  liquid w/pack needed, 16, 134, 135
  methods, dangerous, 13, 39–41, 62–65, 114, 160
  Pressure Canning imperative, 8–9 (bacteria), 10–11 (*pH* rating/acidity), 22–25 (altitude)
  Raw pack, 52–54
  seals, safe, 57–60, 303–04
  spoilage, signs/remedies, 60–61, 78, 109–10, 115–17, 142–43, 162–63, 305, 334
  storage, 59–60
  ills. 7, 15, 30, 45, 51, 55, 87, 97, 110, 213
  see Canner(s): B–W Bath, Pressure; & specific foods
Carrots
  canning, 124
  cookies, orange, 502
  drying, 412
  freezing, 227
  pudding, steamed, 493–94
  root-cellaring, 430
Carrot-Marmalade, Spicy for Game, 317
Carrot-Orange Cookies, 502
Carrot Pudding, Steamed, 493–94
Casseroles
  Eggplant, 468

Mixed Vegetable, 469
Tomato–Corn Pudding, 470
Cauliflower
  brining, 334
  canning, 124
  freezing, 227
  pickles, in, 337–38, 344
  root-cellaring, 430
Celery
  canning, 124–25
  drying (leaves), 412
  freezing, 227
  root-cellaring, 430
  vegetables, mixed and tomatoes with, 177
    ill. 428
Celsius (centigrade) *see* **Metric(s)**
"Checking" skins (fruits/berries)
  canning, drying pre-treatment, 393–94
Cheese
  Chowder, 464
  Cottage, making, 456–57
  freezing, 256
  Greek tarts, 263
  Rinktum Tiddy (w/tomatoes), 471
Chemical additives
  crispers @ pickles, 333
  see Firming agents
Cherries (sweet and sour)
  canning, 81–82
  freezing, 209–10
  juice (canned), 101
  juice (freezing), 209–10
  see also Pies; Preserves; Sulfuring
Cherry leaves @ firming agent, 333
Chicken
  broth, 172–74
  canned, 151–57
  Wonderful "Stretched," 480
Chinese cabbage
  curing, 358, 360
  fermenting, 361, 363
  freezing, 226–27
  root-cellaring, 436
Chili
  peppers, drying, 415
  sauce, 352
Church of Jesus Christ of Latter-day Saints,
    376, 513
Chutney, Indian (relish), 350–51
Cider, Boiled (canned), 181
Citric acid
  about, 288–89
  anti-discoloration treatments, 285
  canning seafood, 287

freezing fruits, 200
  see also Lemon Juice; Vinegar
Clams
  broth, canning, 174
  canning, 168–69
  freezing, 248
Clostridium botulinum, 9, 140, 162, 365, 377
  acidity rating (*pH*), gen'l control, 10
  heat, gen'l control/destruction, 12, 114
  moisture under 35% inhibits growth, 9,
    378
  pickles, 334–35
  sanitation inhibits, gen'l, 11–12, 140
  spores (toxin-producers), gen'l, 32, 104,
    114
  toxin destroyed, 9, 78, 109–10, 117,
    162–63, 287
  Type "E" (fish strain), 9
    ill. 7
  see also **Botulism**
Cobblers, fruit, 492–95
Coconut, freezing, 210
Cod, dried, 417
  drying, 319–30
  recipes, 481–82
  salt-cured, 355
Codfish Cakes (Salt), 481
Codfish Gravy, 482
Color preservatives, commercial, 285
Community Canning Kitchens, 18-19
Conserves
  failures, correcting, 304–05
  gen'l procedure, 294–97
  steps in making, 321
Conserves, recipes
  Blueberry, 322
  Strawberry, 321
  Sweet Cherry, 322
Convenience foods
  canning, 170-85
  freezing, 249-72 *passim*
  see also individual recipes
Cookies, recipes, 500–02
  freezing, 265–66
  "Ice Box," 500–01
Cook-in-pouch freezing
  equipment, 269–71
  what to freeze, 271–72
  ill. 271
  see also Convenience foods, freezing
Cooperative-Extension Service, 505-06
Copper
  (drying trays) destroys Vit. C, 379
  reaction w/pickling liquids, 332

Cordial, Spiced Blackberry, 502–03
Corn, *pH* rating, 10
    canning, 125–27
    cobs, @ smoke-curing, 371
    drying, 412–13
    dry-salting to preserve, 358–59
    freezing, cob/cut, 228–29, 272
    hominy, 128, 445–47
    recipes, 175, 470–71
    relish, 349
    ills. 55, 125
Corn syrup
    in canning fruit, 4, 76
    in jams/jellies, 282–83, 296–97
Corned beef
    canning, 179
    curing, 366
    hash, 473
    smoked/chipped beef, 366–67
Cottage Cheese, making, 456–57
County Agent, how to locate, 505–06
Cow peas, *see* Pea(s), blackeyed
Crab(s)
    canning, 166–67
    meat, freezing, 247
Crabapple(s)
    Butter, 319–20
    jelly, 307
    juice from jelly, 299
    spiced, 323
Cranberries
    canning, 95
    freezing, 205
    juice, 101
    pie, 498
    puréed, 206
    whole, 206
Cranberry Pie, 498
Crisping, pickles, 333
    see also Firming agents
Cucumber(s) for pickles
    blossom end (enzymes) removed, 331
    stem retained, 331
    see also Pickles
Curing, see Salt-curing; Smoke-curing
Currants
    canning, 96
    freezing, 206
    juice, 101, 207
    juice from jelly, 299
Cyclamates (artificial sweetener), 283–
    84

D

Dairy products
    cottage cheese, making
    freezing butter, cream, eggs, 253–56
    milk pasteurizing, 450–51
Dandelions w/Dumplings, 466
Dandelions (greens), 466
Dates
    drying, 406
    freezing, 210
Deer, *see* Venison
Desserts; *see* Cakes; Cobblers; Cookies; Pies;
    Puddings; Sauces
Dewberries
    canning, 965
    drying, 405–06
    freezing, 205
Dicalcium phosphate, 324–25
    see also Low-methoxyl Pectin
"Diet," *see* Sugarless
Diet foods
    canned fruit, 92
    jams, jellies, 327–30
    "Diet" (sugarless) jelly/jam, 327–30
    see also Pectin, low-methoxyl
Dilly Green Beans, 345
Dill Pickles, 340–41, 344
Discoloration, *see* Anti-discoloration
Disinfectants, household gen'l, 11–12, 105,
    142
Drying, defined, 377–78, 385
    altitude (blanching), 26, 220, 224, 395
    climate, general, 385–86
    dryers, man-made, 381–83; *and see* spe-
        cific foods
    equipment (furnishings), 378–80, 384
    indoor, 388, 391
    moisture usu. remaining, 9, 378, 399
    Mormons, 376, 513
    open-air/sun, 385–88; *and see specific
        foods*
    post-drying treatments, 400–01
    pre-drying treatments, 392–99
    storage, 401–02
    sulfuring (SO$_2$), 395–99
    syrup blanching, 286
    tests, dryness, 399–400, 418–20 *passim*
    ills. 381–83, 404, 419
Drying fish, 388, 419–20
    see also Salt-curing; Smoke-curing
Drying fruits
    anti-discoloration/anti-oxidant, 39, 284–
        86, 392–93

blanching, steam, 392, 394
blanching, syrup (confection), 393
Calorie content, 377
"checking" skins, 393, 394
conditioning, 400
cooking, 403
Leathers, 406–07
moisture remaining, 399
storing, 66–67, 401–02
sulfuring (SO₂), *esp. open-air/sun,* 396–99
see also specific fruits
ill. 404
Drying meat (jerky), 377, 417–19
Drying vegetables
altitude, in blanching, 409
blanching (usu. steam), importance, 392, 394–95
conditioning, 400
cooking, 409–410
moisture remaining, 399
pasteurizing, 400–01
storing, 66–67, 400–01
see specific vegs for methods/times
Dry pack, *see under* Freezing, packs
Dry-salting to preserve, ferment, *see* Salt-curing
Dumplings, Cornmeal, 467
Dumplings, Egg, 479
Dumplings, "Master Mix," 445

E

Eels, freezing, 247
EFNEP (Expanded Food and Nutrition Education Program), 35, 506
Egg Cakes (Baked), 483–84
Eggplant
canning, 127
Casserole, 468
freezing, 229
Eggplant Party Casserole, 468
Elderberries
canning, 96
"checking skins," 95
freezing, 205
Elk
butchering (cuts of), 144
canning, 144
ill. 145
see also Beef; Meat
Enzymes
in blossom ends, 105, 33

enzymatic action and heat, 10
role in spoilage, 6
see also Blanching; Drying; Freezing; Pickles
Exhausting (pre-canning step), 51, 140, 160
see Canning Meats, Seafood; "Tin" cans
Extension Service, 505–07 *passim*
see USDA

F

"Fat back," *see under* Salt pork
Fermentation, desirable, 361; *see also* Brining; Pickles; Salt-curing
undesirable (spoilage), 6–8, 78, 109–10, 115, 117, 162, 369
ills. 7, 110
"Fiddleheads" (wild ferns) cooked, 465
freezing, *see* Greens, wild
Figs
canning, 84–85
drying, 406
freezing, 211
Filo (Greek pastry), using, 261–62, 264
cheese tarts, 263
folding, 264
piroshki w/cabbage, 264 & 470
spinach pie, 262
sweet tarts, 264
ill. 264
Firming agents
alum, 291
calcium chloride, 291
calcium hydroxide, 290
cherry leaves, 333
cold, 290
grape leaves, 333
pectin, 291
salt, 290
Fish
canning, 158–69
curing (salting/smoking), 374–75
drying, 419–20
freezing, 245–47
frozen, cooking, 245
pickled fillets, 447–48
ill. 419
see also Shellfish
Fish Chowder, New England, 461
Fish Hash, 482
Fish, recipes for, 461–83 *passim*
Clam Broth, 174
Chowder, 461
Hash, 482

Fish, recipes for (*continued*)
  Shad Roe, 246–47
  Shrimp Stock, 173
Florida mullet
  canning, 165–66
  drying, 419–20
Flounder, freezing 246
Food and Drug Administration (FDA), 67
Food-grade, defined, 194
Freeze, sharp, initial, 186–87, 190
  ill. 7
Freezer(s)
  choosing, how-to, 187
  dry ice in, 192
  inventory of contents, 191
  maintenance, 190–92
  power failure in, 191–92
  safety, 190
  setting temperature, 190
  sizes and types, 188–90
  wrappings, moisture-vapor proof, 195
Freezer burn, defined, 194
  see moisture-vapor proof
Freezer (uncooked) Berry Jellies with Powdered Pectin, 314
Freezer (uncooked) jams, 303–04, 314, 316
Freezing convenience foods
  containers, 250–51
  equipment, 250
  foods that do not freeze well, 252–53
  labeling, 251–52
Freezing food (general)
  defined, 186
  freezer capacity for, 186–87
  packaging for, 193–95
  quality in, 190–01
  role of moisture in, 196
  temperatures for, 190–01
  yield chart, fruits, 199
  yield chart, vegetables, 219
  ills. 198, 220, 239, 271
Freezing specific foods
  baked goods, 265–66
  cook-in-pouch, 269–72
  dairy foods, 255–56
  eggs, 253–55
  fish and shellfish, 243–48
  jams, 303–04
  main dishes, 256–58
  meats, 236–42
  poultry, 240–42
  refreezing, 69–70
  sauces, 259–61
  soups, 265
  vegetables, 218–35

Frozen food
  inadvertently thawed, 192
  refreezing of, 193
  what can be refrozen, 193
Frozen food/freezer plans, 187
Fructose, 283
  see also sweeteners
Fruit Cobblers, Basic Rule, 492–493
Fruit Cobblers, Canned, 495
Fruit cocktail, freezing, 211
Fruit for Special Diets
  canning, 92
  purées, 92–93
  unsweetened, 92
Fruit(s), canning, 72–102 *passim*
  altitude note, 74–75
  juices in, 75–76
  liquids for, 74
  steps in, 77
  sweeteners, 76
  troubles, correcting, 78–79
  ills. 87, 97, 213
  see also specific fruits
Fruit juices, pasteurizing
  altitude, high, 21
Fruit(s), dried, canning of, 83–84
Fruit(s), freezing
  color-holding treatments, 199–201
  general preparation for, 197
  headroom for, 197–98
  use of ascorbic acid in, 199–200
  yields in, 199
Fruits, *see* individual fruits under specific
  method: Canning; Drying; Freezing

G

Game, wild
  canning procedures, 141–157 *passim*
  diseases of, 141
  dressing and cutting, 154
  freezing, 237–40
  ills. 144, 145
  see also Bear; Elk; Venison
Garlic, drying, 413
Gauges, Pressure Canner
  dead-weight/weighted, 23
  dial, 23
  servicing/sources for, 35–36
Gelatin-firmed ("diet") jelly/jam, 327–30
Gelatin, salads (freezing), 267–68
Gooseberries
  canning, 96
  freezing, 205, 207

Government Bulletins, 505-13 *passim*
Grape(s)
  butter (preserve), 319–20
  canning, 85–86
  drying, 406
  freezing, 212
  jams, jellies, 310–328 *passim*
  juice, 101–02, 212
  juice from jelly, 298–99
Grape (Diet) Jam, 328
Grape Jelly (Concord/wild), no added pectin, 308
Grape (sugarless) Jelly, 327–328
Grape Jelly, pectin added, 310
Grape leaves, usu. scruppernong, @ firming agent, 333
Grapefruit
  canning, 86
  freezing, 211–212
Greens (garden and wild)
  canning, 127–28
  drying, 416–17
  freezing, 230
Guacamole Dip (avocado), 489
Guava, in jams, jellies, 297, 299
Gumbo, *see* okra

H

Haddock, freezing, 245
Halibut, freezing, 245
Ham (cured Pork), 367–69, 371–72, 374
  w/Dried Apples, 479
Hash
  canned, 179
  Corned Beef, 473
  Fish, 482
  Red Flannel, 473
  Sausage, 480–81
Head Cheese (fresh Pork in meat jelly), 450
Headroom
  altitude affecting, 54, 79
  canning, general, in cans, 54; jars, 54–55
  freezing, 197–98, 213, 270–71
  jams, 302
  jellies: paraffin-seal, 301; 2-pc modern lids, 301–02
  pickles, etc., 54 (as for B–W Bath)
  Pressure-processing, 54
  swollen food (starchy), 54, 121–122, 125–38 *passim*
  ills. 53, 55, 87, 110, 198, 213, 271

Heat and acidity, 12
  ill. 15
  see also spoilage
Herbs, drying, 414
Hominy (corn dried & hulled), 445–47
  lye, warning, 446; *see also* Soapmaking
Honey
  freezing, 283
  in canning fruit, 76
  in jams/jellies, 297
  see also Sweeteners, about
Hot pack
  boiling, 115
  microwave, 115
  steam, 115
Hot-smoking (cooking), *see* Smoking/Curing, 22
Hot-Water Bath (pasteurizing), 31
  fruit juices, 21
  see also Juices, fruit canning
How to Steam Your Pudding, 494–95
Huckleberries
  canning, 97
  freezing, 205–06

I

Ice cream, re-freezing, 256
Indian Fry Bread, 488
Indian Pudding (canned), 183
  Pueblo, 490
  Yankee, 491
Information sources, 505–513 *passim*
Iron, darkening shellfish, 162
Irradiation (commercial sterilizing) foods, 67

J

Jam(s), *cooked* **procedure, 302–03**
  altitude, 25–26, 299
  B–W Bath finish, 303
  done tests, 26, 300, 303
  equipment, 293–94
  pectin, adding, 302
  pectin, low-methoxyl, 324–7
  sweetening, 296, 302
  troubles/remedies, 304–05
  2-pc lid for seal, 302
  see also Diet foods; Sweeteners
Jam(s), *uncooked* **(freezer) procedure, 303–04**
  B–W Bath *not* for, 292
  gelatin (firming agent), 315, 328–30

Jam(s) (*continued*)
  paraffin seal, 303
  pectin, added, 303
  refrigeration, 204
  spoilage, 303
Jelly(ies), *cooked* **procedure, 294, 298–302**
  altitude, high, 25–26, 299, 301
  B–W Bath finish (non-paraffin), 13, 292
  done tests, 26, 300–01
  equipment, 293–94
  jelling components, 295–97
  juice, cooked, for, 298–99
  pectin, adding, 299, 303
  pectin, low-methoxyl, gen'l, 325–26
  storage, 292, 302
  troubles/remedies, 304–05
  yield, rough, 306
  ills. 300
  see also Jams, etc.
Jelly(ies), "diet," 295, 327–28
Jelly(ies), freezer (uncooked) procedure, 303–04
Jelly(ies), popular fruits for, 297
  acid, natural, test, 296
  condition, 294–95
  pectin, natural, test, 295
  ripe/underripe, ideal ratio, 306
Jelly(ies) w/low-methoxyl pectin, gen'l recipe w/sugar, 325–26
  sugarless (artificial sweetener), 326
Jerky, dried beef/venison, 418–19
Jerusalem artichokes, freezing, 230
Johnson, Dr. Evelyn
  economic feasibility of preserving food, 1, 2
Juices
  canning, 98–99
  extracting for jelly, 298–99
  fruit, 202–17 *passim*
  sweetening, for jelly, 98
  see specific fruits

K

Kedgeree, 482–83
Keely, Jane, 460
Kendall, Prof. Pat, 24–25, 26
Klippstein, Prof. Ruth, 71
  The True Cost of Home Food Preservation, 1, 2
Kohlrabi
  freezing, 230
  root-cellaring, 431

L

Lamb
  butchering, 147
  canning, 144
  freezing, 237–40
  ill. 147
Lard
  rendering, 452–53
  soapmaking, 453–56
  ill. 453
"Leather britches," *see* Beans, green, drying
Leathers, fruit, 403–09 *passim*
Lemon–Honey Jelly, 313
Lemon juice
  about, 289
  as anti-oxidant, 285
  in freezing fruits, 201
  see also Citric acid
"Lemon salt" *see* citric acid
Liver loaf, 478
Lobster
  canning, 167
  freezing, 247
Loganberries, 297
  canning, 97
  freezing, 205
Low-methoxyl pectin, 324–27
Lye
  hominy, in treating, 128, 446–47
  in drying, 393
  soapmaking, 454–56
  see also Hominy

M

McGuckin Hardware Co. (Boulder, Colo.), 36, 509
Mackerel
  canning (small), 165–66
  drying (small), 419–20
  freezing, 243
  King, canning, 164–65
Main dishes, 466–85 *passim*
  canned, 178–81
  frozen, 256–64
Maple syrup, re-canning, 452
  canning liquid, fruits, 76
  freezing, fruits, 203
  pickles, 333
  sweetener, natural, gen'l, 283

Maple Syrup Pie, 500
Marmalade(s), 316–18
  B–W Bath finish, 302
  described, 294
  equipment, 293–94
  troubles & remedies, *see* Jams
  2-pc lids for seal, 302
  see also Jam(s)
Marmalades, recipes for, 316–19
  Classic Orange, 318
  Ginger Squash, 316
  Green Tomato, 317
  Spicy Carrot, for Game, 317
  Yellow Tomato, 318
Mason Jars, *see* Jars, canning
"Master Mix," baking, 444–45
Measurements, standard U.S. converted to
  metrics, 273–77
  see also Metrics for specific procedures by
  chapter
Meats
  broth, 172–74
  canning, 140–57 *passim*
  curing, 357–64
  cuts for, 143–44
  drying, 377, 417–19
  freezing, 236–42
  frozen meats: cooking, 236–37; prepara-
  tion of, 236–42
Meat, canning, 140–57 *passim*
  cuts for, 143–44
  ills. 145–47
Meat(s) recipes for
  Boiled Dinner (corned beef), 472
  Ham and Dried Apples with Egg Dump-
  lings, 479
  Hamburger and Onion Shortcake, 477
  Hash, Corned Beef, 473
  Liver, Baked Loaf, 478
  Pork (Farmers') Sausage, 449
  Pork Head Cheese (Farm-Wife's), 450
  Pork, Salt (Fried with Gravy), 478–79
  Sausage, Bologna-style, 449
  Sausage Hash, 480–81
  Stew, Vegetable/Beef, 474
  Venison roasts, 474
    stews, 476
  ills. 144-47, 153, 239, 372, 373
Melba Sauce (Susan Osgood's), 183
Melon, freezing, 213
Metric(s) conversions, 273–77
  altitude/boiling, 21, 22
  tables @ processing, *see* each preserving

method chapter intro
  ill. 7
Microwave oven
  canning, not for, 4
  cooking in, 460
  for blanching vegetables, 221
Milano Importing, 261
Milk, pasteurizing, 450–51
  freezing, 255
Milkweed, *see* Greens, Wild
Milkweed, stewed/creamed, 465–66
Mince Pie, 499
Mincemeat, 352–53
Minerals, reaction w/canning shellfish, 162,
  166
Minnesota Extension Bulletin, *413, Home
  Canning—Fruits,
  Vegetables and Meats,* 15, 25, 35, 510
  see Wolf; Zottola
Minnesota, 15 *psi* @ sea level, 35, 510
Minnesota, Special Tomato Mixture, Can-
  ning, 177–78
Mint (fresh) Jelly, 313
Mirro Corp. (mfgr, Pressure Canners), 23,
  24, 509
Mixed corn and beans (succotash), 129–30
Mixed vegetables, canning, 129, 176–77
Mochiko (Sweet Rice Flour), 259–61
  alternatives to, 259
  Basic Freezer Sauce, 260
  sources, 259
  see also Sauces
Molasses, as sweetener, gen'l, 283
Molds (fungi)
  aflatoxin, 40
  mycotoxin, 6, 65–66
  role in spoilage, 6
  ill. 7
  see also Poisoning, food
Moose
  butchering (cuts of), 144
  ill. 145
  see also Beef
Mormons, 376
  see also Church of Jesus Christ of Latter-
  day Saints ("L.D.S.")
Muffins, Blueberry, 490
Muffins, "Master mix," 445
Mullet, Florida
  canning, 165–66
  drying, 419–20
Mushrooms
  canning, 130

drying, 414
freezing, 231
Mussels, freezing, 248
Mustard sauce, tart for pickles, 338
Mycotoxins, 6, 65–66
  see also Aflatoxin; Poisoning, food

N

National Presto Industries, Inc. (mfgr,
  Pressure Canners), 23, 24, 509
  see also Wenstadt, Betty
Nectar(s), see specific fruits
Nectarines
  drying, 407
  freezing, 213–14
  see anti-discoloration
Nitrate/Nitrites, 287
  and nitrosamines, 287
  curing meats, 287, 365
Nut meats, in canning, 130–31

O

Okra (gumbo)
  canning, 131
  freezing, 231
Onion Soup, French, 462
Onions, White
  canning, 131–32
  drying, 415
  root-cellaring, 431
  see specific recipes
Onions w/Curry, 472
Open-kettle, defined, 13
  botulism, 40
  disrepute, 13
  failings of, 40
  mold from, 40
  origin, 13
Orange(s)
  acidity (*pH* rating), 10
  canning, sections, 86
  Cookies, and Carrot, 502
  freezing, sections, 211–12
  Marmalade, Classic, 318
Oven(s)
  canning, *never* in, 4
  convection, for drying, 21
  microwave, for blanch, 13, 21
Oysters
  freezing, 248
  see also salsify

P

Packs, gen'l
  dry (freezing), 201
  Hot (canning), 52–54
  Raw (canning), 52–54
  wet (freezing), 202–03
  ills. 53, 55, 87, 97, 125
  see specific foods canned/frozen
Paraffin, sealing jelly, 301
Parasites, 141, 158
  see Game, canning & curing
Parsnips
  canning, 132
  freezing, 231
  root-cellaring, 431
Pasteurizing (usu. simmer)
  altitude, @ high, 21
  dried food, 22
  fruit juices (canning), 22, 99
  milk, 21
Pastries, 261–62, 266, 497
  ill. 264
Pastry for Dessert Pies, 497
Pea(s) (black-eyed)
  canning, 132–33
  drying, 415
  freezing, 231
  root-cellaring, 431
  swell in canning, 54
  see also Beans, lima/shell
Pea(s), green
  canning, 133
  drying, 415
  edible-pod types, 133, 231
  freezing, 231–32
  root-cellaring, 431
  soup, 464
  swell in canning, 54
Peach(es)
  brandied, 88
  butter (preserve), 319–20
  canning, 86–88
  drying, 407–08
  freezing, 214
  leathers, 406–07
  Melba (& Sauce), 87, 183
  nectar, 102
  purée, 93
  ills. 87, 213
  see Anti-discoloration
Peach (Diet) Jam, 328–29
Pears
  botulism @ canned, 66

butter (preserve), 319–20
canning, 88–90
drying, 408
freezing, 215
nectar, 102
purée, 93
Pectin, defined, 295
and sugar, 299
as firming agent, 291
content in fruits, 297
homemade, 295–96
impaired, 295, 306
natural, 299
use in preserves, 295, 299
Pectin-added jelly/jam, 310–16
Pectin, low-methoxyl jelly(ies), gen'l, 323–27
recipe w/sugar 325–26
sources, 324, 512
sugarless (artificial sweetener), 326
Peppers (bell, green, sweet)
canning, 134
drying, 415–16
freezing, 232
Peppers, hot
drying, 415
freezing, 232
root cellaring, 431
see guacamole for recipe
Perch, freezing, 245
Persimmons, freezing, 215
pH **defined, 11**
low acid defined, 10
ratings, 10
relevant to canning, 14
strong acid defined, 10
see also Acidity
Pickled Fish Fillets, 447–48
Pickles, described, 331
B–W Bath finish, 331
brine, fermenting, 335
brine, long (cure/preservative), 333
brine, short (firming), 334
cucumbers, enzymes concentrated, 331
equipment, 332
firming agents, 334
salt (NaCl), 331–32
spices, gen'l, 333–35
spoilage, 334–35
sugar (sucrose), 333
tartness, to reduce, 334–35
vegetables, measuring, 335
vinegar, 332–33
water, 333, 335
Pickles, recipes for

Bread & Butter, 338, 339
Christmas (Dot Robbins's), 343
Dill Cucumber (short-brine), 344
"Dilly" Green Beans, 345
Green Tomato, 346
Little Cucumber Crock, 339
canning, 340–41
Mustard, 337
sauce, tart, 338
Quick Dill, 341
Ripe Cucumber (Miss Russell's), 342
Small-batch Freezer, 341
Sweet Chips, 336
syrup, spiced for canning, 337
Sweet Mustard, 344
Sweet Pumpkin, 339
Watermelon, 342
Zucchini, 343
Pickling Salt, 279–81, 355–57
see Curing; Canning; Pickles
Pickling solution for fresh fish, 448
Pies, dessert, recipes, 497–500
Apple Filling, canned, 182
apple slices for, frozen, 203
Pies
freezing pastry & filling, 266
see specific recipes
Pike, freezing, 245
Pimientos
canning, 134–35
freezing, 233
Pineapple
canning, 90
freezing, 215
Plain Dandelion Greens, 466
Plastics for storing food, 66
Plums
canning, 90–91
drying, 408–09
freezing, 216
juice, 102, 216
juice from jelly, 299
Leather, 406–07
see also Prunes, Italian
Poisoning, food gen'l
aflatoxin 40; *and see* Mycotoxin
bacterial load, 69–70
botulism (*C. botulinum* toxin), 9, 32, 58–59, 103–04, 114
"ptomaine," 8
salmonellosis (Salmonellae), 8, 9, 140, 240–41, 253
"staph" (*Staphlococcus aureus*), 8–9
trichinosis, 141

ills. 7, 110
see also Spoilage
Popcorn, drying, 412
Pork, fresh
  canning, 146
  butchering, 146
  fat rendering (lard), 146
Pork, fresh
  freezing, 237–40
  Head Cheese, 450
  sausage, in canning, 179–80
  ills. 146–47, 453
Pork, salted
  brining, 369
  dry-salting, 367–68
  nitrates/nitrites in cure, 365
  "sweet pickle" for, 369–70
  ills. 367, 368, 369
Pork, smoked, 370–74, *ills. 368, 372*
Potash water, homemade
  in soap, 455
Potatoes, sweet
  canning, 135
  drying, 416
  freezing, 221, 234
  root-cellaring, 431
Potatoes, white
  canning, 135–36
  drying, 416
  mild brine (anti-discoloration), 135, 287
  root-cellaring, 431
Poultry & small game
  broth, 157
  canning, general procedure, 151–57
  cutting, 153
  dressing, 152
  freezing, 241–42
  giblets, 156
  stuffing, recipe, 480
  ills. 55, 153
Potassium nitrite/sodium nitrate, 287
  and nitrosamines, 287
  see Nitrates, nitrites
Preserves
  canning, gen'l procedure, 294–97
  failures, correcting, 304–05
  steps in making, 321
  Strawberry, 321
  Sweet Cherry, 322
Preserves/conserves recipes, 321–23
Pressure Canner, see Canner(s), Pressure
Prunes, fresh
  drying, 408–09
  juice, 102
  see also plums

Prunes, Italian
  canning, 90–91
  drying, 408–09
  juice, 102
  see also Plums
"Ptomaine" (food poisoning), 8
Publications about food handling, 505–13
  passim
Puddings, recipes, 490–95
  canning (Indian Pudding), 183
  see also Cobblers
Pueblo Indian Pudding, 490–91
Pueblo Wild Rose Hip Jelly, 312
Pumpkin(s)
  canning, 136–37
  drying, 416
  freezing, 221, 233
  root-cellaring, 431
Pumpkin Bread, 486
Pumpkin Cookies, 501
Purées, fruit, 92–93
  canning, 92–93
  drying (as leathers), 403–409
  freezing, 203–17 *passim*
  see also specific fruits
Pyracantha (Firethorn) Jelly, 312

Q

Quinces
  butter (preserve), 319–20
  jelly, 306–7
  preserves, 321

R

Rabbit
  canning, 142
  dressing/cutting up, 152–53
  freezing, 240–42
Radiation in food purification, 67
Radishes, winter
  root cellaring, 431
Raspberries
  canning, 97
  freezing, 207–08, 269
  juice, 208
  sauce, 183
  vinegar, 184
  see Jams; Jellies
Raspberry (Frozen Diet) Jam, 329
Raspberry Vinegar (canned drink base), 184
Raw pack, canning
  see Packs, raw

Recchia, Antonio, 261
Red Flannel Hash, 473
Red Currant Jelly, no added pectin, 307
Refrigeration, inhibits spoilage, 6–9, 72, 142, 151, 243
Relishes, procedures for
  B–W Bath finish, 331
  equipment, 332
  precooking, 334
  salt, 331
  spices, 333
  spoilage, 334–35
  sugar (sucrose), etc., 333
  tartness, to reduce, 333, 334–35
  vinegar, 332–33
Relishes, recipes for
  Beet, 347
  Chili Sauce, 352
  Chutney, Indian, 350
  Corn, 349
  Green Tomato, 347
  Piccalilli, 346
  Pickled Pears, 349
  Tomato Ketchup, 351
  Zucchini (Margaret Hawes's), 348
Rendering, *see* Lard; Soapmaking
Rinktum Tiddy (cheese/tomatoes), 471
Rhubarb "Pie plant"
  canning, 91–92
  freezing, 217
  juice (canned), 102
  juice (frozen), 217
  recipes for, 492–500 *passim*
  see Raw pack
Rhubarb–Berry Fool with Yogurt, 492
Rhubarb–Berry Jam, 315
Rhubarb Pie, 500
Rice flour, "sweet," *see* Mochiko
Rios, Roberta (County Agent, NM), 24–25
Roast Venison, 475
Roasts, freezing, 237
Roe, fish, freezing, 246–47
Root-cellaring ("wintering-over" fruits/vegetables)
  equipment, 423
  fruits, 430, 433–35
  humidity/temperature, 430–31
  indoors, 423–26
  outdoors, cold-climate, 429–33
  outdoors, mild-climate, 427–29
  pitfalls, 422–23
  vegetables, 430–31, 435–39
  Walter Needham, 429–30
  ills. 424, 428, 432
Russell, Miss Gertrude "putting-by" epitomized, 2–4

Ripe Cucumber Pickles, 342
Rutabagas
  canning, 137
  drying, 417
  fermenting (curing), 363
  freezing, 233
  see also turnip

S

Saccharin, *see* sweeteners, artificial/non-nutritive
Safety, *see* Spoilage; specific foods and methods
  see also Soapmaking
Salads, gelatin
  freezing, 267–68
Salicylic acid, *see* Aspirin
Salmon
  canning, 164
  drying, 419–20
  salt/smoke curing, 374–75
Salmonella, defined, 8
  in meat processing, 140
  toxin, heat destroys, 9
  see Bacteria; Poisoning, food
Salsify ("Oyster plant")
  anti-discoloration (mild acid-brine), 287
  canning, 137
  "Oyster" Patties, 471
  root-cellaring, 431, 438
Salt, qualities/uses/varieties, 279–82
  contamination from, 70, 281, 356
  seasoning *optimal,* 103–85 *passim,* 460–501 *passim*
  substitutes (artificial), poor @ canning & freezing, 143, 252, 281
  see also Brine; Pickles, etc.; Salt-curing
Salt-curing fish
  cod, pre-drying, 417, 419, 420
  salmon, coko, pre-smoking (*cold*), brining/dry-salting, 375
  ill. 419
  see also Pickled Fish Fillets; Seafood—Canning, Freezing
Salt-curing meat, general, 357, 364
  brining pork (bacon, ham, etc.), 369–70
  dry-salting beef, 366–67, 417–19
  dry-salting pork, 367–69
  equipment, 357–58
  nitrates/nitrites (saltpeter), general, 287, 365
  salt for, 70, 279–81, 356
  troubles, 70, 366, 369
  ills. 367, 368, 369
  see also Drying

Salt-curing vegetables, general, 356-57
  equipment, 357-58
  fermenting, brine (mild), 363-64
  fermenting, dry salt (mild), 361-63
  preserving, brine (strong), 360-61
  preserving, dry salt (strong), 358-60
  see also Brine; Pickles; specific vegetables
Saltpeter (nitrates), 287, 365
Salt pork, "fat back," *see under* Pork, Salt-
    curing
  Fried, & Gravy, 478
  see also Beans, baked
Sand Plum Jelly (Helen Ruth's), 311
Sandwiches, freezing, 266-67
Sanitation
  "bacterial load," 68-70
  disinfectants for, 11-12, 142
  eggs, freezing, 253-54
  importance of, 11
  meats, canning, 142
Saucepans, pressure, for canning limitations,
    32-33
Sauces
  dessert, 182-83
  freezing (*mochiko*), 260
  main-dish/vegetable, 484-85
Sauces, recipes
  Béarnaise, 484-85
  Chili, 352
  Cider, boiled, canned, 182
  Cream/White, freezer, 260
  Greek Lemon, 484
  (Peach) Melba, canned, 183
  Tomato, 485
Sauerkraut, acidity (*pH* rating), 10
  canning, 138
Sausage
  anti-discoloration, 287, 449
  Bologna-style, 449; canned, 180
  Farmer's Pork, 449; canned, 179
  hash, 480-81
Scallops, freezing, 248
Seafood, *see* Fish and Shellfish
Seals, canning, checking, 57-60, 303-04
  ills. 51, 110, 198
Seed, dried (live for germinating), 442
Shad, canning, 164
  drying, 419-20
Shad Roe, poached/frozen/baked, 246-47
Shellfish,
  altitude, canning, 159
  clam broth, canning, 173-74
  clams, canning, 168-69
  clams, freezing, 248

crab, canned, 166 67
crab, frozen, 247
lobster, canned, 167
lobster, freezing, 247
shrimp, canned, 167-68
shrimp, frozen, 247
troubles, canning, 162-63
see also Fish
Shrimp
  canning, 167-68
  freezing, 247-48
  stock, in canning, 173-74
Slaked lime (calcium hydroxide), 290
  see Firming agents
Smelt, freezing, 245
Smoke-curing (*cold*), general, 370-71
  barrel "smokehouse," 372-74
  fuel for (& sources), 370-71
  "hot-smoking," as different from, 370
  pre-salting fish/meat, 366, 367-70, 372,
    375
  sausage, Bologna-style, 449
  troubles, 370-71
  ills. 372, 373
  see also Canning Meat; Salt-curing
Soapmaking, 454-56
  ill. 453
  see Lard, rendering
Sodium silicate (waterglass), 451
Sorghum, 283
  see also Sweeteners
Soup(s)
  canning, 171-73
  freezing, 265, 268
  stock (broth), in canning, 171-78
Soup(s) recipes, 174, 175, 460-64
  canned, 174, 175
  see also Broth(s)
"Sour salt," *see* Citric acid
Soybeans
  canning, 138
  freezing, 233
  sprouting, 442
Spices
  in canning, 171
  in freezing, 252, 268
  in pickles & relishes, used whole, 333, 335
Spinach
  canning, 127
  drying, 416-17
  freezing, 218
  Greek pie, 262
  see also Greens
Spinach Pie, Greek, 262

Spoilage, gen'l, 5–12, 60–61, 70, 369
bacterial load, 69–70, 240–41, 281
refrigeration inhibits, 6–9, 72, 142, 151, 243, 359–70 *passim*
signs of, 78, 109–10, 115, 117, 142–43, 162–63, 334, 366
ills. 7, 110
see also Brine(s); Poisoning, food.
Sprouting (germinating seeds to eat)
freezing, 443
growing seed (& drying), 442
Munroe, Esther, 441
procedures, 442–43
salads, 443–44
sources, edible seeds, 441–42
toxic seeds, 441
Squash (chayote, summer, zucchini)
canning, 138–39
drying, 417
freezing, 234
ills. 53, 55
Squash Marmalade, Ginger, 316
Squash Pie, Old Newfane Inn, 499
Squash (winter)
canning, *cubed only,* 15–16
drying, 416–17
freezing, 234
root-cellaring, 431
see also Pumpkin
Steaks, beef, freezing, 238
Steam Blanching, *see* Blanching
Stew, canning, 180
Stinett's, Jeanne, frozen
corn-on-the-cob, 229
Stock, Brown Classic, 460
Stockpots @ B–W B Kettle, 28–29
Storage
canned food, 60
cured meat, 365
dried food, 401–02
freezer (time span), 196
indoor, 423–26
outdoor, 427–33
root-cellaring, 421–39 *passim*
ills. 424, 427, 428, 432
Strawberries
canning, 97–98
freezing, 208
juice, 208–09
ill. 97
see also Jams; Jellies; Preserves
Strawberry (Frozen) Jam, 316
Strawberry Jam, no added pectin, 309
Strawberry (Sugarless) Jam, 320–330

Strawberry (Sun-cooked) Jam, 309–10
Strietelmier, Mr., 512
Succotash (corn & bean mixture)
canning, 129–30
Sugar, white, *see* sweeteners, about
Sugar, brown, *see* brown sugar
Sugarless jellies & jams, w/gelatin, 327–30
Apple Jelly, 327
Damson Plum Jam, 330
Grape Jam, 328
Grape Jelly, 327–28
Peach Jam, 328
Raspberry Jam, frozen, 329
Strawberry Jam, 329
Sugar substitutes, 282–84
Sulfur, C-enamel cans offset, 49
Sulfur, sulfuring, 395–99, 402, 404 *ff*
box, 397
reaction w/iron @ shellfish, 162
ill. 397
Sun Drying Foods, 404, 513
Sweet-and-Sour Spiced Crabapples, 323
Sweet potatoes, *see* Potatoes, sweet
Sweeteners, about
as preservative, 74
brown sugar, 282
corn syrup, 282–83
fructose, 283
fruit, canning, 76
honey, 283
juice, used as, 72, 75–76
maple syrup, 283
sorghum & molasses, 283
sugar (sucrose), 282
see also Sweeteners, artificial
Sweeteners, artificial/non-nutritive
aspartame, 283
cyclamates, 283–84
saccharin, 284
Sweeteners, jellies, 296–97, 327–30
Switchel, Hay-time, 503
Syrups, sugar
for freezing fruit, 202
for freezing (wet pack), 202
making & canning, 98
syrup blanching, in drying, 286
ill. 87

T

Temperature, *see* Specific food-preservation method
ill. 7
"Tin" cans, 41, 49–52

Tomato(es)
acidity (*pH* rating), 10
canning, 103–13
  botulism in, 66
  processing methods, 106
  spoilage, 109–10
Cocktail (w/vegs), canned, 184–85
Corn Pudding, 470
freezing, 234–35
Jelly, 313
juice, 235
marmalades, 317, 318
mixed w/vegs., canning, 177–78
pressure–processing, 108–09
removing blossom ends, 105
soups, 175, 178, 463
specific products, 110–13 *passim*
stewed, 176–77, 235
troubles, correcting, 109–10
with cheese, 471
ill. 110
Tongue, canned, 151
see Beef
Tortillas, White Flour, 488–89
Trichina spiralis (trichinosis) infestations, in
  pork & bear, 141
Trout
  canning, 165–66
  drying, 419–20
Tularemia in wild game, rabbit, 141
Tuna
  canning, 164–65
  drying, 419–20
Turkey, *see* poultry
Turnips
  canning, 139
  drying, 417
  freezing, 235
  root-cellaring, 431
Turnips, white
  see Rutabagas
"TV Dinners," homemade, 251, 257

                        U

United States Department of Agriculture
  publications (USDA), 507–12 *passim*
US Government Printing Office, 507
US Government Publications Distribution
  Center, 507

                        V

Veal, *see* beef & meats
Vegetables
blanching at high altitudes, 224

canning, 114–39
cooking frozen, 222–23
freezing, 218–35
mixed in canning, 129
stock (broth) in canning, 173
ills. 53, 55, 110, 125, 220, 428
see specific vegetables
Vegetable-Beef Stew (canned), 180–81
Vegetable Broth/Stock (canned), 173
Vegetable (mixed) Casserole, 469
Vegetables, mixed
  beef stew, 180
  canning, 129
  Casserole, 469
  drying, 414
  recipes, 176–78
  soup base, 174–75
  tomato corn pudding, 470
Vegetable(s) recipes for, 176–472 *passim*
Vegetable (Tennessee) Soup Base (canned),
  174
Vegetarian mincemeat, 354
  piroshkis (cabbage), 263, 470
Venison
  canning, 144–45
  drying (jerky), 418–19
  freezing, 237–40
  safety warning, 474
  stewed, roasted, 474–77
  Venison Book, The, 475
Vinegar, 289–90, 332
  reducing proportion @ pickles dangerous,
  103, 333
  see Acid, to add; Anti-discoloration
Vinegar, Raspberry (canned), 184
Vitamin C, *see* Ascorbic acid

                        W

Water, for food preservation, as ingredient
  contaminants in, 278
  minerals in, "hard," 279, 335
  pickles, for, 333, 335
  treatments for, 279
  quality of, 278
Waterglassing eggs (sodium silicate), 451
Wenstadt, Betty (National Presto Ind.), 23,
  24, 61, 509
Whitefish
  canning, 165–66
  drying, 419–20
Wine Jelly, 314
Wolf, Prof. Isabel D., 71, 107, 510

Woodburn, Dr. Margy, 61, 163
Wood stove, for drying, 451
Wrappings, freezing, 239
  ill. 239

                    Y

Yams
  canning, 135
  drying, 416
  freezing, 234
  see Potatoes, sweet
Yankee Indian Pudding, 491
Yeasts, role in spoilage, 6
  see also Fermentation
Yellow Cake, 445
  "Master Mix," 445
Yields in put-by foods
  fish canned, 166–68 *passim*
  fruits canned, 80
  fruits frozen, 199
  fruits/vegs dried, 377
  jelly (fruit juice & sugar), 306
  meat, info sources, 143

  shellfish canned, 166–68 *passim*
  syrups, fruit canning, 75
  tomatoes canned, 104
  vegs canned, 116
  vegs frozen, 219
Youngberries
  canning, 97
  freezing, 205

                    Z

Zinc
  galvanizing, 326, 329
  lids, 44
  ill. 45
Zottola, Dr. Edmund A., 107, 510
Zucchini
  bread, 487
  canning, 138–39
  drying, 417
  freezing, 234
  pickles, 343
  relish, 348
Zucchini Tea Bread, 487

About the authors of *PUTTING FOOD BY:*

RUTH D. HERTZBERG earned her Bachelor of Science degree at the University of Maine. She taught Home Economics in New England high schools and served as County Agent in Home Economics with the Vermont Extension Service for many years.

BEATRICE VAUGHAN wrote nine cookbooks prior to her death in 1972. Some of her heirloom recipes are included in this edition.

JANET GREENE graduated from Stanford University and was a reporter for metropolitan newspapers on the Pacific Coast before joining the United Press where she became a capital-bureau manager. She was Editor-in-Chief of The Stephen Greene Press when the idea for this book was conceived, and she has several books to her credit. At her Brattleboro office, she continues to edit and write; at her farmhouse in the mountains she puts food by.